SHORT BREAKS
IN BRITAIN

Produced by the Publishing Division of the Automobile Association

Maps prepared by the Cartographic Department of the Automobile Association
© The Automobile Association

All the establishments listed in this guide are classified and regularly inspected by the AA's Hotel Inspectorate. This applies to the accommodation and regular hotel services, but not to the short break holidays.

Head of Advertisement Sales:
Christopher Heard tel 0256 491544

Advertisement Production:
Karen Weeks tel 0256 491545

Cover Illustration by Directions Limited

Colour Illustrations by Ian McGill

Typeset by Microset Graphics Ltd., Basingstoke, Hampshire

Colour Reproduction by LC Repro & Sons Ltd., Aldermaston

Printed and bound in Great Britain by
William Clowes Limited, Beccles and London

Every effort is made to ensure accuracy, but the publishers do not hold themselves responsible for any consequences that may arise from errors or omissions. Whilst the contents are believed correct at the time of going to press, changes may have occurred since that time or will occur during the currency of this book.

Published by the Automobile Association, Fanum House Basingstoke, Hampshire RG21 2EA

ISBN 0 74950 200 2

CONTENTS

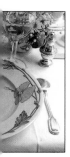

Introduction

T here are times when you need to get away for a few days, nothing too expensive or exotic, just a short break. You might fancy a weekend exploring a part of the country you haven't yet visited, or prefer to spend some time on a favourite hobby with people sharing the same interests, and under the instruction of a qualified tutor or guide.

Whatever your preference, you will find it here, for special interest holidays range from the exciting and energetic to the restful and relaxing. There are hotels offering literary breaks, murder mystery weekends, gastronomic breaks, medieval weekends, music breaks and even self-awareness breaks. You could take flying lessons, learn to sail, improve your painting, visit stately homes, take up wildlife photography, or spend a few days browsing round antique fairs. Just look in the index at the back of the book and take your pick.

Of course, you may not wish to do anything other simply relax in the luxurious surroundings of a first class hotel. You will find that many such establishments offer special rates for short break guests, so your few days away needn't cost the earth.

While you would normally imagine short breaks to be available out of season, this need not necessarily be the case, for many establishments offer special activity holidays and reduced terms throughout the year. Good value weekend breaks are often available in hotels which cater for a business clientele during the week. These hotels are usually in busy towns and cities, and are perfect for shopping sprees and theatre trips. Should you prefer solitude, you could opt for the low season break, when Britain's popular seaside resorts and country towns can be surprisingly tranquil.

Whatever you want from a break, this guide is designed to help you find it, so read on and discover all that Britain has to offer.

❁

"Whatever your preference, you will find it here, for special interest holidays range from the exciting and energetic to the restful and relaxing."

❁

This guide is arranged alphabetically in county order and covers the whole of England, Scotland and Wales, plus the Channel Islands. Within each county, towns are listed in alphabetical order and, where more than one establishment appears under a town heading, these too are arranged alphabetically.

The location atlas at the back of the book pin-points every city, town and village for which there is a gazetteer entry. This is preceded by a Special Interest Index which is designed to assist those who are looking for a particular kind of break. If you want a weekend sailing, painting or visiting stately homes, for example, this will tell you all the places which provide the activity you have in mind.

Each gazetteer entry includes details of its AA classification and the various kinds of classification are explained on page 15. If the hotel is a member of a hotel group, the name of the group is shown in brackets after the address. However, if the group name features as part of the hotel name, we do not repeat the information.

ABOUT THIS BOOK

usually send their brochure, if you enquire in advance, so that you can be sure of what to expect.

Activities

The inclusion of an activity break in our gazetteer is no guarantee that it will take place. Some of the activity breaks offered may depend upon a minimum number of participants and if this is not reached, the break may be cancelled.

Where possible, we have given brief details of what the various activities involve, but a full programme of events

Descriptions of establishments

In each description we have tried to indicate the character of the hotel and to give some examples of the kind of facilities it has to offer, but this is in no way intended to include every detail, and places may well have more amenities than those stated. Establishments will

should be available from the establishment. You should always try to obtain this in advance of your break in case you need to take special equipment with you, and for information that you may need to know. Many hotels can arrange activities for you on an individual basis, but the mention of this

in a gazetteer entry should not be mistaken for an organised activity break. It will usually mean that the hotel staff will book such things as riding, golf, etc., at local establishments.

We must stress that, although all of the accommodation in the guide has been inspected by the AA, this does not apply to any of the activities offered.

Prices

Unless otherwise stated, short break prices refer to bed, breakfast and evening meal per person, per night. So that you can judge for yourself how much of a bargain a short break will be, we have included the establishments' normal prices.

Many of the short-break prices are based upon two people sharing a double or twin-bedded room and a supplement may be charged for single occupancy. In some cases we have been able to show the single supplement, but the absence of such details in a gazetteer entry does not necessarily mean that no supplement is charged. Anyone planning to take a break alone is advised to check the situation when booking.

Children are normally accommodated at a reduced rate, or free, if they share a room with their parents, but this may be further enhanced in the case of a short break. Some hotels will even accommodate children free in their own room, as long as they are accompanied on the break by two adults. Please remember, though, that children's meals must be paid for as taken.

Prices for activity breaks vary considerably and we have tried to give an indication of what is included. For many the price is inclusive of accommodation, meals and any organised activity, but in some cases there may be an extra charge for lunches. Again, it is wise to check in advance.

Please remember that price information is always subject to change and, although all of the details within this guide have been supplied to us in good faith by the proprietors, changes can occur after we go to press or during the currency of the guide.

WEEKEND BREAKS

WITH QUEENS MOAT HOUSES HOTELS

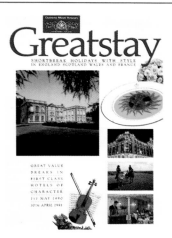

- Hotels of character
- Children free
- Mid-week breaks
- Luxury weekends
- Speciality weekends

- Many popular locations
- Children free
- Extensive leisure facilities
- Luxury weekends
- Speciality weekends

For your free brochure call
0403 741797 (24 hrs)
Please Quote AA Short Breaks in Britain

INTERNATIONAL HOTELIERS

For further information and reservations call
FREE 0800 289331

Queens Moat Houses Reservations
Queens Court • 9-17 Eastern Road • Romford RM1 3NG

The CHOCOLATE Experience

f the many different short breaks available around the country, the editor chose a 'chocaholics' break, dedicating the weekend to the consumption of chocolate and a visit to Cadbury World in Bourneville.

I didn't quite know what to expect from my visit to the chocolate factory. I'd had visions of enormous rooms throbbing with the noise of magnificent machinery mixing, pouring, moulding, chopping and packaging immense quantities of rich, aromatic chocolate. I had half-hoped to see chocolate rivers and candy trees, and be welcomed at the gates by Mr Willy Wonka – or should I say, a mysterious and eccentric Mr Cadbury?

The first thing that struck me as I approached the entrance, was the tempting smell of hot chocolate – although I had only just finished breakfast, my stomach informed me that it was time to indulge. The Cadbury people could tell, and I was handed a free bar immediately on arrival. It

was tucked away in the depths of my bag as I began to psyche myself up for the race ahead. Time and hoards of hungry children were the competition for my self-appointed mission to eat the most chocolate ever consumed by man, woman or child.

But there was no need. After a short wait – visitors enter the exhibition area in groups of about 20 in order that the rooms never become too crowded – I found myself transported to a wonderful tropical rainforest. There I saw the Aztecs of 16th-century Central America growing and trading cocoa beans, and making mind-boggling sacrifices to the God of Rain to ensure the safe harvest of their crops. I even tasted the strange concoction which was a favourite of their Emperor Montezuma. 'Chocolatl' was a mixture of ground cocoa beans, honey and chilli peppers – not to everybody's taste, I admit, but surprisingly palatable.

From the Emperor's temple, I went on to discover how chocolate was introduced to Spain, and then to Britain in the late 17th century. I soon emerged into a cobbled square of Georgian England, outside White's Chocolate House which opened in

1693 and was one of the many which achieved notoriety through the questionable activities of its clientele. To me, hot chocolate is a beverage gently sipped on cold wintry nights, usually before nipping off to bed with a hot water bottle. Not so the dandies of the 18th century, for John Mackay observed in 1722 that 'frivolous young men gamble away thousands at White's and the Chocolate Houses in Covent Garden'. Twenty years later, Horace Walpole was complaining that things had gone too far. 'One of the youths at White's has committed murder, and intends to repeat it. He betted £1,500 that a man could live for twelve hours under water; hired a desperate fellow, sunk him in a ship, by way of experiment, and both ship and man have not appeared since.'

Fortunately, I was not greeted by dandies and wild gamblers as I entered the Cocoa House, but the gentle Mary Cadbury who proudly related the Cadbury story. It was her father, John, who in 1824, started a grocery business in Birmingham, and introduced cocoa and drinking chocolate as a sideline. His sons, Richard and George, not only introduced a new process from Holland for pressing

It was Don Cortez, the Spanish explorer who brought cocoa beans to Europe after meeting with the Aztec Emperor Montezuma.

the cocoa butter from the beans to produce cocoa essence, but they were also responsible for the creation of the Bourneville factory and village, and for the many employee welfare schemes for which the company has been renowned.

Clocking in to the factory brought back memories for many visitors – I'm not sure if they were happy ones as I couldn't help noticing a large group of women laughingly dodge through another entrance, avoiding the clock altogether. Within the stark white walls of this hand-processing unit, we were all shown how the bean is winnowed, roasted, pressed and mixed into thick, oozing dark chocolate. Further on, caramel was being rolled on huge marble slabs, coated in chocolate, and then delicately decorated. There is something tantalisingly irresistible about handmade chocolates, but in this part of the factory, the skilful workers are not encouraged to take their pick. To be honest, they admitted, they didn't really feel like eating chocolate when they were working with it all day.

Should you ever need persuading to indulge your tastebuds, the packaging and advertising of the Cadbury products can usually achieve this. The next section of the exhibition was a fascinating display of boxes and wrappers, from the early pictures painted

Though advertising styles have changed the Cadbury name has always been an integral part of every design.

Early label designs reflect the 'quality and superior style' which marked the Cadbury approach to business.

12

by Richard Cadbury himself, to the modern designs with which we have become familiar. There were video screens showing clips from well-known television advertisements, an amazing collection of posters, a story-board showing how one of the famous Milk Tray commercials was made, and two enormous Creme Eggs!

By this time, with the smell and sight of fresh chocolate, and the promotion material surrounding me, reminding me of all the irresistible bars and boxes available, I knew I had to have something, and soon. As if by magic, I suddenly found myself in paradise – the Cadbury World chocolate shop! The choice was agonising but, having selected only a few choice items, I rewarded myself immediately afterwards in the adjoining ice cream parlour and then continued on my expedition, for it was not yet over.

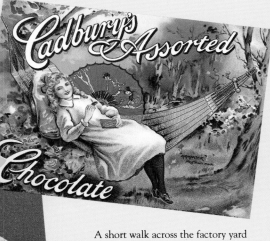

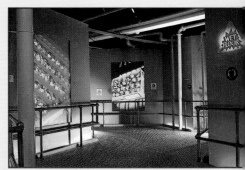

The modern Creme Egg factory shows how 300 million creme eggs are made in a year.

By the time I left, I felt I knew everything there is to know about chocolate, factory reforms in the 19th century, and advertising, but I have since learned that the exhibition is to be extended to include a visit to the moulded chocolate production line and the packaging unit. I'll have to indulge in another Chocolate Break next year; meanwhile, it might be useful to learn a little self-control.

13

A short walk across the factory yard brought me to the Alternative Exhibition which was a display of early machinery, pictures and odd bits and pieces. There were some wonderful notices issued by the Medical Department of Cadbury in 1903, in particular the Ten Commandments of Hygiene, and a superb model of the Bourneville village as it once was. Before long, I was listening to the security guard's tales of life on the factory floor and in the village, many years ago.

The 'Cadbury World Break' is just one of the treats on offer to chocolate lovers, and is available at the following hotels:

The George Hotel, Bird Street, Lichfield, Staffordshire, WS13 6PR Telephone: (0543) 414822

The Manor Hotel, Meriden, Coventry, West Midlands, CV7 7NH Telephone: (0676) 22735

Penns Hall Hotel, Penns Lane, Walmley, Sutton Coldfield, West Midlands, B76 8LN Telephone: (021) 351 3111

* Moor Hall Hotel, Four Oaks, Sutton Coldfield, West Midlands, B75 6LN Telephone: (021) 308 3751

*This break also includes a visit to Tudor in Lichfield, a demonstration of chocolate work by Barry Colenso of Thorntons, and special chocolate dishes on the menu.

Most of the establishments you will find in this book have gained an AA star rating. The criteria by which we decide upon these ratings, are very complex, but here we briefly explain what you can expect from each category:

★ Hotels and inns generally of small scale with good facilities and furnishings. Adequate bath and toilet arrangements will not necessarily include en suite facilities, but some may be available. Meals are provided for residents but their availability to non-residents may be limited.

★★ Hotels offering a higher standard of accommodation and some bedrooms with private bath or shower rooms.

★★★ Well-appointed hotels with more spacious accommodation with the majority of bedrooms containing a private bath or shower room. Fuller meal facilities are provided.

★★★★ Exceptionally well-appointed hotels offering a high standard of comfort and service with bedrooms providing a private bath or shower room.

★★★★★ Luxury hotels offering the highest international standards.

🛏 This symbol is used to denote an AA Country House Hotel where a relaxed informal atmosphere and personal welcome prevail. However, some of the facilities may differ from those found in urban hotels of the same classification. These hotels are often secluded and, though not always rurally situated, are quiet.

(RED) When this appears after a star rating it means that the hotel has been awarded red stars and is considered by our inspectors to be of outstanding merit within its classification.

% A percentage score is awarded to all hotels and is based on quality. It is an indication of where each hotel stands in

HOW WE CLASSIFY ACCOMMODATION

comparison to others within the same star classification. Hotels have been assessed for quality under a number of broad headings: hospitality, cleanliness, services, food, bedrooms, overall impression and the Inspector's personal view. All hotels recognised by the AA may be expected to score at least 50%, and a score of around 61% is considered to be the average benchmark.

The percentage ratings act as a quality gauge within each star classification, and can also be used across the star classification bands, to help you decide, for example, whether to stay at a very good three-star hotel, or at an average four-star hotel.

Please remember that a high percentage score within a star classification does not necessarily mean that there are more facilities and services than at another hotel with a lower score. What it does mean, however, is that the standard of services and facilities it offers is better. In short, the overall standard and quality of the hotel will be higher as the percentage awarded increases.

A small number of hotels have reached such a standard of excellence that they have been awarded red stars – the AA's highest accolade – and no percentages are given for this select category as they are judged to be the very best in their star classification, and therefore outside the scope of the percentage scheme.

Q The quality assessment of guesthouses, farmhouses and inns, is indicated by one to four of these symbols. One symbol means that the establishment offers clean, modest accommodation with adequate bathroom facilities. Two symbols show a higher standard in terms of furnishing, decor and comfort – likely to have some en suite facilities. Three symbols indicate superior accommodation with comfortable public areas and some en suite facilities. Four symbols are a sign of the very best establishments, offering a high degree of comfort, good food and hospitable, caring hosts. Many provide a high proportion of en suite facilities.

GH This indicates that the establishment is a guesthouse, which is different from, but not necessarily inferior to a star–rated hotel. Guesthouses range from simple bed and breakfast accommodation to small private hotels and are generally owned and run by a family. You will usually find a more informal atmosphere and frequently the accommodation is of a very high standard. Many of the bedrooms may have private bath or shower rooms.

FH Farmhouse accommodation has a special quality and is particularly noted for being inexpensive and cosy, with a high standard of good home cooking. Many of those that we list are working farms and you may find that the farmer is willing to let visitors look around the farm, or even help feed the animals. Always check beforehand to make sure this is the case, and remember that a modern farmyard is a potentially dangerous place. Always take great care and never leave children unsupervised around the farm. As with guesthouses, standards vary considerably and are often far above what one might expect. Some

of our listed farmhouses are grand ex-manor houses, furnished with antiques and offering a stylish way of life; others are more simple with a homely atmosphere.

INN We all know what to expect from a traditional inn – a cosy bar, convivial atmosphere, good beer and pub food. The inns in our book will vary in character from picturesque country inns with old beams, to small hotels in busy towns.

Symbols

✶ Dogs are not accepted at these hotels.

& Accommodation is suitable for disabled visitors. It is important that intending visitors should inform the hotel of the extent of their disability in order to be certain that their needs can be met.

Credit cards

1	Access/Euro/Mastercard accepted
2	American Express accepted
3	Barclaycard/Visa accepted
4	Carte Blanche accepted
5	Diners Club card accepted

NB. *If you intend to pay by any of the above credit cards, you would be well advised to check the position when booking.*

Rosettes

These are awarded to hotels and restaurants where our inspector considered that the food and service can be specially recommended:

✿ Where food is of a higher standard than is expected for its classification.

✿✿ Excellent food and service, irrespective of classification.

✿✿✿ Outstanding food and service, irrespective of classification.

ENGLAND

▓ AVON ▓

ALMONDSBURY Avon *Map 3 ST68*

★★★★64% **Aztec** BS12 4TS ☎ (0454) 201090

Normal price: £126 (room)
Short breaks: £196 (room for 2 nights). Single occupancy £52 (bed and breakfast only).

This completely new hotel includes extensive leisure facilities and its own pub, The Black Sheep.

ALVESTON Avon *Map 3 ST68*

★★★69% **Alveston House** BS12 2LJ ☎ (0454) 415050

Normal price: £78.50 room. Dinner £12.75-£15.75 and à la carte
Short breaks: £41.50. Min 2 nights, Fri-Sun
Credit cards ① ② ③ ⑤

Standing beside the A58 between junctions 14 and 16 of the M5, this comfortable hotel has thirty bedrooms all with ensuite facilities and colour television.

★★★58% **Post House** (Trusthouse Forte) Thornbury Road BS12 2LL ☎ (0454) 412521

Normal price: £48.50. Dinner £14.50 and à la carte
Short breaks: £38. Min 2 nights, must include Saturday.
Credit cards ① ② ③ ④ ⑤

An extension to the original Ship Inn, the hotel combines character with modern facilities. All the bedrooms have ensuite bathrooms and colour television and some rooms have been set aside for non-smokers. Guests can make use of the outdoor heated swimming pool, mini golf and pitch and putt. There is a special Christmas programme.

BATH Avon *Map 3 ST76*

GH Q Ashley Villa 26 Newbridge Road BA1 3JZ ☎ (0225) 421683
Closed 2 weeks at Xmas

Normal price: £20-£30
Short breaks: £19-£27 excluding dinner. Min 2 nights, Fri-Sun
Credit cards ① ③

This guest house is comfortably furnished and has a relaxing informal atmosphere. Most of the bedrooms have ensuite facilities, all have colour television and tea/coffee making facilities. In the summer there is a heated outdoor swimming pool.

GH QQ Avon 9 Bathwick Street BA2 6NX ☎ (0225) 446176 & 422226
Closed 25 & 26 Dec

Normal price: £24.75, single £35
Short breaks: £22.50 excluding dinner; single £30. Min 2 nights (ex Bank Holiday weekends)
Credit cards ① ③ ⑤

Centrally situated, close to the shops and tourist sites. All the bedrooms have ensuite facilities, colour television and tea and coffee making facilities. Some rooms are reserved for non-smokers.

★69% Berni Royal (Berni/Chef & Brewer) Manvers Street BA1 1JP ☎(0225) 463134

Normal price: £35. Dinner £8-£15 à la carte
Short breaks: £27.50 excluding dinner. Min 2 nights weekends, min 3 nights midweek
🐾 (ex guide dogs)

Standing opposite the railway station, this hotel has thirty warm, well-equipped bedrooms all with private bath or showers and colour television; there are four family rooms.

GH QQQ Brompton House St John's Road BA2 6PT ☎(0225) 420972 & 448423
Closed Xmas

Normal price: £27.50
Short breaks: £25 excluding dinner. Min 2 nights
🐾 Credit card ①

This delightful Regency residence was once the rectory to St Mary's Church. Each bedroom has colour television and ensuite facilities, and there is one family room.

GH QQ Carfax Great Pulteney Street BA2 4BS ☎(0225) 462089

Normal price: £27.50-£32.50 including dinner
Short breaks: £25.50-£29.50. Min 2 nights
🐾 (ex guide dogs) Credit cards ① ② ③

A large guest house where all bedrooms have colour television and most have ensuite bath or shower rooms. Some rooms are for families and non-smokers. Parking is limited.

QQQ Dorset Villa 14 Newbridge Road BA1 3JZ ☎(0225) 425975

Normal price: £20.50
Short breaks: £19.00 excluding dinner.
Credit cards ① ③

West of the city on the main A4 road, this small hotel has been recently refurbished and provides well-furnished accommodation with good facilities.

★★69% Duke's Great Pulteney Street BA2 4DN ☎(0225) 463512

Normal price: £40. Dinner £10-£15
Short breaks: £47.50. Min 2 nights
Credit cards ① ② ③

Built in 1780, this hotel provides warm service and hospitality. Bedrooms are comfortable and all have ensuite facilities and colour television, including the four family rooms.

★★★61% Francis (Trusthouse Forte) Queen Square BA1 2HH ☎(0225) 424257

Normal price: £56. Dinner £15.50 and à la carte
Short breaks: £56-£62 Thu-Sun
Credit cards ① ② ③ ④ ⑤

A charming and elegant hotel just a short walk from some of the city's shops. Service throughout is helpful and friendly. All the bedrooms have ensuite bathrooms and colour television; some rooms have been set aside for non-smokers. There is a special Christmas programme.

★64% **Gainsborough** Weston Lane BA1 4AB ☎(0225) 311380
Closed Xmas & 1st wk Jan
Normal price: £33. Dinner £10.50
Short breaks: £29 excluding dinner. Min 2 nights
Sep-Apr

On the outskirts of the city, close to the village of Weston lies this small personally-run hotel. All the bedrooms have ensuite facilities and colour television, there are two family rooms and one room has a four-poster bed.

GH QQQ Leighton House 139 Wells Road BA2 4QE ☎(0225) 314769
Normal price: £26-£28. Dinner £12.50
Short breaks: £37.50. Single £52.50. Min 2 nights, Nov-Apr.
✖ Credit card [1]

Hospitality and personal attention are offered at this house on the A367 Exeter Road, ten minutes' walk from the city centre. The comfortable bedrooms have ensuite facilities and colour television and there are two family rooms.

GH QQQ Oldfields 102 Wells Road BA2 3AL ☎(0225) 317984
mid Jan-mid Dec
Normal price: £26
Short breaks: 10% off. Min 4 nights (ex Bank Holidays)
✖ (ex guide dogs)

A restored Victorian family house overlooking Bath and the surrounding hills. Each bedroom has colour television and eight have ensuite facilities.

GH QQQQ Orchard House Warminster Road (A36), Bathampton BA2 6XG ☎(0225) 466115
Normal price: £57 including dinner
Short break: £40

This small hotel, built in 1984, offers a warm welcome and comfortable accommodation with above average facilities. All rooms have ensuite bath or shower rooms and colour television, and those facing the main road are triple-glazed and air conditioned. Guests may use the sauna, solarium and spa bath.

GH QQ Parkside 11 Marlborough Lane BA1 2NQ ☎(0225) 29444
Closed Xmas week
Normal price: £18-£19
Short breaks: £17.50 excluding dinner. Min 2 nights, Sun-Thu Oct-before Easter

This spacious Edwardian house lies on the edge of Victoria Park and is within easy walking distance of the city centre. All the bedrooms have colour television and there is one family room.

★★★★71% **Royal Crescent** (Queens Moat) (Prestige) 16 Royal Crescent BA1 2LS ☎ (0225) 319090

Normal price: £97.50. Dinner £33 & à la carte
Short breaks: £83 excluding dinner. Min 2 nights Sun-Thu
✝ (ex guide dogs)

Formed from two of the largest houses in Bath's magnificent Royal Crescent, this hotel offers mostly spacious bedrooms all with private bath or shower rooms and colour television. Some rooms have four-poster beds and others are reserved for non-smokers. There is a special Christmas programme.

GH QQQQ Somerset House 35 Bathwick Hill BA2 6LD ☎ (0225) 466451

Normal price: £36.55-£44 including dinner
Short breaks: £73.10 for 2 nights, Sun-Thu.
Activity breaks: Brunel Break, £107 for 2 nights including Sun lunch, talk by Brunel expert and transport and fees to places of interest. Chalk and Cheese Break, £140 for 3 nights including one lunch. Visits around the area including a vineyard, a cheese dairy, a paper mill and a stone barrow. Herbs for Health, £102 for 2 nights including Sun lunch, transport and entrance fees. Guest speakers will talk on aromatherapy, herbs in cooking and planning a herb garden. Opera Weekends, £127 for 2 nights including after theatre snacks, Sun lunch, tour of Bath, and stall seats for a production by the Welsh National Opera at Bristol.
Credit cards 1 2 3

A fine period house with a choice of sitting rooms, offering imaginative, well-cooked food. This is a strictly non-smoking establishment.

GH QQQ Tasburgh Bath Warminster Road, Bathampton BA22 6SH ☎ (0225) 425096

Normal price: £27-£29
Short breaks: £25-£27. Min 2 nights, except public holidays.
Single from £30
✝ Credit cards 1 2 3 5

A Victorian house offering a high standard of accommodation and warm hospitality. Most of the bedrooms have ensuite facilities, all have colour/television and some rooms are for families and non-smokers.

GH QQQ Villa Magdala Henrietta Road BA2 6LX ☎ (0225) 466329

Closed January

Normal price: from £26
Short breaks: from £24, Nov-Mar
✝ Credit cards 1 3

This beautifully maintained house stands in attractive grounds just a few minutes' walk from the city centre. There are seventeen bedrooms, all with ensuite facilities and colour television. Children under six are not accommodated.

GH QQQ Wentworth House 106 Bloomfield Road BA2 2AP ☎ (0272) 339193

Normal price: £24
Short breaks: 5% off for 3 nights or more.
Credit cards 1 3

This large, comfortable guest house has a lounge bar and a dining room with a conservatory which overlooks the outdoor swimming pool. All the bedrooms have colour television, most have ensuite facilities and there are two family rooms.

BRISTOL   Avon   Map 3 ST57

★★★65% **Avon Gorge** (Mount Charlotte (TS)) Sion Hill, Clifton BS8 4LD ☎ (0272) 738955

Normal price: £57.25. Dinner from £13 à la carte
Short breaks: £39.50
Credit cards 1 2 3 5

Enjoying fine views of Clifton Suspension Bridge, this hotel provides bedrooms with private bathroom and colour television; two rooms have four-poster beds and there are rooms for non-smokers. There is a special Christmas programme. The hotel plans to provide a much needed car park.

★★62% **Clifton** St Pauls Road, Clifton BS8 1LX ☎(0272) 736882

Normal price: £33. Dinner £9.50-£12.50 & à la carte
Short breaks: £29 includes £8 restaurant voucher,
newspaper. Min 2 nights, Fri-Sun. Single £38
Credit cards [1] [2] [3] [5]

Close to the university and city centre, this hotel offers accommodation with good facilities; most bedrooms have ensuite bath or shower room and all have colour television, with rooms for families and non-smokers. The wine bar and restaurant have a lively, informal atmosphere.

★★★63% **Henbury Lodge** Station Road, Henbury BS10 7QQ (4¹/₂m NW of city centre off B4055)
☎(0272) 502615

Normal price: £37.25. Dinner £14.80
Short breaks: £22 excluding dinner. Single £29.50.
Min 3 nights, Fri-Sun
Credit cards [1] [2] [3] [5]

A Georgian country-style hotel close to the M5, providing imaginative, well-prepared food. Each bedroom has a colour television and ensuite facilities with rooms for non-smokers and families. The hotel has some leisure facilities, and offers a special Christmas programme.

★★★69% **Redwood Lodge & Country Club** Beggar Bush Ln, Failand BS8 3TG (2m W of Clifton Bridge on B3129) ☎(0272) 393901

Normal price: £50. Dinner fr £16.
Short break: £50 Fri-Sun, £55 Mon-Thu. Min 2 nights.
Activity breaks: Christmas Breaks, £260 for 3 nights. New
Year Breaks, £200 for 3 nights. 1990 prices.
✕

Signposted off the A369 west of the city centre this hotel, now extensively refurbished, offers well-equipped bedrooms and an excellent range of leisure facilities.

★★67% **Rodney** Rodney Place, Clifton BS8 4HY ☎ (0272) 735422

Normal price: £40-£46. Dinner £12 & à la carte
Short breaks: £35. Min 2 nights, Fri-Sun
Credit cards [1] [2] [3] [5]

Dating back to the 18th century, this hotel provides attractive, comfortable accommodation in modern bedrooms each with ensuite bath or shower room and colour television. Two rooms are set aside for non-smokers. No parking.

★★★50% **St Vincent Rocks** (Trusthouse Forte) Sion Hill, Clifton BS8 4BB ☎ (0272) 739251

Normal price: approx £41. Dinner £14-£16.95 & à la carte
Short breaks: £40 (subject to review). Min 2 nights, Thu-Sun
Credit cards [1] [2] [3] [4] [5]

Standing near the Avon Gorge and the Clifton Suspension Bridge, this hotel offers friendly, helpful service. Each bedroom has an ensuite bath or shower room and colour television, and some rooms are for non-smokers. There is a special Christmas programme.

★★★52% **Unicorn** (Rank) Prince Street BS1 4QF ☎ (0272) 230333

Normal price: £86 room with Continental breakfast (price
subject to review). Dinner from £14 à la carte
Short breaks: £42.50 (1990 prices). Min 2 nights, Fri-Sun

A modern hotel on the waterfront offering a good range of facilities including a choice of eating options. Bedrooms vary from spacious to more compact, and all have ensuite facilities and colour television. There is a special Christmas programme.

CHELWOOD   Avon   *Map 3 ST66*

★★72% **Chelwood House** BS18 4NH ☎ (0761) 490730
Restricted service 24 Dec-15 Jan

Normal price: £39.50-£47.50. Dinner £16.50-£24 à la carte
Short breaks: £53. Min 2 nights, Fri-Sun. Single £60
🐾 (ex guide dogs) Credit cards ① ② ③ ⑤

A charming 300-year-old building, tastefully
transformed to provide country house-style
accommodation. All the bedrooms have ensuite
facilities and colour television, and three rooms
are furnished with four-poster beds. Children
under ten are not accommodated.

LYMPSHAM   Avon   *Map 3 ST35*

★★ 🐑 **Batch Farm Country** BS24 0EX ☎ (0934) 650371
Closed Xmas

Normal price: £24. Dinner £9-£10 & à la carte
Short breaks: £33. Min 2 nights. £6 single supplement
🐾 Credit cards ① ② ③ ⑤

This small hotel is part of a working farm and is
only a short drive from Weston-super-Mare. All
bedrooms have private bathroom and colour
television and there are rooms for families and
non-smokers. Fishing, croquet and snooker are
available.

MIDSOMER NORTON   Avon   *Map 3 ST65*

★★★59% **Centurion** Charlton Lane BA3 4BD ☎ (0761) 417711

Normal price: £36.50. Dinner £13-£16 & à la carte (1990
price)
Short breaks: £26.50 (£42 for single room) excluding
dinner. Fri-Sat.
🐾 (ex guide dogs) Credit cards ① ② ③ ⑤

This sports club has a 9-hole golf course,
squash, heated indoor swimming pool, sauna
and snooker. The new and pleasant bedrooms
all have an ensuite bath and colour television.

OLD SODBURY   Avon   *Map 3 ST78*

QQ **Dornden** Church Lane BS17 6NB ☎ (0454) 313325

Normal price: £22.50
Short breaks: £20 excluding dinner. Min 2 nights at
weekend (excluding Badminton Horse Trials weekend) or
4 nights in week. (Prices approximate)

A former vicarage set in attractive gardens with
a tennis court, this traditionally furnished
guesthouse has spacious bedrooms, including
four family rooms, all with colour TV and half
with private bath or shower.

PETTY FRANCE   Avon   *Map 3 ST78*

★★★71% **Petty France** GL9 1AF (on A46 S of junc with A333) ☎ (045423)

Normal price: from £75 room. Dinner £16-£30.
Short breaks: from £96 room. Min 2 nights, Thu-Mon.
Activity breaks: Bridge Breaks, £120. Wine Tasting, £250.
Walking Breaks, £96. Shooting, £165. Riding Breaks, £115.
Details from hotel.
Credit cards ① ② ③ ⑤

The former dower house of the Beaufort estate
with its original character enhanced by good
pictures and occasional antiques. Not far from
Badminton.

RANGEWORTHY   Avon   Map 3 ST68

★★ ♠ 64% **Rangeworthy Court** (Exec Hotel) Church Lane, Wotton Road BS17 5ND
☎ (045422) 347 & 473

Normal price: £30-£34. Dinner £15-£17.50.
Short breaks: £35 weekend, £42 weekdays, Apr-May & Nov-Dec. £39 weekend, £46 weekdays, Jun-Oct. Min 2 nights. Single supplement weekends.
Activity breaks: Christmas & New Year Breaks, and Weekend with Box at Cheltenham. Details from hotel.

Dating from the 14th century, this former manor house is in a peaceful setting by the church. Personal attention is provided by the proprietors and their friendly staff.

REDHILL (nr Bristol)   Avon   Map 3 ST46

QQQ **Hailstones Farm** ES18 7JG ☎ (0934) 862209

Normal price: £15-£17.50
Short breaks: from £15 excluding dinner. Nov-Easter.
✗

This welcoming farmhouse with 150 acres of mixed farming land provides comfortable accommodation. The four bedrooms, all no-smoking, include two family rooms and have wash basins or private shower; colour TV is available.

THORNBURY   Avon   Map 3 ST69

★★★(Red) ♠ **Thornbury Castle** (Pride of Britain) BS12 1HH ☎ (0454) 418511
Closed 2-12 Jan

Normal price: £62-£90, single £80. Dinner £25-£29.
Short breaks: Normal rate for first night, 25% discount each extra night. Dinner must be taken in the hotel. Continental breakfast, bottle of champagne on arrival. Min 2 nights, Nov-2nd week Mar.
✗ Credit cards 1 2 3 4 5

Once owned by Henry VIII, this imposing 16th-century castle is now a welcoming and relaxing hotel offering a blend of modern comfort and historical interest. Each bedroom has a private bathroom and colour television and some are furnished with four-poster beds. There is a special Christmas programme. Children under twelve are not accommodated.

TORMARTON   Avon   Map 3 ST77

★★64% **Compass Inn** (Inter-Hotels) GL9 1JB ☎ (045421) 242 & 577

Normal price: £37.25. Dinner £13-£18.
Short breaks: £44.75, min 2 nights. Single supplement Mon-Thu.
Activity breaks: Hot Air Ballooning, Clay Pigeon Shooting and Riding Breaks. Details from hotel.
Credit cards 1 2 3 5

Old family-run inn offering modern facilities. See advertisement on p18.

WESTON-SUPER-MARE   Avon   Map 3 ST36

GH QQ **Baymead** Longton Grove Road BS23 1LS ☎ (0934) 622951

Normal price: £25.
Short breaks: £20, min 2 nights, Feb-Apr & Oct-Nov.
Activity breaks: Old Tyme Dancing, Theatre Visits, Rambling Breaks. Details from hotel.

This large, family-run hotel is close to amenities, and has a popular bar and upgraded bedrooms with modern facilities.

★★64% Beachlands 17 Uphill Road North BS23 4NG ☎ (0934) 621401

Normal price: £25.75. Dinner £9.75.
Short breaks: £29.75, min 2 nights, Oct-1 May.
Activity breaks: Learn to Play Golf, £245 (1990) for 6 nights
including tuition, green fees and club membership.
Credit cards ① ② ③ ⑤

A family-run hotel overlooking the golf course, with particularly friendly, attentive service.

★★60% Berni Royal (Berni/Chef & Brewer) South Parade BS23 1JN ☎ (0934) 623601

Normal price: £35. Dinner £8-£15 à la carte
Short breaks: £27.50 excluding dinner. Min 2 nights
weekends, 3 nights midweek
✖ (ex guide dogs) Credit cards ① ② ③ ⑤

Situated close to the Promenade, this Victorian hotel has been modernised and provides ensuite bedrooms with colour television, popular bars and a grill restaurant.

★★★60% Commodore (Exec Hotel) Beach Road, Sand Bay, Kewstoke BS22 9UZ ☎ (0934) 415778

Normal price: £41 including dinner
Short breaks: £36.50, min 2 nights; £30 min 3 nights. Single
£49.25 min 2 nights; £38.17 min 3 nights. Fri-Sun
✖ (ex guide dogs) Credit cards ① ② ③ ⑤

A modern hotel on the sands at Kewstoke, two miles from the town centre, offering a good choice of imaginative food and well-equipped bedrooms with ensuite facilities and colour television. There are special facilities for children.

★★★65% Grand Atlantic (Trusthouse Forte) Beach Road BS23 1BA ☎ (0934) 626543

Normal price: £48. Dinner from £11.50 & à la carte
Short breaks: £40, £10 single supplement (subject to
review). Min 2 nights
Credit cards ① ② ③ ④ ⑤

A large seafront hotel with comfortable ensuite bedrooms with colour television. Some enjoy impressive sea views and others are for non-smokers. There are special facilities for children. Christmas breaks are available.

GH QQQ Wychwood 148 Milton Road BS23 2UZ ☎ (0934) 27793

Normal price: £19.
Short breaks: £18 excluding dinner. Min 3 nights

Some of the bedrooms at this friendly hotel have ensuite facilities, and all have colour television. There is an outdoor heated pool.

▪ BEDFORDSHIRE ▪

BEDFORD   Bedfordshire   Map 4 TL04

★★★64% Barns (Lansbury) Cardington Road, Fenlake MK44 3SA ☎ (0234) 270044

Normal price: £41. Dinner from £15 and à la carte
Short breaks: £32 excluding dinner. Fri-Sun
✖ (ex guide dogs) Credit cards ① ② ③ ⑤

This hotel offers rooms with private facilities and colour television. Leisure amenities include fishing, sauna, solarium and gymnasium. The hotel has a special Christmas programme.

★★★78% Woodlands Manor Green Lane, Clapham MK41 6EP (2m N A6) ☎ (0234) 363281

Normal price: £50. Dinner £21 & à la carte
Short breaks: £45, min 2 nights, Fri-Sun and Bank Holiday
Monday.
✖

A privately-run Victorian manor house set in wooded grounds and gardens, with an elegant restaurant. All of the bedrooms have ensuite bathroom or shower and colour television. Children under seven are not accommodated.

LEIGHTON BUZZARD Bedfordshire   Map 4 SP92

★★★71% **Swan** High Street LU7 7EA ☎ (0525) 372148

Normal price: £59.50 including dinner.
Short breaks: £37.50, min 2 nights, Fri-Sun.
Activity breaks: Off Road Motor Sports, including Rally Cars, Quad Bikes, Racing Karts, Trial Cars, 4-Wheel Drive Trials and Hovercraft Flying. From £85 (1990). Details from hotel.
✶ (ex guide dogs) Credit cards ① ② ③ ⑤

High standards of service from helpful, willing staff and a relaxing, friendly atmosphere are attractive features of this comfortable Georgian coaching inn.

LUTON Bedfordshire   Map 4 TL02

★★★69% **Strathmore Thistle** (Mount Charlotte (TS)) Arndale Centre LU1 2TR ☎ (0582) 34199

Normal price: £49.75. Dinner from £16 & à la carte
Short breaks: £44 excluding dinner. No single supplement at weekends
✶

This hotel has an attractive restaurant, and a coffee shop which serves less expensive meals. Bedrooms are ensuite with colour television, with some rooms set aside for non-smokers.

■ BERKSHIRE ■

ASCOT Berkshire   Map 4 SU96

★★★★50% **Berystede** (Trusthouse Forte) Bagshot Road, Sunninghill SL5 9JH ☎ (0990) 23311 code due to change to (0344)

Normal price: £60. Dinner from £19.
Short breaks: £57. Min 2 nights, Fri, Sat and Sun.
Activity breaks: Arts & Antiques Break, £146.
Credit cards ① ② ③ ④ ⑤

A popular hotel with both conference and private guests, set in attractive grounds. Bedrooms continue to be upgraded.

GH QQ Highclere Kings Road, Sunninghill SL5 9AD ☎ (0990) 25220 code due to change to (0344)
Restricted service 24 Dec-2 Jan

Normal price: £36
Short breaks: £23, Fri-Sun
Credit cards ① ③

This friendly hotel has eleven bedrooms, most equipped with private showers and there are two rooms for families. All bedrooms have colour television. The hotel has its own putting green.

★★★★56% **Royal Berkshire** (Hilton) London Road, Sunninghill SL5 0PP ☎ (0990) 23322 code due to change to (0334)

Normal price: £80 and £85. Dinner from £23.50.
Short breaks: £57, excluding dinner. Min 2 nights incl Sat. Champagne Weekend, £80 incl champagne on arrival.
Activity breaks: Tennis Coaching, £167 (1990 price).

A large conference-orientated hotel set in several acres of quiet grounds, offering leisure facilities, a formal dining room and a choice of accommodation.

CROWTHORNE Berkshire   Map 4 SU86

★★★55% **Waterloo** (Trusthouse Forte) Duke's Ride RG11 7NW ☎(0344) 777711

Normal price: £44.50 room. Dinner £13.95 & à la carte
Short breaks: £40, single £95. Min 2 nights, Thu-Sun.
All prices subject to review.
Credit cards ① ② ③ ④ ⑤

This hotel provides modern facilities and friendly service. All the bedrooms have ensuite facilities and colour television, some rooms are for non-smokers and one room has a four-poster bed. There is a special Christmas programme.

DATCHET Berkshire Map 4 SU97

★★52% **Manor** (Consort) The Village Green SL3 9EA ☎ (0753) 43442

Normal price: £44.50 room. Dinner £16 & à la carte
Short breaks: £49. Fri-Sun (excluding Christmas)
Credit cards ⊡ ② ③ ⑤

Overlooking the village green and next to the railway station, this hotel has two bars and a restaurant. Bedrooms are equipped with modern facilities, all are ensuite with colour television and one has a four-poster bed. There is a special Christmas programme.

ELCOT Berkshire Map 4 SU36

★★★65% **Elcot Park Resort** (Best Western) RG16 8NJ (1m N off A4) ☎ (0488) 58100

Normal price: £54 including dinner (1990).
Short breaks: £52, min 2 nights, Fri-Sun (1990).
Activity breaks: Murder & Mayhem Weekends. Break the Bank Weekends with roulette and blackjack. Gourmet Evenings, and Bastille Day dinner. Details from hotel.
Credit cards ⊡ ② ③ ⑤

Dating back to 1678, this smart hotel sits within 16 acres of grounds, and offers good views of the surrounding countryside. Interesting menus and fine wines.

HUNGERFORD Berkshire Map 4 SU36

★★★64% **Bear** Charnham Street RG17 0EL ☎ (0488) 682512

Normal price: £44. Dinner from £17.95
Short breaks: £32 excluding dinner. 1990 prices.

This charming hotel has open fires, antiques and exposed beams. The popular restaurant provides a good choice of menus whilst bedrooms are well equipped with modern facilities. There is a special Christmas programme.

HURLEY Berkshire Map 4 SU88

★★★63% **Ye Olde Bell** SL6 5LX ☎ (0628) 825881

Normal price: £49. Dinner from £17.50
Short breaks: £32 excluding dinner (subject to review). Min 2 nights, Fri-Sun
Credit cards ⊡ ② ③ ⑤

This ancient inn traces its history back to 1136 and has retained much of its original character. Bedrooms are comfortable with ensuite facilities and colour television and there is a special Christmas programme.

PANGBOURNE Berkshire Map 4 SU67

★★★72% **Copper Inn** Church Road RG8 7AR ☎ (07357) 2244

Normal price: £47
Short breaks: £42. Min 2 nights, Fri-Sun.
Credit cards ⊡ ② ③ ⑤

This small, welcoming hotel has an attractive bar serving real ale and a restaurant featuring fresh local produce. The elegant bedrooms, including a family room and one with a four-poster bed, all have private bathrooms and colour TV.

READING Berkshire Map 4 SU77

★★★★63% **Caversham** (Queens Moat) Caversham Bridge, Richfield Avenue RG1 8BD ☎ (0734) 391818

Normal price: £60.50. Dinner £18.
Short breaks: £40 excluding dinner. Min 2 nights, Fri-Sun.
Activity breaks: Murder/Mystery Weekends, £165 Mar-Nov. Includes light lunch and full Sun lunch. War and Peace Weekends, £132 Jun-Oct. Paintball games at Mapledurham House, including coffee and lunch. Tour of Shire Horse Centre, cruise to Mapledurham House, visit to The Herb Gardens, wine-tasting and lunch. Taste of England Weekend, £145 May, Jul & Sept. Boating Weekend, £110 Apr-Sept. Either join a leisurely cruise or hire a boat. Luxury hamper provided. All prices 1990.
Credit cards 1 2 3 5

Situated on the banks of the Thames, this hotel offers compact, well-equipped bedrooms, spacious open-plan public rooms, a bright, conservatory-style restaurant serving interesting meals, and good leisure facilities.

★★60% **George** (Berni/Chef & Brewer) King Street RG1 2HE ☎ (0734) 573445

Normal price: £35
Short breaks: £25.50 excluding dinner. Min 2 nights, Fri-Sun.
🏠 (ex guide dogs) Credit cards 1 2 3 5

All bedrooms in this hospitable hotel have private bathrooms and colour TV, and include a couple of family rooms.

QQ **Thames House** 18/19 Thameside RG1 8DR ☎ (0734) 507951

Normal price: £24
Short breaks: £18 excluding dinner. Min 2 nights.
🏠 Credit cards 1 3

Overlooking the river, this peaceful guesthouse formed from two houses made into one provides well-equipped accommodation, with colour TV in all bedrooms, most having private shower and including two family rooms.

SLOUGH Berkshire Map 4 SU97

★★★★64% **Holiday Inn** Ditton Road SL3 8PT ☎ (0753) 44244

Normal price: £63.50. Dinner £17 and à la carte.
Short breaks: £41. Min 2 nights, Fri-Sun. £14 single supplement.
Credit cards 1 2 3 5

A modern hotel conveniently located for the M4 and London. Facilities include large conference rooms, a leisure club and an à la carte restaurant. Lounge service for drinks is enhanced by live music in the evenings. A wide selection of recreational facilities is also available.

STREATLEY Berkshire Map 4 SU58

★★★73% **Swan Diplomat** High Street RG8 9HR ☎ (0491) 873737

Normal price: £62.50. Dinner £19.50-£21.50
Short breaks: from £69.57, single £125. Min 2 nights, Fri-Sun

This tastefully renovated hotel offers spacious bedrooms which are individually decorated and enjoy hill or river views. Other facilities include the riverside restaurant, a boathouse bar and leisure complex. Christmas breaks are available.

THATCHAM Berkshire *Map 4 SU56*

★★★★63% **Regency Park** Bowling Green Road RG13 3RP ☎ (0635) 71555

Normal price: £49.50. Dinner £16.95 & à la carte
Short breaks: £49.50. Min 2 nights, Fri-Sun (excluding Xmas)

This hotel has been extended and refurbished to a high standard. Bedrooms are spacious and well equipped and the attractive modern restaurant features a choice of menus. There are special facilities for children and Christmas breaks are available.

WINDSOR Berkshire *Map 4 SU97*

★★52% **Aurora Garden** 14 Bolton Avenue SL4 3JF ☎ (0753) 868686

Normal price: £37.50. Dinner £16.50-18
Short breaks: £44, single £54. Min 2 nights, Fri-Sun

Situated in a quiet tree-lined avenue only a short distance from the town centre, this hotel offers attractive, comfortable ensuite bedrooms and a cosy bar/lounge area. There is a special Christmas programme.

★★★65% **The Castle** (Trusthouse Forte) High Street SL4 1LJ ☎ (0753) 851011

Normal price: £57.60. Dinner from £18 & à la carte
Short breaks: £60. Min 2 nights, Thu-Sun
Credit cards [1] [2] [3] [4] [5]

This elegant hotel has a Georgian frontage with wrought iron balconies. Large bedrooms, tastefully and comfortably furnished provide all modern amenities. Christmas breaks are available.

★★59% **Ye Harte & Garter** (Berni/Chef & Brewer) High Street SL4 1PH ☎ (0753) 863426

Normal price: £40. Dinner £8-£15 à la carte
Short breaks: £27.50 excluding dinner. Min 2 nights, Fri-Sun
(ex guide dogs) Credit cards [1] [2] [3] [5]

This inn overlooks Windsor Castle and has two restaurants and comfortable bedrooms equipped with modern facilities. There is no parking on the premises.

★★★★73% **Oakley Court** (Queens Moat) (Prestige) Windsor Road, Water Oakley SL4 5UR (2m W A308) ☎ (0628) 74141

Normal price: £74. Dinner from £27.50 & à la carte
Short breaks: £80. £30 single supplement. Min 2 nights. Not available July and August.
Credit cards [1] [2] [3] [5]

A splendid mansion set in landscaped gardens on the banks of the River Thames offers accommodation in the main house and modern Garden and River Wings. There are leisure facilities, and Christmas breaks are available.

★★63% **Royal Adelaide** 46 Kings Road SL4 2AG ☎ (0753) 863916

Normal price: £40. Dinner from £12.75 & à la carte
Short breaks: £35. Min 2 nights, Fri-Sun
Credit cards [1] [2] [3] [5]

Overlooking the Long Walk which runs from the Castle, this Georgian hotel has ensuite bedrooms with colour television and offers special Christmas breaks.

WOKINGHAM Berkshire *Map 4 SU86*

★★60% **Cantley House** Milton Road, RG11 5QG ☎ (0734) 789912

Normal price: £37. Dinner £10-£20 & à la carte
Short breaks: £40 includes £15 dinner allowance. Single £50. Min 2 nights, Fri-Sun

A peaceful, relaxed hotel set in picturesque parkland retaining much of its Victorian character. All the bedrooms have private bathroom and colour television, there is a choice of restaurants, and some leisure facilities are available.

★★★★52% **Reading Moat House** (Queens Moat) Mill Lane, Sindlesham RG11 5DF ☎ (0734) 351035

Normal price: £62. Dinner from £20
Short breaks: £42.50. Min 2 nights, Fri-Sun
Credit cards ① ② ③ ⑤

This modern hotel has ensuite bedrooms, a restaurant, coffee shop and leisure centre among its many facilities.

YATTENDON Berkshire Map 4 SU57

★★65% **Royal Oak** The Square RG16 0UF ☎ (0635) 201325

Normal price: £40. Dinner from £25
Short breaks: £50, includes £15 dinner allowance, champagne with breakfast, newspapers and early morning tea. Min 2 nights, Fri-Sun
Credit cards ① ② ③

An appealing 16th-century inn provides accommodation in charming bedrooms which are individually decorated and furnished. Good food is served in the small restaurant and the lively, popular bar.

▒ BUCKINGHAMSHIRE ▒

AMERSHAM Buckinghamshire Map 4 SU99

★★62% **Crown** (Trusthouse Forte) High Street HP7 0DH ☎ (0494) 721541

Normal price: £45 (room). Dinner £14-£16.95 and à la carte
Short breaks: £42. Min 2 nights, Thu-Sun
Credit cards ① ② ③ ④ ⑤

This Elizabethan inn with a handsome Georgian facade offers a varied menu of good, imaginative cooking. Over half of the bedrooms have private facilities, all have colour television. There is a special Christmas programme.

AYLESBURY Buckinghamshire Map 4 SP81

★★★★73% **Forte** (Trusthouse Forte) Aston Clinton Road HP22 5AA ☎ (0296) 393388

Normal price: £60
Short breaks: from £45. Min 2 nights, Thurs-Sun
Credit cards ① ② ③ ④ ⑤

A modern, comfortable hotel with an indoor heated swimming pool, sauna, solarium and gymnasium. All the bedrooms have ensuite facilities and colour television and some rooms are set aside for families and non-smokers.

★★★(Red) ⚜ **Hartwell House** (Prestige) Oxford Road HP17 8NL ☎ (0296) 747444

Normal price: from £79.50. Dinner £29.50.
Short breaks: from £100, including bottle of champagne. Nov-Apr. Single price from £105.
Activity breaks: Historic House Summer Breaks, fr £100 per night, May-26 October, Sun-Thurs. Includes entry to house of choice – Blenheim Palace, Woburn Abbey, Waddesdon Manor or Claydon House – and early morning tea.
✱ Credit cards ① ② ③ ⑤

An elegant Grade I listed country house with a history dating back to the 16th century. Decor and furnishings throughout are in keeping with the distinguished history of the house.

BEACONSFIELD   Buckinghamshire   Map 4 SU99

★★★56% **Bellhouse** (De Vere) Oxford Road HP9 2XE ☎ (0753) 887211

Normal price: £60. Dinner £17.50.
Short breaks: £45 excluding dinner. Min 2 nights.
Activity breaks: Murder/Mystery Weekend, £150 for three
nights. (1990). Details from hotel.
Credit cards ① ② ③ ④ ⑤

Busy commercial hotel with good business and
conference facilities and comfortable accommodation. Varied menus in the bright modern
bistro and main restaurant.

BURNHAM   Buckinghamshire   Map 4 SU98

★★★67% **Burnham Beeches Moat House** (Queens Moat) Grove Road SL1 8DP ☎ (0628) 603333

Normal price: £45.50-£47.50
Short breaks: £48. Min 2 nights, Fri-Sun
Credit cards ① ② ③ ④ ⑤

Surrounded by 600 acres of forest and parkland
is this former hunting lodge with excellent
leisure facilities including a heated indoor
swimming pool, tennis and a gymnasium. All
the bedrooms have private bathrooms and
colour television, two rooms have four-poster
beds and there are rooms for non-smokers.
Special Christmas programme.

CHENIES   Buckinghamshire   Map 4 TQ09

★★★62% **Bedford Arms Thistle** (Mount Charlotte (TS)) WD3 6EQ ☎ (09278) 3301

Normal price: £47.90. Dinner from £15 à la carte
Short breaks: £42 excluding dinner. No single supplement
at weekends
Credit cards ① ② ③ ④ ⑤

An attractive country hotel in a small peaceful
village, offering good hospitality. There are ten
bedrooms each with private facilities and colour
television, some for families and non-smokers.

GERRARDS CROSS   Buckinghamshire   Map 4 TQ08

★★64% **Ethorpe** (Berni/Chef & Brewer) Packhorse Road SL9 8HY ☎ (0753) 882039

Normal price: £42. Dinner £8-£15 à la carte
Short breaks: £27.50 excluding dinner. Min 2 nights,
Fri-Sun
🦮 (ex guide dogs) Credit cards ① ② ③ ⑤

The bedrooms at this friendly hotel are
comfortable and spacious with co-ordinating
soft furnishings and fabrics, ensuite facilities
and colour television. There are family rooms
and one room has a four-poster bed.

MARLOW   Buckinghamshire   Map 4 SU88

★★★★73% **Compleat Angler** (Trusthouse Forte) Marlow Bridge SL7 1RG ☎ (06284) 4444 due to change
to (0628) 484444

Normal price: £82.50. Dinner £30-£50.
Short breaks: £80, min 2 nights, Fri-Sun. Nov-Mar & Aug.
Single supplement.
Activity breaks: Gourmet Breaks, £250 for 2 nights. Apr &
Nov 1991 & Mar 1992.
Credit cards ① ② ③ ④ ⑤

Ideally situated on the Thames and set in its
own lovely gardens, the hotel offers a relaxing
atmosphere and willing helpful service.

NEWPORT PAGNELL Buckinghamshire Map 4 SP84

★★ **Swan Revived** High Street MK16 8AR ☎ (0908) 610565

Normal price: £30
Short breaks: £19 (£25 for single room) excluding dinner.
Fri or Sat only.
Credit cards ①②③⑤

Nearly all bedrooms in this friendly 15th-century coaching inn have private shower or bath, one with a four-poster bed and all with colour TV.

SAUNDERTON Buckinghamshire Map 4 SP70

★★62% **Rose & Crown** Wycombe Road, Aylesbury HP17 9NP ☎ (08444) 5299 & 2241

Normal price: £47.75, includes dinner (£15-£18.50)
Short breaks: £37.75. Min 2 nights, Thur-Sun.
🕭 Credit cards ①②③⑤

A privately-owned hotel with a warm, friendly atmosphere offering comfortable and well-equipped, though compact, bedrooms. The menus are interesting, specialising in fresh fish, and good bar meals are available.

WOOBURN COMMON Buckinghamshire Map 4 SU98

★★63% **Chequers Inn** Kiln Lane HP10 0JQ (1m W unclass towards Bourne End) ☎ (06285) 29575

Normal price: £35. Dinner from £16 (1990 prices)
Short breaks: £82 for 2 nights. Fri-Sun
🕭 (ex guide dogs) Credit cards ①②③

This busy 17th-century inn has been thoughtfully modernised to provide comfortable en-suite accommodation. Service is friendly and helpful.

▦ CAMBRIDGESHIRE ▦

ALCONBURY Cambridgeshire Map 4 TL17

★★64% **Alconbury House** Alconbury Weston PE17 5JG ☎ (0480) 890807

Normal price: £30. Dinner from £10.50.
Short breaks: £29, min 2 nights, Fri-Sun, except Xmas.
Single supplement.
Activity breaks: Antiques weekend, £85. Birdwatching weekend, £65. Squash, £70. Details from hotel.
Credit cards ①②③⑤

An attractive Georgian house set in its own grounds, with attentive staff and a good range of dishes served in both the bar and restaurant.

BARHILL Cambridgeshire Map 4 TL36

★★★61% **Cambridgeshire Moat House** CB3 8EU ☎ (0954) 780555

Normal price: £40.
Short breaks: £49, includes morning paper. Single supplement of £10.
Activity breaks: Golf break, £45. Tuition, club and buggie hire are all extra.
Credit cards ①②③⑤

Convenient for the city centre, this comfortable hotel offers a very comprehensive range of leisure facilities, including squash courts, swimming pool and an 18-hole championship golf course.

BUCKDEN   Cambridgeshire   Map 4 TL16

★★★62% **George** High Street PE18 9XA ☎ (0480) 810307
Normal price: £40.
Short breaks: £50. Min 2 nights, Fri-Sun
🦮 Credit cards ①②③④⑤

According to legend, Dick Turpin stayed at this 16th-century former coaching inn beside the old Great North Road. Today's travellers will find sixteen bedrooms all with ensuite facilities and colour television, one family room and one with a four-poster bed.

CAMBRIDGE   Cambridgeshire   Map 5 TL45

★★67% **Arundel House** 53 Chesterton Road CB4 3AN ☎ (0223) 67701
Closed 25-26 Dec
Normal price: £32.50. Dinner £11.50 & à la carte
Short breaks: £39.75. Single supplement £9. Min 2 nights, Thu-Sun
Credit cards ①②③⑤

Situated on the edge of Jesus Green and close to the city centre, this hotel offers well-prepared food in the bar and restaurant. All of the bedrooms have colour television, most have ensuite facilities.

★★★61% **Gonville** Gonville Place CB1 1LY ☎ (0223) 66611
Closed 4 days at Xmas
Normal price: £38.50. Dinner £9.75
Short breaks: £40, including dinner allowance of £9.75 and lunch. Min 2 nights, Thu-Sun
Credit cards ①②③④

Located in the city centre, overlooking Parkers Piece, this hotel has spotless ensuite bedrooms with colour television. There are some family rooms.

★★★★55% **Garden House** (Queens Moat) Granta Place, Mill Lane CB2 1RT ☎ (0223) 63421
Normal price: £56. Dinner £18.50-£29.50 & à la carte
Short breaks: £65, including £18.50 dinner allowance. £17.50 single supplement. Min 2 nights, Thu-Mon (excluding Xmas)
🦮 (ex guide dogs)

Approached via Trumpington Street, this modern-style hotel is set in attractive gardens on the River Cam. The ensuite bedrooms are spacious and comfortable, and all have colour television. Some rooms are set aside for non-smokers and families. There is a special Christmas programme.

★★★★55% **Post House** (Trusthouse Forte) Lakeview, Bridge Road, Impington CB4 4PH (2¹/₂m N, on N side of rdbt jct A45/B1049) ☎ (0223) 237000

Normal price: £60.50. Dinner from £16.50 & à la carte
Short breaks: £57 including £16.50 dinner allowance. £5 single supplement. Min 2 nights, must include Saturday
Credit cards ①②③④⑤

All the bedrooms here have ensuite facilities and colour television, with some rooms set aside for families and non-smokers. The hotel has a health and leisure club. There is a special Christmas programme.

★★★★55% **University Arms** (De Vere) Regent Street CB2 1AD ☎ (0223) 351241

Normal price: £45. Dinner from £15.
Short breaks: £46, min 2 nights, Fri-Sun.
Activity breaks: Painting in Watercolours, £104. Antique Appreciation, £160. Details from hotel.
Credit cards ①②③⑤

All the unique features of this famous city centre hotel have been carefully preserved, though the bedrooms have been refurbished and the entrance re-styled.

ELY   Cambridgeshire   Map 5 TL58

★★66% **Lamb** (Queens Moat) 2 Lynn Road CB7 4EJ ☎ (0353) 663574

Normal price: £34. Dinner from £12
Short breaks: £35. Min 2 nights
Credit cards ①②③⑤

Located on a busy central road junction The Lamb offers a choice of bars as well as a restaurant and buttery. Bedrooms are comfortable and well-equipped with ensuite facilities and colour television. There is a special Christmas programme.

HUNTINGDON   Cambridgeshire   Map 4 TL27

★★★61% **George** (Trusthouse Forte) George Street PE18 6AB ☎ (0480) 432444

Normal price: £51.50. Dinner from £15 & à la carte
Short breaks: £46. Min 2 nights, Fri-Sun
Credit cards ①②③④⑤

Parts of this hotel date back to early Stuart times, but modern facilities can be found in all the bedrooms. Chaucer's Restaurant features some traditional English dishes. There is a special Christmas programme.

PETERBOROUGH   Cambridgeshire   Map 4 TL19

★★★56% **Bull** Westgate PE1 1RB ☎ (0733) 61364

Normal price: £39. Dinner from £10.50 & à la carte (1990 price)
Short breaks: Superbreak: £39.50 inc £10.45 dinner allowance. Fri-Sun.
Credit cards ①②③⑤

Behind the 17th-century facade of this former coaching inn is an extensively modernised, quite large hotel, with well-equipped bedrooms all with en suite facilities and colour TV, and including a few family rooms.

★★★65% **Butterfly** (Butterfly) Thorpe Meadows, off Longthorpe Parkway PE3 6GA ☎ (0733) 64240

Normal price: from £35
Short breaks: £35 inc set-price dinner or £11 dinner allowance, Fri-Sun. £15 single supplement. Fri-Sun.
Credit cards ①②③⑤

At the water's edge on Thorpe Meadows, this newly opened modern coaching inn offers comfortable accommodation with fully equipped en suite bedrooms.

★★★66% **Peterborough Moat House** (Queens Moat) Thorpe Wood PE3 6SG ☎ (0733) 260000

Normal price: £59. Dinner £11.95 & à la carte (1990 price)
Short breaks: £37. Min 2 nights, Fri-Sun.
Credit cards ① ② ③ ⑤

On the west side of the city by a golf course, this modern purpose-built hotel has fully equipped en suite bedrooms with colour TV, some non-smoking, and a leisure centre with indoor swimming pool, sauna, solarium, gymnasium, jacuzzi and spa pool.

ST IVES   Cambridgeshire   Map 4 TL37

★★★62% **Dolphin** Bridge Foot, London Road PE17 4EP ☎ (0480) 66966

Normal price: £29. Dinner £11.50 & à la carte.
Short breaks: £36.50. Min 2 nights, Fri-Mon.
Credit cards ① ② ③ ⑤

A modern, purpose-built hotel in the town centre with views of the nearby river and surrounding countryside.

★★64% **St Ives Motel** London Road PE17 4EX ☎ (0480) 63857

Normal price: £27.50. Dinner £10.50 & à la carte.
Short breaks: £30. Min 2 nights, Fri-Sun.
Credit cards ① ② ③ ⑤

Easily located, this small roadside hotel has been extended to create a restaurant and bar with two blocks of bedrooms at the rear. Popular with business people and locals for good value meals.

★★★62% **Slepe Hall** Romsey Road PE17 4RB ☎ (0480) 63122

Normal price: £33.75. Dinner from £11.95 & à la carte.
Short breaks: £30, min 2 nights, Fri-Sun.
Credit cards ① ② ③ ⑤

A small, comfortable hotel set back from the main road.

SIX MILE BOTTOM   Cambridgeshire   Map 5 TL55

★★★74% **Swynford Paddocks** Newmarket CB8 0UE ☎ (063870) 234

Normal price: £45. Dinner from £18.50 & à la carte.
Short breaks: £55-£60 (1990 prices), min 2 nights, Fri-Sun & Bank Hol Mons.
Credit cards ① ② ③ ⑤

A former country mansion set amidst well-maintained gardens, with race horses grazing in its pastures. The house has been carefully restored, and the individually styled bedrooms are furnished to a high standard. The à la carte menu is imaginative and based on fresh produce, and there is a good selection of recreational facilities.

WANSFORD   Cambridgeshire   Map 4 TL09

★★76% **Haycock** PE8 6JA ☎ (0780) 782223

Normal price: £40-£60
Short breaks: £85 for 2 nights includes à la carte dinner on 1 evening. Thu-Mon
Credit cards ① ② ③ ⑤

A 17th-century riverside coaching inn offering comfortable ensuite bedrooms which are tastefully furnished. Freshly prepared dishes are served in the restaurant and buttery. Fishing is available and there is a special Christmas break.

WISBECH   Cambridgeshire   Map 5 TF40

★★55% **White Lion** 5 South Brink, PE13 1JO ☎ (0945) 584813

Normal price: £27.50. Dinner £9.50-£10.50 & à la carte
Short breaks: £34. Min 2 nights, £28 for 3rd night. Fri-Sun.
Single supplement £8.50.
Credit cards ① ② ③ ⑤

Situated close to the town centre and River Nene, this coaching inn has two bars and offers good parking facilities. All the bedrooms have colour television and most are ensuite.

■ CHESHIRE ■

BUCKLOW HILL   Cheshire   Map 7 SJ78

★★★61% **Swan** (De Vere) WA16 6RD ☎ (0565) 830295

Normal price: £41. Dinner £13.75 and à la carte
Short breaks: £35. Min 2 nights
Credit cards ① ② ③ ⑤

The public areas of this historic hotel are situated in the main building, and the bedrooms are in an adjoining stable block. All rooms have ensuite bath or shower rooms and colour television, with rooms for families and non-smokers. Three rooms are furnished with four-poster beds.

CHESTER   Cheshire   Map 7 SJ46

★★★61% **Abbots Well** (Embassy) Whitchurch Road, Christleton CH3 5QL ☎ (0244) 332121

Normal price: from £93 room only. Dinner £13.75 & à la carte
Short breaks: £40. Min 2 nights. Single £40 weekends only
Credit cards ① ② ③ ⑤

A modern hotel in spacious grounds beside the southern by-pass, with a well-equipped leisure centre. All bedrooms are ensuite with colour television, with rooms for families and non-smokers. A Christmas programme is provided.

★★★61% **Blossoms** (Trusthouse Forte) St John Street CH1 1HL ☎ (0244) 323186

Normal price: £56 room. Dinner from £13.95 & à la carte
Short breaks: £50. Min 2 nights
Credit cards ① ② ③ ⑤

This original coaching house made of timber and brick dates back to the 17th century. Situated in the city centre it offers bedrooms which have been well furnished and decorated to a high standard, all with ensuite facilities and colour television. Some rooms are for non-smokers and one has a four-poster bed. There is a special Christmas programme.

GH QQQ Brookside 12 Brook Lane CH2 2AN ☎ (0244) 381943
Closed Xmas week

Normal price: £23.50
Short breaks: £53 weekend. Min 2 nights, £58 midweek.
Min 2 nights
Credit cards ① ③

A large well-furnished hotel with an attractive restaurant and Victorian-style lounges. Bedrooms are well equipped and have ensuite facilities and colour television. The hotel has a gymnasium, sauna and solarium.

❀★★★★(Red) **Chester Grosvenor** (Prestige) Eastgate Street CH1 1LT ☎ (0244) 324024

Normal price: £82.50 room only. Dinner from £17
Short breaks: £65 excluding dinner. £40 single supplement.
Min 2 nights, Fri-Sun
🦮 (ex guide dogs) Credit cards ① ② ③ ④ ⑤

Situated in the centre of this beautiful and historic city this impressive half-timbered hotel offers luxurious accommodation and gourmet menus. All bedrooms have private facilities and colour television, and the hotel has its own gymnasium. No parking.

★★★★71% **Chester International** (Queens Moat) Trinity Street CH1 2BD ☎ (0244) 322330

Normal price: £67.50. Dinner £17-£21 and à la carte
Short breaks: £55. Min 2 nights, Fri-Sun

A large, elegant, modern hotel overlooking the renowned Roodee racecourse. Standards of service and hospitality have been described as exemplary. All rooms have ensuite facilities and colour television, with some rooms set aside for non-smokers. There is a good range of leisure amenities, and a special programme is provided at Christmas.

★★62% **Dene** Hoole Road CH2 3ND ☎ (0244) 321165

Normal price: £23-£24. Dinner £7-£8 and à la carte
Short breaks: £27.50 including £7 dinner allowance. Single £38. Min 2 nights.

Standing in its own grounds on the A56 this hotel offers neat accommodation in the main house and the motel block. All rooms have ensuite facilities and colour television. See advertisement on p35.

**Higher Burwardsley,
Tattenhall, Cheshire
Telephone: (0829) 70434**

The Pheasant is a three hundred year old Inn, nestling on top of the Peckforton Hills just 10 miles from Chester. All bedrooms have central heating, colour TV, radio/alarm and en suite facilities plus panoramic views over the Cheshire plain. Bistro and bar snack menu available 7 days. Fully licensed. Large car park. An ideal centre for touring Cheshire. Under personal management.

Rowton Hall Hotel ★ ★ ★

Whitchurch Road, Rowton, Chester, CH3 6AD

Telephone: Chester (0244) 335262   Telex: 61172 Rowtel   Facsimile: (0244) 335464

A country house hotel with beautiful gardens, set in 8 acres of grounds two miles outside Chester. 42 Bedrooms en suite, hospitality trays, colour TV, telephone, trouser press.
Indoor swimming pool, sauna, steam room, multi gym.
Conference and banqueting facilities (Max 160)
A la carte restaurant and bar open to non residents.

GH Q Eaton 29 City Road CH1 3AE ☎ (0244) 320840

Normal price: £21-£23.50. Dinner £8.95
Short breaks: £27.50-£30, single £34-£39. Min 2 nights

Situated alongside the Shropshire Union Canal and close to the main railway station, this hotel has well-equipped bedrooms, most with ensuite facilities.

GH QQ Eversley 9 Eversley Park CH2 2AJ ☎ (0244) 373744

Normal price: £21.
Short breaks: £50 for 2 nights
✈ Credit cards [1]

Set in a residential area about a mile from the city centre this hotel provides comfortable bedrooms with colour television, most with private facilities.

★★65% **Green Bough** 60 Hoole Road CH2 3NL ☎ (0244) 326241

Normal price: £23.50. Dinner £9-£10
Short breaks: £31. Min 2 nights.
Credit cards [1] [3]

A warm and friendly hotel in a main road position, about a mile from the city centre. Accommodation is delightfully furnished with a good range of facilities. All rooms have ensuite facilities and colour television, and there are family rooms.

★★★64% **Hoole Hall** (Crown & Raven) Warrington Road, Hoole Village CH2 3PD ☎ (0244) 32051

Normal price: £48.25. Dinner from £14.50 & à la carte
Short breaks: £40. £10 single supplement. Min 2 nights, Fri-Sun
Credit cards [1] [2] [3]

An impressive Georgian and Victorian mansion set in five acres of parkland, two miles from the city centre. All bedrooms are ensuite with colour television and some rooms are for non-smokers. There is a special Christmas programme.

★★★65% **Mollington Banastre** (Best Western) Parkgate Road CH1 6NN (A540) ☎ (0244) 851471

Normal price: £44.50-£47.50. Dinner from £16 & à la carte
Short breaks: £49-£54, including £16 dinner allowance. Min 2 nights
Credit cards [1] [2] [3] [5]

Modern extensions have been added to the original house, and there is a leisure complex and a pub called the Good Intent. All bedrooms are ensuite with colour television, with some rooms for non-smokers. There is a special Christmas programme.

★★★58% **Plantation Inn** Liverpool Road CH2 1AG ☎ (0244) 374100

Normal price: £45-£50.50. Dinner £11.50-£13.50 & à la carte
Short breaks: £44. Min 2 nights, Fri-Sun (ex Christmas/ New Year)

Situated within walking distance of the city centre this hotel serves international cuisine in the colourful Coral Reef Restaurant and there is dancing several evenings a week. All rooms have ensuite facilities and colour television. There is a special Christmas programme.

★★★60% **Rowton Hall** (Consort) Whitchurch Road, Rowton CH3 6AD (2m SE A41) ☎ (0244) 335262
Closed 25-26 Dec

Normal price: £43 (1990 prices). Dinner from £12.50 & à la carte
Short breaks: £49 (1990 prices). Min 2 nights, Fri-Sun

Improvements are continually being made at this one-time Georgian country house which has a smart new leisure complex. All bedrooms are ensuite with colour television, and some are furnished with four-poster beds.

DARESBURY Cheshire Map 7 SJ58

★★★67% **Lord Daresbury** (De Vere) Chester Road WA4 4BB ☎ (0925) 67331

Normal price: from £49.50. Dinner £16 & à la carte
Short breaks: £100 for 2 nights. Weekends all year, anytime
Jul & Aug
Credit cards ① ② ③ ⑤

This large and popular modern hotel is set in open countryside close to junction 11 of the M56. It has a very good leisure centre. All bedrooms have ensuite facilities and colour television with rooms for non-smokers and families.

DISLEY Cheshire Map 7 SJ98

★★★62% **Moorside** (Best Western) Mudhurst Lane, Higher Disley SK12 2AP ☎ (0663) 64151

Normal price: from £49.50. Dinner £16-£20 & à la carte
Short breaks: £39. Min 2 nights, Fri-Sun. £10 single supplement.
Credit cards ① ② ③ ⑤

An extensive leisure complex has now opened to complement the other amenities at this hotel which is set in open moorland. All the bedrooms have colour television and most have ensuite bath or shower rooms.

HIGHER BURWARDSLEY Cheshire Map 7 SJ45

IN QQQ **Pheasant** CH3 9PF ☎ (0829) 70434

Normal price: £25
Short breaks: £30 including £10 dinner allowance. Min 2 nights, Fri-Sun
🦮 (ex guide dogs) Credit cards ① ② ③ ⑤

This 300-year-old beamed inn has excellent modern bedrooms in a converted barn, all ensuite with colour television and tea-making facilities. Bar meals and snacks are served in the lounge bar. Children under fourteen are not accommodated. See advertisement on p36.

HOLMES CHAPEL Cheshire Map 7 SJ76

★★★67% **Old Vicarage** Knutsford Road CW4 8EF ☎ (0477) 32041

Normal price: £27. Dinner £13.50-£14.50 & à la carte
Short breaks: £34. Min 2 nights, Fri-Sun
🦮 (ex guide dogs) Credit cards ① ② ③

Situated on the A50 north of Holmes Chapel, this hotel has a choice of restaurants, and modern bedrooms with colour television and ensuite facilities.

KNUTSFORD Cheshire Map 7 SJ77

★★★65% **Cottons** (Shire) Manchester Road WA16 0SU ☎ (0565) 50333

Normal price: £55
Short breaks: £102 for 2 nights. Single £54 excluding dinner per night.
Credit cards ① ② ③ ⑤

Situated in rural surroundings just north-west of Knutsford this hotel has a leisure club with a swimming pool. Each bedroom has a private bath or shower room and colour television, and there are rooms for non-smokers. Christmas breaks are available.

★★72% **Longview** (Exec Hotel) Manchester Road WA16 0SU ☎ (0565) 2119
Closed Xmas & New Year

Normal price: £30. Dinner £12.75
Short breaks: £35, single £40. Min 2 nights, Fri-Sun, Nov-Apr

This delightful, privately-owned hotel has attractive bedrooms with private bathrooms and colour television.

★★57% **Royal George** (Berni/Chef & Brewer) King Street WA16 6EE ☎ (0565) 4151

Normal price: £36. Dinner £8-£15 à la carte
Short breaks: £25.50 excluding dinner. Min 2 nights, Fri-Sun
🛪 (ex guide dogs) Credit cards ①②③⑤

This elegant Georgian hotel offers bedrooms which have been modernised to a high standard with ensuite facilities. Three also have four-poster beds.

MACCLESFIELD Cheshire Map 7 SJ97

★★65% **Park Villa** Park Lane SK11 8AE ☎ (0625) 511428 & 614173

Normal price: £38.50. Dinner from £11.
Short breaks: £27.50 excluding dinner. Min 3 nights, Fri-Sun.
Activity breaks: Bridge, £115 Fri-Mon incl, May & August Bank Holiday Weekends, £160 Christmas Eve-Boxing Day. All breaks include tuition and practice.
Credit cards ①②③⑤

A late Victorian house with a well-tended garden providing particularly comfortable lounges.

MOTTRAM ST ANDREW Cheshire Map 7 SJ87

★★★67% **Mottram Hall** (De Vere) Prestbury SK10 4QT ☎ (0625) 828135

Normal price: £55. Dinner from £17.50.
Short breaks: from £40, min 2 nights, Fri-Sun.
Activity breaks: Golf, details from hotel.
Credit cards ①②③⑤

Georgian mansion built in 1721, standing in formal gardens surrounded by 120 acres of parkland.

NANTWICH Cheshire Map 7 SJ65

★★ **Alvaston Hall** (Associated Leisure) Middlewich Road CW5 6PD ☎ (0270) 624341

Normal price: £79
Short breaks: £56 for 1 night, £77 for 2 nights. £10 single supplement. Fri-Sun.
Credit cards ①②③④⑤

In open countryside just north of the town, this extended Victorian house has en suite facilities and colour television in all bedrooms, and extensive leisure facilities: indoor swimming pool, tennis, squash, sauna, solarium, gymnasium, whirlpool bath; also entertainment. Christmas breaks.

★★ **Cedars Hotel & Restaurant** 136 Crewe Road CW5 6NB ☎ (0270) 626455

Normal price: £15.75 Fri-Sat, £24 Sun-Thu.
Short breaks: £24 inc £10 dinner allowance.
Credit cards ①③

This family-owned house has a good restaurant and pleasantly furnished accommodation with private shower or bath in many bedrooms, all with colour TV and including two family rooms. There is also a pool table.

NORTHWICH Cheshire Map 7 SJ67

★ **Blue Cap** (Berni/Chef & Brewer) 520 Chester Road, Sandiway CW8 2DN ☎ (0606) 883006

Normal price: £26.50
Short breaks: £21 excluding dinner. Fri-Sun.
🛪 (ex guide dogs) Credit cards ①②③⑤

All bedrooms in this small hotel have private bath or shower and colour television, one with a four-poster. The restaurant serves mainly grills.

PARKGATE   Cheshire   Map 7 SJ27

★★62% **Parkgate** (Lansbury) Boathouse Lane L64 6RD ☎ 051-336 5001

Normal price: from £38. Dinner from £14.
Short breaks: £33, min 2 nights, Fri-Sun.
Activity breaks: Details from hotel.
Credit cards [1] [2] [3] [5]

A recently extended and refurbished hotel, well suited to the business traveller. Rooms have private bath or shower and colour TV.

★★★57% **Ship** (Trusthouse Forte) The Parade L64 6SA ☎ 051-336 3931

Normal price: £32.50. Dinner from £12 & à la carte (1990 price)
Short breaks: £38. Fri-Sun
Credit cards [1] [2] [3] [4] [5]

Overlooking the Dee Estuary, this small traditional hotel has well-equipped ensuite bedrooms, all with colour television and including two non-smoking rooms and two with four-poster beds. Christmas breaks.

POTT SHRIGLEY   Cheshire   Map 7 SJ97

★★★★65% **Shrigley Hall Golf & Country Club** Shrigley Park SK10 5SB ☎ (0625) 575757

Normal price: £80 for 2 nights. Dinner £18.50-£21.
Short breaks: £99 for 2 nights including dinner for one night only. Min 2 nights, Fri-Sun.
Activity breaks: Golf Breaks, £115 for 2 nights including one round of golf and one dinner.
Credit cards [1] [2] [3] [4] [5]

A magnificent building set in 260 rolling acres which include an 18-hole championship golf course. Many other sports are offered.

SANDBACH   Cheshire   Map 7 ST76

★★★65% **Chimney House** Congleton Road CW11 0ST ☎ (0270) 764141

Normal price: £44. Dinner from £14 & à la carte.
Short breaks: £38, min 2 nights, Fri-Sun.
Credit cards [1] [2] [3] [5]

Distinguished by its Tudor facade, this hotel is set in spacious grounds on the A534 near junction 17 of the M6. Comfortable bedrooms are exceptionally well-appointed, and versatile conference facilities are available.

★★★62% **Saxon Cross** Homes Chapel Road CW11 9SE ☎ (0270) 763281

Normal price: £35 Mon-Thur, £27 Fri-Sun. Dinner £13.80-£14.20.
Short breaks: £20 excluding dinner. Min 2 nights, Fri-Sun.
Credit cards [1] [2] [3] [5]

This motor hotel stands beside the A5022 just off junction 17 of the M6, and is a popular place for banqueting and functions. Rooms have a light, cheerful decor and are well-equipped, each with colour television. Cars can be parked outside bedrooms.

SANDIWAY Cheshire *Map 7 SJ56*

★★★ ♣ 75% **Nunsmere Hall Country House** Tarporley Road, Northwich CW8 2ES ☎ (0606) 889100

Normal price: £45. Dinner £25-£35
Short breaks: £59, Fri-Sun, includes a bottle of champagne and a newspaper. £20 single supplement.
Credit cards [1] [2] [3] [4] [5]

A beautifully converted Victorian mansion in an idylic setting overlooking a lake, surrounded by 10 acres of gardens and parkland. The accommodation is individual and sumptuously furnished and decorated, and the cuisine is especially recommended.

STOCKPORT Cheshire *Map 7 SJ88*

★58% **Acton Court** Buxton Road SK2 7AB ☎ 061-483 6172

Normal price: £38.50. Dinner £9.50 & à la carte.
Short breaks: £31.50, min 2 nights, Fri-Sun except Dec. £10.50 single supplement.
Credit cards [1] [2] [3] [5]

Set on the A6 Buxton road, close to the town centre and junction 12 of the M63, a converted, gabled Victorian hotel. Recent improvements have considerably enhanced the well-equipped bedrooms. The attractive restaurant provides a good standard of cooking.

STRETTON Cheshire *Map 7 SJ68*

★★69% **Old Vicarage** Stretton Road WA4 4NS ☎ (0925) 73706

Normal price: £40
Short breaks: £40. Fri-Sun.

This old vicarage has been fully modernised and offers ensuite bedrooms and a popular restaurant which overlooks a secluded rear garden. Christmas breaks are available.

TARPORLEY Cheshire *Map 7 SJ56*

★★★69% **Wild Boar** Whitchurch Road, Beeston CW6 9NW (2.5m S off A49) ☎ (0829) 260309

Normal price: £40. Dinner from £16.50 & à la carte
Short breaks: £43, Fri-Sun (includes Sunday lunch)
Credit cards [1] [2] [3] [5]

Modern ensuite bedrooms enjoy views of the beautiful rolling countryside at this hotel. The mock-Tudor restaurant offers a high standard of cuisine. Christmas breaks are available.

WARRINGTON Cheshire *Map 7 SJ68*

★★58% **Patten Arms** (County Inns) Parker Street WA1 1LS ☎ (0925) 36602
Closed Xmas

Normal price: £40 Fri-Sun, £57 Mon-Thu.
Short breaks: £20 excluding dinner, Fri-Sun. Min 2 nights.
Credit cards [1] [2] [3] [5]

Situated opposite Bank Quay station and close to the town centre this hotel offers accommodation in bedrooms with ensuite facilities and colour television.

▪ CLEVELAND ▪

EASINGTON   Cleveland   Map 8 NZ71

★★★ ▲ 72% **Grinkle Park** TS13 4UB (2m S off unclass rd linking A174/A171) ☎ (0287) 40515

Normal price: £72 room. Dinner £14.50 & à la carte
Short breaks: £48, single £58. Min 2 nights, Fri-Mon, max 7 nights.

Located between the coast and moorland, this hotel is set in 35 acres of grounds with a lake and attractive gardens. Individually designed bedrooms are particularly attractive, and have ensuite facilities and colour television. Leisure amenities include fishing and tennis.

MIDDLESBROUGH   Cleveland   Map 8 NZ42

★★ **Highfield** (Berni/Chef & Brewer) 358 Marton Road TS4 2PA ☎ (0642) 817638

Normal price: £27.
Short breaks: £23.50 excluding dinner. Min 2 nights weekends, 3 nights midweek.
🛪 (ex guide dogs) Credit cards ① ② ③ ⑤

This large old house standing in its own grounds offers warm, friendly service and very comfortable accommodation, with ensuite facilities and colour television in all bedrooms.

REDCAR   Cleveland   Map 8 NZ62

★★★67% **Park** Granville Terrace TS10 3AR ☎ (0642) 490888

Normal price: £22.50
Short breaks: £17.50 excluding dinner. Min 2 nights, Fri-Sun. Single supplement.
🛪 (ex guide dogs) Credit cards ① ② ③ ⑤

This elegant hotel just off the seafront provides good value meals and bar snacks and has comfortable bedrooms, all with ensuite facilities and colour TV.

STOCKTON-ON-TEES   Cleveland   Map 8 NZ41

★50% **Claireville** 519 Yarm Road, Eaglescliffe TS16 9BG (3m S A135) ☎ (0642) 780378

Normal price: £32.25 including dinner.
Short breaks: £28.75, min 2 nights, Fri-Sun. Single price £36.75.
Activity breaks: Details from hotel.
Credit cards ① ③ ⑤

A modestly-furnished family-run hotel set in an acre of gardens.

★★★67% **Parkmore** (Best Western) 636 Yarm Road, Eaglescliffe TS16 0DH (3m S A19) ☎ (0642) 786815

Normal price: £32-£36. Dinner £13.50-£15.
Short breaks: £40. Min 2 nights, Fri-Sun.
Activity breaks: Honeymoon/Anniversary, £94. Health and Fitness, £94. Details from hotel.
Credit cards ① ② ③ ⑤

This comfortable hotel provides an excellent leisure centre, and competently prepared meals are served by a friendly, efficient staff.

★★★61% **Post House** (Trusthouse Forte) Low Lane, Thornaby-on-Tees TS17 9LW ☎ (0642) 591213

Normal price: £47. Dinner £16
Short breaks: £41, min 2 nights, Thu-Sun. £36 2-6 nights, Jul-Sep.
Credit cards ① ② ③ ④ ⑤

This is a busy hotel with friendly staff, an a la carte restaurant and a coffee shop. The bedrooms are ensuite with colour television and some are set aside for families and non-smokers.

★★★★55% **Swallow** 10 John Walker Square TS18 1QZ ☎ (0642) 679721
Normal price: £43. Dinner £14.75-£18.50 & à la carte.
Short breaks: £42.50, Fri-Sun, including lunch.
Credit cards ① ② ③ ④ ⑤

An attractive leisure centre is now available in the basement of this modern town centre hotel. A convenient undercover free public car park is behind the hotel.

■ CORNWALL ■

BOSCASTLE *Cornwall & Isles of Scilly* Map 2 SX09

★★63% **Bottreaux House** PL35 0BG ☎ (08405) 231
Closed Dec-Feb (Open Xmas)
Normal price: £28. Dinner £8.50-£12.35 à la carte
Short breaks: £56.50 for 2 nights

Standing on a hill overlooking the picturesque harbour village the small personally-run hotel offers a friendly atmosphere and accommodation in bright, clean bedrooms with ensuite facilities and colour television. There is a special Christmas programme. Children under ten are not accommodated.

GH QQQ Melbourne House New Road PL35 0DH ☎ (08405) 650
Normal price: £38-£42 including dinner.
Short breaks: £35-£39. Min 2 nights, Oct-Apr (ex Bank Holidays)
Credit cards ① ③

In a commanding position overlooking the Jordan Valley and village, this fine house has been tastefully restored to retain its charm and character. Televisions are provided in the bedrooms and one room has an ensuite shower. Children are not accommodated.

GH QQQ Old Coach House Tintagel Road PL35 0AS ☎ (08405) 398
Closed 23 Dec-2 Jan restricted service Nov-Mar
Normal price: £15
Short breaks: £14 excluding dinner. Min 3 nights, Mar-May & Oct-Nov.
🦮 (ex guide dogs) Credit cards ① ② ③

This small guesthouse has four rooms all with private bath or shower rooms and colour television. There is one family room.

GH QQQQ St Christophers Country House High Street PL35 0BD ☎ (08405) 412
Mar-Oct & Xmas
Normal price: £16-£17. Dinner £7 (four course)
Short breaks: £69 for 3 nights. Mar-May & Sep-Oct.
Credit cards ① ③

Enthusiastically-run by experienced owners, this charming cottage-style guesthouse serves imaginative home cooking. Seven of the ten bedrooms have ensuite showers and there is a colour television in the comfortable lounge. Children under twelve are not accommodated.

BUDE *Cornwall & Isles of Scilly* Map 2 SS20

★★65% **Bude Haven** Flexbury Avenue EX23 8NS ☎ (0288) 352305
Normal price: £17-£18. Dinner £6-£7
Short breaks: £19.16-£20.83. Min 3 nights, Oct-May
Credit cards ① ③

Resident proprietors extend a warm welcome to this hotel which offers comfortable bedrooms, all with ensuite bath or shower rooms and colour television.

★★64% Camelot Downs View EX23 8RE ☎ (0288) 352361

Normal price: £22. Dinner £10-£12.
Short breaks: £26, min 3 nights.
Activity breaks: Golf Breaks, £40 per day, £230 per week, plus golf fees.
🛪 Credit cards ① ③

Well-kept owner-run hotel with strong ties to the golf course across the road. Well-equipped bedrooms and a genial atmosphere.

GH QQQ Cliff Maer Down, Crooklets EX23 8NG ☎ (0288) 3110
Apr-Oct

Normal price: from £27 including dinner
Short breaks: from £24. Single supplement £2. Min 2 nights, Apr-Oct

Leisure facilities at this guesthouse include an indoor heated swimming pool, tennis, solarium and indoor spa pool. All the bedrooms have private bathrooms and colour television, including the family rooms.

GH QQQ Corisande 24 Downs View EX23 8RG ☎ (0288) 3473
Closed Xmas

Normal price: £19-£21
Short breaks: £17-£19. Min 3 nights, Jan-May & Sep-Dec
Credit cards ① ③

Close to the beach and overlooking the golf course, this family-run hotel has comfortable bedrooms with good facilities. All rooms have colour television, five have private showers and there are two family rooms. Children under three are not accepted.

★59% Edgcumbe Summerleaze Crescent EX23 8HJ ☎ (0288) 353846

Normal price: £13.50-£16. Dinner from £7
Short breaks: £18.75-£20.50. Min 2 nights, mid Sep-end May (ex 24-31 Dec)
Credit cards ① ③

This personally-run hotel specialises in family holidays and has a pool table. All rooms have colour television, some have private showers and there are rooms set aside for families. There is a special Christmas programme.

★★61% Penarvor Crooklets Beach EX23 8NE ☎ (0288) 352036

Normal price: £35 including dinner.
Short breaks: £29. Min 3 nights, Mar-Nov.
Activity breaks: Golf Breaks, details from hotel.
Credit cards ① ③

A family run hotel set in a quiet location with friendly attentive service and good food. Attractively furnished bedrooms and comfortable public rooms.

GH QQ Pencarrol 21 Downs View EX23 8RF ☎ (0288) 2478 due to change to 352478
1 Jan-30 Nov

Normal price: £11-£12
Short breaks: £10-£10.80. Min 3 nights, Jan-Jun & Oct-Nov

This friendly guest house offers cheerful accommodation and has two bedrooms on the ground floor. One room has an ensuite shower and there are two family rooms.

FALMOUTH   *Cornwall & Isles of Scilly*   Map 2 SW83

GH QQ Cotswold House 49 Melvill Road TR11 4DF ☎ (0326) 312077

Normal price: £16.50. Dinner £6
Short breaks: £22, min 3 nights.

This small, private hotel is in a pleasant position close to Gyllyngvase Beach and the town and harbour. All bedrooms have colour television, and most have private bath or shower room.

★★★69% **Greenbank** Harbourside TR11 2SR ☎ (0326) 312440
Closed 1-15 Jan

Normal price: £80-£115 room. Dinner £15.50 & à la carte
Short breaks: £90 for two. Min 2 nights, Fri-Mon
Credit cards ① ② ③ ⑤

Beautifully situated on the river's edge, this hotel offers spacious accommodation with good facilities. The restaurant overlooks the river and offers a choice of menus. Fishing is available.

★★★62% **Green Lawns** Western Terrace TR11 4QJ ☎ (0326) 312734

Normal price: £32.20 Apr-May, £37.95 Jun-Sept. Dinner £15-£16.
Short breaks: £26 Fri-Mon, £29 Mon-Fri, excluding dinner. Min 2 nights.
Activity breaks: Deep Sea Fishing Breaks, Freshwater Fishing Breaks, Sailing Holidays, Diving, Windsurfing and Water-Skiing Breaks. Details from hotel.
Credit cards ① ② ③ ④ ⑤

Built in 1910 in the style of a French chateau and set amid terraced lawns, the hotel offers purpose-built bedrooms and a modern leisure complex.

GH QQQ Gyllyngvase House Gyllyngvase Road TR11 4DJ ☎ (0326) 312956

Normal price: £35 bed and breakfast, £49 with dinner
Short breaks: £42. Min 3 nights, Mar-15 May & Oct

Standing in its own grounds this small, privately-run hotel is ideally situated for the beaches, town and park. It offers good home cooking and comfortable bedrooms, most with private facilities.

★★★ 🏊 76% **Penmere Manor** Mongleath Road TR11 4PN ☎ (0326) 211411

Normal price: £70-£88 room. Dinner £17-£18 & à la carte
Short breaks: £94-£114 for 2 nights.

Set in five acres of garden and woodland, the hotel features a fitness trail, a children's adventure playground and a leisure club with an indoor pool. All bedrooms are ensuite with colour television. There is a special Christmas programme.

GH QQQ Rathgowry Gyllyngvase Hill TR11 4DN ☎ (0326) 313482
Mar-Oct

Normal price: £28
Short breaks: £14-£18 excluding dinner. Min 3 nights, Mar-May & Sep-Oct

Overlooking the beach, this spacious Edwardian house has comfortable public rooms and ensuite bedrooms with colour television.

45

★★★66% **Royal Duchy** (Brend) Cliff Road TR11 4NX ☎ (0326) 313042

Normal price: £39-£44. Dinner £13.50-£15.
Short breaks: from £40 Nov-Mar, from £44 Apr-May, Sept-Oct, from £48 Jun. Min 2 nights except Jul-Aug.
Activity breaks: Sailing, Apr-May. Details from hotel.

In a good position with fine views of the bay, this hotel has fairly spacious public rooms and a semi-formal restaurant. Bedrooms can be compact or de-luxe suites.

GH QQQ **Westcott** Gyllyngvase Hill TR11 4DN ☎ (0326) 311309

Normal price: £22-£23 including dinner.
Short breaks: £18-£25, Mar-Apr. Single price £17.75-£18.75.
Activity breaks: House and Garden Breaks, £175-£185 per week, Apr-May. Details from hotel.
🐾

Friendly, attentive service is provided by the conscientious owners of this cosy hotel which has views of the bay.

FOWEY   Cornwall   Map 2 SX15

GH QQQQ **Carnethic House** Lambs Barn PL23 1HQ ☎ (072683) 3336

Normal price: £33.50.
Short breaks: £27.50, min 2 nights.
Activity breaks: £55 for 2 nights and Sunday lunch. Various breaks including Golf, Horse Riding and Boat Trips can be organised.
🐾 Credit cards ① ② ③ ⑤

The beautiful gardens of this welcoming house contain a heated swimming pool. Guests can enjoy home cooked dishes, including fresh fish.

★★75% **Marina** Esplanade PL23 1HY ☎ (0726) 833315
Closed Nov-Feb

Normal price: fr £37 with dinner
Short breaks: fr £33. Min 2 nights

In a unique waterfront location, this hotel offers a high standard of accommodation throughout; bedrooms are ensuite with colour television. There are facilities for fishing, windsurfing and sailing. The hotel does not have a car park, but provides courtesy transport when checking out.

GOLANT   Cornwall & Isles of Scilly   Map 2 SX15

★★63% **Cormorant** PL23 1LL ☎ (072683) 3426

Normal price: £33-£38. Dinner from £17
Short breaks: £40, single £43. Min 2 nights, Oct-May
Credit cards ① ③

In a picturesque setting overlooking the Fowey estuary, this hotel offers comfortable accommodation and good food. Bedrooms are thoughtfully furnished, all have private bathrooms and colour television. There is an indoor pool, and a Christmas programme is available.

GUNNISLAKE   Cornwall & Isles of Scilly   Map 2 SX47

GH QQQ **Hingston House** St Anns Chapel PL18 9HB ☎ (0822) 832468

Normal price: £35.25
Short breaks: £31.75. Single £36.75. Min 2 nights

A country house providing friendly service and comfortable accommodation. Most bedrooms have ensuite shower rooms, and all have colour television. There is a croquet lawn and putting green.

GWITHIAN Cornwall & Isles of Scilly Map 2 SW54

★63% **Sandsifter** Godrevy Towans TR27 5ED ☎ (0736) 753314
Normal price: £16.50-£22. Dinner £7.50-£8.50 & à la carte
Short breaks: £25, min 3 nights; £24.75 min 4 nights. All
year (ex Bank Holidays)
🛦 (ex guide dogs) Credit cards ①③

This busy, small hotel on the edge of the sand dunes offers an extensive selection of bar meals in addition to the restaurant menus. All seven bedrooms have ensuite bathroom and colour television. There is a special Christmas programme. Children under twelve are not accommodated.

HAYLE Cornwall & Isles of Scilly Map 2 SW53

★★57% **Hillside** Angarrack TR27 5HZ (1m E of Hayle on unclass rd off A30) ☎ (0736) 752180
Closed 23-31 Dec & wknds Nov-3 Mar
Normal price: £23.50. Dinner £9.75-£12
Short breaks: £28.50. £4 single supplement. Min 2 nights
🛦 (ex guide dogs) Credit cards ①③

Set in a small village a short distance from Hayle, this hotel is personally run and provides a homely atmosphere. Five of the ten bedrooms have ensuite facilities and there are some family rooms.

HELSTON Cornwall & Isles of Scilly Map 2 SW62

★★63% **Gwealdues** Falmouth Road TR13 8JX ☎ (0326) 572808
Normal price: £15. Dinner £8.50 & à la carte
Short breaks: £20, single £30. Min 2 nights, Fri-Sun
Credit cards ①③

The comfortable hotel standing beside the Falmouth road on the outskirts of town, offers private bath or shower rooms in most bedrooms.

LANREATH Cornwall & Isles of Scilly Map 2 SX15

★★58% **Punch Bowl Inn** PL13 2NX ☎ (0503) 20218
Normal price: £17.50. Dinner £8.50 & à la carte (1990
prices)
Short breaks: 3 days £72; 7 days £154 (1990 prices).
Credit cards ①③

A popular early 17th-century coaching inn with a restaurant and cosy bars with log fires. Bedrooms, named after Punch characters, range from antique-furnished to modern in style.

LISKEARD Cornwall & Isles of Scilly Map 2 SX26

★★ ♣ 61% **Country Castle** Station Road PL14 4EB ☎ (0579) 42694
Closed Nov. Restricted service Jan & Feb
Normal price: £60 (room)
Short breaks: £31.50-£36.50. Oct-Jun
Credit cards ①③

Enjoying magnificent views over the Looe Valley, this hotel provides individually-furnished and attractively decorated bedrooms and an elegant lounge. There are some leisure amenities and Christmas breaks are available.

LIZARD, THE   Cornwall & Isles of Scilly   Map 2 SW71

★★66% Housel Bay Housel Cove TR12 7PG ☎ (0326) 290417
Closed Jan-Feb 10

Normal price: £36-£50
Short breaks: £33-£42

Dating from Victorian times this hotel is situated on the cliffside. All the bedrooms are ensuite with colour television, one has a four-poster bed and two are for non-smokers. Christmas breaks are available.

★68% Kynance Bay House TR12 7NR ☎ (0326) 290498

Normal price: £56 for 3 nights
Short breaks: £50 for 3 nights excluding dinner.
Activity breaks: Photographic Courses, £138-£148 for 3 days including packed lunch, tuition, transport.
Credit cards [1] [2] [3] [5]

Commanding fine coastal views from its position at the edge of the village, a well-run hotel with a happy family atmosphere offers comfortable bedrooms, a good choice of meals from its short à la carte menu and the charm of a sheltered hidden garden.

LOOE   Cornwall & Isles of Scilly   Map 2 SX25

★★65% Fieldhead Portuan Road PL13 2DR ☎ (05036) 2689
Closed Dec-Jan

Normal price: £26. Dinner £10.75 & à la carte
Short breaks: £33. Min 2 nights
✻ Credit cards [1] [2] [3]

Comfortable accommodation, home-cooked dishes and friendly service are available at this hotel. There is a heated outdoor pool in the terraced garden. Children under five are not accommodated.

GH Q Kantara 7 Trelawney Terrace PL13 2AG ☎ (05036) 2093

Normal price: £9-£12.
Short breaks: £32 for 2 nights.
Activity breaks: Accompanied Walking Holidays, £110 per week. Reflexology Tuition, Positive Thinking Courses, Self Awareness Courses and Counselling Courses, all £150 per week.
Credit cards [1] [3]

A pre-war mid-terrace house where guests enjoy a hearty breakfast, and a relaxed atmosphere is created by the friendly, caring proprietor.

LOSTWITHIEL   Cornwall & Isles of Scilly   Map 2 SX15

★★67% Restormel Lodge (Consort) Hillside Gardens, PL22 0DD ☎ (0208) 872223

Normal price: £54 room. Dinner £10-£14 & à la carte
Short breaks: £35, single £42. Min 2 nights
Credit cards [1] [2] [3] [5]

A friendly and relaxed hotel providing well-equipped bedrooms and a popular restaurant serving table d'hôte and à la carte meals. There is an outdoor heated pool, and Christmas breaks are available.

MARAZION   Cornwall & Isles of Scilly   Map 2 SW53

★★ Mount Haven (Minotels) Turnpike Road TR17 0DQ ☎ (0736) 710249

Normal price: £22. Dinner from £10.50 (1990 price)
Short breaks: £30. Min 2 nights, Oct-Mar.
Credit cards [1] [2] [3]

A former coaching inn, this friendly family-run hotel has a galleried restaurant and comfortable bedrooms, including family rooms, all with colour television and ensuite facilities. There is free golf on a nearby course.

MAWNAN SMITH   Cornwall & Isles of Scilly   Map 2 SW72

★★★62% **Trelawne** TR11 5HS ☎ (0326) 250226

Normal price: £69-£76 room and breakfast. Dinner £14.90 & à la carte.
Short breaks: £39.50-£48. Min 2 nights, Mar-Dec.
Credit cards 1 2 3 5

Standing in 2 acres of gardens within easy reach of the sea, this homely family-run hotel serves imaginative food and has an indoor swimming pool and games room. All bedrooms have colour television and most have ensuite bath or shower. Christmas breaks. See advertisement on p45.

MEVAGISSEY   Cornwall & Isles of Scilly   Map 2 SX04

QQQ **Mevagissey House** Vicarage Hill PL26 6SZ ☎ (0726) 842427

Normal price: £18-£21
Short breaks: £26-£29. Min 3 nights, Mar-May, Sep-Oct.
£4 single supplement 3 nights, £2 5-7 nights.
🦮 (ex guide dogs) Credit cards 1 3

This large detached guesthouse, a former rectory, has views across the harbour and four of its six bedrooms, including two family rooms, have private bath or shower and all have colour television. No children under 7.

QQQ Mrs A Hennah **Treleaven Farm** PL26 6RZ (SX008454) ☎ (0726) 842413

Normal price: £27
Short breaks: £25. Min 2 nights, Apr-May, Sep-Oct.
🦮 Credit cards 1 3

This large detached farmhouse on a hill with 200 acres of mixed farmland has private shower and colour television in all six bedrooms, plus a lawned garden, heated outdoor swimming pool, putting green and games room.

★★ **Tremarne** Polkirt Hill PL26 6UY ☎ (0726) 842213

Normal price: £25-£29. Dinner £12.25 (1990 price)
Short breaks: £24. Min 2 nights, Mar-May, Sep-Nov.
🦮 (ex guide dogs) Credit cards 1 3

This friendly hotel with a pleasant garden and fine views serves good food, and offers ensuite bath or shower and colour television in all bedrooms, including two family rooms. There is an outdoor heated swimming pool. No children under 3.

★★ **Trevalsa Court** Polstreath PL26 6TH ☎ (0726) 842468 & 843794

Normal price: £46. Dinner from £9.50 (1990 price)
Short breaks: £40-£54 including £10 dinner allowance and bar snacks or packed lunch. Min 2 nights, Jun-Sep 3 nights. Not available mid Nov-mid Mar. Single supplement.
Credit cards 1 2 3 5

Overlooking the sea, this peaceful country house hotel has ensuite facilities and television in all bedrooms, including two family rooms, with opportunities for fishing trips, shooting and horse riding. No children under 10.

MOUNT HAWKE Cornwall & Isles of Scilly Map 2 NZ20

★ **Tregarthen Country Cottage** Banns Road TR4 8BW ☎ (0209) 890399

Normal price: £35
Short breaks: £30. Min 2 nights.
✕ (ex guide dogs)

On the edge of the village, this charming small hotel with a garden and comfortable lounges serves wholesome food and all bedrooms have ensuite facilities, one with a corner spa bath.

MOUSEHOLE Cornwall & Isles of Scilly Map 2 SW42

★★ **Carn Du** Raginnis Hill TR19 6SS ☎ (0736) 731233

Normal price: £20-£25. Dinner from £11.45 (1990 price)
Short breaks: from £30. Min 3 nights.
✕ Credit cards ① ② ③

This small, personally run hotel with a garden and panoramic views across Mount's Bay serves home-cooked food, particularly fish and vegetables, and most bedrooms have private shower and television. Christmas breaks.

★★ **The Lobster Pot** South Cliff TR19 6QX ☎ (0736) 731251

Normal price: £29.50 plus 10% service charge. Dinner £13.75 & à la carte (1990 price)
Short breaks: from £28.60. Min 2 nights weekend, 3 nights midweek. Closed 3 Jan-1 Feb.
Credit cards ① ② ③

Overhanging the small village harbour, this characterful hotel and restaurant has private bath or shower and colour television in most bedrooms. Some of them, including family rooms, are situated in the annexe. Christmas breaks.

MULLION Cornwall & Isles of Scilly Map 2 SW61

QQ **Henscath House** TR12 7EP ☎ (0326) 240537

Normal price: £27-£29 including dinner
Short breaks: £26-£28. Min 6 nights, excluding Xmas/New Year.

All main rooms have magnificent views; good atmosphere and good food.

★★ **Mullion Cove** TR12 7EP ☎ (0326) 240328

Normal price: £39.50.
Short breaks: £28. Min 3 nights. Mar-June, Sep-Oct.
Credit cards ① ③ ⑤

This friendly hotel with sweeping views over Mount's Bay has colour television in all bedrooms, many with private bath or shower, and includes family rooms. There is an outdoor heated swimming pool, hard tennis court, sauna and solarium. Christmas breaks.

NEWQUAY   Cornwall & Isles of Scilly   Map 2 SW86

★★★62% **Bristol** Narrowcliff TR7 2PQ ☎ (0637) 875181

Normal price: £41. Dinner £13.50 & à la carte (1990 price)
Short breaks: £80 for 2-night weekend, £175 for 5-day
break. 22 Sep-18 May.
Credit cards ① ② ③ ⑤

Directly overlooking Tolcarne beach, this hotel has been under the same ownership since 1927. It has ensuite bath in most bedrooms, all with colour television including family rooms. Leisure facilities include an indoor swimming pool, snooker, sauna and solarium. Christmas breaks.

★★ **Cumberland** 8-10 Henver Road TR7 3BJ ☎ (0637) 873025

Normal price: £50
Short breaks: £40 excluding dinner (£6 extra).
Credit cards ①

A short walk from the beach and town centre, this convivial modern hotel with a ballroom and cocktail bar has ensuite bedrooms with colour television, an outdoor swimming pool and solarium. No children.

Q Fistral Beach Esplanade Road, Pentire TR7 1QA ☎ (0637) 873993 due to change to 850626

Normal price: £49 approx.
Short breaks: £42 approx. Min 2 nights, Mar-May, Sep-Nov.
Single supplement.
Credit cards ① ③

This purpose-built modern guesthouse with an outdoor swimming pool has magnificent sea views and easy access to the beach. All bedrooms have colour television and most, including two family rooms, have private shower.

★★ **Philema** 1 Esplanade Road TR7 1PY ☎ (0637) 872571

Normal price: £48
Short breaks: £44. Min 2 nights, Mar-May, Sep-Nov.
Credit cards ① ③

This comfortable friendly hotel overlooking the golf course has many family bedrooms, en suite facilities and colour television, plus a four-poster bed. Leisure facilities include an indoor swimming pool, sauna, solarium, table tennis and pool table. Christmas breaks.

QQQ Porth Enodoc 4 Esplanade Road, Pentire TR7 1PY ☎ (0637) 872372

Normal price: £15.75. Dinner £6.50
Short breaks: £20. Min 2 nights. Estr-25 May, 28 Sep-Oct.
£3 single supplement.
✱

Set it its own gardens, this attractive, friendly guesthouse with glorious sea view has comfortable, well-equipped bedrooms, including some family rooms, all with private shower and colour television.

★★★54% **Riviera** Lusty Glaze Road TR7 3AA ☎ (0637) 874251

Normal price: £34.75. Dinner from £12.50.
Short breaks: £22.50, min 2 nights, Fri-Sun. Oct-May.
Activity breaks: Bridge Weeks, £225 plus £14 single
supplement. Apr & Oct.
Credit cards ① ② ③

Good interesting food is a feature of this comfortable, proprietor-run cliff-top hotel.

GH QQ Rolling Waves Alexandra Road, Porth TR7 3NB ☎ (0637) 873236

Normal price: £119.60-£165 per week half-board
Short breaks: £19.95, min 2 nights, Sept-May.
Activity breaks: Heritage Breaks, including visits to
National Trust properties throughout Cornwall. Details
from hotel.
✱ Credit cards ① ③

Overlooking Porth Beach and the putting green, this bungalow-style house has comfortable accommodation and a convivial atmosphere.

QQQ Tir Chonaill Lodge 106 Mount Wise TR7 3NB ☎ (0637) 876492

Normal price: £14.75
Short breaks: £13.75 excluding dinner (£5 extra). Min 2 nights, Oct-May.

This modern terraced guesthouse close to the gown centre and beaches offers friendly personal service. It offers bright bedrooms, including many family rooms, all with ensuite facilities and colour television.

★64% **Trevone** Mount Wise TR7 2BP ☎ (0637) 873039

Normal price: £14-£17. Dinner £7.50-£8.50.
Short breaks: £52 for 3 nights (Spring), £55 (Autumn). Min 3 nights, Mon-Thu.
Activity breaks: Birdwatching, £140 per week. 20-27 Apr, £145 12-19 Oct. These weeks are run as house parties. Wild Flower & Garden, £145. 27 Apr-4 May.

Small family hotel situated close to the town centre and beaches.

★★ **Water's Edge** Esplanade Road, Pentire TR7 1QA ☎ (0637) 872048

Normal price: £29.50-£40. Dinner from £11.95 (1990 price)
Short breaks: £27.50-£39. Min 2 nights, May-Oct.
🏌 (ex guide dogs) Credit cards ①③

Overlooking Fistral Bay and close to a golf course, this small friendly hotel serves home-made food and most bedrooms, including a new family room and one with a four-poster, have private bathrooms; all have colour television.

PADSTOW *Cornwall & Isles of Scilly* Map 2 SW97

QQQ Dower House Fentonluna Lane PL28 8BA ☎ (0841) 532317

Normal price: £30-£44 (1990 prices)
Short breaks: £1 off per person per night, Oct, 1-19 Apr; £1.50 off, Nov-Mar.
Credit cards ①

This friendly characterful guesthouse with countryside views and situation close to the beach has comfortable bedrooms, most with ensuite facilities and including three family rooms.

★★★58% **Metropole** (Trusthouse Forte) Station Road PL28 8DB ☎ (0841) 532486

Normal price: £100 room. Dinner £13.75.
Short breaks: £55, min 2 nights. Single supplement.
Activity breaks: Painting in Watercolour. Details from hotel.
Credit cards ①②③④⑤

Large detached hotel in an elevated position overlooking the river estuary.

PENZANCE   Cornwall & Isles of Scilly   Map 2 SW43

QQ Camilla Regent Terrace TR18 4DW ☎ (0736) 63771

Normal price: £15-£17.50
Short breaks: £21-£23. Min 2 nights, Oct-Apr excluding Xmas & Easter.

This friendly family-run guesthouse in a regency building overlooking the seafront has comfortable bedrooms, some ensuite and half with colour television.

★ **Estoril** 46 Morrab Road TR18 4EX ☎ (0736) 62468 & 67471 & 69811

Normal price: £24. Dinner £8.50 (1990 price)
Short breaks: £27.50 inc morning coffee and afternoon tea. Min 2 nights, Feb-May, Oct-Nov.
✙ Credit cards ① ③

A small homely hotel in the town centre with comfortable, well-equipped bedrooms, all with ensuite facilities and colour television.

★★★60% **Mount Prospect** (Exec Hotel) Britons Hill TR18 3AE ☎ (0736) 63117

Normal price: £39.10. Dinner from £10.35 (1990 price)
Short breaks: £32.20. Min 2 nights, Oct-Mar.
Credit cards ① ② ③ ⑤

Overlooking Mount's Bay and Penzance harbour, this comfortable hotel with its own gardens and outdoor swimming pool has ensuite facilities and colour television in all bedrooms, which include a few family and non-smoking rooms.

Q Mount Royal Chyandour Cliff TR14 3LQ ☎ (0736) 62233

Normal price: £17-£19
Short breaks: £12-£14 excluding dinner. Min 2 nights, Mar-Jun. £17 for single occupancy.

Facing the sea and the harbour, this small family hotel has washing or ensuite facilities in all bedrooms, which include some family rooms.

★★★52% **Queen's** The Promenade TR18 4HG ☎ (0736) 62371

Normal price: £40
Short breaks: £38 excluding dinner for 3 nights; £36.50 excluding dinner for 5 nights. Special rates for single occupancy.
Credit cards ① ② ③ ⑤

Standing on the seafront with fine views over Mount's Bay, this large Victorian hotel provides traditional service and atmosphere. All bedrooms, including family rooms, have ensuite bathrooms and colour television, and there is a sauna, solarium and gymnasium. Christmas breaks.

★ **Tarbert** (Minotels) 11-12 Clarence Street TR18 2NU ☎ (0736) 63758

Normal price: £19.50-£22.50. Dinner from £10.50 & à la carte (1990 price).
Short breaks: £28.75-£31.75. Min 2 nights, Oct-Nov & 15 Jan-10 May.
✙ Credit cards ① ② ③ ⑤

This small hotel in the town centre serves good food, and has comfortable bedrooms, all with en suite facilities and colour television. No children under 12.

PERRANPORTH   Cornwall & Isles of Scilly   Map 2 SW75

Q Cellar Cove Droskyn Way TR6 0DS ☎ (0872) 572110

Normal price: from £14
Short breaks: £40 excluding dinner for 3 nights, late May-Aug.
Credit cards ① ③

This friendly hotel with views over the bay provides simple, good-value accommodation, with colour television in most bedrooms, which include family rooms and a few ensuite. There is also an outdoor swimming pool, table tennis and pool table.

Q Fairview Tywarnhayle Road TR6 0DX ☎ (0872) 572278

Normal price: £26
Short breaks: £16.50. Min 3 nights, Apr-June, Sep.
Credit cards [1] [3]

A comfortable family hotel with good views and pleasant bedrooms, including family and non-smoking rooms, all with washing facilities and some with private shower.

POLBATHIC   *Cornwall & Isles of Scilly*   Map 2 SX35

QQ Old Mill PL11 3HA ☎ (0503) 30596

Normal price: £36 for 3 nights.
Short breaks: £32.50 excluding dinner for 3 nights. Min 3 nights.

This friendly family-run guesthouse has comfortable bedrooms, including two family rooms, all with washing facilities and one with colour television.

POLMASSICK   *Cornwall & Isles of Scilly*   Map 2 SW94

QQQ Kilbol House PL26 6HA ☎ (0726) 842481

Normal price: £33 room & breakfast.
Short breaks: £65.55 for 3 nights. Min 3 nights, Oct-Easter.

This well-maintained guesthouse provides comfortable accommodation and attentive service, with half the bedrooms, including a family room, having private bathrooms.

POLPERRO   *Cornwall & Isles of Scilly*   Map 2 SX25

★66% **Claremont** Fore Street PL13 2RG ☎ (0503) 72241

Normal price: £17-£23. Dinner £10.95-£16.50.
Short breaks: £14.50 & £17.25 excluding dinner, Apr-14 Jun and 15 Sept-Apr. £16.50 & £19.50 excluding dinner 15 Jun-14 Sept. Min 3 nights.
Activity breaks: French Conversation, £126 for 3 nights, including classes for near beginners and wine with dinner. Apr-May.
Credit cards [1] [3]

A small holiday hotel with a warm French influence providing comfortable accommodation and well-cooked food.

PORT GAVERNE   Cornwall & Isles of Scilly   Map 2 SX08

★★ Headlands PL29 3SH ☎ (0208) 880260

Normal price: £37-£45. Dinner from £9.50 & à la carte
(1990 price)
Short breaks: £33-£40. Min 3 nights.
Credit cards 1 2 3 5

This friendly 17th-century inn spectacularly sited above a rocky inlet serves good varied food, and offers comfortable public rooms and ensuite bedrooms with colour television. Also a sauna. Christmas breaks.

PORTHOWAN   Cornwall & Isles of Scilly   Map 2 SW64

GH QQ Beach TR4 8AE ☎ (0209) 890228

Normal price: £18.50. Dinner £8.
Short breaks: £23, min 3 nights, Sept-Jun.
Activity breaks: Christmas Break, £258, 24-28 Dec. Details from hotel.
Credit cards 1 2 3 5

This family holiday hotel enjoys spectacular views from its elevated position.

PORT ISAAC   Cornwall & Isles of Scilly   Map 2 SW98

★★68% Archer Farm Trewetha PL29 3RU ☎ Bodmin (0208) 880522

Normal price: £25-£27.50. Dinner £15.
Short breaks: £19-£21 excluding dinner. Min 2 nights, Apr, end Sept & Oct.
Activity breaks: Health & Beauty Weekend, details from hotel.

Standing on the outskirts of the village and extended from a farmhouse, the hotel provides comfortable bedrooms, good home cooking and friendly owners.

Q Bay 1 The Terrace PL29 3SG ☎ (0208) 880380

Normal price: £22.50 or £27.50 en suite, including dinner.
Short breaks: £19 or £23.50 en suite. Min 3 nights, Easter-Jun, Sep-Oct.

In an elevated position overlooking the sea, this double-fronted friendly guesthouse has several family rooms and a few bedrooms with private bath.

★★ Castle Rock PL29 3SB ☎ (0208) 880300

Normal price: £35. Dinner from £11.50 (1990 price)
Short breaks: £33. Min 2 nights, Mar-Jun, Sep-Dec, excluding bank hols.
Credit cards 1 5

This friendly clifftop hotel with a garden and fine sea views has bright public rooms and comfortable, well-equipped bedrooms, including family rooms, many with private bath or shower and colour television.

QQ St Andrews The Terrace PL29 3SG ☎ (0208) 880240

Normal price: £21.50
Short breaks: £30.45. Min 2 nights, Oct-Jun.
✕ (ex guide dogs)

This personally run guesthouse overlooking the sea serves good food and has comfortable public rooms and bright bedrooms, including two family rooms, some with private bath or shower and some non-smoking.

PORTSCATHO   Cornwall & Isles of Scilly   Map 2 SW83

★★★63% Rosevine Porthcurnick Beach TR2 5EW ☎ (087258) 206 & 230

Normal price: from £25. Dinner £17 (1990 price)
Short breaks: £33. Min 3 nights, 3 Apr-23 May, 21 Sept-12 Oct. Some rooms unavailable.
Credit cards 1 3

Close to the beach and set in landscaped gardens, this small and bright hotel offers spacious public rooms and comfortable bedrooms with private bath or shower and colour television, including two family rooms.

PRAA SANDS   Cornwall & Isles of Scilly   Map 2 SW52

★★ **Prah Sands** Chy An Dour Road TR20 9SY ☎ (0736) 762438

Normal price: £28-£33 for half-board
Short breaks: £70 for 3 nights, £90 for 4 nights. Min 3 nights, Oct-Apr.
Credit cards ①③

This family hotel on the water's edge has a garden with a tennis court, croquet lawn and swimming pool, and many of the bedrooms are family rooms, all with colour television and over half with private bathrooms.

REDRUTH   Cornwall & Isles of Scilly   Map 2 SW64

★★★58% **Penventon** TR15 1TE ☎ (0209) 214141

Normal price: £24.50
Short breaks: £17.50 excluding dinner. Min 2 nights, Fri-Sun. Single supplement.
Credit cards ①②③

This family-owned Georgian manor house has a choice of restaurants and bars, a discoteque in the grounds and children's and leisure facilities, including indoor swimming, snooker, sauna, solarium and gymnasium. Bedrooms have ensuite facilities and colour television.

ROCK   Cornwall & Isles of Scilly   Map 2 SW97

Q **Roskarnon House** PL27 6LD ☎ (020886) 2329

Normal price: £25
Short breaks: £75 for 3 nights.
✗

Set in an acre of grounds overlooking the Camel Estuary, this detached guesthouse has an attractive dining room and several family rooms among the bedrooms, about half of which have ensuite facilities and colour television.

RUAN HIGH LANES   Cornwall & Isles of Scilly   Map 2 SW93

★★71% **Hundred House** TR2 5JR ☎ (0872) 501336

Normal price: £35-£41. Dinner £14 (1990 price)
Short breaks: £30-£38.50. Min 3 nights, Mar-Oct.
Credit cards ①③

This friendly, personally run Georgian house with a garden has cosy comfortable bedrooms with colour television, and private bath or shower. No children under 10.

ST AGNES   Cornwall & Isles of Scilly   Map 2 SW75

★★ 🏨 61% **Rose in Vale Country House** Rose in Vale, Mithian, TR5 0QD ☎ (087255) 2202

Normal price: £29.95 including dinner.
Short breaks: £27.45, Mar-May and Oct, min 2 nights.
Credit cards ①③

This peacefully situated, attractive Georgian house with a modern extension offers a good variety of leisure facilities. Most bedrooms have ensuite bathrooms, and all have colour television.

★67% **Sunholme** Goonvrea Road TR5 0NW ☎ (087255) 2318
Closed Nov-March

Normal price: £39-£42 room and breakfast.
Short breaks: £81 3 nights Apr-mid Jul, mid Sept-end Oct.
Credit cards ①③

This hotel is set in well-tended grounds and commands magnificent views of both coast and countryside. There are three well-presented, interconnecting lounges and neat bedrooms.

ST AUSTELL *Cornwall & Isles of Scilly* Map 2 SX05

★★★★61% **Carlyon Bay** (Brend) Sea Road, Carlyon Bay PL25 3RD ☎ (072681) 2304

Normal price: £53-£59. Dinner £16.
Short breaks: fr £52, Nov-Mar, fr £58, Apr-May, Sept-Oct, fr £60 May-Jun. Min 2 nights.
Activity breaks: Garden Holidays, Mar & Apr. Historic Houses, Jun. Golf Tuition Holidays, Apr, May, Sept, Oct. Details from hotel.
Credit cards [1] [2] [3] [5]

Set in 250 acres, this hotel has superb indoor and outdoor leisure facilities including its own golf course. Most bedrooms have excellent sea views.

★★★63% **Cliff Head** Sea Road, Carlyon Bay PL25 3RB ☎ (072681) 2345

Normal price: £68.80. Dinner £10.95
Short breaks: £126.50 for 2 nights, £189.18 for 3 nights, £252.42 for 4 nights. Includes lunch and £10.95 dinner allowance. Single, 2 nights £77.62.
Credit cards [1] [2] [3] [5]

A comfortable cliff-top hotel with a private beach. All bedrooms have a private bathroom and colour television, and there is a good range of leisure facilities.

★★★63% **Porth Avallen** Sea Road, Carlyon Bay PL25 3SG ☎ (072681) 2802 & 2183
Closed Christmas and New Year

Normal price: £33.30. Dinner £15-£18.
Short breaks: £37.15, min 2 nights, Fri-Sat, including Sunday lunch before departure. £12 single supplement.
Credit cards [1] [2] [3] [5]

A privately-owned resort hotel overlooking Carlyon Bay. The sound English cooking is nicely prepared and service is friendly and helpful. Most bedrooms have ensuite facilities and all have colour television.

ST IVES *Cornwall & Isles of Scilly* Map 2 SW54

★★58% **Boskerris** Boskerris Road, Carbis Bay TR26 2NQ ☎ (0736) 795295

Normal price: £62-£83.50 room, breakfast & dinner.
Short breaks: £26.50, min 3 nights, Sept, Oct, Apr & Etr.
Activity breaks: Golfing Breaks, details from hotel.
Credit cards [1] [3] [5]

A country house style hotel enjoying glorious coastal views. Meals are carefully cooked and well balanced.

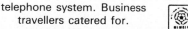

★★★58% **Carbis Bay** Carbis Bay TR26 2NP ☎ (0736) 795311

Normal price: £60 room & breakfast. Dinner from £16 à la carte.
Short breaks: £30, min 2 nights, Easter-Nov.
Credit cards ① ② ③ ⑤

A large, detached hotel in a prominent position overlooking its own private beach and the bay. The recently upgraded bedrooms are comfortable and the service from local staff is friendly. There is also a heated swimming pool.

★★59% **Chy-An-Dour** Trelyon Avenue TR26 2AD ☎ (0736) 796436

Normal price: £29-£33. Dinner £9-£11.50
Short breaks: £61 for 2 nights, Jan-June and Sep-Dec.
£5 single supplement.
✿ Credit cards ① ③

A friendly holiday hotel in a peaceful setting with superb views of St Ives and the bay. Public rooms are comfortable and the bedrooms, though compact, are well equipped.

★★★61% **Chy-An-Drea** The Terrace TR26 2BP ☎ (0736) 795076
Closed Dec-12 March

Normal price: £26.95-£36. Dinner £13-£14
Short breaks: £30, min 3 nights, Mar-Oct excluding Bank Holidays.
Credit cards ① ② ③ ⑤

A popular hotel offering a homely atmosphere and prompt, friendly service.

★ **Dunmar** Pednolver Terrace TR26 2EL ☎ (0736) 796117

Normal price: £19.50
Short breaks: £17.50, min 2 nights, Oct-May.
Credit cards ① ③

A small friendly hotel overlooking the town and the bay.

★★★64% **Garrack** Higher Ayr TR26 3AA ☎ (0736) 796199
Normal price: £35.50. Dinner from £13 & à la carte.
Short breaks: £33 any 2-5 nights Oct-May.
Credit cards 1 2 3 4 5

A country house atmosphere prevails in this secluded family-run hotel which enjoys panoramic views over St Ives Bay. It has a heated indoor swimming pool and leisure complex and the small restaurant provides commendable cooking.

GH QQQ Hollies 4 Talland Road, TR26 2DF ☎ (0736) 796605
Normal price: £34 room.
Short breaks: £30 room. Single £15. Min 2 nights Oct-May.
✖

A friendly, well-furnished guesthouse providing good, home-cooked meals and comfortable ensuite bedrooms with colour television.

★★★67% **Porthminster** The Terrace TR26 2BN ☎ (0736) 795221
Normal price: £45. Dinner £13.75 & à la carte.
Short breaks: £37, min 2 nights, Oct-May (excluding Christmas, New Year & Easter), includes buffet lunch.
Credit cards 1 2 3 4 5

A traditional hotel in a commanding position overlooking St Ives Bay with direct access to a safe, sandy beach from the gardens. There is a good selection of leisure facilities.

★59% **Trecarrell** Carthew Terrace TR26 1EB ☎ (0736) 795707
Closed March
Normal price: £21.50-£24.50. Dinner £5.50-£7.
Short breaks: £16.50-£18.50, min 3 nights, Mar-June, mid Sep, end Oct.
✖ Credit cards 1 3

This personally-managed, small Victorian hotel is located in a quiet position above the town and offers good value for money.

QQ White House The Valley, Carbis Bay TR26 2QY ☎ (0736) 797405
Normal price: £30
Short breaks: £128.25 for 3 nights, £213.75 for 5 nights Dec-Jun, Sept & Oct.
✖ Credit card 1

Comfortable bedrooms and cosy public areas are complemented by home-cooked food in this pleasantly located detached house at the foot of a wooded valley, 150 yards from safe, sandy beaches and a mile from St Ives.

ST MAWES   Cornwall & Isles of Scilly   Map 2 SW83

★★60% **St Mawes** The Seafront, TR2 5DW ☎ (0326) 270266
Closed Dec and Jan
Normal price: £40. Dinner £14-£25 à la carte.
Short breaks: £37, includes £14 dinner allowance.
Credit cards 1 3

A small, comfortable, quayside hotel dating from the 17th century, which offers thoughtfully-equipped cottagey bedrooms and a bar with great character.

SANDPLACE   Cornwall & Isles of Scilly   Map 2 SX25

GH QQQ Polraen Country House PL8 1PJ ☎ (05036) 3956
Normal price: £24 bed and breakfast, £35.25 with dinner
Short breaks: £30-£33, single £35.25. Min 3 nights
Credit cards 1 3

This attractive and comfortable country house was built of Cornish stone in the early 1700s. Each bedroom is ensuite with colour television.

SENNEN   Cornwall & Isles of Scilly   Map 2 SW32

★★★66% **State House** TR19 7AA ☎ (0736) 871844

Normal price: £99 room. Dinner £14-£18.50
Short breaks: £99 for two, single £49.50 with £15
supplement. Min 3 nights
🐕 (ex guide dogs) Credit cards ①②③

This hotel has thirty-four bedrooms all with private bathroom and colour television; three rooms are furnished with four-poster beds. Christmas breaks are available.

TALLAND BAY   Cornwall & Isles of Scilly   Map 2 SX25

★★★ 🍴 71% **Talland Bay** (Inter-Hotels) PL13 2JB ☎ (0503) 72667

Normal price: £50 including dinner.
Short breaks: £45, min 2 nights. 2-30 Apr & 22 Oct-22 Dec.
Activity breaks: Riding, Sailing, Water Skiing, Golf, Tennis,
Fishing and Walking Breaks. Details from hotel.
Credit cards ①②③⑤

Lovely gardens surround this charming hotel whose rooms have excellent sea views. The food is good, the staff helpful, and the hotel has access to the beach.

TINTAGEL   Cornwall & Isles of Scilly   Map 2 SX08

★★561% **Atlantic View** Treknow PL34 0EJ ☎ (0840) 770221

Normal price: £35. Dinner £11.50 & à la carte (1990 prices)
Short breaks: £30. £6.50 single supplement. Min 3 nights,
Oct-Easter
Credit cards ①③

A small personally-run hotel with comfortable lounges and fine sea views. Some of the bedrooms have four-poster beds, and all are ensuite with colour television. Children under two are not accommodated.

★★62% **Bossiney House** PL34 0AX ☎ (0840) 770240
Closed Nov-Feb (except 5 days at Xmas)

Normal price: £31. Dinner £8.25-£10.25
Short breaks: £26.50. Min 3 nights, Mar-May, part Jun & Oct
Credit cards ①②③⑤

This modern holiday hotel is situated in its own grounds and has good leisure facilities including an indoor heated pool. Most of the bedrooms have private bath or shower rooms. Christmas breaks are available.

GH Q Trevervan Trewarmett, PL34 0ES ☎ (0840) 770486

Normal price: £14
Short breaks: £54 for 3 nights
🐕 (ex guide dogs) Credit cards ①③

This personally-run guesthouse is situated in the village of Trewarmett, two miles south on the B3263. It offers comfortable accommodation with rooms for families and non-smokers.

GH QQQ Trewarmett Lodge PL34 0ET ☎ (0840) 770460

Normal price: £25
Short breaks: £22.50, single £25.50. Min 2 nights, Mar-Oct
Credit cards ①③⑤

Standing in a small hamlet one mile from Tintagel, this small hotel has a popular and busy restaurant and comfortable accommodation.

TORPOINT   Cornwall & Isles of Scilly   Map 2 SX45

★67% **Whitsand Bay** Portwrinkle PL11 3BU (5m W, off B3247) ☎ (0503) 30276

Normal price: £35. Dinner £12.50.
Short breaks: £32. Single supplement.
Activity breaks: Golf Break, £50 per night including one
hour's tuition and one round of golf.

A popular family and golfing hotel commanding unrestricted sea views. It offers an attractive new leisure complex adjacent to the golf course.

TRENEAR (nr Helston)   Cornwall & Isles of Scilly   Map 2 SW63

FH Q Longstone TR13 0HG ☎ (0326) 572483
Normal price: £11-£12.
Short breaks: £10.50. Sep, Oct, & Feb-Apr (not Easter)

This farmhouse is set in beautiful countryside and has a playroom and sun lounge.

TRURO   Cornwall & Isles of Scilly   Map 2 SW84

★★★63% Brookdale (Inter-Hotels) Tregolls Road TR1 1JZ ☎ (0872) 73513 & 79305
Closed Xmas week
Normal price: £31. Dinner £14.50
Short breaks: £38, single £50. Min 2 nights, Fri-Sun
Credit cards 1 2 3 5

A small and well-managed hotel pleasantly situated in the centre of Truro. Each bedroom has a private bath or shower room and colour television, and the restaurant offers imaginative dishes.

WATERGATE BAY   Cornwall & Isles of Scilly   Map 2 SW86

★★59% Tregurrian TR8 4AB ☎ (0637) 860280
Closed Nov-Feb
Normal price: £14.50 (1990 prices)
Short breaks: 5% reduction for 3 nights, 10% reduction for 5 nights, (except Jul & Aug)
Credit cards 1 3

This family-run hotel is close to the beach, and offers special facilities for children and leisure amenities which include an outdoor heated pool. Most of the bedrooms are ensuite, and all have colour television.

WIDEGATES   Cornwall & Isles of Scilly   Map 2 SX25

GH QQQ Coombe Farm PL13 1QN ☎ (05034) 223
Mar-Oct
Normal price: £16.50-£18.50
Short breaks: £2 nights £51-£54, 3 nights £76
✕ (ex guide dogs)

This delightful country house is set in ten acres of lawns, woods, streams and ponds. It has a heated outdoor swimming pool, a games room, and large, comfortable family bedrooms. Children under five are not accommodated.

▒ CUMBRIA ▒

AMBLESIDE   Cumbria   Map 7 NY30

★★64% Borrans Park Borrans Road LA22 0EN ☎ (05394) 33454
Closed three days at Xmas
Normal price: £52-£64 (room). Dinner £13
Short breaks: £35, min 2 nights, Nov-Mar
✕ Credit cards 1 3

This fine Georgian house is set in its own landscaped gardens on the southern outskirts of town. All the bedrooms have ensuite bath or shower rooms and colour television, there are two family rooms and seven rooms have four-poster beds. Children under seven are not accommodated.

GH QQ Compston House Compston Road LA22 9DJ ☎ (05394) 32305

Normal price: £21.50 room and breakfast
Short breaks: £17.50. Min 2 nights, Sun-Thu, Nov-Mar
✗ (ex guide dogs)

This family-run hotel has a very friendly atmosphere. Accommodation includes a bright attractive dining rom, a lounge and bar. All the bedrooms have private showers, there is one family room and two for non-smokers. Children under five are not accepted.

★★63% **Elder Grove** Lake Road LA22 0DB (on A591 ¹/₂m S) ☎ (05394) 32504
Closed mid Nov-mid Feb

Normal price: £32.50
Short breaks: £33.50 low season. Min 2 nights.

This family-run hotel has twelve pleasantly decorated bedrooms all with private bath or shower room and colour television. There is one family room and one room with a four-poster bed.

★★60% **Glen Rothay** Rydal LA22 9LR ☎ (05394) 32524

Normal price: £35 bed and breakfast, £45 including dinner
Short breaks: £124.50 for 3 nights
Credit cards [1] [3]

This quaint, historic hotel offers ensuite facilities and colour televisions in all bedrooms, including the family rooms and those with four-poster beds. Fishing is available, and there is a special programme of events at Christmas.

GH QQQQ Grey Friar Lodge Country House Brathay LA22 9NE (1m W off A593) ☎ (05394) 33158
Mar-Oct

Normal price: £37.50
Short breaks: £35. Min 3 nights, Mar-Oct
✗

Superb hospitality and cooking are the hallmarks of this excellent country house. Ensuite bath or shower rooms and colour television are provided in all of the eight bedrooms. Children under twelve are not accommodated.

★★70% **Kirkstone Foot Country House** Kirkstone Passs Road LA22 9EH ☎ (05394) 32232

Normal price: £44.50-£53.50 including dinner.
Short breaks: £35-£45.
Activity breaks: Wines of the World Weekend, £120 for 2 nights including all tasting wines and dinner wine. Various wine suppliers to speak and host the events. 15th, 22nd & 29th November. Christmas & New Year breaks, details on application.
✗

A converted 17th-century manor house in an attractive position above town, with well-kept grounds. A 5-course dinner is served at 8pm with the emphasis on traditional English food.

QQQ Lyndhurst Wansfell Road LA22 0EG ☎ (05394) 32421

Normal price: £26.50 including dinner.
Short breaks: £70.00 for 3 days.

This compact, modern guesthouse has well-equipped bedrooms, two of which are in an adjacent building just 10 yards away.

★★ 🐾 72% **Nanny Brow Country House** Clappersgate LA22 9NF ☎ (05394) 32036

Normal price: £43-£78. Dinner £18.50.
Short breaks: £38-£65, min 4 nights incl Fri, Sat & Sun. Nov-May.
Activity breaks: Theme weekends, £25 on top of normal room rates. Oct-Mar.

Attractive Edwardian country house sitting in its own grounds high above the A593. Traditional rooms in the main house are complemented by a garden wing of suites and studio bedrooms.

★★69% **Riverside** Under Loughrigg, Rothay Bridge LA22 9LJ ☎ (05394) 32395
Closed Dec-Jan

Normal price: £26.50
Short breaks: from £20. Min 2 nights, available all year except Bank Holidays
🕱

Looking out across the River Rothay to Loughrigg Fell is this attractive, comfortable hotel. All rooms have ensuite bathrooms and colour television, there are two family rooms and one room with a four-poster bed. Children under eight are not accepted. The hotel has fishing facilities.

GH QQQQ Rothay Garth Rothay Road LA22 0EE ☎ (05394) 32217

Normal price: £88-£104 room, including dinner.
Short breaks: £70-£89 for 2 people. Min 2 nights, Jan-part Aug & part Oct-Dec

A delightful hotel offering attentive service and wholesome, fresh cuisine. All the bedrooms have colour television, most have private bath or shower, and some are set aside for non-smokers. The hotel has special facilities for children.

★★70% Skelwith Bridge Skelwith Bridge LA22 9NJ (2¹/₂m W A593) ☎ (05394) 32115

Normal price: £19 Nov-Mar, £34 Apr-Oct
Short breaks: from £25, Nov-Mar, min 2 nights; from £40, Apr-May, min 2 nights; from £37.50 Jun-Aug.
Credit cards ① ③

Set in picturesque surroundings this 17th-century inn retains a wealth of charm and character. There are twenty-three comfortable bedrooms all with ensuite bath and shower facilities and colour television. Three are family rooms, two have four-poster beds and some are set aside for non-smokers. Fishing is available.

GH Q Thrang House Compston Road LA22 9DJ ☎ (05394) 32112
Mar-Dec

Normal price: £28
Short breaks: £25-£30. Min 2 nights, Sun-Thu, Mar-Jun
✻

Good, hearty breakfasts are served at this slate built house. There are six bedrooms all with colour television, and two have private showers. Children under nine are not accommodated.

★★76% Wateredge Borrans Road, Waterhead LA22 0EP ☎ (05394) 32332
Closed mid Dec-early Feb

Normal price: from £110 including dinner
Short breaks: from £84 Sun-Thu; from £94 including dinner Fri-Sat. Available early Feb-mid May (excluding Easter week and Bank Holidays), and Nov-mid Dec. Prices are for 2 people.

Two 17th-century cottages form the heart of this skilfully extended, comfortable hotel on the edge of Windermere. All rooms have ensuite facilities and colour television. A rowing boat is available for guests' use. Children under seven are not accommodated.

ALSTON   Cumbria   Map 12 NY74

★★67% Lowbyer Manor Country House CA9 3JX ☎ (0434) 381230

Normal price: £50.50 room. Dinner £13.15-£18.85 à la carte
Short breaks: £75 room. Min 2 nights, Nov-Jun
Credit cards ① ② ③ ⑤

An interesting period house on the A686, one mile north of the town centre, offering comfortable accommodation. It has eleven bedrooms, some in an annexe, and all with ensuite bath or shower rooms and colour television. There is a special Christmas programme.

APPLEBY-IN-WESTMORLAND   Cumbria   Map 12 NY62

★★★ ⚘ 68% Appleby Manor Country House (Best Western) Roman Road CA16 6JD ☎ (07683) 51571

Normal price: £35.50-£42. Dinner £13-£14.50.
Short breaks: £46-£49. Min 2 nights. Single supplement.
Activity breaks: Romance break, £66. Cycling break, £53. Hangover break – whisky tasting, £58. All prices for 2 nights.

Red sandstone building in its own grounds in an elevated position overlooking the town. A relaxed and informal style of service is provided.

★★59% White Hart Boroughgate CA16 6XG ☎ (07683) 51598

Normal price: £22.50. Dinner £9 and à la carte
Short breaks: £20-£25. Min 2 nights excluding Bank Holidays, Jul, Aug and Fair Week

This small, modernised hotel dates from the 18th century. All the bedrooms have colour television and some have ensuite facilities. Smoking is not permitted in the bedrooms.

BARROW-IN-FURNESS   Cumbria   Map 7 SD16

★★66% **Lisdoonie** 307/309 Abbey Road LA14 5LF ☎ (0229) 27312
Closed Xmas & New Year

Normal price: £45 room with breakfast, single £36 (1990
prices)
Short breaks: room with breakfast £33, single £22. Min 2
nights, Fri-Sat (1990 prices)
Credit cards 1 2 3

A compact, homely hotel on the main road. All rooms have private facilities and colour television and there are two family rooms.

BASSENTHWAITE   Cumbria   Map 11 NY23

★★★★ ₩ 58% **Armathwaite Hall** CA12 4RE ☎ (059681) 551

Normal price: £50-£85. Dinner from £23.95.
Short breaks: £55 or £62.50. Min 2 nights, Fri, Sat & Sun,
Nov-Apr excluding Xmas, New Year & Easter.
Activity breaks: Four-star Riding Holiday, £135 or £145 for
2 nights, including 2 hours daily riding. Sauna, Swimming
and Fishing Break, details on request. Other activities
available based on a minimum of 10 people.
Credit cards 1 2 3 5

A pleasant country house atmosphere is enhanced by helpful service and willing staff at this large hotel with fine views across the lake.

FH QQ Bassenthwaite Hall (East) CA12 4QP ☎ (059681) 393
Apr-Oct restricted service Jan & Dec

Normal price: £15
Short breaks: £12.50. Min 2 nights.

A fully modernised 17th-century farmhouse in a picturesque village close to a quiet stream. There are two bedrooms, one a family room. Children under two are not accommodated.

★★★59% **Castle Inn** (Best Western) CA12 4RG ☎ (059681) 401

Normal price: £39.50. Dinner £12.95 & à la carte
Short breaks: £47. Single £57. Min 2 nights.
Credit cards 1 2 3 5

This former coaching inn stands beside the A591 at the head of Bassenthwaite Lake. The hotel has extensive leisure amenities, special facilities for children and provides a special Christmas programme.

★★ ₩ 67% **Overwater Hall** Ireby CA5 1HH ☎ (059681) 566
Closed 24 Dec-23 Feb

Normal price: £40 room and breakfast
Short breaks: £33 Sun-Thu, £35 Fri-Sat; single £38 Sun-Thu,
£40 Fri-Sat. Min 2 nights, Feb-Jun
Credit cards 1 3

Set in splendid seclusion near Overwater, north of Bassenthwaite, this family-run hotel is popular locally for dinner. Most of the bedrooms have unspoilt views of the countryside; there are family rooms and some rooms with four-poster beds.

BEETHAM   Cumbria   Map 7 SD47

★62% **Wheatsheaf** LA7 7AL ☎ (05395) 62123

Normal price: £35 room with breakfast. Dinner £7.50 & à la
carte
Short breaks: £22, Oct-Apr (except Easter).
Credit cards 1 3

An attractive, oak-beamed village inn close to Lakeland, noted for its bar food. There are six cosy bedrooms, all with private facilities and colour television.

BORROWDALE   Cumbria   Map 11 NY21

★★★69% **Borrowdale** CA12 5UY ☎ (059684) 224

Normal price: £70-£90 room. Dinner from £15.50.
Short breaks: £230 for two, min 4 nights, Sun-Thu.
Activity breaks: Winter Walking Weekends, £95-£120 including full day's walking with experienced guide, packed lunch and Sunday lunch.
Credit cards 1 3

A former coaching inn, carefully modernised to provide comfortable, well-equipped bedrooms, with friendly and efficient young staff.

★★★66% **Borrowdale Gates Country House** CA12 5UQ ☎ (059684) 204 & 606 due to change to (07687) 77204

Normal price: £34-£39 including dinner. Single £37-£42
Short breaks: £100 for 3 nights, Thu-Sun; single £107; £122.50 for 4 nights, Sun-Thu. Single £130. Nov-Mar. 1990 prices.
🐾 (ex guide dogs) Credit cards 1 3

Set amid beautiful Lakeland scenery this delightful hotel offers comfortable, well-equipped ensuite bedrooms, relaxing lounges and good food. There are special facilities for children and a Christmas programme is available.

★★★★72% **Lodore Swiss** (Stakis) CA12 5UX ☎ (059684) 285
Closed 4 Jan-14 Feb

Normal price: £55 including dinner
Short breaks: from £50 including £22 dinner allowance.
Min 7 nights
Credit cards 1 2 3 5

Located at the head of the Borrowdale valley, this hotel has an excellent range of leisure facilities including two swimming pools, tennis, squash and a gymnasium. All the comfortable bedrooms have ensuite facilities and colour television, and some rooms are for families.

BRAMPTON   Cumbria   Map 12 NY56

✿★★ (Red) 🏵 **Farlam Hall** (Relais et Châteaux) Hallbankgate CA8 2NG (2³/₄m SE A689)
☎ (06976) 234 & 357 Closed Feb (Rosette awarded for dinner only)

Normal price: £130-£180 room with dinner
Short breaks: £110-£160. Min 2 nights. Nov-Jan & Mar-Apr (except Bank Holidays)
Credit cards 1 3

Situated in delightful wooded grounds with a gently flowing river, this part 17th- and part 19th-century house offers courteous service and mainly traditional British cooking. There are thirteen comfortable bedrooms all with ensuite facilities and colour television, and one room has a four-poster bed. Children under five are not accommodated.

★★69% **Tarn End** Talkin Tarn CA8 1LS (2m S off B6413) ☎ (06977) 2340
Closed Feb Restricted service Oct-Jan

Normal price: £29.75. Dinner £15.50-£25.50 à la carte
Short breaks: £45. Min 2 nights
🐾 (ex guide dogs) Credit cards 1 2 3 5

This friendly, peaceful, family-run hotel on the banks of Talkin Tarn is justifiably proud of the standard of its French haute cuisine. All six bedrooms have ensuite bath or shower rooms and colour television and there is one family room. There are facilities for fishing and rowing. A special Christmas programme is offered.

BROUGH   Cumbria   Map 12 NY71

★★57% **Castle** Main Street CA7 4AX ☎ (09304) 252

Normal price: £17.50. Dinner £5.50-£11 and à la carte
Short breaks: £15. Min 3 nights, Nov-Mar. Single £20
🍴 (ex guide dogs) Credit cards ①③

This hotel offers fourteen bedrooms ranging from the spacious and traditional to more modern and compact. All have ensuite facilities and colour television, and there are two family rooms. There is a special Christmas programme.

BROUGHTON IN FURNESS   Cumbria   Map 7 SD28

★★61% **Eccle Riggs** Foxfield Road LA20 6BN ☎ (0229) 716398 & 716780

Normal price: £64.50 room with breakfast. Dinner £10.50 and à la carte (1990 prices)
Short breaks: £43.50 for two

Set in parkland one mile from the village, this Victorian mansion has bedrooms equipped with ensuite facilities and colour television; some rooms are set aside for families. The hotel has an indoor heated swimming pool, a 9-hole golf course and solarium. There is a special Christmas programme.

BUTTERMERE   Cumbria   Map 11 NY11

★★66% **Bridge** CA13 9UZ ☎ (059685) 252 & 266

Normal price: £46 including dinner
Short breaks: £39. Min 2 nights, Sun-Thu, Nov-Mar and other months as available

A warm and friendly hotel providing accommodation in comfortably furnished bedrooms with modern facilities. All rooms have private bathrooms and two have four-poster beds. There is a special Christmas programme.

CARLISLE   Cumbria   Map 11 NY45

★★★63% **Central Plaza** (Inter-Hotels) Victoria Viaduct CA3 8AL ☎ (0228) 20256

Normal price: £66 room. Dinner from £14.50 & à la carte
Short breaks: £45. Single supplement £6. Min 2 nights
Credit cards ①②③⑤

All the bedrooms at this city centre hotel have ensuite bath or shower rooms and colour television. There is a special Christmas programme.

★★★68% **Cumbrian** Court Square CA1 1QY ☎ (0228) 31951

Normal price: £87.50 room. Dinner £16.50 & à la carte
Short breaks: £90 for two. Min 2 nights
Credit cards ①②③⑤

This totally renovated hotel stands next to the railway station and offers first class accommodation and spacious lounges and bars. All bedrooms are ensuite with colour television. There is a special Christmas programme.

CARTMEL   Cumbria   Map 7 SD37

★★58% **Aynsome Manor** LA11 6HH (1m N on unclass rd) ☎ (05395) 36653
Closed 2-28 Jan

Normal price: £88-£98 room. Dinner £16
Short breaks: £67-£73 midweek, £73-£80 weekends for two. Min 2 nights
Credit cards ①②③

This lovely old manor house is surrounded by farmland. Bedrooms have their own style and character, all have colour television and most have private baths or showers. There is a special Christmas programme.

CASTERTON Cumbria Map 7 SD67

★★66% **Pheasant Inn** LA6 2RX ☎ (05242) 71230

Normal price: £25-£27.50. Dinner £11-£13.50 & à la carte
Short breaks: £35.
Credit cards ☐1☐ ☐3☐

A comfortable village inn popular for its restaurant dinners and bar lunches. Annexe bedrooms are contained in a modernised coaching house, and all have private facilities and colour television. There are special facilities for children. A Christmas programme is available.

COCKERMOUTH Cumbria Map 11 NY13

★★56% **Globe** (Consort) CA13 9LE ☎ (0900) 822126

Normal price: £35. Dinner from £13
Short breaks: £30. Min 2 nights
Credit cards ☐1☐ ☐2☐ ☐3☐ ☐5☐

Originally a coaching inn, this hotel has practical bedrooms with colour television, most with private facilities. There is a special Christmas programme.

GH QQQQ Low Hall Country Brandlingill CA13 0RE (3m S on unclass off A5086) ☎ (0900) 826654
Etr-Nov restricted service New Year

Normal price: £38-£46 room. Dinner £11
Short breaks: £63-£76 for two. Min 3 nights, Easter – Nov
Credit cards ☐1☐ ☐3☐

A delightful 17th-century converted farmhouse set in a peaceful location. Bedrooms are individually furnished and decorated with Laura Ashley designs, and some have ensuite facilities. Children under ten are not accommodated.

★★★61% **Trout** Crown Street CA13 0EJ ☎ (0900) 823591

Normal price: £30. Dinner £13.95-£16.95 & à la carte
Short breaks: £35. Min 2 nights, Fri-Sun (ex Bank Holidays). Single £80 for 2 nights

An attractive hotel with immaculate side gardens running down to the River Derwent where the hotel has fishing rights. Bedrooms have recently been improved, and all have colour television and ensuite facilities. There is a special Christmas programme.

CONISTON   Cumbria   Map 7 SD39

★66% **Black Bull** Yewdale Road LA21 8DU ☎ (05394) 41335

Normal price: £30. Dinner from £9.50 à la carte
Short breaks: £25 excluding dinner. Min 3 nights
Credit cards ① ③

A charming country inn at the centre of the village offering a good standard of cooking. All bedrooms are ensuite with colour television. There are facilities for sailing and pony trekking, and there is a special Christmas programme.

QQQQ Coniston Lodge Sunny Brow, LA21 8HH ☎ (05394) 41201

Normal price: £27.50
Short breaks: £20.62, min 4 nights.
Credit cards ① ③

A magnificent extension to a family home has been furnished and decorated to the highest standard. It is both attractive and comfortable, and all six bedrooms are thoughtfully equipped. This is a non-smoking house.

★★65% **Coniston Sun** LA21 8HQ ☎ (05394) 41248

Normal price: £30-£35. Dinner £15.50-£18
Short breaks: £27 excluding dinner. Sun-Thu, Nov-Mar
(ex Christmas and Bank Holidays)
Credit cards ① ③

Standing high above the village, this spaciously comfortable family-run hotel offers enjoyable cordon bleu meals. Most bedrooms are ensuite, all have colour television and two are furnished with four-poster beds.

★★63% **Yewdale** Yewdale Road LA21 8LU ☎ (05394) 41280

Normal price: £18.95-£26.95. Dinner £12.50-£13.50
Short breaks: £107.50 for 4 nights, Sun-Thu
Credit cards ① ③

A charming little village-centre hotel dating back to 1896, offering attractive accommodation and a warm welcome. All bedrooms have colour television, and most have ensuite facilities.

CROOKLANDS   Cumbria   Map 7 SD58

★★★65% **Crooklands** (Best Western) LA7 7NW ☎ (04487) 432

Normal price: £50. Dinner £8.50-£18.50 & à la carte
Short breaks: £53. Min 2 nights (except Xmas)
🎄 Credit cards ① ② ③ ⑤

A former 16th-century Croft and Ale house with low beamed ceilings and stone walls in the public areas, and a modern bedroom wing. All rooms have colour television, and some have ensuite baths. There is a special Christmas programme.

CROSBY-ON-EDEN   Cumbria   Map 12 NY45

★★★56% **Newby Grange** CA6 4RA ☎ (022873) 645 due to change to (0228) 573645

Normal price: £81.90 room. Dinner £10.95 & à la carte
Short breaks: £30. Min 2 nights weekends, 4 nights
midweek (except December)
Credit cards ① ③

Offering efficient and friendly service, this hotel is set in five acres of attractive grounds. All bedrooms have ensuite facilities and colour television. Fishing is available and there is a special Christmas programme.

★★★ 🐾 69% **Crosby Lodge Country House** High Crosby CA6 4QZ ☎ (022873) 618 due to change to
(0228) 573618 Closed 24 Dec-mid Jan Restricted service Sun

Normal price: £60.50 room & breakfast. Dinner £20.50-
£24.50 & à la carte
Short breaks: £43.75. Min 2 nights, Fri-Sat, Oct-Apr
(except Bank Holidays)
Credit cards ① ② ③

Elegantly furnished, spacious, comfortable bedrooms with ensuite facilities and colour television are a feature of this relaxing family-owned hotel. The restaurant provides a high standard of cuisine.

ELTERWATER   Cumbria   Map 7 NY30

★★ ♨ 68% **Eltermere Country House** LA22 9HY (on unclass rd between A593 & B5343)
☎ (09667) 207 Closed 25-26 Dec Restricted service mid Nov-mid Feb

Normal price: £28.50. Dinner £13.95
Short breaks: from £35 (1990 price). Min 3 nights midweek, min 4 nights if includes weekend. Mid Feb-23 Aug (except Bank Holiday weeks)

This charming country house overlooks Elterwater and the surrounding fells. Most of the attractive bedrooms have ensuite facilities, and all have colour television.

ESKDALE GREEN   Cumbria   Map 6 NY10

★★61% **Bower House Inn** (Best Western) CA19 1TD ☎ (09403) 244

Normal price: from £25. Dinner from £15
Short breaks: £35, single £40. Min 2 nights, Fri-Mon.
✕ Credit cards [1] [3]

This country inn is popular with tourists and hillwalkers. Most of the bedrooms are contained in two annexe buildings and have ensuite facilities and colour television. There are some family rooms. A special Christmas programme is available.

FAUGH   Cumbria   Map 12 NY55

★★★54% **String of Horses Inn** CA4 9EG ☎ (0228) 70297
Closed 24-25 Dec

Normal price: from £66 room. Dinner from £14.95 & à la carte
Short breaks: from £52 for two excluding dinner. Min 2 nights, Oct-Apr. Single 10% reduction
Credit cards [1] [2] [3] [5]

A charming village inn with oak beams and roaring log fires. The bedrooms are very elaborate, most with canopied or four-poster beds and double sunken baths. There is a swimming pool.

GLENRIDDING   Cumbria   Map 11 NY31

★★63% **Glenridding** (Best Western) CA11 0PB ☎ (07684) 82228
Closed 4-23 Jan

Normal price: £32.50. Dinner from £17.50.
Short breaks: £47 min 2 nights, £45 min 3 nights.
Credit cards [1] [2] [3] [5]

This friendly tourist hotel situated in the centre of the village has a dining room, bar and budget restaurant. Each bedroom has colour television and private bath or shower room, and two rooms have four-poster beds. A Christmas programme is available.

GRANGE-OVER-SANDS   Cumbria   Map 7 SD47

★68% **Clare House** Park Road LA11 7HQ ☎ (05395) 33026 & 34253
Closed Nov-Mar

Normal price: £23-£26. Dinner £14
Short breaks: £30. Min 4 nights, Apr.

Warm, comfortable accommodation is available at this family-run hotel overlooking Morecambe Bay. Most bedrooms are ensuite, and some have balconies and sea views. Guests can enjoy croquet and putting. No children under five years.

★★★65% **Grange** (Consort) Lindale Road, Station Square, LA11 6EJ ☎ (05395) 33666

Normal price: £62 room with breakfast. Dinner £13.50 & à la carte
Short breaks: £129 for two for 3 nights. Single supplement £5
Credit cards 1 2 3 5

A substantial Victorian building overlooking the town and bay from its well-tended gardens. Each room has colour television and ensuite bath or shower. There are special facilities for children, and a Christmas programme is provided.

★★69% **Netherwood** Lindale Road LA11 6ET ☎ (05395) 32552

Normal price: from £32.75. Dinner £10-£13 & à la carte
Short breaks: £35. Min 2 nights, Nov-Mar.

Overlooking Morecambe Bay estuary, this hotel has an indoor heated swimming pool and a gymnasium, and offers special facilities for children. All bedrooms have colour television, most have ensuite bath or shower room and there are rooms for non-smokers.

GRASMERE *Cumbria* Map 11 NY30

★★★65% **Gold Rill Country House** Red Bank Road LA22 9PU ☎ (09665) 486
Closed Jan

Normal price: £40. Dinner £16-£17
Short breaks: £36-£38, min 3 nights, Feb-Aug & Nov-Dec

This comfortable hotel lies just to the west of the village and is enthusiastically-run by resident proprietors. Bedrooms vary in size, all are ensuite with colour television and one has a four-poster bed. There are some leisure amenities and a Christmas programme is provided.

★★67% **Grasmere** Broadgate LA22 9TA ☎ (09665) 277
Closed Jan

Normal price: from £28. Dinner from £14
Short breaks: £32. Min 2 nights. Apr, Nov, Dec, Feb & Mar (except Bank Holidays)
Credit cards 1 3

This friendly hotel is set in its own gardens with lawns leading down to the river. Comfortable bedrooms are equipped with colour television and ensuite facilities, and one room has a four-poster bed. There are special facilities for children over seven, but children under seven are not accommodated.

★★67% **Oak Bank** (Guestaccom) Broadgate LA22 9TA ☎ (09665) 217
Closed Xmas-Jan

Normal price: £37-£40.
Short breaks: £60, 2 nights midweek; £66, 2 nights weekend. Feb-Easter & Nov-Dec
Credit cards [1] [3]

This hotel has an attractive conservatory dining room where guests can enjoy a four-course dinner. The comfortable bedrooms are all ensuite with colour television, and two are furnished with four-poster beds. See advertisement on p71.

★★★64% **Prince of Wales** (Mount Charlotte (TS)) LA22 9PR ☎ (09665) 666

Normal price: £70 (room). Dinner from £12.50
Short breaks: £44.50, single occupancy £54.50. Min 2 nights, all year (except Xmas & New Year). 1990 Prices.
Credit cards [1] [2] [3] [4] [5]

Situated on the shore of the lake, this hotel provides friendly service and comfortable accommodation in ensuite bedrooms with colour television. Fishing is available.

★★★61% **Red Lion** (Consort) Red Lion Square LA22 9SS ☎ (09665) 456

Normal price: £36-£46
Short breaks: £28.80-£36.80. Min 5 nights, Sun-Thu (except Easter, Xmas & New Year)
Credit cards [1] [2] [3] [5]

Set at the heart of this popular village this tourist hotel has fine views over the surrounding countryside. All bedrooms are ensuite with colour television and there are some family rooms. There is a special Christmas programme.

★★★★64% **Wordsworth** LA22 9SW ☎ (09665) 592

Normal price: £48. Dinner £16.
Short breaks: £45 Sun-Thu, £56 Fri & Sat. Min 2 nights. Single supplement.
Activity breaks: Champagne Breaks: July-Aug Bank Hol Weekend. Details from hotel. Valentine Weekend, £105 (1990) February.
🏌

The hotel has steadily improved since reopening under private ownership in 1987, and now offers some splendid bedrooms, and a sun lounge extension to the attractive swimming pool. See advertisement in colour section.

GRIZEDALE   Cumbria   Map 7 SD39

★★70% **Grizedale Lodge** LA22 0QL ☎ (09666) 532
Closed Jan-mid Feb

Normal price: £40 with dinner
Short breaks: £75 2 nights Fri-Sun; £68 2 nights midweek. £6 single supplement. Feb, Mar, Nov, Dec
🏌 Credit cards [1] [3]

A peaceful, relaxing hotel providing skilfully prepared meals and comfortable accommodation in ensuite bedrooms with colour television. Smoking is not permitted in the bedrooms. There is a special Christmas programme.

HAWKSHEAD (near Ambleside)   Cumbria   Map 7 SD39

★★ 🛥 75% **Field Head House** Outgate LA22 0PY ☎ (09666) 240
Closed 14 Jan-8 Feb Restricted service Tue

Normal price: £52.50-£57.50
Short breaks: £47.50-£52.50. Min 2 nights, Wed-Mon

A small country house hotel with seven bedrooms all offering ensuite facilities and colour television (smoking is not permitted in the bedrooms). A special Christmas programme is provided.

★★ 🏩 73% **Highfield House** Hawkshead Hill LA22 0PN ☎ (09666) 344
Closed 24-26 Dec

Normal price: £64-£80 room with dinner
Short breaks: £58-£72 for two. Single occupancy from
£29.70. Min 2 nights, Dec-Mar.
Credit cards ③

Set in its own grounds just outside the village,
this country house has comfortable bedrooms,
most ensuite and all with colour television. The
inventive country cooking offers excellent
value for money.

INN Q Kings Arms LA22 0NZ ☎ (09666) 372

Normal price: £17-£20.50
Short breaks: £15 excluding dinner. Sun-Thu, Dec-Easter
(except 24 Dec-3 Jan)
Credit cards ① ③

Overlooking the village square, this 16th-
century inn has oak beams and an open fire.
Some bedrooms have ensuite shower rooms,
and all have colour television.

★★63% **Queen's Head** Main Street LA22 0NS ☎ (09666) 271

Normal price: £25. Dinner £12-£17 à la carte
Short breaks: £63 for 3 nights excluding dinner. Sun-Thu
🐾 Credit cards ① ② ③

An historic inn at the centre of the village,
popular for its bar meals and à la carte dinners.
Most bedrooms are ensuite with colour
television. A Christmas programme is available.
Children under eight are not accommodated.

★★★ 🏩 56% **Tarn Hows** Hawkshead Hill LA22 0PR ☎ (09666) 330

Normal price: £50. Dinner from £16.50 & à la carte
Short breaks: £45. Min 2 nights
Credit cards ① ② ③ ⑤

Situated at Tarn Hows on an unclassified road,
this comfortable hotel offers peace and
tranquility along with friendly attentive service.
All bedrooms are ensuite with colour television.
There are some leisure amenities and a
Christmas programme is available.

KENDAL   Cumbria   Map 7 SD59

★★69% **Garden House** Fowl-ing Lane LA9 6PH ☎ (0539) 731131
Closed 4 days at Xmas

Normal price: £31.50. Dinner £14.75-£16.50
Short breaks: £43, min 2 nights. Single £43, Fri-Sun only
🐾 (ex guide dogs) Credit cards ① ② ③ ⑤

This pleasant Regency-style house is situated
off the A685 to the north east of the town
centre. Bedrooms are individually decorated
and particularly well equipped, and most are
'non-smoking'.

GH QQQQ Lane Head Country House Helsington LA9 5RJ (0.5m S off A6) ☎ (0539) 731283/721023

Normal price: £25-£29
Short breaks: £38. Min 2 nights, Nov-Apr
Credit cards ① ③

Set on a hillside overlooking Kendal this
hotel provides comfortable, well-equipped
accommodation and imaginative three or four
course dinners. Children under five are not
accommodated.

★★★69% **Riverside** Stramongate Bridge LA9 4BZ ☎ (0539) 724707

Normal price: £37. Dinner £13.50 & à la carte
Short breaks: £44, single £54. Min 2 nights
🐾 (ex guide dogs) Credit cards ① ② ③ ⑤

This newly-built hotel, a former tannery, is set
on the banks of the River Kent and has
comfortable bedrooms all with ensuite
facilities. The restaurant provides a high
standard of cuisine, with lighter dishes served
in the Buttery. Christmas breaks are available.

★★60% Woolpack Stricklandgate LA9 4ND ☎ (0539) 723852

Normal price: from £75 room. Dinner £13.50-£15 & à la carte
Short breaks: £47.50, single £57.50. Min 2 nights includes lunch on day of departure
Credit cards ① ② ③

This modernised coaching inn has character bars and a popular coffee house. Bedrooms are all ensuite with colour television, with rooms for families and non-smokers. Christmas breaks are available.

KESWICK Cumbria Map 11 NY22

★★★73% Brundholme Country House Brundholme Road CA12 4NL ☎ (07687) 74495

Normal price: £35. Dinner £16.
Short breaks: £47.25, min 2 nights, except bank holidays and Sept-Oct.
Activity breaks: Mountain Biking and Fell Wandering Breaks. Details from hotel.
Credit cards ① ③

Converted to a stylish country house hotel in 1988, this fine Georgian mansion commands superb views across the town to the surrounding hills. The emphasis is on quality throughout.

★★66% Chaucer House Ambleside Road CA12 4DR ☎ (07687) 72318 & 73223

Normal price: £27.50. £32.50 en suite. Dinner £9.30.
Short breaks: £22.50. £26.50 en suite, min 2 nights, Sun-Thu, Mar-May & Oct. Single price £24. £28.50 en suite.
Activity breaks: Free Golf Break, normal rate, Mon-Thu. Walking Breaks, details on request.
Credit cards ① ② ③ ④

A friendly comfortable hotel with several spacious lounges - one with a real fire - and attractive dining room and lounge bar.

GH QQQ Dalegarth House Country Portinscale CA12 5RQ ☎ (07687) 72817

Normal price: £22 bed and breakfast, £32 with dinner
Short breaks: £29.50 with 6-course dinner. Dec-May.
🕇 (ex guide dogs) Credit cards ① ③

Set in its own gardens, this detached house near Keswick has an attractive dining room and residents bar. All bedrooms are 'no-smoking', and facilities include private bath or shower room and colour television. Children under five are not accommodated.

★★★57% Derwentwater (Consort) Portinscale CA12 5RE ☎ (07687) 72538

Normal price: £56.45. Dinner £12.95-£14.50.
Short breaks: £46.50, min 2 nights. Single price £52.75.
Activity breaks: Murder Weekends, £125 for two nights including wine reception, morning coffee Sat & Sun, and buffet lunch Sat. 22 & 29 Nov 1991, 17, 24 & 31 Jan and 7 & 14 Feb 1992

This hotel looks towards Derwentwater from its setting of neat lawns and gardens, and has recently been improved by an upgrading programme.

GH QQ Foye House 23 Eskin Street CA12 4DQ ☎ (07687) 73288

Normal price: £42-£44 (room) with dinner
Short breaks: £120 (room) with dinner for 3 nights. Single
£60 for 3 nights. Jan-Jun & Oct-Dec (ex Bank Holidays)
🐾 (ex guide dogs)

Bright bedrooms (all are 'no-smoking') and cosy, comfortable public rooms are features of this guesthouse.

★67% **Latrigg Lodge** Lake Road CA12 5DQ ☎ (07687) 73545

Normal price: £22-£24, £34-£36 including dinner
Short breaks: £30, single £35 (includes £13 dinner
allowance). Min 2 nights

This is essentially a restaurant with bedrooms and is situated in the centre of town. All rooms are well furnished and have ensuite facilities and colour television, and there is a quiet comfortable lounge. Christmas breaks are available. See advertisement in colour section.

★67% **Linnett Hill** 4 Penrith Road, CA12 4HF ☎ (07687) 73109

Normal price: £18. Dinner £8.50 & à la carte
Short breaks: £24, single £26. Min 2 nights, Nov-Mar
(ex Bank Holidays)
Credit cards ① ③

This small, friendly hotel has a small bar, cosy lounge, a private car park and ensuite bedrooms with colour television. Children under five are not accommodated.

★★62% **Queen's** (Exec Hotel) Main Street CA12 5JF ☎ (07687) 73333
Closed 24-26 Dec

Normal price: £21-£27. Dinner £10.50-£12
Short breaks: £27.50-£34. Min 2 nights (ex Bank Holidays)
🐾 Credit cards① ② ③ ⑤

Standing in the centre of town, this early Victorian former posting house has ensuite bedrooms with colour television, many are family rooms. See advertisement on p75.

GH QQQ Ravensworth 29 Station Street CA12 5HH ☎ (07687) 72476
Feb-Dec

Normal price: £18
Short breaks: £24, single £30. Min 3 nights
🐾 (ex guide dogs) Credit cards ① ② ③ ⑤

This comfortable private hotel offers personal service. Some of the bedrooms have ensuite facilities.

★★ 🏨 66% **Red House** Underskiddaw CA12 4QA (on A591) ☎ (07687) 72211

Normal price: £39 Apr-mid May, Nov-Dec. £44 mid May-
Oct. Dinner £15.
Short breaks: £35 (£39) dates as above. Min 3 nights. Single
supplement.
Activity breaks: Painting Breaks, £260 for 5 nights. Spring
and early autumn.
Credit cards ① ③

Set amidst 8 acres of woodlands just north of Keswick, this Victorian country house commands superb views of northern Lakeland. Its games cellar is popular on wet days.

GH QQ Richmond House 37-39 Eskin Street CA12 4DG ☎ (07687) 73965

Normal price: £19.50.
Short breaks: £17, min 3 nights winter & spring.
Activity breaks: Photographic Breaks, £189 for 6 days
including packed lunches and tuition. 26 Oct-1 Nov. Caters
for the beginner to the advanced enthusiast. Run by a
professional landscape photographer.
🐾 Credit cards ① ③

A comfortable guesthouse set in a residential area close to the town centre.

★★61% Skiddaw Main Street CA12 5BN ☎ (07687) 72071
Normal price: £25.50. Dinner £11-£15.
Short breaks: £35.50, min 2 nights, Nov-Mar.
Activity breaks: Art Holidays, £192 for 4 nights. Jun-Oct.

A stay at this well-run hotel in the town centre represents good value for money, with a wide range of bar meals and an extensive à la carte menu in the evening. See advertisement on p74.

GH QQ Squirrel Lodge 43 Eskin Street CA12 4DG ☎ (07687) 73091
Closed Nov

Normal price: from £12.50.
Short breaks: £17.50. Min 2 nights, mid Oct-Easter
Credit cards ① ③

A lovely little family-run guesthouse offering well-appointed bedrooms and good food. This is a non-smoking establishment. Children under ten are not accommodated. There is no parking on the premises.

GH QQQ Thornleigh 23 Bank Street CA12 5JZ ☎ (07687) 72863
Normal price: £18
Short breaks: £16 bed and breakfast. Min 3 nights, Sun-Thu, Nov-Mar
Credit cards ① ③

Set in a residential area close to the town centre, this guesthouse offers ensuite bedrooms, first class home cooking and a friendly welcome. Children under sixteen are not accommodated.

★★63% Walpole Station Road CA12 4NA ☎ (07687) 72072
Normal price: £34 with dinner.
Short breaks: £30. Min 2 nights, Nov-Mar.
Credit cards ① ③

Good food and friendly service are features of this traditional tourist hotel. Most bedrooms have ensuite facilities, all have colour television. There is a special Christmas programme.

KIRKBY LONSDALE   *Cumbria*   Map 7 SD67

GH QQQ Abbot Hall LA6 2AB ☎ (05242) 71406
Normal price: £16.
Short breaks: £22.30, min 3 nights, Mar-May, Sept-Oct.
✱

This former farmhouse with its colourful window boxes, has oak beams and flagstone floors to add to its character. Home cooked meals are served on an impressive antique oak table.

INN QQQ Whoop Hall Skipton Road LA6 2HP ☎ (05242) 71284
Normal price: £25
Short breaks: £32.50, min 2 nights except Xmas & Bank Hols.
✱ Credit cards ① ③

Farm buildings from 1618 provide the shell for this attractive modern inn. Bedrooms are pleasant with many extras, and there is a split-level restaurant.

LONGTOWN   *Cumbria*   Map 11 NY36

FH QQ New Pallyards Hethersgill CA6 6HZ (5.5m E off the A6071 Brampton-Longtown rd, take unclass rd) ☎ (022877) 308 due to change to (0228) 577308

Normal price: £49 including dinner.
Short breaks: £129 for 3 nights.
Activity breaks: Fishing Breaks, from £43 per day, May-Sept. Horse Riding, from £59. Details from hotel.

A modern farmhouse situated 5.5 miles east of Longtown on the Stapleton road, with pretty bedrooms, comfortable lounges and a friendly atmosphere.

NEWBY BRIDGE   *Cumbria*   Map 7 SD38

★★★67% **Lakeside** (Consort) LA12 8AT ☎ (05395) 31207

Normal price: £50. Dinner £16.50.
Short breaks: £55, min 2 nights.
Activity breaks: Water Sports. Details from hotel.

A comfortable hotel set right on the shore at the southern end of Lake Windermere with many fine views. Helpful service is given by friendly young staff.

★★★63% **Swan** (Exec Hotel) LA12 8NB ☎ (05395) 31681

Normal price: £37. Dinner £15.50-£18.
Short breaks: from £42 (summer), from £44 (winter). Min 2 nights, must include Sat. 2 Apr-20 Aug, Nov-Mar. Single supplement.
Activity breaks: Weekend of Antiques, £100 (1990). Floral Art Weekend, £135, Weekend of Gilbert & Sullivan, £125.
🕱

Guests may arrive by car, boat or helicopter at this modernised coaching inn set on the River Leven at the southern end of Lake Windermere. Bedrooms are spacious and well-furnished.

★★★69% **Whitewater** The Lakeland Village LA12 8PX ☎ (05395) 31133

Normal price: £85 for 2 people.
Short breaks: £106 including £29.90 dinner allowance for 2 people (£63 for 1 person on 2-night stay).
🕱 (ex guide dogs) Credit cards ① ② ③ ⑤

A converted mill by the turbulent River Leven, this smart hotel and leisure club complex has spacious ensuite bedrooms and colour television, including a four-poster bed and family rooms. Leisure facilities include tennis, indoor swimming pool, squash, sauna, solarium, gymnasium, putting; also entertainment. Christmas breaks are available.

PENRITH   *Cumbria*   Map 12 NY53

★★ **George** Devonshire Street CA1 7SU ☎ (0768) 62696

Normal price: £49.50. Dinner from £9.75 (1990 price)
Short breaks: £60. Min 2 nights, Fri-Sun, Nov-Apr.
Supplement for single occupancy.
Credit cards ① ③

This former coaching inn provides courteous service and all bedrooms, which include a family room, have private bath or shower and colour television.

QQ **Grotto** Yanwath CA10 2LF ☎ (0768) 63288

Normal price: £32
Short breaks: £29. Min 2 nights, Nov-Mar.
🕱

This attractive modernised stone guesthouse is set in a secluded garden by the west coast railway line. Three of its six bedrooms are family rooms, most with private shower and all with colour television.

Q Limes Country Redhills, Stainton CA11 0DT (2m W A66) ☎ (0768) 63343

Normal price: £16. Dinner £9.
Short breaks: £22.50. Min 2 nights, Apr-May, Oct-Mar, except Bank Hols. £25 for single occupancy.
✱ Credit card ③

This friendly family-run guesthouse provides excellent breakfasts. The bedrooms, half of them family rooms, all having washing facilities and some have private shower.

★★★73% **North Lakes** (Shire) Ullswater Road CA11 8QT ☎ (0768) 68111

Normal price: £54. Dinner £15-£18 & à la carte (1990 price)
Short breaks: £61 including £16 dinner allowance. Min 2 nights, Fri-Sun. Supplement for single occupancy.
Credit cards ① ② ③ ⑤

This very comfortable modern hotel, well situated for exploring the Lake District, has a pleasant restaurant and bar, and attractive ensuite bedrooms all with colour television. Extensive leisure facilities include swimming, squash, gymnasium, sauna, solarium and snooker. Christmas breaks are available.

RAVENGLASS   Cumbria   Map 6 SD09

★ **Pennington Arms** CA18 1SD ☎ (06577) 222 & 626

Normal price: £22
Short breaks: £13.50 excluding dinner. Min 4 nights or 2 nights at weekends. £15.50 for single occupancy.

This friendly inn situated in a quiet village on the estuary of three rivers provides quite simple accommodation, with some bedrooms having private bath or shower and including family rooms in the annexe.

RAVENSTONEDALE   Cumbria   Map 7 NY70

★★73% **Black Swan** CA17 4NG ☎ (05873) 204

Normal price: £27. Dinner from £16.
Short breaks: £90 for 2 nights including Sunday lunch. Fri-Sat only, Oct-May. 3rd night free excluding meals, Nov, Dec & May. Single supplement.
Activity breaks: Fishing Breaks, £120 for 2 nights including tuition.

A delightful hotel in a quiet picturesque village setting, with charming accommodation enhanced by some thoughtful finishing touches.

★★65% **Fat Lamb** (Guestaccom) Cross Bank CA18 4LL ☎ (05873) 242

Normal price: £36.50. Dinner £11.50 & à la carte (1990 price)
Short breaks: £36.50 including dinner and lunch on day of departure. Min 2 nights, except Bank Hols.

Set in the dales, this peaceful 17th-century inn and former farmhouse is traditionally furnished and has pleasant, compact bedrooms, including two family rooms, all with modern ensuite bathrooms. Christmas breaks are available.

ROSTHWAITE   *Cumbria*   *Map 11 NY21*

★★★60% **Scafell** CA12 5XB ☎ (059684) 208

Normal price: £45 including dinner.
Short breaks: £34-£40. Fri-Mon, 7 Apr-16 May, Jul & Aug.
Activity breaks: Guided Fell Walks, Nov-Dec, Feb-Etr.
Details from hotel.

Located in the heart of Borrowdale and surrounded by misty fells, this very pleasant hotel offers warm hospitality and a high standard of food.

SAWREY   *Cumbria*   *Map 7 SD38*

GH QQQ Ees Wyke Country House LA22 0JZ ☎ (09666) 393
Mar-Dec

Normal price: £26
Short breaks: £24 bed and breakfast. Min 3 nights Sun-Thu, Nov-Mar (except Xmas)
🗶

Standing in its own grounds overlooking Esthwaite Water, this striking Georgian house offers six comfortable and individually furnished bedrooms all with ensuite facilities. Children under twelve are not accommodated.

SEDBERGH   *Cumbria*   *Map 7 SD69*

★★64% **Oakdene Country House** Garsdale Road LA10 5JN ☎ (05396) 20280

Normal price: £27. Dinner £10.50 & à la carte.
Short breaks: £24.30, min 2 nights, Mon-Fri, dinner not included. Closed Jan & Feb.

A small, family-run hotel enjoying delightful views of the surrounding countryside. All bedrooms are refurbished and comfortable.

SHAP   *Cumbria*   *Map 12 NY51*

★★62% **Shap Wells** Penrith (situated 3 miles SW of Shap Village off A6) CA10 3QU ☎ (09316) 628 & 744. Closed 2 Jan-14 Feb

Normal price: £27.50-£37.50. Dinner £11.50 & à la carte.
Short breaks: £25-£32.50 Nov-Dec, £30-£40 Apr-Nov, min 2 nights. £5-£10 supplement for single occupancy Apr-Nov.
Credit cards 1 2 3 5

Peacefully set in its own extensive grounds, this large hotel is conveniently located near the A6 and M6. Improvements are continually being created to this long-established family-run hotel, and social events and conferences are now well catered for. The newer bedrooms are very comfortable and well appointed, and there is a selection of recreational facilities. See advertisement p78.

SILLOTH   *Cumbria*   *Map 11 NY15*

★★66% **Golf** Criffel Street CA5 4AB ☎ (06973) 31438

Normal price: from £38.50. Dinner from £12.50.
Short breaks: from £35.50. Single supplement.
Activity breaks: Golf Package, £43.50 per day plus £11 green fee (1990). Offer includes a full day's golf at Silloth-on-Solway Golf Club.
Credit cards 1 2 3 5

Situated close to the southern shore of the Solway Firth, a championship golf course, and the tourist attractions of the lake District, an ideal tourist hotel.

TEMPLE SOWERBY   Cumbria   Map 12 NY62

★★74% Temple Sowerby House CA10 1RZ ☎ (07683) 61578

Normal price: £56 room and breakfast. Dinner £18.50.
Short breaks: £40.50, min 2 nights.
Activity breaks: Champagne Breaks in Four-Poster Rooms, details from hotel.
Credit cards ①③

This former 17th-century farmhouse is now a well-furnished and comfortable hotel of charm and comfort. Staff are thoughtful and friendly.

THORNTHWAITE   Cumbria   Map 11 NY22

★★61% Ladstock Country House CA12 5RZ ☎ (059682) 210
Closed Jan

Normal price: £36-£64. Dinner £11.95-£12.95
Short breaks: £31.50-£41.50, single £37.50. Min 3 nights
🐾 (ex guide dogs) Credit cards ①③

This period house is set in attractive gardens 2.5 miles north-west of Keswick. All the bedrooms have colour television, most have four-poster beds. Christmas breaks are available.

★★ 🛏 65% Thwaite Howe CA12 5SA ☎ (059682) 281
Closed Nov-Feb

Normal price: £25 bed and breakfast, £33 with dinner
Short breaks: £28.50, £10 maximum supplement for single occupancy. Min 2 nights Mar, Apr, Jul & Aug (ex Bank Holidays).

A charming Lakeland house set in delightful gardens, offers well-furnished, comfortable bedrooms and a good standard of home cooking. Children under twelve are not accommodated.

ULVERSTON   Cumbria   Map 7 SD27

★★58% Sefton House Queen Street LA12 7AF ☎ (0229) 52190

Normal price: £30. Dinner from £13
Short breaks: £38.50. Min 2 nights, Fri-Sun
🐾 (ex guide dogs) Credit cards ①③

Just off the A590, close to the town centre, this hotel offers a friendly, informal atmosphere and pleasant service. Most of the bedrooms are ensuite, all have colour television.

WASDALE HEAD   Cumbria   Map 11 NY10

★★67% Wasdale Head Inn CA20 1EX ☎ (09406) 229
Closed mis Nov-mid Mar

Normal price: £40 including dinner
Short breaks: £38.50 (1990 prices) Min 4 nights
Credit cards ①③

Remotely situated amongst spectacular mountain scenery, this small country inn is popular with walkers and climbers and those wishing to 'get away from it all'. It offers hearty home cooking and ensuite bedrooms.

WATERMILLOCK   Cumbria   Map 12 NY42

★★★ 🛏 75% Leeming House (Trusthouse Forte) CA11 0JJ ☎ (07684) 86622

Normal price: £63.75. Dinner £29.50
Short breaks: £80, single £90. Min 2 nights
Credit cards ①②③④⑤

A charming country house set on the western shore of Lake Ullswater. Bedrooms are tastefully furnished and have good facilities and the elegant restaurant serves a six course dinner menu. Christmas breaks are available.

✿ ★★★ 🏨 73% **Rampsbeck Country House** CA11 0LP ☎ (07684) 86442 & 86688
Closed 6 Jan-24 Feb (Rosette awarded for dinner only)

Normal price: £30-£42.50, dinner £23-£30
Short breaks: Winter breaks £40-£55 min 2 nights Mar,
Nov & Dec (ex Bank Holidays). Midweek breaks £45-£60
min 2 nights, Sun-Thu, Apr-Jun & Oct. Single £45-£60

A warm, friendly hotel where the elegant, comfortable accommodation is complemented by the superb cooking. Fishing and croquet are available. There is a special Christmas programme. Children under five are not accommodated.

WETHERALL   Cumbria   Map 12 NY45

★★★66% **Crown** (Shire) CA4 8ES ☎ (0228) 61888

Normal price: £100 (room)
Short breaks: £200, 2 nights for 2 people.
Single £53 bed and breakfast. Fri-Sun

This former 18th-century fishing inn has been extended and carefully modernised to provide comfortable and well-appointed accommodation with a leisure complex. Christmas breaks are available.

WIGTON   Cumbria   Map 11 NY24

★★59% **Greenhill Lodge** Red Dial CA7 8LS (2m S off A595) ☎ (06973) 43304

Normal price: £46 room. Dinner £15-£16.50
Short breaks: £22.50 min 2 nights, Fri-Sun
Credit cards ① ③

This former 18th-century mansion is now a family-owned, well-run hotel offering a good range of food and comfortable accommodation in ensuite bedrooms with colour television. Christmas breaks are available.

WINDERMERE   Cumbria   Map 7 SD49

GH QQ **Archway** College Road LA23 1BY ☎ (09662) 5613

Normal price: £34.50
Short breaks: £32 Min 2 nights, Fri-Sun, Dec-Apr (ex Bank Holidays)
🐾

A neat and cosy guesthouse on a quiet side street near the town centre. The bedrooms are all non-smoking, some have ensuite showers, and the food is imaginative and well cooked. Children under twelve are not accommodated.

★★★60% **Belsfield** (Trusthouse Forte) Kendal Road LA23 3EL ☎ (09662) 2448

Normal price: from £93 (room). Dinner £14-£15.50 & à la carte
Short breaks: from £62, for 2 people
Credit cards ① ② ③ ④ ⑤

An elegant Victorian residence overlooking Lake Windermere. Public rooms are comfortable and enjoy fine views, whilst bedrooms have all modern amenties. Leisure amenities include an indoor heated pool and there is a special Christmas programme.

GH QQQ **Brooklands** Ferry View, Bowness LA23 3JB ☎ (09662) 2344

Normal price: £17-£19
Short breaks: £15-£17 bed and breakfast. Min 2 nights, Nov-Mar (ex Xmas & New Year). Single £17

A very pleasant, peaceful and comfortable house with a warm and friendly atmosphere. Some rooms have ensuite showers.

★★★62% **Burn How Garden House** Back Belsfield Road LA23 3HH ☎ (09662) 6226

Normal price: £29-£35, dinner £15 & à la carte
Short breaks: 2 nights £75-£95, 4 nights £115-£180. Single 2 nights £95-£115, 4 nights £135-£200. Sun-Fri
🐾 (ex guide dogs)

Delightfully situated above Lake Windermere, this hotel offers accommodation in family chalets, a modernised Victorian house or a purpose-built wing with sun balconies and four-poster beds. Leisure facilities are available, and there is a Christmas programme.

★★★63% **Burnside** Kendal Road LA23 3EP ☎ (09662) 2211

Normal price: £38. Dinner £13-£14
Short breaks: £45. Min 2 nights, Oct-Apr.
Credit cards ①②③⑤

This large Victorian house is steadily being enlarged and improved to provide spacious comfortable bedrooms. New leisure facilities are also part of a time-share complex situated within the hotel grounds. Christmas breaks are available.

★★74% **Cedar Manor** (Exec Hotel) Ambleside Road LA23 1AX ☎ (09662) 3192

Normal price: £84 room with dinner
Short breaks: £195-£216 for 3 nights, double room with dinner. £7 single supplement. All year (excl Bank Hols).
Credit cards ①③

This charming and peaceful hotel has a cosy bar and attractive dining room. Bedrooms are spacious and well appointed; two are situated in the converted coach house. Christmas breaks are available.

GH QQQ Cranleigh Kendal Road LA23 3EW ☎ (09662) 6226
Mar-Nov

Normal price: £42-£50 room
Short breaks: £60-£70 2 nights
Credit cards ①③

This attractive Victorian house has ensuite bedrooms with colour television and hairdryers. One of the lounges is reserved for non-smokers. Children under five are not accommodated.

GH QQQQ Hawksmoor Lake Road LA23 2EQ ☎ (09662) 2110

Normal price: £19-£25. Dinner £9.50
Short breaks: £25, Sun-Thu, Nov & Jan-Apr. Single £22.50 & £9.50 dinner. Jan-Apr, Nov
🐕 (ex guide dogs)

This guesthouse offers a high standard of accommodation, all rooms have ensuite facilities and are tastefully decorated and furnished. Good home cooking is served in the delightful dining room.

83

★★68% Hideaway Phoenix Way LA23 1DB ☎ (09662) 3070

Normal price: £70-£90 (room). Dinner £12.50
Short breaks: £66-£84 for 2 people. Min 4 nights

Peacefully situated on the west side of the village this house has attractive and comfortable public rooms and pretty well equipped bedrooms. Christmas breaks are available.

★★ ♨ 84% Holbeck Ghyll Country House Holbeck Lane LA23 1LU ☎ (05394) 32375

Normal price: £45-£60 including dinner.
Short breaks: £40-£50, min 2 nights, Nov-May.
Activity breaks: Snooker and Putting Breaks, also Rock Climbing Absailing and Canoeing. Details from hotel.
Credit cards [1] [3]

Froms its splendid position high on a hillside, this former shooting lodge offers wonderful views of Lake Windermere, and a spontaneous friendliness from the staff.

★★★ Hydro (Mount Charlotte (TS)) Helm Road LA23 3BA ☎ (09662) 4455

Normal price: £64.50
Short breaks: £42.50 £9.50 single supplement. Min 2 nights (ex Xmas, New Year & Easter)
Credit cards [1] [2] [3] [5]

A modernised Victorian hotel overlooking Lake Windermere. All rooms have ensuite facilities andcolour television and there are some family rooms. Christmas breaks are available.

★★★ ♨ 64% Langdale Chase LA23 1LW ☎ (05394) 32201

Normal price: £84-£110 double room. Dinner from £19
Short breaks: £47-£62. Min 2 nights, Oct-Apr.

This impressive country house hotel has gardens running down to Lake Windermere. Most of the bedrooms are ensuiite, all have colour television. Leisure amenities include tennis and rowing boats, and a special Christmas programme is available.

★★★58% Low Wood (Best Western) LA23 1LP (3m N A591) ☎ (05394) 33338

Normal price: from £56. Dinner from £17.
Short breaks: from £58, min 2 nights.
Activity breaks: Windsurfing, Water Skiing, and Romance Breaks. Details from hotel.
Credit cards [1] [2] [3] [5]

A large, recently refurbished hotel standing on the shore of Lake Windermere, with extensive leisure amenities including a water ski and windsurfing school.

★ ♨ 67% Quarry Garth Country House Troutbeck Bridge, LA23 1LF ☎ (09662) 88282

Normal price: £50 including dinner
Short breaks: £40. Min 2 nights, Sun-Thu (ex Xmas, New Year & Easter)
Credit cards [1] [2] [3] [5]

Set in eight acres of gardens between Windermere and Ambleside, this small country house offers enjoyable meals and comfortable ensuite bedrooms with colour television. Fishing is available and there are Christmas breaks.

GH QQQ Rosemount Lake Road LA23 2EQ ☎ (09662) 3739

Normal price: £17.50-£22
Short breaks: £16.50 bed and breakfast. Min 2 nights, Nov-Mar
✶ Credit cards [1] [3]

Friendly and personal attention is provided by the enthusiastic owners of this guesthouse. Situated between the village and the Lake it offers warm and comfortable accommodation, all bedrooms are 'no smoking'.

★★62% Royal (Best Western) Queens Square, Bowness LA23 3DB ☎ (09662) 3045 Telex no 65273 Fax (09662) 2498

Normal price: £33.50. Dinner £13.
Short breaks: from £39, min 2 nights
Activity breaks: Whodunnit Weekends, £108 approx.
Details from hotel.
Credit cards [1] [2] [3] [4] [5]

A hotel reputed to be the oldest establishment in the Lake District, and one which numbers many famous names among its guests over the years.

★★★69% **Wild Boar** (Best Western) Crook LA23 3NF (2.5m S of Windermere on B5284 Crook road)
☎ (09662) 5225

Normal price: £44 Apr, £50 Sept. Dinner £18.
Short breaks: from £44-£45 Apr & £60-£62 Sept. Min 2 nights.
Activity breaks: Golfing Breaks, £98 for 2 nights midweek Apr, £120 for 2 nights midweek Sept. Includes one day's free golf. Details from hotel.
Credit cards ①②③④⑤

This 18th-century country hotel, in a secluded setting of woodland and fell, has a good atmosphere and personal attention and service.

WITHERSLACK Cumbria Map 7 SD48

★(Red) 🐗 **Old Vicarage Country House** LA11 6RS ☎ (044852) 381
Closed Xmas week

Normal price: £70-£120 (room). Dinner £23.50
Short breaks: £107-£157 room with dinner. Min 3 nights
Credit cards ①②③⑤

Set away from the more popular Lakeland towns this delightful hotel makes an excellent base for holidays. Lavish five-course dinners are served in the elegant dining rooms and the comfortable bedrooms are all ensuite with colour television. Children under twelve are not accommodated.

WORKINGTON Cumbria Map 11 NX92

★★★55% **Cumberland Arms** Belle Isle Street CA14 2XQ ☎ (0900) 64401

Normal price: £65.
Short breaks: £62.50, min 2 nights. Single supplement.
Activity breaks: Golfing Break, £65, Mon-Thu. Details from hotel.
Credit cards ①②③⑤

A large hotel close to the railway station, offering a good standard of carefully prepared meals.

★★★67% **Washington Central** Washington Street CA14 3AW ☎ (0900) 65772
Closed 1 Jan

Normal price: £43 includes dinner
Short breaks: £30, single £35. Min 2 nights, Fri-Sun
🐾 (ex guide dogs) Credit cards ①②③

This modern town centre hotel is built around a small enclosed courtyard. Bedrooms are pleasant and cosy with ensuite facilities, and friendly staff serve well-prepared meals.

▦ DERBYSHIRE ▦

ASHBOURNE Derbyshire Map 7 SK14

★★★69% **Ashbourne Lodge** (Best Western) Derby Road, DE6 1XH ☎ (0335) 46666

Normal price: £68 room with breakfast. Dinner £15 and à la carte
Short breaks: £44. Min 2 nights
Credit cards ①②③⑤

A modern hotel on the main Derby road with fifty-one bedrooms, all with private bathrooms and colour television. Some rooms are set aside for families and non-smokers. There is a special Christmas programme.

★★★59% **Beresford Arms** Station Road DE6 1AA ☎ (0335) 300035

Normal price: £30. Dinner £12.50-£15.
Short breaks: £40, min 2 nights. Single occupancy £62.
Activity breaks: Details from hotel.
🐾 Credit cards ①②③

A fully renovated town centre hotel, personally run by Karen and Peter Wells. Tastefully furnished bedrooms and a quality restaurant.

★★ 🏮 74% **Callow Hall** Mappleton Road DE6 2AA ☎ (0335) 43403 & 43164
Closed 25-26 December & 2 wks February

Normal price: £80-£110 room with breakfast. Dinner from £21.50 and à la carte
Short breaks: £195, 2 people for 2 nights. Single room by arrangement
🐕 (ex guide dogs) Credit cards ① ② ③ ⑤

Situated half a mile from the town centre, this small hotel provides well designed, comfortable bedrooms, each with its own private bath or shower room and colour television. Fishing is available.

ASHFORD-IN-THE-WATER   Derbyshire   Map 7 SK17

★★73% **Ashford** Church Street DE4 1QB ☎ (0629) 812725

Normal price: £70-£75 room with breakfast. Dinner £17 and à la carte
Short breaks: £63-£68 for two excluding dinner. £50 single room excluding dinner. Min 4 nights
Credit cards ① ③

This comfortable little hotel provides a friendly and informal atmosphere. The bedrooms are decorated in a delightful rustic style, and are equipped with modern facilities including ensuite facilities and colour television. The restaurant offers an interesting selection of dishes. There is a special Christmas programme.

★★ 🏮 73% **Riverside Country House** Fennel Street DE4 1QF ☎ (0629) 814275

Normal price: £45. Dinner £27.50
Short breaks: £65
Credit cards ① ② ③

This charming ivy-clad Georgian country house has seven bedrooms, all with ensuite bath or shower rooms and colour television. There are two rooms with four-poster beds. Smoking is not allowed in the bedrooms. The hotel has facilities for fishing and horse riding.

BAKEWELL   Derbyshire   Map 8 SK26

★★ 🏮 77% **Croft Country House** Great Longstone DE4 1TF ☎ (062987) 278
Closed 22 Dec-Feb

Normal price: £36. Dinner £16
Short breaks: £48. Single £55. Min 2 nights
🐕 (ex guide dogs)

Comfortable lounges and charming gardens are features of this country house. It offers attractive bedrooms with colour television, and most rooms have private facilities.

★★★52% **Rutland Arms** (Best Western) The Square DE4 1BT ☎ (0629) 812812

Normal price: £57 room with breakfast. Dinner £15.95 and à la carte
Short breaks: £38, Mon-Thu; £40, Fri-Sun. Min 2 nights

Situated in the town centre, this large former coaching inn dates from 1804. The modern well-equipped bedrooms have private bathrooms and colour television, and there are two family rooms. There is a special Christmas programme.

BASLOW   Derbyshire   Map 8 SK27

★★★(Red) **Cavendish** DE4 1SP ☎ (0246) 582311

Normal price: £75
Short breaks: £65 excluding dinner. Min 2 nights, Fri-Sun, Oct-Mar
🐕 Credit cards ① ② ③ ⑤

In a superb setting and enjoying views of the Chatsworth estate, this hotel has comfortable and tastefully furnished bedrooms with ensuite bath or shower rooms and colour television. One room has a four-poster bed. Fishing is available and there is a putting green. A special Christmas programme is available.

BRETBY Derbyshire Map 8 SK22

★★★64% **Stanhope** (Lansbury) Ashby Road East DE15 0PU ☎ (0283) 217954

Normal price: £76 room. Dinner from £14 and à la carte
Short breaks: £28. Fri-Sun
🐾 (ex guide dogs) Credit cards ① ② ③ ⑤

Standing in well-maintained gardens on the A50, this hotel has warm, comfortable bedrooms all with colour television and ensuite facilities. There is one family room, and the hotel has special facilities for children. Some rooms are for non-smokers. There is a special Christmas programme.

BUXTON Derbyshire Map 7 SK07

GH QQ Buxton View 74 Corbar Road SK17 6RJ ☎ (0298) 79222
Mar-Nov

Normal price: £30 room with breakfast
Short breaks: 10% off. Min 7 nights

This house is set in a residential area with commanding views over the town. The comfortable bedrooms all have colour television and there are some rooms with ensuite facilities. There is one room for families.

★★★66% **Lee Wood** (Best Western) 13 Manchester Road SK17 6TQ ☎ (0298) 23002 & 70421
Closed 24-29 Dec

Normal price: £70-£80 room with breakfast. Dinner £15-£17.50 and à la carte
Short breaks: £48. Min 2 nights. No single supplement at weekends and some weekdays
Credit cards ① ② ③ ⑤

Situated close to the town centre in delightful gardens, this hotel offers comfortable, well-equipped bedrooms all with private facilities and colour television. Two rooms are for families, and the hotel has special facilities for children.

★★★60% **Palace** (Trusthouse Forte) Palace Road SK17 6AG ☎ (0298) 22001

Normal price: £107 room. Dinner from £14 & à la carte
Short breaks: £90 for 2 people

This impressive Victorian building overlooking the spa town has comfortable bedrooms with ensuite bathrooms and colour television. There are rooms for families and non-smokers. Leisure facilities include a swimming pool and gymnasium. There is a special Christmas programme.

★★66% **Portland** 32 St John's Road SK17 6XQ ☎ (0298) 71493

Normal price: £50 room with breakfast. Dinner £13
Short breaks: £40. Min 2 nights (except Bank Holidays, Easter and Christmas)

A welcoming family-run hotel with ensuite facilities and colour television in all bedrooms; there are rooms for families and non-smokers and two rooms have four-poster beds.

Templeton 13 Compton Road SK17 9DN ☎ (0298) 25275

Normal price: £30-£34 room and breakfast.
Short breaks: £32.50 for two.

Templeton provides bright, warm and well-equipped accommodation close to the town centre. Good home-cooked meals are provided and there is ample parking space.

CHESTERFIELD Derbyshire Map 8 SK37

★★★63% **Chesterfield** (Best Western) Malkin Street S41 7UA ☎ (0246) 271141

Normal price: £35. Dinner £10.95.
Short breaks: £36, min 2 nights, Fri-Sun.
Activity breaks: Golf, Theatre and Heritage Weekends, included in short break price.

A fully modernised hotel with 1920's style interior and facilities including a smart function room. Situated adjacent to the station.

★★61% Portland West Bars S40 1AY ☎ (0246) 234502 & 234211

Normal price: £28.50. Dinner £5-£10
Short breaks: £28.50 including £8 dinner allowance. Min 2
nights, Fri-Sun. Single £35.
🛪 (ex guide dogs) Credit cards [1] [3]

A comfortable, friendly, city centre hotel
offering a good choice of eating options at
lunchtime. All bedrooms have colour television,
and most have ensuite facilities.

DERBY   Derbyshire   Map 8 SK33

★★★61% International (Consort) Burton Road (A5250) DE3 6AD ☎ (0332) 369321

Normal price: £27. Dinner £11.50-£12.80
Short breaks: £35, includes Sunday lunch. Min 2 nights,
Fri & Sat, may be extended to include Thu & Sun. Jan-Nov
Credit cards [1] [2] [3] [5]

Some of the bedrooms here are situated in an
annexe, and all are extremely well-equipped
with private facilities and colour television. The
hotel has a gymnasium, speciality evenings are
a feature and there is a Christmas programme.

DRAYCOTT   Derbyshire   Map 8 SK43

★★★56% Tudor Court (Best Western) Gypsy Lane DE7 3PB ☎ (03317) 4581

Normal price: £72.
Short breaks: £40 Mon-Tues, £35 Fri-Sun. Min 2 nights.
Single supplement.
Activity breaks: Romantic Breaks, £80 including flowers,
chocolates and champagne. Theme Park Weekends, £80
including day passes to Alton Towers and American
Adventure.

Standing in eight acres of grounds, this modern
hotel, built in traditional style, has a popular
night club within the complex.

DRONFIELD   Derbyshire   Map 8 SK37

★★53% Manor 10 High Street S18 6PY ☎ (0246) 413971
Restricted service Sun evenings

Normal price: £31.10. Dinner £12.50 & à la carte
Short breaks: £21.50 excluding dinner. Single £35.25. Min 2
nights, Fri-Sun
Credit cards [1] [2] [3] [5]

A small, proprietor-run hotel situated in Old
Dronfield, and dating from the 16th and 18th
centuries. The restaurant offers good \a la carte
and daily menus. All the bedrooms are ensuite
with colour television.

GRINDLEFORD   Derbyshire   Map 8 SK27

★★★67% Maynard Arms Main Road S30 1HN ☎ (0433) 30321

Normal price: £64 room and breakfast
Short breaks: £40 excluding dinner. Free morning paper.
Min 2 nights
Credit cards [1] [2] [3] [5]

This busy hotel has a comfortable lounge with
views across the gardens to the Derwent
Valley. Most of the bedrooms are ensuite, all
have colour television and two are furnished
with four-poster beds. There is a special
Christmas programme.

HATHERSAGE   Derbyshire   Map 8 SK28

***64% **Hathersage Inn** (Best Western) Main Street S30 1BB ☎ (0433) 50259

Normal price: £30. Dinner £12.50.
Short breaks: £41 (1990 price). Min 2 nights, including one afternoon tea. Single supplement.
Activity breaks: Cycling Breaks, £80, 6 Nov-28Mar; £92, 30 Mar-5 Nov. Walking Breaks, £90 and £100, dates as above.
Credit cards 1 2 3 5

A charming old inn in the centre of the village, with particularly comfortable bedrooms in the adjacent Morley House.

KIRK LANGLEY   Derbyshire   Map 8 SK23

63% **Meynell Arms (Minotels) Ashbourne Road DE6 4NF ☎ (033124) 515

Normal price: £19-£26. Dinner £10-£15 à la carte
Short breaks: £25, min 2 nights. Single supplement.
Credit cards 1 3

A Georgian manor house hotel, well known locally for its value-for-money bar snacks, on the A52 close to Derby.

MATLOCK   Derbyshire   Map 8 SK36

QQ **Farley Farm** Farley Village DE4 5LR ☎ (0629) 582533

Normal price: £24
Short breaks: £25. Min 5 nights, Oct-Mar.

Set high in the Derbyshire hills, this stone-built, part 17th-century farmhouse has riding stables and 225 acres of arable and dairy land. Its three bedrooms, one with colour television, have hot and cold water facilities and include a family room.

***52% **New Bath** (Trusthouse Forte) New Bath Road DE4 3PX (2m S A6) ☎ (0629) 583275

Normal price: £90 room, £7 breakfast. Dinner from £12.25 (1990 price)
Short breaks: £55 including £13.50 dinner allowance. Min 2 nights.
Credit cards 1 2 3 4 5

This much extended Georgian-style building high above the A6 has colour television and ensuite bath in all bedrooms, 11 of them non-smoking. Leisure facilities include a garden, swimming pool, sauna, solarium and thermal pool. Christmas breaks are available.

** **Red House** Old Road, Darley Dale DE4 2ER (2.5m N A6) ☎ (0629) 734854

Normal price: £30-£36. Dinner £14.50-£16.50 (1990 price)
Short breaks: £44. Min 2 nights.
Credit cards 1 2 3 5

This small friendly hotel with a garden has private bath or shower and colour television in all its bedrooms.

***70% **Riber Hall** (Pride of Britain) DE4 5JU ☎ (0629) 582795

Normal price: £81. Dinner from £23 à la carte
Short breaks: £115-£139 for 2 nights inc lunch and £22 dinner allowance. £20 single supplement. Min 2 nights, Nov-Apr.
✱ (ex guide dogs) Credit cards 1 2 3 4 5

This quiet country house hotel dating from Elizabethan times has four-poster beds in most of its bedrooms. All rooms are in the annexe and offer ensuite bath and colour television. Interesting food and wines are served, and there is a tennis court. No children under 10.

ROWSLEY   Derbyshire   Map 8 SK26

** **East Lodge** DE4 2EF ☎ (0629) 734474

Normal price: £30-£36. Dinner £12.50 (1990 prices)
Short breaks: £38. Min 2 nights, Nov-Mar, excluding Bank Hols. Single supplement.
Credit cards 1 3

Set in 10 acres of grounds, this stonebuilt former lodge of Haddon Hall provides a personal, friendly service and well-equipped and furnished accommodation, with colour television in the six bedrooms. Christmas breaks are available.

★★★53% **Peacock** (Embassy) DE4 2EB ☎ (0629) 733518
Normal price: £45.50. Dinner £21-£28 (1990 price)
Short breaks: £45 winter, £55 summer. Min 2 nights,
Fri-Sun.
Credit cards ① ② ③ ⑤

Situated on the River Derwent with its own garden, this relaxing hotel has a popular restaurant and several family bedrooms housed in a cottage annexe. All bedrooms have colour television and those in the main building offer private bath or shower. Christmas breaks are available.

SANDIACRE   Derbyshire   Map 8 SK43

★★★52% **Post House** Bostocks Lane NG10 5NJ ☎ (0602) 397800
Normal price: £93 room. Dinner £13.50-£17.75 & à la carte
Short breaks: £35, min 2 nights, Fri-Sun
Credit cards ① ② ③ ④ ⑤

A modern, purpose-built hotel with a restaurant and a coffee shop which serves snacks and grills throughout the day.

SHARDLOW   Derbyshire   Map 8 SK43

★★63% **Lady in Grey** Wilne Lane DE7 2HA ☎ (0332) 792331
Normal price: £25. Dinner from £10 & à la carte.
Short breaks: £16.25. Min 1 night, Fri-Sun, excluding
dinner.
✱ Credit cards ① ② ③ ⑤

This fully restored old house offers comfortable accommodation in modern, well-equipped bedrooms. The restaurant, which overlooks attractive gardens, emphasises Spanish cuisine and offers a good, reasonably-priced wine list.

SOUTH NORMANTON   Derbyshire   Map 8 SK45

★★★62% **Swallow** Carter Lane East DE55 2EH ☎ (0773) 812000
Normal price: £86 (1990 prices).
Short breaks: £90, min 2 nights, includes lunch on
departure day.
Credit cards ① ② ③ ④ ⑤

This large, modern hotel has been recently extended and refurbished to provide more comfortable lounge and bar areas and banqueting/meeting rooms. There is a choice of snacks or à la carte menus, and the comprehensive indoor leisure facilities are popular at weekends.

THORPE (Dovedale)   Derbyshire   Map 7 SK15

★★★65% **Peveril of the Peak** (Trusthouse Forte) DE6 2AW ☎ (033529) 333
Normal price: £51.50. Dinner fr £15.50.
Short breaks: £55, min 2 nights.
Activity breaks: Clay Pigeon Shooting, £200, 19-21 Apr.
Credit cards ① ② ③ ④ ⑤

Eccentric and rambling, this comfortable hotel sits in 11 acres of gardens and grounds at the foot of Thrope Cloud, and it makes a popular retreat.

DEVON

ASHBURTON   Devon   Map 3 SX77

FH Q Bembridge Woodland TQ13 7JX (2m E unclass towards Denbury) ☎ (0364) 52426
Closed Dec
Normal price: £15 bed and breakfast, £18.50 including
dinner
Short breaks: £15. Min 3 nights, Mar-Oct

Five rooms are available for guests at this comfortable farmhouse, one room has an ensuite bathroom and there are three family rooms.

★★ 🏨 69% **Holne Chase** (Inter-Hotels) TQ13 7NS ☎ (03643) 471

Normal price: fr £40. Dinner £19.50.
Short breaks: fr £55, min 2 nights
Activity breaks: Winter Walking Holidays, Nov-Mar. Short breaks rate plus £5 per day.

An attractive period house in a magnificent setting with most impressive views.

BAMPTON Devon Map 3 SS92

GH Q Bridge House Luke Street EX16 9NF ☎ (0398) 31298

Normal price: fr £19.
Short breaks: fr £16, min 3 nights.
Activity breaks: Fly Fishing, Clay Pigeon Shooting and Riding on Exmoor Breaks, £145. Game Shooting, Sept-Jan. Details from hotel.
✶ Credit cards ① ③

This attractive family-run hotel and restaurant is set in the centre of Bampton, and offers an imaginative menu.

INN QQQ Exeter Tiverton Road EX16 9DY ☎ (0398) 31345

Normal price: £28.45. Dinner fr £8.95.
Short breaks: £27, min 2 nights. Single price £28.50.
Activity breaks: Salmon & Trout Fishing, short breaks price plus £10 per rod per day. Clay Pigeon Shooting, and Game Shooting, details from hotel.
✶ Credit cards ① ③

This ancient country inn offers food in the bar and the more formal restaurant. Stabling is available for guests' horses.

BANTHAM Devon Map 3 SX64

INN QQ Sloop TQ7 3AJ ☎ (0548) 560489 & 560215

Normal price: £40-£44 room and breakfast. Dinner £6.50-£11 and à la carte
Short breaks: £28.50-£31.50

This 16th-century inn provides a high standard of accommodation and food. Most bedrooms have ensuite facilities, all have colour television and there are two family rooms.

BARNSTAPLE Devon Map 2 SS53

GH QQ Cresta 26 Sticklepath Hill EX31 2BU ☎ (0271) 74022 Closed Xmas

Normal price: £12-£14
Short breaks: £22, 2 nights; £30, 3 nights; single £24, 2 nights; £33, 3 nights. Fri-Sun

Situated on the main Barnstaple to Bideford road one mile from Barnstaple town centre, this guest house has ensuite facilities in two bedrooms and colour television in all.

★★ 🐾 68% **Downrew House** Bishops Tawton EX32 0DY ☎ (0271) 42497 & 46673

Normal price: from £54.42-£66.50 including dinner
Short breaks: £51.60. Min 2 nights, Feb-Mar & Nov-20 Dec

Dating from 1640, this small, cosy house stands in twelve acres of meadowland just outside the town. All the bedrooms have ensuite facilities and colour television, and there are two family rooms. Leisure amenities include snooker, a heated outdoor swimming pool, and a private 15-hole pitch and putt course. There is a special Christmas programme. Children under seven are not accommodated.

★★★64% **Imperial** (Trusthouse Forte) Taw Vale Parade EX32 8NB ☎ (0271) 45861

Normal price: £43. Dinner from £14.50 and à la carte
Short breaks: £51. Min 2 nights
Credit cards ① ② ③ ④ ⑤

Staff are pleasant and friendly at this town centre hotel. There are fifty-six comfortable bedrooms, all with ensuite facilities and colour television; some rooms are for families and non-smokers. There is a special Christmas programme.

★★★62% **Park** (Brend) Taw Vale EX32 8NJ ☎ (0271) 72166

Normal price: £34. Dinner £10-£14 and à la carte
Short breaks: from £38, min 2 nights (except Xmas). £10 single supplement

The Park offers comfortable accommodation in bedrooms which all have private facilities and colour television. There is a special Christmas programme.

★★ **Royal & Fortescue** (Brend) Boutport Street EX31 1HG ☎ (0271) 42289

Normal price: £30. Dinner £10-£12 and à la carte
Short breaks: £35. Min 2 nights (except Xmas)

A bustling town centre hotel providing friendly service. There is colour television in all the bedrooms, and thirty-five have ensuite facilities. Four rooms are for families. There is a special Christmas programme.

BEER   Devon   *Map 3 SY28*

★★60% **Anchor Inn** EX12 3ET ☎ (0297) 20386
Closed 1 week Xmas

Normal price: £24
Short breaks: 15% reduction. Min 2 nights, Mon-Thu, Nov-Mar
🎋 Credit cards ① ③

Informal and friendly service is a feature of this hotel which faces the slipway to the beach. Bedrooms are warm and cosy, all have colour television and some have ensuite facilities. Children under ten are not accommodated.

BERRYNARBOR   Devon   *Map 2 SS54*

GH QQ **Lodge Country House** EX34 9SG (Berrynarbor 1¹/₂m W of A399) ☎ (0271) 883246
Jan-Dec Closed Xmas

Normal price: £13.50-£16.50
Short breaks: £19. Min 2 nights, Oct-Spring Bank Holiday week (except Easter)

A family-run hotel set in beautiful grounds overlooking the Sterridge Valley. All rooms have tea-making facilities and colour television, and some have ensuite facilities. Children under two are not accommodated.

BIDEFORD   Devon   Map 2 SS42

GH Q Kumba Chudleigh Road, East-the-Water EX39 4AR ☎ (02372) 71526 due to change to (0237) 471526

Normal price: £14
Short breaks: £12.50. Min 2 nights, Jan-Jun & Sep-Dec (except Bank Holidays)

A comfortable, family-run guest house overlooking the River Torridge, with special facilities for children. Five of the nine bedrooms are family rooms, and two rooms have colour television.

GH QQ Mount Northdown Road EX39 3LP ☎ (02372) 73748

Normal price: £15.50-£19.50
Short breaks: £22-£26. Single £23.50-£29, (1990 prices). Min 2 nights
🛪 Credit cards ① ③

This Georgian building of character is situated close to the town centre and quay. It provides accommodation in comfortable bedrooms, some of which have private facilities. There are two family rooms and one is set aside for non-smokers.

GH QQQ Pines at Eastleigh Old Barnstaple Road, Eastleigh EX39 4PA (3m E off A39 at East-the-Water) ☎ (0271) 860561

Normal price: £18.
Short breaks: £50 for 2 nights. Single price £55.
Activity breaks: Painting Holidays, 2 nights fr £80. Various artists teach painting with a variety of media. Details from hotel.
Credit cards ① ③

Surrounded by gardens on the edge of the village, this 200-year-old house offers a choice of home-cooked meals and good service.

★★60% Riversford (Inter-Hotels) Limers Lane EX39 2RG ☎ (0237) 474239

Normal price: £97.60-£107.60, room with dinner
Short breaks: £84 for 2 people. Min 2 nights

A family-managed hotel about a mile from the town centre. Leisure amenities include a solarium, badminton and putting. There are special facilities for children and a special Christmas programme is provided.

★★★66% Royal (Brend) Barnstaple Street EX39 4AE ☎ (0237) 472005

Normal price: £34. Dinner £10-£12.
Short breaks: £39. Min 2 nights, excluding Xmas & New Year. Single supplement.
Activity breaks: Murder/Mystery Weekends, April. Details on application.

A traditional older-style hotel with comfortable, spotlessly clean bedrooms and stylish public rooms. Recently upgraded and refurbished.

★★69% Sonnenheim Heywood Road EX39 2QA ☎ (0237) 474989
Closed Nov-Feb

Normal price: £38 room with breakfast. Dinner £12.50-£15 & à la carte
Short breaks: £35 for two. Single £22. Min 3 nights, Mar-Oct
Credit cards [1] [3]

The personally-run country house-style hotel provides comfortable public areas and a friendly atmosphere throughout. Most of the pleasant bedrooms have ensuite facilities, all are equipped with colour television and one room is set aside for families.

★★ 🏤 58% Yeoldon House Durrant Lane, Northam EX39 2RL ☎ (0237) 474400

Normal price: £104.50 room, breakfast and dinner.
Short breaks: £67. Min 3 nights, Sun-Thu.
Activity breaks: Water Skiing, £280, 3 nights. Apr-Sept. Golf Lessons, £280, 3 nights. Painting Breaks, £280, 3 nights 1-8 March. Wine Tasting, £240, 3 nights, 29 Nov-2 Dec.

A country house style hotel commanding an expansive view over the River Torridge - to which its lawns slope down - and across woodland to the village beyond. See advertisement on p93.

BIGBURY-ON-SEA Devon Map 3 SX64

★69% Henley (Minotels) TQ7 4AR ☎ (0548) 810240

Normal price: £39-£45 room and breakfast; £64-£68 with dinner
Short breaks: £62 2 days, £87 3 days
Credit cards [1] [3]

In a commanding cliff-top position the hotel has a private path to the beach and gardens. Most of the six well-equipped bedrooms have ensuite bath or showers, and all have colour television. There are two family rooms. A special programme is arranged for Christmas.

BISHOPSTEIGNTON Devon Map 3 SX97

★★58% Cockhaven Manor TQ14 9RF ☎ (0626) 775252

Normal price: £24
Short breaks: £26 including £6 dinner allowance. Min 2 nights
Activity breaks: Rock climbing, Mountain Biking, Sailing, Abseiling, all £50.00 per day.
Credit cards [1] [3]

Situated in a small village a short drive from Teignmouth, Torquay and Paignton, this hotel dates back to the 16th century. The bars are lively and the à la carte restaurant offers steak and fish dishes. Bedrooms and public areas are at present undergoing complete refurbishment.

BOVEY TRACEY   Devon   Map 3 SX87

GH QQ Blenheim Brimley Road TQ13 9DH ☎ (0626) 832422
Restricted service 25 & 26 Dec

Normal price: £22 bed and breakfast, £32 with dinner
Short breaks: £29. Min 2 nights, Oct-Mar

Situated on the outskirts of the village, this fine detached Victorian house has six comfortable bedrooms all with ensuite showers and colour television. There is one family room. Children under five are not accommodated.

★★53% **Coombe Cross** (Inter-Hotels) Coombe Cross TQ13 9EY ☎ (0626) 832476

Normal price: £37.90. Dinner fr £15.95.
Short breaks: £34. Min 2 nights. Single supplement.
Activity breaks: Bridge Breaks, Gardening Breaks, details from hotel.

Comfortable   traditional   country   hotel, personally run.

BRANSCOMBE   Devon   Map 3 SY18

GH QQ Bulstone EX12 3BL ☎ (029780) 446
Feb-Nov Restricted service Dec-Jan

Normal price: £30 including dinner
Short breaks: £25. Fri-Sun, Feb-Mar & Oct-Nov
✗

This comfortable guest house has special facilities for children. Most of the bedrooms are family rooms and some have private bathrooms. Smoking is not permitted in the bedrooms.

BRENDON   Devon   Map 3 SS74

GH Q Brendon House EX35 6PS ☎ (05987) 206
Closed Xmas week. Restricted service Jan-Mar

Normal price: £16. Dinner £9
Short breaks: £25. Min 2 nights
Credit card [1]

In an ideal location for touring Exmoor and the North Devon coast, this house on the edge of the village offers friendly service. There is a lounge with colour television, and some bedrooms have ensuite facilities.

BRIXHAM   Devon   Map 3 SX95

★★★61% **Quayside** (Inter-Hotels) King Street TQ5 9TJ ☎ (08045) 55751
Closed Xmas & New Year

Normal price: £68 room and breakfast. Dinner from £13.95
& à la carte
Short breaks: £78 for two. Min 2 nights

Overlooking the harbour with views to Torquay, this hotel has compact bedrooms with ensuite facilities and colour television; two rooms are furnished with four-poster beds. Interesting menus feature local fish. Car parking is available 500 yards from the hotel.

BUCKFAST   Devon   Map 3 SX76

GH Q Furzeleigh Mill Country House Dart Bridge TQ11 0JP ☎ (0346) 43476

Normal price: £30.20 room high season
Short breaks: £21.55-£28.95, min 3 days.
Credit cards ①②③

Standing in its own gardens on the edge of the village, this guest house offers comfortable accommodation; most rooms have ensuite facilities, and all have colour television. There are two family rooms.

CHAGFORD   Devon   Map 3 SX78

★★63% **Easton Court** Easton Cross, TQ13 8JL (1¹/₂m E A382) ☎ (0647) 433469
Closed January

Normal price: £36, £52 with dinner
Short breaks: £42. Min 3 nights
Credit cards ①②③⑤

This part-thatched hotel is run in a friendly and informal manner and offers ensuite bedrooms with colour television. Two rooms have four-poster beds. There is a special Christmas programme. Children under 14 are not accommodated.

★★★73% **Teignworthy** Frenchbeer TG13 8EX ☎ (0647) 433355

Normal price: £185 room, breakfast and dinner
Short breaks: £175 for two. Single occupancy £97.50 Nov – Easter.
Credit cards ①③

A granite and slate country hotel, tucked away in an elevated position and commanding views across Dartmoor, provides personal service and a tranquil atmosphere. Cosy public rooms and attractively furnished bedrooms alike - both in the main building and the adjacent cottage - are generously supplied with books, magazines, flowers and chocolates. The restaurant's table d'hôte menu changes daily and makes full use of seasonal produce and locally grown ingredients in its imaginative dishes.

CHERITON FITZPAINE   Devon   Map 3 SS80

FH QQ Brindiwell EX17 4HR ☎ (03636) 357

Normal price: £24 room and breakfast
Short breaks: £10.
Activity breaks: Landscape Painting, details from hotel.
✗

Period farmhouse with oak beams and panelling, on the side of a valley with views of the Exe Valley and Dartmoor.

CLAWTON Devon *Map 2 SX39*

★★ ♣ 68% **Court Barn Country House** (Exec Hotel) EX22 6PS ☎ (040927) 219

Normal price: £46 including dinner.
Short breaks: £76 for 2 nights. Min 2 nights.
Activity breaks: Croquet Break, short break price plus £10 tuition. Jun-Sept. Pheasant Shooting, late Oct-Mar. Golfing Breaks, short break price plus £10-£12 per round. Painting and Drawing Breaks, short break price plus £25.
Credit cards ①②③⑤

Dating back to around the 14th century and re-built in 1853, this hotel stands in 5 acres of grounds and gardens. Personally run, it offers spotlessly clean bedrooms.

COLYFORD Devon *Map 3 SY29*

GH QQQQ Swallows Eaves Swan Hill Road EX13 6QJ ☎ (0297) 53184

Normal price: £37-£41
Short breaks: £32.50. Min 2 nights
🛏 (ex guide dogs)

A comfortable little hotel offering a warm welcome. All the bedrooms have ensuite facilities and colour television, and excellent home-cooked dinners are served in the elegant dining room. Children under six are not accommodated.

COLYTON Devon *Map 3 SY29*

★★65% **White Cottage** Dolphin Street EX13 6NA ☎ (0297) 52401
Closed 2 weeks at Xmas

Normal price: £27.50. Dinner £12.50-£19.50 à la carte
Short breaks: £37. Min 2 nights, Oct-Mar
Credit cards ①③

This is a Grade II listed building offering an interesting choice of dishes in the charming dining room. Bedrooms retain some of the original features, and all have ensuite facilities and colour television. One room is furnished with a four-poster bed.

COMBE MARTIN Devon *Map 2 SS54*

GH QQQ Channel Vista EX34 0AT ☎ (027188) 3514
Easter-Oct & Xmas

Normal price: £17 including dinner
Short breaks: £23. Min 3 nights, Apr-Jun
🛏 (ex guide dogs)

This charming Edwardian house is only 150yds from the picturesque cove. It provides home cooking and friendly service. All bedrooms are ensuite and some have colour television. Children under three are not accepted.

CROYDE Devon *Map 2 SS43*

★★65% **Croyde Bay House** Moor Lane, Croyde Bay EX33 1PA ☎ (0271) 890270
Closed mid Nov-Feb

Normal price: £37 including dinner
Short breaks: £33.50. Mon-Wed, Mar-May & Oct-Nov

Personal service is provided by friendly proprietors at this hotel which overlooks Croyde Bay. All bedrooms have private bath or shower and colour television, and there are two family rooms.

★★66% **Kittiwell House** St Mary's Road EX33 1PG ☎ (0271) 890247

Normal price: £45 including dinner.
Short breaks: £40. Min 2 nights, Jul-Sept. Single supplement.
Activity breaks: Golf Breaks, short breaks price plus £12-£18 per day green fees. Horse Riding Breaks, short breaks price plus £5 for one hour's riding over beach and moorland, or £7.50 for one hour's instruction. Clay Shooting Breaks, short breaks price plus £12 min charge. Christmas House Party, £290 for 4 nights. New Year Break, £145 for 2 nights. Walking/Wildlife Legends. Details from hotel. All prices 1990.

This thatched longhouse stands on the edge of the village within walking distance of the excellent surfing beaches. The heavily beamed restaurant offers a choice of menus.

GH QQQQ **Whiteleaf at Croyde** EX33 1PN ☎ (0271) 890266

Normal price: £24. Dinner around £15.00
Short breaks: £38.33. Min 3 nights. £5 single supplement

Built in the 1930s and standing in its own attractive grounds, the Whiteleaf offers individually-styled bedrooms with ensuite facilities.

DARTINGTON   Devon   *Map 3 SX76*

INN QQ **Cott** TQ9 6HE ☎ (0803) 863777

Normal price: £32.50.
Short breaks: £40, includes £15 dinner allowance. Min 2 nights, Oct-Mar
Credit cards ① ② ③ ⑤

This rambling thatched inn dates from 1324 and offers a good standard of food and accommodation. Some of the cottage-style bedrooms have private bathrooms, and all are non-smoking. Children under ten are not accommodated.

DARTMOUTH   Devon   *Map 3 SX85*

★★★62% **Dart Marina** (Trusthouse Forte) Sandquay TQ6 9PH ☎ (0803) 832580

Normal price: from £86 room. Dinner £15-£20
Short breaks: from £47. Min 2 nights
Credit cards ① ② ③ ④ ⑤

From its beautiful situation beside the River Dart, the hotel enjoys beautiful views across to Kingswear. The bedrooms provide a high standard of decor and furnishings; all are ensuite with colour television. There is a special Christmas programme.

DAWLISH   Devon   *Map 3 SX97*

GH Q **Mimosa** 11 Barton Terrace EX7 9QH ☎ (0626) 863283

Normal price: £11
Short breaks: £10, Sep-May.

This family-run guesthouse is set close to the town centre and beaches. Children under three are not accommodated.

DODDISCOMBSLEIGH   Devon   *Map 3 SX88*

INN QQ **Nobody Inn** EX6 7PS ☎ (0647) 52394

Normal price: £47. Dinner £12-£15.
Short breaks: £43 excluding dinner. Min 4 nights.
Activity breaks: Salmon, Trout and Sea Fishing, Clay Shooting, Pheasant Shooting and Rough Shooting. Details from hotel.
🐾 Credit cards ① ③

Full of character, with an inglenook fireplace and exposed beams, this popular inn offers bar meals and an à la carte restaurant.

EXETER   Devon   *Map 3 SX99*

★★★61% **Countess of Wear Lodge** (Queens Moat) Topsham Road, Exeter Bypass EX2 6HE
☎ (0392) 875441

Normal price: £30. Dinner £7-£10.
Short breaks: £36, including dinner allowance of £14. Min 2
nights, Fri-Sun.
Activity breaks: Murder/Mystery Weekends, £105 Oct-Apr,
£115, May-Sept. Bird Watching, £90, 11-13 Jan including
packed lunches, cruise up the Exe Estuary and visit to a
reserve.
Credit cards ① ② ③ ⑤

A motel-style hotel situated just outside the city,
with ground floor bedrooms, the majority set
around an open car park. Good choice of food.

★★★54% **Devon Motel** (Brend) Exeter Bypass, Matford EX2 8XU ☎ (0392) 59268

Normal price: £30. Dinner £11-£13 & à la carte
Short breaks: £38. £10 single supplement. Min 2 nights,
Fri-Sun (except Xmas & New Year)

This modern hotel offers a choice of standard
and well-equipped executive rooms all with
ensuite facilities and colour television. Meals
are taken in the adjacent former manor house
where the eating options include a lunchtime
carvery.

★★★57% **Gipsy Hill** (Consort) Gipsy Hill Lane, Pinhoe EX1 3RN (3m E on B3181) ☎ (0392) 65252
Closed 25-30 December

Normal price: from £31. Dinner £12
Short breaks: £38.50-£43.50. £10 single supplement. Min 2
nights, Thu-Sun

Set in attractive gardens, the hotel has twenty
bedrooms with ensuite facilities and colour
television. Two rooms have four-poster beds.

★★58% **Red House** 2 Whipton Village Road EX4 8AR ☎ (0392) 56104

Normal price: £32.50, includes 3-course carvery dinner
Short breaks: £27 includes 3-course carvery dinner, single
£32. Min 2 nights, Fri-Sun
Credit cards ① ②

Guests can choose between \a la carte, carvery
and bar snack menus at this small, family-run
hotel on the outskirts of the city. Bedrooms are
all ensuite with colour television.

★★★67% **Rougemont** (Mount Charlotte (TS)) Queen Street EX4 3SP ☎ (0392) 54982

Normal price: £41.25. Dinner from £12.50 & à la carte
Short breaks: £36.50. (£28 single occupancy midweek).
Min 2 nights. (1990 prices)

Located in the heart of the city opposite Exeter
central station, this character hotel has bright
modern bedrooms, all with ensuite facilities
and colour television; some rooms are for
families and non-smokers. There is a special
Christmas programme.

★★67% St Andrews (Exec Hotel) 28 Alphington Road EX2 8HN ☎ (0392) 76784
Closed 24 Dec-1 Jan

Normal price: £30. Dinner from £11 & à la carte
Short breaks: £21 excluding dinner. Min 2 nights, Fri-Sun.
Single £26.50
Credit cards [1] [2] [3]

This long-established family-run hotel offers comfortable accommodation, good home-cooked meals and friendly service. All bedrooms are ensuite with colour television, and there are two family rooms.

★★★66% St Olaves Court Mary Arches Street EX4 3AZ ☎ (0392) 217736
Closed 25 Dec-4 Jan

Normal price: £33. Dinner from £14.95 & à la carte
Short breaks: £30. Min 2 nights, Fri-Sun

Tucked away in secluded grounds at the heart of the city, this Georgian hotel has an attractive restaurant serving French cuisine. Annexe bedrooms are spacious, and offer the luxury of ensuite jacuzzis.

★★★63% White Hart 65 South Street EX1 1EE ☎ (0392) 79897
Closed 25-26 Dec

Normal price: £71 room. Dinner £11.40-£23 à la carte
Short breaks: £40 for two excluding dinner. Single £33.
Min 2 nights, Fri-Sun
🐾 (ex guide dogs) Credit cards [1] [2] [3] [5]

This former coaching inn is steeped in history and offers a good choice of eating options. Bedrooms, both those in the main building and the new wing, are well-equipped with modern furnishings and facilities; most are ensuite, and all have colour television.

EXMOUTH   Devon   Map 3 SY08

★58% Aliston House 58 Salterton Road EX8 3EW ☎ (0395) 274119

Normal price: £56-£60 room and breakfast. Dinner £7
Short breaks: £52-£56. Min 2 nights

A friendly, welcoming hotel offering attractive accommodation and good service. All bedrooms have colour television, and most have ensuite facilities. There is a special Christmas programme.

★★65% Barn Foxholes Hill, off Marine Drive EX8 2DF ☎ (0395) 274411

Normal price: £24.50. Dinner from £12
Short breaks: £22 excluding dinner. Min 2 nights, Oct-Apr.
🐾 Credit cards [1] [3]

Set in its own well-kept gardens, this hotel has a comfortable lounge and informal reception bar. Bedrooms are clean and bright, and all have private facilities and colour television. The hotel has some leisure amenities.

GH QQQ Carlton Lodge Carlton Hill EX8 2AJ ☎ (0395) 263314

Normal price: £24.50
Short breaks: £22.50 excluding dinner. Min 2 nights, Oct-Apr (except Bank Holidays)
Credit cards [1] [3]

A pleasant, fully-licensed hotel just off the seafront. Bedrooms are comfortable, all have colour television and most have private bath or shower room.

★★★58% Imperial (Trusthouse Forte) The Esplanade EX8 2SW ☎ (0395) 274761

Normal price: £50. Dinner from £13.25
Short breaks: £47. Min 2 nights
Credit cards [1] [2] [3] [4] [5]

Set in grounds which include an outdoor pool, this popular family hotel offers good amenities and friendly service. All bedrooms are ensuite with colour television. There is regular enter-tainment, and a special Christmas programme is available.

★★★59% **Royal Beacon** (Best Western) The Beacon EX8 2AF ☎ (0395) 264886

Normal price: fr £39.
Short breaks: £40 with sea views, £34 side views. Min 2 nights, Sept-Apr.
Activity breaks: Golf Breaks, short breaks price plus green fee.
Credit cards ①②③④⑤

A modernised Georgian posting house overlooking the sea.

FAIRY CROSS   Devon   Map 2 SS42

★★★ 🏮 69% **Portledge** (Best Western) EX39 5BX (off A39) ☎ (02375) 262 & 367

Normal price: £43, Apr-25 May & Sept-Dec. £52.50, 26 May-Aug. Dinner £18.
Short breaks: £45, Apr-18 May & 6 Nov-28 Mar. £50, 31 Aug-5 Nov. Min 2 nights.
Activity breaks: Whodunnit Weekends and Horror Weekends. Details from hotel.
Credit cards ①②③⑤

Steeped in history and surrounded by beautiful Devonshire countryside, this 13th-century manor house was converted to a hotel in 1947. Public areas are elegant and charming.

FENNY BRIDGES   Devon   Map 3 SY19

★64% **Fenny Bridges** EX14 0BQ ☎ (0404) 850218

Normal price: £19.75. Dinner from £4.45 & à la carte
Short breaks: £15, single £20. Min 3 nights, Fri-Sun
Credit cards ①②③⑤

This roadside inn maintains its busy bar trade, and offers attractive ensuite bedrooms with excellent facilities. Meals are available in the dining area of the lounge bar. Fishing is available.

★61% **Greyhound Inn** (Berni/Chef & Brewer) EX14 0BJ ☎ (0404) 850380

Normal price: £25. Dinner £8-£15 à la carte
Short breaks: £23.50 excluding dinner. Min 2 nights, Fri-Sun.
🐾 (ex guide dogs) Credit cards ①②③⑤

This small hotel has ten bedrooms, all with ensuite facilities and colour television. One room is furnished with a four-poster bed.

FROGMORE   Devon   Map 3 SX74

INN QQ **Globe** TQ7 2NR ☎ (0548) 531351

Normal price: £15
Short breaks: £17. Oct-Mar (except Xmas)
Credit cards ①②③⑤

Situated three miles from Kingsbridge on the A379, the Globe has a good reputation for food and offers comfortable rooms with many facilities for children.

HALWELL   Devon   Map 3 SX75

GH Q **Stanborough Hundred** TQ9 7JG ☎ (054852) 236
20 Mar-Oct

Normal price: £18.50 bed and breakfast, £29 with dinner
Short breaks: £108-£118, two people for 2 nights, Apr-mid Oct
🐾 (ex guide dogs)

This charming small hotel stands in sheltered gardens, and offers a friendly welcome and comfortable accommodation.

HARBERTONFORD   Devon   *Map 3 SX75*

★★★67% **Old Mill Country House** TQ9 7SW ☎ (080423) 349

Normal price: £58 room. Dinner £14.95
Short breaks: £135-£155, two people for 2 nights.
✻ Credit cards 1 3

This former mill, peacefully located in a riverbank setting, has been tastefully converted to provide comfortable bedrooms with private bath and colour television. The restaurant offers interesting dishes and is popular locally. Fishing is available. Children under twelve are not accommodated.

HONITON   Devon   *Map 3 ST10*

★★66% **Home Farm** Wilmington EX14 9JR (2m E) ☎ (040483) 278
Closed Dec-Jan

Normal price: £75 for 2 nights with dinner
Short breaks: £65 for 2 nights, single £70. Oct-Nov & Feb-Apr

A cottage-style family-run hotel, three miles from the town, with individually decorated bedrooms, some of them located in an annexe. The informal restaurant offers an \a la carte menu. There are golf practice nets for guests' use.

INN QQ Monkton Court Monkton EX14 9QH (2m E A30) ☎ (0404) 42309

Normal price: £22.50
Short breaks: £21 excluding dinner. Min 3 nights
✻ (ex guide dogs) Credit cards 1 3

Each bedroom at this inn has tea/coffee making facilities and colour television, and most have ensuite bath or shower room.

HOPE COVE   Devon   *Map 3 SX64*

★★68% **Cottage** Inner Hope Cove TQ7 3HJ ☎ (0548) 561555
Closed 2-30 Jan

Normal price: £79-£102 (room with dinner)
Short breaks: £29.70-£35. Nov-Easter

Beautifully set in its own grounds overlooking Hope Cove, this hotel offers a warm welcome and friendly service. Most of the bedrooms are ensuite with colour television. There is a special Christmas programme.

★61% **Greystone** TQ7 3HH ☎ (0548) 561233

Normal price: £14-£17.50
Short breaks: from £46 (2 nights) to £130 (5 nights). Not mid July-end Aug.
Credit cards 1 3

Substantial home-prepared meals and friendly informal service make for an enjoyable stay at this hotel where most of the bedrooms have private bath or shower room. There is a special Christmas programme. Children under seven are not accommodated.

HORRABRIDGE   Devon   *Map 2 SX57*

★★66% **Overcombe** PL20 7RN ☎ (0822) 853501

Normal price: £18.
Short breaks: £26.50.
Activity breaks: Discovering Dartmoor, £61.50 for the weekend including packed lunches and transport.
Credit cards 1 3

A village centre hotel close to the main road, with comfortable bedrooms and open fires burning in public areas in the colder months. Relaxed friendly service.

ILFRACOMBE Devon Map 2 SS54

GH QQ Cavendish 9-10 Larkstone Terrace EX34 9NU ☎ (0271) 863994

Normal price: from £13.
Short breaks: from £17, min 3 nights, Easter-Oct. Single
supplement
Credit cards ① ② ③

This family hotel enjoys an elevated position with panoramic views. The bedrooms are comfortable and the service friendly.

★★65% Elmfield Torrs Park EX34 8AZ ☎ (0271) 863377

Normal price: £32. Dinner £9.50 & à la carte
Short breaks: £29, min 3 nights, Mar-Oct.
✗ Credit cards ① ③

A friendly hotel in an elevated position overlooking Ilfracombe and the surrounding countryside.

★★57% Ilfracombe Carlton (Consort) Runnacleave Road EX34 8AR ☎ (0271) 862446

Normal price: from £40. Dinner £10.50.
Short breaks: £25 low season, £30.50 high season. Min 2
nights.
Activity breaks: Modern Sequence Dancing, £58 for 2
nights. Feb-Apr. Taste of the West Country, £58 for 2
nights. Details from hotel.
✗ Credit cards ① ② ③

A popular holiday hotel offering easy access to both town centre and beaches, and featuring daily entertainment in the season.

GH QQ Strathmore 57 St Brannocks Road EX34 8EQ ☎ (0271) 862248

Normal price: £15.
Short breaks: £40 for 3 days.
Credit cards ① ② ③ ⑤

This comfortable family-run guesthouse is conveniently placed for all the amenities of Ilfracombe. Interesting menus are offered.

★57% Torrs Torrs Park EX34 8AY ☎ (0271) 862334

Normal price: £23.50. Dinner £8.50 & à la carte
Short breaks: £21, min 3 nights. Mar 9-May 17 & Sept 21-
Oct 31
Credit cards ① ② ③ ④ ⑤

A family-run resort hotel in an elevated position enjoying views over the town, sea and countryside.

★★61% Tracy House Belmont Road EX34 8DR ☎ (0271) 863933 & 868979

Normal price: from £22. Dinner £8.50.
Short breaks: £23.33, min 3 nights, Mar-May, Sept-Oct
Credit cards ① ② ③

An informally-run hotel with comfortable public areas, situated close to the town centre yet within walking distance of the beaches.

GH QQQ Westwell Hall Torrs Park EX34 8AZ ☎ (0271) 862792

Normal price: £27.50 including dinner.
Short breaks: £25, min 4 nights.
Credit cards ③

An elegant detached Victorian property with lovely views of the town and coastline. Imaginative home-cooked meals are served in the intimate dining room.

INSTOW Devon Map 2 SS43

★★★61% Commodore Marine Parade EX39 4JN ☎ (0271) 860347

Normal price: £45. Dinner £16 & alc
Short breaks: £39, min 2 nights, Nov-Mar.
✗ Credit cards ① ② ③

A modern hotel in a commanding position with views across the river to Appledore. Bedrooms are comfortable and public areas relaxing. See advertisement on p93.

JACOBSTOWE   Devon   Map 2 SS50

FH QQ Higher Cadham EX20 3RB ☎ (083785) 647

Normal price: £16.50.
Short breaks: £15. Min 3 nights, Sept-Nov & Feb-May.
✗

Well-decorated and comfortably furnished 16th-century farmhouse, an ideal base for touring.

KENNFORD   Devon   Map 3 SX98

★★61% **Fairwinds** EX6 7UD ☎ (0392) 832911

Normal price: from £31 including dinner.
Short breaks: from £29, min 2 nights. Single supplement.
✗ Credit cards ① ③

A friendly hotel offering cosy bedrooms, and run in an informal manner by the resident owners.

KINGSBRIDGE   Devon   Map 3 SX74

★★★ ➡ 76% **Buckland-Tout-Saints** (Prestige) Goveton TQ7 2DS (2.5m NE on unclass rd)
☎ (0548) 853055

Normal price: £52.50. Dinner £25-£30.
Short breaks: £75, min 2 nights.
✗ Credit cards ① ② ③ ④ ⑤

A charming Queen Anne house offering true country house hospitality, and commanding views of the South Devon countryside.

★★62% **Kings Arms** (Exec Hotel) Fore Street TQ7 1AB ☎ (0548) 852071

Normal price: £25. Dinner £12-£18 à la carte
Short breaks: £35, min 2 nights. Single price £37.50.
Credit cards ① ③

KINGSTEIGNTON Devon *Map 3 SX87*

★★★71% **Passage House** Hackney Lane TQ12 3QH ☎ (0626) 55515

Normal price: £47-£52 approx. Dinner £13.75.
Short breaks: £48, min 2 nights, Fri-Sun. Single price £53.
Activity breaks: Romantic Weekend, £115 (1990) including
four-poster bed, flowers and champagne. Action Breaks,
with choice of Horse Riding, Pony Trekking, Golf, Fishing,
Rough and Clay Shooting, Squash, Tennis, Walking,
Rambling and Rock Climbing – prices from hotel. Bird
Watching Break, prices from hotel. Escape to Dartmoor
Break, £95 (1990). Wet Weekends, £105 (1990) including
sailing, water skiing, wind surfing and rowing. Fly/Drive
Weekends, £245 for 3 nights (1990), including flight to
Exeter airport and three day's car hire.
Credit cards ①②③⑤

A modern hotel with leisure complex including
swimming pool, jet stream, jacuzzi, sauna and
solarium. Overlooks the Teign Estuary and its
wildlife.

LODDISWELL Devon *Map 3 SX74*

GH QQQ **Woolston House** TQ7 4DU ☎ (0548) 550341

Normal price: £74-£88 room, breakfast and dinner
Short breaks: £32, min 2 nights Nov-23May.
⚹

A Georgian country house catering especially
for children, and set in 30 acres of grounds with
a heated pool, tennis court and adventure
playground.

LYDFORD Devon *Map 2 SX58*

★★ 🐾 67% **Lydford House** (Minotels) EX20 4AU ☎ (082282) 347

Normal price: £26. Dinner from £11.
Short breaks: £31.50, min 2 nights, 2 Jan-30 Apr & Oct-22
Dec.
Activity breaks: Take A Riding Break, £72 for 2 nights
including one 2-hour escorted ride on Dartmoor.
Introduction to the Horse, £78.50 for 2 nights including one
45-minute private lesson in the hotel's outdoor school and a
one-hour escorted ride on Dartmoor. Four Poster
Pampering, £186 for 2 nights including bottle of
champagne, flowers and breakfast in bed. First Night
Special, £86.50 for 1 night including four-poster,
champagne, flowers and breakfast in bed.
Credit cards ①②③⑤

This delightful, granite-built country house was
formerly the home of the Victorian artist
William Widgery, whose scenes of Dartmoor
still hang in the cosy residents' lounge.

LYNMOUTH Devon *Map 3 SS74*

★★59% **Bath** (Exec Hotel) Sea Front EX35 6EL ☎ (0598) 52238

Normal price: £24-£31.50. Dinner from £13.
Short breaks: from £30, min 2 nights, Mar-Jun, part Jul-Oct.
Activity breaks: Water Painting Holidays, from £230 for 6
nights. May & Oct.
Credit cards ①②③⑤

Set beside the harbour at the centre of this
attractive village, a family-run hotel with many
rooms having views over the harbour to the sea
beyond. Friendly service.

★★69% Rising Sun Harbourside EX35 6EQ ☎ (0598) 53223

Normal price: £35-£45. Dinner £16.50 & à la carte
Short breaks: £44-£48, min 2 nights, Oct-Jun except Bank Hols.
Credit cards 1 2 3

A 14th-century thatched smugglers' inn beside the harbour with thick walls, crooked ceilings and uneven floors, and all modern comforts.

★ Rock House EX35 6EN ☎ (0598) 53508

Normal price: £32. Dinner £11 & à la carte
Short breaks: £28.33, min 3 nights.
Credit cards 1 2 3 5

Delightful little Georgian hotel overlooking the harbour, where a busy tea garden is one of the attractions.

LYNTON   Devon   Map 3 SS74

GH QQQ Alford House Alford Terrace EX35 6AT ☎ (0598) 52359

Normal price: £27.
Short breaks: £25, min 3 nights.
✕ Credit cards 1 3

A warm welcome awaits guests at this 1840's house which overlooks Lynton and the sea beyond.

★★59% Crown (Inter-Hotels) Sinai Hill EX35 6AG ☎ (0598) 52253

Normal price: from £29.50. Dinner from £13.50 & à la carte
Short breaks: from £35.50, min 2 nights.
Credit cards 1 2 3 5

A coaching inn dating back to 1760, with a reputation for fine beer. It combines cosy bedrooms with a popular restaurant.

★★69% Gordon House Lee Road EX35 6BS ☎ (0598) 53203

Normal price: £21. Dinner £9.
Short breaks: £27, min 2 nights, Mar-Nov.

A well proportioned, detached Victorian house, which has been sympathetically restored to provide comfortable, modern facilities. There is a choice of two lounges, and bedrooms are well-equipped.

GH QQQ Hazeldene Lee Road EX35 6BP ☎ (0598) 52364

Normal price: £27.
Short breaks: £25, min 3 nights, Apr, May, Oct, Nov, Jan & Feb
Credit cards 1 2 3

Standing on the edge of the town centre, this small hotel is an ideal base from which to tour Exmoor and the north Devon coast.

★★62% Neubia House (Guestaccom) Lydiate Lane EX35 6AH ☎ (0598) 52309 & 53644

Normal price: £36.75 including dinner.
Short breaks: £30.50, 15 Feb-24 May; £35.50, 28 May; £33.25, 27 Aug-25 Nov. Min 2 nights.
Credit cards ① ③

A small, secluded house with brightly-decorated bedrooms and a cheerful dining room serving good home-cooked meals with particularly delectable puddings. A good base from which to tour North Devon and Exmoor.

GH Q Retreat 1 Park Gardens, Lydiate Lane EX35 6DF ☎ (0598) 53526

Normal price: £13.
Short breaks: £19, min 2 nights, Oct-Feb.

This small, friendly guesthouse offers pleasant, spotlessly clean accommodation. Good value for money.

★65% Rockvale Lee Road EX35 6HW ☎ (0598) 52279 & 53343

Normal price: £30 including dinner.
Short breaks: £27, min 2 nights, Dec-Feb. High season single supplement.
Credit cards ① ③

A former Bristol merchant's holiday home, the hotel is comfortable and modernised.

★★57% Sandrock Longmead EX35 6DH ☎ (0598) 53307

Normal price: £37-£45. Dinner from £13.50 & à la carte
Short breaks: £21.50-£23.50, min 2 nights.
Credit cards ① ② ③

A friendly little touring and holiday hotel which has been owned by the same family for many years.

GH QQQQ Waterloo House Lydiate Lane EX35 6AJ ☎ (0598) 53391

Normal price: £21.50.
Short breaks: £29.16, min 3 nights
✶

Combining the spirit of the 19th century with today's modern comforts, this gracious hotel is one of the oldest lodging houses in Lynton.

MORETONHAMPSTEAD   Devon   Map 3 SX78

QQQ Cookshayes 33 Court Street TQ13 8LG ☎ (0647) 40374

Normal price: £26-£30
Short breaks: £23.50-£27. Min 2 nights, Mar-Apr, Oct.
Credit cards ① ③

Standing on the edge of Dartmoor amid secluded gardens which include a putting green, this stylish guesthouse serves fresh country food. Bedrooms include a family room, all have colour television and most offer private shower. No children under 5.

★★ White Hart (Minotels) The Square TQ13 8NF ☎ (0647) 40406

Normal price: £53, room and breakfast. Dinner £9.75-£10.25 (1990 price)
Short breaks: £36.50. Min 2 nights. £3 single supplement.
Credit cards ① ② ③ ⑤

Built in 1637, this traditional, friendly inn serves varied dishes in the restaurant and beamed bar, and has cosy bedrooms, some for families, all with ensuite bath and colour television; also a snooker room. No children under 10. Christmas breaks are available.

MORTEHOE   Devon   Map 2 SS44

QQQQ Sunnycliffe EX34 7EB ☎ (0271) 870597

Normal price: £19.50-£20
Short breaks: £23.50-£33. Min 2 nights, Feb-Nov.
✶

Set on a hillside by open moorland, this charming family-run guesthouse serves traditional English cuisine and has comfortable public rooms and bedrooms (half non-smoking), all with ensuite facilities and colour television. No children.

NEWTON ABBOT   Devon   Map 3 SX87

★★ Queens Queen Street TQ12 2EZ ☎ (0626) 63133 & 54106

Normal price: £33. Dinner £10.95-£11.95 & à la carte (1990 price)
Short breaks: £66 for 2 nights, Fri-Sat only.
Credit cards [1] [3]

This characteristic family-run hotel convenient for the station, town centre and racecourse, offers spotless comfort and traditional Devon cooking. Most bedrooms have private bath and all have colour television. Christmas breaks are available.

NORTH HUISH   Devon   Map 3 SX57

★★ Brookdale House TQ10 9NR ☎ (054882) 402 & 415

Normal price: £37.50-£47.50. Dinner £23 (1990 price)
Short breaks: £55-£65 including afternoon tea. Min 2 nights, Nov-Easter. £15 single supplement.
ϰ Credit cards [1] [3]

Situated in a wooded valley, this small and charming family-run hotel serves imaginative, quality food. The comfortable bedrooms, two in the annexe, have spacious well-equipped bathrooms and colour television. No children under 10. Christmas breaks are available.

OTTERY ST MARY   Devon   Map 3 SY19

QQ Fluxton Farm Fluxton EX11 1RJ ☎ (0404) 812818

Normal price: £27.50
Short breaks: £50 for 2 nights, Oct-June.

In a peaceful setting south of the town, this owner-run 16th-century Devon longhouse offers neat accommodation. The many bedrooms, among them two family rooms, offer private bath or shower. Snooker and fishing facilities available.

★★★58% Salston (Best Western) EX11 1RQ (1m SW off B3174 towards West Hill) ☎ (0404) 815581

Normal price: £52.50. Dinner £15.
Short breaks: £45, min 2 nights.
Activity breaks: Golf, Fishing, Clay Pigeon Shooting and Swimming Breaks, details from hotel.
Credit cards [1] [2] [3] [5]

An 18th-century country house with modern extensions enjoying lovely views over the East Devon countryside. There are some recreational facilities.

PAIGNTON   Devon   Map 3 SX86

QQ Channel View 8 Marine Parade TQ3 2NU ☎ (0803) 522432

Normal price: £26
Short breaks: £22.50. Min 2 nights. Extra charge for sea view rooms.
ϰ (ex guide dogs) Credit card [1]

Standing on the seafront, this small friendly hotel has bright, compact bedrooms all with ensuite bathrooms and colour television.

QQ Cherra 15 Roundham Road TQ4 6DN ☎ (0803) 550723

Normal price: £18
Short breaks: £15. Min 2 nights, Mar-Jun, Sept-Oct.

This friendly family-run hotel close to the harbour has a garden with a putting green and colour television in all bedrooms, half of them family rooms and many with private shower.

★★67% Sunhill (Inter-Hotels) Alta Vista Road TQ4 6DA ☎ (0803) 557532

Normal price: £25-£34. Dinner fr £12.
Short breaks: £32.50-£37.50, min 4 nights, Jan-May, Oct-Dec.
Activity breaks: Bridge Weekends, 17-19 May, 1-3 Nov, 29 Nov-1 Dec. Racing Breaks. Details from hotel.

An hotel overlooking and having direct access to Goodrington Sands. Meals are freshly cooked, and experienced staff offer friendly service.

PARKHAM   Devon   *Map 2 SS32*

★★★64% **Penhaven Country House** EX39 5PL ☎ (02375) 388 & 711

Normal price: £42.50 including dinner.
Short breaks: £39.50. Min 2 nights, Fri-Sat; Jan-May, Oct-Dec.
Credit cards ① ② ③ ⑤

Set in woods on the edge of the village, this comfortable restored Victorian rectory serves good local dishes in the small restaurant. The country-style bedrooms all have private bathrooms and colour television. No children under 10. Christmas breaks are available.

PLYMOUTH   Devon   *Map 2 SX45*

★★65% **Camelot** 5 Elliot Street, The Hoe PL1 2PP ☎ (0752) 221255

Normal price: £33.50
Short breaks: £20. Min 2 nights, Fri-Sun, Oct-Mar. £33 for single occupancy.
Credit cards ① ② ③ ⑤

Close to the Hoe and Barbican, this informal terraced hotel offers comfortable bedrooms and compact public areas. The atmosphere is lively, and the cosy dining room serves an imaginative menu.

★★★★63% **Copthorne** (Best Western) Armada Centre, Armada Way PL1 1AR ☎ (0752) 224161

Normal price: £50.50
Short breaks: £33 excluding dinner. Fri-Sun. £45 for single occupancy.
Credit cards ① ② ③ ⑤

This modern hotel in the city centre provides prompt pleasant service, a choice of interesting menus and comfortable well-equipped bedrooms, including family and non-smoking rooms, all ensuite and with colour television. Leisure facilities include snooker, indoor swimming, sauna, solarium and gymnasium.

★ **Drake** 1&2 Windsor Villas, Lockyer Street, The Hoe PL1 2QD ☎ (0752) 229730

Normal price: £19-£22.50
Short breaks: £16-£19 excluding dinner. Min 2 nights, Fri-Sun.
Credit cards ① ② ③ ⑤

This friendly hotel offers sound food and good facilities, with colour television in all bedrooms. Most rooms have ensuite facilities, and there are some family rooms.

★ **Imperial** Lockyer Street, the Hoe PL1 2QD ☎ (0752) 227311

Normal price: £34.75. Dinner £9.75-£11.25 (1990 price)
Short breaks: £29. Min 2 nights.
🐾 Credit cards ① ② ③ ⑤

This detached Victorian hotel has pleasant public rooms, including a games room, and provides friendly service. All bedrooms, which include some family rooms, have colour television and most have ensuite facilities.

★★★66% **Mayflower Post House** (Trusthouse Forte) Cliff Road, The Hoe PL1 3DL ☎ (0752) 660974

Normal price: £88 room.
Short breaks: £45 including set-price dinner or £13 dinner allowance. Min 2 nights.
Credit cards ① ② ③ ④ ⑤

Overlooking Plymouth Sound, this purpose-built hotel has a garden with an outdoor swimming pool and provides fine views from the attractive restaurant and coffee shop. All bedrooms, including many family rooms and some non-smoking, are ensuite and offer colour television. Christmas breaks are available.

★★★61% **New Continental** Millbay Road PL1 3LD ☎ (0752) 220782

Normal price: £35
Short breaks: £37.50 (1990), including set-price dinner or £12.75 dinner allowance. Min 2 nights, Fri-Sun. £10 single supplement.
Credit cards ① ② ③ ⑤

This refurbished hotel gives friendly service and has well-equipped bedrooms, all ensuite and with colour television. There are good leisure facilities including an indoor swimming pool, sauna, solarium, gymnasium and games room.

★★★★58% **Plymouth Moat House** (Queens Moat) Armada Way PL1 2HJ ☎ (0752) 662866

Normal price: £49. Dinner £12.50 & à la carte (1990 price)
Short breaks: £41.50 including dinner or £12 dinner allowance.
Credit cards ① ② ③ ⑤

This 12-storey purpose-built hotel with a variety of restaurants and bars has attractive, spacious bedrooms, all ensuite and with colour television; 5th-floor rooms are non-smoking. The small leisure centre includes an indoor swimming pool, sauna, solarium and gymnasium. Christmas breaks are available.

★★ **Strathmore** (Consort) Elliot Street, The Hoe PL1 2PP ☎ (0752) 662101

Normal price: £27.50. Dinner from £10.50 (1990 price)
Short break: £30. Min 2 nights, Fri-Sun. £40 for single occupancy.
Credit cards ① ② ③ ⑤

Part of a terrace on Plymouth Hoe, this popular hotel provides comfortable, recently modernised accommodation with all bedrooms, which include family rooms, having private bathrooms and colour television. Christmas breaks.

POUNDSGATE   Devon   Map 3 SX77

GH QQ **Leusdon Lodge** TQ13 7PE ☎ (03643) 304

Normal price: £30 including dinner.
Short breaks: £50 for 2 nights, Oct-Easter.
Activity breaks: Guided Walking Weekends, £63, Apr-Jun & Sept-Nov. Details from hotel.
Credit cards ① ② ③ ⑤

Standing on the edge of Dartmoor with panoramic views, this 150-year-old granite-built guesthouse offers friendly service and traditional fare.

PRINCETOWN   Devon   Map 2 SX57

✿★★ ♨71% **Prince Hall** Two Bridges PL20 6SA ☎ (082289) 403

Normal price: £25-£27
Short breaks: £40.50-£42.50 including set-price dinner or £17.50 dinner allowance. Min 2 nights.
Credit cards ① ② ③ ⑤

The hotel, in the heart of Dartmoor National Park, commands breathtaking views and retains the atmosphere of a family home, with spacious bedrooms and intimate public areas.

★★50% **Two Bridges** Princetown PL20 6SW ☎ (082289) 581

Normal price: £18-£35
Short breaks: £20.50-£35.50 including £11 dinner allowance. Min 2 nights. Single supplement.
Credit cards ① ② ③ ⑤

Dating from the 18th century, this hotel provides an ideal base for exploring Dartmoor. Spacious public areas include a character bar and comfortable lounge with an open fire. Bedrooms have been recently upgraded, with pretty soft furnishings ensuring their original charm and character is not lost.

ROUSDON   Devon   Map 3 SY29

★★57% **Orchard Country** DT7 3XW ☎ (02974) 2972

Normal price: £25. Dinner £12.50.
Short breaks: £29, min 2 nights Apr, May & Oct. Single
supplement.
Activity breaks: Organised Walks and Hikes, £58 for 2
nights, Apr, May & Oct.
Credit cards 1 3

A personally run little hotel offering friendly,
informal service in a relaxed atmosphere. Set
in quiet rural surroundings between Lyme
Regis and Seaton.

SALCOMBE   Devon   Map 3 SX73

★★68% **Grafton Towers** Moult Road, South Sands TQ8 8LG ☎ (054884) 2882

Normal price: from £36. Dinner from £12.50
Short breaks: from £34, min 3 nights, Apr, May & Oct.
Credit cards 1 3

There are panoramic views of the Salcombe
estuary from this Victorian house which stands
in a secluded, elevated position. The service is
friendly, and some bedrooms have ensuite
facilities and a television.

★63% **Knowle** Onslow Road TQ8 8HY ☎ (054884) 2846

Normal price: fr £34.50 including dinner.
Short breaks: £59.80 for 2 nights, Mar-May & Oct.
Credit cards 1 3

Small, personally-run hotel in an elevated
position with modest accommodation.

QQQ Lyndhurst Bonaventure Road TQ8 8BG ☎ (054884) 2481

Normal price: £28-£32
Short breaks: £27, min 2 nights, Jan-May & Oct-Nov.
excluding Easter & Bank Holidays.
✗

A charming hotel which enjoys views of the bay and offers new accommodation to a fine standard. Smoking is not permitted in the bedrooms, which are well-equipped and all have colour television.

★★★72% **Soar Mill Cove** Soar Mill Cove, Malborough TQ7 3DS ☎ (0548) 561566

Normal price: £54-£59 (1990 prices). Dinner £25-£35 & à la carte.
Short breaks: £43-£57 excluding dinner. Min 3 nights. Half board breaks are also available. £8 single supplement in summer.
Credit cards ☐1☐ ☐3☐

Situated 300 yards from the beautiful Soar Mill Cove, this family-run hotel has been modernised and extended to provide high standards of comfort combined with attentive, friendly service. Bedrooms are spacious and well equipped with sun patios, and the restaurant offers imaginative dishes using local produce, complemented by a well-balanced wine list. Good recreational facilities are also provided.

★★★79% **Tides Reach** South Sands TQ8 8LJ ☎ (054884) 3466

Normal price: £57 low season, £80 high season. Dinner fr £22.50.
Short breaks: £54-£60, min 2 nights, Mar-May, Oct & Nov.
Activity breaks: Bridge Breaks, Mar. Details from hotel.

Perched right on the water's edge with glorious views of the estuary and coastline. An indoor leisure complex with health and beauty spa enhances the hotel's facilities. See advertisement on p111.

★ **Woodgrange** Devon Road TQ8 8HJ ☎ (054884) 2439 and 2006
Closed November-April

Normal price: £42-£48 room & breakfast. Dinner £10-£15
Short breaks: £54 for two, min 2 nights. April-May 14 (not Easter). Single £27
Credit cards ☐1☐ ☐2☐ ☐3☐ ☐5☐

This small 16th-century hotel and restaurant is neatly tucked away in the narrow streets of the town and close to the beach. Accommodation is compact but very comfortable and full of character. There is a cosy restaurant, small non-smoking lounge and library, and a residents' and diners' bar. Good, imaginative dishes are served in the restaurant.

SAUNTON Devon Map 2 SS43

★★★★57% **Saunton Sands** (Brend) EX33 1LQ ☎ (0271) 890212

Normal price: £52 low season, £58 high season. Dinner £15
Short breaks: from £40, Nov-Apr; from £58, Apr, May, Sept, Oct; from £60, Jun. Min 2 nights. Single supplement.
Activity breaks: Brian Barnes Golf Week, details from hotel.
✗

Beautifully situated hotel enjoying panoramic sea views and direct access to the beach. Extensive leisure and recreational facilities include a large indoor pool and squash courts.

SIDMOUTH Devon Map 3 SY18

★★62% **Applegarth** Church Street, Sidford EX10 9QP ☎ (0395) 513174

Normal price: £28.50. Dinner from £9.50 & à la carte.
Short breaks: £26.50, min 2 nights.
✗ Credit cards ☐1☐ ☐3☐

A charming little 16th-century family-run hotel standing in its own grounds about a mile from the sea. Cottage-style bedrooms are spotlessly clean, with bright décor and pine furnishings. The compact, comfortably furnished public areas include a restaurant where fresh, quality home cooking is complemented by friendly personal service.

★★★★69% **Belmont** The Esplanade ☎ (0395) 512555
Normal price: £47. Dinner £14.50 & à la carte.
Short breaks: from £44, min 2 nights Apr; from £46 Nov-
Apr; from £48 May, Oct, except Bank Holidays. £5 single
supplement.
🐾 Credit cards ① ② ③ ⑤

A totally refurbished hotel with fine sea views
stands at the quieter end of the promenade.
Bedrooms and public areas alike are
comfortable and well-equipped, while friendly,
efficient service is provided in all areas.

★★ 🐾 70% **Brownlands** Sid Road EX10 9AG ☎ (0395) 513053
Normal price: £35.50-£44.50. Dinner £14.95
Short breaks: £33.50-£42.50, Fri-Sun, includes Sunday
lunch.

Set in seven acres, enjoying panoramic views
over Sidmouth and Lyme Bay, this attractive
Victorian hotel has been sympathetically
restored, providing a new oak-panelled dining
room and restful conservatory overlooking the
grounds. The bedrooms are comfortable,
freshly decorated and well furnished, and, like
the public rooms, spotlessly clean.

★★★61% **Fortfield** Station Road EX10 8NU ☎ (0395) 512403
Normal price: £32-£50. Dinner £12.50 & à la carte.
Short breaks: £37-£40, min 2 nights Apr-early May, and Oct-
Mar excluding Easter, Christmas & New Year.
Credit cards ① ② ③

A family managed hotel run on traditional lines
offering elegant, comfortable lounges
furnished with fine antiques. Bedrooms are
simply decorated and furnished but well
equipped, each with colour television, and
there is a small leisure centre in the extensive
grounds, overlooking the sea.

★★65% **Littlecourt** Seafield Road EX10 8HF ☎ (0395) 515279
Normal price: £30, Apr-5 May; £34, 4 Oct-1 Nov; £27.50,
Nov-1 Apr. Dinner £9.50-£10.50.
Short breaks: £27.50, Apr-3 May, Nov-1 Apr; £31.50 4 Oct-1
Nov. Min 2 nights.
Activity breaks: Christmas House Party, 23-30 Dec. Details
from hotel.
Credit cards ① ③

This attractive character property is within
walking distance of the seafront and the town
centre. Public areas combine comfort and
modern quality.

★★68% **Mount Pleasant** Salcombe Road EX12 8JA ☎ (0395) 514694
Normal price: £27.
Short breaks: £28. Min 2 nights, Apr-May, excluding Easter.
Includes 1 night free.

Originally the 18th-century home for the vicar
of Salcombe Regis, the hotel overlooks the
river from a delightful position near the town
centre. Careful improvements have produced
cosy individual bedrooms and public areas
which include a small, intimate dining room.

★★★78% **Riviera** The Esplanade EX10 8AY ☎ (0395) 515201
Normal price: £41-£57. Dinner £17.50 & à la carte.
Short breaks: £40-£54, min 4 nights, Oct-May.
Credit cards ① ② ③ ⑤

Situated in a prime position off the sea front,
this fine Georgian hotel has been totally
refurbished to provide comfortable public areas
and particularly well equipped quality
bedrooms. Staff are friendly and efficient, and a
good room service is available.

★★★60% **Royal Glen** Glen Road EX10 8RW ☎ (0395) 513221 & 578124

Normal price: from £36-£46. Dinner from £9.50
Short breaks: from £46, min 2 nights, Nov-end Apr
Credit cards ① ② ③

Once the residence of Queen Victoria's parents, the Duke and Duchess of Kent, this beautiful house stands in its own grounds and offers a wealth of history and character. Bedrooms are compact but all furnished in Victorian style, with colour televisions adding a modern touch. A heated indoor pool completes the transformation.

★★63% **Royal York & Faulkner** Esplanade EX10 8AZ ☎ (0395) 513043 & 513184

Normal price: from £25-£43.50 including dinner.
Short breaks: £72 for 2 days, 2 May-1Jun, Oct-1Nov.
Activity breaks: Bridge Weekend and Chess Weekends, details from hotel.
Credit cards ① ③

Regency-style building, personally run, on the seafront close to shopping facilities.

★★★★64% **Victoria** Esplanade EX10 8RY ☎ (0395) 512651

Normal price: £50 low season, £60 high season. Dinner £16-£18 & à la carte.
Short breaks: £42-£55, according to season. Min 2 nights, Jan-May & Oct-Dec, excluding Bank Holidays. £10 single supplement.
✵ Credit cards ① ② ③ ⑤

Set in a prime position overlooking the sea, this fine Victorian hotel offers spacious, comfortable public rooms together with a range of leisure activities that includes both indoor and outdoor swimming pools.

★★50% **Westbourne** Manor Road EX10 8RR ☎ (0395) 513774

Normal price: £33.55. Dinner £10.
Short breaks: £31.50, min 2 nights, Mar-May & Oct.
Credit cards ① ③

A family-run Victorian house in its own grounds, quietly situated within easy reach of beaches and the town centre. A choice of meals is served from a single table d'hôte menu in the gracious dining room.

★★★68% **Westcliff** Manor Road EX10 8RU ☎ (0395) 513252

Normal price: £42-£50.50, according to season. Dinner from £16.50 & à la carte.
Short breaks: £40-£48.50 according to season. Min 2 nights, Apr, May, Aug & Oct, includes early morning tea.
✵ Credit cards ① ③

A popular, family owned and run hotel which commands good sea views from a setting amidst two acres of gardens. Recent upgrading of the public rooms has brought them to a commendable standard, with the addition of a new cocktail bar, and there is a wide selection of recreational facilities.

SOUTH BRENT   Devon   Map 3 SX66

FH QQ Great Aish TQ10 9JG ☎ (0364) 72238

Normal price: £14.
Short breaks: £12, min 5 nights.
✵

Home-cooked produce from the extensive kitchen garden features on the menu at this spacious Victorian farmhouse close to Dartmoor National Park.

SOUTH MOLTON   Devon   Map 3 SS72

★★73% **Marsh Hall** (1¼ miles N towards North Molton) EX36 3HQ ☎ (07695) 2666

Normal price: £30. Dinner £15.95
Short breaks: £37, min 3 nights.
Credit cards ① ③

An elegant Victorian house set in peaceful grounds with terraced lawns. The bedrooms are spacious, tastefully decorated and well equipped, with magnificent views. The menus are carefully prepared, and the service is friendly and warm.

SOUTH ZEAL   Devon   Map 3 SX69

GH QQQ Poltimore EX20 2PD ☎ (0837) 840209

Normal price: from £17.
Short breaks: from £15, min 3 nights.
Credit cards [1] [3]

This pretty thatched cottage stands in its own gardens on the fringe of Dartmoor with simple but comfortable bedrooms.

STAVERTON   Devon   Map 3 SX76

★69% **Sea Trout Inn** TQ9 6PA ☎ (080426) 274

Normal price: £24-£26. Dinner £12-£13 & à la carte.
Short breaks: £33-£36, min 2 nights.
Credit cards [1] [3]

A comfortable village inn in a peaceful situation offering attentive service from the resident owners.

STOKE CANON   Devon   Map 3 SX99

★★★73% **Barton Cross** Huxham EX5 4EJ ☎ (0392) 841245 & 841584

Normal price: £38.50-£41.50. Dinner £18.50-£23 & à la carte.
Short breaks: £47, Fri-Sun. Single price £55.50.
Credit cards [1] [2] [3] [4] [5]

Dating back to the 17th century, this hotel has attractive inglenook fireplaces, exposed beams and a thatched roof. See advertisement on p99.

TAVISTOCK   Devon   Map 2 SX47

★★★57% **Bedford** (Trusthouse Forte) Plymouth Road PL19 8BB ☎ (0822) 613221

Normal price: £97 room only. Dinner from £13.95.
Short breaks: £47, min 2 nights.
Activity breaks: Pony Trekking Breaks, from £110 (1990) including trekker's lunch on one day and six hours riding through Dartmoor over two days.
Credit cards [1] [2] [3] [4] [5]

A stone-built hotel on the original site of Tavistock Abbey.

TEIGNMOUTH   Devon   Map 3 SX97

★55% **Drakes** Northumberland Place TQ14 8UG ☎ (0626) 772777

Normal price: £35. Dinner £5.50-£7.50 & à la carte.
Short breaks: £50 for 2 nights, Jun-Aug.
Credit cards [1] [3]

This small, tastefully appointed and comfortable hotel offers an interesting choice of well-cooked food throughout the day.

GH QQ Glen Devon 3 Carlton Place TQ14 8AB ☎ (0626) 772895

Normal price: £11-£11.50.
Short breaks: £9.50 excluding dinner, Oct-Mar.
✸

A simply appointed, family-run hotel with compact, brightly decorated bedrooms and comfortable public areas.

★63% **Glenside** (Guestaccom) Ringmoor Road, Shaldon TQ14 0EP (1m S off A379) ☎ (0626) 872448

Normal price: fr £34. Dinner £9-£10.
Short breaks: £53.50 for 2 nights, Dec-Apr & Oct.

A well-proportioned house which has been successfully converted to provide a hotel with bright, comfortable public areas.

GH QQ Hill Rise Winterbourne Road TQ14 8JT ☎ (0626) 773108

Normal price: £14.50.
Short breaks: £13 excluding dinner. Min 3 nights, Oct-Apr.
✸

A large detached Edwardian house located in a residential area, offering bright bedrooms and comfortable public areas.

★★70% **Ness House** Marine Drive, Shaldon TQ14 0HP ☎ (0626) 873480

Normal price: £32.50. Dinner £12-£20 à la carte.
Short breaks: £20 excluding dinner. Min 2 nights, Oct-May.
✚ Credit cards ①②③

A comfortable Regency hotel with good sea views. The attractive restaurant offers a commendable standard of cooking.

THURLESTONE Devon Map 3 SX64

★★★★68% **Thurlestone** TQ7 3NN ☎ (0548) 560382

Normal price: £72 including dinner.
Short breaks: £55 midweek, £65 Fri-Sat. Min 2 nights, Nov-Mar.
Activity breaks: The Wines of the Rhone, £190, 12-14 Apr. Hunting on Dartmoor, £175 for 2 nights, winter and spring. Horse riding experience essential. National Trust Gardens Tour, £340 2-7 Jun, including visits to Cothele, Saltram House, Killerton, Knightshayes and Castle Drogo.
Credit cards ①③⑤

Spacious hotel, built, owned and managed by the Grose family for 90years, with fine country and sea views.

TIVERTON Devon Map 3 SS91

★★61% **Hartnoll** Bolham EX16 7RA (1.5m N on A396) ☎ (0884) 252777

Normal price: £37 including dinner.
Short breaks: £26.75, min 2 nights. Single price £39.50.
Credit cards ①②③⑤

A Georgian building in its own well-kept gardens just one mile from the town centre and close to the North Devon link road.

★★★60% **Tiverton** Blundells Road EX16 4DB ☎ (0884) 256120

Normal price: £60 room and breakfast.
Short breaks: from £35, min 2 nights. Single supplement.
Activity breaks: Bridge Weekends, £105 (1990), including sherry reception, buffet lunch and tea on Saturday, lunch on Sunday – November. Rambling Breaks, £93 (1990) for 3 nights including guided walks, sherry reception, packed lunches and talks – October.
Credit cards ①②③⑤

A good range of leisure facilities is available at this hotel off the new Link Road, on the outskirts of town.

TORCROSS Devon Map 3 SX84

★66% **Grey Homes** TQ7 2TH ☎ (0548) 580220

Normal price: £54. Dinner £11.
Short breaks: £62, min 2 nights, Mar-Nov. Single supplement.
Credit cards ①③

A small, comfortable hotel in an elevated position overlooking the unique freshwater lake beside the sea and the little fishing village of Torcross.

TORQUAY Devon Map 3 SX96

★★★69% **Abbey Lawn** Scarborough Road TQ2 5UQ ☎ (0803) 299199

Normal price: £64, Apr-May. £67, Oct-Dec. £72, Jun-Sept. Dinner from £15.
Short breaks: £39, Apr-May, £42, Oct-Dec, £46, Jun-Sept. Min 2 nights.
Activity breaks: Classical Music Weekends, £200, May & Oct. Historic Houses Weekends, £200, May & Oct. Murder/Mystery Weekends, £185, Nov. Details from hotel.

Complete refurbishment has restored this fine hotel to its former Georgian elegance and glory. Spotlessly clean throughout.

★★64% Albaston House 27 St Marychurch Road TQ1 3JF ☎ (0803) 296758

Normal price: £38.
Short breaks: £30. Min 2 nights, Jan-May, Sept-Nov.
Credit cards ① ③

Small family-run hotel occupying a main road position half a mile from the town centre.

★★65% Ansteys Lea Babbacombe Road, Wellswood TQ1 2QJ ☎ (0803) 294843

Normal price: from £15.50. Dinner £5.
Short breaks: from £16.30. Min 3 nights, Oct-May except Xmas & Easter. Single price from £17.80.

A tastefully restored, large Victorian villa, with attractive gardens containing a small secluded swimming pool.

★★58% Balmoral Meadfoot Sea Road TQ1 2LQ ☎ (0803) 293381 & 299224

Normal price: £26. Dinner £9.50.
Short breaks: £23.50, min 2 nights, Oct-Jun.
Credit cards ① ③

This large Victorian house is close to the Meadfoot beach, and offers small but well-equipped bedrooms and spacious public rooms.

★★★60% Belgrave Seafront TQ2 5HE ☎ (0803) 296666

Normal price: £35. Dinner £9.
Short breaks: £39. Min 2 nights, Fri-Sun, Oct-mid May.
Credit cards ① ③ ⑤

Situated in a good position overlooking the bay, the hotel offers bright, modern public rooms and attractive bars.

★★57% Bowden Close Teignmouth Road, Maidencombe TQ1 4TJ ☎ (0803) 328029

Normal price: £20. Dinner £8.50 & à la carte.
Short breaks: £24. Min 2 nights, 7 Jan-Jun & 30 Sept-14 Dec.
Credit cards ① ③

A large extended Victorian house set off the A379 at Maidencombe provides comfortable public areas and clean, bright bedrooms.

GH QQQ Braddon Hall Braddons Hill Road East TQ1 1HF ☎ (0803) 293908

Normal price: £20.
Short breaks: £20, min 3 nights.

Within easy reach of the harbour and beaches, this quietly set hotel has ensuite facilities and public areas of a high standard.

GH QQQ Burley Court Wheatridge Lane, Livermead TQ2 6RA ☎ (0803) 607879

Normal price: £18-£23.
Short breaks: £24-£28, min 3 nights, Apr-Oct.
🕇

Situated in an elevated position overlooking Livermead Beach, Burley Court has an indoor leisure complex and a heated outdoor pool.

★★59% Bute Court Belgrave Road TQ2 5HQ ☎ (0803) 293771

Normal price: £27. Dinner £7.50-£9 à la carte.
Short breaks: £24. Single supplement £1.50.
Credit cards ① ② ③ ⑤

A resort hotel with easy access to the seafront and town centre. Entertainment is provided during the season.

117

★★61% **Carlton** Falkland Road TQ2 5JJ ☎ (0803) 291166

Normal price: £30. Dinner £9.50-£12.
Short breaks: £22.50, Oct-Mar.
🦅 Credit cards ①③

A family hotel offering clean, brightly decorated bedrooms and spacious public areas. Entertainment is provided in the lively bars. See advertisement on p117.

GH QQQ **Chesterfield** 62 Belgrave Road TQ2 5EY ☎ (0803) 292318

Normal price: £12-£15.
Short breaks: £15-£18, min 2 nights, Oct-May.
Credit cards ①③

This charming house is part of a terrace close to the seafront. The public rooms still have their original carved ceilings.

★★★70% **Corbyn Head** Torquay Road, Sea Front, Livermead TQ2 6RH ☎ (0803) 213611

Normal price: £30-£96 room and breakfast. Dinner £12.50-£15.50 & à la carte
Short breaks: £44, min 3 nights
Credit cards ①②③⑤

A modern hotel in a commanding position opposite Livermead Beach, with spacious public rooms and a choice of restaurants.

GH QQQ **Craig Court** 10 Ash Hill Road, Castle Circus TQ1 3HZ ☎ (0803) 294400

Normal price: £22.
Short breaks: £59 for 3 nights, 2 Apr-22 May.
🦅

A spacious and detached early Victorian house with large comfortable bedrooms and a choice of two lounges.

★70% **Fairmount House** (Guestaccom) Herbert Road, Chelston TQ2 6RW ☎ (0803) 605446

Normal price: £21 to May 24, £24 from May 25. Dinner £9.50.
Short breaks: £56.50 for 2 nights Mar-24 May, £62 from Oct.
Credit cards ①②③

This attractive little hotel is surrounded by beautifully kept gardens, and a warm welcome and friendly service are assured.

★★67% **Frognel Hall** Higher Woodfield Road TQ1 2LD ☎ (0803) 298339

Normal price: from £23.50. Dinner £7.95-£10.95.
Short breaks: £21.15 excluding dinner. Min 3 nights, Mar-May & Oct-Nov.
Credit cards ①③

An owner-managed hotel with fine bay views from its elevated position. A private house until 1980, it provides good modern facilities whilst retaining many original features.

GH QQQQ **Glenorleigh** 26 Cleveland Road TQ2 5BE ☎ (0803) 292135

Normal price: £20.
Short breaks: £36 for 2 nights (1990), Jan-Spring Bank Hol.
🦅

A perpetual award winner, this friendly family hotel offers a flower-filled garden with an inviting swimming pool. The bedrooms are freshly decorated and beautifully kept.

★★★★50% **Grand** Sea Front TQ2 6NT ☎ (0803) 296677

Normal price: £50. Dinner from £16.50 and à la carte.
Short breaks: £55 (1990). Min 2 nights.
Credit cards ① ③ ⑤

An imposing Victorian hotel on the seafront, undergoing extensive improvements. Public rooms are spacious and comfortable, and the bedrooms well-equipped. Recreational facilities include heated outdoor and indoor pools, sauna, solarium and jacuzzi. There is a special Christmas and New Year programme.

★★★61% **Kistor** Belgrave Road TQ2 5HF ☎ (0803) 212632

Normal price: £27-£35.
Short breaks: £36.50, Mar-May; £40, mid Sept-Oct; £35, Nov to 22 Dec. Prices include lunch. Min 2 nights.
Credit cards ① ② ③ ⑤

Commercial and tourist hotel close to the beach, offering personal attention. See advertisement in colour section.

★★57% **Lansdowne** Babbacombe Road TQ1 1PW ☎ (0803) 299599

Normal price: £51 including dinner.
Short breaks: £90 for 2 nights, Sept-May Spring Bank Hol. Includes bar lunches.
Activity breaks: Christmas Breaks, £160 for 4 nights. Throughout December excluding Xmas. Easter, Valentine, Hallowe'en and Guy Fawkes Breaks, fr £51 per night.
Credit cards ① ② ③

A hotel very well geared to the needs of holidaymakers with friendly service from owners and staff.

★★★58% **Lincombe Hall** Meadfoot Road TQ1 2JX ☎ (0803) 213361

Normal price: £43. Dinner £12.95 & à la carte.
Short breaks: £68 for 2 nights (1990).
Credit cards ① ② ③ ⑤

Built in 1882 as a summer residence, this hotel has retained the elegance and classical simplicity of the period.

★★★57% **Livermead House** (Best Western) Torbay Road TQ2 6QJ ☎ (0803) 294361

Normal price: £46 including dinner.
Short breaks: £41, min 2 nights.
Activity breaks: Anniversary Break £120 for 2 nights including fruit, flowers and champagne. A Date with Agatha Christie, £76-£82. Single Parent Breaks. Details from hotel. Prices for breaks listed are for 1990.
🛧

This hotel, conveniently situated for the town and beaches, has indoor and outdoor leisure facilities.

GH QQQQ Mapleton St Lukes Road North TQ2 5PD ☎ (0803) 292389

Normal price: £16.
Short breaks: £19.50, min 3 nights, Oct-May.
🛧 Credit cards ① ③

Surrounded by its own grounds, with glorious views across the bay, this hotel extends a warm welcome to its guests and provides attractive rooms.

GH QQQ Olivia Court Upper Braddon Hill Road TQ1 1HD ☎ (0803) 292595

Normal price: £25 including dinner.
Short breaks: £19.25, min 2 nights, Oct-Mar.
Credit cards ① ③

This picturesque property is in a quiet residential area close to the town centre. Meals are served in the elegant dining room.

★★68% **Oscar's** 56 Belgrave Road TQ2 5HY ☎ (0803) 293563

Normal price: £16.50-£22.50. Dinner £6.50-£8.50 & à la carte.
Short breaks: £20.50. Min 2 nights, Jan-Jun & Oct-mid Nov.
🛧 Credit cards ① ③ ④

A tall, Victorian terraced house, tastefully converted, Oscar's is in the Belgravia area of Torquay. Bedrooms are comfortable, and the intimate bistro is open from March to October.

★★★64% **Overmead** (Consort) Daddyhole Road TQ1 2EF ☎ (0803) 297633 & 295666

Normal price: £39.50. Dinner £14-£16.
Short breaks: £34.50, min 2 nights, Fri-Mon.
Activity breaks: Murder/Mystery Weekends, details from hotel.
Credit cards ①②③

Stone-built, split level hotel with a modern wing extension, set in a quiet position.

★★66% **Red House** Rousdown Road, Chelston TQ2 6PB ☎ (0803) 607811

Normal price: £15.50-£27.50. Dinner £7.25-£7.95.
Short breaks: £23, min 2 nights, Sept-May. Single price £27.
Credit cards ①③

As its name suggests, this is an attractive red brick hotel within easy reach of the town and beaches. The hotel offers excellent leisure facilities.

GH QQQ Richwood 20 Newton Road TQ2 5BZ ☎ (0803) 293729

Normal price: £12 low season, £21 high season.
Short breaks: £44 for weekend, min 2 nights, Sept-May.
Activity breaks: Dancing Breaks, £44 for weekend. Details from hotel.
Credit cards ①③

An ideal family hotel, with cosy bedrooms that are brightly furnished and decorated. Meals are served in the relaxing dining room.

★★63% **Roseland** Warren Road TQ2 5TT ☎ (0803) 213829

Normal price: £33.50. Dinner £14.50.
Short breaks: £22.50, min 3 nights, Nov-Apr.
Activity breaks: Gourmet Weekends, £90; Jan-Apr, Oct-Dec.

In an elevated setting enjoying breathtaking views across the bay to Paignton and Brixham.

★★★62% **Sefton** Babbacombe Downs Road, Babbacombe TQ1 3LH ☎ (0803) 328728 & 326591

Normal price: £32.50, Apr-mid Jun; £35.50, mid Jun-Sept; £31.50, Sept-Mar. Dinner £9.50-£13.50 & à la carte.
Short breaks: £29.70, min 2 nights, Oct-Mar except Christmas, New Year and Easter.
Credit cards ① ② ③

The Powell family, assisted by a young, friendly staff, have made this Babbacombe hotel popular. There is a large entertainments room.

GH QQQ Sevens 27 Morgan Avenue TQ2 5RR ☎ (0803) 293523

Normal price: £22-£28.
Short breaks: £20-£26 excluding dinner. Min 3 nights except Jul, Aug & Dec.
✶

A small hotel with simply appointed bedrooms and a spacious bar where guests can play pool and darts.

GH Q Skerries 25 Morgan Avenue TQ2 5RR ☎ (0803) 293618

Normal price: £10.50.
Short breaks: £9.50 excluding dinner. Min 3 nights, Oct-May.

Family-run, cosy private hotel with comfortable public rooms and compact bedrooms. Conveniently close to the town centre.

★64% **Sunleigh** Livermead Hill TQ2 6QY ☎ (0803) 607137

Normal price: £44. Dinner £8.75.
Short breaks: £42, Mar-May & Oct; £48, Jun & Sept. Min 3 nights, Mar-Jun, Sept-Oct.

Spaciously comfortable public areas are provided by this large detached Victorian house overlooking Livermead Bay.

GH QQQ Tregantle 64 Bampfylde Road TQ2 5AY ☎ (0803) 297494

Normal price: £29.
Short breaks: £25, min 3 nights.
✶ Credit cards ① ③

Close to the Riviera Centre, this spacious detached house offers friendly and attentive service, and quality, imaginative food.

TOTNES Devon   Map 3 SX86

GH QQQQ Old Forge Seymour Place TQ9 5AY ☎ (0803) 862174

Normal price: £17.50-£25.
Short breaks: £15.50-£23, min 4 nights excluding dinner. Cream teas included. Nov-Mar.
Activity breaks: Blacksmithing Courses for Beginners, 600-year-old forge on premises. Details from hotel.
✶ Credit cards ① ③

An attractive licensed property standing in a walled garden, the Old Forge is over 600 years old, and of great historic interest.

★★59% **Royal Seven Stars** TQ9 5DD ☎ (0803) 862125 & 863241

Normal price: from £24. Dinner £12.75-£15.
Short breaks: from £34.50 including champagne on arrival and Sunday lunch. Min 2 nights, Fri-Sun except Easter, Xmas & New Year. Single price from £44.50.
Credit cards ①③⑤

Originally a coaching inn dating back to 1660, this hotel offers a popular restaurant and a quiet residents' lounge.

WEST BUCKLAND   Devon   Map 3 SS73

FH QQ Huxtable EX32 0SR ☎ (05986) 254

Normal price: £17.
Short breaks: 5% discount 3-6 nights, Sept-Jun.
🛪

The present house was built in 1520 and retains much of its original character and charm. Early childrens' suppers are served in a separate dining room.

WEST DOWN   Devon   Map 2 SS54

GH QQQQ Long House EX34 8NF ☎ (0271) 863242

Normal price: £62, room and dinner.
Short breaks: £60 for two, min 2 nights. Mid Mar-mid Nov.
🛪 Credit card ①

The former forge and post office of this sleepy North Devon village have been converted to provide four individually furnished bedrooms.

GH QQQ Sunnymeade Country House Dean Cross EX34 8NT (1m W on A361) ☎ (0271) 863668

Normal price: £23.50 including dinner.
Short breaks: £22, min 3 nights, Feb-Jul & Sept-Nov.
🛪 Credit cards ①②③⑤

A modern guesthouse offering bright, attractive ensuite bedrooms and spacious, comfortable public areas.

WOODY BAY   Devon   Map 3 SS64

★★77% **Woody Bay** EX31 4QX ☎ (05983) 264

Normal price: £46 including dinner.
Short breaks: £41, min 2 nights, Nov-Mar.
Activity breaks: Bird Watching, early May. Details from hotel. £12 extra over 3 days.
Credit cards ①③

Set in a magnificent spot overlooking the bay on the edge of Exmoor National Park, this spacious Victorian house offers comfortable bedrooms, many with sea views.

WOOLACOMBE   Devon   Map 2 SS44

★★68% **Little Beach** The Esplanade EX34 7DJ ☎ (0271) 870398

Normal price: from £32. Dinner £11.50.
Short breaks: from £27, min 2 nights, Feb-May.
Credit cards ①③

Enjoying a prime position overlooking the bay, the hotel offers imaginative meals and friendly service. Public areas are enhanced by good antiques.

★★★68% **Watersmeet** Mortehoe EX34 7EB ☎ (0271) 870333

Normal price: £40.70. Dinner from £19.50.
Short breaks: £40.55, min 2 nights, Oct-May. Single supplement.
Activity breaks: Painting Breaks, May. Bridge Breaks, May & Oct. Details from hotel.
🛪

Beautifully situated on the headland of Mortehoe, this hotel provides relaxing public areas including a restaurant with fine panoramic views.

YARCOMBE   Devon   Map 3 ST20

★★69% **Belfry** (Minotels) EX14 9BD ☎ (040486) 234 & 588

Normal price: £29. Dinner £14.90 and à la carte.
Short breaks: £37.50-£38.50, min 2 nights. Single prices
£47.50-£48.50.
✱ Credit cards [1] [2] [3] [5]

This hotel, built in 1872, is the former village school, and still retains some original features. Recently refurbished, the hotel features comfortable, well-equipped bedrooms and compact, intimate public areas.

YELVERTON   Devon   Map 2 SX56

★★★70% **Moorland Links** (Forestdale) PL20 6DA ☎ (0822) 852245

Normal price: £77-£84.70 room and breakfast. Dinner £15-
£23 & à la carte.
Short breaks: £47.50, min 2 nights.
Credit cards [1] [2] [3] [5]

Set in nine acres of grounds with breathtaking views across the Tamar Valley, this hotel provides attractive public areas.

▪ DORSET ▪

ABBOTSBURY   Dorset   Map 3 SY58

★★66% **Ilchester Arms** 9 Market Street ☎ (0305) 871243

Normal price: £55-£65. Dinner £3.50-£8.50 à la carte
Short breaks: £120 for 2 nights, Nov-Feb (except Xmas)
Credit cards [1] [3]

The character bars and conservatory restaurant of this village inn serve bar snacks and imaginative daily 'specials'. All the attractive bedrooms have ensuite facilities and colour television.

BLANDFORD FORUM   Dorset   Map 3 ST80

★★★64% **Crown** (Consort) 1 West Street DT11 7AJ ☎ (0258) 456626

Normal price: £32. Dinner £6-£10.
Short breaks: £37.50. Min 2 nights, Tues-Thurs.
Activity breaks: Special Interest Tours on Thomas Hardy,
£105 including 2 nights stay, transport, guide and lecture.
Other tours also available – details on request. Coarse
Fishing Breaks, short breaks price plus day ticket.
Credit cards [1] [2] [3] [5]

A hotel with majestic panelled public rooms and spacious bedrooms, close to the town centre yet overlooking open countryside. Skilfully cooked food.

BOURNEMOUTH   Dorset   Map 4 SZ09

During the currency of this guide some Bournemouth telephone numbers are liable to change.

GH QQ Alum Bay 19 Burnaby Road BH4 8JF ☎ (0202) 761034

Normal price: £17 bed and breakfast, £24 with dinner
Short breaks: 2 days £41. Min 2 nights, Jan-Jun & Sep-Dec
Credit cards [1] [3]

Within a few minutes' walk of Alum Chine and the beach, this Victorian house offers accommodation in comfortable bedrooms with colour television; some rooms have ensuite facilities.

★★65% **Arlington** Exeter Park Road BH2 5BD ☎ (0202) 552879 & 553012
Restricted service Jan-Mar
Normal price: £28.50. Dinner £9.50
Short breaks: £27. Min 2 nights, Jan-Mar & Nov-Dec
🕇 Credit cards ①③

This friendly family-run hotel overlooks the Central Gardens and is within walking distance of the sea, shops and BIC. Bedrooms, though small, are neat and well-equipped and have ensuite facilities, most have colour television. There is a special Christmas programme. Children under two are not accommodated.

GH QQQ Braemar 30 Glen Road BH5 1HS ☎ (0202) 36054
Normal price: £14
Short breaks: £18. Min 3 nights, Mar-May & Oct
🕇

Some of the bedrooms at this hotel, situated near Boscombe Pier, have ensuite facilities; all have colour television. There are four family rooms.

GH QQ Carisbrooke BH2 5NT ☎ (0202) 290432
Feb-Dec
Normal price: £25 including dinner
Short breaks: £23
🕇 (ex guide dogs) Credit cards ①②③

A modern, family-run hotel near the Winter Gardens, providing comfortable bedrooms all with colour television and most equipped with ensuite facilities.

★★★63% **Chesterwood** (Inter-Hotels) East Overcliff Drive BH1 3AR ☎ (0202) 558057
Normal price: £37 including dinner.
Short breaks: £32.50, min 2 nights, Nov-May. Single supplement.
Activity breaks: Christmas Break, £360 for 4 nights. New Year Break, £195 for 3 nights.
🕇 Credit cards ①②③⑤

Seafront hotel with a ballroom where guests can dance to live music, and a sheltered terrrace and swimming pool which are popular in the summer months.

★★★67% **Chine** Boscombe Spa Road BH5 1AX ☎ (0202) 396234
Normal price: £35-£45. Dinner £15-£18
Short breaks: from £45. Min 2 nights, Oct-Dec
🕇 (ex guide dogs)

This large well-maintained hotel has both indoor and outdoor swimming pools, offers special facilities for children and has a special Christmas programme. All the bedrooms have ensuite bath or shower roms and colour television, and there are some family rooms.

★★66% **Chinehurst** 18-20 Studland Road, Westbourne BH1 8JA ☎ (0202) 764583

Normal price: £31. Dinner £9.50
Short breaks: £25. Min 2 nights
Credit cards [1] [2] [3] [5]

This well-managed family-run hotel has thirty-one bedrooms all with private bath or shower rooms and colour television. There are four family rooms and one with a four-poster bed. The hotel has a games room and there is a special Christmas programme.

★★★63% **Connaught** West Hill Road, West Cliff BH2 5PH ☎ (0202) 298020

Normal price: £78 room and breakfast. Dinner from £16.50 and à la carte
Short breaks: £84 for two
Credit cards [1] [2] [3] [5]

Service is friendly and helpful at this hotel set amidst sheltered lawns and gardens. All the bedrooms have colour television and private facilities, with rooms set aside for families and non-smokers. The hotel also provides extensive leisure amenities, special facilities for children and there is a Christmas programme.

★★★50% **County** Westover Road BH1 2BT ☎ (0202) 552385

Normal price: £60 room with breakfast
Short breaks: £50 for two. Min 2 nights, Oct-Mar
Credit cards [1] [2] [3]

Close to the pier, gardens and shops this hotel has a lively disco and has a special Christmas programme. The modern bedrooms have colour television, and most have ensuite facilities. There are family rooms. No parking.

★★★66% **Courtlands** (Best Western) 16 Boscombe Spa Road, East Cliff BH5 1BB ☎ (0202) 302442

Normal price: £84 room and breakfast. Dinner £13.50-£15
Short breaks: £73 for two. Min 2 nights
Credit cards [1] [2] [3] [5]

A popular hotel with newly decorated and furnished bedrooms which are well equipped and comfortable. All have ensuite facilities and colour television and there are family rooms. The hotel has a range of leisure amenities. There is a special Christmas programme.

GH QQ Cransley 11 Knyveton Road BH1 3QG ☎ (0202) 290067

Normal price: £108-£120 for 3 nights including dinner
Short breaks: £100-£112 for 3 nights. Min 3 nights, Apr, May & Oct
Credit cards [1] [3]

Most of the bedrooms at this hotel have private bath or shower rooms, all have colour television, and two rooms are set aside for families.

★★★62% **Cumberland** East Overcliff Drive BH1 3AF ☎ (0202) 290722

Normal price: £35.50-£38.50. Dinner £13.95-£14.95
Short breaks: £38-£41. Min 2 nights, Nov-Apr
🛪 (ex guide dogs) Credit cards [1] [3]

This is a spacious seafront hotel with a sheltered pool and terrace, offering helpful service in an informal atmosphere. All the bedrooms have ensuite facilities and colour television, and there are family rooms and rooms furnished with four-poster beds. The hotel has a special Christmas programme.

★★★56% **Durley Hall** (Consort) Durley Chine Road, West Cliff BH2 5JS ☎ (0202) 766886

Normal price: £54. Dinner £14.50 & à la carte
Short breaks: from £44.50 for 2 nights, Fri-Sat (except Christmas, New Year, Easter)
Credit cards [1] [2] [3] [5]

This recently extended hotel has a coffee shop, new indoor sports facilities and a sun lounge. The bedrooms have colour television and ensuite facilities, one room is furnished with a four-poster bed and there is a good choice of family rooms. A Christmas programme is provided.

★★★68% **Durlston Court** Gervis Road, East Cliff BH1 3DD ☎ (0202) 291488

Normal price: £48. Dinner £9.50
Short breaks: £46. Min 2 nights, Sun-Thu (except Bank Holidays, Christmas and New Year)
Credit cards ① ② ③ ⑤

Now completely refurbished, this small hotel has a series of small lounges and bars and some leisure amenities. All the bedrooms have ensuite facilities and colour television and there are some family rooms. There is a special Christmas programme.

★★63% **Durly Chine** Chine Crescent, West Cliff BH2 5LB ☎ (0202) 551926

Normal price: £28.50 including dinner
Short breaks: 2 nights from £49.50; 3 nights from £68.50; 4 nights from £87.50. Oct-May
Credit cards ① ③

A family-owned and run hotel in its own grounds offering friendly service and a relaxing atmosphere. Most of the modern bedrooms have ensuite facilities, all have colour television and there are family rooms. The hotel has an outdoor heated swimming pool. A special Christmas programme is provided. Children under five years are not accommodated.

★★★67% **East Anglia** 6 Poole Road BH2 5OX ☎ (0202) 765163

Normal price: £40-£45
Short breaks: £70 for 2 nights, Apr-24 May. Single rooms only available Fri-Sun
Credit cards ① ② ③ ⑤

A homely atmosphere prevails throughout this friendly and well-run hotel. Leisure amenities include a heated outdoor swimming pool and there is a special programme at Christmas. All the bedrooms, including those in the annexe, have ensuite facilities and colour television and there are family rooms.

★★55% **Fircroft** 4 Owls Road, Boscombe BH5 1AE ☎ (0202) 309771

Normal price: £30. Dinner from £11.
Short breaks: £29. Min 2 nights, Oct-May
Credit cards ① ③

Bedrooms at this hotel have ensuite facilities and colour television, with a good choice of family rooms. There are facilities for squash and there is a special Christmas programme.

GH QQQ Golden Sands BH4 8HR ☎ (0202) 763832
Feb-Nov

Normal price: £20.50-£24
Short breaks: £24.50-£28.50. Single room 20% extra. Min 2 nights
✸

Attractive guest house close to Alum Chine with comfortable bedrooms, all with ensuite facilities and colour television. There are two family rooms. Children under four are not accommodated.

★★65% **Hartford Court** 48 Christchurch Road BH1 3PE ☎ (0202) 551712 & 293682

Normal price: £23. Dinner £7.50
Short breaks: £24. Min 2 nights, Oct-Apr
Credit cards ① ③

Most of the bedrooms at this hotel have ensuite facilities, all are equipped with colour television and there are six family rooms. There is a special Christmas programme. Children under ten are not accommodated.

★★★58% **Hermitage** Exeter Road BH2 5AH ☎ (0202) 557363

Normal price: £72-£84 room and breakfast
Short breaks: £45
Credit cards ① ② ③ ⑤

This hotel is in an excellent position with easy access to the sea, shops and BIC. Public rooms are comfortable, and bedrooms vary from spacious and well furnished to smaller, modest rooms.

GH QQ Highclere 15 Burnaby Road BH4 8JF ☎ (0202) 761350
Apr-Sep

Normal price: £24-£26
Short breaks: £23. Min 2 nights

A neat, well-maintained hotel with sea views and within easy walking distance of Alum Chine and the beach. All eight rooms have ensuite facilities and colour television and there are five family rooms. Children under three are not accommodated.

★★★★61% **Highcliff** (Best Western) West Cliff BH2 5DU ☎ (0202) 55702

Normal price: £120 room and breakfast
Short breaks: £100 for two. Single occupancy £55
🕭 (ex guide dogs) Credit cards ① ② ③ ⑤

This hotel, with its fine sea views and commanding position, has recently been refurbished and extended to include fifty new bedrooms and a conference room. Easter, Christmas and New Year programmes.

★★71% **Hinton Firs** (Exec Hotel) Manor Road, East Cliff BH1 3HB ☎ (0202) 555409

Normal price: £40.25. Dinner £8.25 and à la carte
Short breaks: £34.50. Min 2 nights, Nov-Apr (except Christmas, New Year & Easter)
🕭 (ex guide dogs) Credit cards ① ② ③

An appealing hotel set in neat gardens, with both indoor and outdoor pools. All the bedrooms are very well equipped, all have ensuite facilities and most have colour television. There are nineteen family rooms. There is a special Christmas programme.

GH Q Mae-Mar 91/95 West Hill Road BH2 5PQ ☎ (0202) 23167

Normal price: £30-£44
Short breaks: £27.50-£40 including £6.50 dinner allowance. Min 3 nights, Sun-Thu, Jul-Aug

In the heart of the West Cliff hotel area, Mae-Mar provides comfortable accommodation with colour television in all the bedrooms. Some rooms have private showers and there are family rooms. No parking facilities.

★★61% **Mansfield** West Cliff Gardens BH2 5HL ☎ (0202) 552659
Closed 28 Dec-17 Jan

Normal price: £28-£30. Dinner £7.25
Short breaks: £26-£28 for the first two nights, £19-£23 each extra night. Min 2 nights, Oct-Apr
🕭 Credit cards ① ③

Friendly and attentive resident owners provide personal service at this hotel. There are thirty comfortable bedrooms all with ensuite facilities and colour television, some of the rooms are for families and one is furnished with a four-poster bed. The hotel has a special Christmas programme. See advertisement on p128.

★★★62% **Marsham Court** Russell Cotes Road BH1 3AB ☎ (0202) 552111

Normal price: £42. Dinner £13.50 & à la carte
Short breaks: £45. Min 2 nights. £5 single supplement
🦮 (ex guide dogs)

A large hotel with good sea views providing accommodation in comfortable, mostly spacious bedrooms. All have ensuite facilities and colour television, including the family rooms. The hotel has a heated outdoor swimming pool and a snooker table. There is a special Christmas programme.

GH QQ Mayfield 46 Frances Road BH1 3SA ☎ (0202) 21839
Closed Dec
Normal price: £12-£14
Short breaks: £15.50. Min 2 nights Apr, Oct-Nov, Jan-Mar.

This hotel, situated in a quiet area within easy walking distance of the beach, has some rooms with private showers. Children under seven are not accommodated.

★★★57% **Melford Hall** St Peters Road BH1 2LS ☎ (0202) 551516

Normal price: £25-£27.50 Double room.
Short breaks: £24.75 Double room and Dinner.
Credit cards ①②③⑤

This large holiday hotel offers excellent value for money. Colour television is provided in all the bedrooms, including the family rooms, and most have ensuite facilities. The hotel has a range of leisure amenities and there is a special Christmas programme.

★★★50% **Miramar** East Overcliff Drive, East Cliff BH1 3AL ☎ (0202) 556581

Normal price: £50, including 4-course dinner
Short breaks: £41, single £46. Min 2 nights, Nov-Mar
🦮 (ex guide dogs) Credit cards ①②③

A warm comfortable hotel enjoying fine sea views. All the bedrooms have ensuite facilities and colour television and there are some family rooms. Guests may use the leisure facilities at the Carlton Hotel (5 minutes' walk). There is a special Christmas programme.

★★★64% **Moat House** (Queens Moat) Knyveton Road BH1 3QQ ☎ (0202) 293311

Normal price: £80 room with breakfast. Dinner £13.50
Short breaks: £48. Min 2 nights, Fri-Sun
Credit cards ①②③⑤

Standing in a quiet area of the town this hotel has a range of leisure facilities including a new indoor pool, snooker and gymnasium. Bedrooms have ensuite baths or showers and colour television and there are family rooms. A special Christmas programme is provided.

★★★64% **New Durley Dean** Westcliff Road BH2 5HE ☎ (0202) 557711

Normal price: £42.50-£49.50. Dinner £14.50.
Short breaks: £36.25-£39.25. Min 2 nights, Oct-Jun.
Activity breaks: Christmas Party Break, £36.45 per night
including dancing. 30 Nov-6 Jan.
✱ Credit cards [1] [2] [3]

An elegant Victorian red-brick hotel, recently
refurbished and re-opened. Leisure facilities
include an indoor pool with whirlpool spa,
Turkish steam room and 'trymnasium'.

★★★★70% **Norfolk Royale** Richmond Hill BH2 6EN ☎ (0202) 551521

Normal price: £55.
Short breaks: £55, min 2 nights, Fri-Sun.
Activity breaks: Wine Appreciation, from £65 per night.
Antique Collectors Break, from £130 per weekend, details
on request. Dry Skiing, from £55 per night. Motor
Cruising Instruction, from £250. Other breaks on request.
✱

Splendid 1920's building, recently refurbished
to a very high standard. Staff throughout are
smart and amiable. Bedrooms provide luxuries
like bathrobes and toiletries.

GH QQ Oak Hall Private 9 Wilfred Road BH5 1ND ☎ (0202) 395062

Normal price: £24.75 including dinner.
Short breaks: £63 for 3 nights, Jan-1 Jun.
Activity breaks: Details from hotel.
Credit cards [1] [3]

This detached house in a pleasant area of the
resort offers modern facilities and comfortable
hospitality.

★★★62% **Pavilion** 22 Bath Road BH1 2NS ☎ (0202) 291266

Normal price: £27. Dinner £12-£14
Short breaks: £30. Min 2 nights
Credit cards [1] [2] [3] [5]

This small, smartly decorated hotel has an
attractive lounge and dining room. All the
bedrooms have colour television and ensuite
facilities, there are four family rooms and two
rooms with four-poster beds. The hotel has
special facilities for children and there is a
Christmas programme.

★★★67% **Piccadilly** Bath Road BH1 2NN ☎ (0202) 552559

Normal price: £40. Dinner from £10.95 & à la carte
Short breaks: £35. Min 2 nights
✱ (ex guide dogs) Credit cards [1] [2] [3] [5]

Centrally situated and with friendly staff, this
hotel provides bedrooms all equipped with
ensuite facilities and colour television. One
room is furnished with a four-poster bed and
there are two family rooms. There is a special
Christmas programme.

★★★59% **Queens** Meyrick Road, East Cliff BH1 3DL ☎ (0202) 554415

Normal price: £79-£85 room and breakfast. Dinner £15.95
Short breaks: from £73 for two. Min 2 nights, Oct-Apr
Credit cards [1] [3]

A large hotel with some leisure facilities, and
offering a five-course dinner menu of fresh
dishes. Ensuite bath or shower rooms and
colour television are provided in all bedrooms,
there are family rooms and one room has a
four-poster bed. There is a special Christmas
programme.

★★★★★62% **Royal Bath** (De Vere) Bath Road BH1 2EW ☎ (0202) 555555

Normal price: from £130 room with breakfast. Dinner from
£21.10 & à la carte
Short breaks: from £130 for two. Min 2 nights
✱ (ex guide dogs) Credit cards [1] [2] [3] [4] [5]

A spacious and elegant hotel in a commanding
position overlooking the sea. It has a new
leisure complex and lively dinner dances take
place in the main restaurant on Saturday
evenings. All the bedrooms have ensuite
bathrooms and colour television and two are
furnished with four-poster beds. There is a
special Christmas programme.

★★63% Royal Exeter (Berni/Chef & Brewer) Exeter Road BH2 5AG ☎ (0202) 290566 & 290567

Normal price: £30. Dinner £8-£15 à la carte
Short breaks: £27.50 excluding dinner. Min 2 nights, Fri-Sun; min 3 nights, Mon-Thu
✕ (ex guide dogs)

Situated opposite the BIC and near the sea, this hotel offers a choice of popular restaurants during the summer. The attractive bedrooms all have ensuite showers and colour television, and there are ten family rooms.

★★57% Russell Court (Inter-Hotels) Bath Road BH1 2EP ☎ (0202) 295819

Normal price: £37. Dinner from £7.50
Short breaks: £17.50 excluding dinner. Min 2 nights, Nov-Mar

In a central location this hotel provides personal, friendly service. All the bedrooms have colour television and most have ensuite facilities. There is a special Christmas programme.

★★★60% Savoy West Hill Road BH2 5EJ ☎ (0202) 294241

Normal price: £45. Dinner £9.95-£18
Short breaks: £46.25 weekend break per night; following Sun night £29.75. Any 3 nights £44.50 per night. Single from £42, min 3 nights

This large clifftop hotel has a sun lounge and comfortable dining room. All the bedrooms have ensuite facilities and colour television, and there are ten family rooms. Leisure amenities include a swimming pool and games room. There is a special Christmas programme.

GH QQ Sorrento 16 Owls Road BH5 1AG ☎ (0202) 394019
Mar-Nov. Restricted service Xmas

Normal price: £19-£25.50
Short breaks: £16.33-£24.17. Min 3 nights

This attractive hotel midway between Boscombe shopping centre, the beach and pier provides comfortable accommodation; some of the bedrooms have ensuite facilities and there is a colour television in the lounge.

★★61% St George West Cliff Gardens BH2 5HL ☎ (0202) 26075 due to change to 556075
Cl;osed 3 Jan-2nd week Mar

Normal price: £22-£28. Dinner £3.50
Short breaks: 2 nights £49-£51; 3 nights £74-£77; 4 nights £95-£98. Mar-mid May & mid Oct-Christmas

Peacefully situated on the West Cliff overlooking the bay, this hotel is just ten minutes' walk from the town centre and pier. Most of the bedrooms have ensuite facilities, all have colour television and there are some family rooms. There is a pool table for guests' use.

GH QQ St John's Lodge 10 St Swithun's Road South BH1 3RQ ☎ (0202) 290677

Normal price: £22.50-£23.50
Short breaks: £21-£22. Min 4 nights
Credit cards ① ③

Close to the shops and within walking distance of the Chine and pier, this hotel has comfortable bedrooms equipped with colour television; some rooms have ensuite showers. Amenities include a sauna and jacuzzi.

★★59% **Sun Court** West Hill Road BH2 5PH ☎ (0202) 551343

Normal price: £26.50-£30. Dinner £13 & à la carte
Short breaks: £27-£31. Min 2 nights, Apr-May
Credit cards ① ② ③ ⑤

This modern hotel has a smart cocktail bar, a separate lounge and a range of leisure amenities. Bedrooms range from small budget-priced rooms to spacious ones with balconies, and all have ensuite facilities and colour television. There is a special Christmas programme.

★★★63% **Trouville** Priory Road BH2 5DH ☎ (0202) 552262

Normal price: £77 room
Short breaks: £59 for two including dinner allowance of £11.95. Min 2 nights, Oct-Apr £11.95
Credit cards ① ③

A family-owned hotel, convenient for the BIC and the Winter Gardens, and with some leisure facilities. All the bedrooms have ensuite bath or shower rooms and colour television, and there are family rooms.

★★63% **Ullswater** West Cliff Gardens BH2 5HW ☎ (0202) 555181

Normal price: £21-£28
Short breaks: £48-£54. Min 2 nights, Sep-May
🐾 (ex guide dogs) Credit cards ① ③

A friendly hotel providing comfortable bedrooms with ensuite facilities and colour television. Guests can play table tennis, and there is a special Christmas programme.

★★61% **West Cliff Hall** (Best Western) 14 Priory Road BH2 5DN ☎ (0202) 299715

Normal price: £48-£70 room. Dinner £6-£8
Short breaks: £22. Min 2 nights, Nov-25 Mar
Credit cards 1 2 3 5

A busy holiday hotel centrally situated and just a short walk from West Cliff. All bedrooms have ensuite facilities and colour television and there are family rooms. The hotel has a relaxed atmosphere and offers good value for money. There is a special Christmas programme.

★★61% **Whitehall** Exeter Park Road BH2 5AX ☎ (0202) 554682
Closed 6 Nov-Feb

Normal price: £24-£30. Dinner from £8.50
Short breaks: £27. Min 2 nights, Mar-May & Oct.
Credit cards 1 2 3 5

A quiet holiday hotel in an elevated position close to the town centre. Most of the bedrooms have ensuite bath or shower rooms, all have colour television and there are family rooms.

★★62% **Winterbourne** Priory Road BH2 5DJ ☎ (0202) 296366

Normal price: £38. Dinner from £10.
Short breaks: £31. Min 2 nights, Nov-Apr.
Activity breaks: Golfing Breaks, details from hotel.
Credit cards 1 3

Friendly hotel with an informal atmosphere and excellent views of the town and the sea, ideal for holidaymakers.

BRIDPORT Dorset *Map 3 SY49*

★56% **Bridport Arms** West Bay DT6 4EN (2m S off B3157 Weymouth Rd) ☎ (0308) 22994

Normal price: £27.50. Dinner £8.50-£12.95 à la carte
Short breaks: £32 including £10 dinner allowance. Min 2 nights, Sun-Thu, Oct-Mar
Credit cards 1 3

A thatched inn situated right on the beach offering modest accommodation and warm, friendly service. There are eight bedrooms; all have colour television, some have ensuite facilities and two are family rooms.

GH QQQ Britmead House 154 West Bay Road, DT6 4EG ☎ (0308) 22941

Normal price: £14-£20
Short breaks: £13.50-£19. Single room £17-£25. Min 3 nights
Credit cards 1 2 3 5

This comfortable, family-run establishment offers good home cooking and friendly service. There are seven spacious bedrooms (five have ensuite facilities), all with colour television, tea-making facilities, hair dryers and mini bar. Children under five are not accommodated.

★★67% Eype's Mouth Country Eype DT6 6AL (2m SW) ☎ (0308) 23300

Normal price: £26. Dinner from £10.50 & à la carte
Short breaks: £28.75. Min 2 nights
Credit cards [1] [3]

A friendly hotel in rural surroundings just five minutes from the sea and coastal footpath. Dinner dances are held in the dining room and there is a special Christmas programme. All the bedrooms have ensuite facilities and colour television, and one room is furnished with a four-poster bed.

★★★62% Haddon House West Bay DT6 4EL (2m S off B3157 Weymouth Rd) ☎ (0308) 23626 & 25323

Normal price: £22.50 (winter), £27.50 (summer). Dinner £14.50
Short breaks: £32.50-£37.50, 2 and 5 night breaks
Credit cards [1] [2] [3] [5]

A Regency-style hotel providing spacious bedrooms with many personal extras and colour television. The attractive dining room offers a varied menu, local fish being a speciality. There is a special Christmas programme. The hotel is close to the picturesque harbour, and opposite is an 18 hole golf course which offers reduced rates to guests.

★★68% Roundham House (Exec Hotel) Roundham Gardens, West Bay Road DT6 4BD ☎ (0308) 22753 & 25779 Closed mid Nov-Jan

Normal price: £24.15. Dinner £12-£13.50
Short breaks: £33.75, single £42, includes newspaper or glass of wine
🗶 Credit cards [1] [2] [3] [5]

Personally-run by resident proprietors who provide friendly service and a well-priced dinner menu. There are eight comfortable bedrooms with colour television, and most have ensuite facilities.

CHARMOUTH Dorset *Map 3 SY39*

GH QQ Newlands House Stonebarrow Lane DT6 6RA ☎ (0297) 60212 Mar-Oct

Normal price: from £35 room. Dinner £8.50
Short breaks: 3-day break from £73; 5-day break from £122

A 16th-century farmhouse, standing on the edge of National Trust land, only minutes' walk from the beach. All the bedrooms have colour television and most have ensuite facilities. Smoking is not permitted in the bedrooms. Children under six are not accommodated.

★★57% Queen's Arms The Street DT6 6QF ☎ (0297) 60339 Closed 2nd week Nov-2nd week Feb

Normal price: £32
Short breaks: £29, Min 2 nights. Feb-Jun & Oct
Credit cards [1] [3]

This hotel has low, beamed ceilings and comfortable rooms. All bedrooms are 'non-smoking', most have private facilities, and all have colour television. Children under five are not accommodated.

★★69% White House 2 Hillside, The Street DT6 6PJ ☎ (0297) 60411 Closed Dec-Feb, restricted service Mar

Normal price: £55 including dinner
Short breaks: £45. Min 3 nights
Credit cards [1] [3]

A charming little Regency house providing comfortable bedrooms with colour television. Most also have ensuite facilities. Children under fourteen years are not accommodated.

CHRISTCHURCH   Dorset   Map 4 SZ19

★★65% Fisherman's Haunt Salisbury Road, Winkton BH23 7AS (2.5m N on B3347)
☎ (202) 477283 & 484071 Closed 25 Dec

Normal price: £26. Dinner £15-£20 à la carte
Short breaks: £28.50 with £6 dinner allowance. Min 2 nights, Oct-Mar

This attractive, busy hotel is set in its own grounds near the River Avon, and provides an ideal base for fishermen. Most of the bedrooms are ensuite, all have colour television and two are furnished with four-poster beds.

★★★72% Waterford Lodge (Best Western) 87 Bure Lane, Friars Cliff, Mudeford BH23 4DN (2m E off B3059) ☎ (0425) 272948 & 278801

Normal price: £35-£38. Dinner £14.50 & à la carte
Short breaks: £46-£49. Min 2 nights
Credit cards ① ② ③ ⑤

Family-run and providing a warm and friendly atmosphere, this hotel offers comfortable accommodation, with spacious bedrooms all with ensuite facilities and colour television. There is a special Christmas programme.

CORFE CASTLE   Dorset   Map 3 SY98

★★70% Mortons House East Street BH20 5EE ☎ (0929) 480988

Normal price: £40. Dinner from £18 à la carte
Short breaks: £50-£60. £10 single supplement. Min 2 nights (ex Christmas)
Credit cards ① ③

A charming listed Elizabethan manor house in the middle of the picturesque village, with delightful well-equipped bedrooms all with ensuite facilities and colour television. One room is furnished with a four-poster bed.

EVERSHOT   Dorset   Map 3 ST50

★★(Red) Summer Lodge DT2 0JR ☎ (0935) 83424
Closed 2-18 Jan

Normal price: from £50. Dinner from £23
Short breaks: from £53, single £63, includes cream tea. Min 3 nights, Sun-Thu, mid Oct-Easter (except Xmas)
Credit cards ① ② ③

A charming Georgian house standing in delightful grounds and gardens. The public rooms have a pleasant, comfortable atmosphere and the bedrooms vary in size and style. All are tastefully furnished and have ensuite facilities and colour television. There are some leisure amenities and a Christmas programme is available. Children under eight are not accommodated.

GH QQQ Rectory House Fore Street DT2 0JW ☎ (093583) 273
Closed Xmas

Normal price: £23-£25
Short breaks: £6 per couple reduction for 2 nights; or 3 nights for the price of 2. Min 2 nights, Jan-Apr & Nov-Dec

Standing in the centre of the peaceful village, this charming stone house offers English-style cooking and a friendly atmosphere. Each bedroom has colour television and ensuite bathroom. Children under twelve are not accommodated.

FERNDOWN   Dorset   Map 4 SU00

★★60% Coach House Inn (Consort) Tricketts Cross BH22 9NW (junc A31/A348) ☎ (0202) 861222

Normal price: £53 room. Dinner £8.25 and à la carte
Short breaks: £31, single supplement £8. Min 2 nights, Fri-Sun
Credit cards ① ② ③ ⑤

A modern hotel with a friendly informal atmosphere and attentive staff. All the bedrooms are ensuite with colour television, and are contained in four blocks outside the main building.

★★★★61% **Dormy** (De Vere) New Road BH22 8ES ☎ (0202) 872121

Normal price: £60. Dinner £15-£16.
Short breaks: £70, min 2 nights. Every weekend except
Bank Hols, and any night in Aug.
Activity breaks: Golf Week, £425 for 6 days including golf.
1 Apr.
Credit cards ①②③④⑤

Attractive hotel offering some accommodation
in individual bungalows in the hotel's extensive
grounds.

HORTON   Dorset   *Map 4 SU00*

INN QQQ Horton Cranborne Road BH21 5AD ☎ (0258) 840252

Normal price: £55
Short breaks: £40 excluding dinner. Min 2 nights, Mon-Fri
✱ Credit cards ①③

A large detached inn on the crossroads offers
good food and very well-equipped bedrooms,
some with ensuite facilities.

LYME REGIS   Dorset   *Map 3 SY39*

★★★65% **Alexandra** Pound Street DT7 3HZ ☎ (02974) 2010 & 3229

Normal price: £90 room and dinner.
Short breaks: £80 for two, min 2 nights. Feb-May, Nov &
Dec.
Credit cards ①③

Built in 1735, this hotel occupies a prime
position with beautiful views over Lyme Bay.
The table d'hôte menu of fresh English dishes
changes daily.

★★65% **Buena Vista** Pound Street DT7 3HZ ☎ (02974) 2494

Normal price: £38 including dinner.
Short breaks: £30, Oct-Apr.
Credit cards ① ② ③ ⑤

This attractive Regency building offers fine views of the bay, and homely accommodation with some modern facilities.

★★65% **Dorset** Silver Street DT7 3HX ☎ (02974) 2482

Normal price: £21. Dinner from £11.
Short breaks: £27.66, min 3 nights, Mar-Oct.
Credit cards ① ③

Georgian in style but with later additions, this hotel is set high above the town with views over Golden Cap. Ideal holiday accommodation.

GH QQQ **Kersbrook** Pound Road DT7 3HX ☎ (02974) 2596 & 2576

Normal price: £40-£45 including dinner.
Short breaks: £35-£37.50, min 2 nights, Feb-May & Oct.
Credit cards ① ③

Set in picturesque gardens with views over the town and sea, this thatched house offers meals with a strong local following.

★★★62% **Mariners** Silver Street DT7 3HS ☎ (02974) 2753

Normal price: £40. Dinner £14 & à la carte.
Short breaks: £38, min 2 nights.
Credit cards ① ② ③ ⑤

A 17th-century coaching inn with a friendly and relaxing atmosphere, personally supervised by the owners. The attractive restaurant specialises in fresh local fish dinners. See advertisement on p135.

★★62% **Royal Lion** Broad Street DT7 3QF ☎ (02974) 5622

Normal price: £30-£33. Dinner £11.50-£12.50.
Short breaks: £35, min 2 nights.
Credit cards ① ② ③ ⑤

A 16th-century coaching inn with 20th-century additions, in the heart of the town yet close to the sea. There is a range of leisure facilities.

PIDDLETRENTHIDE   Dorset   Map 3 SY79

★★ **Old Bakehouse** DT2 7QR ☎ (03004) 305

Normal price: £20.50-£23.50. Dinner £13-£16 à la carte (1990 price).
Short breaks: £34. Min 2 nights, Oct-May. £2 supplement for four-poster and single rooms.
Credit cards ① ③

This friendly owner-run hotel converted from a former bakehouse has a galleried restaurant serving well-prepared food. All bedrooms, most of them located in the annexe and some with four-poster beds, have private facilities and colour television. No children under 12.

POOLE   Dorset   Map 4 SZ09

★★ **Antelope** High Street BH15 1BP ☎ (0202) 672029

Normal price: £37.50.
Short breaks: £42. Min 2 nights, Fri-Sun.
🛠 (ex guide dogs) Credit cards ① ② ③ ④ ⑤

Situated in the High Street not far from the quay, this renovated hotel has a cheerful, rustic-style restaurant and fully equipped bedrooms, all ensuite and with colour television, and including a family room and some non-smoking rooms.

★★★56% **Dolphin** High Street BH15 1DU ☎ (0202) 673612

Normal price: £34
Short breaks: £27 excluding dinner, Fri-Sun. Special rate also available for Sun night. £32.30 for single occupancy.
Credit cards ① ② ③ ⑤

This friendly, informal hotel in the main shopping area has a choice of good eating places and all bedrooms, including one with a four-poster bed, have private bathrooms and colour television.

★★★73% **Harbour Heights** 73 Haven Road, Sandbanks BH13 7LW ☎ (0202) 708594

Normal price: £35. Dinner £12.50-£15 & à la carte (1990 prices)
Short breaks: £40 including £10.50 dinner allowance. Fri-Sun. £10 single supplement.
Credit cards ①②③⑤

Set in attractive gardens high above Poole Harbour, this hotel has very comfortable bedrooms, all ensuite and with colour television, and many with balconies. There is a choice of formal restaurant or carvery, plus a cocktail bar.

★★★★53% **Hospitality Inn** (Mount Charlotte) The Quay BH15 1HD ☎ (0202) 666800

Normal price: £87.50 room
Short breaks: £42.50
Credit cards ①②③④⑤

Overlooking the harbour, this modern well-equipped hotel has a spacious restaurant and comfortable bedrooms, all ensuite and with colour television.

★★★75% **Mansion House** Thames Street BH15 1JN ☎ (0202) 685666

Normal price: £45.50
Short breaks: £53.50 including set-price dinner or £17.50 dinner allowance and early tea. Min 2 nights.
Credit cards ①②③⑤

Close to the quay, this elegant Georgian town-house provides friendly service, good honest food and comfortable ensuite bedrooms with colour television and other amenities.

★★★59% **Sandbanks** Banks Road, Sandbanks BH13 7PS ☎ (0202) 707377

Normal price: £40-£50. Dinner from £14.
Short breaks: from £45. Min 2 nights, Apr, Oct-Dec.
🦮 (ex guide dogs) Credit cards ①②③⑤

This modern family hotel right on the beach has ensuite bedrooms with colour television, many with balconies, and extensive children's and leisure facilities, including a children's restaurant and nursery, an indoor swimming pool, sauna, steam room, solarium and gymnasium. Christmas breaks are available.

QQ **Sheldon Lodge** 22 Forest Road, Branksome Park BH13 6DH ☎ (0202) 761186

Normal price: £27 including dinner Oct-May. £29 Jun-Sept.
Short breaks: 5% off normal rate. Min 2 nights, Oct-May.
Credit cards ①③

This detached guesthouse in a quiet area has roomy public areas, including a bar, sun lounge and snooker room. Compact ensuite bedrooms, some non-smoking and one a family room, offer colour television and modern facilities.

PORTLAND   Dorset   Map 3 SY67

★★★52% **Portland Heights** (Best Western) Yeates Corner DT5 2EN ☎ (0305) 821361

Normal price: £33. Dinner £10.80 & à la carte (1990 price)
Short breaks: £44 including set-price dinner or £13 dinner allowance. Min 3 nights, Jun-Sep. £10 single supplement.
Credit cards ①②③⑤

Overlooking Chesil Beach, this modern hotel has well-equipped bedrooms, a few of them family rooms, with private bathrooms and colour television. The good leisure amenities include an outdoor swimming pool and gymnasium. Christmas breaks are available.

ST LEONARDS   Dorset   Map 4 SZ19

★★★67% **St Leonards** BH24 2NP ☎ (0425) 471220

Normal price: £78 room and breakfast. Dinner from £11 à la carte.
Short breaks: £44, min 2 nights, Fri-Sun.
🦮 Credit cards ①②③⑤

A warm and friendly atmosphere prevails at this hotel. Public areas are limited, but the bright, relaxing restaurant serves well-prepared dishes, and there are some exceptionally good bedrooms, each with colour television.

SHAFTESBURY   Dorset   *Map 3 ST82*

★★★56% **Grosvenor** (Trusthouse Forte) The Commons SP7 8JA ☎ (0747) 52282

Normal price: £50 room. Dinner £11 & à la carte.
Short breaks: £39, min 2 nights, Fri-Sun. Single price £40.
Credit cards ① ② ③ ④ ⑤

A former coaching inn with a friendly, informal atmosphere and bedrooms which have now been upgraded.

★★★64% **Royal Chase** (Best Western) Royal Chase Roundabout SP7 8DB ☎ (0747) 53355

Normal price: from £64.
Short breaks: £44-£50, min 2 nights including morning tea, and newspaper. Single supplements midweek.
Activity breaks: Romance/Celebration Breaks, £55-£63 per night including champagne and flowers on arrival. Horse Riding Breaks, lessons and hacking at nearby BHS approved centre. Clay Pigeon Shooting. Christmas Breaks, 3 nights for £250. Thomas Hardy Motortrail, including sketch map and tour leaflet for Hardy places. All prices 1990.

Formerly a monastery, this privately-owned hotel has been furnished to maintain some of its original character. The attractive restaurant offers an interesting menu.

STUDLAND   Dorset   *Map 4 SZ08*

★★ 🏨 66% **Manor House** BH19 3AU ☎ (092944) 288

Normal price: £84.75-£105.50 room, breakfast and dinner.
Short breaks: Prices on application.
Credit cards ① ③

Gothic-style manor house with secluded gardens and grounds overlooking the sea and cliffs.

GH QQ Studholme Ferry Road BH19 3AQ ☎ (092944) 271

Normal price: £28.
Short breaks: from £81 for 3 days, Sun-Thu, mid Mar-Oct.
✕

A pleasant detached hotel situated in its own gardens close to Studland Beach, and offering good home cooking and an informal atmosphere.

SWANAGE   Dorset   *Map 4 SZ07*

QQQ Chines 9 Brolington Road BH19 1LR ☎ (0929) 422457

Normal price: £18.40-£21.85, according to season.
Short breaks: £16-£19, min 3 nights, Mon-Fri, Apr-Oct.
✕

A compact 2-storeyed house in a quiet road near the beach and the town. There is colour television in each bedroom.

★★★62% **Grand** (Best Western) Burlington Road BH19 1LU ☎ (0929) 423353

Normal price: fr £40. Dinner £12.95-£13.95 & à la carte.
Short breaks: £36-£49 (1990), min 2 nights.
Credit cards ① ② ③ ⑤

Occupying an excellent cliff-top position, this family resort hotel has been upgraded, and offers good leisure amenities.

GH QQQ Havenhurst 3 Cranbourne Road BH19 1EA ☎ (0929) 424224

Normal price: £21.
Short breaks: £26, min 2 nights, Oct-Mar except Xmas & New Year.
✼

Pleasant guesthouse in a quiet area, with neat bedrooms.

★★★55% **Pines** Burlington Road BH19 1LT ☎ (0929) 425211

Normal price: £46 including dinner (1990).
Short breaks: £35, min 2 nights, Oct-May except Xmas & Easter
Credit cards ① ③

A family-run resort hotel with an excellent cliff-top location offering spacious, comfortable lounges and a friendly attentive staff.

WAREHAM Dorset Map 3 SY98

★★68% **Kemps Country House** East Stoke BH20 6AL ☎ (0929) 462563

Normal price: £37.50. Dinner from £14.95 & à la carte.
Short breaks: £99 for 2 nights.
✼ Credit cards ① ② ③ ④ ⑤

A Victorian country house with a pleasantly informal atmosphere and good views across open countryside. Interesting dishes are served in the restaurant. See advertisement on p140.

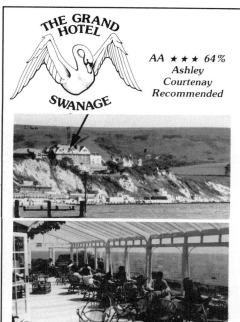

THE GRAND HOTEL SWANAGE

AA ★ ★ ★ 64%
Ashley Courtenay Recommended

Set in a superb clifftop position on Dorset's Heritage Coast, steps from the lawn lead down to the secluded clean sandy beach.

The spacious lounge, sun lounge, bars and restaurant combine the best traditions of hospitality, comfort, excellent cuisine and entertainment; all have breathtaking views.

A lift serves all floors.

The Burlington Club, within the Hotel, offers its full facilities to residents — exercise plunge pool, spa bath, steam room, sauna, solarium, and gymnasium/fitness centre.

The Hotel, 7 miles from Bournemouth via the ferry, is an ideal centre for water sports, golf, walking and bird watching, or simply relaxing!

Special Breaks from £33.00 dinner, bed & breakfast (minimum 2 night stay).

The Grand Hotel, Burlington Road, Swanage, Dorset BH19 1LU
Telephone: Swanage (0929) 423353

★★★67% **Springfield Country** Grange Road, Stoborough BH20 5AL (1.5m S off A351)
☎ (0929) 552177 & 551785

Normal price: £46. Dinner £12 & à la carte.
Short breaks: £50, min 2 nights. Single price £60.
Credit cards ① ② ③

A family-run hotel set in attractive gardens, now upgraded to provide comfortable accommodation and two restaurants serving skilfully prepared dishes.

WEST BEXINGTON   Dorset   Map 3 SY58

★★67% **Manor** Beach Road DT6 9DF ☎ (0308) 897616

Normal price: £29.95-£33.50. Dinner £17.45
Short breaks: £89.50 for 2 nights.
🛏 Credit cards ① ② ③ ⑤

An attractive stone-built hotel which stands close to the sea and Chesil beach offers a pleasant informal atmosphere and attractive bedrooms with ensuite facilities and colour television. Meals are available in the formal dining room and the cellar bar.

WEST LULWORTH   Dorset   Map 3 SY88

★★62% **Cromwell House** BH20 5RJ ☎ (092941) 253

Normal price: £30-£31. Dinner £8.50-£9.50 & à la carte.
Short breaks: £28.50-£29.50, min 2 nights. Single price £30-£33.
Credit cards ① ③

This comfortably furnished hotel is situated in an elevated position with splendid coastal and country views. There is a cosy bar, the bedrooms are well-furnished, and it is happy and relaxed.

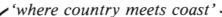

★★61% Gatton House BH20 5RU ☎ (092941) 252
Normal price: £25.
Short breaks: £34.50, min 2 nights, Nov-Mar.
Credit cards ⬚1⬚ ⬚3⬚

A small hotel which commands splendid views over surrounding countryside from its position high on a hill.

★65% Shirley BH20 5RL ☎ (092941) 358
Normal price: £19.25-£22.25
Short breaks: 2-4 nights: £24-£28.30. 5+ nights: £22.55-£27.45.
Activity breaks: Guided walks. Apply for details.
Credit cards ⬚1⬚ ⬚3⬚

The hotel has been in the hands of the same proprietors for twenty years, and their good-natured, natural hospitality creates an informal atmosphere which make it ideal for the holiday-maker. Bedrooms, though small in many cases, are fully equipped with modern facilities, books and games are available in the modern lounge, and the garden contains a sheltered pool and giant chess set.

WEYMOUTH   Dorset   Map 3 SY69

GH Q Beechcroft 128-129 Esplanade DT4 7EU ☎ (0305) 786608
Normal price: £15.41-£16.10.
Short breaks: £59.16 3 nights (low season); £62.44 4 nights (high season). (1990 prices)
Credit cards ⬚1⬚ ⬚3⬚

Located on the seafront with continental awnings.

★★61% Crown 51-52 St Thomas Street DT4 8EQ ☎ (0305) 760800
Normal price: £42. Dinner £5.95-£8.
Short breaks: £24, min 2 nights, Fri-Sun.
Activity breaks: Painting Weekends, £75 for 2 nights full board. Bridge Weekends, £70 for 2 nights full board. Details from hotel.
🍗 Credit cards ⬚1⬚ ⬚2⬚ ⬚3⬚ ⬚5⬚

A busy coaching hotel of imposing appearance offering good value accommodation, comfortable bedrooms and simple fare.

★★62% Glenburn 42 Preston Road DT3 6PZ (3m NE A353) ☎ (0305) 832353
Normal price: £41. Dinner fr £12.
Short breaks: £37.50, min 2 nights, Oct-Apr except Bank Hols.
🍗 Credit cards ⬚1⬚ ⬚3⬚

Situated away from the noise and bustle of the town centre, this family-run hotel has a friendly atmosphere and very clean bedrooms.

★★63% Rex 29 The Esplanade DT4 8DN ☎ (0305) 760400
Normal price: £40 including dinner.
Short breaks: £76 for 2 nights.
Activity breaks: Bridge Breaks, £85 for 2 days. Details from hotel.
Credit cards ⬚1⬚ ⬚2⬚ ⬚3⬚

A family holiday hotel overlooking the seafront. Guests are assured of efficient service from friendly, helpful staff.

★★66% Streamside 29 Preston Road DT3 6PX ☎ (0305) 833121
Normal price: £29. Dinner £10.50 & à la carte.
Short breaks: £35, min 2 nights, Oct-Apr. Single price £40-£45.
Credit cards ⬚1⬚ ⬚2⬚ ⬚3⬚ ⬚5⬚

This privately-owned mock Tudor hotel has a friendly, informal atmosphere, and offers small bedrooms and comfortable public rooms.

GH QQQ Sunningdale 52 Preston Road, Overcombe DT3 6QD ☎ (0305) 832179
Normal price: £40-£49.60 room and breakfast.
Short breaks: £65 for 3 nights, Sept-Jun.

Hotel set back off main Preston road enjoying elevated position.

WIMBORNE MINSTER   Dorset   Map 4 SZ09

★★★57% **King's Head** (Trusthouse Forte) The Square BH21 1JA ☎ (0202) 880101

Normal price: £75 room. Breakfast £7. Dinner £13.50-£18.35.
Short breaks: £52. 2-6 nights.
Credit cards ①②③④⑤

A busy country town hotel offering comfortable public areas, an attractive restaurant and good sized bedrooms. Friendly, willing service.

GH Q Riversdale 33 Poole Road BH21 1QB ☎ (0202) 884528

Normal price: £30-£50 room and breakfast
Short breaks: £90, 3 night break.
Credit cards ①

Detached guesthouse with neat accommodation on the edge of the town centre.

WINTERBOURNE ABBAS   Dorset   Map 3 SY69

★★61% **Whitefriars** Copyhold Lane DT2 9LT ☎ (0305) 889206

Normal price: £30-£35. Dinner £13-£16 à la carte.
Short breaks: £45, min 3 nights.
Credit cards ①②③⑤

Skilfully prepared meals based on good, fresh produce add to the attractions of this charming hotel. The atmosphere is warm and relaxing.

▓ CO DURHAM ▓

DARLINGTON   Co Durham   Map 8 NZ21

★★★61% **King's Head** (Swallow) Priestgate DL1 1NW ☎ (0325) 380222

Normal price: £40. Dinner from £11.50
Short breaks: £40 including lunch one day. Min 2 nights, Fri-Sun, Jul & Aug.
Credit cards ①②③⑤

Situated in the town centre, this Victorian hotel has sixty bedrooms all with ensuite facilities and colour television; some rooms are set aside for non-smokers. There is a special Christmas programme.

DURHAM   Co Durham   Map 12 NZ24

★★★69% **Ramside Hall** (Consort) Belmont, DH1 1TD (3m NE A690) ☎ 091-386 5282

Normal price: from £44. Dinner £9.50-£12.50 & à la carte
Short breaks: from £45, single £62. Min 3 nights
🐾 (ex guide dogs)

Lying in extensive grounds off the A690, this hotel offers a choice of restaurants and some luxury bedrooms. All rooms have ensuite facilities and colour television, with some rooms set aside for non-smokers and families (there are special facilities for children).

★★★★68% **Royal County** (Swallow) Old Elvet DH1 3JN ☎ 091-386 6821

Normal price: £89-£95 room. Dinner from £16.50
Short breaks: £95-£125 for two includes 1 lunch. Min 2 nights, Fri-Sun

Recently extended and refurbished to a very high standard, this hotel has a variety of restaurants and excellent leisure facilities. Bedrooms are all ensuite with colour television, and some rooms are for families and non-smokers. There is a special Christmas programme.

★★★67% **Hallgarth Manor** (Best Western) Pittington DH6 1AB (3m E between A690 & B2183) ☎ 091-372 1188

Normal price: £71-£77 room. Dinner from £14 & à la carte
Short breaks: £45-£48
Credit cards ① ② ③ ⑤

A relaxing atmosphere prevails at this attractive hotel in a country location. Bedrooms feature genuine antique furniture, and all have ensuite facilities and colour television.

FIR TREE   Co Durham   Map 12 NZ13

GH QQQ **Greenhead Country House** Greenhead DL15 8BL ☎ (0388) 763143

Normal price: £21
Short breaks: £19 excluding dinner, single £28. Min 2 nights
🐾 (ex guide dogs) Credit cards ① ③

Traditional farmhouses have been tastefully converted into this small, beautifully appointed establishment. The attractive bedrooms are modern with ensuite facilities, and most have colour television. Children under thirteen are not accommodated.

GRETA BRIDGE   Co Durham   Map 12 NZ01

★★63% **Morritt Arms** DL12 9SE ☎ (0833) 27232 & 27392

Normal price: £32.50. Dinner £18
Short breaks: £37.50-£42.50, single £45-£50. Min 2 nights
Credit cards ① ② ③ ⑤

This old coaching inn retains its Dickensian character. All seventeen bedrooms have private bath and colour television and one room has a four-poster bed. Fishing is available and there is a special Christmas programme.

HASWELL PLOUGH   Co Durham   Map 12 NZ34

GH Q **The Gables** Front Street DH6 2EW ☎ 091-526 2982

Normal price: £35 room and breakfast.
Short breaks: £15, min 2 nights, Fri-Sun.
Activity breaks: Heavy Horse Driving with Covered Wagon, short breaks price plus £25.

A licensed property situated on the B1283 6 miles east of Durham. The bar and dining room are particularly attractive.

NEASHAM   Co Durham   Map 8 NZ31

★★★63% **Newbus Arms** (Best Western) Hurworth Road DL2 1PE ☎ (0325) 721071

Normal price: £80 room and breakfast. Dinner £4.50-£25.
Short breaks: from £45, min 2 nights. Single supplement.
Activity breaks: Bank Holiday Special, £69.98. Sheer Bliss,
£130 for 2 nights. Golf Breaks, £140.
Credit cards 1 2 3 5

An elegant period house in its own gardens with impressive public and conference areas.

ROMALDKIRK   Co Durham   Map 12 NY92

★★70% **Rose & Crown** DL12 9EB ☎ (0833) 50213

Normal price: £27.50. Dinner £15-£18 (1990 price)
Short breaks: £37.50. Min 2 nights, Fri-Sat, Oct-Apr.
Credit cards 1 3

This charming old village inn serves a choice of meals and all the bedrooms, half of them in an annexe, have en suite facilities and colour television, with four-poster beds in nearly all of them. Christmas breaks are available.

RUSHYFORD   Co Durham   Map 8 NZ22

★★★59% **Eden Arms** (Swallow) DL17 0LL ☎ (0388) 720541

Normal price: £40
Short breaks: £90 for 2 nights including set-menu dinner or
£11.50 dinner allowance and £8.25 Sunday lunch. Min 2
nights, Fri-Sun.
Credit cards 1 2 3 5

This well-equipped hotel just two miles from the A1(M) has a leisure centre with indoor swimming pool, sauna, solarium and gymnasium. There are ensuite facilities and colour television in all bedrooms, including some family and no-smoking rooms and one with a four-poster bed. Christmas breaks are available.

SEDGEFIELD   Co Durham   Map 8 NZ32

★★66% **Crosshill** 1 The Square, Stockton-on-Tees TS21 2AB ☎ (0740) 20153 & 21206

Normal price: £40. Dinner £15-£17 & à la carte.
Short breaks: £40, Fri-Sun, includes £14 dinner allowance
and Sunday lunch. £10 single supplement.
Credit cards 1 2 3

A friendly family-run hotel in the centre of the village. The attractive restaurant is renowned for its high standard of cuisine, and bar meals are also available in the comfortable lounge bar. Bedrooms are nicely decorated and thoughtfully equipped.

TEES-SIDE AIRPORT   Co Durham   Map 8 NZ31

★★★64% **St George** (Mount Charlotte (TS)) Middleton St George DL2 1RH ☎ (0325) 332631

Normal price: £65 room Fri-Sun, £70 Mon-Thurs. Dinner
from £11.75 & à la carte
Short breaks: £32.50, min 2 nights. Single supplement Mon-
Thurs.
Credit cards 1 2 3 5

Modern hotel within airport complex.

THORNLEY   Co Durham   Map 8 NZ33

★★63% **Crossways** Dunelm Road DH6 3HT (5m SE of Durham City) ☎ (0429) 821248

Normal price: £27.50. Dinner £8.50 & à la carte.
Short breaks: £32.50, min 2 nights except Christmas & New
Year. Single price £47.50.
Credit cards 1 2 3 5

A modern, family-run hotel with a choice of bars and an attractive, small dining room serving good-value meals.

■ ESSEX ■

BRAINTREE   Essex   *Map 5 TL72*

★★66% **White Hart** (Lansbury) Bocking End CM7 6AB ☎ (0376) 21401

Normal price: £72 room. Dinner from £9 à la carte
Short breaks: £24 excluding dinner. Min 2 nights, Fri-Sun
🏋 (ex guide dogs) Credit cards ① ② ③ ⑤

This popular inn has been a focal point of the town since the 15th century. The Beefeater Steakhouse offers a range of popular dishes and guests are assured of a warm welcome. All bedrooms have private facilities and colour television, and rooms have been set aside for non-smokers and families.

BROXTED   Essex   *Map 5 TL52*

★★★ **Whitehall** (Pride of Britain) Church End CM6 2BZ ☎ (0279) 850603

Normal price: £80. Dinner from £29.
Short breaks: £70. Min 2 nights, Oct-1 Apr.
Activity breaks: Gourment Evenings and Clay Pigeon Shooting. Details from hotel.
🏋 Credit cards ① ② ③ ⑤

A delightful country manor house with some unrivalled rural views and an atmosphere of peace and tranquility. The historic restaurant has several exposed beams.

BUCKHURST HILL   Essex   *Map 5 TQ49*

★★57% **Roebuck** (Trusthouse Forte) North End IG9 5QY ☎ 081-505 4636

Normal price: £58
Short breaks: £44. Min 2 nights
Credit cards ① ② ③ ④ ⑤

All bedrooms at this hotel have private bathrooms and colour television, and five rooms are set aside for non-smokers. There is a special Christmas programme.

CHELMSFORD   Essex   *Map 5 TL70*

★★★74% **Pontlands Park** West Hanningfield Road, Great Baddow CM2 8HR ☎ (0245) 76444
Closed 28 Dec-4 Jan

Normal price: £102 plus 10% service charge, room with breakfast. Dinner £24
Short breaks: £84 plus 10% service charge, for two excluding dinner. Fri-Sun
🏋 (ex guide dogs) Credit cards ① ② ③ ⑤

This country house hotel has individually-furnished bedrooms and spacious suites all with private baths and colour television. Some rooms are furnished with four-poster beds. Within the beautiful grounds is 'Trimmers' health and leisure centre.

COLCHESTER   Essex   *Map 5 TL92*

★★65% **Kings Ford Park** Layer Road, Layer De La Haye CO2 0HS (2.5m S B1026) ☎ (0206) 34301
Restricted service Sunday

Normal price: £70 room. Dinner £11.95-£13.45 & à la carte
Short breaks: £82 for 2 nights including £10.90 dinner allowance. Min 2 nights, Fri-Sat
Credit cards ① ② ③ ⑤

A comfortable Regency house in a woodland park. All bedrooms have private bath or shower rooms and colour television, there are family rooms and one room has a four-poster bed. There is a special Christmas programme.

EPPING   Essex   Map 5 TL40

★★★57% **Post House** (Trusthouse Forte) High Street, Bell Common CM16 4DG ☎ (0378) 73137

Normal price: £39.50 (1990). Dinner from £16.
Short breaks: £41, min 2 nights, Fri-Sun.
Activity breaks: Murder/Mystery, £159. Apr 26-28.
Credit cards ① ② ③ ④ ⑤

A carefully modernised old coaching inn with annexe accommodation, and a choice of menus in the 'Turpins' restaurant where the service is attentively friendly.

CHESTERFORD, GREAT   Essex   Map 5 TL54

★★59% **Crown House** CB10 1NY ☎ (0799) 30515

Normal price: £35. Dinner from £17 & à la carte
Short breaks: £24 excluding dinner. Single £26
✗ (ex guide dogs) Credit cards ① ③

A friendly and personally-owned hotel with two dining rooms offering a choice of carefully-prepared dishes. Bedrooms are generally spacious, and all are ensuite with colour television. There is a special Christmas programme.

DUNMOW, GREAT   Essex   Map 5 TL62

★★52% **Saracen's Head** (Trusthouse Forte) High Street CM6 1AG ☎ (0371) 873901

Normal price: £45. Dinner £12.95 & à la carte
Short breaks: £43. Min 2 nights, Fri-Sun.
Credit cards ① ② ③ ④ ⑤

A 17th-century inn, now a well-run hotel with cosy lounges and spacious, comfortable ensuite bedrooms, some set aside for non-smokers. Christmas breaks are available.

HARLOW   Essex   Map 5 TL41

★★★70% **Churchgate Manor** (Best Western) Churchgate Street, Old Harlow ☎ (0279) 420246

Normal price: £32.50-£36. Dinner from £14.95 & à la carte
Short breaks: £42. Min 2 nights, Fri-Sun
Credit cards ① ② ③ ⑤

Set in its own landscaped gardens this charming hotel, built in the 17th century as a chantry house, has an indoor swimming pool and leisure centre. Each bedroom has a private bathroom and colour television, and there are family rooms. Christmas breaks are available.

★★★51% **Green Man** (Trusthouse Forte) Mulberry Green, Old Harlow CM17 0ET ☎ (0279) 442521

Normal price: £47. Dinner from £14.50 & à la carte
Short breaks: £82 for 2 nights (must include Sat) (please enquire for details)
Credit cards ① ② ③ ④ ⑤

This character coaching inn has an interesting beamed restaurant and comfortable ensuite bedrooms which are situated in an annexe. Christmas breaks are available.

★★★65% **Harlow Moat House** (Queens Moat) Southern Way CM18 7BA ☎ (0279) 22441 due to change to 422441 Closed 24 Dec-3 Jan

Normal price: £55-£80 room. Dinner from £13.50 & à la carte
Short breaks: £38. £12 single supplement. Min 2 nights, Fri-Sun
✗ (ex guide dogs)

A large hotel with modern and well-equipped bedrooms; all are ensuite with colour television and some are for non-smokers.

HARWICH   Essex   Map 5 TM23

★★53% **Cliff** Marine Parade, Dovercourt CO12 3RD ☎ (0255) 503345

Normal price: £53 room. Dinner from £9.50
Short breaks: weekend break Fri & Sat night £110 for two,
£85 single. Includes Sat & Sun lunch
Credit cards ①②③④⑤

An informal seafront hotel with friendly staff and a popular bar. Bedrooms all have ensuite facilities and colour television.

SOUTHEND-ON-SEA   Essex   Map 5 TQ88

QQQ **Tower** 146 Alexandra Road SS1 1HE ☎ (0702) 348635

Normal price: £25
Short breaks: £20, min 2 nights, excluding dinner. £10-£12
single supplement.
Credit cards ①②③⑤

First used as a hotel in 1923, this fully modernised house lies in a quiet residential area, close to the cliff. Some rooms are compact but all are well equipped, each with colour television.

THAXTED   Essex   Map 5 TL63

★★56% **Four Seasons** Walden Road CM6 2RE ☎ (0371) 830129

Normal price: £75 room. Dinner £15-£20.
Short breaks: £50, Fri & Sat only.
🏌 Credit cards ①②③

A pleasant, hospitable welcome awaits guests at this hotel where the owners personally supervise the service. A choice of freshly-prepared, popular dishes is offered.

★★65% **Swan** Bullring, Watling Street CM6 2PL ☎ (0371) 830321

Normal price: £75 room. Dinner £19.95 & à la carte.
Short breaks: £42.50, min 2 nights, Fri-Sun. Single
supplement.
Credit cards ①②③

The original timber-framed structure of this building is concealed by an elegant Georgian façade. It stands beside the great parish church, and bedrooms and public areas are comfortable and full of character.

WALTHAM ABBEY   Essex   Map 5 TL30

★★★★60% **Swallow** (Swallow) Old Shire Lane EN9 3LX ☎ (0992) 717170

Normal price: £98 room. Dinner £14.50-£20 & à la carte
Short breaks: £105 including lunch one day, min 2 nights,
Fri-Sun.
Credit cards ①②③⑤

This hotel and leisure club offers a brasserie and formal restaurant, and public areas are all air-conditioned. Close to junction 26 of the M25.

WITHAM   Essex   Map 5 TL81

★★58% **White Hart** (Berni/Chef & Brewer) Newland Street CM8 2AF ☎ (0376) 512245

Normal price: £26.50. Dinner £8-£15
Short breaks: £23.50 excluding dinner. Min 2 nights, Fri-
Sun.
🏌 Credit cards ①②③⑤

This former coaching inn is situated in the busy centre of Witham. Upgrading is planned for the already comfortable, but compact bedrooms. The atmosphere is relaxed and informal, and the popular carvery restaurant features exposed beams.

◼ GLOUCESTERSHIRE ◼

AMBERLEY   Gloucestershire   Map 3 SO80

★★68% **Amberley Inn** (Best Western) GL5 5AF ☎ (0453) 872565

Normal price: £68. Dinner £13.50-£15.
Short breaks: £41. Min 2 nights.
Activity breaks: Hot Air Ballooning, £211. Golf break, from £122. Gliding break, from £116. Horse riding break, from £101. All prices per person for 2 nights.
Credit cards ①②③

A stone-built inn at the heart of the village with log fires during the winter months. An attractive cottage annexe offers four bedrooms.

BERKELEY   Gloucestershire   Map 3 ST69

★★56% **Berkeley Arms** Canonbury Street GL13 9BG ☎ (0453) 810291

Normal price: £23. Dinner from £11.50 & à la carte
Short breaks: £33. Min 2 nights, Fri-Mon
Credit cards ①②③⑤

Set in the centre of town this small hotel, formerly a coaching inn, offers a good choice of bar meals, a buffet lunch and evening set price menus. The bedrooms all have ensuite facilities and colour television and there is one family room.

FH QQQ Greenacres Breadstone GL13 9HF (2m W off A38) ☎ (0453) 810348
3 Jan-Nov

Normal price: £33.
Short breaks: £89 for 3 nights (1990 prices)

A 16th-century house with beams and inglenook fireplaces.

★★63% **Old Schoolhouse** Canonbury Street GL13 9BG ☎ (0453) 811711
Closed 22 Dec-7 Jan

Normal price: £52 room. Dinner £9-£15 à la carte
Short breaks: £36 for two

A small hotel offering friendly, personal service. All seven bedrooms have ensuite bath or shower rooms and colour television and there is one family room.

BIBURY   Gloucestershire   Map 4 SP10

★★ ♠ 67% **Bibury Court** GL7 5NT ☎ (028574) 337
Closed 24-30 Dec

Normal price: £66-£70 room with Continental breakfast. Dinner £15-£20 à la carte
Short breaks: £89 for 2 nights
Credit cards ①③

Set within landscaped walled grounds this fine period building is now a hotel of charm and character. All the eighteen bedrooms have private baths and colour television and ten rooms are furnished with four-poster beds. Fishing is available.

BIRDLIP   Gloucestershire   Map 3 SO91

★★★59% **Royal George** (Lansbury) GL4 8JH ☎ (0452) 862506

Normal price: £40. Dinner from £14 & `a la carte
Short breaks: £46. Min 2 nights, Fri-Sun.
🎋 (ex guide dogs) Credit cards ①②③⑤

Standing in rural surroundings on the edge of the village, the hotel has a sauna, solarium and 9-hole putting green. All the bedrooms have colour television, most have ensuite facilities and rooms have been set aside for families and non-smokers. There is a special Christmas programme.

BLEDINGTON Gloucestershire *Map 4 SP22*

INN QQQ Kings Head The Green OX7 6HD ☎ (060871) 365

Normal price: £49 room with breakfast. Dinner £3.95-£8 and à la carte
Short breaks: £80 for two people for 2 nights excluding dinner. £39 each additional night. Nov-1 Mar
✗ (ex guide dogs)

This delightful 15th-century inn looks out over the quiet village green. There are six comfortable bedrooms, all with ensuite bathrooms and colour television; some rooms have been set aside for families and non-smokers. The inn has a popular restaurant.

BOURTON-ON-THE-WATER Gloucestershire *Map 4 SP12*

★★64% **Chester House** (Minotels) Victoria Street GL54 2BS ☎ (0451) 20286
Closed mid Dec-mid Feb

Normal price: £30 with Continental breakfast. Dinner £14.95
Short breaks: £40.45. Min 2 nights. Mid Feb-Apr & Oct-mid Dec. £8 single supplement

This building of character and charm provides modern facilities in both the traditional and motel-style bedrooms. All rooms have ensuite bathrooms and colour television, there are family rooms and one room has a four-poster bed.

CHARINGWORTH   Gloucestershire   Map 4 SP13

✿★★★ ₪ **Charingworth Manor** GL55 6NS (on B4035 3m E of Chipping Campden) ☎ (0386) 78353

Normal price: from £95 room and breakfast. Dinner £24.50 & à la carte
Short breaks: from £70. Min 2 nights, Sun-Thu.
Credit cards ① ② ③ ⑤

This former 14th-century manor is now a hotel of charm incorporating all the modern comforts one would expect. All the ensuite bedrooms have colour television and two are furnished with four-poster beds. Staff are attentive and hardworking. There is a special Christmas programme.

CHELTENHAM   Gloucestershire   Map 3 SO92

GH QQ Beaumont House 56 Shurdington Road GL53 0JE ☎ (0242) 245986

Normal price: £22
Short breaks: £20 excluding dinner. Single £22. Min 2 nights, Oct-Jun.

This listed Victorian building is set in a picturesque garden close to the town centre. All rooms have colour television and tea/coffee making facilities, and some are ensuite.

★★★65% **Carlton** Parabola Road, GL50 3AQ ☎ (0242) 514453

Normal price: £72 room. Dinner from £11.50 & à la carte
Short breaks: £37 including £11.50 dinner allowance. Min 2 nights, Fri-Sun
Credit cards ① ② ③ ⑤

A large double-fronted late Georgian house close to the promenade. All bedrooms have ensuite bath or shower rooms and colour television, and some are furnished with four-poster beds. There is a special Christmas programme.

★★★★56% **Golden Valley Thistle** (Mount Charlotte (TS)) Gloucester Road GL51 0TS ☎ (0242) 232691

Normal price: £46.75. Dinner from £14.50 & `a la carte
Short breaks: £41 excluding dinner. No single supplement at weekends

Easily accessible from junction 11 of the M5, this hotel has a new Leisure Club and offers special facilities for children. The modern bedrooms all have ensuite bathrooms and colour television, and some rooms are set aside for families and non-smokers.

✿★★★(Red) ₪ **Greenway** (Pride of Britain) Shurdington GL51 5UG ☎ (0242) 862352

Normal price: £57.50-£97.50. Dinner from £25.
Short breaks: £75-£117.50, including early morning tea and newspaper. Min 2 nights. Single supplement.
Activity breaks: Racing at Cheltenham, £280. Transport can be provided to race meetings by taxi or helicopter, and club badges can be bought in advance. Bird Safaris, £280.
✼ Credit cards ① ② ③ ④ ⑤

Tree-lined hills provide a pleasing backdrop to this delightful Cotswold hotel with its comfortable informality and professional staff. Superb bedrooms with attendant luxuries.

GH QQ Hallery House 48 Shurdington Road GL53 0JE ☎ (0242) 578450

Normal price: £16.50-£22. Dinner £10
Short breaks: £23-£27. Single supplement £3. Min 2 nights (except Cheltenham Gold Cup Week)

Situated on the main Stroud road out of Cheltenham, this is a lovely Victorian Grade II listed building. All rooms have colour and satellite television, and some have ensuite facilities.

GH QQQ Hannaford's 20 Evesham Road GL52 2AB ☎ (0242) 515181

Normal price: £22. Dinner around £7.50
Short breaks: £30 including free bottle of house wine. Min 2 nights, Thu-Sat.
✼ Credit cards ① ③

An attractive comfortable terrace house near the centre and public car park. Most of the bedrooms have private facilities, and all have colour television. Children under seven are not accommodated. No parking.

GH QQQ Hollington House 115 Hales Road GL52 6ST ☎ (0242) 519718
Closed Xmas

Normal price: from £19. Dinner £6.50
Short breaks: from £25. Min 2 nights, Thu-Sat (except
Christmas, Easter and Gold Cup Week – mid-Mar)
Credit cards ①③

This attractive Cotswold-stone detached house
is set in small, pleasant gardens. All bedrooms
have colour television and most have private
showers.

★★★65% **de la Bere** (Trusthouse Forte) Southam GL52 3NH (3m NE A46) ☎ (0242) 237771

Normal price: £91 room. Dinner from £17.
Short breaks: £54, min 2 nights including Sat.
Activity breaks: Murder/Mystery Weekends, £150 approx.
Details from hotel.
Credit cards ①②③④⑤

A Tudor mansion with many original features
intact, including fine oak panelling and beams
in both public areas and bedrooms. Extensive
well-tended grounds and good leisure facilities.

GH QQQ North Hall Pittville Circus Road GL52 2PZ ☎ (0242) 520589
Closed Xmas

Normal price: £21.75. Dinner £4.75
Short breaks: £25. Min 2 nights, Oct-May. £6 single
supplement

This detached house has large bedrooms with
colour television, and most have ensuite
facilities.

★★68% **Prestbury House** The Burgage, Prestbury GL52 3DN (2m NE A46) ☎ (0242) 529533 & 30106

Normal price: £32.50. Dinner £16.50-£18.50.
Short breaks: £33.75, min 2 nights, Fri & Sat, Jul-Sept.
Activity breaks: Croquet, £1 per game, May-Sept. Hill
Walking, £16 for a guide per 6 people. Horse Riding and
Golf Breaks. Details from hotel.

This hotel is popular for its peaceful situation
and friendly owners and staff. All bedrooms
have modern facilities, but those in the annexe
are more compact in size.

★★★★54% **Queen's** (Trusthouse Forte) Promenade GL50 1NN ☎ (0242) 514724

Normal price: £100 room. Dinner £17.95-£18.95 & à la carte
Short breaks: £110 for two. Min 2 nights, Fri-Sun
Credit cards 1️⃣ 2️⃣ 3️⃣ 4️⃣ 5️⃣

A large traditional-style hotel in a central position overlooking the town gardens. All the bedrooms have ensuite facilities and colour television, with some rooms for families and non-smokers. There is a special Christmas programme.

★★★63% **White House** Gloucester Road, Staverton GL51 0FT (3m W off B4063) ☎ (0452) 713226

Normal price: £82 room. Dinner £13.50 & à la carte
Short breaks: £40. Fri-Sun
🦮 (ex guide dogs) Credit cards 1️⃣ 2️⃣ 3️⃣ 5️⃣

Comfortable and attractively decorated, this hotel provides modern bedrooms with ensuite bathrooms and colour television. Two rooms are furnished with four-poster beds. There is a special Christmas programme.

★★★69% **Wyastone** Parabola Road GL50 3BG ☎ (0242) 516654 & 245549

Closed 24 Dec-2 Jan
Normal price: £77 room. Dinner £13.25-£16.95
Short breaks: £42.50. Min 2 nights, Fri-Sun.
🦮

A small hotel run by caring proprietors and their friendly staff. The ensuite bedrooms all have colour television, and one room has a four-poster bed. See advertisement on p151.

CHIPPING CAMPDEN Gloucestershire *Map 4 SP13*

★★★70% **Cotswold House** The Square GL55 6AN ☎ (0386) 840330

Normal price: £80-£142 room and breakfast. Dinner £19.50.
Activity breaks: Christmas Break, from £86 for 2 nights.
New Year Break, £130 for 3 nights. Lazy Weekend, £136 for 2 nights including champagne.
🦮

A Regency town house recently restored to its former elegance and splendour. Well presented imaginative cuisine is served in the charming dining room.

★★64% **Noel Arms** (Exec Hotel) High Street GL55 6AT ☎ (0386) 840317

Normal price: £110 room with dinner.
Short breaks: £90 for two. Min 2 nights.

This former 14th-century coaching inn offers clean and well-maintained bedrooms with ensuite facilities and colour television. Two rooms have four-poster beds. There is a special Christmas programme.

CIRENCESTER Gloucestershire Map 4 SP00

★★★65% **Crown of Crucis** Ampney Crucis GL7 5RS ☎ (0285) 851806
Closed 25 Dec

Normal price: £29. Dinner £9.50-£12.50 & `a la carte
Short breaks: £23 excluding dinner. Min 2 nights, Fri-Sun
Credit cards [1] [2] [3]

Now completely refurbished, this 16th-century inn, situated on the A417 three miles east of the town, offers a wide range of food and comfortable ensuite bedrooms with colour television. A Christmas programme is provided.

★★★69% **Fleece** Market Place GL7 2NZ ☎ (0285) 658507

Normal price: £41.50. Dinner from £13.95.
Short breaks: £32 excluding dinner. Min 2 nights, Fri-Sun.
Activity breaks: To be arranged, contact hotel for details.
Credit cards [1] [2] [3] [5]

A Tudor inn in the town centre offering a high standard of bedroom accommodation and a comfortable lounge. Staff are friendly and courteous.

★★★65% **King's Head** (Best Western) Market Place GL7 2NR ☎ (0285) 653322
Closed 27-30 Dec

Normal price: £76 room. Dinner from £14 & à la carte
Short breaks: £78 for two including dinner allowance of £14.
Min 2 nights

Situated in the market square, this hotel provides friendly and attentive service and bedrooms with ensuite facilities and colour television. Guests can play table tennis and skittles. There is a special Christmas programme.

CLEEVE HILL Gloucestershire Map 3 SO92

★★★57% **Rising Sun** (Lansbury) GL52 3PX ☎ (0242) 676281

Normal price: £38. Dinner from £14 & à la carte
Short breaks: £46. Min 2 nights, Fri-Sun.
Credit cards [1] [2] [3] [5]

In a commanding position overlooking the Malvern Hills, four miles south of Cheltenham, this hotel has a popular restaurant. Bedrooms have ensuite facilities and colour television, with some rooms set aside for non-smokers. There is a special Christmas programme.

COLEFORD Gloucestershire Map 3 SO51

★★69% **Lambsquay House** GL16 8QB ☎ (0594) 33127
Restricted service January

Normal price: £42 room. Dinner £8-£19.50 & à la carte
Short breaks: £26.50-£33 including £11 dinner allowance.
Single £34-£40. Min 2 nights (except Bank Holidays).

A small attractive Georgian house on the outskirts of town with well-equipped ensuite bedrooms with a good range of facilities. Good home cooking and friendly attentive service is also provided. There is a special Christmas programme.

★★63% **Speech House** (Trusthouse Forte) Forest of Dean GL16 7EL ☎ (0594) 822607

Normal price: £90 room and breakfast. Dinner £11.50-£12.95.
Short breaks: fr £45, min 2 nights.
Activity breaks: Pony Trekking Breaks, £118.
Credit cards [1] [2] [3] [4] [5]

In the heart of the Forest of Dean, well outside the town, this 17th-century house is signposted from all directions. Some bedrooms contain massive four-poster beds.

COLESBOURNE   Gloucestershire   Map 3 SO91

INN QQQ Colesbourne GL53 9NP ☎ (024287) 376 & 396

Normal price: £24. Dinner £18
Short breaks: 2 nights £75; 3 nights £110; 4 nights £135.
Single 2 nights £85; 3 nights £120; 4 nights £150.
🐾 (ex guide dogs) Credit cards ① ② ③ ⑤

A traditional Cotswold coaching inn with comfortable bedrooms sited in a converted stable block. All rooms have private bath or shower rooms and colour television. Christmas and New Year breaks are available.

FAIRFORD   Gloucestershire   Map 4 SP10

★★★60% **Hyperion House** (Consort) London Street GL7 4AH ☎ (0285) 712349
Restricted service

Normal price: £80 room. Dinner £20
Short breaks: £100 for two. Single £65. Min 2 nights
(except Christmas, New Year and Cheltenham Gold Cup)
Credit cards ① ② ③ ⑤

Situated in the heart of the village, this Cotswold stone house provides attractive public areas and well-equipped bedrooms with ensuite facilities and colour television. There is a special Christmas programme.

FOSSEBRIDGE   Gloucestershire   Map 4 SP01

★★65% **Fossebridge Inn** GL54 3JS ☎ (0285) 720721

Normal price: £65 room. Dinner £10.50-£24.50
Short breaks: £49.50. Min 2 nights
Credit cards ① ② ③ ⑤

A comprehensive range of bar snacks is served in the characterful Bridge Bar which dates back to the original 15th-century inn. Some bedrooms are situated in an annexe, and all are ensuite with colour television. Fishing is available.

GLOUCESTER   Gloucestershire   Map 3 SO81

★★★68% **Gloucester** (Embassy) Robinswood Hill GL4 9EA (2.5m SE off B4073) ☎ (0452) 25653

Normal price: £52. Dinner £14-£14.50.
Short breaks: £56.
Activity breaks: Golf Breaks, about £65. Ski Breaks. Details from hotel.
Credit cards ① ② ③ ⑤

Squash courts, golf courses, a dry ski slope and a swimming pool are among the facilities provided by this large, well-managed complex three miles from the city.

★★★75% **Hatton Court** Upton Hill, Upton St Leonards GL4 8DE (3m SE B4073) ☎ (0452) 617412

Normal price: £92-£110 room and breakfast. Dinner from £19.50 & à la carte
Short breaks: £52.50. Min 2 nights
🐾 (ex guide dogs) Credit cards ① ② ③ ⑤

A popular hotel set in 37 acres of gardens and pasture land with views of the Severn Valley. All bedrooms are ensuite with colour television, and two rooms are furnished with four-poster beds. There is a croquet lawn and outdoor pool, and a Christmas programme is available.

★★63% **Twigworth Lodge** Tewkesbury Road, Twigworth GL2 9PG ☎ (0452) 730266

Normal price: £56-£64 room. Dinner £10-£18 & à la carte
Short breaks: £60 for two, with £10 dinner allowance per person. Min 2 nights, Fri-Sun, all year (except Christmas).
£7 single supplement

Set in three acres of farmland alongside the A38 north of the city centre, this hotel provides bedrooms with ensuite bath or shower room, an indoor heated pool and snooker facilities.

LOWER SLAUGHTER   Gloucestershire   Map 4 SP12

★★76% **Grapevine** (Best Western) Sheep Street GL54 1AU ☎ (0451) 30344

Normal price: from £45. Dinner from £16.95.
Short breaks: from £49.50 including welcoming glass of
sherry. Min 2 nights. Single price from £70.50.
🦮 Credit cards ① ② ③ ⑤

In the heart of a charming Cotswold village, the
Grapevine offers a relaxed and informal
atmosphere, enhanced by the friendly, willing
service of the staff.

★★★(Red) 🏨 **Lower Slaughter Manor** (Prestige) GL54 2HP ☎ (0451) 20456

Normal price: £49.50-£85. Dinner from £25.95.
Short breaks: £88, min 2 nights except Christmas, New
Year and Cheltenham Festival Week. Single price £105.
Credit cards ① ② ③ ⑤

This elegant manor house stands beside the
Parish Church at the heart of an unspoilt
Cotswold village, and offers an atmosphere of
rest and peace.

LYDNEY   Gloucestershire   Map 3 SO60

★★59% **Feathers** High Street GL15 5DN ☎ (0594) 842815 & 842826

Normal price: £24.75. Dinner £6-£10 & à la carte.
Short breaks: £27.50, min 2 nights. Single price £30.
Credit cards ① ② ③

There is a friendly atmosphere in this popular
town centre hotel, which offers a choice of \a la
carte dining room or carvery, and good bar
menus.

MICKLETON   Gloucestershire   Map 4 SP14

★★★64% **Three Ways** (Inter-Hotels) GL55 6SB ☎ (0386) 438429

Normal price: £62-£72 room and breakfast. Dinner £12.50-
£15.50 (1990 prices)
Short breaks: £41 including £13.50 dinner allowance for 2
nights, £35 for 3 nights. Min 2 nights, Fri-Sun. £10 single
supplement.
Credit cards ① ② ③ ⑤

Convenient for touring, this hotel has an
attractive restaurant and modern bedroom
wing with some family rooms, ensuite facilities
and colour television. It also has a garden, and
sometimes musical entertainment. Christmas
breaks are available.

MORETON-IN-MARSH   Gloucestershire   Map 4 SP23

QQQ **Horse & Groom Inn** Upper Oddington GL56 0XH ☎ (0451) 30584

Normal price: £22. Dinner £10-£12
Short breaks: £30. Min 2 nights, Nov-Feb.
🦮 (ex guide dogs) Credit cards ①

Set in the attractive Cotswold village of
Oddington, this 16th-century family-run inn has
a cosy dining room and beamed bars. All
bedrooms have ensuite facilities and colour
television.

★★ **Redesdale Arms** High Street GL56 0AW ☎ (0608) 50308

Normal price: £47.95
Short breaks: £42.50
🦮 (ex guide dogs) Credit cards ① ② ③

This comfortable, well-run hotel has a good
restaurant and all bedrooms, half in the annexe
including two family rooms, have ensuite
facilities and colour television. Christmas
breaks are available.

NORTH NIBLEY   Gloucestershire   Map 3 ST79

QQQ **Burrows Court** Nibley Green, Dursley GL11 6AZ ☎ (0453) 546230

Normal price: £34
Short breaks: £30. Min 2 nights. £38 for single room.
🦮 Credit cards ① ③

A converted 18th-century weaving mill set in an
acre of gardens, this attractive guesthouse has
ensuite bathrooms and colour television in all
bedrooms, plus an outdoor swimming pool. No
children under 5 are accommodated.

STOW-ON-THE-WOLD Gloucestershire Map 4 SP12

✿★★★ ⚘ 77% **Wyck Hill House** Burford Road GL54 1HY ☎ (0451) 31936

Normal price: £24. Dinner from £27.50 & à la carte
Short breaks: £67.50, min 2 nights except Xmas, New Year
and Cheltenham Festival.
Credit cards ① ② ③ ⑤

Attractive country house hotel with an excellent local reputation for its meals. Chef Ian Smith works mostly with good British produce to devise an imaginative menu.

STROUD Gloucestershire Map 3 SO80

★★★56% **Bear of Rodborough** (Trusthouse Forte) Rodborough Common GL5 5DE ☎ (0453) 878522

Normal price: £49. Dinner £14.
Short breaks: £49, min 2 nights.
Activity breaks: Badger Watching Breaks, £125, May.
Wildflower Breaks, £125, May. Botanical Drawing, £125,
June. Details from hotel.
Credit cards ① ② ③ ④ ⑤

Situated on the edge of the common with fine views over the surrounding countryside, this historic inn offers good food and friendly, attentive service.

★★★ ⚘ 65% **Burleigh Court** Brimscombe GL5 2PF (2.5m SE off A419) ☎ (0453) 883804

Normal price: £37. Dinner £17.25-£23.50 à la carte
Short breaks: £49.50 including £16 dinner allowance. Min 2
nights, except Bank Hols.
🛏 Credit cards ① ② ③ ⑤

A fine Georgian house in a commanding position overlooking the surrounding countryside. Good food and friendly service from the Benson family and their staff.

★★64% **Imperial** (Berni/Chef & Brewer) Station Road GL5 3AP ☎ (0453) 764077

Normal price: £29. Dinner £8-£15 à la carte.
Short breaks: £25.50, excluding dinner. Min 2 nights
weekends, or 3 midweek nights.
🛏 Credit cards ① ② ③ ⑤

A Georgian coaching inn clad in colourful creeping ivy, with a ground floor restaurant featuring the popular `new look' Berni menu.

★★68% **London** 30-31 London Road GL5 2AJ ☎ (0453) 759992

Normal price: £20-£30. Dinner £11.95 & à la carte.
Short breaks: £28.50-£36, Fri-Sun.
🛏 Credit cards ① ② ③ ④ ⑤

On the A419 east of the town centre, this hotel has undergone major improvements, and most of the modern bedrooms have ensuite facilities.

TETBURY Gloucestershire Map 3 ST89

✿★★★(Red) ⚘ **Calcot Manor** (Pride of Britain) Calcot GL8 8YJ (3m W at junc A4135/A46)
☎ (0666) 890391

Normal price: from £50. Dinner £30-£38.
Short breaks: from £70, min 2 nights. Midweek only
summer months. Single price from £100 including dinner.
Activity breaks: Clay Pigeon Shooting, short breaks price
plus £60. Archery Breaks, short break plus £50.
Ballooning, short break plus £90.
🛏 Credit cards ① ② ③ ⑤

A charming and comfortable Cotswold-stone hotel with a relaxed and unpretentious style. The cooking is a highlight.

★★★77% **Close** (Prestige) Long Street GL8 8AQ ☎ (0666) 502272

Normal price: £55-£85. Dinner £17-£27.50.
Short breaks: £70-£90, min 2 nights except Mar & May 1-9.
Single price £110.
🛏 Credit cards ① ② ③ ⑤

A discreet façade which blends beautifully with its High Street neighbours gives no hint of the internal proportions of this most unusual hotel.

★★★62% **Hare and Hounds** (Best Western) Westonbirt GL8 8QL ☎ (066688) 233

Normal price: £37.50. Dinner £16.50-£18.50.
Short breaks: £45, min 2 nights. Single price £65 Mon-Thu.
Activity breaks: Hot Air Ballooning, £215. Includes an hour
long balloon flight over the Cotswolds with champagne on
landing. Golf Breaks, from £126. Includes two day's golf at
Minchinhampton. Gliding, from £120. Includes one 20-
minute flight. Horse Riding, from £105. Includes a two-
hour ride.
Credit cards ①②③

A family-owned and managed country hotel standing in grounds which extend to almost ten acres, including large, well-tended lawns.

★★★71% **Snooty Fox** Market Place GL8 8DD ☎ (0666) 502436

Normal price: £84-£110 (room). Dinner from £18 & à la
carte
Short breaks: £98-£120 including newspaper. Min 2 nights
except Bank Hols, Cheltenham Gold Cup and Badminton
Horse Trials. Single price £78.
🛪 Credit cards ①②③⑤

Honey coloured Cotswold stone building facing the old Market Hall. This popular hotel has been ambitiously refurbished to a high standard.

TEWKESBURY   Gloucestershire   Map 3 SO83

★★★64% **Bell** (Best Western) Church Street GL20 5SA ☎ (0684) 293293

Normal price: £35.
Short breaks: £20 per night for 3 night stay including Sun,
from £40 min 2 nights.
Credit cards ①②③⑤

A distinctive black and white building dating from Victorian times standing on the western side of town. Bedrooms vary in size, but all are modern.

★★★65% **Tewkesbury Park Golf & Country Club** Lincoln Green Lane GL20 7DN ☎ (0684) 295405

Normal price: £52. Dinner £15.
Short breaks: £55 Mon-Thu, £50 Fri-Sun. Min 2 nights.
Activity breaks: Golf Breaks and Golf Tuition Breaks.
Details from hotel.
🛪 Credit cards ①②③④⑤

This modern hotel and leisure complex is surrounded by grounds containing a golf course, tennis courts and parkland. Indoor facilities include a swimming pool.

★★★66% **Tewkesbury Hall** Puckrup GL20 6EL (3m N A38) ☎ (0684) 296200

Normal price: £45. Dinner £19.50-£21.50.
Short breaks: £49.50, min 2 nights, Fri-Sun.
Activity breaks: Ballooning, short break plus £120. Theatre
Breaks, short break plus ticket price. Clay Shooting, £250
approx.
Credit cards ①②③⑤

Forty acres of grounds surround this country house-style hotel which is within easy reach of the M5/M10 junction.

★★65% **Tudor House** High Street GL20 5BH ☎ (0684) 297755

Normal price: £32.50 (1990). Dinner from £10.95.
Short breaks: £32, min 2 nights, Fri-Sun.
🛪 Credit cards ①②③⑤

A fine old Tudor building with an elegant Queen Anne staircase, and a priest's hole. Bedrooms meticulously preserve the original character of the building.

UPPER SLAUGHTER   Gloucestershire   Map 4 SP12

★★70% **Fosse Manor** (Consort) GL54 1JX ☎ (0451) 30354

Normal price: £38. Dinner from £16.95 & à la carte
Short breaks: from £47, min 2 nights, no weekends Apr-Aug.
Credit cards ①②③⑤

An attractive hotel set in its own grounds with comfortable accommodation and willing service from the friendly staff. The character of the original old manor house remains.

❀ ★★★ 🍺 77% **Lords of the Manor** GL54 2JD ☎ (0451) 20243

Normal price: from £100 room. Dinner £25 & à la carte.
Short breaks: from £62.50 Oct to May. Oct-May 1992 on application. Min 2 nights.
🦅 Credit cards ①②③⑤

A magnificent 17th-century former rectory, now converted into a hotel of considerable character. A meal here is a truly memorable experience.

★★63% **Old Stocks** The Square GL54 1AF ☎ (0451) 30666

Normal price: £30. Dinner £8.95-£14.95.
Short breaks: £33, Sun-Thurs, £36, Fri-Sat. Min 2 nights, except Jul-Oct.
Credit cards ①②③

This hotel next to the green consists of three 16th and 17th century buildings which have been tastefully upgraded and refurbished.

WILLERSEY   Gloucestershire   Map 4 SP13

GH QQQQ **Old Rectory** WR12 7PN ☎ (0386) 853729

Normal price: £29.50.
Short breaks: £20 excluding dinner. Min 2 nights, Oct-Mar.
🦅 Credit cards ①③

The Old Rectory is a haven of peace and tranquility, tucked away alongside the church. Accommodation is exceptional with many extras, and guests are made to feel very welcome.

▣ HAMPSHIRE ▣

AMPFIELD   Hampshire   Map 4 SU32

★★★62% **Potters Heron** (Lansbury) SO51 9ZF ☎ (0703) 266611

Normal price: £90 (room). Dinner from £11 and à la carte
Short breaks: £46. Min 2 nights, Fri-Sun
🦅 Credit cards ①②③⑤

This is a picturesque thatched hotel with a modern bedroom block at the rear. All rooms have ensuite facilities and colour television, some are set aside for non-smokers and one room has a four-poster bed. Amenities include a gymnasium and sauna, and there is a special Christmas programme.

ANDOVER   Hampshire   Map 4 SU34

★★★63% **Ashley Court** Micheldever Road SP11 6LA ☎ (0264) 57344

Normal price: £33-£44. Dinner £9.50-£14.50.
Short breaks: £22 excluding dinner. Min 1 night, Fri, Sat or Sun.
Activity breaks: Murder/Mystery Weekend, £75 for 2 nights (1990 price). Fishing Breaks, Clay Pigeon Shooting, Pyjama Weekends, Go Karting, Survival Weekends. Details from hotel.
Credit cards ①②③

Quietly situated hotel now offering new bedrooms. The Rendezvous Restaurant provides an à la carte lunch and dinner menu, and service is friendly.

★★61% **Danebury** High Street SP10 1NX ☎ (0264) 23332

Normal price: £71 (room). Dinner £12 and à la carte
Short breaks: £32. Min 2 nights, Fri-Sun
🦅 Credit cards ①②③⑤

Parts of this town centre hotel date back to the 16th century, but its comfortable bedrooms provide all modern facilities including colour television and private bathrooms. One room has a four-poster bed. The public bars are popular with the locals and there is a special Christmas programme.

AVON   Hampshire   Map 4 SZ19

★★★66% **Tyrrells Ford Country House** BH23 7BH (4m S of Ringwood on B3347) ☎ (0425) 72646

Normal price: £32.50-£45. Dinner £14.95-£17.95 and à la carte
Short breaks: £40-£55. Single room £55-£65. Min 2 nights
✹ (ex guide dogs) Credit cards ①③

Situated on the edge of the New Forest, this Georgian house offers comfortable accommodation. All sixteen bedrooms have ensuite bath or shower rooms and colour television.

BARTON-ON-SEA   Hampshire   Map 4 SZ29

★★65% **Cliff House** Marine Drive West, BH25 7QL ☎ (0425) 619333 & 610014

Normal price: £66-£80 room with breakfast. Dinner £11.50
Short breaks: £85 for 2 people. £20 single supplement. Min 2 nights, Oct-Mar (ex Christmas and Easter).
✹

This fresh clean little hotel enjoys uninterrupted sea views. All the bedrooms have ensuite facilities and colour television; smoking is not permitted in the bedrooms or dining room. There is a special Christmas programme.

BASINGSTOKE   Hampshire   Map 4 SU65

★★★57% **Hilton Lodge** (Hilton) Old Common Road, Black Dam RG21 3PR ☎ (0256) 460460

Normal price: £86. Dinner from £15.50.
Short breaks: £40 excluding dinner. (1990 prices). Min 2 nights, Thu-Sun.
Activity breaks: Bird-Watching, £109. 6-7 July.

A modern purpose-built hotel with twenty four plaza rooms providing extra touches like chocolates and bathrobes. Service is helpful and friendly.

★★55% **Red Lion** (Trusthouse Forte) 24 London Street RG21 1NY ☎ (0256) 28525

Normal price: £40 including dinner.
Short breaks: £64 for 2 nights

In a central position with good car parking, this hotel has sixty-two bedrooms all with ensuite amenities and colour television; there are two family rooms and some for non-smokers, but no lounge. There is a special Christmas programme.

BEAULIEU   Hampshire   Map 4 SU30

★★★73% Montagu Arms SO42 7ZL ☎ (0590) 612324

Normal price: £43-£75. Dinner £22.50 & à la carte
Short breaks: £56.50 (meal in Wine Press Bar); £72.50
(meal in restaurant). Min 2 nights. (1990 prices).
🛇 (ex guide dogs) Credit cards ① ② ③ ⑤

This creeper-clad listed building in the centre of the picturesque village has individually furnished and decorated bedrooms which include three rooms with four-poster beds and three suites. All have ensuite facilities and colour television. There is a special Christmas programme.

BROCKENHURST   Hampshire   Map 4 SU20

★★★62% Balmer Lawn (Hilton) Lyndhurst Road SO42 7ZB ☎ (0590) 23116

Normal price: £47.50. Dinner £14-£15
Short breaks: £40 excluding dinner. Single £50. Min 2
nights
Credit cards ① ② ③ ④ ⑤

This former hunting lodge enjoys views over the New Forest and has good leisure facilities. Bedrooms have colour television and ensuite facilities, with rooms set aside for families and non-smokers. There is a special Christmas programme.

★★★69% Careys Manor Lyndhurst Road SO4 7RH ☎ (0590) 23551

Normal price: £49.95. Dinner £19.95-£24.95.
Short breaks: £53.85, min 2 nights.
Activity breaks: Gourmet Breaks, and Health/Fitness
Assessment Breaks, about £127.70. Details from hotel.
Credit cards ① ② ③

Features of this hotel include modern bedroom wings with a choice of accommodation, a French-staffed cafe/bar restaurant, and a well-run health and leisure centre.

★★★60% Forest Park (Forestdale) Rhinefield Road SO4 7ZG ☎ (0590) 22844

Normal price: £70 bed and breakfast, £90 including dinner
Short breaks: from £90 for 2 people. Single £62.50. Min 2
nights.
Credit cards ① ② ③ ④ ⑤

A pretty roadside hotel on the outskirts of Brockenhurst providing straightforward cuisine, relaxed service and a good range of leisure facilities. Each bedroom has ensuite bath or shower room and colour television, with rooms set aside for families and non-smokers.

★★67% Cottage Sway Road SO42 7SH ☎ (0590) 22296

Normal price: £84-£86 for 2 people including dinner
Short breaks: £72-£76. Min 2 nights, Nov-Mar (ex Bank
Holidays). Single £82-£86
🛇 Credit cards ① ③

A cosy cottage hotel personally run by resident proprietors, and offering friendly and helpful service. All six bedrooms have ensuite facilities and colour television. Children under sixteen are not accommodated. There is a special Christmas programme.

★★ 🌢 69% Whitley Ridge Beaulieu Road SO4 7QL ☎ (0590) 22354

Normal price: from £44
Short breaks: from £42. Min 2 nights
Credit cards ① ② ③ ⑤

A former 18th-century Royal Hunting Lodge offering individually-styled bedrooms all with ensuite bath or shower rooms and colour television; one room has a four-poster bed. The restaurant is popular with residents and locals alike.

EASTLEIGH   Hampshire   Map 4 SU41

★★★63% **Crest** (Trusthouse Forte) Leigh Road, Passfield Avenue SO5 5PG ☎ (0703) 619700

Normal price: £44-£48 (room).
Short breaks: £50 (1990 price), min 2 nights, Fri-Sun.
Activity breaks: Archery Breaks, £68 per night. Archery in the New Forest including target archery, archery darts and shooting at the clout. Flight Training Weekends, £90 per night excluding dinner, including trial flying lesson in a light aircraft
Credit cards ① ② ③ ④ ⑤

An attractive and well-designed modern hotel with friendly service and particularly good standards of cooking in the Beatrix Restaurant.

EMSWORTH   Hampshire   Map 4 SU70

★★★64% **Brookfield** Havant Road PO10 7LF ☎ (0243) 376342
Closed 25 Dec-1 Jan

Normal price: £32. Dinner £11.50 & à la carte
Short breaks: £35. Min 2 nights, Fri-Sun.
🕇 (ex guide dogs) Credit cards ① ② ③ ⑤

This friendly, family-run hotel has now been by-passed by the new road. The Hermitage Restaurant overlooks the gardens and provides menus which represent good value for money. All the bedrooms are ensuite with colour television.

FAREHAM   Hampshire   Map 4 SU50

★★63% **Maylings Manor** 11A Highlands Road PO16 7XJ ☎ (0329) 286451

Normal price: £32. Dinner £8.75-£10 & à la carte
Short breaks: £32. Min 2 nights, Fri-Sun.

An Edwardian manor house set in 2 ¹/₂ acres of gardens on the western edge of town. The restaurant offers a choice of menus, and light meals are served in the bar. All the bedrooms have colour television and most have ensuite bathrooms; two rooms have a four-poster bed.

★★66% **Red Lion** (Lansbury) East Street PO16 0BP ☎ (0329) 822640

Normal price: £82 (room). Dinner from £11 & à la carte
Short breaks: £42. Min 2 nights, Fri-Sun
Credit cards ① ② ③ ⑤

This former coaching inn has beams and exposed brickwork in the public areas and offers bar meals as well as the restaurant menu. Bedrooms are ensuite with colour television, with rooms set aside for non-smokers; one room has a four-poster bed.

FLEET   Hampshire   Map 4 SU85

★★★56% **Lismoyne** Church Road GU13 8NA ☎ (0252) 628555

Normal price: £80 (room). Dinner £12.95 & à la carte
Short breaks: £53.50 (room), less 10% if lunch or dinner is taken each day. Single £49.60. Min 2 nights, Fri-Sun (ex Xmas)
Credit cards ① ② ③ ④ ⑤

Staff are pleasant and friendly at this Victorian hotel set in two acres of gardens in a residential area. Each bedroom has an ensuite bath or shower room and colour television, and one is furnished with a four-poster bed.

FORDINGBRIDGE   Hampshire   *Map 4 SU11*

★★66% **Ashburn** (Minotels) Station Road SP6 1JP ☎ (0425) 652060

Normal price: £62 (room). Dinner £10.50 & à la carte
Short breaks: £72 for 2 people. £5 single supplement. Min 2 nights
Credit cards ① ③

Set on a quiet hillside on the edge of town, this hotel offers a choice of original and modern new wing bedrooms with views over the lawn and swimming pool. All are ensuite with colour television. Service is friendly and the cooking very reliable.

HAVANT   Hampshire   *Map 4 SU70*

★★★60% **Bear** (Lansbury) East Street PO9 1AA ☎ (0705) 486501

Normal price: from £85 (room). Dinner from £11 & à la carte
Short breaks: £44. Min 2 nights, Fri-Sun
🛇 (ex guide dogs) Credit cards ① ② ③ ⑤

This 16th-century coaching inn offers well-equipped ensuite bedrooms, with rooms for families and non-smokers. The restaurant serves grills and a range of more imaginative dishes. Christmas breaks are available.

HEDGE END   Hampshire   *Map 4 SU41*

★★★64% **Botleigh Grange** (Best Western) SO3 2GA ☎ (0489) 787700

Normal price: £36.75-£44.25. Dinner £9-£12 & à la carte
Short breaks: £39. Min 2 nights in September.
Credit cards ① ② ③ ⑤

This 17th-century building has a modern wing of bedrooms with two four-poster rooms. Putting and fishing is available. There are special Christmas breaks.

HOOK   Hampshire   *Map 4 SU75*

★★60% **Raven** (Lansbury) Station Road RG27 9HS (0.75m N of M3 Junc 5 on B3349) ☎ (0256) 762541

Normal price: £85 (room). Dinner from £11 & à la carte
Short breaks: £38. Min 2 nights, Fri-Sun
🛇 (ex guide dogs) Credit cards ① ② ③ ④ ⑤

Conveniently located near the station this hotel has a spacious, lively bar lounge and a busy restaurant. Bedrooms are ensuite with colour television, with rooms for families and non-smokers. Christmas breaks are available.

LYMINGTON   Hampshire   *Map 4 SZ39*

GH QQ Albany House Highfield SO41 9GB ☎ (0590) 671900

Normal price: £16-£24.
Short breaks: £24-£30, min 2 nights, Nov-Apr except
Christmas, New Year & Easter. Single price £28.

A 3-storey Regency house overlooking the municipal park. The delightful lounge is comfortable and restful, and the dinner menus are imaginative.

LYNDHURST   Hampshire   Map 4 SU03

GH QQQ Knightwood Lodge Southampton Road SO4 7BU ☎ (0703) 282502

Normal price: £21-£23. Dinner £13 & à la carte
Short breaks: £19 excluding dinner. Min 2 nights, Oct-May.
🎠 Credit cards ① ② ③ ⑤

Run by an experienced, enthusiastic young couple, this hotel offers a steam room and sauna, and value for money meals.

★★★60% **Lyndhurst Park** (Forestdale) High Street SO43 7NL ☎ (0703) 283923

Normal price: £80 (room). Dinner £13 & à la carte
Short breaks: £90, min 2 nights, Fri-Sun.
Credit cards ① ② ③ ④ ⑤

A Georgian mansion, sympathetically modernised to offer a choice of bedrooms, restaurant, bar and games room. Set in its own grounds.

MIDDLE WALLOP   Hampshire   *Map 4 SU23*

★★ **Fifehead Manor** SO20 ☎ (0264) 781565

Normal price: £42.50.
Short breaks: £100 for 2 nights. Min 2 nights, Nov-Good Fri
Credit cards ① ② ③ ⑤

A small manor house on the fringe of the village serving sophisticated French food in the restaurant and with comfortable bedrooms, some in the annexe, all with private bath and colour television. There is croquet in the lawned garden.

MILFORD-ON-SEA   Hampshire   *Map 4 SZ29*

★★★72% **South Lawn** Lymington Road SO41 0RF ☎ (0590) 643911

Normal price: £51. Dinner from £12.25
Short breaks: £41.25-£42.50. Min 2 nights, Nov-May exc bank holidays.
🏋 Credit cards ① ③

Set in well-kept grounds, this former dower house has a restaurant with a good menu and wine list, and comfortable, spacious accommodation. All bedrooms have ensuite facilities and colour television. No children under 7 accommodated.

★★★64% **Westover Hall** Park Lane SO41 0PT ☎ (0590) 643044

Normal price: £32.50. Dinner £12.95-£16.95 (1990 price)
Short breaks: £47
Credit cards ① ② ③ ⑤

This friendly Swiss-managed Victorian hotel with a garden and fine sea views serves well-prepared food and the bedrooms all have private bath and colour television. There are special facilities for children. Christmas breaks are available.

NORTH WALTHAM   Hampshire   *Map 4 SU54*

★★ **Wheatsheaf** (Lansbury) RG25 2BB ☎ (0256) 398282

Normal price: £42.50. Dinner from £12.50 (1990 price)
Short breaks: £42. Min 2 nights, Fri-Sun.
Credit cards ① ② ③ ④ ⑤

This skilfully modernised 18th-century inn retains its historic atmosphere and has ensuite facilities and colour television in all bedrooms, including a family room and one with a four-poster bed.

PORTSMOUTH AND SOUTHSEA   Hampshire   *Map 4 SZ69*

GH QQ **Birchwood** 44 Waverley Road PO5 2PP ☎ (0705) 811837

Normal price: £140 per week including dinner. (Double per night – £27-£35)
Short breaks: £126 per week, min 4 nights.
🏋 Credit cards ① ③

This Victorian terraced house overlooks the grassy municipal garden. The seafront is a 5-minute walk away, and the accommodation is cosy and comfortable.

★★★67% **Holiday Inn** Southampton Road, North Harbour PO6 4SH ☎ (0705) 383151

Normal price: £118 (room)
Short breaks: £44 bed and breakfast Fri-Sun. £20 single supplement
Credit cards ① ② ③ ④ ⑤

This very comfortable hotel has well-equipped ensuite bedrooms with colour television, including non-smoking and many family rooms. Extensive leisure facilities include indoor swimming, squash, sauna, solarium, gymnasium and children's adventure playground. Christmas breaks are available.

★★★55% **Hospitality Inn** (Mount Charlotte (TS)) St Helens Parade PO4 0RN ☎ (0705) 731281

Normal price: £83.40 (room). Dinner from £11.95 & à la carte
Short breaks: £36.50, min 2 nights, Thurs-Sun
Credit cards ① ② ③ ⑤

This impressive and spacious seafront hotel has limited lounge facilities, but the gracious restaurant features fine chandeliers.

RINGWOOD   *Hampshire*   Map 4 SU10

QQQQ Little Forest Lodge Poulner Hill BH24 3HS ☎ (0425) 478848

Normal price: from £20
Short breaks: from £27.50. Min 2 nights, Oct-Apr. Single
supplement.

Set in 3 acres of gardens, this elegantly furnished house provides friendly personal service and good quality accommodation, with five generous-sized bedrooms, some of them family rooms, all ensuite and with colour television.

★ **Moortown Lodge** 244 Christchurch Road BH24 3AS ☎ (0425) 471404

Normal price: £27
Short breaks: £35, including set-price dinner or £8.50 dinner allowance. Min 2 nights. £10 single supplement.
🗶 Credit cards ① ② ③

This hospitable small hotel serves good home-cooked meals and has pleasant compact and well-equipped bedrooms, all with colour television and nearly all with private bath or shower.

ROTHERWICK   *Hampshire*   Map 4 SU75

★★★★ 🛏 79% **Tylney Hall** (Prestige) RG27 9AJ ☎ (0256) 764881

Normal price: £110 approx. Dinner from £23.50.
Short breaks: £145 for 2 people, min 2 nights, Mon-Thu.
Activity breaks: Clay Pigeon Shooting, short break rate plus £40. Hot Air Ballooning, short break rate plus £140. Horse Riding, short break plus £20. Archery, short break plus £20.
🗶 Credit cards ① ② ③ ⑤

A magnificent country mansion set within 60 acres of pleasant gardens and woodland, with many of the splendid bedrooms contained in former coach houses and gardeners' cottages.

ROMSEY   *Hampshire*   Map 4 SU32

★★★61% **White Horse** (Trusthouse Forte) Market Place SO5 8NA ☎ (0794) 512431

Normal price: £70-£80. Dinner from £12.95.
Short breaks: £50, min 2 nights.
Activity breaks: Music at Leisure, £126, 26-28 Apr. Heritage Tours, £169 (1990).
Credit cards ① ② ③ ④ ⑤

Part-Tudor coaching inn with Georgian façade offering elegance at the Lucella Dixon restaurant and a flower-filled courtyard for summer bar meals or drinks.

SOUTHAMPTON   *Hampshire*   Map 4 SU41

★★63% **Elizabeth House** 43-44 The Avenue SO1 2SX ☎ (0703) 224327

Normal price: £27. Dinner from £11.75 à la carte.
Short breaks: £20, Fri-Sun, excluding September.
Credit cards ① ② ③ ⑤

A small family owned and run hotel with a friendly atmosphere. Bedrooms are furnished in a utilitarian manner, but provided with modern facilities including colour television. There is a smart dining room and a cellar bar.

★★★50% **Polygon** Cumberland Place SO9 4DG ☎ (0703) 330055

Normal price: £55. Dinner £18.30 & à la carte.
Short breaks: £45, min 2 nights, Fri-Sun. £10 single supplement.
Credit cards ① ② ③ ④ ⑤

This city centre commercial hotel has fine conference facilities and a spacious restaurant offering a choice of menus; the bedrooms are in the process of being upgraded to similar standards.

★★57% **Star** High Street SO9 4ZA ☎ (0703) 339939

Normal price: £25-£35. Dinner £10-£15 à la carte.
Short breaks: £20-£25 excluding dinner. Min 2 nights, Fri-Sun, Nov-Aug. £10-£15 single supplement.
Credit cards ① ② ③ ⑤

This centrally-situated, family-run hotel provides well equipped bedrooms, and is continually being refurbished and upgraded. There is a choice of carvery and à la carte menus, and the service is friendly.

SOUTHSEA   Hampshire   Map 4 SZ69

QQQ Upper Mount House The Vale, Clarendon Road PO5 2EQ ☎ (0705) 820456

Normal price: £15-£20
Short breaks: £20-£30, min 2 nights.
Credit cards ① ③

A listed 3-storey building set to the rear of a main road, in a quiet lane.

STOCKBRIDGE   Hampshire   Map 4 SU33

★★★61% **Grosvenor** High Street SO20 6EU ☎ (0264) 810606

Normal price: £78 room and breakfast. Dinner from £11 & `a la carte.
Short breaks: £44, min 2 nights, Fri-Sun.
✗ Credit cards ① ② ③ ⑤

Set in an attractive old market village in the Test Valley, the hotel offers particularly well equipped bedrooms. The standard of cuisine is high, under the close personal supervision of the resident manager.

SWAY   Hampshire   Map 4 SZ29

★★60% **White Rose** (Exec Hotel) Station Road SO41 6BA ☎ (0590) 682754

Normal price: £43 including dinner.
Short breaks: £35-£38, min 2 nights, Oct-Jul. Single supplement.
Credit cards ① ③

Substantial red brick house standing in 6 acres of grounds, with an attractive bar serving good value imaginative bar meals.

WINCHESTER   Hampshire   Map 4 SU42

✿★★★ 🌑 78% **Lainston House** (Prestige) Sparsholt SO21 2LT (3m NW off A272) ☎ (0962) 63588

Normal price: £64. Dinner £26-£40 à la carte.
Short breaks: £90, min 2 nights, Fri-Sun.
Credit cards ① ② ③ ④ ⑤

This attractive William and Mary period house is set in 63 acres of parkland. Bedrooms are individually designed, and provide quality bed linen and bathrobes.

★★★★58% **Wessex** (Trusthouse Forte) Paternoster Row SO23 9LQ ☎ (0962) 61611

Normal price: £56.70. Dinner £19 & à la carte
Short breaks: £51, min 2 nights, Thurs-Sun, except Easter & Christmas.
Credit cards ① ② ③ ④ ⑤

A modern hotel next to the Cathedral precinct, offering a choice of meals from the coffee shop and Waltons Restaurant.

★★★61% **Winchester Moat House** (Queens Moat) (Consort) Worthy Lane SO23 7AB ☎ (0962) 68102

Normal price: £55. Dinner £16.50-£18.
Short breaks: £45, min 2 nights, Fri-Sun. Single price £55.
Credit cards ① ② ③ ⑤

Sited on the former coach station, this purpose-built hotel is close to a car park. The restaurant features table d'hôte menus.

■ HEREFORD & WORCESTER ■

ABBERLEY   Hereford & Worcester   Map 7 SO76

★★★ 👪 77% **Elms** (Queens Moat) (Prestige) (on A443) WR6 6AT ☎ (0299) 896666

Normal price: £50-£62.50. Dinner £20
Short breaks: £70. Min 2 nights, Fri-Sun (Mon-Thu on request). Not available Christmas or New Year.
🦮 (ex guide dogs) Credit cards ① ② ③ ④ ⑤

An attractive avenue of limes leads to this lovely Queen Anne house which has recently been completely restored. All the bedrooms, including those in the annexe, have ensuite facilities and colour television. Tennis, putting and croquet are available. There is a special Christmas programme.

ADFORTON   Hereford & Worcester   Map 7 SO47

GH QQQ Lower House SY7 0NF ☎ (056886) 223
Open Etr-Nov

Normal price: £18
Short breaks: £23. Min 2 nights
🦮

Two of the four bedrooms at this guesthouse are set aside for families, and one room has an ensuite shower.

BEWDLEY   Hereford & Worcester   Map 7 SO77

★★53% **Black Boy** Kidderminster Road DY12 1AG ☎ (0299) 402119
Closed 25 Dec

Normal price: £41.80-£59.40 room with breakfast. Dinner £10.75
Short breaks: £66-£90 room with breakfast for 2 nights. Single £41.80-£60.50, Fri & Sat or Sat & Sun.
Credit cards ① ② ③

An 18th-century inn, standing on the A456 close to the River Severn and the town centre, with a pleasant bar and small cosy restaurant. Some bedrooms are equipped with ensuite amenities and colour television and there are two family rooms.

BREDWARDINE   Hereford & Worcester   Map 3 SO34

GH QQQQ Bredwardine Hall HR3 6DB ☎ (09817) 596
Mar-Nov

Normal price: £22
Short breaks: £61 for 2 nights; £212 for 7 nights. Single supplement £6. Mar-Nov

A warm and friendly welcome is assured here and the owners provide personal service. Most bedrooms have ensuite bath or shower rooms, all have colour television and there is one family room. Children under ten are not accommodated.

BROADWAY   Hereford & Worcester   Map 4 SP03

★★★62% **Broadway** (Inter-Hotels) The Green WR12 7AB ☎ (0386) 852401

Normal price: £42.50. Dinner £17-£18.50 and à la carte
Short breaks: £45. Min 2 nights, Nov-Mar
🦮 Credit cards ① ② ③ ⑤

Set in the heart of the village this former 16th-century building has log fires, original timbers and a gallery. Most bedrooms, including those in the annexe, have ensuite facilities, all have colour television and there are rooms for families and non-smokers. One room is furnished with a four-poster bed. A special Christmas programme is available.

★★ 🏨 70% **Collin House** Collin Lane WR12 7PB ☎ (0386) 858354 & 852544

Normal price: £38-£43.50. Dinner £15-£17 à la carte
Short breaks: £48.75-£54.70 including £17 dinner allowance.
Single £53. Min 2 nights, Nov-Mar. £259-£286 for a five-night midweek break, Sun-Thu, Apr-Oct, including £17 dinner allowance.
🏸 Credit cards ① ③

This lovely 16th-century Cotswold stone house is situated in eight acres of grounds and is full of charm and character. Most of the seven bedrooms have ensuite facilities and two are furnished with four-poster beds. There is a special Christmas programme.

★★★68% **Dormy House** Willersey Hill WR12 7LF (2m E off A44 in Gloucestershire) ☎ (0386) 852711
Closed 25 & 26 Dec

Normal price: £54. Dinner £24.95 & à la carte
Short breaks: £66, Mon-Thu; Champagne Weekenders. Available Cheltenham Gold Cup in mid Mar & Mackeson Cup in mid Nov. Min 2 nights

A privately-owned hotel enjoying fine views of the Vale of Evesham from its superb elevated location. Bedrooms are individually-decorated and furnished, and all have ensuite facilities and colour television. Two rooms have four-poster beds.

EVESHAM Hereford & Worcester Map 4 SP04

★★★66% **Evesham** Coopers Lane, off Waterside WR11 6DA ☎ (0386) 765566
Closed 25 & 26 Dec

Normal price: £39. Dinner £14-£21 à la carte
Short breaks: £40-£56 depending on season. Min 2 nights, all week in summer, Thu-Mon in winter. Single supplement midweek
Credit cards ① ② ③ ⑤

Situated close to the river and convenient for the town centre, this is a pleasant family-run hotel offering comfortable accommodation and an imaginative menu. All bedrooms are ensuite with colour television. The hotel has an indoor heated swimming pool.

★★★65% **Northwick Arms** Waterside WR11 6BT ☎ (0386) 40322

Normal price: from £55 (room). Dinner £12-£15 & à la carte
Short breaks: £64 room with £10 dinner allowance. £7
single supplement. Min 2 nights, Fri-Sun, all year (ex
Christmas)

A small hotel set next to the River Avon, south-east of the town centre. Bedrooms are modern and comfortable with ensuite facilities and colour television, one room has a four-poster bed.

★★77% **Riverside** The Parks, Offenham Road WR11 5JP ☎ (0386) 446200
Restricted service Nov-Feb

Normal price: £30-£35. Dinner £15.95-£17.95
Short breaks: £37.50
✖ (ex guide dogs) Credit cards ①③

The cottage-style hotel and its riverside moorings can be found by following the signs for Offenham, as there is no access to the hotel from the by-pass. Public rooms and bedrooms are pretty and comfortable enjoying views of the River Avon. All bedrooms are ensuite with colour television. Fishing is available and the hotel has a special Christmas programme.

★★73% **Waterside** 56 Waterside WR11 6JZ ☎ (0386) 442420

Normal price: £27.35. Dinner £14.50
Short breaks: £32.50. Min 2 nights, Fri-Sun. Single £42.50
Credit cards ①②③

The proprietors offer a warm welcome and comfortable accommodation which is well equipped with an array of modern facilities. Most bedrooms are ensuite with colour television. Fishing is available.

FOWNHOPE   Hereford & Worcester   Map 3 SO53

GH QQQ Bowens Country House HR1 4PS ☎ (043277) 430
Closed Xmas & New Year

Normal price: £17 bed and breakfast, £26.50 with dinner
Short breaks: £52 for 2 nights (ex Bank Holidays) 1990
prices

Attractive grounds and gardens surround this 17th-century house which provides comfortable accommodation including two annexe rooms in a converted coach house. There is a putting green and tennis court. Not suitable for children under ten.

HEREFORD   Hereford & Worcester   Map 3 SO54

HEREFORD   Hereford & Worcester   Map 3 SO54

★★61% Castle Pool (Exec Hotel) Castle Street HR1 2NR ☎ (0432) 356321

Normal price: £30. Dinner from £15
Short breaks: £39, single £50. Min 2 nights, Fri-Sun, Apr-Sep 1991. Available all week, Oct 1991-Mar 1992
Credit cards ①②③⑤

In a tranquil setting in attractive gardens which extend to what was once the moat of Hereford Castle, this hotel has twenty-six ensuite bedrooms all with colour television. Two rooms have four-poster beds. Christmas breaks are available.

★★★61% Green Dragon (Trusthouse Forte) Broad Street HR4 9BG ☎ (0432) 272506

Normal price: £70 (room). Dinner £15.50 & à la carte
Short breaks: £52 for two. £5 single supplement. Min 2 nights
Credit cards ①②③④⑤

A city centre hotel with an attractive oak-panelled restaurant. Each bedroom has a private bath and colour television, two rooms have four-poster beds and there are rooms for non-smokers. Christmas breaks are available.

★★75% Merton (Minotels) Commercial Road HR1 2BD ☎ (0432) 265925

Normal price: £32. Dinner from £15.
Short breaks: £40, including early morning tea or coffee and newspaper. Min 2 nights, Fri-Sun.
Activity breaks: Self Awareness Breaks, including courses on self defence, health and fitness. Details from hotel.
Credit cards ①②③⑤

A very pleasant private hotel close to the city centre, with attractive accommodation and the popular Grosvenor Restaurant.

★★ 🐾 64% Netherwood Country House Tupsley HR1 1UT ☎ (0432) 272388

Normal price: £68. Dinner from £15.
Short breaks: £75, min 2 nights.
Activity breaks: Air Sports including Ballooning, Flying, Gliding, Hang Gliding, Microlighting, Paragliding and Powerchuting. Water Sports including Sailing, Wind-surfing, Kayak and Canadian canoeing. Ball Sports including Golf, tennis, squash, bowls and indoor bowls. Motor Sports including Autograss, Car Rallying, Driving Courses, four-wheel off-road driving, go-karting, micro-trike grand prix, quad biking. Arts and Crafts, Festivals, Field Sports and Specialist Pursuits. Murder/Mystery Weekends. Brochure on request from hotel.
🎠 Credit cards ①②③

A charming early Victorian country house in two acres of grounds and gardens, once owned by the Baskerville family, and reputed to be the setting for Conan Doyle's famous novel.

FH Q Orchard Mordiford HR1 4EJ (Mordiford 3m E off B4224) ☎ (043273) 253 due to change to (0432) 870253

Normal price: £25.
Short breaks: £38, min 2 nights, Nov-Easter Thurs.
Activity breaks: Wine and Cider Tasting Tours, £100 for 2 days including all meals (except night of arrival), transport, entrance to all vineyards, cider factories and tastings.

A 17th-century stone-built farmhouse set in a quiet location with fine views of the surrounding countryside.

HOW CAPLE   Hereford & Worcester   Map 3 SO63

★★62% How Caple Grange HR1 4TR ☎ (098986) 208

Normal price: £61.50 (room). Dinner £9 & à la carte
Short breaks: £74 for 2 people. Min 2 nights

Dating back to 1730, this impressive stone-built house has spacious bedrooms and a range of leisure amenities.

KIDDERMINSTER   Hereford & Worcester   Map 7 SO87

★★68% **Gainsborough House** (Consort) Bewdley Hill, DY11 6BS ☎ (0562) 820041

Normal price: £32. Dinner £11.95-£12.95.
Short breaks: £34.50, Fri-Sun.
Activity breaks: England's Heritage Break, £36 per night.
Steam Safari, £36.75 per night. Details from hotel.
Credit cards ① ② ③ ⑤

A popular hotel located between Kidderminster and Bewdley with relaxing and comfortable accommodation and many quality attributes.

★★★★55% **Stone Manor** Stone DY10 4PJ (2m SE on A448) ☎ (0562) 777555

Normal price: £46.50. Dinner £16.25-£30.
Short breaks: £47.75 (1990), min 2 nights, Fri-Sun.
Credit cards ① ② ③ ⑤

An attractive mock Tudor hotel standing in 25 acres of woodland and gardens. Most bedrooms are modern and bright, but a few older ones are beginning to show their age.

KINGTON   Hereford & Worcester   Map 3 SO25

★★66% **Burton** (Exec Hotel) Mill Street HR5 3BQ ☎ (0544) 230323

Normal price: £24. Dinner from £12.50.
Short breaks: £32.50, min 2 nights. Single price £44.50.
Activity breaks: Family History Weekends, £95 including talks, demonstrations, practical help sessions and family tree DIY pack. Herefordshire County Archivist and the Curator of the Kington Museum are among the organisers.
Credit cards ① ② ③ ⑤

A combination of friendly service, bright public areas and good bedrooms make this old town centre inn popular with both tourists and business people alike.

LEDBURY   Hereford & Worcester   Map 3 SO73

★★★52% **Feathers** High Street HR8 1DS ☎ (0531) 5266

Normal price: £75.
Short breaks: £45, min 2 nights, Fri-Sun. Single price £50.
Credit cards ① ② ③ ⑤

This High Street hotel retains much of the character of its Elizabethan origins, with sloping floors and exposed beams. The busy bar is popular with locals.

LEOMINSTER   Hereford & Worcester   Map 3 SO45

★★60% **Royal Oak** (Minotels) South Street HR6 8JA ☎ (0568) 2610

Normal price: £19-£21. Dinner £13-£14 & à la carte.
Short breaks: £17.25 excluding dinner. Min 2 nights.
Credit cards ① ② ③ ⑤

A former Georgian coaching inn with simple but comfortable accommodation and informal service. Close to the town centre.

★★★53% **Talbot** (Best Western) West Street HR6 8EP ☎ (0568) 6347

Normal price: £35-£42. Dinner £14-£16 & à la carte
Short breaks: £40, min 2 nights.
✻ Credit cards ① ② ③ ⑤

Parts of this town-centre hotel date back to the 15th century, and much of its original charm and character has been retained despite large scale improvements.

LUGWARDINE   Hereford & Worcester   Map 3 SO53

★★★ ♨ 64% **Longworth Hall** HR1 4DF ☎ (0432) 850223

Normal price: £37.40. Dinner from £13.95.
Short breaks: £39.10. Min 2 nights. Single supplement.
Activity breaks: Games Convention, Sept-Oct. Walking
Weekend, May-Sept. Outdoor Pursuits including Clay
Pigeon Shooting, £7.50 per hour, Horse Riding and Paint
Ball Adventure, £40. Madley Music Festival and Bromyard
Folk Festival. Details from hotel.
Credit cards ③ ⑤

Dating from 1788 and set in its own pleasant grounds, this friendly family-run hotel commands panoramic views of the surrounding countryside.

MALVERN   Hereford & Worcester   Map 3 SO74

★★ **Broomhill** West Malvern Road, West Malvern WR14 4AY (2m W B4232) ☎ (0684) 564367

Normal price: £19.75
Short breaks: £22-£27. Min 2 nights.

This three-storey Victorian house set high on the slopes of the Malvern Hills has fine views and bedrooms with colour television and private, separate bath or shower. Service by the proprietors is friendly and informal. No children under 5 are accommodated.

★★★64% **Colwall Park** (Inter-Hotels) Colwall WR13 6QG (3m SW B4218) ☎ (0684) 40206

Normal price: from £55.
Short breaks: from £45, min 2 nights.
Activity breaks: Painting Courses from £250 (1990) for 5
nights. Morning coffee, lunch, tea and tuition included.
Credit cards ① ② ③

A privately-owned hotel with a relaxing atmosphere making it ideal for a weekend break. The interesting menu makes good use of fresh produce.

★★★63% **Cottage in the Wood** (Consort) Holywell Road, Malvern Wells WR14 4LG (3m S A449)
☎ (0684) 573487

Normal price: from £36. Dinner £16-£25 (1990 price)
Short breaks: from £42.50 including £18 dinner allowance
(£55 single price). Min 2 nights. Not available mid-Mar,
mid-June, Christmas & New Year.
Credit cards ① ③

Set in 7 acres of grounds high in the Malvern Hills, this peaceful owner-run Georgian country house hotel serves traditional English food and all its bedrooms, half of them in annexes, have ensuite facilities and colour television. Christmas breaks are available.

★★★60% **Foley Arms** (Best Western) Worcester Road WR14 4QS ☎ (0684) 573397

Normal price: £72
Short breaks: £45. Min 3 nights, Fri-Sun. £15 single supplement.
Credit cards ①②③⑤

This family-run hotel in the town centre has a comfortable lounge overlooking the River Severn and all its bedrooms, including a family and a no-smoking room, have ensuite facilities and colour television.

★★ **Holdfast Cottage** Welland, Malvern Wells WR13 6NA (4m SE) ☎ (0684) 310288

Normal price: £36-£39. Dinner £18-£24 (1990 price)
Short breaks: £39 (£48 single price). Min 2 nights.
✗ (ex guide dogs) Credit cards ①

There is a cottage atmosphere in this 17th-century country house, which serves locally grown produce and has pretty bedrooms with bath or shower facilities and colour television. Croquet. No children under 10. Christmas breaks are available.

★★ **Malvern Hills** Wynds Point WR13 6DW (4m S A449) ☎ (0684) 40237

Normal price: £57.50. Dinner from £11.
Short breaks: £85 inc buffet lunch and £12 dinner allowance. Min 2 nights. Single supplement.
Credit cards ①③

Situated between Malvern and Ledbury and a good base for exploring the area, this hotel has comfortable bedrooms, including a family room, all with colour television and private bath or shower. Facilities include a garden and solarium. Christmas breaks are available.

★★63% **Mount Pleasant** Belle Vue Terrace WR14 4PZ ☎ (0684) 561837

Normal price: £28.75-£31.50. Dinner £9.95-£10.95 & à la carte.
Short breaks: £37 min 2 nights. Single price £43-£45.
✗ Credit cards ①②③⑤

Set in attractive gardens, this large Georgian house is run in a friendly and informal manner. The small intimate restaurant offers a mainly Spanish theme menu.

★★ **Royal Malvern** (Minotels) Graham Road WR14 2HN ☎ (0684) 563411

Normal price: £27.50. Dinner from £12.75 (1990 price)
Short breaks: £22.50 excluding dinner. Min 2 nights, Fri-Sun. Single supplement.
Credit cards ①②③⑤

A comfortable 18th-century hotel in the town centre with colour television in all bedrooms, most with private bath.

173

MUCH BIRCH   Hereford & Worcester   Map 3 SO53

★★★61% **Pilgrim** HR2 8HJ ☎ (0981) 540742

Normal price: £34. Dinner £16.75 & à la carte
Short breaks: £45. Min 2 nights
Credit cards ① ② ③ ⑤

A former rectory, now a privately-owned hotel, with a modern bedroom extension. Staff are genuinely friendly and welcoming. There are some leisure facilities. Christmas breaks are available.

PERSHORE   Hereford & Worcester   Map 3 SO94

★★ **Avonside** Main Road, Wyre Piddle WR10 2JB (2m NE on B4084) ☎ (0386) 552654

Normal price: £28. Dinner from £13 (1990 price)
Short breaks: £38. Min 2 nights except Christmas.
🦮 Credit cards ① ③

Set by the river in the village of Wyre Piddle, this small, relaxing hotel with a garden and outdoor swimming pool has colour television and ensuite facilities in all bedrooms, which include a few family rooms. Fishing facilities available. No children under 7. Christmas breaks are available.

REDDITCH   Hereford & Worcester   Map 7 SP06

★★★63% **Southcrest** (Best Western) Pool Bank B97 4JG ☎ (0527) 41511

Normal price: £25-£35. Dinner £11-£11.50 & à la carte
Short breaks: £34 including set-price dinner or £11 dinner allowance. Fri-Sun. Single supplement.
Credit cards ① ② ③ ⑤

Set in 7 acres of grounds, this much extended former country house half a mile south of the town centre has well-equipped comfortable bedrooms, all with private bathrooms and colour television and including two family rooms and two with four-poster beds.

ROSS-ON-WYE   Hereford & Worcester   Map 3 SO62

QQ **Arches Country House** Walford Road HR9 5PT ☎ (0989) 63348

Normal price: £14.50
Short breaks: £13.50 excluding dinner. Min 2 nights.

On the southern outskirts of the town, this attractive modern detached house set in half an acre of lawned garden provides friendly service and comfortable bedrooms with colour television and wash basins, some of them family rooms or having private shower.

★ **Bridge House** Wilton HR9 6AA (adjacent A40/A49 junc) ☎ (0989) 62655

Normal price: £24-£25. Dinner from £8.95 & à la carte
Short breaks: £30-£32. Min 2 nights, exc bank hols. £35-£37
for single occupancy.
🛪 Credit cards ① ③

This small and friendly family-run hotel with a garden offers wholesome meals and has colour television and private bath or shower in all bedrooms, including one with a four-poster bed. Christmas breaks are available.

QQ Brookfield House Ledbury Road HR9 7AT ☎ (0989) 62188

Normal price: £13.50
Short breaks: £12.50 excluding dinner. Min 3 nights, exc
Bank Hols.
Credit cards ① ③

This large early 18th-century house is hospitably run and provides comfortable accommodation with all bedrooms having wash basins and colour television and some private bath or shower. Breakfast available only.

★★★61% **Chase** (Consort) Gloucester Road HR9 5LH ☎ (0989) 763161

Normal price: £46.50. Dinner £15 & à la carte (1990 price)
Short breaks: £55 including early morning tea, newspaper
and afternoon tea. Min 2 nights, (except Christmas/New
Year and Cheltenham race week).
🛪 (ex guide dogs) Credit cards ① ② ③ ⑤

Set in 11 acres of grounds on the outskirts of town, this former country house provides good service and comfortable accommodation, with all bedrooms, including two family rooms and two with four-poster beds, having private bath and colour television. Christmas breaks are available.

★★58% **Chasedale** Walford Road HR9 5PQ ☎ (0989) 62423

Normal price: £25
Short breaks: £34 including set-menu dinner or £10.50
dinner allowance. Min 2 nights. Single supplement.
Credit cards ① ③ ④ ⑤

This friendly family-run hotel, in a detached house with pleasant gardens on the southern outskirts of town, has private bath and colour television in all bedrooms, which include some family rooms. Christmas breaks are available.

★★ 🛦 71% **Glewstone Court** Glewstone HR9 6AW ☎ (098984) 367

Normal price: from £32. Dinner from £17.
Short breaks: £44. Min 2 nights.
Activity breaks: Hot Air Ballooning and Multi Activity
Breaks. Details from hotel.
Credit cards ① ② ③

A delightful hotel, transformed since 1987 from delapidation to elegance and comfort. The imaginative meals make the most of local produce.

★★66% **Hunsdon Manor** Gloucester Road, Weston-under-Penyard HR9 7PE (2m E A40)
☎ (0989) 62748 & 63376

Normal price: £22. Dinner £9.50 (1990 price)
Short breaks: £32. Not available Gold Cup week in March.
Supplement for single occupancy.
Credit cards ① ② ③ ⑤

Standing in two acres of gardens, this manor house dating from the 16th century offers a varied menu in the restaurant. It offers bedrooms with colour television and modern amenities, most with private bath. There's also a solarium and sauna.

★★66% **Orles Barn** Wilton HR9 6AE ☎ (0989) 62155

Normal price: £25-£35. Dinner £8.25-£9.25 & à la carte
(1990 price)
Short breaks: £35. Min 2 nights. £10 single supplement.
Credit cards ① ② ③ ⑤

This small family-run hotel with a garden that includes a swimming pool serves home-cooked meals and has children's facilities. All bedrooms, several of them family rooms, have colour television and most have private bathroom or shower.

★★★ ⬥ 65% **Pengethley Manor** (Best Western) HR9 6LL (4m N on A49 Hereford rd) ☎ (098987) 211

Normal price: £50. Dinner from £18.50.
Short breaks: £60, min 2 nights. Single supplement.
Activity breaks: Romantic Break, £170 for 2 nights including champagne and flowers.
Credit cards [1] [2] [3] [5]

This country house hotel is set in attractive, extensive grounds with superb views across the beautiful Herefordshire countryside. Service is professional and hospitable.

★★★65% **Royal** (Trusthouse Forte) Palace Pound HR9 5HZ ☎ (0989) 65105

Normal price: £55. Dinner from £14.
Short breaks: £50, min 2 nights. Single supplement.
Activity breaks: Bridge Weekends, £110. Fly Fishing Weekends, £200. Heritage Weekends, £150. Details from hotel.
Credit cards [1] [2] [3] [4] [5]

The Royal was built in 1837, and occupied a prime elevated position with views across the horseshoe bend of the River Wye.

ST OWEN'S CROSS   *Hereford & Worcester*   Map 3 SO52

FH QQQ Aberhall HR2 8LL ☎ (098987) 256

Normal price: £25-£29 (room).
Short breaks: £24-£28, Nov-Feb.
🕱

Set in the Wye Valley with some superb views, this 17th-century farmhouse is ideal for energetic visitors who can use the hard tennis court, or enjoy the basement games room.

SHRAWLEY   *Hereford & Worcester*   Map 7 SO86

★★★64% **Lenchford** Worcester WR6 6TB ☎ (0905) 620229

Normal price: £55. Dinner £12-£17.50 & à la carte.
Short breaks: £35, min 2 nights, Fri-Sun; includes £11 dinner allowance.
🕱 Credit cards [1] [2] [3] [5]

This family-run hotel enjoys an idyllic setting on the banks of the River Severn, in a quiet rural location six miles north of Worcester. Several of its spacious bedrooms have balconies with river views, and the service is relaxed and informal. There is a heated outdoor pool, and fishing is available.

SYMONDS YAT (EAST)   *Hereford & Worcester*   Map 3 SO51

★★65% **Royal** HR9 6JL ☎ (0600) 890238

Normal price: £39.50 including dinner.
Short breaks: £34.50, min 2 nights, Sun-Thurs, except Bank Hols.
🕱 Credit cards [1] [2] [3]

This peaceful hotel in a superb location on the banks of the River Wye is ideally placed for touring the Wye Valley.

SYMONDS YAT (WEST)   *Hereford & Worcester*   Map 3 SO51

★★64% **Paddocks** HR9 6BL ☎ (0600) 890246

Normal price: £28.50. Dinner £9.20-£17.45 à la carte
Short breaks: £40, min 2 nights.
Credit cards [1] [3] [5]

This large hotel, set in one of the most popular and picturesque parts of the Wye Valley, is easily reached from the A40.

QQ Woodlea Ross-on-Wye HR9 6BL ☎ (0600) 890206

Normal price: From £19.75.
Short breaks: £26-£28.75 (en suite), min 2 nights. Midweek only Easter-end Oct, excluding Bank Holidays.
Credit cards [1] [3]

This pleasant and cosy house is quietly situated at the end of a lane above the Wye rapids, with lovely views across the valley to wooded hills. Many of the bedrooms have ensuite facilities, and there is a congenial bar.

ULLINGSWICK   Hereford & Worcester   Map 3 SO54

GH QQQQ Steppes HR1 3JG ☎ (0432) 820424

Normal price: £27.50.
Short breaks: £39, min 2 nights.

The Steppes is a charming small hotel in a tiny hamlet with plenty of character from the dining room to the fascinating cellar bar. The appetising gourmet menu changes daily.

UPTON-UPON-SEVERN   Hereford & Worcester   Map 3 SO84

GH QQQ Pool House WR8 0PA ☎ (06846) 2151

Normal price: £23.50.
Short breaks: £29.50, min 2 nights, Apr-May.
✶ Credit cards ① ③

A lovely Queen Anne residence with a delightful garden area leading down to the River Severn. Accommodation is attractive and spacious.

★★★56% **White Lion** (Exec Hotel) High Street WR8 0HJ ☎ (06846) 2551

Normal price: £46. Dinner from £13.50 & à la carte.
Short breaks: £40. Single price £49.
Credit cards ① ② ③ ⑤

A former 16th-century coaching inn with many original features such as beams and sloping floors. An intimate restaurant serves a range of traditional dishes.

VOWCHURCH   Hereford & Worcester   Map 3 SO33

GH QQQQ Croft Country House HR2 0QE ☎ (0981) 550226

Normal price: £40 room and breakfast.
Short breaks: from £59 for 2 nights, Oct-Mar.
✶ Credit cards ① ③

A delightful small country house dating from the 18th century, and furnished with comfort in mind. Lovely gardens with summerhouse and lily pond are a feature.

WHITCHURCH   Hereford & Worcester   Map 3 SO51

INN Q Crown HR9 6DB ☎ (0600) 890234

Normal price: £22.50.
Short breaks: £45-£50 for 2 nights, £66-£70 for 3 nights.
Single supplement.
Credit cards ① ② ③ ⑤

A large character inn offering a range of bar meals both at lunchtime and in the evening. Bedrooms are modest but well-equipped.

GH QQ Portland HR9 6DB ☎ (0600) 890757

Normal price: £16.
Short breaks: £23.50, min 2 nights. Single supplement.

The Portland guest house is ideal for touring as it is close to Ross-on-Wye, Goodrich and Symonds Yat.

WHITNEY-ON-WYE   Hereford & Worcester   Map 3 SO24

INN QQQQ Rhydspence HR3 6EU (2m W A438) ☎ (04973) 262

Normal price: £23-£25. Dinner £10-£20 à la carte.
Short breaks: £37, min 2 nights, Sun-Thurs. Oct-Mar.
✶ Credit cards ① ② ③

A lovely 14th-century inn set exactly on the border between England and Wales, with congenial bars and a very attractive restaurant.

WORCESTER Hereford & Worcester Map 3 SO85

★★★71% **Fownes** City Walls Road WR1 2AP ☎ (0905) 613151

Normal price: £53.50. Dinner £15.95.
Short breaks: £32 excluding dinner. Min 2 nights, Fri-Sun.
Single price £42.
Activity breaks: Elgar Trail and Cider Trail Breaks. Details
from hotel.
✂ Credit cards ① ② ③ ⑤

This former glove factory offers good-size bedrooms, and the restaurant and 'all day' brasserie allow a choice of eating style.

★★★56% **Giffard** (Trusthouse Forte) High Street WR1 2QR ☎ (0905) 726262

Normal price: £38.
Short breaks: £45, min 1 night.
Credit cards ① ② ③ ④ ⑤

This busy modern hotel is located in the city centre. The restaurant offers good views of Worcester Cathedral, and there is a coffee shop for light meals and refreshments.

★★★69% **Star** (Crown & Raven) Foregate Street WR1 1EA ☎ (0905) 24308

Normal price: £34.65. Dinner from £11.55 & à la carte
Short breaks: £46, min 2 nights, Fri-Sun.
Credit cards ① ② ③

This 16th-century inn has recently been extensively improved, and now offers three luxurious 'executive' rooms, and two rooms suitable for disabled guests.

★★63% **Ye Olde Talbot** (Lansbury) Friar Street WR1 2NA ☎ (0905) 23573

Normal price: £38. Dinner from £14 & à la carte
Short breaks: £38, min 2 nights, Fri-Sun.
✂ Credit cards ① ② ③ ⑤

A warm and pleasant atmosphere pervades this 13th-century coaching inn, and the staff are particularly caring and friendly.

▪ HERTFORDSHIRE ▪

BUSHEY Hertfordshire Map 4 TQ19

★★★58% **Hilton National** Elton Way, Watford Bypass WD2 8HA ☎ (0923) 35881

Normal price: £55 (room). Dinner £15.75-£17.50.
Short breaks: £40 excluding dinner. Min 2 nights, Thu-Sun,
must include Sat.
Activity breaks: Chelsea Flower Show, Horse of the Year
Show, and Patchwork Breaks. Details from hotel. Gliding
Breaks, £190 for 2 nights. Other breaks, details from hotel.
Credit cards ① ② ③ ⑤

A conference centre and leisure complex are features of this large, modern hotel. Bedrooms are being refurbished, and the restaurant and bar are due to be extended.

CHIPPERFIELD Hertfordshire Map 4 TL00

★★66% **Two Brewers Inn** (Trusthouse Forte) The Common WD4 9BS ☎ King's Langley (0923) 265266

Normal price: £50. Dinner £15.50 & à la carte
Short breaks: £47. Min 2 nights, Fri-Sun
Credit cards ① ② ③ ④ ⑤

A charming and cosy 17th-century inn overlooking the village green offering well equipped, modern accommodation. All the bedrooms have private facilities and colour television, with some rooms for non-smokers. There is a special Christmas programme.

HARPENDEN   Hertfordshire   Map 4 TL11

★★★66% **Harpenden Moat House** (Queens Moat) 18 Southdown Road AL5 1PE ☎ (0582) 764111
Closed 26-31 Dec

Normal price: £63-£95 (room).
Short breaks: £47.25 for 2 people. Min 2 nights, Fri-Sun.
£15 single supplement.
Credit cards ①②③⑤

Dating back to the Georgian period, this hotel offers modern bedrooms with private bathrooms and colour television. Two rooms have four-poster beds, and others are for non-smokers. There are some leisure amenities.

HATFIELD   Hertfordshire   Map 4 TL20

★★★57% **Comet** (Embassy) 301 St Albans Road West AL10 9RH (junc A1/A414) ☎ (0707) 265411
Restricted service Xmas

Normal price: £42.95 with dinner.
Short breaks: £31.50. Min 2 nights, Fri-Sun.

The hotel provides accommodation in bedrooms which are generally spacious. Most rooms have private bathrooms, and all have colour television. There is a popular carvery restaurant.

HEMEL HEMPSTEAD   Hertfordshire   Map 4 TL00

★★★55% **Post House** (Trusthouse Forte) Breakspear Way HP2 4UA ☎ (0442) 51122

Normal price: £94 room only. Dinner £16 & à la carte
Short breaks: £27 excluding dinner. Fri-Sun
Credit cards ①②③④⑤

Situated about two miles from the town centre, this hotel offers ensuite bedrooms with colour television, with rooms set aside for non-smokers. A special Christmas programme is available.

HERTFORD   Hertfordshire   Map 4 TL31

★★★61% **White Horse** (Trusthouse Forte) Hertingfordbury SG14 2LB (1m W on A414)
☎ (0992) 586791

Normal price: £50. Dinner £13.95-£15.95 & à la carte
Short breaks: £45. Min 2 nights, Fri-Sun
Credit cards ①②③④⑤

This is a pleasant hotel with a warm atmosphere. Bedrooms provide a good standard of modern accommodation and the attractive restaurant offers a well balanced menu. Christmas breaks are available.

HITCHIN   Hertfordshire   Map 4 TL12

★★★55% **Blakemore Thistle** (Mount Charlotte (TS)) Little Wymondley SG4 7JJ (3m SE A602)
☎ (0438) 355821

Normal price: £45.25. Dinner from £13.50 & à la carte
Short breaks: £40 excluding dinner. No single supplement
at weekends
Credit cards ①②③④⑤

Originally a Georgian house, this popular hotel has been extended to provide modern bedroom accommodation. There is a games room and outdoor heated pool.

REDBOURN   Hertfordshire   Map 4 TL11

★★★60% **Aubrey Park** Hemel Hempstead Road AL3 7AF ☎ (058285) 2105

Normal price: £45-£50 excluding breakfast
Short breaks: £50 including dinner. Fri-Sun. £5 single supplement.
Credit cards ①②③④⑤

Set in 6 acres of grounds which includes a swimming pool, this pleasant hotel has a choice of traditional and international style restaurants, a spacious bar and ensuite bedrooms with colour television and all modern facilities.

ST ALBANS   Hertfordshire   Map 4 TL10

★★★69% **Noke Thistle** (Mount Charlotte (TS)) Watford Road AL2 3DS (2.75m S at junct A405/B4630) ☎ (0727) 54252

Normal price: £50.25. Dinner from £17.50 & à la carte
Short breaks: £45 excluding dinner. No single supplement at weekends. Credit cards ①②③④⑤

A comfortable, elegant hotel with modern bedrooms and attentive staff. Enterprising French and English cuisine is served in the restaurant.

STEVENAGE   Hertfordshire   Map 4 TL22

★★★60% **Hertford Park** Danestrete SG1 1EJ ☎ (0438) 350661

Normal price: £38. Dinner from £10.75.
Short breaks: £35, min 2 nights, Fri-Sun.
Credit cards ①②③④⑤

Situated in the heart of the town centre, this large modern hotel offers functional, well equipped accommodation. There is a pleasant restaurant on the first floor, and an open plan bar.

TRING   Hertfordshire   Map 4 SP91

★★62% **Rose & Crown** (Lansbury) High Street HP23 5AH ☎ (044282) 4071

Normal price: £44. Dinner from £13.25 & à la carte
Short breaks: £34 excluding dinner, Fri-Sun.
✕ Credit cards ①②③⑤

The variety of accommodation at this popular coaching inn ranges from four-posters to more compact singles. The atmosphere throughout is lively.

WARE   Hertfordshire   Map 5 TL31

INN QQQ Feathers (Berni/Chef & Brewer) Wadesmill SG1 2TN ☎ (0920) 462606

Normal price: £30.50. Dinner £8-£15.
Short breaks: £27 excluding dinner, Min 2 nights.
✕ Credit cards ①②③⑤

The Feathers has a busy and very popular bar and Berni carvery. The bedrooms are all new and attractive, with co-ordinated decor and many extras.

WATFORD   Hertfordshire   Map 4 TQ19

★★★63% **Dean Park** (Queens Moat) 30-40 St Albans Road WD1 1RN ☎ (0923) 229212

Normal price: £42.50. Dinner £14 & à la carte
Short breaks: £40, min 2 nights, Fri-Sun (1990 prices)
✕ Credit cards ①②③④⑤

A modern purpose-built hotel with a pleasant first floor cocktail bar and restaurant offering both à la carte and table d'hôte menus.

◼ HUMBERSIDE ◼

BARMBY MOOR   Humberside   Map 8 SE74

GH QQQQ Barmby Moor Country Hull Road YO4 5EZ (2m W off A1079) ☎ (0759) 302700
Normal price: £25
Short breaks: £34. Single £50. Mon-Sat, Jan-Xmas
🦅 Credit cards 1 2 3

A converted and restored 17th-century coaching inn with a pleasant mixture of modern and antique features. The original stables and stableyard now contain a heated swimming pool. All four bedrooms have ensuite shower rooms and colour television.

BEVERLEY   Humberside   Map 8 TA03

★★★59% **Beverley Arms** (Trusthouse Forte) North Bar Within HU17 8DD ☎ (0482) 869241
Normal price: £52. Dinner fr £14.95.
Short breaks: £47. Min 2 nights, Thu-Mon.
Activity breaks: Treasures of Yesteryear – Sculpture and Furniture. £140 for 2 nights including lectures and presentations.
Credit cards 1 2 3 4 5

A modernised coaching inn with functional, up-to-date bedrooms and traditional public rooms.

BRIDLINGTON   Humberside   Map 8 TA16

GH QQ Bay Ridge Summerfield Road YO15 3LF ☎ (0262) 673425
Feb-Oct
Normal price: £18.50.
Short breaks: £18. Min 3 nights.

A spacious, well-designed conversion of two semi-detached houses close to South Bay, providing fourteen bedrooms. Most have ensuite facilities and all have colour television. Guests can play bar billiards and darts.

★★67% **Monarch** (Consort) South Marine Drive YO15 3JJ ☎ (0262) 67447
Closed 18 Dec-7 Jan
Normal price: £27.50. Dinner £12-£14 & à la carte
Short breaks: £35-£38.50, single £40-£43. Min 2 nights
Credit cards 1 2 3 5

This comfortable friendly sea-front hotel offers very good value menus. All the bedrooms have colour television, most have ensuite facilities and there are some family rooms. The hotel has special facilities for children.

★★★66% **Expanse** North Marine Drive YO15 2LS ☎ (0262) 675347

Normal price: £32. Dinner £11.
Short breaks: £37. Min 2 nights.
Activity breaks: Arts Festival Break, from £37 per night,
4-11 May. In conjunction with Bridlington Arts Festival.
✈

Comfortable bedrooms, several cosy lounges and particularly friendly service are the attractions of this large seafront hotel. See advertisement on p181.

★★66% **New Revelstoke** 1-3 Flamborough Road YO15 2HY ☎ (0262) 672362

Normal price: £60 room with breakfast. Dinner £10.50 & à la carte
Short breaks: £60 for two people. Min 2 nights, Nov-May, except Bank Holidays (1990 prices)
✈

Situated close to the town's amenities and North Sands this hotel has generally spacious bedrooms. Most have private bath or shower rooms, and all have colour television.

DRIFFIELD, GREAT   Humberside   Map 8 TA05

★★★67% **Bell** (Best Western) 46 Market Place, YO25 7AP ☎ (0377) 46661

Normal price: £75-£82.50 room and breakfast. Dinner £12-£15.
Short breaks: £60, including morning tea and newspaper. Min 2 nights, Fri-Sun.
Activity breaks: Nautilus Fitness Weekend, £150 for 2 nights. Supervised individual exercise programme with use of leisure and relaxation facilities.
✈ Credit cards ① ② ③ ⑤

A carefully modernised coaching inn with its historic character and atmosphere preserved. Accommodation is comfortable with appealing decor.

HULL   Humberside   Map 8 TA02

★★63% **Pearson Park** Pearson Park HU5 2TQ ☎ (0482) 43043
Closed 24 Dec-1 Jan

Normal price: £27. Dinner £9 & à la carte
Short breaks: £28.50, Thu-Mon

In a peaceful situation in a well-kept public park, just one mile from the city centre, this hotel offers comfortable bedrooms, most with private facilities and colour television.

★★★57% **Royal** (Consort) Ferensway HU1 3UF ☎ (0482) 25087

Normal price: £29.25. Dinner £11.75-£14.75 & à la carte
Short breaks: £34. Min 2 nights, Fri-Sun

This is a city centre hotel with spacious public rooms. Each bedroom has a private bathroom and colour television, and there are rooms for families and non-smokers. The hotel has its own gymnasium. Christmas breaks are available.

LITTLE WEIGHTON   Humberside   Map 8 SE93

★★★ ⚓ 66% **Rowley Manor** Rowley Road HU20 3XR ☎ (0482) 848248

Normal price: £46. Dinner £14.95-£16.50 & à la carte
Short breaks: £44, min 2 nights, Thurs-Sun.
Credit cards ① ② ③ ⑤

Tranquilly set amid attractive gardens which include a croquet lawn, the hotel offers friendly, courteous service and a range of interesting menus.

SCUNTHORPE *South Humberside* *Map 8 SE81*

★★★60% **Wortley House** Rowland Road DN16 1SU ☎ (0724) 842223

Normal price: £35. Dinner from £9 and à la carte.
Short breaks: £25, min 2 nights, Fri-Sun. £10 single supplement.
Credit cards [1] [2] [3] [4] [5]

The large house, suitably converted and extended, stands near the town centre; spacious public areas of comfort and style are complemented by up-to-date bedrooms.

SLEDMERE *Humberside* *Map 8 SE96*

Q Triton Driffield YO25 0XQ ☎ (0377) 86644

Normal price: £28 with en suite facilities, £22 without. Dinner from £7 & à la carte.
Short breaks: £46 with en suite facilities, £34 without. Min 2 nights.
Credit cards [1] [3] [5]

A period inn offering good value accommodation in this attractive estate village.

SUTTON UPON DERWENT *Humberside* *Map 8 SE74*

★★63% **Old Rectory** YO4 5BX ☎ (090485) 548

Normal price: £21.
Short breaks: £29. Min 2 nights.
Credit cards [1]

A former rectory offering peace and quiet and freshly prepared meals. All the bedrooms have colour television, and some have ensuite showers.

WILLERBY *Humberside* *Map 8 TA03*

★★★75% **Grange Park** (Best Western) Main Street HU10 6EA ☎ (0482) 656488

Normal price: £35.50 Fri-Sun, £43 Mon-Thu. Dinner £15 and à la carte.
Short breaks: £42.50, min 2 nights, Fri-Sun. Single supplement.
Credit cards [1] [2] [3] [5]

Extensive leisure facilities and a creche are popular features of this very comfortable hotel. The intimate French restaurant and more formal Italian one offer good value meals.

KENT

ASHFORD *Kent* *Map 5 TR04*

GH QQ Downsview Willesborough Road, Kennington TN24 9QP ☎ (0233) 621953

Normal price: £28
Short breaks: £60 for 2 people. Single supplement £5. Min 2 nights, Fri-Mon.
Credit cards [1] [2] [3] [5]

This family run hotel stands in mature grounds with views across the Stour Valley to the North Downs. Most of the bedrooms have ensuite facilities, and all have colour television.

★★★★(Red) **Eastwell Manor** (Queens Moat) (Prestige) Eastwell Park, Boughton Lees TN25 4HR ☎ (0233) 635751

Normal price: £110-£215 room with breakfast. Dinner from £22
Short breaks: £97. Min 2 nights (except Christmas and New Year)

Surrounded by extensive grounds, this imposing country house hotel offers a choice of French and English cuisine in the elegant dining room. Leisure amenities include a billiards room, croquet and tennis. The twenty-three elegant bedrooms all have private bathroom and colour television.

BROADSTAIRS Kent Map 5 TR36

★★65% Castlemere Western Esplanade CT10 1TD ☎ (0843) 61566

Normal price: £45. Dinner £12
Short breaks: £38.50. Min 2 nights, Thu-Sun
Credit cards ① ③

A long-established, family-run hotel facing the sea with an attractive restaurant, good bar and lounge. Most bedrooms have ensuite facilities, all have colour television and there are family rooms. A special Christmas programme is provided.

GH QQ Devonhurst 13 Eastern Esplanade CT10 1DR ☎ (0843) 63010

Normal price: £17.50
Short breaks: £15.50 excluding dinner. Min 3 nights, Oct-May
✶ (ex guide dogs)

This family-run hotel extends a warm welcome to guests, with a friendly atmosphere and comfortable rooms. The first floor lounge has a balcony affording magnificent views of the sea and coastline. Children under 5 are not accommodated.

★★67% Royal Albion (Consort) Albion Street CT10 1LO ☎ (0843) 68071

Normal price: £47 including dinner
Short breaks: £43. Min 2 nights
✶ (ex guide dogs) Credit cards ① ② ③ ⑤

A cosy family-run hotel providing friendly service. Each bedroom has a colour television and ensuite facilities, and one room has a four-poster bed. There is a special Christmas programme.

CANTERBURY Kent Map 5 TR15

★★60% Canterbury 71 New Dover Road CT1 3DZ ☎ (02274) 450551

Normal price: £29. Dinner from £11.50 and à la carte
Short breaks: £30-£31. £10 single supplement. Min 2 nights, Oct-Jun
Credit cards ① ② ③ ⑤

A pleasant Georgian-style hotel with a friendly atmosphere. Each bedroom has an ensuite bath or shower room and colour television and there are family rooms.

★★★54% Chaucer (Trusthouse Forte) Ivy Lane CT1 1TU ☎ (0227) 464427

Normal price: £100 (room only). Dinner £13-£14.
Short breaks: £52, min 2 nights, except Jul & Aug, and mid week.
Activity breaks: Arts & Antiques. £134 Feb 22-24. £150 Nov. Heritage Breaks, £180, May-Oct. Details from hotel.
Credit cards ① ② ③ ④ ⑤

A large hotel, mostly rebuilt since the war, offering compact bedrooms and some larger double rooms. The restaurant is spacious, and there is a pleasant lounge bar.

GH QQQ Ebury New Dover Road CT1 3DX ☎ (0227) 768433
Closed 25 Dec-14 Jan

Normal price: £28. Dinner £10
Short breaks: £33 including £10 dinner allowance. Min 2 nights, Mon-Sat
Credit cards ① ② ③

A large Victorian building in two acres of grounds. All the cheerfully decorated, spacious bedrooms have ensuite facilities and colour television and there are family rooms. The hotel has an indoor heated swimming pool and spa bath.

★★★60% Falstaff (Lansbury) St Dunstans Street CT2 8AF ☎ (0227) 462138

Normal price: £85 (room). Dinner from £11 and à la carte
Short breaks: £48, min 2 nights, Fri-Sun
Credit cards ① ② ③ ⑤

A skilfully-modernised 16th-century coaching inn near the Westgate Tower offering ensuite bedrooms with colour television. There are rooms for families and non-smokers and some rooms are furnished with four-poster beds. There is a special Christmas programme.

GH QQQ Magnolia House 36 St Dunstan's Terrace CT2 8AX ☎ (0277) 765121

Normal price: £40-£48 room with breakfast
Short breaks: £36-£40 for two excluding dinner. Single £20-£24 bed and breakfast. Min 2 nights, Nov-Feb
🖾

A friendly, family-run Georgian house set in a quiet street close to the Westgate Tower. All bedrooms are 'no-smoking' and some have ensuite facilities.

GH QQQ Pointers London Road CT2 8LR ☎ (0227) 456846
Closed Xmas and New Year

Normal price: £21-£26
Short breaks: £29-£31. Min 2 nights

Situated only a few minutes' walk from the city centre and cathedral is this family-run Georgian hotel. All the bedrooms have ensuite bath or shower rooms and colour television.

CRANBROOK   Kent   Map 5 TQ73

★★ 🖾 70% **Kennel Holt Country House** Goudhurst Road TN17 2PT ☎ (0580) 712032

Normal price: £86.25 room. Dinner £19.75 & à la carte
Short breaks: £47.50, includes afternoon tea. Min 3 nights, Nov-Apr (ex Xmas & Easter)
Credit cards ①③

Set in six acres of gardens with its own duck pond and paddock, this Elizabethan manor house offers individually furnished bedrooms with ensuite facilities and colour television. Two rooms have four-poster beds. Leisure amenities include mini golf and croquet. There is a special Christmas programme. Children under six are not accommodated.

DOVER   Kent   Map 5 TR34

GH QQ Castle House 10 Castle Hill Road CT16 1QW ☎ (0304) 201656

Normal price: £24-£34 room with breakfast
Short breaks: £42 2 nights, £60 3 nights for 2 excluding dinner. Sun-Wed, Nov-Feb
🖾 Credit cards ③

This cosy family-run guesthouse is in a convenient position, close to all amenities. All bedrooms have colour television, and some have ensuite showers.

GH QQQ Number One 1 Castle Street CT16 1QH ☎ (0304) 202007

Normal price: £30-£35 room with breakfast
Short breaks: £26-£30 room with breakfast. Min 2 nights, Jan-May & Sep-Dec

Conveniently situated for the town, ferries and hoverport, this is a friendly guesthouse with a cosy atmosphere. Most of the bedrooms have ensuite facilities, and all have colour television.

★★★54% **White Cliffs** (Waterloo Crescent) Marine Parade, CT17 9BW ☎ (0304) 203633
Closed 24-26 Dec

Normal price: £35-£40. Dinner £8-£11 & à la carte
Short breaks: £30-£36. Min 2 nights

A long-established hotel offering a choice of bedrooms, some with uninterrupted sea views; all have ensuite facilities and colour television.

DYMCHURCH   Kent   Map 5 TR12

GH QQ Chantry Sycamore Gardens TN29 0LA ☎ (0303) 873137

Normal price: £15
Short breaks: £22. Min 2 nights, Jan-Apr & Oct-Dec

This guesthouse has comfortable bedrooms, some with ensuite facilities, and a pleasant television lounge. Not suitable for children under three.

FOLKESTONE   Kent   Map 5 TR23

★★★63% **Clifton** (Consort) The Leas CT20 2EB ☎ (0303) 851231

Normal price: £32.50. Dinner £14.50-£15.95 & à la carte
Short breaks: £36.50-£41.50. Min 2 nights

Situated in a commanding cliff-top location, this hotel offers bedrooms with ensuite facilities and colour television. There is a solarium and games room, and a special Christmas programme is available. No parking on the premises.

GOUDHURST   Kent   Map 5 TQ73

★★71% **Star & Eagle** High Street TN17 1AL ☎ (0580) 211512

Normal price: £33-£40. Dinner £15-£20 & à la carte
Short breaks: £22.50-£27.50 excluding dinner. Min 2 nights, Mon-Thu, Oct-Mar.
Credit cards ① ② ③

Parts of this attractive hotel date back to the 14th century. Bedrooms are particularly well furnished, all have colour television and most are ensuite; two have four-poster beds. There is a special Christmas programme.

HADLOW   Kent   Map 5 TQ65

★★62% **Leavers Manor** Goose Green TN11 0JH ☎ (0732) 851442

Normal price: £42. Dinner £10
Short breaks: £33. Min 2 nights, Fri-Sun (ex Easter & Xmas)
🕊 (ex guide dogs) Credit cards ① ② ③ ⑤

A charming Georgian house providing comfortable accommodation, including some rooms in a new bedroom wing, and well-cooked meals.

HAWKHURST   Kent   Map 5 TQ73

★★68% **Tudor Court** (Best Western) Rye Road TN18 5DA ☎ (0580) 752312

Normal price: £41-£43.50. Dinner from £12.50 & à la carte
Short breaks: £46.50. Single £58.50. Min 2 nights

This charming hotel has a pleasant welcoming atmosphere. Accommodation, which includes five recently-built bedrooms, provides modern facilities and comforts. There are leisure amenities, and Christmas breaks are available. See advertisement under Surrey.

HYTHE   Kent   *Map 5 TR13*

★★★★66% **Hythe Imperial** (Best Western) Princes Parade CT21 6AE ☎ (0303) 267441

Normal price: £110 room. Dinner £17-£20 & à la carte
Short breaks: £50. Min 2 nights, Fri-Sun (ex Bank Holidays).
🕭 (ex guide dogs) Credit cards ① ② ③ ⑤

A large seafront hotel offering an extensive range of sports and leisure amenities. The comfortable bedrooms are all ensuite with colour television. There are special facilities for children, and Christmas breaks are available.

★★★60% **Stade Court** (Best Western) West Parade ☎ (0303) 268263

Normal price: £75 room. Dinner from £14.50 & à la carte
Short breaks: £85. Single £45. Min 2 nights
Credit cards ① ② ③ ⑤

In a pleasant seafront location this hotel features a range of accommodation from family suites to singles; some rooms even have their own small sun lounges. There are extensive leisure amenities and Christmas breaks are available.

LARKFIELD   Kent   *Map 5 TQ65*

★★★60% **Larkfield** (Trusthouse Forte) London Road ME20 6HJ ☎ (0732) 846858

Normal price: £55. Dinner £14.50.
Short breaks: £43, min 2 nights, Thu-Sun.
Activity breaks: Golf Breaks, £110 for 2 nights. Heritage Breaks, £150 for 2 nights. Details from hotel.
Credit cards ① ② ③ ④ ⑤

A skilfully extended modern hotel with a choice of bedrooms, and good food served in the restaurant by friendly staff.

MAIDSTONE   Kent   *Map 5 TQ75*

★★ **Grange Moor** St Michael's Road ME16 8BS (off A26) ☎ (0622) 677623 & 57222

Normal price: £62. Dinner £10 and à la carte (1990 price)
Short breaks: £42. Min 2 nights, Fri-Sun
Credit cards ① ③

This friendly family-run hotel has a Tudor-style restaurant and compact but attractive bedrooms, including family rooms. All have ensuite facilities and colour television.

MARGATE   Kent   *Map 5 TR57*

QQ **Beachcomber** 3-4 Royal Esplanade, Westbrook CT9 5DL ☎ (0843) 221616

Normal price: £15.50.
Short breaks: £21.85. Min 4 nights.
🕭

Overlooking the bay, this friendly guesthouse has a cosy bar and charming bedrooms, including a few family rooms, with hot and cold water facilities.

QQQ **Greswolde** 20 Surrey Road, Cliftonville CT9 2LA ☎ (0843) 223956

Normal price: £14.50
Short breaks: £13 excluding dinner. Min 2 nights, 1 Oct-15 Mar.
🕭 Credit cards ① ③

This small, well-run guesthouse has colour television in all bedrooms, including 2 family rooms. Most have private shower.

RAMSGATE   Kent   *Map 5 TR36*

QQ **St Hilary** 21 Crescent Road CT11 9QU ☎ (0843) 591427

Normal price: £12-£16
Short breaks: £10-£12 excluding dinner. Min 2 nights, Jan-Jun, Sep-Dec. £13 for single occupancy.
🕭 Credit cards ①

This cheerful guest house in a residential area has a basement dining room and bright compact bedrooms, including family rooms. All have wash basins and some have private shower.

ROCHESTER Kent *Map 5 TQ76*

★★★75% **Bridgewood Manor** (Best Western) Bridgewood Roundabout, Maidstone Road ME5 9AX
☎ (0634) 201333

Normal price: £90 room and breakfast. Dinner from £17.50.
Short breaks: £45, min 2 nights, Fri-Sun.
Activity breaks: Biggles Break, £125. Summer Ski
Weekend, £125 May-Sept. Romantic Weekend, £120.
Details from hotel.
Credit cards ① ② ③ ⑤

A quantity of intricate old woodwork has been used in the design of this purpose-built hotel which overlooks a courtyard. Public areas include leisure facilities.

SEVENOAKS Kent *Map 5 TQ55*

★★66% **Royal Oak** Upper High Street TN14 5PG ☎ (0732) 451109

Normal price: £78. Dinner from £16.50.
Short breaks: £42.50, min 2 nights, Mon-Thur.
Credit cards ① ② ③ ⑤

Originally a coaching inn, this popular hotel has been tastefully refurbished to provide a choice of individually styled bedrooms, comfortable modern lounges, a Victorian bar and an elegant restaurant. Standards of cuisine are high, and service is friendly and attentive.

TUNBRIDGE WELLS (ROYAL) Kent *Map 5 TQ53*

★★62% **Royal Wells Inn** Mount Ephraim TN4 8BE ☎ (0892) 511188

Normal price: £37.50. Dinner £14.50-£16 & à la carte
Short breaks: £50, min 2 nights, must include a weekend
night. Single price £60.
Credit cards ① ② ③ ⑤

An attractive restaurant with interesting menus of skilfully prepared dishes is offered at this family-run hotel with a friendly, informal atmosphere.

★★61% **Russell** (Inter-Hotels) 80 London Road TN1 1DZ ☎ (0892) 544833

Normal price: £44-£50 room only, Fri-Sun. £55 room only,
Mon-Thurs. Dinner from £13.
Short breaks: £77 for two, Fri-Sun, £88 for two, Mon-Thurs,
min 2 nights.
✗ Credit cards ① ② ③ ⑤

A friendly, comfortable hotel with enthusiastic and willing staff. The dinner menu offers a good choice of mostly traditional dishes.

★★★73% **Spa** (Best Western) Mount Ephraim TN4 8XJ ☎ (0892) 20331

Normal price: £74.50 including dinner.
Short breaks: £55, Fri-Sun.
Activity breaks: Romance and Celebration, £130. Fitness Weekends, £110. Single Parent Weekends, £55. Details from hotel.
Credit cards 1 2 3 4 5

An elegant Georgian mansion set in 14 acres of landscaped gardens with a lake. Meals are served in a charming restaurant.

TONBRIDGE   Kent   Map 5 TQ54

★★64% **Rose and Crown** (Trusthouse Forte) High Street TN9 1DD ☎ (0732) 357966

Normal price: £45. Dinner £12.95.
Short breaks: £40, min 2 nights.
Activity breaks: Murder & Mystery Weekends, £160 for 2 nights
Credit cards 1 2 3 4 5

A former posting and coaching house dating from the 16th century with many heavy oak beams and attentive, friendly service.

WATERINGBURY   Kent   Map 5 TQ65

★★★59% **Wateringbury** (Lansbury) Tonbridge Road ME18 5NS ☎ (0622) 812632

Normal price: £44. Dinner from £11 & à la carte
Short breaks: £42, min 2 nights, Fri-Sun.
🎗 Credit cards 1 2 3 5

This busy hotel provides comfortable accommodation with a cosy bar and lively restaurant. The menu offers a variety of popular dishes.

WROTHAM Kent *Map 5 TQ65*

★★★★54% **Post House** (Trusthouse Forte) London Road, Wrotham Heath TN15 7RS ☎ (0732) 883311

Normal price: £66. Dinner £16.60-£18.80 & à la carte
Short breaks: £52, min 2 nights.
Credit cards ① ② ③ ④ ⑤

A second generation of Post House with a carvery-style à la carte restaurant and good leisure facilities. The car parking is excellent.

■ LANCASHIRE ■

ACCRINGTON Lancashire *Map 7 SD72*

★★★61% **Dunkenhalgh** (Character) Blackburn Road, Clayton le Moors BB5 5JP (adj to junc 7 M65)
☎ (0254) 398021

Normal price: £41
Short breaks: £85, 2 nights including Sunday lunch. Single room £95, 2 nights. Fri-Sun
Credit cards ① ② ③ ⑤

Extensive leisure facilities at this impressive country house include an indoor heated swimming pool, snooker, a gymnasium and sauna. All the bedrooms have a private bath or shower room and colour television, and one room has a four-poster bed. There is a special programme of events for Christmas.

BLACKBURN Lancashire *Map 7 SD62*

★★★57% **Blackburn Moat House** (Queens Moat) Preston New Road BB2 7BE ☎ (0254) 64441

Normal price: £72 room. Dinner £11.95-£12.95
Short breaks: £69 for 2 nights, must include Sat. (1990 prices)
Credit cards ① ② ③ ④ ⑤

A modern functional hotel, with a distinctive gabled roof. All bedrooms have private bath or shower rooms and colour television, with some rooms set aside for non-smokers.

★★76% **Millstone** (Shire) Church Lane, Mellor BB10 7JR (3m NW) ☎ (0254) 813333

Normal price: £80 room with breakfast
Short breaks: £148 for 2 people. Min 2 nights, Fri-Sat.
Single £40 excluding dinner.
Credit cards ① ② ③ ⑤

Good, interesting food is served in the attractive dining room of this charming village inn. There are twenty bedrooms all with ensuite bath or shower rooms and colour television; some rooms are for families and non-smokers. There is a special Christmas programme.

BLACKPOOL Lancashire *Map 7 SD33*

GH QQ Brooklands 28-30 King Edward Avenue FY2 9TA ☎ (0253) 51479

Normal price: £29 room with breakfast
Short breaks: From £90-£108 3 nights
🦮 (ex guide dogs)

An attractive hotel set in a quiet side road off the North Promenade. All the bedrooms have colour television, some have ensuite showers, and there are three family rooms.

GH QQ Burlees 40 Knowle Avenue FY2 9QT ☎ (0253) 54535
Feb-Nov

Normal price: £24 including dinner
Short breaks: £19.75 Feb-Apr; £20.75 May-Jun. Min 3 nights
🦮 Credit cards ① ③

Pleasantly situated family-run hotel just a short walk from the promenade. Most of the bedrooms have ensuite shower rooms and colour television, and there are three family rooms.

★★52% **Claremont** 270 North Promenade FY1 1SA ☎ (0253) 293122

Normal price: from £34. Dinner £9-£10.50
Short breaks: from £24. Min 3 nights
✷ (ex guide dogs)

This large busy hotel is on the sea front and close to the centre of town. Bedrooms have ensuite bathrooms and colour television and there is a choice of family rooms. A special programme is available at Christmas.

QQ **Cliff Head** 174 Queens Promenade FY2 9JN ☎ (0253) 591086

Normal price: £25-£31 room
Short breaks: £45-£69 for 2 people, 3 nights

This neat and well maintained property enjoys sea views, is situated at the northern end of Queens Parade, and is convenient for the Cavendish Road tram stop. The bedrooms are fairly compact, but are comfortable and well equipped.

★★59% **Cliffs** Queens Promenade FY2 9SG ☎ (0253) 52388

Normal price: from £28.50. Dinner £10-£11
Short breaks: 3 nights £99, 4 nights £124, 5 nights £145, 6 nights £162
Credit cards ①②③

This large sea front hotel to the north of the town has an all-day coffee shop, a leisure complex and entertainment. All the bedrooms have ensuite bath or shower rooms and colour television, one has a four-poster bed and there are family rooms. A Christmas programme is available.

GH QQ **Derwent** 8 Gynn Avenue FY1 2LD ☎ (0253) 55194
Mar-3 Nov

Normal price: £11.50
Short breaks: £25 for 2 people. Min 4 nights, June
✷

A friendly, well-furnished hotel in a quiet road offering comfortable bedrooms, some with ensuite showers. Two are family rooms.

GH QQ **Hartshead** 17 King Edward Avenue FY2 9TA ☎ (0253) 53133 & 57111

Normal price: £14
Short breaks: £13.80. Single £16. Min 3 nights, May-Jun.

Friendly proprietors and home cooked food are features of this small hotel. There are ten comfortable bedrooms all with colour television, and some have ensuite facilities. Children under three are not accommodated.

★★67% **Headlands** 611-613 South Promenade FY4 1NJ ☎ (0253) 41179

Normal price: midweek £60, weekends £66 room and breakfast.
Short breaks: midweek £194 (4 nights), weekends £70. Min 2 nights, includes dinner, afternoon tea, morning coffee. Weekends include Sunday lunch
Activity breaks: Dancing (4 days) April or May: £194
Credit cards ①③

A reasonably-priced, long-established hotel at the southern end of the promenade is very popular with holiday-makers, some of whom return year after year. Accommodation has been refurbished to create comfortable, well-equipped ensuite bedrooms, and service throughout is hospitable and friendly.

★★★★50% **Imperial** North Promenade FY1 2HB ☎ (0253) 23971

Normal price: £136 room and breakfast
Short breaks: £54
Activity breaks: Murder/Mystery Weekend £170, including extras. Contact hotel for dates
Credit cards ①②③④⑤

Imposing Victorian building overlooking sea with spacious public areas and elegant, modern palm court restaurant.

★65% **Kimberley** New South Promenade FY4 1NQ ☎ (0253) 41184
Closed 3-13 Jan
Normal price: £30 including dinner
Short breaks: 25% discount. Min 3 nights, Sun-Thurs

A friendly, informal hotel standing in a crescent off the seafront. Light snacks are served throughout the day at the Coffee Shop. All the bedrooms have colour television, most have private facilities and some rooms have been set aside for families. Guests can play table tennis, and there is a special Christmas programme.

GH QQ **Mimosa** 24A Lonsdale Road FY1 6EE ☎ (0253) 41906
Normal price: £15
Short breaks: £13.50. Min 3 nights, Sun-Thu, Nov-Jun.
Credit cards ☐1 ☐3

This modern establishment has spacious bedrooms complete with ensuite facilities and colour television. Breakfast is served in guests' rooms.

★★★63% **New Clifton** Talbot Square, FY1 1ND ☎ (0253) 21481
Normal price: £85 room and breakfast
Short breaks: £33
Activity breaks: Superbowl/Clifton Breaks; £33 including admission and shoe hire. Theatre breaks; £37.50
Credit cards ☐1 ☐2 ☐3 ☐5

Centrally sited and overlooking the sea, the hotel has well-furnished bedrooms and public areas.

★★★★67% **Pembroke** North Promenade FY1 2JQ ☎ (0253) 23434
Normal price: £53. Dinner £12.50 & à la carte
Short breaks: £53, including £13.50 dinner allowance.
Single £63. Min 2 nights
Credit cards ☐1 ☐2 ☐3 ☐4 ☐5

A large, impressive seafront hotel with extensive leisure facilities and attentive, friendly service. Bedrooms have ensuite facilities and colour television, and some are for families and non-smokers. There is a special Christmas programme.

★★65% **Sheraton** 54-62 Queens Promenade FY2 9RP ☎ (0253) 52723
Normal price: from £27.50
Short breaks: £89.50 4 night break, Mon-Thu, Apr-Jun; £95 in Nov; including 2 half day coach trips, depending on weather.

A friendly hotel overlooking the sea with an indoor heated swimming pool, sauna and solarium. All bedrooms have ensuite facilities and colour television and there are plenty of family rooms, making this ideal for family holidays. There is a special Christmas programme.

GH Q **Sunny Cliff** 98 Queens Promenade, Northshore FY2 9NS ☎ (0253) 51155
Normal price: £25 room and breakfast
Short breaks: £16

In a quiet position overlooking the sea and north shore cliffs, this hotel provides comfortable accommodation with tea and coffee making facilities in all rooms. There is a TV lounge, sun lounge and lounge bar.

GH QQQQ **Sunray** 42 Knowle Avenue, Queens Promenade FY2 9QT ☎ (0253) 51937
Closed 15 Dec-5 Jan
Normal price: £42 room with breakfast
Short breaks: 10% discount. Min 2 nights, Nov-Mar

A friendly, welcoming guest house offering bright bedrooms all with ensuite facilities, colour television, direct-dial telephones and hairdryers. There are two family rooms.

★★64% **Warwick** 603-609 New South Promenade FY4 1NG ☎ (0253) 42192

Normal price: £51.50 room, Dinner £12.50
Short breaks: £68.50 for two people. Min 2 nights. Single supplement.
Credit cards [1] [2] [3] [5]

This hotel overlooks the seafront and offers bedrooms which, although of varying sizes, are all freshly decorated and well-equipped. Pleasant public areas include a comfortable bar and attractive restaurant.

BURNLEY   Lancashire   Map 7 SD83

★★★63% **Keirby** Keirby Walk, BB11 2DH ☎ (0282) 27611
Closed 24-26 Dec

Normal price: £29.25. Dinner £11.75-£14.25 and à la carte
Short breaks: £35. Min 2 nights, Fri-Sun

Situated in the town centre, this hotel has well-equipped bedrooms all with private baths and colour television. Some rooms are set aside for non-smokers.

★★★71% **Oaks** (Shire) Colne Road, Reedley BB10 2LF ☎ (0282) 414141

Normal price: £90 room
Short breaks: £180 for 2 people, for 2 nights, Fri-Sun. Single £48 with breakfast

A country house has been sympathetically converted to offer comfortable accommodation. All bedrooms have ensuite bath or shower rooms and colour television, with rooms for families and non-smokers. Two rooms have four-poster beds. Leisure amenities include an indoor heated swimming pool, tennis, squash, snooker and gymnasium. There is a special Christmas programme.

CHARNOCK RICHARD M/WAY SERVICE AREA (M6)   Lancashire   Map 7 SD51

★★54% **Welcome Lodge** (Trusthouse Forte) Mill Lane PR7 5LR ☎ (0257) 791746

Normal price: £40 room. £30 single price
Short breaks: £31 for two excluding dinner. £24 single. Fri-Sun
Credit cards [1] [2] [3] [4] [5]

Functional but comfortable accommodation with ensuite facilities and colour television is situated in the service area complex. Meals and drinks are available to Lodge residents. Accessible from both carriageways of the M6.

FLEETWOOD   Lancashire   Map 7 SD34

★★★60% **North Euston** The Esplanade FY7 6BN ☎ (03917) 6525

Normal price: £26.50. Dinner £11.50
Short breaks: £32.50, Min 2 nights, Fri-Sun, Sep & Oct
🐾 (ex guide dogs) Credit cards [1] [2] [3] [5]

Dating from 1841 and in a prominent position overlooking the Wyre Estuary, this hotel has a restaurant and bistro. All the attractive bedrooms have colour television, and most have ensuite facilities. Guests can play table tennis and pool, and there is a special Christmas programme.

GARSTANG   Lancashire   Map 7 SD44

★★68% **Crofters** (Consort) Cabus PR3 1PH ☎ (0995) 604128

Normal price: £24.75. Dinner £13 and à la carte
Short breaks: £33, single £45. Min 2 nights
Credit cards [1] [2] [3] [5]

Service is courteous and friendly at this modern hotel which has attractive public areas and provides interesting menus. Each bedroom has a private bathroom and colour television. There is a special Christmas programme.

★★ 🐾 **Pickerings** Garstang Road, Catterall PR3 0HA (2m S B6430) ☎ (0995) 602133
Restricted service 26 & 27 Dec

Normal price: £30. Dinner £16-£25
Short breaks: from £40, includes £16.50 dinner allowance, champagne with dinner, complimentary drinks and chocolates. Fri-Sun
🐾 (ex guide dogs)

A small, personally-run hotel which offers interesting menus featuring fresh local produce. Bedrooms are particularly spacious, and all have colour television and private bath or shower room. There is a special Christmas programme.

GISBURN   Lancashire   Map 7 SD84

★★★61% **Stirk House** (Consort) BB7 4LJ ☎ (0200) 445581

Normal price: £76. Dinner £15.50
Short breaks: £90 for 2 nights, Thu-Sun
🐾 (ex guide dogs) Credit cards ①②③④⑤

The 16th-century manor house offers comfortable accommodation with private bath or shower room and colour television. The sports complex has an indoor swimming pool, squash courts and an exercise room among its facilities.

HURST GREEN   Lancashire   Map 7 SD63

★★77% **Shireburn Arms** BB6 9QJ ☎ (025486) 518

Normal price: £31.25. Dinner £11.50
Short breaks: £79 for 2 nights

A delightful country inn offering friendly service, character bars and lounges, and good value menus. The comfortable ensuite bedrooms have many thoughtful extras. Christmas breaks are available.

LANCASTER   Lancashire   Map 7 SD46

★★★67% **Royal Kings Arms** Market Street LA1 1HP ☎ (0524) 32451

Normal price: £35. Dinner from £12 & à la carte
Short breaks: £37.50, min 2 nights, Fri-Sun. Any 2 nights in Jul/Aug.
Credit cards ①②③⑤

A comfortable city centre hotel with spacious public rooms and modern bedrooms. Service is cheerful and courteous.

LANGHO   Lancashire   Map 7 SD34

★★★64% **Mytton Fold Farm** Whalley Road BB6 8AB ☎ (0254) 240662

Normal price: £50-£73 room and breakfast
Short breaks: £62.50 min 2 nights, Fri-Sun
🐾 Credit cards ① ③

This family run hotel provides comfortable bedrooms, friendly service, and a very good restaurant.

LEYLAND   Lancashire   Map 7 SD52

★★★56% **Penguin** Leyland Way PR5 2JX ☎ (0772) 422922

Normal price: £35. Dinner from £11.25 & à la carte.
Short breaks: £23, min 1 night, Fri-Sun.
Credit cards ①②③⑤

Functional modern hotel just off junction 28 of the M6.

LYTHAM ST ANNES   Lancashire   Map 7 SD32

★★★68% **Bedford** (Exec-Hotel) 307-311 Clifton Drive South FY8 1HN ☎ (0253) 724636

Normal price: £25. Dinner from £12.50 & à la carte
Short breaks: £32.50, min 2 nights except Xmas & New
Year. Single price £35.
Credit cards [1] [3]

A very friendly hotel with a choice of eating options in the main restaurant, a coffee shop and a quaint lower-ground-floor bistro.

★★69% **Chadwick** South Promenade FY8 1NP ☎ (0253) 720061

Normal price: £32.75 including dinner.
Short breaks: £29.40, Nov-May.
✚ Credit cards [1] [2] [3] [5]

Good leisure facilities and friendly service are provided at this sea front hotel.

★★★★61% **Clifton Arms** (Lansbury) West Beach, Lytham FY8 5QJ ☎ (0253) 739898

Normal price: £46-£50. Dinner from £14 & à la carte
Short breaks: £48, min 2 nights except during Blackpool
Illuminations.
Credit cards [1] [2] [3] [5]

Guests will experience delightfully courteous service in every area of this comfortable hotel.

★61% **Lindum** 63-67 South Promenade FY8 1LZ ☎ (0253) 721534 & 722516

Normal price: £27. Dinner £8.50.
Short breaks: £47 for 2 nights, Nov-May.
Credit cards [1] [2] [3]

Dinner represents good value at this seafront hotel which provides friendly, unobtrusive service under the supervision of its resident owners.

★★62% **New Glendower** (Consort) North Promendade FY8 ☎ (0253) 723241

Normal price: £27.50. Dinner £11.95-£12.50.
Short breaks: £36, min 2 nights, Nov-Aug.
Credit cards [1] [2] [3] [5]

A large seafront hotel, refurbished to provide pleasant public areas. Those bedrooms overlooking the sea are more spacious and attractive.

MELLING   Lancashire   Map 7 SD57

★★ **Melling Hall** (Exec Hotel) LA6 2RA ☎ (05242) 21298

Normal price: £22.50. Dinner £10.50 and à la carte.
Short breaks: £27.50 (£35 for single occupancy). Min 2
nights. Not available bank holidays.
Credit cards [1] [2] [3] [5]

In open country on the edge of the village, this converted 17th-century manor house has comfortable bedrooms, including a family room, most with ensuite bath or shower and all with colour television. Christmas breaks are available.

MORECAMBE   Lancashire   Map 7 SD46

Q **Ashley** 371 Marine Road, Promenade East LA4 5AH ☎ (0524) 412034

Normal price: £20 including dinner
Short breaks: £18.50. Min 3 nights. Single supplement.
Credit cards [1] [3]

This small family-run guesthouse on the sea front has colour television in all bedrooms, and private bath or shower in most.

★★ **Clarendon** Promenade, West End LA4 4EP ☎ (0524) 410180

Normal price: £20
Short breaks: £18 excluding dinner. Min 2 nights, Fri-Sun,
Nov-Apr.
Credit cards [1] [2] [3] [4] [5]

On the sea front, this hotel has a games room and the bedrooms include some family rooms, all with colour television and most with private bath or shower.

QQ Craigwell 372 Promenade East LA4 5AH ☎ (0524) 410095 & 418399

Normal price: £18-£20
Short breaks: £24-£29. Min 3 nights.
Credit cards ☐1☐ ☐3☐

This friendly, personally-run small hotel enjoys views over Morecambe Bay's sands. The bedrooms are generally compact but comfortably furnished and well equipped, and all have modern facilities. Dinner features a choice of home cooked dishes, including vegetarian items.

Q Ellesmere 44 Westminster Road LA4 4JD ☎ (0524) 411881

Normal price: £12
Short breaks: £13. Min 4 nights.
✷ (ex guide dogs) Credit cards ☐1☐ ☐3☐

A small friendly guesthouse within walking distance of the seafront, with colour television and hot and cold water facilities in all bedrooms, which include a no-smoking room and two family rooms.

★★★ Elms (Consort) Bare LA4 6DD ☎ (0524) 411501

Normal price: £35. Dinner £10.25-£11.50 and à la carte
Short breaks: £42.50. Min 2 nights, Fri-Sun.
✷ Credit cards ☐1☐ ☐2☐ ☐3☐ ☐4☐ ☐5☐

This pleasant comfortable hotel with a garden serves home-grown English food and all bedrooms, including a family room and a four-poster bed, have ensuite bathrooms. Christmas breaks are available.

QQQ Prospect 363 Marine Road East LA4 5AQ ☎ (0524) 417819

Normal price: £15
Short breaks: £18.50. £24 for single room. Min 3 nights.
Credit cards ☐3☐

Overlooking the bay, this modern well-furnished guesthouse has ensuite bathrooms and colour television in all bedrooms, with many family rooms.

QQ Wilmslow 374 Marine Road East LA4 5AH ☎ (0524) 417804

Normal price: £19
Short breaks: £23. Min 3 nights.
✷ Credit cards ☐1☐ ☐3☐

A family-run promenade guesthouse serving home-cooked meals and with comfortable bedrooms, including two family rooms. All have colour television and many have private shower.

PRESTON   Lancashire   Map 7 SD52

★68% **Brickhouse** Chipping PR3 2QH ☎ (0995) 61316

Normal price: £22.25
Short breaks: £77 for 2 people for 2 days including set-dinner or £14.95 dinner allowance and lunch on day of departure. Min 2 nights, Tue-Sat.
Credit cards ☐1☐ ☐3☐

This hotel takes its name from the original construction of the building, and parts of the bar-restaurant still retain the original exposed beams and old brickwork. The bedrooms are comfortable and well-equipped and most offer pleasant views of the countryside. The restaurant features a wide range of innovative and interesting dishes, using only the best fresh ingredients.

★★★68% **Tickled Trout** (Associated Leisure) Preston New Road, Samlesbury PR5 0UJ ☎ (077477) 671

Normal price: £40. 1990 prices.
Short breaks: £30 including set-price dinner or approx £15 dinner allowance. Fri-Sun, Jan-Oct. Single supplement.
Credit cards ☐1☐ ☐2☐ ☐3☐ ☐5☐

This comfortable hotel with an old world restaurant and lounge has modern ensuite bedrooms with colour television. Many of them are family and no-smoking rooms, and two offer four-poster beds. Leisure facilities include fishing, sauna, steam room, solarium and gymnasium. Christmas breaks are available.

★★★61% **Swallow Trafalgar** Preston New Road, Samlesbury PR5 0UL ☎ (0772) 877351

Normal price: £42. Dinner from £11.75 (1990 price)
Short breaks: £46 including dinner & Sunday lunch. Min 2 nights, Fri-Sun, Sep-Jun.
Credit cards 1 2 3 5

This modern hotel provides helpful service and pleasant bedrooms, including some no-smoking, with private bath or shower and colour television. The leisure facilities include indoor swimming, squash, sauna, solarium, gymnasium, steam room and spa pool. Christmas breaks are available.

SALFORD Lancashire Map 7 SJ89

★61% **Beaucliffe** 254 Eccles Old Road, Pendleton M6 8ES ☎ 061-789 5092

Normal price: £27. Dinner £8.50-£16 à la carte
Short breaks: £19.50, min 1 night, Fri-Sat; dinner not included. £4.50 single supplement.
🛦 Credit cards 1 2 3 5

Well-situated for Manchester city centre and the motorway network, opposite Hope Hospital close to junction 2 of the M602, this is a friendly well-established hotel. It is furnished with antiques which give character to its comfortable lounge and other public areas. Guests are provided with secure parking.

★61% **Inn of Good Hope** 226 Eccles Old Road M6 8AG ☎ 061-707 6178

Normal price: £26.50. Dinner £8-£15.
Short breaks: £21 excluding dinner. Min 2 nights, Fri-Sun.
🛦 Credit cards 1 2 3 5

Particularly well-appointed bedrooms with ensuite facilities are provided by this popular pub, situated on the A578 close to its junction with the M602, within easy reach of both city centre and motorway network.

SLAIDBURN Lancashire Map 7 SD75

QQQQ **Parrock Head** Woodhouse Lane, Clitheroe BB7 3AH ☎ (02006) 614

Normal price: £27.50
Short breaks: From £106 for 3 nights, Mon-Thur & Sun except Bank Hol. Includes £12 allowance towards à la carte dinner.
Credit cards 1 2

A peacefully situated 17th-century longhouse carefully converted to provide a most comfortable and relaxing place to stay. The bedrooms are appointed to a very high standard, and a delightful first floor lounge enjoys lovely views of the surrounding countryside. The attractive restaurant serves freshly cooked local produce complemented by a well chosen wine list.

TODMORDEN Lancashire Map 7 SD92

★★★ 🍜 70% **Scaitcliffe Hall** Burnley Road OL14 7DQ ☎ (0706) 818888

Normal price: £28.50 room.
Short breaks: £69 for 2 nights, £99 for 3 nights, Fri-Sun. Single supplement.
Credit cards 1 2 3 5

This attractive country house which dates back to 1666 is set in its own well-tended grounds. It offers comfortable accommodation and well-prepared food.

◼ LEICESTERSHIRE ◼

CASTLE DONINGTON Leicestershire Map 8 SK42

★★★60% **Donington Manor** High Street DE7 2PP ☎ (0332) 810253
Closed 27-30 Dec

Normal price: £56.70 room with breakfast
Short breaks: £48 room with breakfast. Single £28. Min 2 nights, Fri-Sun (ex during motorcycle Grand Prix).
🗙 (ex guide dogs) Credit cards ① ② ③ ⑤

Set on the edge of the village and convenient for the East Midland Airport this hotel offers value for money. All the bedrooms have colour television, most have ensuite bathroom, and some rooms are furnished with a four-poster bed.

★★★66% **Donington Thistle** (Mount Charlotte (TS)) East Midlands Airport DE7 2SH ☎ (0332) 850700

Normal price: £50.25. Dinner from £13 and à la carte
Short breaks: £45 excluding dinner. No single supplement at weekends
Credit cards ① ② ③ ⑤

This modern purpose-built hotel on the perimeter of the East Midlands Airport has an up-to-date leisure club and offers special facilities for children. Each bedroom has an ensuite bath or shower room and colour television, and there are rooms for families and non-smokers.

KEGWORTH Leicestershire Map 8 SK42

★★★61% **Yew Lodge** 33 Packington Hill DE7 2DF ☎ (0509) 672518

Normal price: £67 (£56 at weekends). Dinner from £12.50
Short breaks: £30, excluding dinner. Min 1 night, Fri-Sun.
Credit cards ① ② ③ ⑤

A busy hotel just off the A6, conveniently close to junction 24 of the M1, and within easy reach of East Midlands Airports.

LEICESTER Leicestershire Map 4 SK50

★★★65% **Belmont** (Best Western) De Montfort St LE1 7GR ☎ (0533) 544773

Normal price: £25. Dinner £12.95.
Short breaks: £40 including champagne. Fri-Sun.
Activity breaks: Theatre Nights, details from hotel.
Credit cards ① ② ③ ⑤

A busy, popular, privately-owned hotel, located close to both city centre and railway station. Many of the bedrooms have recently been refurbished.

★★★★58% **Grand** (Embassy) Granby Street LE1 6ES ☎ (0533) 555599

Normal price: £41 midweek, room only per person. £30 weekend (1990 prices). Dinner £7.95-£10.95.
Short breaks: £42 approx. Min 2 nights, must include Fri, Sat or Sun.
Credit cards ① ② ③ ④ ⑤

Impressive Victorian city-centre building standing on the main A6.

★★★★60% **Holiday Inn** St Nicholas Circle LE1 5LX ☎ (0533) 531161

Normal price: £47.50 midweek. Dinner from £14.75 & à la carte.
Short breaks: £40 excluding dinner.
Credit cards ① ② ③ ④ ⑤

Large, modern purpose-built hotel close to the city centre, adjacent to a multi-storey car park.

★★★60% **Leicester Forest Moat House** (Queens Moat) Hinckley Road, Leicester Forest East LE3 3GH
☎ (0533) 394661

Normal price: £66 room. Dinner £10.50 & à la carte.
Short breaks: £30 including newspaper, min 2 nights. Single supplement.
Credit cards ① ② ③ ⑤

A busy hotel with modern accommodation, with executive-style bedrooms planned during 1990. The refurbished bar provides flexible eating options.

★★★65% **Leicestershire Moat House** (Queens Moat) Wigston Road, Oadby LE2 5QE (3m SE A6)
☎ (0533) 719441

Normal price: £21. Dinner £11.50 & à la carte
Short breaks: £30, min 2 nights Fri-Sun. Single price £35.
Credit cards [1] [2] [3] [5]

New bedrooms have proved popular at this hotel, and existing rooms have been refurbished to a similar standard. The Csars restaurant has a carvery and à la carte menu.

★★64% **Old Tudor Rectory** Main Street, Glenfield LE3 8DG ☎ (0533) 320220

Normal price: £46. Dinner from £8.95.
Short breaks: £36.80 excluding dinner. Fri-Sun.
Credit cards [1] [3]

This former rectory has sections which date back to the 16th century. Hospitality is warm and friendly, and accommodation simple.

★★★61% **Park International** Humberstone Road LE5 3AT ☎ (0533) 620471

Normal price: £25. Dinner £8.55.
Short breaks: £20, min 2 nights Fri-Sun. Single price £25.
Credit cards [1] [2] [3] [4] [5]

A large, busy city centre hotel catering mainly for business people and conference delegates.

★★★61% **Post House** (Trusthouse Forte) Braunstone Lane East LE3 2FW ☎ (0533) 630500

Normal price: £39 room only. Dinner from £14 and à la carte.
Short breaks: £38.
Credit cards [1] [2] [3] [4] [5]

A large and busy hotel on the A6, conveniently placed for access to the M1, M69 and city centre. It offers a choice of restaurants.

★★★62% **Saint James** Abbey Street LE1 3TE ☎ (0533) 510666

Normal price: £43. Dinner from £10.50.
Short breaks: £38.
Credit cards [1] [2] [3] [5]

Located on top of a multi-storey car park in the city centre, this recently refurbished hotel has comfortable bedrooms and public areas.

★★★62% **Stage** (Consort) 299 Leicester Road, Wigston Fields LE8 1JW (on A50) ☎ (0533) 886161

Normal price: £31. Dinner £9.95 and à la carte.
Short breaks: £26.
🦮 Credit cards [1] [2] [3] [4] [5]

An attractive split-level, open-plan area contains the restaurant and lounge bar at this pleasant hotel which has recently been extensively improved.

LOUGHBOROUGH Leicestershire Map 8 SK51

★★54% **Great Central** (Minotels) Great Central Road LE11 1RW ☎ (0509) 263405

Normal price: £35-£50 room. Dinner £9.95-£12 and à la carte.
Short breaks: £55 for 2 nights, min 2 nights, Fri-Sat.
Credit cards [1] [2] [3] [5]

A small hotel close to the Old Great Central Railway line. The modest accommodation has a relaxed, informal atmosphere.

★★★63% **King's Head** (Embassy) High Street LE11 2QL ☎ (0509) 233222

Normal price: £79 room. Dinner from £11.50.
Short breaks: £29.50 (1990 price). Min 2 nights, Fri-Sun.
Activity breaks: Canals and Railways in East Midlands, £103, June. City of Lincoln Break, £105, 12-14 October. Richard III Road to Bosworth Field, £105, 29 Jun-1 Jul.
Credit cards [1] [2] [3] [4] [5]

A popular hotel for weekend breaks, situated in the town centre and only 3 miles from the M1.

LYDDINGTON Leicestershire Map 4 SP89

★★★54% **Marquess of Exeter** (Best Western) Main Road LE15 9LT ☎ (0572) 822477

Normal price: £35. Dinner £12.95 and à la carte.
Short breaks: £42, min 2 nights, Fri-Sun. Single supplement.
🦮 Credit cards [1] [2] [3] [5]

Charming 17th-century rural village inn, with modern bedrooms in the annexe.

MARKET HARBOROUGH Leicestershire Map 4 SP78

★★★61% **Three Swans** (Best Western) 21 High Street LE16 7NJ ☎ (0858) 466644

Normal price: £77-£81 room and breakfast. Dinner from £13.95 (1990 price)
Short breaks: £39 including £16.75 dinner allowance. Min 2 nights, Fri-Sun.
🐾 (ex guide dogs) Credit cards ① ② ③ ④ ⑤

This historic inn in the town centre dates from the 15th century and all bedrooms, nearly a third of them non-smoking, have bath or shower facilities and colour television.

MARKFIELD Leicestershire Map 8 SK41

★★★72% **Field Head** Markfield Lane LE6 0PS ☎ (0530) 245454

Normal price: £84 room.
Short breaks: £28 excluding dinner. Fri-Sun.
Credit cards ① ② ③ ⑤

A farmhouse dating back to 1672 has been sympathetically extended and restored to create a modern hotel which offers comfortable, well-appointed public areas and good-sized, fully-equipped, attractively decorated bedrooms. The entrance is off the B5327 from its roundabout junction with the A50, and one mile from junction 22 of the M1. The entrance is not obvious, and if the turning off the A50 is missed a long detour cannot be avoided, as it is very dangerous to make a U-turn on this road.

MELTON MOWBRAY Leicestershire Map 8 SK71

★★62% **Sysonby Knoll** Asfordby Road LE13 0HP ☎ (0664) 63563

Normal price: £21. Dinner from £8 (1990 price)
Short breaks: £22.50. Min 3 nights, Fri-Sun.
Credit cards ① ③

On the outskirts of the market town with views over the River Eye and the countryside, this comfortable little hotel with garden and swimming pool has ensuite facilities in most of its bedrooms, plus colour television.

NARBOROUGH Leicestershire Map 4 SP59

★★63% **Charnwood** 48 Leicester Road LE9 5DF (off A46 2m S M1 junc 21) ☎ (0533) 862218

Normal price: £30
Short breaks: £20 excluding dinner. Fri-Sun.
Credit cards ① ② ③

A friendly hotel with a large garden, and private bath or shower and colour television in all bedrooms.

NORMANTON Leicestershire Map 8 SK84

★★★ ♨ 72% **Normanton Park** LE15 8RP (1m E unclass rd on S shore of Rutland Water)
☎ (0780) 720315

Normal price: £66 room and breakfast. Dinner £15-£17.50.
Short breaks: £80 for 2 people. Min 2 nights.
Activity breaks: Cycling, Fishing, Walking, Sailing, Bird
Watching and Clay Pigeon Shooting Breaks. Details from
hotel.
Credit cards [1] [2] [3] [5]

Converted from a magnificent coach house, the hotel has modern accommodation and a popular restaurant. Using the A606, follow signs for South Shore then Normanton Park.

OAKHAM Leicestershire Map 4 SK80

★★★76% **Barnsdale Country Club** Exton LE15 8AB ☎ (0572) 757901

Normal price: £127 room and breakfast.
Short breaks: £135 for two including continental breakfast
and £30 dinner allowance. Min 2 nights.
Credit cards [1] [2] [5]

Originally built in 1890 for the Earl Fitzwilliam family, Barnsdale Hall is now at the centre of a luxurious time-share development set in 60 acres of grounds which reach the edge of Rutland Water. As well as the time-share apartments, there are two blocks of good quality, well-equipped hotel rooms and the range of leisure facilities is extensive.

★★63% **Boultons** 4 Catmose Street LE15 6HW ☎ (0572) 722844

Normal price: £30. Dinner from £10 and à la carte (1990
price)
Short breaks: £31.25. Sat-Sun only. £10 single supplement.
Credit cards [1] [2] [3] [5]

A comfortable hotel in the centre of this old market town, with ensuite facilities and colour television in all bedrooms. Half of them are non-smoking and there are two family rooms. Christmas breaks are available.

✿★★★ ♨ 82% **Hambleton Hall** (Relais et Chateaux) LE15 8TH (3m E off A606) ☎ (0572) 756991

Normal price: £98-£200 room and breakfast. Dinner £35
Short breaks: Weekends only, contact hotel for details. Min
3 nights, Nov-Apr.
Credit cards [1] [2] [3] [4] [5]

Acclaimed for its high-quality cuisine, this charming Victorian country house hotel set in unspoilt countryside has bedrooms equipped with every convenience, including one with a four-poster bed. The quiet gardens include a tennis court. Christmas breaks are available.

★★★68% **Whipper-in** Market Place LE15 6DT ☎ (0572) 756971

Normal price: £40. Dinner from £16.95 & à la carte (1989
price)
Short breaks: £42.50 including £18.95 dinner allowance.
Min 2 nights, Fri-Sun.
Credit cards [1] [2] [3] [5]

This 17th-century inn furnished with antiques has been transformed into a comfortable hotel with private bath and colour television in all bedrooms, including two with four-poster beds. The popular restaurant serves good British food. Christmas breaks are available.

UPPINGHAM Leicestershire Map 4 SP89

★★★67% **Falcon** (Inter-Hotels) High Street LE15 9PY ☎ (0572) 823535

Normal price: £37.50. Dinner £10.50-£12.50 & à la carte
Short breaks: £44.50, min 2 nights, Fri-Sun.
Credit cards [1] [2] [3] [5]

Former coaching inn situated in the attractive town centre.

★★67% **Lake Isle** High Street East LE15 9PZ ☎ (0572) 822951

Normal price: £31. Dinner from £17.
Short breaks: £46, Fri-Sun.
Credit cards [1] [2] [3] [5]

This high street hotel provides attentive, friendly service. The food and extensive wine list are proving popular with residents and locals alike.

▪ LINCOLNSHIRE ▪

BRANSTON   Lincolnshire   Map 8 TF06

★★★54% **Moor Lodge** (Consort) LN4 1HU ☎ (0522) 791366

Normal price: £37.40. Dinner from £15.30 and à la carte
Short breaks: £41.80, single £48.40. Min 2 nights
Credit cards ① ② ③ ⑤

This interesting hotel offers a choice of newly refurbished bedrooms with modern facilities and older more functional rooms. All bedrooms have ensuite facilities and colour television, there are family rooms and one room has a four-poster bed. There is a special Christmas programme.

DUNHOLME   Lincolnshire   Map 8 TF07

★★★50% **Four Seasons** Southern Lane LN2 3QP ☎ (0673) 60108

Normal price: £50 room and breakfast. Dinner £8.95-£9.95 and à la carte
Short breaks: Mini-weekend of 1 night dinner, dance and cabaret, bed, breakfast and Sunday lunch from £80 per couple. Long weekend as before plus 1 extra night and dinner allowance £135 per couple. Single mini-weekend from £55, long weekend £110.
Credit cards ① ② ③

Located on the A46 Lincoln/Grimsby road, this is a purpose built motel block with the adjacent main building providing the hotel services. Bedrooms are all ensuite with colour television. There is a special Christmas programme.

GRANTHAM   Lincolnshire   Map 8 SK93

★★★65% **Angel & Royal** (Trusthouse Forte) High Street NG31 6PN ☎ (0476) 65816

Normal price: £48.50. Dinner from £13.95.
Short breaks: £42, min 2 nights, Fri-Sun.
Activity breaks: Medieval Weekends, £130.
Credit cards ① ② ③ ④ ⑤

Built some time prior to the 13th century and steeped in history, the hotel is approached through a 15th-century stone archway.

★★56% **Kings** North Parade NG31 8AU ☎ (0476) 590800

Normal price: £55 room and breakfast. Dinner £9.25-£13.95 & à la carte
Short breaks: £50 for two. Single £35. Min 2 nights, Fri, Sat, Sun.
Credit cards ① ② ③ ⑤

Situated on the outskirts of the town centre, this Georgian house has a comfortable lounge, a choice of restaurants and well-equipped bedrooms. There is a tennis court.

HEMSWELL   Lincolnshire   Map 8 SK99

★★64% **Hemswell Cliff** Lancaster Green, Hemswell Cliff DN21 5TU ☎ (042773) 8181 & 8182

Normal price: £60 room and breakfast. Dinner £10.50-£16 and à la carte
Short breaks: £75 for two. Min 2 nights, Sat & Sun.
🐕 (ex guide dogs)

This former RAF Officers' Mess has been modernised and now offers up-to-date accommodation and spacious public rooms. There are facilities for squash, and Christmas breaks are available.

LINCOLN   Lincolnshire   Map 8 SK97

GH QQQQ D'isney Place Eastgate LN2 4AA ☎ (0522) 538881

Normal price: £28.50.
Short breaks: £22.50.
Credit cards ① ② ③ ⑤

This small luxury hotel is ideally situated for exploring. Substantial, well-presented breakfasts are served in the bedrooms.

★★59% Duke William 44 Bailgate LN1 3AP ☎ (0522) 533351

Normal price: £30. Dinner £7.95-£9.95.
Short breaks: £25-£26, Fri-Sun. £36 single price.
🕇 Credit cards ① ② ③ ⑤

Situated close to the castle, this hotel has friendly staff. There is a popular public bar, and a restaurant with a small table d'hôte menu.

★★★58% Eastgate Post House (Trusthouse Forte) Eastgate LN2 1PN ☎ (0522) 520341

Normal price: £47. Dinner from £14.
Short breaks: £42, min 2 nights, Thu-Sun.
Activity breaks: Golf Breaks, £124. Details from hotel.
Credit cards ① ② ③ ④ ⑤

Ideal for both holiday and commercial guests. The Palatinate Restaurant overlooks the Cathedral and offers an interesting menu.

★★71% Hillcrest (Guestaccom) 15 Lindum Terrace LN2 5RT ☎ (0522) 510182

Normal price: £24.95. Dinner £7.50-£12 & à la carte
Short breaks: £32, min 2 nights, Thurs-Sun. Single supplement.
Credit cards ① ③

The hotel stands in an elevated position in a quiet residential area to the north-east of Lincoln, and guests can enjoy views of part of the city.

GH QQQ Tennyson 7 South Park LN5 8EN ☎ (0522) 521624

Normal price: £20.
Short breaks: £25, min 2 nights except Xmas.
🕇 Credit cards ① ② ③

This pair of Victorian houses has been extensively modernised to provide good accommodation.

★★★ 🛏 67% Washingborough Hall Country House (Minotels) Church Hill, Washingborough LN4 1BE (3m E B1190) ☎ (0522) 790340

Normal price: £29.50. Dinner £12.50 & à la carte.
Short breaks: £36, min 2 nights except Christmas & New Year. Single price £48.
Credit cards ① ② ③ ⑤

Situated within sight of the Cathedral, this hotel is set in three acres of gardens and woodlands. Decor and furnishings, though modest, are well cared for.

OSBOURNBY   Lincolnshire   Map 4 TF03

★39% **Whichcote Arms** London Road NG34 0DG ☎ (05295) 239 & 500

Normal price: £21
Short breaks: £17 excluding dinner (£20 for single room).
Min 2 nights.

This detached stone building on the A15, six miles south of Sleaford, is a former farm manager's house of the Whychcote Estate. Accommodation is modest and the restaurant serves good standard, popular dishes. There are good car parking and banqueting facilities.

SKEGNESS   Lincolnshire   Map 9 TF56

★★53% **Vine** Vine Road, Seacroft PE25 3DB ☎ (0754) 3018 & 610611

Normal price: £50 room and breakfast. Dinner £15.
Short breaks: £70-£145, 2-5 nights min, includes £6 dinner allowance.
Credit cards ①②③⑤

A 17th-century smuggling inn set in its own grounds in a quiet residential area close to the seafront. The accommodation is simply furnished, with old-fashioned but comfortable public area, and the restaurant offers a choice of menus.

SPALDING   Lincolnshire   Map 8 TF22

★★69% **Woodlands** 80 Pinchbeck Road PE11 1QF ☎ (0775) 769933

Normal price: £58 room and breakfast. Dinner £17-£23 à la carte
Short breaks: £35 for 2 excluding dinner. Min 2 nights, Fri-Sat.
Credit cards ①②③⑤

A tastefully converted Edwardian house just north of the town centre, recently extended to offer a new wing of bedrooms, a larger restaurant and upgraded public areas.

STAMFORD   Lincolnshire   Map 4 TF00

★★★69% **Garden House** St. Martin's PE9 2LP ☎ (0780) 63359

Normal price: £37.50. Dinner from £15.
Short breaks: £40, min 2 nights, Fri-Sun.
Credit cards ①②③

A charming 18th-century house sympathetically improved to provide modern comforts; aptly-named, the hotel has particularly attractive gardens and a delightful, well-stocked conservatory. Home-produced dishes of good quality are served in an elegant dining room, and the standard of hospitality, together with professional service, is an outstanding feature.

★★62% **Lady Anne's** 37-38 High Street, St. Martin's PE9 2LJ ☎ (0780) 53175

Normal price: £70 room and breakfast. Dinner £9.50-£12.50.
Short breaks: £70 for two. Min 2 nights, Oct-May.
Credit cards ①②③④⑤

An 18th century stone built house set in 3 acres of grounds on the B1081, easily accessible from the A1. Personally supervised by the proprietors, it is a popular venue.

SUTTON-ON-SEA   Lincolnshire   Map 4 TF58

★★60% **Grange & Links** Mablethorpe LN12 2RA ☎ (0507) 441334

Normal price: £65 room and breakfast
Short breaks: £45 for 2 people. £10 single supplement.
Activity breaks: Golf: £55
Credit cards ①②③⑤

An hotel popular with residents and locals alike, providing sound accommodation and good public areas. It offers a particularly warm welcome to the golfers who avail themselves of its course (situated a short distance from the hotel).

■ LONDON ■

E1 Stepney and east of the Tower of London

★★★★60% **Tower Thistle** (Mount Charlotte (TS)) St Katharine's Way E1 9LD ☎ 071-488 4134

Normal price: £64.95. Dinner from £24 and à la carte.
Short breaks: £56 excluding dinner. Single supplement weekdays.
✕ Credit cards ①②③④⑤

Overlooking Tower Bridge from its spectacular location on the banks of the Thames, this large modern hotel normally teems with activity. Service aims to please.

NW3 Hampstead and Swiss Cottage

★★★59% **Charles Bernard** 5-7 Frognal, Hampstead NW3 6AL ☎ 071-794 0101

Normal price: £43.50. Dinner £9-£15.75 à la carte.
Short breaks: £32, min 2 nights, Fri-Sun. Single price £52.
✕ Credit cards ①②③⑤

Close to Central London, this commercial hotel offers nicely-appointed, well-equipped bedrooms.

★★★★65% **Holiday Inn Swiss Cottage** 128 Henry's Road, Swiss Cottage NW3 3ST ☎ 071-722 7711

Normal price: £76.50 room only (1990 price). Dinner £9-£15 à la carte.
Short breaks: £47.50 excluding dinner (1990). Min 2 nights, Fri-Sun & Bank Hols. Single price £85.
Credit cards ①②③④⑤

A modern, multi-storey hotel with a leisure club and indoor heated pool. Bedrooms are spacious, and the split-level lounge and cocktail bar are extremely comfortable.

★★★58% **Post House** (Trusthouse Forte) Haverstock Hill NW3 4RB ☎ 071-794 8121

Normal price: From £56. Dinner from £11.95 and à la carte
Short breaks: From £35.50 excluding dinner. Min 2 nights, Thu-Sun. Single supplement
Credit cards ①②③④⑤

This hotel has comfortable surroundings and fine south-west views across the city. In the restaurant the daily roast is recommended.

NW7 Mill Hill

★★62% **Welcome Lodge** (Trusthouse Forte) M1 Scratchwood Service Area, Mill Hill NW7 3HB (Access from Motorway only) ☎ 081-906 0611

Normal price: £31.
Short breaks: £15.50 excluding dinner, Fri-Sun. Single price £24.
Credit cards ①②③⑤

This motorway lodge provides comfortable bedrooms and a small restaurant offering short à la carte and carvery menus. Staff are friendly and efficient.

SW1 Westminster

★★★★63% **Cavendish** (Trusthouse Forte) Jermyn Street SW1Y 6JF ☎ 071-930 2111

Normal price: £82.50. Dinner £20 and à la carte.
Short breaks: £45-£55 excluding dinner, min 2 nights, Thurs-Sun. Single supplement £15.
Credit cards ①②③④⑤

The Cavendish is undergoing refurbishment designed to improve the comfort of the bedrooms. Traditional afternoon tea can be ordered in the gallery lounge.

★★★★★72% **Hyatt Carlton Tower** Cadogan Place SW1X 9PY ☎ 071-235 5411

Normal price: £132.50. Dinner £22-£35 and à la carte.
Short breaks: £86.25 room only Fri-Sun.
✕ Credit cards ①②③④⑤

A somewhat regimented modern hotel with a new health centre, that also has a relaxing lounge. Bedrooms are modestly furnished and prices comparatively expensive.

★★★63% **Royal Horseguards Thistle** (Mount Charlotte (TS)) Whitehall Court SW1A 2EJ
☎ 071-839 3400

Normal price: £58.45. Dinner from £15.75 and à la carte
Short breaks: £50 excluding dinner. Single supplement weekdays
✻ Credit cards ① ② ③ ④ ⑤

Guests of many nationalities frequent this large, imposing hotel, with its majestic lounge and elegant reception area. All bedrooms have modern facilities.

★★★★67% **Royal Westminster Thistle** (Mount Charlotte (TS)) 40 Buckingham Palace Road SW1W 0QT
☎ 071-834 1821

Normal price: £74.25. Dinner from £15.95 & à la carte.
Short breaks: £65 excluding dinner. Single supplement on weekdays.
✻ Credit cards ① ② ③ ④ ⑤

Spacious bedrooms, an impressive lobby and a comfortable lounge are features of this hotel. The two eating options are the formal restaurant and the more casual Café St Germain.

SW5   Earl's Court

★★★67% **Swallow International** Cromwell Road SW5 0TH ☎ 071-973 1000

Normal price: £57.50. Dinner £15 & à la carte.
Short breaks: £49.50 winter, £57.50 summer, min 2 nights. Single supplement.
Credit cards ① ② ③ ⑤

This hotel has an exclusive leisure club, and the Fountain Brasserie is open throughout the day. Blayne's Restaurant and piano bar feature a traditional menu.

SW7   South Kensington

★★★★65% **Gloucester** (Rank) 4-18 Harrington Gardens SW7 4LH ☎ 071-373 6030

Normal price: £78.75.
Short breaks: £55 including 15% dinner allowance. Fri-Sun. Single supplement.
Credit cards ① ② ③ ④ ⑤

A pleasant modern hotel with open-plan foyer/lounge and two restaurants. Bedrooms are spacious, and cheerful staff provide 24-hour service.

SW19   Wimbledon

★★★★63% **Cannizaro House** (Mount Charlotte (TS)) West Side, Wimbledon Common SW19 4UF
☎ 081-879 1464

Normal price: £57.50. Dinner from £16.50 and à la carte.
Short breaks: £51 excluding dinner. Single supplement weekdays.
Credit cards ① ② ③ ④ ⑤

Set in its own beautiful parkland, this historic Georgian mansion provides guests with all the peace and tranquility of the countryside.

W1   West End

★★★★(Red) **Athenaeum** (Rank) (Pride of Britain) Piccadilly W1V 0BJ ☎ 071-499 3464

Normal price: £94.50
Short breaks: £75 including 15% dinner allowance. Must include Fri, Sat or Sun night. Single supplement midweek. 1990 prices
✻ Credit cards ① ② ③ ④ ⑤

Standards of customer care here could be a model for other hotels, and contribute much to the attractions of this friendly hotel. The drawing room and restaurant are equally attractive.

★★★★(Red) **Brown's** (Trusthouse Forte) Albemarle Street, Dover Street W1A 4SW ☎ 071-493 6020

Normal price: £104.25. Dinner £29.95-£30.95.
Short breaks: £90 excluding dinner, including half bottle of champagne, fruit and chocolates. Min 2 nights, must include Sat. Single price £135.
✗ Credit cards ① ② ③ ④ ⑤

Newly arrived guests are greeted as old and valued customers at this hotel in the heart of Mayfair. The response to requests for room service is both prompt and courteous.

★★★70% **Chesterfield** 35 Charles Street W1X 8LX ☎ 071-491 2622

Normal price: £75 room only.
Short breaks: £56 excluding dinner. Min 2 nights, Fri-Sun. Single price £80.
✗ Credit cards ① ② ③ ⑤

Traditional hotel in the centre of Mayfair with colourful bedrooms furnished to a high standard. A warm atmosphere is created by flowers and antiques.

★★★★★66% **Churchill** 30 Portman Square W1A 4ZX ☎ 071-486 5800

Normal price: £117.87 room only. Dinner from £30 and à la carte
Short breaks: £68 excluding dinner. Fri-Sun only.
Credit cards ① ② ③ ④ ⑤

The flower-filled lobby, attractive arcade of shops and sunken lounge where afternoon tea is served to the accompaniment of a harp, are some of the attractions of this hotel.

★★★★58% **Cumberland** (Trusthouse Forte) Marble Arch W1A 4RF ☎ 071-262 1234

Normal price: £75-£86 (1990) room only. Dinner £19-£35.
Short breaks: £53-£57 excluding dinner. Min 2 nights, Thu-Sun, Apr-Dec.
✗ Credit cards ① ② ③ ④ ⑤

This popular hotel offers a choice of restaurants, including a carvery and a coffee shop as well as the main restaurant and, for those who like the exotic, one in Japanese style.

★★★★★78% **Inn on the Park** (Prestige) Hamilton Place, Park Lane W1A 1AZ ☎ 071-499 0888

Normal price: £107.50 room. Dinner £24.50-£38.50 and à la carte.
Short breaks: £90 (1990), excluding dinner, including champagne & car parking. Min 2 nights, Fri-Sun, Nov-Apr & Aug.
✗ Credit cards ① ② ③ ④ ⑤

Possibly the best modern hotel in London, certainly elegant and attractive, with every attention paid to the comfort and convenience of guests.

✿★★★★★73% **Inter-Continental** Hamilton Place, Hyde Park Corner W1V 0QY ☎ 071-409 3131

Normal price: £120.87 (1990). Dinner £40 and à la carte.
Short breaks: £120 including Continental breakfast, excluding dinner. Fri-Sun.
✗ Credit cards ① ② ③ ④ ⑤

This hotel maintains high standards of service in all departments, and rooms are smartly furnished. Three restaurants offer a range of eating choices.

★★★★★59% **London Hilton** 22 Park Lane W1A 2HH ☎ 071-493 8000

Normal price: £123.62 room only. Dinner £45 and à la carte.
Short breaks: £70 excluding dinner. Min 2 nights, Fri-Sun. 1990 prices
Credit cards ① ② ③ ④ ⑤

From its prime position at the heart of Mayfair the Hilton's rooms command superb views over Hyde Park. Staff are cosmopolitan, well trained and very helpful.

★★★★73% **Montcalm** Great Cumberland Place W1A 2LF ☎ 071-402 4288

Normal price: £104.95. Dinner £21.95 and à la carte.
Short breaks: £64.50, excluding dinner, including bottle of champagne, newspaper and car parking. Min 2 nights, Fri-Sun.
✗ Credit cards ① ② ③ ④ ⑤

This terraced Georgian building has been tastefully modernised. The Celebrities restaurant offers an interesting menu of skilfully prepared dishes.

★★★★55% **Ramada** 10 Berners Street W1A 3BA ☎ 071-636 1629

Normal price: £75 (1990) room only.
Short breaks: £65 (1990) excluding dinner. Min 2 nights, Fri-Sun.
🗙 Credit cards ① ② ③ ④ ⑤

A magnificent lounge and dining room are the key features of this hotel, which offers a successful carvery lunch and à la carte menu, and popular afternoon teas.

★★★★50% **St George's** (Trusthouse Forte) Langham Place W1N 8QS ☎ 071-580 0111

Normal price: From £80. Dinner £18.50 and à la carte.
Short breaks: From £49, excluding dinner. Min 2 nights, Mon-Wed. Single price from £65.
🗙 Credit cards ① ② ③ ④ ⑤

The hotel shares its building with the BBC, and bedrooms are all above the ninth floor. The Summit Restaurant affords panoramic views over London.

★★★★68% **Selfridge** (Mount Charlotte (TS)) Orchard Street W1H 0JS ☎ 071-408 2080

Normal price: £81.75. Dinner from £16.95 and à la carte.
Short breaks: £73, excluding dinner. Single supplement on weekdays.
🗙 Credit cards ① ② ③ ④ ⑤

A modern hotel with fine public rooms and two restaurants - one formal and very comfortable and the other very informal. Bedrooms tend to be small.

★★★★63% **Westbury** (Trusthouse Forte) Bond Street, Conduit Street W1A 4UH ☎ 071-629 7755

Normal price: £210 room only. Dinner £20.50-£22.50.
Short breaks: £60 approx, excluding dinner. Min 2 nights, Thu-Sun. Single price £80 including breakfast.
Activity breaks: Bridal Shopping Spree, £72.50 for Sat night.
Credit cards ① ② ③ ④ ⑤

An attractive hotel, ideally set in Mayfair, which greets winter guests with a glowing fire in its marbled foyer. The Polo Lounge serves refreshments 24 hours a day.

W2   Bayswater, Paddington

GH QQQQ Byron 36-38 Queensborough Terrace W2 3SH ☎ 071-243 0987

Normal price: £40.
Short breaks: £37.50 excluding dinner. Min 3 nights. Single price £65.
🗙 Credit cards ① ② ③ ⑤

Setting the highest standards, this hotel recreates the style and elegance of the Victorian era. Helpful, friendly staff assist in creating a relaxing atmosphere.

★★★59% **Hospitality Inn Bayswater** (Mount Charlotte (TS)) 104-105 Bayswater Road W2 3HL ☎ 071-262 4461

Normal price: £55-£59. Dinner £12-£17 à la carte
Short breaks: £41 excluding dinner. Single supplement weekdays
Credit cards ① ② ③ ④ ⑤

Some rooms in this Bayswater hotel overlook the park. Staff are friendly and service is willing throughout the hotel. Bedrooms are equipped with every modern convenience.

★★★62% **Park Court** (Mount Charlotte (TS)) 75 Lancaster Gate, Hyde Park W2 3NN ☎ 071-402 4272

Normal price: £53.75. Dinner from £14.
Short breaks: £40 excluding dinner.
Credit cards ① ② ③ ④ ⑤

A very popular tour hotel with its own garden and barbecue area. The lower ground floor Park Brasserie offers informal buffet-style meals.

★★★★67% **Royal Lancaster** (Rank) Lancaster Terrace W2 2TY ☎ 071-262 6737

Normal price: £88 (Continental breakfast). Dinner £20-£23 and à la carte
Short breaks: £61 (1990) including dinner allowance of 15%. Fri-Sun. Single supplement.
🗙 Credit cards ① ② ③ ④ ⑤

Overlooking Hyde Park, there are some unrivalled views of the Italian Gardens. The Rosette restaurant offers a choice of menus, and the Pavement Cafe a more informal atmosphere.

GH QQ Slavia 2 Pembridge Square W2 4EW ☎ 071-727 1316

Normal price: £28.50.
Short breaks: £22 excluding dinner. Min 2 nights.
Credit cards ① ② ③ ⑤

Hotel offering reasonably priced simple accommodation.

★★★★72% **White's** (Mount Charlotte (TS)) Lancaster Gate W2 3NR ☎ 071-262 2711

Normal price: £105. Dinner from £15.50 and à la carte.
Short breaks: £65.50 excluding dinner. Min 2 nights. Single price £93.50.
✱ Credit cards ① ② ③ ④ ⑤

This small hotel which overlooks Hyde Park offers high standards of service, cuisine and accommodation, and enjoys a club-like atmosphere.

W4   Chiswick

GH QQQ Chiswick 73 Chiswick High Road W4 2LS ☎ 081-994 1712

Normal price: £33 (Continental breakfast).
Short breaks: £24 excluding dinner. Min 2 nights, Fri-Sun.
Single price £38.
Credit cards ① ② ③ ⑤

This hotel offers attractive accommodation and good service. The restaurant has a residential bar, and the standard of cooking is high.

W5   Ealing

★★★70% **Carnarvon** (Consort) Ealing Common W5 3HN ☎ 081-992 5399

Normal price: £58.45.
Short breaks: £39 excluding dinner. Min 2 nights, Fri-Sun.
Single supplement.
✱ Credit cards ① ② ③ ⑤

A modern hotel on the edge of Ealing Common with spacious, bright and comfortable accommodation. Staff are well-organised and personable, and standards are high.

W8   Kensington

★★★62% **Kensington Close** (Trusthouse Forte) Wright's Lane W8 5SP ☎ 071-937 8170

Normal price: £62.50. Dinner £3.50-£13.95.
Short breaks: £40-£45 excluding dinner, min 2 nights, Thu-Sun. Single price £45-£53.50.
Activity breaks: Theatre Breaks, £53.50-£60.50. Dining Breaks, £50 approx. Theatre and Dining Breaks, £60.50-£68.
Credit cards ① ② ③ ④ ⑤

A large quietly situated hotel with a health and fitness club including a swimming pool, two squash courts and a gymnasium.

★★★★68% **Kensington Palace Thistle** (Mount Charlotte (TS)) De Vere Gardens W8 5AF
☎ 071-937 8121

Normal price: £60.25 . Dinner from £17.50 & à la carte.
Short breaks: £53 excluding dinner. Single supplement weekdays
✱ Credit cards ① ② ③ ④ ⑤

The rooms in this busy hotel have been upgraded, and the restaurant offers interesting and enjoyable dishes. Service is attentive and efficient.

★★57% **Lexham** 32-38 Lexham Gardens W8 5JU ☎ 071-373 6471

Normal price: £20.75. Dinner from £8.25.
Short breaks: £27.34, min 2 nights, Nov-Mar. Single price £38.15.
✱ Credit cards ① ③

A traditional hotel with good-value accommodation. There is no bar but a choice of two lounges, and the staff are pleasant and cheerful.

★★★★★61% **Royal Garden** (Rank) Kensington High Street W8 4PT ☎ 071-937 8000

Normal price: £92.95.
Short breaks: £68 (1990) including dinner allowance of 15%.
Single supplement.
✺ Credit cards ① ② ③ ④ ⑤

Suites, studios and bedrooms are all tastefully furnished and equipped to five-star standard, and offer views over Kensington Gardens and Hyde Park or Kensington High Street.

W11   Holland Park, Notting Hill

★★★73% **London Kensington Hilton** Holland Park Avenue W11 4UL ☎ 071-603 3355

Normal price: £84. Dinner £20-£35
Short breaks: £49 excluding dinner. Min 2 nights, Fri-Sun.
Credit cards ① ② ③ ④ ⑤

Large and exceptionally comfortable hotel with a distinctly international flavour. There is a choice of three places to eat, several shops and car parking for 100.

WC1   Bloomsbury, Holborn

★★★60% **Bonnington** 92 Southampton Row WC1B 4BH ☎ 071-242 2828

Normal price: £50. Dinner from £12 and à la carte.
Short breaks: £40 excluding dinner. Fri-Sun.
Credit cards ① ② ③ ⑤

In a prime position between the City and the West End, the Bonnington offers good quality food in the Bonnington Grill and the lounge bar. Staff are polite and friendly.

★★★★61% **Russell** (Trusthouse Forte) Russell Square WC1B 5BE ☎ 071-837 6470

Normal price: from £77.50. Dinner from £14.50 and à la carte.
Short breaks: £45 (1990), excluding dinner. Min 2 nights, Fri-Sun. Single price £55.
Credit cards ① ② ③ ④ ⑤

Large hotel with imposing entrance hall, comfortable bedrooms and good service. Two eating choices in an informal, colourful brasserie and a carvery with à la carte menu.

WC2   Covent Garden

★★★67% **Drury Lane Moat House** (Queens Moat) 10 Drury Lane WC2B 5RE ☎ 071-836 6666

Normal price: £78.50-£85.75. Dinner from £17.50.
Short breaks: £57.50 including early morning tea and newspaper. Min 2 nights, Fri-Sun. Single supplement £30.
Activity breaks: Theatre Breaks, £160 including theatre ticket, champagne and chocolates.
Credit cards ① ② ③ ④ ⑤

A stylish, purpose-built hotel conveniently situated for the theatre, Covent Garden and the Opera House. Efficient service prevails throughout.

★★★56% **Royal Trafalgar Thistle** (Mount Charlotte (TS)) Whitcomb Street WC2H 7HG ☎ 071-930 4477

Normal price: from £58.45. Dinner from £12 and à la carte.
Short breaks: £50 excluding dinner. Single supplement weekdays.
Credit cards ① ② ③ ④ ⑤

Real ale and lunchtime snacks are served in the traditional atmosphere of this hotel's pub, in total contrast to the French-style brasserie.

★★★55% **Strand Palace** (Trusthouse Forte) Strand WC2R 0JJ ☎ 071-836 8080

Normal price: £60.50. Dinner £14.95-£15.95 and à la carte.
Short breaks: £46.50 (1990 price), excluding dinner. Min 2 nights, Thu-Sun. Single price £51.50.
Credit cards ① ② ③ ④ ⑤

Facilities at this theatreland hotel include two popular bars, a carvery, a coffee shop and a variety of shops. Bedrooms offer a variety of styles.

★★★★69% **Waldorf** (Trusthouse Forte) Aldwych WC2B 4DD ☎ 071-836 2400

Normal price: from £90. Dinner £22.50-£24.50 and à la carte. *Short breaks:* £50-£59 excluding dinner. Min 2 nights, must include a Sat. Single price £72-£85.
🍗 Credit cards ① ② ③ ④ ⑤

Edwardian elegance is the keynote of this hotel, now combined with modern amenities. Outstanding attractions include the Palm Court, the two bars and the Waldorf Restaurant.

CROYDON   Greater London   Map 4 TQ36

★★57% **Briarley** 8 Outram Road, Croydon CR0 6XE ☎ 081-654 1000

Normal price: £32.50. Dinner from £10.50 and à la carte. Single £55
Short breaks: £20 excluding dinner. Single £30. Fri-Sun (must include Sat)
Credit cards ① ② ③ ⑤

Standing in a residential area off the A215 West Wickham road, this hotel offers a choice of bedrooms in the main house or the rear annexe. All have private facilities and colour television.

★★★★62% **Selsdon Park** (Best Western) Sanderstead, Croydon CR2 8YA (3m SE off A2022) ☎ 081-657 8811

Normal price: £78. Dinner from £21 and à la carte
Short breaks: £86. Single £95. Min 2 nights, Fri-Sun. Special rates all week Jul-Aug

A mansion set in beautiful gardens amid 200-acre grounds offering both indoor and outdoor leisure facilities. All the bedrooms have ensuite facilities and colour television and one room is furnished with a four-poster bed. There is a special Christmas programme. See advertisement under Surrey.

ENFIELD   Greater London   Map 4 TQ39

★★54% **Holtwhites** 92 Chase Side, Enfield EN2 0QN ☎ 081-363 0124

Normal price: £97 room and breakfast. Dinner £10-£20 à la carte
Short breaks: £35 excluding dinner. Single £45. Min 2 nights, Fri-Sun
Credit cards ① ② ③ ⑤

A busy hotel offering a choice of well-equipped bedrooms with colour television. Most have ensuite bath or shower room. Children under five are not accommodated.

HAYES   Greater London   Map 4 TQ07

★★★60% **Ariel** Hayes, Middlesex UB3 5AJ ☎ 081-759 2552

Normal price: £110 room and breakfast.
Short breaks: £35 Fri, Sat, Sun only
Activity breaks: Theatre breaks: from £78.20-£91.30
Credit cards ① ② ③ ④ ⑤

A popular hotel on the A4 with quick access to the airport. The ground floor has been completely upgraded to include a new foyer, lounge, bar, carvery and fish restaurant. Service is well managed and friendly and the porterage is very helpful.

HEATHROW AIRPORT (LONDON)   Greater London   Map 4 TQ07

★★★★64% **Excelsior** (Trusthouse Forte) Bath Road, West Drayton UB7 0DU (adj M4 spur at junc with A4) ☎ 081-759 6611

Normal price: £115-£135 room and breakfast. Dinner £13.95 and à la carte
Short breaks: £35 excluding dinner. Min 2 nights, Fri-Sun. 1990 prices
Credit cards ① ② ③ ④ ⑤

Stylish and extensive refurbishment has transformed this popular hotel which has a good range of leisure facilities. All bedrooms are ensuite with colour television, with rooms set aside for non-smokers. There is a special Christmas programme.

★★★★64% **Heathrow Penta** Bath Road, Hounslow TW6 2AQ ☎ 081-897 6363

Normal price: £107 room and breakfast. Dinner £14.24 and à la carte
Short breaks: £68-£75 for two. Single £63-£68 excluding dinner.
🐾 (ex guide dogs) Credit cards ① ② ③ ⑤

Bedrooms at this airport hotel are air-conditioned and double-glazed. Room service and the coffee shop offer 24-hour service and there is a popular leisure complex and swimming pool. There is a special Christmas programme.

★★★★61% **Holiday Inn** Stockley Road, West Drayton UB7 9NA (2m N junc M4/A408) ☎ (0895) 445555

Normal price: £115-£122 room
Short breaks: £80 for two. Single £60. Fri & Sat 1990 prices
Credit cards ① ② ③ ④ ⑤

This modern hotel has good leisure facilities and offers a choice of eating options. The bedrooms are spacious, all are ensuite with colour television, and there are rooms for families and non-smokers.

HORNCHURCH Greater London Map 5 TQ58

★★★59% **Hilton National** Southend Arterial Road, Hornchurch RM11 3UJ ☎ (04023) 46789

Normal price: £87 room. Dinner £10.50-£32.20.
Short breaks: £52-£55, min 2 nights, Fri-Sun.
Activity breaks: Motor Racing, £130 for 2 nights. Dry Skiing, £90.
Credit cards ① ② ③ ⑤

A modern hotel with comfortable bedrooms and a new leisure centre. The popular 'Palms' cocktail bar and eating house has been enlarged.

OSTERLEY Greater London Map 4 TQ17

★★56% **Osterley** (Consort) 764 Great West Road, Osterley TW7 5NA ☎ 081-568 9981

Normal price: £30. Dinner £8.50 and à la carte (1990 price)
Short breaks: £25 including continental breakfast, excluding dinner. Min 2 nights, Fri-Sun.
Credit cards ① ② ③ ⑤

A friendly hotel with well-equipped comfortable bedrooms, all with private bar or shower and colour television.

WOODFORD GREEN Greater London Map 4 TQ49

★★★68% **Woodford Moat House** (Queens Moat) Oak Hill, Woodford Green IG8 9NY ☎ 081-505 4511

Normal price: £46. Dinner £14.25-£28.65 and à la carte.
Short breaks: £42.50, min 2 nights, Fri-Sun.
🐾 Credit cards ① ② ③ ⑤

Ideally situated on the edge of Epping Forest, this hotel offers tempting set and à la carte meals in the attractive wood-panelled restaurant.

▪ MANCHESTER ▪

ALTRINCHAM Manchester Map 7 SJ78

★★★63% **Bowdon** Langham Road, Bowdon WA14 2HT ☎ 061-928 7121
Restricted service 25 & 26 Dec

Normal price: £23. Dinner £11.50 and à la carte
Short breaks: £32. Single £32. Min 2 nights, Fri-Sun.

Well placed for access to Manchester, the airport and the M56, this hotel has been modernised and now provides comfortable bedrooms all with ensuite facilities and colour television.

★★63% **Cresta Court** (Best Western) Church Street WA14 4DP ☎ 061-927 7272

Normal price: £51.50 room
Short breaks: £34.50 room (1990)

A modern hotel with good car parking facilities situated at the junction of the A56/A560. All the bedrooms have colour television and ensuite facilities, and there are some family rooms.

BOLTON Manchester Map 7 SD70

★★★63% **Egerton House** (Character) Blackburn Road, Egerton BL7 9PL (3m N A666) ☎ (0204) 57171

Normal price: £65 room with breakfast
Short breaks: £86 for 2 nights including Sunday lunch. Min 2 nights, Fri-Sun. Single £88
✘ (ex guide dogs) Credit cards ① ② ③ ⑤

In secluded grounds and gardens, this comfortable hotel provides attractive bedrooms with private bath or shower rooms and colour television. Some rooms are for families.

★★★64% **Last Drop** (Character) Hospital Road, Bromley Cross BL7 9PZ (3m N off B6472) ☎ (0204) 591131

Normal price: £85 room with breakfast. Dinner £16-£30 and à la carte
Short breaks: £82 for 2 people, with £12.50 dinner allowance. Min 2 nights, Fri-Sun
Credit cards ① ② ③ ⑤

This unique hotel, together with tea room, craft shop and pub, forms part of a village created in 1964 from derelict farm buildings, and is now a popular tourist attraction. An outstanding leisure complex has an indoor heated swimming pool and a large gymnasium. There is a special Christmas programme.

★★★61% **Pack Horse** (De Vere) Bradshawgate, Nelson Square BL1 1DP ☎ (0204) 27261

Normal price: £85 room and breakfast. Dinner £12.50-£14.
Short breaks: £72. Min 2 nights, any nights Jul & Aug, any 2 weekend nights throughout the year.
Activity breaks: Ballroom Dancing Breaks, £75. Dry Ski Weekends, £85. Leisure Break, £68 including one complimentary ticket per family for entry to Granada Studios Tour.
Credit cards ① ② ③ ⑤

In a town centre position yet within easy reach of the national motorway network stands a traditional hotel with an attractive Georgian façade.

MANCHESTER Manchester Map 7 SJ89

★★★★66% **Holiday Inn** Crowne Plaza, Peter Street M60 2DS ☎ 061-236 3333

Normal price: £112 per room
Short breaks: £40 excluding dinner (£60 single occupancy) for 1 night only Fri/Sat; £74 (£99 single occupancy) for 2 nights, Fri-Sun.
Credit cards ① ② ③ ⑤

This large and elegant modernised Edwardian hotel in the city centre has ensuite facilities and colour television in all bedrooms, with family and no-smoking rooms. Apart from 3 restaurants, there is a heated swimming pool, squash, sauna, solarium and gymnasium. Christmas breaks are available.

★★★★66% **Piccadilly** (Embassy) Piccadilly M60 1QR ☎ 061-236 8414

Normal price: £105 room, Mon-Thu; £52.50, Fri-Sun.
Short breaks: £55. Min 2 nights, Fri-Sun.
Credit cards ① ② ③ ④ ⑤

Situated in the city centre, this large, comfortable hotel with two elegant restaurants has ensuite facilities and colour television in all bedrooms, including no-smoking rooms. Facilities include a heated swimming pool, sauna, solarium and gymnasium. Christmas breaks are available.

★★★★64% **Portland Thistle** (Thistle) 3-5 Porland Street, Piccadilly Gardens M1 6DP ☎ 061-228 3400

Normal price: £56 room only
Short breaks: £35 excluding dinner. Single supplement on weekdays.
Credit cards ① ② ③ ④ ⑤

An attractive, centrally situated hotel with a good restaurant, extensive champagne and whisky lists, and ensuite facilities and colour television in all bedrooms, which include family and no-smoking rooms. Leisure facilities include a heated swimming pool, sauna, solarium, gymnasium, whirlpool and hairdresser.

★★★★65% **Ramada Renaissance** Blackfriars Street M3 2EQ ☎ 061-835 2555

Normal price: £97.50 room
Short breaks: £27.50, min 1 night, Fri-Sun. Single price £55.
Activity breaks: Ballroom Dancing, £89-£105. Murder/Mystery, details from hotel.
Credit cards ① ② ③ ④ ⑤

A large, modern, city-centre hotel with spacious bedrooms, and a young staff provide service in a cheerful and helpful manner.

★★★60% **Willow Bank** 340-342 Wilmslow Road, Fallowfield M14 6AF ☎ 061-224 0461

Normal price: £34.50 room.
Short breaks: £16 room, Fri-Sun. £25 single occupancy.
✗ (ex guide dogs) Credit cards ① ② ③ ⑤

Situated 3 miles from the city centre, this hotel has comfortable public rooms and colour television in all bedrooms, which have separate private bath or shower. There is also live entertainment.

MANCHESTER AIRPORT   Manchester   Map 7 SJ88

★★★59% **Wilmslow Moat House** (Queens Moat) Altrincham Road SK9 4LR ☎ (0625) 529201

Normal price: £94 room. Dinner £12
Short breaks: £79 for 2 people. Min 2 nights, Fri-Sun. Single £39.50
Credit cards ① ② ③ ⑤

Behind its distinctive Swiss Chalet exterior, this hotel offers every modern amenity, including excellent leisure facilities. Each bedroom has a private bathroom and colour television, and two have four-poster beds.

★★★★57% **Excelsior** (Trusthouse Forte) Ringway Road M22 5NS ☎ 061-437 5811

Normal price: £103 room and breakfast. Dinner from £14.50 (1990 price)
Short breaks: £49, min 2 nights, Thu-Sun (must include Sat)
Credit cards ① ② ③ ④ ⑤

This large hotel in the airport complex has colour television and ensuite facilities in all bedrooms, some of them non-smoking. It incorporates a leisure centre with heated swimming pool, sauna, solarium, gymnasium and health and fitness centre.

★★★★67% **Manchester Airport Hilton** Outwood Lane, Ringway M22 5WP ☎ 061-436 4404

Normal price: from £135 room and breakfast. Dinner £8.50-£40.
Short breaks: from £60, min 2 nights, Fri-Sun.
Activity breaks: Motor Racing Breaks, from £144. A chance to drive at Oulton Park racing circuit. Mersey River Festival and Royal Lancaster Show, Chorley. Details from hotel.

A large modern hotel which features lots of greenery and an attractive little stream running through its public areas. Enhanced by an appealing leisure complex.

MARPLE   Manchester   Map 7 SJ98

★ **Springfield** Station Road SK6 6PA ☎ 061-449 0721

Normal price: £48 room and breakfast
Short breaks: £39 for two excluding dinner. £30 single. Fri-Sun.
Credit cards ① ② ③ ⑤

This small friendly hotel in a pleasant residential area within easy reach of motorway and airport links serves good home cooking, and all bedrooms have colour television and private bath or shower.

OLDHAM   Manchester   Map 7 SD90

★★★62% **Smokies Park** (Consort) Ashton Road, Bardsley OL8 3HX ☎ 061-624 3405

Normal price: £65 room
Short breaks: £38. Min 2 nights, Fri-Sun and Bank Holiday Mons.
✖ (ex guide dogs) Credit cards ① ② ③ ⑤

This new hotel midway between Ashton-under-Lyne and Oldham provides full modern comforts, all bedrooms having ensuite bathrooms and colour television.

RAMSBOTTOM   Manchester   Map 7 SD71

★★★62% **Old Mill** Springwood BL10 9DS ☎ (070682) 2991

Normal price: £23-£29.50. Dinner from £10.50 & à la carte (1990 price)
Short breaks: £33, 1-3 nights, Fri-Sun. £38.50 for single occupancy.
✖ Credit cards ① ② ③ ④ ⑤

This recently extended hotel has a comfortable lounge bar and beamed restaurant, and a leisure centre with indoor swimming pool, sauna, solarium and gymnasium. All bedrooms, which include a few family rooms and some with a four-poster bed, are ensuite with colour television. Christmas breaks are available.

ROCHDALE   Manchester   Map 7 SD91

★★★65% **Norton Grange** (Associated Leisure) Manchester Road OL11 2XZ ☎ (0706) 30788

Normal price: £42.50
Short breaks: £41.50 including set-price dinner or £15 dinner allowance and luncheon. Fri-Sun.
Credit cards ① ② ③ ④ ⑤

This modernised and extended Victorian mansion with a garden provides comfortable accommodation. All bedrooms are ensuite and with colour television, including many family rooms and one with a four-poster bed. Christmas breaks are available.

STANDISH   Manchester   Map 7 SD51

★★★69% **Kilhey Court** Chorley Road WN1 2XN (on A5106 1.5 miles north of A49/A5106 junction) ☎ (0257) 472100

Normal price: £63-£103 (suite) weekday, £45 weekend. Dinner £15-£20 and à la carte.
Short breaks: £40, min 2 nights, Fri-Sun.
Credit cards ① ② ③ ⑤

Situated in 10 acres of grounds and gardens with a lake, this extended Victorian mansion provides comfortable accommodation and excellent cuisine. Conference facilities are available, and a new wing provides more bedrooms and a leisure complex.

▓ MERSEYSIDE ▓

BEBINGTON   Merseyside   Map 7 SJ38

★★61% **Bridge Inn** Bolton Road, Port Sunlight L62 4UQ ☎ 051-645 8441

Normal price: £30
Short breaks: £25 excluding dinner. Single £30. Min 2 nights, Fri-Sun.
✖

This popular inn, standing close to the church in the unique setting of Port Sunlight Village provides comfortable accommodation. All the bedrooms have private facilities and colour television, there are two family rooms and one is furnished with a four-poster bed.

BLUNDELLSANDS   Merseyside   Map 7 SJ39

★★★59% **Blundellsands** (Lansbury) Serpentine L23 6TN ☎ 051-924 6515

Normal price: £38. Dinner from £14 and à la carte
Short breaks: £35 with dinner. Min 2 nights, Fri-Sun.
Credit cards ①②③⑤

.Situated in a residential area of Crosby beside the railway station, this is an extended Victorian building offering ensuite bedrooms with colour television. Some rooms are for families and non-smokers.

BOOTLE   Merseyside

★★★54% **Park** Park Lane West L30 3SU ☎ 051-525 7555

Normal price: £22.50
Short breaks: £30 including £10 dinner allowance. (1990 prices)
Credit cards ①②③④⑤

Situated beside the busy A5036 not far from Aintree and convenient for the M57 and M58, this commercial and conference hotel is gradually being improved. Those bedrooms which have been refurbished are attractively appointed and well-equipped.

BROMBOROUGH   Merseyside   Map 7 SJ38

★★★64% **Cromwell** (Lansbury) High Street L62 7HZ ☎ 051-334 2917

Normal price: £39 room. Dinner from £14 and à la carte
Short breaks: £36. Min 2 nights, Fri-Sun
Credit cards ①②③⑤

A town centre hotel providing an ensuite bathroom and colour television in all bedrooms; some rooms are set aside for families and non-smokers and one has a four-poster bed. The hotel has a sauna, solarium and gymnasium.

HAYDOCK   Merseyside   Map 7 SJ59

★★★66% **Post House** (Trusthouse Forte) Lodge Lane, Newton-Le-Willows WA12 0JG (adj to M6 junc 23) ☎ (0942) 717878

Normal price: £92 room. Dinner from £10.50 and à la carte
Short breaks: £38. Min 2 nights, Fri-Sun
Credit cards ①②③④⑤

A purpose-built hotel with a wing of superior bedrooms and a modern keep-fit complex with a swimming pool. Christmas breaks are available.

LIVERPOOL   Merseyside   Map 7 SJ39

★★★★57% **Liverpool Moat House** (Queens Moat) Paradise Street L1 8JD ☎ 051-709 0180

Normal price: £99 room and breakfast. Dinner £17.60-£19.80.
Short breaks: £87. Min 2 nights, Fri-Sun. Single price £68.50.
Activity breaks: Soccer City, Aug-May. Details from hotel.
Credit cards ①②③④⑤

Modern purpose-built hotel close to the city centre.

RAINHILL   Merseyside   Map 7 SJ49

★ **Rockland** View Road L35 0LG ☎ 051-426 4603

Normal price: £27
Short breaks: £18.50 excluding dinner. Min 2 nights, Fri-Sun. £25 single price.
Credit cards ①③

Just off the A57, this detached Georgian house set in its own grounds has comfortable annexe bedrooms, half of them family rooms, with private bathrooms and colour television.

SOUTHPORT Merseyside Map 7 SD31

★★64% **Bold** Lord Street PR9 0BE ☎ (0704) 32578

Normal price: £25. Dinner £13.40–£21.40 and à la carte, (1990 prices).
Short breaks: £15 excluding dinner. Min 2 nights Fri-Sun.
🗡 Credit cards ① ② ③ ④ ⑤

A completely refurbished Victorian hotel providing attractive bedrooms and public areas. The elegant restaurant offers many tantalising dishes, and a competitively priced wine list complements the delicious food.

QQ Crimond 28 Knowsley Road PR9 0HN ☎ (0704) 536456

Normal price: £30
Short breaks: £21 includes a £5 dinner allowance. Min 2 nights, Fri-Sun.
Credit cards ① ② ③ ⑤

This family-run hotel situated in a quiet residential area is popular with business people for its conference and leisure facilities. The bedrooms very in size and style, and all are well equipped.

★★60% **Lockerbie House** 11 Trafalgar Road, Birkdale PR8 2EA ☎ (0704) 65298

Normal price: £24. Dinner from £8.50.
Short breaks: £22 excluding dinner. Min 3 nights. £3 single supplement.
Credit cards ① ② ③ ⑤

Situated in a quiet residential area close to Birkdale station and the famous golf course, this small hotel is run in a friendly and informal manner by the enthusiastic proprietors. Bedrooms continue to be improved, and most are spacious and comfortable.

★★55% **Metropole** Portland Street PR8 1LL ☎ (0704) 36836

Normal price: £26.75. Dinner from £8.75.
Short breaks: £24, min 2 nights Oct '91-Apr '92, excluding Christmas and New Year. £6 single supplement.
Credit cards ① ② ③

A pleasant, family-run hotel.

★★★★54% **Prince of Wales** (Trusthouse Forte) Lord Street PR8 1JS ☎ (0704) 536688

Normal price: £80 room. Dinner £10.50–£13.50.
Short breaks: from £47, min 2 nights, Mon-Wed.
Activity breaks: Murder Weekends, £164. Golfing Breaks, £107. Horse Racing Weekends, £151. Details from hotel.
Credit cards ① ② ③ ⑤

A large hotel in Southport's famous Lord Street, set close to both seafront and main shopping areas.

★★★62% **Royal Clifton** Promenade PR8 1RB ☎ (0704) 33771

Normal price: £75-£85 room and breakfast. Dinner from £12.50
Short breaks: from £45, min 2 nights.
Credit cards ① ② ③ ⑤

A large seaside hotel overlooking the promenade and gardens. Leisure facilities include pool, sauna and solarium.

★★★61% **Scarisbrick** Lord Street PR8 1NZ ☎ (0704) 43000

Normal price: £35. Dinner £11.25-£13.50.
Short breaks: £35, min 2 nights, Fri-Sun. Single price £45.
Activity breaks: Golfing Breaks, £150 for 2 nights.
Credit cards ① ② ③ ⑤

A modernised former coaching inn, the Scarisbrick still retains some of its original character with Victorian-style furnishing and decor.

★★61% **Stutelea** Alexandra Road PR9 0NB ☎ (0704) 544220

Normal price: £37.40. Dinner £9.90–£14 à la carte.
Short breaks: £34.50, min 2 nights.
🗡 Credit cards ① ② ③ ⑤

Situated within easy reach of the town centre, this family-run hotel offers comfortable accommodation, with well tended gardens creating a relaxing atmosphere. Amenities include a leisure club with a well equipped gymnasium and an indoor pool.

GH QQ White Lodge Talbot Street PR8 1HP ☎ (0704) 536320

Normal price: £15-£17. Dinner £6.
Short breaks: £13.50-£15.50 excluding dinner. Sept-Jun.
✕

Pleasant, well-maintained accommodation is offered at this family-run guesthouse, including an attractive basement lounge bar. Convenient for the town centre.

▪ NORFOLK ▪

BLAKENEY Norfolk Map 9 TG04

★★61% **Manor** NR25 7ND ☎ (0263) 740376
Closed 4-27 Dec

Normal price: £34. Dinner from £9.50
Short breaks: £70 for 2 nights

Overlooking Blakeney Quay and point, the 16th-century Manor Hotel provides well-equipped warm bedrooms with ensuite facilities and colour television. Most rooms are in a courtyard annexe offering accommodation on ground level. There are two family rooms and one with a four-poster bed. Children under ten are not accommodated.

BUNWELL Norfolk Map 5 TM19

★★ 🛦 62% **Bunwell Manor** Bunwell Street NR16 1QU ☎ (095389) 8304

Normal price: £30. Dinner £10 and à la carte
Short breaks: £35. Min 2 nights
Credit cards ①③

Dating from the 16th century this hotel offers a warm welcome and tasty, wholesome food. There are ten bedrooms all with colour television and ensuite facilities; two rooms are set aside for families. Special facilities for children.

CROMER Norfolk Map 9 TG24

GH QQ Sandcliff Runton Road NR27 9AS ☎ (0263) 512888
Feb-10 Dec

Normal price: £21
Short breaks: from £19.20, including £5 dinner allowance.
Min 3 nights

Friendly private hotel on the coast road and convenient for the town centre. Some of the bedrooms have ensuite bath and shower, and colour television.

DEREHAM Norfolk Map 5 TF91

★★64% **King's Head** Norwich Street NH19 1AD ☎ (0362) 693842 & 693283

Normal price: £24.50
Short breaks: £28 including £10.50 dinner allowance. Min 2 nights
Credit cards ①②③⑤

A 16th-century hotel only a few minutes from the town centre. There is a walled garden, and accommodation is well-equipped and carefully maintained. Staff are courteous and efficient.

DOWNHAM MARKET   Norfolk   Map 5 TF60

★★56% **Castle** High Street PE38 9HF ☎ (0366) 384311

Normal price: £21. Dinner from £9.90 and à la carte
Short breaks: £28. Min 2 nights
Credit cards ①②③⑤

A 300-year-old coaching inn standing in the centre of town offering freshly prepared meals. All the bedrooms have colour television, most have ensuite bath or shower rooms and two have four-poster beds. There is a special Christmas programme.

GH QQQ Crosskeys Riverside Hilgay PE38 0LN ☎ (0366) 38777
Closed 23 Dec-23 Jan

Normal price: £21.27
Short breaks: 2 nights £27.13, 3 nights £26, 4 nights £25.41, 5 nights £25.02, 6 nights £24.71, 7 nights £24.43.

This former coaching inn, situated on the banks of the River Wissey, has comfortable bedrooms with private bathrooms and colour television. Fishing is available.

★57% **Crown** Bridge Street PE38 9DH ☎ (0366) 382322

Normal price: £42 room and breakfast.
Short breaks: 2 days 10% off room and restaurant; 3 days 12½% off
Credit cards ①②③⑤

A town-centre hotel, dating back to the 17th century, offering well-prepared food, real ale and bedrooms with good facilities.

GARBOLDISHAM   Norfolk   Map 5 TM08

GH QQ Ingleneuk Lodge Hopton Road IP22 2RQ ☎ (095381) 541
Restricted service 1-16 Oct & Xmas

Normal price: £14.75-£19.75. Dinner £11
Short breaks: £23.75-£28.75. Single (must include Fri or Sat night) £29.75-£34.75. Min 2 nights.
🖾 Credit cards ①③

A modern bungalow set in ten acres of quiet wooded countryside. Most bedrooms have ensuite facilities, and all have colour television. Fishing is available.

GREAT YARMOUTH   Norfolk   Map 5 TG50

GH QQ Balmoral 65 Avondale Road NR31 6DJ ☎ (0493) 662538

Normal price: £15-£19
Short breaks: £13 excluding dinner. Single £15. Min 3 nights, Jun-Sep

This family-run establishment provides compact, modern accommodation in a residential area. Two rooms have ensuite showers and there are family rooms. There is no parking on the premises.

★★63% **Burlington** 11 North Drive NR30 1EG ☎ (0493) 844568 & 842095
Closed Jan-Feb Restricted service Dec

Normal price: £32.50. Dinner £9.50
Short breaks: £34-£44. Mar-Oct
Credit cards ①③

This family-owned hotel stands at the quieter end of the seafront. Some of the bedrooms have fine sea views, all have colour television and most are ensuite. Leisure amenities include a swimming pool and gymnasium. There is a Christmas programme.

GH QQ Georgian House NR30 4EW ☎ (0493) 842623
Closed Xmas Restricted service Nov-Etr

Normal price: £18.50-£20
Short breaks: £16-£17.50 excluding dinner. Min 2 nights, Spring and Autumn; min 3 nights Summer. Fri-Mon

Most of the bedrooms have private bath or shower rooms, and all have colour television. Children under five are not accommodated.

★★69% **Imperial** North Drive NR30 1EQ ☎ (0493) 851113

Normal price: £30. Dinner £13.50.
Short breaks: £42, min 2 nights. Must include Sat.
Activity breaks: Golf Breaks, £52.50 per night.
Credit cards [1] [2] [3] [4] [5]

This imposing Victorian hotel, set at the quieter end of the seafront, offers a high standard of English cuisine.

GH QQ Jennis Lodge 63 Avondale Road NR31 6DJ (2m S off A12) ☎ (0493) 662840

Normal price: £17-£22
Short breaks: £15. Oct-Apr

Situated in a quiet residential road close to Marine Parade and steps to the promenade and beach, this guesthouse offers comfortable accommodation with a choice of family rooms. There is no parking on the premises.

★★★60% **Meridian Dolphin** Albert Square NR30 3JH ☎ (0493) 855070

Normal price: £41. Dinner from £9.50 and à la carte
Short breaks: £35. Min 2 nights, Fri-Mon
Credit cards [1] [2] [3] [5]

Situated off Marine Parade close to the popular attractions of the Pleasure Beach, this hotel provides full ensuite facilities and every modern convenience in the light and attractively furnished rooms. There are some leisure amenities, and a Christmas programme is available.

GRIMSTON   Norfolk Map 9 TF72

★★★(Red) ✿ ♨ **Congham Hall Country House** (Pride of Britain) Lynn Road PE32 1AH
☎ (0485) 600250

Normal price: £47.50 room.
Short breaks: £150 for 2 nights, Sat & Sun. Single price £175.
Activity breaks: Shooting Breaks, £40 per half day's shooting. Ballooning, Helicopter Flights and Flying Lessons, details from hotel.
✻ Credit cards [1] [2] [3] [5]

An elegant Georgian house set in 40 acres of parkland with orchards, a paddock and colourful gardens. A resident pianist performs on the grand piano at weekends.

HETHERSETT   Norfolk Map 5 TG10

★★★70% **Park Farm** NR9 3DL ☎ (0603) 810264
Closed 25-29 Dec

Normal price: from £32.50. Dinner £10.50-£11.50 and à la carte
Short breaks: from £30 excluding dinner. Single from £47. Min 2 nights (ex Bank Holidays)
✻ (ex guide dogs) Credit cards [1] [2] [3] [4] [5]

This hotel, a former farm with outbuildings, provides well-equipped accommodation in an informal courtyard arrangement. The elegant restaurant offers a good selection of menus. Leisure amenities include an indoor heated pool. See advertisement on p222.

HOLT   Norfolk Map 9 TG03

GH QQQ Lawns Station Road NR25 6BS ☎ (0263) 713390

Normal price: £25
Short breaks: £36, min 2 nights, Mon-Thu. Single price £40.
Activity breaks: Bird Watching Breaks, details from hotel.
Credit cards [1] [2] [3]

Built as a farmhouse, and later used as a dormitory for Gresham School, The Lawns is now a highly recommended hotel.

HORNING   Norfolk Map 9 TG31

★★★62% **Petersfield House** Lower Street NR12 8PF ☎ (0692) 630741

Normal price: £32.50. Dinner from £14 and à la carte
Short breaks: £43. No single supplement at weekends. Min 2 nights
Credit cards ① ② ③ ⑤

A family-run hotel, in landscaped gardens close to the River Bure, provides friendly service and comfortable ensuite bedrooms. Fishing is available and there are Christmas breaks.

HORSHAM ST FAITH   Norfolk Map 9 TG21

GH QQQ Elm Farm Chalet Norwich Road NR10 3HH ☎ (0603) 898366
Restricted service 25-26 Dec

Normal price: £21.18-£24.75
Short breaks: £20.18-£23.75 excluding dinner. 7 nights Apr-Oct, min 2 nights, Nov-Mar (ex Bank Holidays)
🐾 (ex guide dogs)

This guesthouse has an annexe of bedrooms with ensuite showers and colour television.

HUNSTANTON   Norfolk Map 9 TF64

GH QQQ Pinewood 26 Northgate PE36 6AP ☎ (04853) 33068 due to change to 533068

Normal price: £15-£18
Short breaks: £42-£48 for 2 nights (except Aug)
Credit cards ① ③

This well-run guesthouse offers high standards throughout. Bedrooms are attractively furnished and decorated, and some have sea views and ensuite facilities.

GH QQQ Sutton House 24 Northgate PE36 6AP ☎ (04853) 2552

Normal price: £17-£25
Short breaks: £25-£30. Min 2 nights
Credit cards ① ③

Situated just a few minutes' walk from the town centre, this guesthouse offers good value for money with above average accommodation and well-chosen daily menus.

KING'S LYNN   Norfolk Map 9 TF62

★★★60% **Duke's Head** (Trusthouse Forte) Tuesday Market Place PE30 1JS ☎ (0553) 774996

Normal price: £49. Dinner from £14.
Short breaks: from £40, min 2 nights
Activity breaks: Heritage Tours and Steam Weekends. Details from hotel.
Credit cards ① ② ③ ④ ⑤

Situated in the town centre facing Tuesday Market Place, this hotel has a particularly comfortable and attractive lounge. Service is generally friendly and efficient.

★★64% **Globe** (Berni/Chef & Brewer) Tuesday Market Place PE30 1EZ ☎ (0553) 772617

Normal price: £30. Dinner £8-£15
Short breaks: £25.50 excluding dinner. Min 2 nights weekends, 3 nights midweek.
🐾 Credit cards ① ② ③ ⑤

The Globe is a popular meeting place where the bars and restaurants offer reasonably priced Berni dishes. Bedrooms are modestly furnished and well-equipped.

★★★69% **Knights Hill** (Best Western) Knights Hill Village, South Wootton PE30 3HQ (junc A148/A149) ☎ (0553) 675566

Normal price: from £38.50. Dinner from £15.50.
Short breaks: from £50, min 2 nights.
Activity breaks: Sandringham Shooting Breaks, from £115. Details from hotel
Credit cards ① ② ③ ⑤

Accommodation is provided in both the main building - a former hunting lodge - and the converted courtyard buildings which include the Farmers Arms Inn and Restaurant.

★★69% Stuart House Goodwins Road PE30 5QX ☎ (0553) 772169

Normal price: £20-£27.50.
Short breaks: £30.50, min 2 nights, Fri-Sun. Single price £33
✻ Credit cards ① ② ③

A hotel with spotlessly clean rooms, plain but interesting cuisine, a warm friendly welcome and enthusiastic service. Set in a quiet residential area.

★★64% Tudor Rose St Nicholas Street, off Tuesday Market Place PE30 1LR ☎ (0553) 762824

Normal price: £24.
Short breaks: £30, min 2 nights.
Credit cards ① ② ③ ⑤

Comfortable, modestly furnished rooms and good service from a small team of staff are offered at this 15th-century inn. Bars and restaurants feature beamed ceilings.

NEATISHEAD Norfolk Map 9 TG32

QQ Regency Neatishead Post Office Stores NR12 8AD ☎ (0692) 630233

Normal price: from £14
Short breaks: £5 off normal tariff for 3-night stay; £7 off per week. Min 3 nights.

In the centre of a quiet village at the heart of Norfolk Broads, this friendly 17th-century guesthouse offers comfortable accommodation with colour television and hot and cold water in all bedrooms, one a family room.

NORWICH Norfolk Map 5 TG20

★★★64% Arlington (Best Western) 10 Arlington Lane, Newmarket Road NR2 2DA ☎ (0603) 617841

Normal price: £35. Dinner from £7.95 (1990 price)
Short breaks: £35
Credit cards ① ② ③ ⑤

Close to the city centre, this hotel has two restaurants and compact, well-equipped bedrooms including a few family rooms and one with a four-poster bed, all with ensuite bathrooms and colour television. Christmas breaks are available.

★★★62% Maids Head (Queens Moat) Tombland NR3 1LB ☎ (0603) 761111

Normal price: £43. Dinner from £10.25 and à la carte (1990 price)
Short breaks: £49. Min 2 nights, Thu-Sun.
Credit cards ① ② ③ ⑤

This partly 13th-century hotel by the cathedral has three bars and many lounge areas. All bedrooms, including a family room and one with a four-poster bed, have private bathrooms and colour television. Christmas breaks are available.

★★★63% **Nelson** Prince of Wales Road NR1 1DX ☎ (0603) 760260

Normal price: £40. Dinner £10.50 and à la carte (1990 price)
Short breaks: £41 including £11.50 dinner allowance. Min 2 nights. £30 for Sun special. £203 for 7-night special Jul-Sep. Single room bargain breaks available only Thu-Sun.
🛧 (ex guide dogs) Credit cards ① ② ③ ④ ⑤

Set on the River Wensun with two riverside restaurants, this modern hotel has well-equipped ensuite bedrooms, including family rooms, all with colour television. There is a sauna. Christmas breaks are available.

★★★63% **Norwich** (Best Western) 121-131 Boundary Road NR3 2BA ☎ (0603) 787260

Normal price: £32.50. Dinner £10.50-£12.25 and à la carte (1990)
Short breaks: £35 including £11 dinner allowance. Min 2 nights. Single rooms available Fri-Sun only.
🛧 (ex guide dogs) Credit cards ① ② ③ ⑤

This pleasing modern hotel to the north-west of the city offers a good range and quality of facilities. All bedrooms, which include some non-smoking and many family rooms, have ensuite bathrooms and colour television. Christmas breaks are available.

★★65% **Oaklands** 89 Yarmouth Road, Thorpe St Andrews NR7 0HH ☎ (0603) 34471

Normal price: £32.50. Dinner £9.95-£18 (1990 prices)
Short breaks: £35 including £10.95 dinner allowance (1990 prices). Min 2 nights, Fri-Sun.
Credit cards ① ② ③ ⑤

In a secluded position in a leafy suburb with views of the River Yare valley, this hotel has simply furnished, comfortable bedrooms, including family rooms. Most are ensuite and all have colour television. The restaurant has a carvery. Christmas breaks are available.

★★★68% **Post House** (Trusthouse Forte) Ipswich Road NR4 6EP ☎ (0603) 56431

Normal price: £49. Dinner from £13.95 and à la carte.
Short breaks: £49 including £13.95 dinner allowance. Min 2 nights, Thu-Sun.
Credit cards ① ② ③ ④ ⑤

On the city outskirts, this reliable hotel has well-equipped ensuite bedrooms all with colour television. The leisure facilities include an indoor swimming pool, sauna, solarium, gymnasium and health and fitness centre. Christmas breaks are available.

★★★63% **Sprowston Manor** (Best Western) Wroxham Road, Sprowston NR7 8RP (2m NE A1151) ☎ (0603) 410871

Normal price: £37.50 or £50
Short breaks: £45 or £55 including £13 dinner allowance. Min 2 nights, Fri-Sun.
Credit cards ① ② ③ ⑤ .

Set in 10 acres of grounds by a golf course, this 16th-century country house hotel has a bar and restaurant, and a croquet lawn. All bedrooms, including a family room and two with four-poster beds, have private bath or shower and colour television.

★★64% **Wroxham** Hoveton NR12 8AJ

Normal price: £48
Short breaks: £38 including £9.50 dinner allowance and dinner dance Sat nights. Min 2 nights, Fri-Sun.
Credit cards ① ② ③ ⑤

Many rooms have their own balconies overlooking the water at this hotel, which enjoys an enviable position at the heart of the broads. Extensive public areas include the Riverside Bar, which is particularly popular for lunchtime snacks, and a restaurant which offers a wide à la carte selection as well as its table d'hôte menu.

SHERINGHAM Norfolk Map 9 TG14

★★64% **Beaumaris** South Street NR26 8LL ☎ (0263) 822370

Normal price: £25.50. Dinner from £11.95 and à la carte.
Short breaks: £35, min 2 nights.
Credit cards ① ② ③

A gradually improving hotel in a quiet area within walking distance of the town centre and beach. Guests are treated to traditional care and attention.

SHIPDHAM Norfolk Map 5 TF90

★★69% **Shipdham Place** Church Close IP25 7LX ☎ (0362) 820303

Normal price: From £22-£42. Dinner £18.50-£22.50.
Short breaks: From £40-£58, min 2 nights, includes 5 course dinner and early morning tea or coffee. £10-£22 single supplement.
Credit cards ① ③

Originally a 17th-century rectory, the hotel offers charming bedrooms individually decorated, in relaxing and peaceful surroundings. Comfortable lounge areas are tastefully furnished, and a table d'hôte menu makes good use of quality fresh ingredients.

SWAFFHAM Norfolk Map 5 TF80

★★★61% **George** (Consort) Station Road PE37 7LJ ☎ (0760) 721238

Normal price: £29.50. Dinner from £11.50 and à la carte.
Short breaks: £34, min 2 nights. Single price £50.
Credit cards ① ② ③ ④ ⑤

This tastefully restored Georgian house serves a variety of freshly prepared dishes in the bar and restaurant. A family team of owners provides willing service throughout.

THETFORD Norfolk Map 5 TF88

★★★59% **Bell** (Trusthouse Forte) King Street IP24 2AZ ☎ (0842) 754455

Normal price: £48.25. Dinner £14.25-£16.50.
Short breaks: £47, min 2 nights, Thu-Sun.
Activity breaks: Clay Pigeon Shooting, £182.
Credit cards ①②③④⑤

This 15th-century coaching house has been carefully converted to an elegant, comfortable hotel.

★★57% **Historical Thomas Paine** (Best Western) White Hart Street IP24 1AA ☎ (0842) 755631

Normal price: £28. Dinner £12-£15 and à la carte
Short breaks: £34 weekends, £36 midweek, min 2 nights
Credit cards ①②③⑤

Partly Georgian hotel, reputed to be the birthplace of Thomas Paine, a famous son of Thetford.

TITCHFIELD Norfolk Map 9 TF74

★★70% **Titchfield Manor** (Best Western) PE31 8BB ☎ (0485) 210221 & 210284

Normal price: £35. Dinner £14.50-£20.
Short breaks: £42, min 2 nights.
Activity breaks: Golf Breaks, Bird Watching, Cycling, Walking and Sailing Breaks. Details from hotel.
Credit cards ①②③⑤

A flintstone building, typical of the area, enjoying views of the nature reserve and the sea.

TOTTENHILL Norfolk Map 9 TF61

GH QQ Oakwood House PE33 0RH ☎ (0553) 810256

Normal price: £22.
Short breaks: £31, min 2 nights except Christmas & New Year. Single supplement.
Credit cards ①③

This family-run hotel just 5 miles south of King's Lynn is set in very attractive lawns, woodland and gardens. Bedrooms are very comfortable.

WELLS-NEXT-THE-SEA Norfolk Map 9 TF94

GH QQQ Scarborough House Clubbs Lane NR23 1DP ☎ (0328) 710309 & 711661

Normal price: £18. Dinner £10.95.
Short breaks: £54 for 2 nights. Oct-Apr.
Credit cards ③

This Victorian detached house is in a quiet lane a few minutes' walk from the town centre, and a mile from the beach. The flintstone restaurant is housed in the former stable block.

WROXHAM Norfolk Map 9 TG31

★62% **King's Head** (Berni/Chef & Brewer) Station Road NR12 8UR ☎ (0603) 782429

Normal price: £25. Dinner £8-£15 and à la carte.
Short breaks: £23.50, min 2 nights weekend, 3 nights midweek.
🐾 Credit cards ①②③⑤

Set in gardens leading down to the river, the hotel offers well-equipped, comfortable rooms, and a popular carvery restaurant in addition to the new bar/café in the Water Front Rooms.

WYMONDHAM Norfolk Map 5 TG10

★★62% **Abbey** (Best Western) Church Street NR18 0PH ☎ (0953) 602148

Normal price: £30. Dinner £11.50-£12 and à la carte.
Short breaks: £38, min 2 nights. Single supplement.
Credit cards ①②③

A sympathetically updated hotel retaining some of its 16th-century and Victorian features. Guests have use of the excellent leisure/golf facilities at a sister hotel.

▪ NORTHAMPTONSHIRE ▪

FLORE Northamptonshire Map 4 SP66

★★★64% **Heyford Manor** (Lansbury) The High Street, NN7 4LP ☎ (0327) 349022

Normal price: £88 room and breakfast. Dinner from £16.25 and à la carte
Short breaks: £28 excluding dinner. Min 2 nights, Fri-Sun.
🐕 (ex guide dogs) Credit cards ① ② ③ ⑤

The hotel has an attractive lounge and bar area, and a restaurant serving imaginative dishes. All bedrooms are ensuite with colour television, and some rooms are set aside for non-smokers. There is a gymnasium, and a special Christmas programme is available.

NORTHAMPTON Northamptonshire Map 4 SP76

★★★70% **Northampton Moat House** (Queens Moat) Silver St, Town Centre NN1 2TA ☎ (0604) 22441

Normal price: £42.50. Dinner from £11 and à la carte (1990 price)
Short breaks: £37 including £12 dinner allowance. Min 2 nights, Fri-Sun. £10 single supplement.
Credit cards ① ② ③ ④ ⑤

Centrally located, this large hotel has an attractive restaurant serving varied meals, two bars and a comfortable open-plan lounge. All bedrooms, with a few family rooms, have ensuite facilities and colour television; leisure facilities include sauna, solarium, gymnasium and jacuzzi.

★★★★55% **Swallow** (Swallow) Eagle Drive NN4 0HW (off A5 between A428 & A508)
☎ (0604) 768700

Normal price: £100 room and breakfast. Dinner from £11.25 (1990 price)
Short breaks: £100 for two including £13.50 dinner allowance and £12 lunch. Min 2 nights, Fri-Sun (any day in August).
Credit cards ① ② ③ ⑤

An imaginatively designed modern hotel with well equipped ensuite bedrooms with colour television including many no-smoking rooms. There are two restaurants and a good leisure centre with indoor swimming pool, sauna, solarium, gymnasium, jacuzzi and steam room.

★★★69% **Westone Moat House** (Queens Moat) Ashley Way, Weston Favell NN3 3EA (3m E off A45)
☎ (0604) 406262

Normal price: £37
Short breaks: £25 excluding dinner. Fri-Sun.
Credit cards ① ② ③ ⑤

This hotel offers comfortable modern facilities, with ensuite bath and colour television in all bedrooms. Many, including a few family rooms, are in the annexe; facilities include sauna, solarium and gymnasium, and croquet and putting in the gardens. Christmas breaks are available.

WEEDON   Northamptonshire   Map 4 SP65

★★★70% **Crossroads** (Best Western) NN7 4PX ☎ (0327) 40354

Normal price: £90 room and breakfast. Dinner £15-£25.
Short breaks: £42 (1990), min 2 nights, Fri-Sun. Single supplement.
Activity breaks: Motor Racing Tuition, normal rates plus £80. Details from hotel.
✶ Credit cards ① ② ③ ⑤

A hotel brimming with antiques and interesting bric a brac, providing a friendly and hospitable atmosphere. Standing where the A5 and the A45 cross.

★66% **Globe** (Inter-Hotels) High Street NN7 4QD ☎ (0327) 40336

Normal price: £19.75. Dinner £10-£13 and à la carte
Short breaks: £17.38 excluding dinner. Min 2 nights, Fri-Sun. Single price £31.
Credit cards ① ② ③ ⑤

This 18th-century coaching house stands where the A5 crosses the A45. All of its attractively furnished rooms have ensuite facilities.

WELLINGBOROUGH   Northamptonshire   Map 4 SP86

★61% **Columbia** (Consort) 19 Northampton Road NN8 3HG ☎ (0933) 229333

Normal price: £21.50 Fri & Sat, £29 Sun (1990). Dinner £9.50-£11.50 & à la carte.
Short breaks: £30, min 2 nights, Fri-Sun, Jan-Nov. Single price £36.
✶ Credit cards ① ② ③

A popular privately-owned hotel close to the town centre, with friendly, helpful staff and an amiable atmosphere. The small restaurant offers an extensive range of dishes.

★★★50% **Hind** (Queens Moat) Sheep Street NN8 1BY ☎ (0933) 222827

Normal price: £27.50 weekends, £37 midweek. Dinner from £10.95 and à la carte.
Short breaks: £38 including newspaper. Min 2 nights, Mon-Thu.
Credit cards ① ② ③ ④ ⑤

The Hind dates back to the 17th century and offers modern accommodation in rooms which retain their old character.

▪ NORTHUMBERLAND ▪

ALNMOUTH   Northumberland   Map 12 NU21

GH QQQQ Marine House 1 Marine Drive NE66 2RW ☎ (0665) 830349

Normal price: £33.
Short breaks: £57 for 2 nights, Feb-Apr.
Activity breaks: Golf Breaks. As short breaks plus reduced fees at Dunstanburgh Castle and Seahouses golf clubs. Details from hotel.

A comfortable seafront hotel with the advantage of delightful views over the golf links to the bay beyond.

ALNWICK   Northumberland   Map 12 NU11

★★★59% **White Swan** Bondgate Within NE66 1TD ☎ (0665) 602109

Normal price: £56 including dinner.
Short breaks: £95 for 2 nights.
Activity breaks: Bird Watching break, details on application.
Credit cards ① ② ③ ⑤

A business and tourist hotel at the centre of town with views of the castle to the rear. Bedrooms vary in style.

BAMBURGH   Northumberland   Map 12 NU13

★★69% **Lord Crewe Arms** Front Street NE69 7BL ☎ (06684) 243
Closed Dec-Mar

Normal price: £29. Dinner £15.50-£17
Short breaks: £40. Single £44. Min 2 nights
Credit cards ①③

Managed by friendly resident proprietors, this attractive hotel is set in the centre of the village. Most of the pretty bedrooms have ensuite facilities, all have colour television and there is one family room. No children under five years accommodated.

★57% **Sunningdale** 21-23 Lucker Road NE69 7BS ☎ (06684) 334

Normal price: £20. Dinner £9
Short breaks: from £12 excluding dinner. Single from £15. Min 3 nights, Oct-Apr.
Credit cards ①③

A family-managed hotel providing friendly service. Some bedrooms have ensuite facilities, there are three family rooms, and two rooms for non-smokers. The hotel has a games room, and a special programme is arranged at Christmas.

★★55% **Victoria** Front Street NE69 7BP ☎ (06684) 431

Normal price: £42. Dinner £14-£15.50
Short breaks: £30-£35. Min 2 nights, Oct-Apr
Activity breaks: Wildlife/Painting Breaks. Bird-Watching Breaks, Nov & Mar. Country Pursuits, Oct. Details on application.

Family-run hotel, recently refurbished to offer modern bedrooms and character public rooms.

BARDON MILL   Northumberland   Map 12 NY76

★65% **Vallum Lodge** Military Road, Twice Brewed NE47 7AN ☎ (0434) 344248

Normal price: £17.50. Dinner £10-£12
Short breaks: £24. Min 2 nights, Mar-mid Jun & Sept-Nov. Single price £25.50.
Activity breaks: Cycling & Walking Holidays, with or without guides, tailored to suit individual needs. Details on request. Excursions from the hotel to places of interest, from £6.50-£12. Includes 30 minute scenic flight over Northumbrian coast and Tyne Valley, £18 per person. Details on request.

A small hotel with bright, comfortable accommodation in a friendly, informal atmosphere, standing on part of Hadrian's Wall.

BELFORD   Northumberland   Map 12 NU13

★★70% **Blue Bell** (Consort) Market Place NE70 7NE ☎ (0668) 213543
Restricted Service 13 Jan-21 Feb

Normal price: £35
Short breaks: £25 excluding dinner. Min 2 nights, Fri-Sun. Nov, Jan, Feb, Mar (ex Bank Holidays)
Credit cards ①②③⑤

This 18th-century coaching inn has been carefully modernised to retain much of its original character. Bedrooms are individually decorated and those overlooking the attractive gardens are more spacious and comfortable. All have ensuite facilities and colour television, one has a four-poster bed and some are set aside for families and non-smokers. Children under six are not accommodated.

BELLINGHAM Northumberland Map 12 NY88

★★64% **Riverdale Hall** (Exec Hotel) NE48 2JT ☎ (0434) 220254

Normal price: £44.50. Dinner £13-£15.
Short breaks: £39.
Activity breaks: Cricket Festivals, Sun-Thurs, middle week in June, 1st and 3rd weeks July, 1st week August. Golf Festivals, Sun-Thurs, middle week May, last week Sept. No extra charge for festivals.
Credit cards ① ② ③ ⑤

Just outside the village, this hotel overlooks its own cricket pitch and the River Tyne. Friendly and attentive service is assured from the resident proprietors.

BERWICK-UPON-TWEED Northumberland Map 12 NT95

★★★53% **Turret House** (Inter-Hotels) Etal Road, Tweedmouth TD15 2EG ☎ (0289) 330808

Normal price: £57-£65 room and breakfast. Dinner £14.50
Short breaks: £39.50. 2 nights
Credit cards ① ② ③ ⑤

An elegant hotel in its own grounds with comfortable bedrooms, all with ensuite facilities and colour television; there is one family room.

BLANCHLAND Northumberland Map 12 NY95

★★67% **Lord Crewe Arms** DH8 9SP ☎ (0434675) 251

Normal price: £42. Dinner £17.50-£21 and à la carte
Short breaks: £51, including £19 dinner allowance. Single £67.50
Credit cards ① ② ③ ⑤

Situated in the heart of the village near the abbey, this hotel has flagstone floors, original stonework and vaulted ceilings. Some of the bedrooms are in an annexe across the square, all rooms have private facilities and colour television, there are three family rooms and one with a four-poster bed. A special Christmas programme is provided. There are no parking facilities.

CHOLLERFORD Northumberland Map 12 NY97

★★★65% **George** (Swallow) NE46 4EW ☎ (0434681) 611

Normal price: £82 room. Dinner £14.95.
Short breaks: £96 for 2 nights, includes one lunch.
Credit cards ① ② ③ ⑤

Set on the banks of the River North Tyne, this hotel offers a choice of modern and traditional bedrooms all with ensuite facilities and colour television. There are family rooms, and one room is furnished with a four-poster bed. Leisure amenities include an indoor heated swimming pool and putting.

CORNHILL-ON-TWEED Northumberland Map 12 NT83

★★★ 🏨 58% **Tillmouth Park** TD12 4UU ☎ (0890) 2255

Normal price: £35. Dinner £14.75.
Short breaks: £45, min 2 nights. Single price £55.
Activity breaks: Fishing Breaks – Spring £690 including 6 days fishing and all meals, Summer £575, Autumn £1,150. Contact hotel for details.
Credit cards ① ② ③ ④ ⑤

Set in extensive grounds 3 miles north-east of the village, this Victorian mansion retains its traditional character. Popular with the fishing community.

FALSTONE   Northumberland   Map 12 NY78

INN QQQ Pheasant Stannersburn NE48 1DD ☎ (0660) 40382

Normal price: £28.35 including dinner
Short breaks: £25. Min 2 nights, Nov-Mar.

Situated at the eastern tip of Keilely Water this cosy, stone-built inn offers attractive and comfortable accommodation and delicious home-cooked evening meals. There is a pool room.

GREENHEAD   Northumberland   Map 12 NY66

FH QQ Holmhead Hadrians Wall CA6 7HY ☎ (06972) 402 due to change to 47402

Normal price: £35 room and breakfast. Dinner £10.
Short breaks: £68 for 4 nights excluding dinner. Single supplement.
Activity breaks: Explore Hadrian's Wall, £165. Golf Special, £115 for 7 nights excluding dinner. Elope to Gretna, £93 for 3 nights. Transport, flowers, cake and photograph extra. Dinner Party Weekends, £55. Fri-Sat, Nov-Feb. Cycle the Wall Breaks, £149 for 6 nights excluding dinner. Cycle maps and itinerary provided.
✟ Credit cards 1 2 3

A traditional Northumbrian farmhouse offering warmth and comfort, and an excellent selection of breakfast dishes. The Roman Wall runs beneath the house.

HALTWHISTLE   Northumberland   Map 12 NY76

FH QQQQ Broomshaw Hill Willia Road NE49 9NP ☎ (0498) 20866 due to change to (0434) 320866 Apr-30 Oct

Normal price: £28 room
Short breaks: £25 excluding dinner. Min 3 nights, Sun-Thu.

Although close to the town centre, this 18th-century farmhouse is in an attractive rural setting one mile from Hadrian's Wall. The comfortable accommodation includes an elegant dining room and spacious bedrooms.

HAYDON BRIDGE   Northumberland   Map 12 NY86

★★60% Anchor (Exec Hotel) John Martin Street NE47 6AB ☎ (0434) 684227

Normal price: £24. Dinner £13-£15 à la carte
Short breaks: £30, single £36. Min 2 nights.
Credit cards 1 2 3 5

Situated on the south side of the River Tyne this former inn has comfortable bedrooms, most with private showers and all with colour television. Fishing is available.

GH QQQQ Langley Castle Langley-on-Tyne NE5 5LU ☎ (043484) 8888

Normal price: £25-£52
Short breaks: £90 for 2 nights. Nov 1991-Mar 1992
Credit cards 1 2 3 5

Carefully restored over several centuries, this historic castle has bedrooms equipped with every modern convenience and superb public rooms. Horse riding is available.

HEXHAM   Northumberland   Map 12 NY96

★★61% County Priestpopple NE46 1PS ☎ (0434) 602030

Normal price: £26.50. Dinner £10 and à la carte
Short breaks: £32.50 includes £10 dinner allowance and one lunch. Min 2 nights, Fri-Sun, Oct-Apr.
Credit cards 1 2 3

This warm, comfortable, small hotel serves good wholesome food. All nine bedrooms have ensuite facilities and colour television, and there are three family rooms.

★★62% **Royal** (Consort) Priestpopple NE46 1PQ ☎ (0434) 602270

Normal price: £57 room and breakfast. Dinner £12 and à la carte
Short breaks: £72 for two people, min 2 nights.
Credit cards ① ② ③ ⑤

A family-run hotel in the town centre with an attractive restaurant, a bistro and comfortable ensuite bedrooms with colour television.

LONGHORSLEY Northumberland Map 12 NZ19

★★★★74% **Linden Hall** (Prestige) NE65 8XF ☎ (0670) 516611

Normal price: £55. Dinner from £19.50.
Short breaks: £65, min 2 nights, Tues-Thu. All week Jul-Aug, Nov-Feb. Single supplement.
Activity breaks: Clay Pigeon Shooting, short break price plus £15. Hot Air Ballooning, short break price plus £95.
Credit cards ① ② ③ ⑤

Dating from the early 19th century, Linden Hall is a beautiful ivy-clad mansion set in 300 acres of fine park and woodland. Bedrooms vary from palatial to compact.

NEWTON Northumberland Map 12 NZ06

Q **Crookhill Farm** NE43 7UX ☎ (0661) 843117

Normal price: £12.50
Short breaks: £10.50 excluding dinner. Min 3 nights.
✠

Overlooking open countryside and conveniently close to the A69, this comfortable stone-built farmhouse with 23 acres of cattle and sheep farmland offers bed and breakfast, and has three bedrooms, one a family room.

POWBURN Northumberland Map 12 NU01

✿★★ 🛥 75% **Breamish House** NE66 4LL ☎ (066578) 266 & 544

Normal price: £64-£94 room.
Short breaks: £45-£57.50 for 2 people. £40 for single room.

Set in well-tended peaceful grounds, this elegant Georgian country house hotel offers very comfortable, high-standard accommodation throughout, with all bedrooms ensuite and with colour television. No children under 12 are accommodated.

ROTHBURY   Northumberland   Map 12 NU00

★★63% **Coquet Vale** Station Road NE65 9QN ☎ (0669) 20305

Normal price: £20. Dinner £8.95-£10.50 and à la carte (1990 price)
Short breaks: £22.50. Min 2 nights.
🦮 (ex guide dogs) Credit cards ①③

Overlooking the valley, this detached greystone building with a garden provides friendly service and has many family rooms among the bedrooms. All have colour television and most have private shower or bath. Christmas breaks are available.

SEAHOUSES   Northumberland   Map 12 NU23

★★74% **Beach House** Sea Front NE68 7SR ☎ (0665) 720337

Normal price: £38-£40. Dinner £14.75.
Short breaks: £37, Apr, May & Oct.
Activity breaks: Bird Watching Weekend, £83 including guide. First Fri & Sat of November.
Credit cards ①③

A warm welcome is extended by the owners of this very pleasant hotel, and bedrooms have good views towards the Farne Islands.

WOOLER   Northumberland   Map 12 NT92

★★53% **Tankerville Arms** (Minotels) Cottage Road NE71 6AD ☎ (0668) 81581

Normal price: £47 room and breakfast. Dinner £14.75-£18.
Short breaks: from £35 excluding dinner. Min 3 nights.
Single price fr £40.
Credit cards ①③⑤

This large comfortable inn is managed by resident proprietors who maintain a high level of service.

▪ NOTTINGHAMSHIRE ▪

NEWARK-ON-TRENT   Nottinghamshire   Map 8 SK75

★63% **South Parade** 117-119 Baldertongate NG24 1RY ☎ (0636) 703008

Normal price: £24.75. Dinner £12.50-£14.
Short breaks: £32 including £10 dinner allowance. Min 2 nights, Thu-Sun. £5 single supplement.
Credit cards ①③

Simple, clean, comfortable accommodation and well-presented, mainly English meals are provided by this privately-owned hotel - a red brick, detached Georgian house standing on the Balderton road - which caters mainly for commercial users.

NOTTINGHAM   Nottinghamshire   Map 8 SK54

★★★★56% **Nottingham Moat House** Mansfield Road NG5 2BT ☎ (0602) 602621

Normal price: £40.95
Short breaks: £22.50-£34 excluding dinner. (£29.50 for single room). Fri-Sun.
Credit cards ①②③⑤

This large, busy, modern hotel stands less than a mile from the city centre and provides good parking facilities.

QQ Park Waverley Street NG7 4HF ☎ (0602) 786299 & 420010

Normal price: £38
Short breaks: £29 excluding dinner. (£40 for single room). Min 2 nights, Fri-Sun.
🦮 (ex guide dogs) Credit cards ①③

A short distance from the town centre, this large guesthouse has an attractive restaurant and comfortable bedrooms, including a family room. Many offer ensuite showers and all have colour television.

★★★★61% **Royal Moat House International** (Queens Moat) Wollaton Street NG1 5RH
☎ (0602) 414444

Normal price: £49.95
Short breaks: £45 including £8.95 dinner allowance. 1990.
Credit cards [1] [2] [3] [5]

This large, well-equipped city-centre hotel has four restaurants and all bedrooms, including many family and no-smoking rooms, are ensuite with colour television. Leisure facilities include squash, solarium and gymnasium.

★★★62% **Stakis Victoria** Milton Street NG1 3PZ ☎ (0602) 419561

Normal price: £81 room.
Short breaks: £30 excluding dinner. £10 single supplement. Min 2 nights.
Credit cards [1] [2] [3] [5]

This former railway hotel in an attractive red-brick building in the city centre has spacious public areas and well-equipped, differently styled bedrooms, including family and no-smoking rooms, all with ensuite facilities and colour television. Christmas breaks are available.

★★★61% **Strathdon Thistle** (Thistle) Derby Road NG1 5FT ☎ (0602) 418501

Normal price: £43.75. Dinner from £10.75 and à la carte (1990 price)
Short breaks: £38. Single supplement on weekdays.
Credit cards [1] [2] [3] [4] [5]

A modern hotel in the city centre with a high standard of cuisine. All bedrooms have private bath or shower and colour television, including some family and no-smoking rooms.

RETFORD (EAST)   Nottinghamshire   Map 8 SK78

★★★65% **West Retford** (Character) 24 North Road DN22 7XG (Situated on A638) ☎ (0777) 706333

Normal price: £40-£43. Dinner from £15.50.
Short breaks: £42 including Sunday lunch. Min 1 night, Fri-Sun. Single supplement.
Activity breaks: Details from hotel.
Credit cards [1] [2] [3] [5]

The comfortable rooms of this 18th-century manor house are complemented by bedrooms of a high standard in an adjoining modern annexe.

SOUTHWELL   Nottinghamshire   Map 8 SK75

★★★62% **Saracen's Head** (Trusthouse Forte) Market Place NG25 0HE ☎ (0636) 812701

Normal price: £48.25. Dinner from £15.
Short breaks: £45, min 2 nights, Thu-Sun.
Credit cards [1] [2] [3] [4] [5]

Timber-framed and dating back to the reign of Charles I, this warm comfortable hotel retains exposed beams and wood panelling. Modern comforts are also provided.

▪ OXFORDSHIRE ▪

ABINGDON   Oxfordshire   Map 4 SU49

★★★61% **Abingdon Lodge** (Consort) Marcham Road OX14 1TZ ☎ (0235) 553456
Closed 25-26 Dec

Normal price: £34 (weekend per day), £51.50 (weekday). Dinner £7.95-£10.50
Short breaks: £37.50. Min 2 nights, Fri-Sun. Single supplement £12
🦮 (ex guide dogs) Credit cards [1] [2] [3] [5]

Conveniently situated at the junction of the A34/A415 this new hotel offers comfortable bedrooms, all with private bathrooms and colour television.

INN QQQ Barley Mow (Berni/Chef & Brewer) Clifton Hampden, OX14 2EH (through village on road to Didcot) ☎ (086730) 7847

Normal price: £26
Short breaks: £23. Min 2 nights
🦮 (ex guide dogs) Credit cards 1️⃣ 2️⃣ 3️⃣ 5️⃣

Standing next to the river in the pretty village of Clifton Hampden, this thatched inn has popular bars and an attractive restaurant. There are five comfortable bedrooms with colour television, and one room has a private shower.

★★61% **Crown & Thistle** (Berni/Chef & Brewer) Bridge Street OX14 3HS ☎ (0235) 522556

Normal price: £75 room and breakfast.
Short breaks: £26, single £33. Min 2 nights, Fri-Sun.
🦮 (ex guide dogs) Credit cards 1️⃣ 2️⃣ 3️⃣ 5️⃣

A small, friendly hotel with a popular Berni grill restaurant. All twenty-one bedrooms have ensuite facilities and colour television, there are three family rooms and one room has a four-poster bed.

★★★59% **Upper Reaches** (Trusthouse Forte) Thames Street OX14 3JA ☎ (0235) 522311

Normal price: £85 room.
Short breaks: £50. Min 2 nights, must include Sat.
Credit cards 1️⃣ 2️⃣ 3️⃣ 4️⃣ 5️⃣

Formerly an abbey cornmill, the hotel overlooks the River Thames on one side and old mill stream on the other. All twenty-six bedrooms have ensuite bathrooms and colour television, and four bedrooms have been set aside for non-smokers. There is a special programme of events at Christmas.

BANBURY   Oxfordshire   Map 4 SP44

★★60% **Lismore** (Minotels) 61 Oxford Road OX16 9AJ ☎ (0295) 267661
Closed 24 Dec-3 Jan

Normal price: £30. Dinner £11.50-£13.50
Short breaks: £35. Single £50. Min 2 nights
Credit cards 1️⃣ 2️⃣ 3️⃣

This homely hotel offers good food and well-equipped bedrooms, most with ensuite facilities, and all with colour television. One room has a four-poster bed and there are family rooms.

★★★66% **Whately Hall** (Trusthouse Forte) Banbury Cross OX16 0AN ☎ (0295) 263451

Normal price: £61. Dinner from £14.50.
Short breaks: £45-£50. Min 2 nights, Fri, Sat or Sun.
Activity breaks: Murder/Mystery Weekend, £164. 1-3 Mar. Heritage Historic Houses Tour, £172. 15-17 Jun. Easter Break, £65. 29 Mar.
Credit cards 1️⃣ 2️⃣ 3️⃣ 4️⃣ 5️⃣

Dating in part from the 17th century, the hotel has been upgraded to provide modern facilities. An interesting restaurant offers meals prepared with flair and imagination.

BLOXHAM   Oxfordshire   Map 4 SP43

★★64% **Olde School** (Inter-Hotels) Church Street OX15 4ET ☎ (0295) 720369

Normal price: £75. Dinner £16-£17.
Short breaks: £78. Min 2 nights, Fri-Mon.
Activity breaks: Cycling £90. Painting, £110. Horse Riding, £100. Golf, £120.
🦮 Credit cards 1️⃣ 2️⃣ 3️⃣ 5️⃣

One-time village school with small, well-equipped bedrooms and professionally-run restaurant.

BURFORD   Oxfordshire   Map 4 SP21

★★63% **Cotswold Gateway** Cheltenham Road OX8 4HX ☎ (0993) 822695

Normal price: £35. Dinner £12.50-£18.50
Short breaks: £45. Min 2 nights, Fri-Sun. Single £60
Credit cards ① ② ③ ⑤

Complete refurbishment has provided well-equipped, modern bedrooms all with private bathrooms and colour television; there are four family rooms. The hotel has an all day coffee shop.

★★63% **Golden Pheasant** High Street OX8 4RJ ☎ (099382) 3223

Normal price: £35-£44. Dinner £12.95-£20.95
Short breaks: £90 for 2 people. Min 2 nights. Additional nights less £5 per person. Single £60.50

A small family-owned hotel with original beams, stonework and large fireplaces. Cottage-style bedrooms combine character with modern facilities, all have ensuite bath or shower rooms and colour television, and one room has a four-poster bed. There is a special Christmas programme.

CHADLINGTON   Oxfordshire   Map 4 SP32

★★62% **Chadlington House** OX7 3LZ ☎ (060876) 437
Closed Jan & Feb

Normal price: from £39.50. Dinner £15-£20
Short breaks: from £75 for 2 nights. Min 2 nights
🐾 (ex guide dogs) Credit cards ① ③

In a rural location, this delightful hotel offers homely accommodation and good cooking. All bedrooms have colour television, most have private facilities and one is furnished with a four-poster bed.

CHARLBURY   Oxfordshire   Map 4 SP31

★★62% **Bell** (Best Western) Church Street OX7 3AP ☎ (0608) 810278

Normal price: £37.50. Dinner £12-£25.
Short breaks: £49. Min 2 nights except Christmas & New Year.
Activity breaks: Clay Pigeon Shooting from £77. Gliding from £77. Hot Air Ballooning, from £149. Horse Riding from £59. Details from hotel.
Credit cards ① ② ③ ④ ⑤

A 17th-century hotel with a warm and cosy atmosphere and some attractive bedrooms. Well-prepared dishes are served in the intimate dining room.

CHISELHAMPTON   Oxfordshire   Map 4 SU59

INN QQQQ Coach & Horses Stadhampton Road OX9 7UX ☎ (0865) 890255

Normal price: £37-£38. Dinner £10.45 and à la carte.
Short breaks: £34.25-£35, single £44-£46.50. Min 2 nights, Fri-Sat.
🐾 (ex guide dogs) Credit cards ① ② ③ ⑤

The attractive stone-built 'olde worlde' coaching inn offers hospitable service in comfortable surroundings. A courtyard annexe has bright ensuite bedrooms with modern facilities.

DEDDINGTON   Oxfordshire   Map 4 SP43

★★66% **Holcombe** (Best Western) High Street OX5 4SL ☎ (0869) 38274

Normal price: £35-£42.50. Dinner £16.95-£18.95.
Short breaks: £47. Min 2 nights.
Activity breaks: Golfing Breaks, Horse Riding Breaks, Fly Fishing Breaks, Clay Pigeon Shooting, Archery Breaks. Prices and details on application.
Credit cards ① ② ③ ⑤

In a picturesque village setting this small 17th-century family-run hotel has undergone complete refurbishment. The restaurant offers thoughtfully prepared dishes.

DORCHESTER-ON-THAMES Oxfordshire Map 4 SU59

★★65% **George** High Street OX9 8HH ☎ (0865) 340404
Closed 1 wk Xmas
Normal price: £41. Dinner £16-£28
Short breaks: £50. Min 2 nights, Fri-Sun

Reputedly one of the oldest coaching inns in England, the hotel offers a warm, friendly atmosphere and good food. The comfortable bedrooms have ensuite bath or shower rooms and colour television, and two rooms have four-poster beds.

HENLEY-ON-THAMES Oxfordshire Map 4 SU78

★★★62% **Red Lion** Hart Street RG9 2AR ☎ (0491) 572161
Normal price: £51. Dinner £18-£28
Short breaks: £68, single £90. Min 2 nights, Fri-Sun, Oct-Apr.
⚔ Credit cards 1 2 3

A character hotel in a riverside setting at the heart of town. Public rooms are comfortable and attractively decorated, and most of the bedrooms have private bathroom and colour television.

HORTON-CUM-STUDLEY Oxfordshire Map 4 SP51

❋★★★ 🐴 67% **Studley Priory** (Consort) OX9 1AZ ☎ (086735) 203 & 254
Normal price: £88 room and breakfast. Dinner £28-£38
Short breaks: £105 for 2 nights. Single £135.
⚔ Credit cards 1 2 3 4 5

Surrounded by woods and parkland, this former Benedictine nunnery is now a very comfortable hotel with a notable restaurant. Leisure facilities include tennis and clay pigeon shooting. Christmas breaks are available.

KINGHAM Oxfordshire Map 4 SP22

★★★69% **Mill House** OX7 6UH ☎ (060871) 8188
Normal price: £52. Dinner from £16.95 and à la carte.
Short breaks: £46, min 3 nights. Single price £56.
⚔ Credit cards 1 2 3 4 5

A delightful Cotswold-stone hotel with commendable standards of cuisine. The Mill House enjoys delightful rural surroundings with a mill stream running through its attractive grounds.

LEW Oxfordshire Map 4 SP30

FH QQQQ **Farmhouse** (SP322059) University Farm OX8 2AU ☎ (0993) 850297 & 851480
Normal price: from £21.
Short breaks: £33 midweek, £34.50 weekends, min 2 nights.
⚔ Credit cards 1 3

Tastefully and sympathetically modernised, this delightful 17th-century farmhouse offers individually decorated rooms of great original charm. There's a popular cosy restaurant.

MIDDLETON STONEY Oxfordshire Map 4 SP52

★★65% **Jersey Arms** OX6 8SE ☎ (086989) 234 & 505
Normal price: £34.75. Dinner £15-£21 à la carte (1990 price)
Short breaks: £47.50 including £17.50 dinner allowance. Min 2 nights, except Christmas & New Year. Single supplement.
⚔ Credit cards 1 2 3 5

Service is friendly at this charming Cotswold inn with beams and open fires, an attractive restaurant, quiet lounge and garden. Bedrooms in the courtyard annexe are more spacious but all have ensuite bath and colour television.

MILTON COMMON   Oxfordshire   Map 2 SP60

★★★64% **Belfry** (Inter) Brimpton Grange OX9 2JW ☎ (0844) 279381

Normal price: £70. Dinner £14.50 and à la carte (1990 price)
Short breaks: £42.50 including £16 dinner allowance. Min 2 nights, Fri-Sun
Credit cards [1] [2] [3] [5]

This large half-timbered country house in extensive grounds has private bath or shower and colour television in all bedrooms. Leisure facilities include an outdoor swimming pool, volley ball and Saturday night dinner dances.

MILTON-UNDER-WYCHWOOD   Oxfordshire   Map 4 SP21

QQQQ **Hillborough** The Green OX7 6JH (off A424 Burton-Stow village centre) ☎ (0993) 830501

Normal price: £24
Short breaks: £32, including £13 dinner allowance. Min 2 nights, Mon-Sat.
Credit cards [1] [2] [3] [5]

This charming Victorian guesthouse, with a cocktail bar and restaurant serving a good range of dishes, has spacious, well-furnished bedrooms, including a family room, with ensuite facilities and colour television; also a croquet pitch.

NORTH STOKE   Oxfordshire   Map 4 SU68

★★★74% **Springs** Wallingford Road OX9 6BE ☎ (0491) 36687

Normal price: £60-£70. Dinner from £22 à la carte (1990 price)
Short breaks: £70 including £25 dinner allowance. Min 2 nights, Fri-Sun, except Christmas/New Year.
Credit cards [1] [2] [3] [4] [5]

Set in woodland with a lake, this attractive country house hotel serves quality meals. The comfortable, individually styled bedrooms offer ensuite facilities and colour television, including 2 four-poster beds and a few family rooms. Also an outdoor swimming pool, tennis, sauna, croquet and putting. Christmas breaks are available.

OXFORD   Oxfordshire   Map 4 SP50

★★★57% **Eastgate** (Trusthouse Forte) The High OX1 4BE ☎ (0865) 248244

Normal price: £90 room. Dinner £14-£15.50 & à la carte (1990 price)
Short breaks: £96 for two including set-dinner or £12 dinner allowance. Thu-Sun.
Credit cards [1] [2] [3] [4] [5]

At the heart of the city, this cheerful hotel has elegant public rooms, a smart carvery restaurant and busy bar. All bedrooms, a few non-smoking, have ensuite bathrooms and colour television, and one has a four-poster bed. Christmas breaks are available.

★★★62% **Inn for All Seasons** Little Barrington OX8 4TN

Normal price: £46.45
Short breaks: £39. Min 2 nights.
Credit cards [1] [3]

Retaining much of the original character and charm, with old stone walls and exposed beams, well-furnished bedrooms and good standards of food.

★★★58% **Linton Lodge** (Hilton) Linton Road OX2 6UJ ☎ (0865) 53461

Normal price: £65. Dinner £13.50-£14.50.
Short breaks: £40 excluding dinner, min 2 nights, Fri-Sun.
Activity breaks: Details from hotel.
Credit cards [1] [2] [3] [5]

Situated just north of the city, this commercial style hotel has recently been refurbished, and offers a blend of modern and traditional accommodation.

★★★63% **Oxford Moat House** (Queens Moat) Godstow Road Wolvercote Rbt OX2 8AL ☎ (0865) 59933

Normal price: £55. Dinner from £12 (1990 price)
Short breaks: £52 including £18 dinner allowance. Min 2 nights, Fri-Sun.
Credit cards ① ② ③ ⑤

This comfortable modern hotel on the city outskirts has well-equipped ensuite bedrooms with colour television, including family rooms, plus extensive leisure amenities: indoor swimming pool, squash, snooker, sauna, solarium, gymnasium, whirlpool, pitch & putt.

★★★★56% **Randolph** (Trusthouse Forte) Beaumont Street OX1 2LN ☎ (0865) 247481

Normal price: £64. Dinner £20-£21.
Short breaks: £70, min 2 nights, must include Sat.
Activity breaks: Gourmet, Music and Garden Breaks, approx £175. Details from hotel.
Credit cards ① ② ③ ④ ⑤

Major refurbishment is in progress at this splendid old city centre hotel. The improvement of the public areas has been completed, and all now offer a high degree of comfort.

★★56% **Victoria** 180 Abingdon Road OX1 4RA ☎ (0865) 724536

Normal price: £55.50.
Short breaks: £52.50 excluding dinner. Min 2 nights, Fri-Sun.
Credit cards ① ③

Standing in a residential area with convenient access to the city, this small family-run hotel has homely bedrooms equipped with modern facilities, all including colour television and many with private bath.

QQQ Westwood Country Hinksey Hill Top OX1 5BG ☎ (0865) 735408

Normal price: £33.
Short breaks: £44. Min 2 nights. Price includes free entry to Cotswold Wildlife Park, winter only.
🕇 (ex guide dogs) Credit cards ① ② ③ ⑤

Standing in 3 acres of woodland on the city outskirts, this small family-run hotel has well-equipped bedrooms, including some family rooms, all with ensuite bathrooms and colour television; plus a sauna, jacuzzi and mini-gym.

SHIPTON-UNDER-WYCHWOOD Oxfordshire Map 4 SP21

★★63% **Shaven Crown** OX7 6BA ☎ (0993) 830330

Normal price: £31. Dinner £16.50-£19.50 à la carte.
Short breaks: £43, min 2 nights, except Bank Holiday weekends or Cheltenham Gold Cup festival.
🕇 Credit cards ① ③

Formerly a 14th-century hospice to Bruern Abbey and retaining many of its original features, this small family-run hotel and restaurant offers individually styled bedrooms with modern facilities, an intimate candle-lit restaurant and a good selection of buffet and bar food.

WESTON-ON-THE-GREEN Oxfordshire Map 4 SP51

★★★66% **Weston Manor** (Best Western) OX6 8QL ☎ (0869) 50621

Normal price: £52.50. Dinner £17.50-£20.
Short breaks: £55, min 2 nights. Single supplement.
🐕 Credit cards [1] [2] [3] [5]

This 14th-century manor house, once the ancestral home of earls and later a monastery, is now a stylish hotel with a unique, oak-panelled restaurant with minstrel's gallery.

WITNEY Oxfordshire Map 4 SP30

★★67% **Witney Lodge** (Consort) Ducklington Lane OX8 7TS ☎ (0993) 779777

Normal price: £39.50. Dinner £9.75-£11 and à la carte.
Short breaks: £39, min 2 nights except Christmas. Single price £49 weekends.
🐕 Credit cards [1] [2] [3] [4] [5]

An attractive, recently opened, Cotswold-style hotel offers particularly good bedrooms with tiled, bright bathrooms, and a homely restaurant with good, value-for-money food.

WOODSTOCK Oxfordshire Map 4 SP41

★★★67% **Bear** (Trusthouse Forte) Park Street OX7 1SZ ☎ (0993) 811511

Normal price: £125 room. Dinner £19.50-£25.50.
Short breaks: £70, min 2 nights, Thu-Mon.
Activity breaks: Arts and Antiques, £160. Details from hotel.
Credit cards [1] [2] [3] [4] [5]

A busy town centre hotel of some character. Carefully prepared dishes are served in the attractive restaurant.

★★70% **Feathers** Market Street OX7 1SX ☎ (0993) 812291

Normal price: £72.50 (Continental breakfast). Dinner £29.50-£34.50.
Short breaks: From £70 including early morning tea and newspaper. Min 2 nights, Nov-Mar.
Credit cards [1] [2] [3] [5]

This delightful, beautifully restored hotel dates from the 17th century. The open fires which burn in the public rooms in season and lovely flowers set the tone.

WROXTON Oxfordshire Map 4 SP44

★★★67% **Wroxton House** (Best Western) OX15 6QB ☎ (0295) 730482 & 730777

Normal price: £47.50. Dinner £24.50-£26.50.
Short breaks: £53. Min 2 nights.
Activity breaks: Romance Break, £120 for 2 nights including champagne, roses and chocolates. Stratford Theatre Break, £120 including matinee seats at Royal Shakespeare Theatre. Any Fri-Sat. Revolution Treasure Hunt Break, £120 including champagne, gifts and entry to Warwick Castle. Learn to Race at Silverstone, £175 including two hour's racing tuition at Silverstone. Drive a race-prepared saloon car or a single seater.
Credit cards [1] [2] [3] [4] [5]

A small country house hotel boasting some fine period furniture and paintings. The restaurant, in three sections, creates an intimate atmosphere.

▪ SHROPSHIRE ▪

BRIDGNORTH *Shropshire* *Map 7 SO79*

★68% **Croft** (Guestaccom) St Mary's Street WV16 6DW ☎ (0746) 762416

Normal price: £24. Dinner £9.95-£13.95
Short breaks: £29. Min 2 nights.
Credit cards ① ② ③

A small town-centre hotel offering warm hospitality and satisfying, nourishing meals. Each bedroom has a colour television, most have ensuite facilities and there are family rooms. No parking.

★★61% **Falcon** St John Street, Lowtown WV15 6AG ☎ (0746) 763134

Normal price: £23. Dinner £10.50-£25 à la carte
Short breaks: £20 excluding dinner. Min 3 nights (ex Bank Holidays). 20% discount on single room rate

This old coaching inn, in Lowtown, is close to the River Severn. Most of the bedrooms have ensuite facilities, all have colour television and there are three family rooms.

CRAVEN ARMS *Shropshire* *Map 7 SO48*

FH QQ Strefford Hall SK7 8DE ☎ (0588) 672383
Closed Christmas & New Year

Normal price: £25
Short breaks: £39. Min 3 nights

A large, comfortable, stone-built Victorian farmhouse, north of the town off the A49. Smoking is not permitted in the bedrooms.

CHURCH STRETTON *Shropshire* *Map 7 SO49*

★★69% **Mynd House** (Exec Hotel) Little Stretton SY6 6RB (2m S B4370) ☎ (0694) 722212

Normal price: From £24, Dinner £12.50-£14.50.
Short breaks: From £35, min 2 nights, excluding Aug. Single supplement.
Activity breaks: Industrial Heritage Break, from £80 for 2 nights. Countryside Heritage Break, from £100 for 3 nights, Spring & Autumn. Romantic Interlude, from £120 for 2 nights. Wine Tasting Breaks, from £120 for 2 nights, min 4 people.
Credit cards ① ③

A large Edwardian house set high in pleasant gardens in the peaceful picturesque village of Little Stretton. It offers modern accommodation and a warm welcome.

CLEOBURY MORTIMER *Shropshire* *Map 7 SO67*

★★69% **Redfern** (Minotels) DY14 8AA ☎ (0299) 270395

Normal price: £27.50. Dinner £14.50.
Short breaks: £35, including cold buffet or packed lunch on one day. Min 2 nights. Single price £44.
Activity breaks: Severn Valley Steam Holidays, £85. Carp Fishing Holidays, £71. Trout Fishing Holidays, £74.
Credit cards ① ② ③ ⑤

A busy village hotel with good quality bedrooms and a friendly atmosphere. Generous portions of well prepared food are served in the country kitchen style restaurant.

HODNET   Shropshire   Map 7 SJ62

★★65% Bear TF9 3NH ☎ (063084) 214 & 787

Normal price: £49. Dinner £7-£12.
Short breaks: 10% discount off normal price. Min 2 nights.
Activity breaks: Medieval Banquets, £47.25 per night.
Alternate Saturdays.
✻ Credit cards ① ③

The character and quality of this quaint village inn have been retained and enhanced to create compact, well-equipped bedrooms for the tourist and business traveller alike.

HUGHLEY   Shropshire   Map 7 SO59

FH QQ Mill SY5 6NT ☎ (074636) 645

Normal price: £18.
Short breaks: £15, min 2 nights Mon-Fri, except Jul & Aug.
Activity breaks: Riding Holidays, 5-day for children, or tailored break to suit all ages. Details from farm.
✻

Lovely old house in a pleasant rural area beneath Wenlock Edge.

LUDLOW   Shropshire   Map 7 SO57

GH QQ Cecil Sheet Road SY8 1LR ☎ (0584) 2442

Normal price: £15.50-£18.
Short breaks: £18, min 2 nights, Nov-Apr.
Credit cards ① ③

This modern bungalow has bright, warm rooms, and the comfortable lounge overlooks a mature rear garden. It is a friendly, family-run base.

★★★65% Feathers At Ludlow Bull Ring SY8 1AA ☎ (0584) 875261

Normal price: £61.
Short breaks: £48, min 2 nights, Nov-Apr. Single supplement.
✻ Credit cards ① ② ③ ④ ⑤

This fine example of timber-framed Jacobean architecture stands at the centre of the historic market town. Its charm and character make it understandably popular.

MUCH WENLOCK   Shropshire   Map 7 SO69

★★72% Wheatland Fox TF13 6AD ☎ (0952) 727292

Normal price: £27.50-£32.50.
Short breaks: £37.50. Min 2 nights.
Credit cards ① ② ③

Set on the edge of the town yet with the atmosphere of a country house, this small personally run hotel offers very comfortable bedrooms and freshly prepared meals.

NEWPORT   Shropshire   Map 7 SJ71

★★64% Royal Victoria (Crown & Raven) St Mary's Street TF10 7AB ☎ (0952) 820331

Normal price: £31.50-£40.
Short breaks: £20. Min 2 nights, Fri-Sun.
Credit cards ① ② ③

This 18th-century hotel in the town centre provides simple comfortable accommodation. All bedrooms have private bath or shower and colour television; also a family bedroom.

NORTON   *Shropshire*   Map 7 SJ70

★★76% **Hundred House** (Exec Hotel) Bridgnorth Road TF11 9EE ☎ (095271) 353

Normal price: £32.50
Short breaks: £42.50 (£65 for single occupancy)
🏋 Credit cards ① ② ③

This small friendly roadside hotel has a busy bar and restaurant serving well-prepared food and the attractive bedrooms, half of them family rooms, have ensuite bathrooms and colour television.

OSWESTRY   *Shropshire*   Map 7 SJ22

★★★64% **Wynnstay** Church Street SY11 2SZ ☎ (0691) 655261

Normal price: from £40.50
Short breaks: from £43. Min 2 nights. Price includes free entry to 2 places of local interest. Single supplement Mon-Thu.
Credit cards ① ② ③ ④ ⑤

This Georgian traditional-style hotel in the town centre, with a crown bowling green, has comfortable modernised bedrooms, nearly half of them non-smoking, all with ensuite bath and colour television, and two with four-poster beds.

ROWTON   *Shropshire*   Map 7 SJ61

QQ **Church Farm** TF6 6QY (1m along unclass road, off A442 Whitchurch to Telford rd) ☎ (0952) 770381

Normal price: £12.50-£15.
Short breaks: £11-£13.33 excluding dinner. Min 3 nights, Oct-Apr.

This 300-year-old farmhouse with 35 acres of dairy, pig and sheep farm has children's facilities and provides simple but comfortable accommodation. There are wash basins in the four bedrooms, all non-smoking and including a family room and one with private shower.

SHIFNAL   *Shropshire*   Map 7 SJ70

★★★★54% **Park House** (Character) Silvermere Park, Park Street TF11 9BA ☎ (0952) 460128

Normal price: £95. Dinner £12.50-£19.45.
Short breaks: £90 for 2 nights including Sunday lunch. Single price £80. Min 1 night.
Activity breaks: Midsummer Ball, Summer Barbecue, Shropshire Historic Tour, Chinese Evening, Italian and French Evenings. Details from hotel.
Credit cards ① ② ③ ⑤

This extensive complex of leisure accommodation was formed by linking two country houses and their grounds. The hotel has a well-deserved reputation for high standards.

SHREWSBURY   *Shropshire*   Map 7 SJ41

★★★★61% **Albrighton Hall** Albrighton SY4 3AG (2.5 miles N on A528) ☎ (0939) 291000

Normal price: £80 weekdays, £70 weekends. Dinner from £15 and à la carte.
Short breaks: £60, min 1 night, £98, min 2 nights, Apr-end Sep; £62, min 1 night, £93, min 2 nights, Oct-end Mar, Fri-Sun. Includes a £13.50 dinner allowance. £15 single supplement.
Credit cards ① ② ③ ⑤

A beautifully preserved 17th-century house, set in 14 acres of gardens and grounds, providing high standards of accommodation and facilities for conferences and functions, together with a wide selection of leisure facilities.

★★★60% **Lion** (Trusthouse Forte) Wyle Cop SY1 1UY ☎ (0743) 53107

Normal price: £48. Dinner £13.50-£17.50.
Short breaks: £51, min 2 nights. Single supplement.
Activity breaks: Music at Leisure, Heritage Tour, Arts &
Antiques and Gardens Breaks, details from hotel.
Credit cards 1 2 3 4 5

A 14th-century hotel with comfortable lounge foyer areas. The Shires Restaurant offers traditional English cuisine and friendly attentive service.

★★★61% **Radbrook Hall** Radbrook Road SY3 9BQ ☎ (0743) 236676

Normal price: £31. Dinner £8-£15 à la carte.
Short breaks: £25.50 excluding dinner. Min 2 nights
weekends, 3 nights mid week.
✕ Credit cards 1 2 3 5

This extended hotel offers guests well-equipped bedrooms, a grill-style restaurant and a leisure and health centre offering a wide selection of recreational facilities.

★★59% **Shrewsbury** Bridge Place, Mardol SY1 1TU ☎ (0743) 231246

Normal price: £25. Dinner £8.95-£10.95
Short breaks: £30, min 2 nights weekends, 5 nights
weekdays. £12.50 single supplement.
Credit cards 1 2 3 5

This family-run hotel near the Welsh Bridge and the town centre has recently been completely refurbished to provide a choice of bars, a small but comfortable lounge and compact bedrooms which are well furnished and equipped, all with colour television.

QQ Sydney House Coton Crescent, Coton Hill SY1 2LJ ☎ (0743) 3829 due to change to 343829

Normal price: £24 with en suite facilities, £18 without.
Short breaks: £29.50 with en suite facilities, £24.50 without,
min 2 nights Nov-Mar, excluding Christmas week. £5.50-
£11.50 single supplement.
✕ Credit cards 1 3

A family-run Victorian house standing on the northern edge of the town, offering fully modernised rooms, each with colour television.

STIPERSTONES   Shropshire   Map 7 SJ30

GH QQ Tankerville Lodge SY5 0NB ☎ (0743) 791401

Normal price: £19 including dinner.
Short breaks: £17, min 2 nights except Easter, Christmas &
New Year. Single price £19.

Set in a lovely area, this hotel is found off the A488 near Minsterley from the north, and via Shelve and Pennerley from the south. Guests will be rewarded with comfortable rooms.

TELFORD   Shropshire   Map 7 SJ60

★★★62% **Buckatree Hall** (Best Western) Wellington TF6 5AL ☎ (0952) 641821

Normal price: £34.87. Dinner from £10.50.
Short breaks: £36-£37.50, min 2 nights, Fri-Sun.
Activity breaks: Romeo and Juliet Weekends, £89 for 2
nights. Step Back in Time Weekends, £76 for 2 nights.
Country House Christmas, £225 for 4 nights. Easter Break,
£104 for 3 nights. All prices approximate.
Credit cards 1 2 3 5

Nine acres of woodland surround this modern hotel at the foot of the Wrekin, with a popular international-style restaurant.

★★★68% **Telford Moat House** (Queens Moat) Foregate, Telford Centre TF3 4NA ☎ (0952) 291291

Normal price: £46.50. Dinner from £14.75 and à la carte.
Short breaks: £41, min 2 nights, Fri-Sun. Single supplement.
Credit cards ① ② ③ ④ ⑤

A modern yet relaxing hotel with a leisure complex. The restaurant offers carvery, a la carte, vegetarian and diabetic menus. Close to the main shopping centre.

WHITCHURCH   Shropshire   Map 7 SJ54

★★★56% **Dodington Lodge** (Inter-Hotels) Dodington SY13 1EN ☎ (0948) 2539

Normal price: £37.50. Dinner from £9.75 and à la carte.
Short breaks: £24, min 2 nights.
Credit cards ① ③

This roadside hotel situated at the junction of the A41 and A49 is also popular with the locals who make full use of the small function room.

WORFIELD   Shropshire   Map 7 SJ40

★★★ 🏨 68% **Old Vicarage** WV15 5JZ ☎ (07464) 497

Normal price: £34.75. Dinner £24.50.
Short breaks: £42.50, min 2 nights.
Credit cards ① ② ③

The tasteful modernisation and extension of this Edwardian house has resulted in a successful combination of character and the comforts of up-to-date facilities.

▪ SOMERSET ▪

BILBROOK   Somerset   Map 3 ST04

★★72% **Dragon House** TA24 6HQ ☎ (0984) 40215

Normal price: £60-£72.50 room with breakfast. Dinner £13.95 and à la carte.
Short breaks: £30.
Credit cards ① ② ③ ⑤

Set in 2¹/₂ acres of beautiful gardens beside the A39, this 17th-century character property has ten bedrooms all with private bath or shower and colour television. One room is furnished with a four-poster bed and there is one family room. There is a special Christmas programme.

BRENT KNOLL   Somerset   Map 3 ST35

★★62% **Battleborough Grange** (Exec Hotel) Bristol Road TA9 4HJ ☎ (0278) 760208

Normal price: £27.50. Dinner £4.50
Short breaks: £30. Single supplement £10 for 2 nights. Min 2 nights, Nov-May.
✖

An attractive, detached hotel set in its own grounds providing modern accommodation and attentive service. All of the bedrooms offer colour television and some have ensuite facilities and four-poster beds. There is a special Christmas programme. Children under eight are not accommodated.

BRIDGWATER   Somerset   Map 3 ST33

★★64% **Friarn Court** St Mary Street TA6 3LX ☎ (0278) 452859

Normal price: £30. Dinner £8-£10.
Short breaks: £20, excluding breakfast and dinner. Min 2 nights, Fri- Sun.
Activity breaks: Taste of Somerset Break, £100 3 nights, including cream tea on arrival, pre-dinner drink, cider-tasting, and two outings of choice. Packages include Gardens, Railways and several others.
✻ Credit cards ①②③⑤

The proprietor runs this hotel personally with warm hospitality, and offers quality bedrooms with modern facilities.

★★★68% **Walnut Tree Inn** (Best Western) North Petherton TA6 6QA (3m S A38) ☎ (0278) 662255

Normal price: £32. Dinner £7.50-£13.
Short breaks: £23 excluding dinner. Min 2 nights, Fri-Sun. Single price £35.
Activity breaks: Jazz Weekend, £120. Who Dunnit Weekend, £150. Details from hotel.
✻

A warm welcome and cosy atmosphere are the hallmarks of this busy, commercial hotel. Once a coaching inn, it now includes a range of accommodation.

CHARDSTOCK   Somerset   Map 3 ST30

★★★71% **Tytherleigh Cot** EX13 7BN ☎ (0460) 21170

Normal price: £51.50 including dinner.
Short breaks: £45. Min 2 nights, Sun-Thu.
Credit cards ①③

This charming listed building dates from the 14th century, and offers bedrooms in carefully converted stables and barns, all providing high standards of comfort and excellent facilities. Some rooms have four-poster beds. There are some leisure amenities and a special Christmas programme is available. Children under twelve are not accommodated.

DULVERTON   Somerset   Map 3 SS92

★★(Red) ➹ **Ashwick House** TA22 9QD (3m NW off B3223) ☎ (0398) 23868

Normal price: £62.50 including dinner
Short breaks: £58. Min 2 nights. 5 night breaks also available
✻

A charming Edwardian hotel high on Exmoor offering beautifully furnished and well-equipped accommodation. There are six spacious bedrooms all with private bath and colour television. A Christmas programme is available. Children under eight are not accommodated.

DUNSTER   Somerset   Map 3 SS94

★★67% **Exmoor House** West Street TA24 6SN ☎ (0643) 821268
Closed Dec & Jan

Normal price: £36-£38 includes dinner
Short breaks: £33-£35. £7.50 single supplement. Min 2 nights
Credit cards ①②③⑤

A small, village hotel provides an excellent standard of hospitality and a menu of good, fresh local dishes. Bedrooms are well kept and very clean, and all have ensuite facilities and colour television. Smoking is not permitted in the bedrooms. Children under twelve are not accommodated. There is no parking on the premises.

★★★62% **Luttrell Arms** (Trusthouse Forte) High Street TA24 6SG ☎ (0643) 821555

Normal price: £97 room. Dinner £15 and à la carte
Short breaks: £63 for 2 people
Credit cards 1 2 3 4 5

Dating back to the 15th century this hotel has a welcoming, family-run atmosphere. All bedrooms have ensuite facilities and colour television and four are furnished with four-poster beds. There is a special Christmas programme.

FROME   Somerset Map 3 ST74

★★★62% **Mendip Lodge** (Best Western) Bath Road BA11 2HP ☎ (0373) 63223

Normal price: £70-£80 room with Continental breakfast. Dinner from £18 and à la carte
Short breaks: from £42.50, single supplement £10. Min 2 nights
Credit cards 1 2 3 5

The original Edwardian building has a motel block of bedrooms, all with ensuite bathroom and colour television. There are special facilities for children, and staff are friendly and helpful throughout.

GLASTONBURY   Somerset   Map 3 ST53

FH QQQQ **Berewall Farm** Cinnamon Lane BA6 8LL ☎ (0458) 31451

Normal price: from £19.50. Dinner from £9.50
Short breaks: £50 2 nights, Oct-May (ex Bank Holidays)

In a peaceful location one mile from Glastonbury, this farmhouse has simply furnished ensuite rooms, each with colour television. Friendly hospitality and excellent home cooking are provided by the Nurse family. There is an outdoor swimming pool, tennis court and horse riding.

HOLFORD   Somerset   Map 3 ST14

★★ 🏨 69% **Combe House** TA5 1RZ ☎ (027874) 382
Closed Jan. Restricted service mid Nov-Dec & Feb-mid Mar

Normal price: £96.50 room with dinner
Short breaks: £57-£63 for 2 nights, late Sep-late May.

A country house situated in a secluded valley of the Quantock Hills. Most of the bedrooms are ensuite with colour television, and one room has a four-poster bed. Other attractions include a heated indoor swimming pool and a tennis court.

ILMINSTER   Somerset   Map 3 ST31

★★60% **Shrubbery** (Consort) TA19 9AR ☎ (0460) 52108

Normal price: £35.
Short breaks: £25, min 2 nights.
Credit cards 1 2 3 4 5

An ancient Ham-stone building on the outskirts of town. Facilities have recently been refurbished, and there is a good range of eating options.

KILVE   Somerset   Map 3 ST14

INN QQQQ **Hood Arms** TA5 1EA ☎ (027874) 210

Normal price: £28. Dinner £6-£12 à la carte.
Short breaks: £35, min 2 nights, Fri-Sun. Single price £40.
Credit cards 1 3

This popular inn stands beside the A39, and the resident proprietors have a reputation for their friendly hospitality. Bedrooms have many thoughtful extras.

MARTOCK Somerset Map 3 ST41

★★72% **Hollies** Bower Hinton TA12 6LG ☎ (0935) 822232

Normal price: £27.50
Short breaks: £22.50 excluding dinner. Min 2 nights, Fri-Sun. £30 for single occupancy.
Credit cards [1] [3]

A converted farm building which still retains original features such as exposed beams and open fireplaces. Spacious annexe bedrooms have excellent facilities, and the à la carte menu has been carefully planned to make the most of fresh local produce.

MINEHEAD Somerset Map 3 SS94

★★61% **Beaconwood** Church Road, North Hill TA24 5SB ☎ (0643) 702032

Normal price: £50. Dinner £10 (1990 price)
Short breaks: £52.50, Mar-May, Oct.
Credit cards [1] [3]

This peaceful family-run hotel outside the town centre has a heated outdoor swimming pool, grass tennis court and special facilities for children. All bedrooms, among them a few family rooms, have colour television and most have ensuite facilities.

★★★70% **Benares** (Consort) Northfield Road TA24 5PT ☎ (0643) 704911

Normal price: £34. Dinner £13.50 (1990 price)
Short breaks: £41.50 (£43.50 for single room). Min 2 nights, Mar-Oct
Credit cards [1] [2] [3] [5]

Set in fine gardens, this friendly hotel has a good restaurant and bedrooms with private bath and colour television. There are special facilities for children. Christmas breaks are available.

GH QQQ Marston Lodge St Michaels Road TA24 5JP ☎ (0643) 702510

Normal price: £19.
Short breaks: £23, min 2 nights, mid Oct-Etr.
Activity breaks: Golf Holidays, short breaks price plus £10 green fees. Riding Holidays, details from hotel.
🛪 Credit cards [1] [3]

Standing high above the town with a terraced garden and enjoying splendid views, Marston Lodge offers a warm welcome.

QQQ Mayfair 25 The Avenue TA24 5AY ☎ (0643) 702719

Normal price: £28
Short breaks: £27 (£31 for single room). Min 3 nights.

This cheerful guesthouse midway between shops and sea has well-equipped bedrooms including many family rooms. Some are in an annexe across the road, and all offer ensuite facilities and colour television. No children under 5 are accommodated.

MONTACUTE   Somerset   Map 3 ST41

★★64% Kings Arms Inn TA15 6UU ☎ (0935) 822513

Normal price: £60. Dinner from £12.50 à la carte
Short breaks: £75 (£95 for single occupancy) for 2 nights.
Min 2 nights.
Credit cards ①②③

This attractive 16th-century stone coaching inn at the centre of the village serves popular modern dishes. All the compact but smart bedrooms, one with a four-poster bed, have ensuite bathrooms and colour television. See advertisement on p247.

PORLOCK   Somerset   Map 3 SS84

★★71% Oaks Doverhay TA24 8ES ☎ (0643) 862265

Normal price: £45, dinner £12-£13.50 (1990 price)
Short breaks: £42.50. Min 2 nights.

Set in its own grounds with fine views of the Bristol Channel, this peaceful little hotel serves good fresh food and provides comfortable accommodation. All bedrooms, two of them family rooms, offer private bath or shower and colour television.

SHIPHAM   Somerset   Map 3 ST45

★★★ ⚜ 63% Daneswood House Cuck Hill BS25 1RD ☎ (093483) 3145 & 3945

Normal price: £37.50. Dinner £16.95-£19.95 à la carte.
Short breaks: £49.50, min 2 nights, Fri-Sun.
✻ Credit cards ①②③⑤

This friendly, personally-run Edwardian hotel is in a quiet woodland setting in the Mendip Hills commanding rural views across its terraced gardens and the valley beyond. Recently upgraded, it offers spacious, comfortable bedrooms with pleasing décor and complementary fabrics. Food standards are notable for their imaginative treatment of quality ingredients and local produce.

★50% Penscot Farmhouse The Square, Winscombe BS25 1TW ☎ (093483) 2659

Normal price: from £27
Short breaks: from £24.85, min 2 nights. £5 single supplement.
Credit cards ①②③⑤

A small village hotel popular with ramblers and tourists, with a comfortable lounge bar.

SIMONSBATH   Somerset   Map 3 SS73

★★ ⚜ 69% Simonsbath House TA24 7SH ☎ (064383) 259

Normal price: £46
Short breaks: £43 excluding dinner. Min 2 nights, Feb-end Nov.
✻ Credit cards ①②③⑤

A fine 17th-century house providing a high degree of comfort and hospitality, augmented by freshly prepared food. Bedrooms are furnished in keeping with the style of the house, but with modern facilities, and most have fine countryside views of Exmoor.

STOKE ST GREGORY   Somerset   Map 3 ST32

QQ Jays Nest Taunton TA3 6HZ ☎ (0823) 490250

Normal price: from £16.50
Short breaks: £21, min 3 nights, Oct-Mar.
Credit cards ②

Conference facilities are available at this cottage style property. Bedrooms are bright and comfortable, some with ensuite facilities, and the recently extended public areas are tastefully furnished and decorated.

STON EASTON   Somerset Map 3 ST65

★★★(Red) ♨ Ston Easton Park (Relais et Châteaux) BA3 4DF ☎ (076121) 631

Normal price: £57.50-£142.50. Dinner £32
Short breaks: £85-£120. Single £115-£145. Min 2 nights,
Nov-Apr (ex Xmas, New Year & Easter)
Credit cards ① ② ③ ⑤

A beautiful Palladian mansion set in large grounds and offering extremely high standards throughout. There are facilities for snooker, croquet and hot air ballooning. Christmas breaks are available. Children under twelve are not accommodated.

STREET   Somerset   Map 3 ST43

Bear 53 High Street BA16 0EF ☎ (0458) 42021

Normal price: £30 midweek, £25 weekends. Dinner £15-£25
à la carte.
Short breaks: £33.75, min 2 nights, Fri-Sun.
Credit cards ① ② ③

An attractive stone hotel with some grounds offering bedrooms of a good size, and a pleasant atmosphere throughout. Public areas are small but cosy.

TAUNTON   Somerset   Map 3 ST22

★★65% Falcon (Exec Hotel) Henlade TA3 5DH (3m E A358) ☎ (0823) 442502

Normal price: £27.50. Dinner from £11.50 and à la carte.
Short breaks: £19 excluding dinner. Min 2 nights, Mon-
Thurs. Single price £25.
✗ Credit cards ① ③

Guests are assured of a warm welcome at this small, pleasantly informal hotel. Bedrooms are particularly well equipped, and the food is simple but well-cooked.

★★★64% Rumwell Manor Rumwell TA4 1EL ☎ (0823) 461902

Normal price: £29.50. Dinner from £13.50 and à la carte.
Short breaks: £37.50, min 2 nights. Single price £54.
Credit cards ① ② ③ ⑤

An imposing Georgian mansion set in its own grounds with views across the Somerset countryside. Bedrooms are spacious and individually decorated.

TEMPLECOMBE   Somerset   Map 3 ST72

★★59% **Horsington House** Horsington BA8 0EG (1m N A357) ☎ (0963) 70721

Normal price: £34.50. Dinner £15-£20.
Short breaks: £42, min 2 nights. Single price £52.
Activity breaks: Bridge Weekends, £115 for 2 nights including all meals with ladies international Elaine Pencharz on hand to help with problems. Mid-week Bridge Breaks, £190 for 4 nights, including three full-day tours to places of interest and evenings of bridge.
Credit cards ①②③

A country house of honey-coloured stone standing in eight acres of grounds with facilities for tennis and croquet. Bridge parties are a speciality.

WATERROW   Somerset   Map 3 ST02

INN QQ Rock TA2 2AX ☎ (0984) 23293

Normal price: £16.50 Nov-Apr, £19.50 May-Oct.
Short breaks: £42 Nov-Apr, £45 May-Oct. Min 2 nights.
Credit cards ①③

A 400-year-old inn offering a character bar and modern bedrooms. Situated on the A361 approximately 2 miles from Wiveliscombe. See advertisement on p249.

WELLS   Somerset   Map 3 ST54

★57% **Ancient Gate House** Sadler Street BA5 2RR ☎ (0749) 72029

Normal price: £23. Dinner £11.75-£12.75 and à la carte.
Short breaks: £32, min 2 nights.
Credit cards ①②③⑤

A hotel with plenty of character situated close to the Cathedral. The Italian cooking is of a good standard, and service friendly and efficient.

FH QQQ Littlewell (ST536445) Coxley BA5 1QP (2m SW on A39) ☎ (0749) 77914

Normal price: £16.50-£18.50.
Short breaks: £26 including dinner wine. Mid Nov-Mar.
✱

Comfortable cottage guesthouse close to Wells. Bedrooms are tastefully decorated and the atmosphere is friendly.

★★★62% **Swan** (Best Western) Sadler Street BA5 2RX ☎ (0749) 78877

Normal price: £37.50. Dinner from £14.50.
Short breaks: from £47.50, min 2 nights. Single supplements weekends.
Activity breaks: Whodunnit Breaks, £160 for 2 nights including Sun lunch. Golf Tuition, £275 for 5 nights. Details from hotel.

A 16th-century and Victorian hotel overlooking the West Front of the cathedral. Amenities include a bar and lounge with log fires.

GH QQ Tor Tor Street BA5 2US ☎ (0749) 72322

Normal price: £16-£18.
Short breaks: £14-£16 excluding dinner, min 3 nights, Oct-Mar.

This charming 17th-century house, close to the Cathedral, is being thoughtfully restored. The owners offer a warm welcome to their guests.

WHEDDON CROSS   Somerset   Map 3 SS93

GH QQQ Higherley TA24 7EB ☎ (0643) 841582

Normal price: £16.75.
Short breaks: £48 for 2 nights including early morning tea. Min 2 nights, winter only.

Higherley is an attractive modern detached building standing in pleasant gardens alongside 6 acres of smallholdings. Bedrooms enjoy superb country views.

WILLITON   Somerset   *Map 3 ST04*

✿★★71% **White House** Long Street TA4 4QW ☎ (0984) 32306 & 32777

Normal price: £26-£27.50. Dinner £26.
Short breaks: £143-£151, 2 people for 3 nights. Single £154-£170 for 3 nights.

An attractive Georgian hotel with a warm, friendly atmosphere, noted for its cuisine. The cooking has a welcome honesty and lack of pretention.

WINCANTON   Somerset   *Map 3 ST72*

★★ 🛌 63% **Holbrook House** Holbrook BA9 8BS ☎ (0963) 32377

Normal price: £36. Dinner £13.50-£20.
Short breaks: £42, min 2 nights.
✗ Credit cards ①②③

Popular for quiet breaks away in the winter, this peaceful country house with extensive outdoor leisure facilities has a charming and courteous staff.

WINSFORD   Somerset   *Map 3 SS93*

★★75% **Royal Oak Inn** (Best Western) Exmoor National Park TA24 7JE ☎ (064385) 455

Normal price: £38.
Short breaks: £52.25, min 2 nights, Fri-Sat.
Credit cards ①②③⑤

Interesting beamed bedrooms are available in the main building of this thatched and picturesque hotel. Public rooms include three very comfortable lounges.

WIVELISCOMBE   Somerset   *Map 3 ST02*

✿★(Red) **Langley House** Langley Marsh TA4 2UF (1m N on unclass rd) ☎ (0984) 23318

Normal price: £37.50-£46.50 (1990). Dinner £19.75-£23.50.
Short breaks: £32.50-£41.50 excluding dinner, min 2 nights.
Credit cards ①②③

Langley House is a delightful 16th-century hotel where guests will appreciate the comforts of the attractive sitting room. The set 5-course dinners will linger pleasantly in the memory.

■ STAFFORDSHIRE ■

CANNOCK Staffordshire Map 7 SJ91

★★★60% **Roman Way** (Crown & Raven) Watling Street, Hatherton WS11 1SH (on A5) ☎ (0543) 572121

Normal price: £68.75 room. Dinner from £11.50 and à la carte
Short breaks: £35, single £40. Min 2 nights, Fri-Sun
Credit cards ① ② ③ ⑤

A modern hotel close to junctions 11 and 12 of the M6. All the bedrooms have ensuite facilities and colour television, and there is a choice of bars.

HANCHURCH Staffordshire Map 7 SJ84

★★★79% **Hanchurch Manor** ST4 8SD ☎ (0782) 643030

Normal price: £47.50-£52.50. Dinner £19-£25 and à la carte
Short breaks: £55 including early morning tea and newspaper. Min 2 nights, Fri-Sun. Single price £75.
✻ Credit cards ① ② ③ ⑤

A distinguished country house in charming rural surroundings, yet within easy reach of the motorway. There are two menus - a fixed price gourmet menu and a seasonal à la carte.

HIMLEY Staffordshire Map 7 SO89

★★68% **Himley House** (Berni/Chef & Brewer) DY3 4LD (on A449 N of Stourbridge) ☎ (0902) 892468

Normal price: £34. Dinner £8-£15 and à la carte
Short breaks: £25.50 excluding dinner. Min 2 nights, Fri-Sun.
✻ (ex guide dogs) Credit cards ① ② ③ ⑤

Originally dating from the 17th century, this hotel has well-furnished ensuite bedrooms and friendly, helpful staff.

LEEK Staffordshire Map 7 SJ95

★★58% **Jester At Leek** 81 Mill Street ST13 8EU (0538) 383997

Normal price: £19.75. Dinner £6.25-£12.55 and à la carte
Short breaks: £18 excluding dinner. Min 2 nights, Fri-Sun.
Credit cards ① ③

A popular restaurant serving generous portions of freshly prepared food, and accommodation in warm if compact bedrooms, are the attractions of this family-run hostelry.

LICHFIELD Staffordshire Map 7 SK10

★★72% **Angel Croft** Beacon Street WS13 7AA ☎ (0543) 258737

Normal price: £33. Dinner £9.25-£16.
Short breaks: £26 excluding dinner. Mon-Thurs.
✻ Credit cards ① ③ ⑤

This Georgian house with well-tended gardens at the rear offers friendly, helpful service, warm, spacious bedrooms and freshly prepared cuisine.

★★★59% **George** (Embassy) Bird Street WS13 6PR ☎ (0543) 414822

Normal price: £66 room (1990). Dinner from £13.50.
Short breaks: £34 (1990). Min 2 nights including Fri, Sat or Sun. Single supplement weekdays.
Activity breaks: Alton Towers, short break price plus entrance fee £7 adults, £6 children. Mar 25-Nov 5. Cadbury World, £72.50 for 2 nights including one adult ticket, exhibition guide book, chunky chocolate mug and chocolate bar voucher.
Credit cards ① ② ③ ④ ⑤

An 18th-century hotel situated close to the town centre and cathedral, catering for both tourist and business clientele alike. Cosy open plan lounge and bar areas.

★★★60% **Little Barrow** Beacon Street WS13 7AR ☎ (0543) 414500

Normal price: £32.50. Dinner from £11.50 and à la carte.
Short breaks: £30, min 2 nights, Fri-Sun.
🏌 Credit cards ① ② ③ ⑤

This popular hotel is close to the Cathedral and just a short distance from the town centre. Bedrooms are well designed, and Carters Restaurant enjoys a good reputation.

NEWCASTLE-UNDER-LYME *Staffordshire* Map 7 SJ84

★★★60% **Post House** (Trusthouse Forte) Clayton Road ST5 4DL ☎ (0782) 717171

Normal price: £83 room. Dinner £16.50-£18.75
Short breaks: £41, min 2 nights, Fri-Sun.
Activity breaks: Alton Towers Break, £48 per night, Apr-Oct.
Credit cards ① ② ③ ④ ⑤

A hotel which provides a popular meeting place for travellers, and offers a choice of restaurants and the amenities of a new leisure complex.

PATTINGHAM *Staffordshire* Map 7 SO89

★★★56% **Patshull Park** Patshull WV6 7HR (1.5m W of Pattingham) ☎ (0902) 700100

Normal price: £74-£85. Dinner from £11.75.
Short breaks: £70, min 2 nights. Single price £60.
Activity breaks: Golf Breaks, Fishing Breaks, £70. Clay Pigeon Shooting, details from hotel.
Credit cards ① ② ③ ⑤

Popular for functions and golfing breaks, with an 18-hole golf course, 65-acre fishing lake and a large leisure/fitness complex within the spacious grounds.

STAFFORD *Staffordshire* Map 7 SJ92

★★55% **Albridge** 73 Wolverhampton Road ST17 4AW ☎ (0785) 54100

Normal price: £95.85 room Friday pm-Monday am. Dinner £6.30-£9.80.
Short breaks: £63.90 room Fri. pm-Mon. am, min 3 nights Fri-Sun, Oct-Mar.
Credit cards ① ② ③ ⑤

A commercial hotel set beside a busy road leading into the town centre. A popular feature is the games room with a pool table.

★★65% **Garth** Wolverhampton Road, Moss Pit ST17 9JR ☎ (0785) 56124

Normal price: £69.30. Dinner £10.55 and à la carte
Short breaks: £35, min 2 nights, Fri-Sun.
Credit cards ① ② ③

An attractive house set in its own grounds, situated just off junction 13 of the M6. Popular with commercial trade, the hotel provides well-equipped accommodation and a restaurant with a set menu, augmented by a more extensive à la carte selection.

★★63% **Swan** Greengate Street ST16 2JA ☎ (0785) 58142

Normal price: £30. Dinner £8-£15 and à la carte.
Short breaks: £25.50 excluding dinner. Min 2 nights, Fri-Sun.
🏌 Credit cards ① ② ③ ⑤

This popular hotel in the centre of town is 400 years old and retains many of its original features. The well-equipped bedrooms are decorated in Laura Ashley designs, with complimentary furnishings.

★★62% **Vine** Salter Street ST16 2JU ☎ (0785) 51071

Normal price: £60.50 room
Short breaks: £36 room, min 2 nights, Fri-Sun.
Credit cards ① ② ③

A busy town-centre inn which is reputedly the oldest licensed house in Staffordshire. The bedrooms are full of character and have all modern amenities including colour television, and there is a very popular bar.

STOKE-ON-TRENT Staffordshire Map 7 SJ84

★★55% **George** Swan Square, Burslem ST6 2AE ☎ (0782) 577544

Normal price: from £42.50 room and breakfast, single from £23.50.
Short breaks: £49 for two nights, single £47 for two nights, Fri-Sun. £70 for 2 people, single £47, Sun-Thurs. Min 2 nights.
Activity breaks: Pottery Factory Tours, details from hotel.
✕

A busy commercial hotel offering both carvery and à la carte meals supplemented by a popular lunch-time bar-snack menu.

★★★67% **Stakis Grand** (Stakis) 66 Trinity Street, Hanley ST1 5NB ☎ (0782) 202361

Normal price: £45 room only.
Short breaks: £45, min 2 nights except Christmas & New Year. Single supplement.
✕ Credit cards ① ② ③ ⑤

A traditional style hotel that has recently been completely and sympathetically refurbished. It has a popular carvery-style restaurant.

STONE Staffordshire Map 7 SJ93

★★★62% **Stone House** (Lansbury) ST15 0BQ ☎ (0785) 815531

Normal price: £44. Dinner from £14 and à la carte.
Short breaks: £38, min 2 nights, Fri-Sun.
Credit cards ① ② ③ ⑤

An Edwardian house, one mile south of the town, recently extended to include extra bedrooms and a leisure and conference complex.

WATERHOUSES Staffordshire Map 7 SK05

GH QQ **Croft House Farm** Waterfall ST10 3HZ (1m NW unclass) ☎ (0538) 308553

Normal price: £15.50.
Short breaks: £23, min 2 nights. Single price £27.
✕

A stone-built house which lies surrounded by farmland in the moorland village of Waterfall. Cheerful bedrooms enhance the warm friendly atmosphere.

▪ SUFFOLK ▪

ALDEBURGH Suffolk Map 5 TM45

★★★58% **Brudenell** (Trusthouse Forte) The Parade IP15 5BU ☎ (0728) 452071

Normal price: £38. Dinner £11.95-£13.50.
Short breaks: £46, min 2 nights. Single supplement.
Activity breaks: Bridge breaks, £50 per person per night. Nov. Jazz weekend, £46 per person per night. Feb, Jul & Oct.
Credit cards ① ② ③ ④ ⑤

A seafront hotel with excellent views from many of its rooms, and comfortable public areas. A particularly friendly team of staff offers good service.

★★62% **Uplands** Victoria Road IP15 5DX ☎ (0728) 452420
Closed 23-30 Dec

Normal price: £40.50. Dinner from £13 and à la carte.
Short breaks: £37.50. Min 2 nights, Apr, May, Oct-Dec.
✕ (ex guide dogs) Credit cards ① ② ③ ⑤

Set in its own beautifully maintained walled garden on the approach road to town, the hotel dates from 1800 and provides neat tidy accommodation. Most of the bedrooms (some are sited in an annexe) have ensuite facilities and colour television. Children under twelve are not accommodated.

★★★67% **White Lion** (Best Western) Market Cross Place IP15 5BJ ☎ (0728) 452720

Normal price: £65 (room). Dinner £14.95-£15.95 and à la carte
Short breaks: £38-£45 per night. Min 2 nights, except Xmas, New Year and Easter
Credit cards ☐1 ☐2 ☐3 ☐5

In an attractive position on the sea front the White Lion, which dates from 1563, is Aldeburgh's oldest hotel. It has a popular restaurant and a Buttery Bar which serves snacks and light meals. All the bedrooms have ensuite facilities, there is one family room and two rooms have four-poster beds. There is a special Christmas programme.

BRANDON Suffolk Map 5 TL78

★★★70% **Brandon House** (Minotels) High Street IP27 0AX ☎ (0842) 810171

Normal price: £59. Dinner £11.95 and à la carte
Short breaks: £66. Min 2 nights
Credit cards ☐1 ☐2 ☐3

A detached Georgian house in its own grounds and set back from the main road. All bedrooms have ensuite facilities, colour television and tea and coffee making facilities.

BROME Suffolk Map 5 TM17

★★ 🏮 67% **Oaksmere** IP23 8AJ ☎ (0379) 870326

Normal price: £38. Dinner £16-£18 and à la carte
Short breaks: £54.50, including a bottle of Champagne on arrival. Min 2 nights, Christmas and New Year

Set in its own grounds, this faithfully restored Victorian house offers comfortable accommodation. All eleven bedrooms have ensuite bath or shower rooms and colour television, there are three family rooms and four with four-poster beds. The hotel has a special Christmas programme.

BURY ST EDMUNDS Suffolk Map 5 TL86

★★★76% **Angel** Angel Hill IP33 1LT ☎ (0284) 753926

Normal price: £59.50 (1990). Dinner £14.50.
Short breaks: £39 excluding dinner. Min 3 nights, Fri-Sun.
Activity breaks: Literary Weekends, £145. With literary guest and tour around selected sites.

A 15th-century ivy-clad hotel of long standing repute, where hospitality and good personal services are readily provided. Run by the Gough family with great pride and genuine pleasure.

GH QQQ Chantry 8 Sparhawk Street IP33 1RY ☎ (0284) 767427
Restricted service weekends

Normal price: £24.50
Short breaks: £22 excluding dinner. Min 2 nights, Fri-Sun
Credit cards ☐1 ☐3

This listed 18th-century house has been sympathetically restored to offer comfortable accommodation in well-furnished rooms. All bedrooms have colour television, most have ensuite facilities and there are some family rooms.

★★★ 🏮 76% **Ravenwood Hall** Rougham IP30 9JA (3m E off A45) ☎ (0359) 70345

Normal price: £42.75
Short breaks: £53.50. Min 3 nights. Single £74
Credit cards ☐1 ☐2 ☐3 ☐5

A Tudor country house, standing in seven acres of woodland just outside the town, with a heated swimming pool, tennis, croquet and horse riding. Shooting parties can be arranged. All seven bedrooms have private bathrooms and colour television, and one room has a four-poster bed. There is a special Christmas programme.

CLARE Suffolk Map 5 TL74

★★70% **Bell** (Minotels) Market Hill CO10 8NN ☎ (0787) 277741

Normal price: £35.25. Dinner £16.50
Short breaks: £46.50. Min 2 nights, Fri-Sun, Oct-Apr

This hotel is a former inn with traditional accommodation centred around a courtyard. Most bedrooms have private facilities, and all have colour television.

FELIXSTOWE Suffolk Map 5 TM33

★★66% **Marlborough** Sea Front IP11 8BJ ☎ (0394) 285621

Normal price: £32.75. Dinner £11.95 and à la carte
Short breaks: £35. Min 2 nights, Thu-Sun. £8 single supplement
Credit cards ①②③⑤

Situated on the seafront, the hotel offers a choice of menus, a popular 'joint of the day' carvery, and comfortable ensuite bedrooms with colour television. There are facilities for windsurfing, and a Christmas programme is available.

★★★69% **Orwell Moat House** (Queens Moat) Hamilton Road IP11 7DX ☎ (0394) 285511

Normal price: £90 room. Dinner £15 and à la carte
Short breaks: £87 for 2 nights, Fri-Sun, includes Sun lunch.
Credit cards ①②③⑤

Located close to the railway station this hotel offers a choice of bars, restaurants and lounges. Bedrooms are pleasantly decorated and furnished, and all have ensuite facilities and colour television, including the family rooms.

FRAMLINGHAM Suffolk Map 5 TM26

★★68% **The Crown** (Trusthouse Forte) Market Hill IP13 9AN ☎ (0728) 723521

Normal price: £96 room. Dinner £14 and à la carte
Short breaks: £51
Credit cards ①②③④⑤

A comfortable small hotel dating from the 16th century and situated in the centre of town. Bedrooms are particularly good, most are spacious and all have warm, modern bathrooms and colour television. Christmas breaks are available.

HINTLESHAM   Suffolk   Map 5 TM04

❋ ★★★(Red) ♨ **Hintlesham Hall** (Relais & Chateaux) IP8 3NS ☎ (047387) 334 & 268

Normal price: from £45. Dinner £25-£35.
Short breaks: from £82.50 for 2 nights including champagne
and luncheon voucher of £20. Jul-Aug & Oct.
Activity breaks: Cookery Classes, Herb Days, Golf, Flower
Arrangements and Antique Breaks. Details of all breaks
from the hotel.
Credit cards [1] [2] [3] [5]

A beautiful country house with charming
façade and reputation for excellent cuisine.
High standards of service and hospitality have
been maintained despite a change of hands.

IPSWICH   Suffolk   Map 5 TM14

★★★61% **Ipswich Moat House** (Queens Moat) London Road, Copdock, IP8 3JD (just off A12 near
Copdock village) ☎ (047386) 444

Normal price: £40. Dinner £12.75-£13 and à la carte
Short breaks: £45, min 2 nights, Thu-Sun. Single price £52.
Credit cards [1] [2] [3] [4] [5]

This modern hotel is set in landscaped
gardens, and attracts those in search of leisure.
Staff are pleasant and helpful.

★★★71% **Marlborough** Henley Road IP1 3SP ☎ (0473) 257677

Normal price: £105 room and breakfast. Dinner £16-£19.
Short breaks: £42.50, min 2 nights, Fri-Sun.
Activity breaks: Tutored Wine Weekends, £95, twice
monthly. Black Tie Dinner Weekends, £115, two per year.
Details from hotel.

The two outstanding features of this hotel are
the standard of hospitality and the 'good table'
it provides. Comfortable accommodation and a
high standard of cleanliness.

★★★62% **Novotel Ipswich** Greyfriars Road IP1 1UP ☎ (0473) 232400

Normal price: £58 room.
Short breaks: £72, min 2 nights, Fri-Sun. Single supplement.
Activity breaks: Fun for Children, £26 including bed and
breakfast and entrance to Kessingland Wildlife Park.
Children under 16 free bed and breakfast when sharing
parents' room. Details from hotel.

Located on the edge of the town centre, this
hotel has open plan public areas and spacious
bedrooms well equipped for the business
traveller and families alike.

★★★53% **Post House** (Trusthouse Forte) London Road IP2 0UA ☎ (0473) 690313

Normal price: £36 room only. Dinner £13.50 & à la carte.
Short breaks: £35, min 2 nights. Must include Sat.
Credit cards [1] [2] [3] [4] [5]

Located about two miles north of the town and
giving easy access to the A45 at its junction
with the A1071, this hotel offers a choice of
menus in its restaurant.

LAWSHALL   Suffolk   Map 5 TL85

★★65% **Corders** Bury Road IP29 4PJ ☎ (0284) 830314

Normal price: £44.
Short breaks: £39, min 2 nights except Christmas period.
🏹 Credit cards [1] [2] [3] [5]

A family-owned hotel where guests are offered
a warm welcome and genuine hospitality. Many
rooms enjoy views over open countryside.

LEISTON   Suffolk   Map 5 TM46

★67% **White Horse** Station Road IP16 4HD ☎ (0728) 830694

Normal price: £26. Dinner £8-£13 & à la carte
Short breaks: £26.25, min 2 nights, Fri-Sun.
Credit cards [1] [3]

This comfortable hotel in the centre of the town
now includes a children's play area in its large
garden. It offers warm hospitality, and modest
but clean and tidy bedrooms.

LONG MELFORD   Suffolk   Map 5 TL84

★★★59% **Bull** (Trusthouse Forte) Hall Street CO10 9JG ☎ (0787) 78494

Normal price: £51. Dinner £15.25-£18.80 and à la carte.
Short breaks: £52, min 2 nights.
Credit cards ①②③④⑤

This former posting house close to the village green offers every modern convenience amidst the comfort and charm of open fireplaces, wooden rafters and carvings.

★★59% **Crown Inn** Hall Street CO10 9JL ☎ (0787) 77666

Normal price: £22.50.
Short breaks: £27.50, min 2 nights. Single price £30.
Credit cards ①③

Set among the 18th and 19th-century buildings of this lovely village's main street, the hotel offers a friendly, convivial atmosphere.

LOWESTOFT   Suffolk   Map 5 TM59

GH QQQ Rockville House Pakefield Road NR33 0HS ☎ (0502) 581011 or 574891

Normal price: £18.75. Dinner £8.
Short breaks: £26.25, min 3 nights.
Activity breaks: Footpaths and Wildlife, and Antique Breaks, £78.75 for 3 nights.
🛪 Credit cards ①③

This quiet retreat, minutes from the seafront, offers quality accommodation.

★★★57% **Victoria** Kirkley Cliff Road NR33 0BZ ☎ (0502) 574433

Normal price: £34.25. Dinner £9.95 and à la carte.
Short breaks: £33, min 3 nights. Single price £30.
Credit cards ①②③⑤

This family hotel, with comfortable old fashioned stile accommodation, is on an elevated position on the sea front. The restaurant offers a good selection of dishes.

MILDENHALL   Suffolk   Map 5 TL77

★★62% **Bell** (Best Western) High Street IP28 7EA ☎ (0638) 717272

Normal price: £27.50-£30. Dinner £9-£14 à la carte (1990 price)
Short breaks: £32.50 including £10 dinner allowance. Min 2 nights, Fri-Sun.
Credit cards ①②③⑤

This inn in the heart of Mildenhall partly dates from the 1600s and has a large bar and reasonable accommodation, with colour television in all bedrooms, most with private bath or shower and including a few family rooms. Christmas breaks are available.

★★★62% **Riverside** (Best Western) Mill Street IP28 7DP ☎ (0638) 717274

Normal price: £30. Dinner £11-£17.
Short breaks: £40.50 weekends, £39.50 mid-week. Min 2 nights. Single supplement at weekends only.
Activity breaks: Bridge Breaks, £90 for 2 nights including Sunday lunch, informal duplicate bridge on two evenings and tournament on Sunday afternoon.
Credit cards ①②③⑤

Popular with families from the nearby Air Force Base, this listed red brick house stands at the end of the town's main road with its rear lawns reaching to the River Lark.

★★★61% **Smoke House Inn** Beck Row IP28 8DH ☎ (0638) 713223

Normal price: £45. Dinner £10-£12 and à la carte (1990 price)
Short breaks: £30 including £10 dinner allowance. £60 for single occupancy. Min 2 nights, except bank holidays.
🛪 (ex guide dogs) Credit cards ①②③

In the centre of the village, this busy old inn has a range of modern buildings including a restaurant and cocktail bar, and musical entertainment. All bedrooms, including 20 family rooms, have private bath and colour television. Christmas breaks are available.

NEWMARKET   Suffolk   Map 5 TL66

★★★62% **Newmarket Moat House** (Queens Moat) Moulton Road CB8 8DY ☎ (0638) 667171

Normal price: £40
Short breaks: £40. Fri-Sun. £10 single supplement.
Credit cards ① ② ③ ⑤

Close to both 'the Gallops' and the town centre, this comfortable hotel, popular for conferences, has well-equipped bedrooms with ensuite bath and colour television, including 2 family rooms.

ORFORD   Suffolk   Map 5 TM44

QQ Kings Head Inn Front Street IP12 2LW ☎ (0394) 450271

Normal price: £34-£36. Dinner £10-£22 à la carte
Short breaks: £39-£41 including £8 dinner allowance, Oct-May. Min 2 nights. £27-£30 including £8 dinner allowance, Nov. Min 3 nights except Sat.
Credit cards ⑤

This small family-run inn dating from the 13th century with its beamed bar and candle-lit dining room has comfortable bedrooms, one a family room, with washing facilities and colour television.

STOWMARKET   Suffolk   Map 5 TM05

★★60% **Cedars** Needham Road IP14 2AJ ☎ (0449) 612668

Normal price: £25. Dinner £7.50-£15 à la carte
Short breaks: £32.50, min 2 nights, Fri-Sun.
Credit cards ① ② ③

Pleasant service and a good standard of cleanliness are the hallmarks of a hotel which offers easy access to the A45. Bedrooms are neatly finished.

WOODBRIDGE   Suffolk   Map 5 TM24

★★62% **Crown** (Trusthouse Forte) Thoro'fare IP12 1AD ☎ (03943) 4242

Normal price: £42.50. Dinner £14 and à la carte
Short breaks: £50 including lunch and bar snacks. Min 2 nights, Fri-Sun.
Credit cards ① ② ③ ④ ⑤

This former coaching inn retains traces of its 16th-century origins like the oak beamed restaurant with open fireplace. Freshly-prepared dishes are served here.

★★★ 🐎 73% **Seckford Hall** IP13 6NU ☎ (0394) 385678

Normal price: £40-£47.50. Dinner £14-£18.50 and à la carte
Short breaks: £52.50-£57.50 (1990), min 2 nights.
Credit cards ① ② ③ ⑤

This picturesque Elizabethan manor has been tastefully converted, retaining linenfold panelling, carved doors and massive stone fireplaces.

▪ SURREY ▪

BAGSHOT   Surrey   Map 4 SU96

✿★★★★ 🐎 70% **Pennyhill Park** (Prestige) London Road GU19 5ET ☎ (0276) 71774

Normal price: £142. Dinner from £30.
Short breaks: £175 includes champagne, flowers and chocolates. Min 2 nights, Tues-Thurs only. Single supplement.
Activity breaks: Horse Riding Break, from £210. Clay Shooting Break, from £210. Polo Break and Stress Management Break, details on application.
🌟

Impressive manor house surrounded by acres of gardens and parkland, including its own golf course. Some bedrooms in a tastefully designed annexe. See advertisement on p260.

BURGH HEATH Surrey Map 4 TQ25

★★58% **Heathside** Brighton Road KT20 6BW ☎ (0737) 353355

Normal price: £40. Dinner from £10
Short breaks: £160 for 2 people for 2 nights, Fri-Sun
Credit cards ①②③⑤

This hotel offers modern accommodation, all rooms have ensuite baths or showers and colour television and there are some family rooms. Breakfast is available in the Happy Eater. The hotel has an indoor heated swimming pool, sauna and gymnasium. There is a special Christmas programme.

DORKING Surrey Map 4 TQ14

★★★★65% **Burford Bridge** (Trusthouse Forte) Burford Bridge, Box Hill RH5 6BX (2m NE A24)
☎ (0306) 884561

Normal price: £120 room, £157 with dinner
Short breaks: £126 for 2 people. Min 2 nights, Thu-Sun.
Credit cards ①②③④⑤

Set amidst beautiful gardens on the banks of the River Mole, this hotel offers a warm welcome and comfortable accommodation. All bedrooms have private bath and colour television, with rooms set aside for non-smokers. There is an outdoor heated pool, and Christmas breaks are available.

★★★56% **White Horse** (Trusthouse Forte) High Street RH4 1BE ☎ (0306) 881138

Normal price: £87 room only. Dinner £15 and à la carte
Short breaks: £92 for 2 people. 2-4 nights (must include Saturday night)
Credit cards ①②③④⑤

Centrally situated 16th-century coaching inn now offering modern facilities in well-equipped bedrooms. Some rooms are set aside for non-smokers. There is an indoor heated pool, and Christmas breaks are available.

EAST HORSLEY Surrey Map 4 TQ05

★★★63% **Thatchers Resort** Epsom Road KT24 6TB ☎ (04865) 4291

Normal price: £47. Dinner from £16.50
Short breaks: £42 (subject to review)
✖ (ex guide dogs) Credit cards ①②③⑤

The hotel has a choice of modern and very well-equipped bedrooms and a summer poolside annexe. All rooms are ensuite with colour television, and some rooms are for families and non-smokers.

EGHAM Surrey Map 4 TQ07

★★★★64% **Runnymede** Windsor Road TW20 0AG ☎ (0784) 436171

Normal price: £110 room only. Dinner £16.95-£18.45 and à la carte
Short breaks: £36 (all meals extra), Fri-Sun.

Now completely refurbished, this hotel has a new style restaurant and bar, and offers a classic menu. Bedrooms are all ensuite with colour television and there are family rooms. A special Christmas programme is available.

FARNHAM Surrey Map 4 SU84

★★56% **Trevena House** Alton Road GU10 5ER ☎ (0252) 716908
Closed 24 Dec-4 Jan

Normal price: £30. Dinner £10-£15 and à la carte
Short breaks: £33, includes £10 dinner allowance. Min 2 nights. Single £25, weekends only, min 2 nights.
✖ Credit cards ①②③⑤

This country house style of motel retains many of its original Gothic-Victorian features. All bedrooms have private bath or shower room and colour television. There is a tennis court and swimming pool.

GUILDFORD   Surrey   Map 4 SU94

GH QQ Blanes Court Albury Road GU1 2BT ☎ (0483) 573171
Closed 1 week Christmas

Normal price: £25-£30
Short breaks: £25 excluding dinner. Min 2 nights, Sat & Sun.
Credit cards ①②③

A quietly-situated hotel offering elegant accommodation and a welcoming atmosphere. Most rooms have ensuite facilities, and all have colour television.

★★★★64% **Post House** (Trusthouse Forte) Egerton Road GU2 5XZ ☎ (0483) 574444

Normal price: £63. Dinner £16.50.
Short breaks: £50, min 2 nights, Fri-Sun.
Activity breaks: Clay Pigeon Shooting, £382. Details from hotel.
Credit cards ①②③④⑤

HASLEMERE   Surrey   Map 4 SU93

★★★67% **Lythe Hill** Petworth Road GU27 3BQ (1.25m E B2131) ☎ (0428) 51251 due to change to 651251

Normal price: £99-£164 room. Dinner £16 and à la carte
Short breaks: £49.50. Min 2 nights, Fri-Sun.

Now a charming hotel, this former farmhouse has spacious, modern and comfortable rooms with ensuite facilities and colour television. Leisure amenities include tennis, fishing and pitch and putt. There is a special Christmas programme.

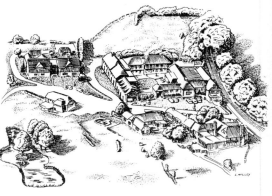

NUTFIELD   Surrey   Map 4 TO35

★★★74% **Nutfield Priory** RH1 4EN ☎ (0737) 822066

Normal price: £107. Dinner £15.50-£20.
Short breaks: £115 including early morning tea and
newspaper. Min 2 nights, Fri-Sun.
Activity breaks: Victorian Evening, Oct. Caribbean
Evenings, Jun, Jul & Aug. Wine & Gourmet Evenings.
Details from hotel.
Credit cards ① ② ③ ⑤

Set high on the Nutfield Ridge, and dating from
1872, this hotel offers fine food and wines and a
leisure centre. Extensive views over Surrey and
Sussex.

STAINES   Surrey   Map 4 TQ07

★★★57% **Thames Lodge** (Trusthouse Forte) Thames Street TW18 4SF ☎ (0784) 464433

Normal price: £47.50 room
Short breaks: £47 (1990), min 2 nights, Thu-Sun.
Credit cards ① ② ③ ④ ⑤

A riverside setting and good car parking make
this a popular venue, and the ten superior Club
Rooms overlook the river. An attractive
restaurant, bar and riverside terrace are
offered.

WEYBRIDGE   Surrey

★★★64% **Ship Thistle** (Mount Charlotte (TS)) Monument Green KT13 8BQ ☎ (0932) 848364

Normal price: £52.75. Dinner from £13.75 and à la carte.
Short breaks: £47 excluding dinner. Single supplement
midweek.
Credit cards ① ② ③ ④ ⑤

A friendly hotel offering comfortable
bedrooms, relaxing bar and lounge areas, and
an elegant restaurant serving both \a la carte
and table d'hôte meals.

▪ SUSSEX, EAST ▪

ALFRISTON   East Sussex   Map 5 TQ50

★★★57% **Star** (Trusthouse Forte) BN26 5TA ☎ (0323) 870495

Normal price: £50. Dinner £13.50.
Short breaks: £50, min 2 nights. Single supplement.
Activity breaks: Golf breaks, £65.
Credit cards ① ② ③ ④ ⑤

An ancient inn with massive oak beams and
inglenook fireplaces, open lounges and a
candlelit restaurant. Choice of bedrooms
including some in a modern wing.

BATTLE   East Sussex   Map 5 TQ71

★★74% **Burntwood** Powdermill Lane TN33 0SU ☎ (04246) 5151

Normal price: £32.50-£37.50. Dinner from £15.50.
Short breaks: £45. Min 2 nights. Single occupancy £55.
Activity breaks: Riding, short break rate plus £7 per hour.
Archery Break, short break rate plus £15 per hour. Fishing
Breaks, short break rate plus £15 per day. Game Shooting
£125-£250 per day including gun hire. Nov-Feb. Clay
Shooting short break rate plus £40 per hour.
Credit cards ① ② ③ ⑤

A delightful small Edwardian country house set
in 18 acres of rolling Sussex countryside. A
high level of service and hospitality is this
hotel's strength.

FH QQQ Little Hemingfold Farmhouse Telham TN33 0TT (2¹/₂m SE on N side of A2100)
☎ (04246) 4338

Normal price: £25-£30. Dinner from £10
Short breaks: £36-£42. Min 2 nights
Credit cards ① ③

Peacefully situated beside a small lake, with forty acres of woodland walks, guests at this farmhouse can also enjoy lawn tennis and trout fishing. Bedrooms are individually furnished, some have ensuite bathrooms and all are equipped with colour television. Children under eight are not accommodated.

QQQ Netherfield Hall Netherfield TN33 9PQ ☎ (04246) 4450

Normal price: £15-£20
Short breaks: £12.50-£17. Dinner not included. Single £15

This attractive coach house has been adapted to offer pleasant, comfortable accommodation, and is situated in a village surrounded by woodlands. As Mr Blake deals in giftware, there is a large selection of pictures and china to choose from as a souvenir. The house has a family atmosphere and pleasant, informal style.

★★★(Red) **Netherfield Place** (Pride of Britain) Netherfield TN33 9PP (3m NW B2096) ☎ (04246) 4455
Closed 2 wks Christmas & New Year

Normal price: £40. Dinner from £17.50 and à la carte
Short breaks: £55 Nov-Easter.
Credit cards ① ② ③ ⑤

Built in 1924, this hotel is a fine example of a Georgian country house. There are fourteen individually-decorated bedrooms all with private bathrooms and colour television; one room is for families and one has a four-poster bed. Guests can play tennis and croquet.

★★72% **La Vieille Auberge** (Minotels) 27 High Street TN33 0EA ☎ (04246) 5171

Normal price: £22.50. Dinner £16-£21.95 and à la carte
Short breaks: £70-£80 for 2 nights, Oct-May
✹ Credit cards ① ② ③

This small auberge with the ambience of a French provincial hotel has seven individually furnished bedrooms; all have colour television, most have ensuite facilities and one is furnished with a four-poster bed. There is a special Christmas programme. The hotel has no parking.

BEXHILL-ON-SEA   East Sussex   Map 5 TV70

★★★64% **Granville** Sea Road TN40 1EE ☎ (0424) 215437

Normal price: £32.75. Dinner from £12.50.
Short breaks: £38.25. Min 2 nights. Single occupancy £49.25.
Activity breaks: Christmas House Party, £275 for 3 nights.
New Year 1960's Break, £99 for 2 nights.
Credit cards ① ② ③ ⑤

A friendly hotel offering peace and charm, with helpful staff led by the personal involvement of the proprietor. The accommodation has been refurbished and modernised.

BOREHAM STREET   East Sussex   Map 5 TQ61

★★★60% **White Friars** (Best Western) BN27 4SE ☎ (0323) 832355

Normal price: £43-£55. Dinner £14.25-£16.50 and à la carte
Short breaks: £48-£60. Single £53-£60. Min 2 nights.
Credit cards ① ② ③ ⑤

This 18th-century manor house has beamed lounges, log fires and quaint bedrooms with further accommodation available in the cottage annexe. All rooms have ensuite facilities and colour television and one is furnished with a four-poster bed. There is a special Christmas programme.

BRIGHTON & HOVE *East Sussex* *Map 4 TQ30*

GH QQQQ Adelaide BN1 2FF ☎ (0273) 205286
Closed Christmas-mid January

Normal price: £27.50, four-poster £35
Short breaks: £22.50, four-poster £28, excluding dinner. Min 2 nights, Fri-Sun (ex Bank Holidays and some conference weekends)
✗ Credit cards 1 2 3 5

Conveniently situated in a quiet position in the Square, this elegant and beautifully-furnished hotel offers a choice of bedrooms with ensuite facilities and colour television. Room service is extensive.

GH QQ Cavalaire House 34 Upper Rock Gardens BN2 1QF ☎ (0273) 696899
Closed Xmas-Feb

Normal price: £29-£38 room
Short breaks: £26-£33 excluding dinner. Min 3 nights (ex Jul-Sep, Bank Holidays and Easter)

A cheerful little terraced house close to the seafront. Each bedroom has a colour television and some have ensuite showers. Children under nine years are not accommodated. No parking.

GH QQ Evercliff House BN2 1QF ☎ (0273) 681161

Normal price: £21-£24
Short breaks: £19.50-£22 excluding dinner. Min 2 nights, Oct-Apr

A neat and attractive guesthouse situated on a hillside away from the seafront, offering well-equipped modern bedrooms with colour television. Some rooms have ensuite facilities, and there are rooms for families and non-smokers. Children under four are not accommodated.

GH QQQ Prince Regent BN1 2FH ☎ (0273) 29962
Closed Christmas Eve & New Years Eve

Normal price: £24
Short breaks: £20.50, single £20, excluding dinner. Min 2 nights, Fri-Sun.
✗ (ex guide dogs) Credit cards 1 3 5

A choice of bedrooms is available here, all with ensuite facilities and colour television, one with a four-poster bed and one for non-smokers. The lounge is furnished with antiques. Children under twelve are not accommodated. No parking.

★★62% **St Catherines Lodge** (Inter-Hotels) Seafront, Kingsway BN3 2RZ ☎ (0273) 778181

Normal price: £32.50. Dinner £9.50-£13.50 and à la carte
Short breaks: £40, single £50. Min 2 nights

Situated opposite the Hove Leisure Centre, this Regency-style hotel has an attractive restaurant and comfortable bedrooms, most with ensuite facilities. A Christmas programme is available.

★★70% **Whitehaven** 34 Wilbury Road BN3 3JP ☎ (0273) 778355

Normal price: £34.50. Dinner £13.50-£16.50
Short breaks: £37.50, min 2 nights, Fri-Sat
✗ Credit cards 1 2 3 5

A welcoming hotel with an elegant restaurant, cosy bar and modern ensuite bedrooms with colour television. Children under eight are not accommodated.

COODEN BEACH *East Sussex* *Map 5 TQ70*

★★★65% **Cooden Resort** TN39 4TT ☎ (04243) 2281

Normal price: £39. Dinner from £16.50
Short breaks: £32 excluding dinner. Min 2 nights, Fri-Sun. (1990 prices)
Credit cards 1 2 3 5

Situated close to the beach, this hotel has good leisure facilities. All bedrooms are ensuite with colour television, with rooms for families and non-smokers. There is a special Christmas programme.

EASTBOURNE   East Sussex   Map 5 TV69

GH QQQ Bay Lodge 61 & 62 Royal Parade BN22 7AQ ☎ (0323) 32515
Mar-Oct

Normal price: £25
Short breaks: £22, includes £6.75 dinner allowance. Min 2
nights, Mar-May & Oct.

A seafront hotel, next to the bowling green and
the Redoubt Gardens, with a small bar and sun
lounge. The bedrooms are spacious, most have
ensuite facilities, and all have colour television.
Children under seven are not accommodated.

★★★★61% **Cavendish** (De Vere) Grand Parade BN21 4DH ☎ (0323) 410222

Normal price: £115-£150 room. Dinner from £16 à la carte
Short breaks: £240 for 2 people for 2 nights

An elegant hotel in a fine seafront position. The
large restaurant is complemented by a cocktail
bar and popular sun lounge, whilst all bedrooms are ensuite with colour television. There
are some leisure amenities and a Christmas
programme is available.

★★★57% **Chatsworth** Grand Parade BN21 3YR ☎ (0323) 411016
Closed Jan-mid Mar

Normal price: £70 room. Dinner from £11.50
Short breaks: £85
Credit cards ① ③

A superb seafront location is the setting for this
hotel which offers friendly services and
comfortable accommodation in ensuite
bedrooms with colour television. A Christmas
programme is available. There is no parking on
the premises.

★65% **Downland** (Minotels) 37 Lewes Road BN21 2BU ☎ (0323) 32689
Closed Jan

Normal price: £29.50-£37.50. Dinner from £14.50 and à la
carte
Short breaks: £40, includes £15 dinner allowance. Min 2
nights.
🖈 (ex guide dogs) Credit cards ① ② ③ ⑤

Guests enjoy a good standard of
accommodation in comfortable bedrooms with
ensuite bath or shower room and colour
television; one room has a four-poster bed. The
chef/proprietor prepares meals with flair and
imagination. A Christmas programme is
available.

GH QQQ Far End 139 Royal Parade BN22 7LH ☎ (0323) 25666
Apr-Oct

Normal price: £32-£36 room
Short breaks: £120-£132 for 2 people for 3 nights. Apr-Jun &
Sep-Oct

A cosy and friendly hotel with bright modern
bedrooms, sea views and easy access to Princes
Park.

GH QQQ Flamingo 20 Enys Road BN21 2DN ☎ (0323) 21654
Closed Nov

Normal price: £55 room with dinner
Short breaks: £49.50 2 nights, £121 5 nights. Easter-Oct
🖈 Credit cards ① ③

Situated in a residential area, this large
Victorian house has comfortable rooms and a
friendly atmosphere. All bedrooms have
ensuite facilities and colour television. There is
no parking on the premises. Children under
eight are not accommodated.

★★★★★60% **Grand** (De Vere) King Edwards Parade BN21 4EQ ☎ (0323) 412345

Normal price: £65. Dinner from £22.50.
Short breaks: £60, £80 with sea view. Min 2 nights, Fri-Sun.
Activity breaks: Music Break, 3-6 May. Details from hotel.

The sheer grandeur of this white, palatial hotel
at one end of Eastbourne's promenade is a
visual delight. Inside the young staff provide a
friendly, welcoming atmosphere.

★★73% **Langham** Royal Parade BN22 7AH ☎ (0323) 31451
Closed 13 Nov-21 Mar

Normal price: £199-£213 per week. Dinner from £8.95
Short breaks: £26-£29. Min 2 nights.
Credit cards [1] [3]

A privately-run hotel overlooking the sea, and offering high levels of service and reliable standards of cooking. There is regular entertainment during the evenings. All bedrooms are ensuite with colour television.

★★★★61% **Lansdowne** (Best Western) King Edward's Parade BN21 4EE ☎ (0323) 25174

Normal price: £35-£37. Dinner from £13.50.
Short breaks: £42.50 including one newspaper. Min 2 nights, 28 Oct-5 May.
Activity breaks: Golf Break, £116-£120 for 2 nights except Sept. Contract Bridge Weekends, £125.50 for 3 nights, 19-22 Apr, 17-20 May, also Nov & Dec to be arranged. Rambling Weekend, £90, 10-12 May.

In a prime seafront position this fine, well managed hotel has been owned by the same family since 1912, and they provide traditional hospitality and service.

★61% **Oban** King Edward's Parade BN21 4DS ☎ (0323) 31581
Closed Dec-Etr restricted service Nov

Normal price: from £44 room
Short breaks: from £25

A friendly family-run hotel standing next to the Wish Tower features a lounge and bar area, and a basement restaurant. The ensuite bedrooms have colour television. There is no parking on the premises.

★★★56% **Queens** (De Vere) Marine Parade BN21 3DY ☎ (0323) 22822

Normal price: £57.50. Dinner from £14
Short breaks: £55. Min 2 nights, Fri-Sun, Jul & Aug any 2 nights.
Credit cards [1] [2] [3] [5]

A popular hotel situated opposite the pier, with a large restaurant, feature bars and helpful service. The good-sized bedrooms are ensuite with colour television, and some face the sea. There is a special Christmas programme.

★★69% **West Rocks** Grand Parade BN21 4DL ☎ (0323) 25217
Closed mid Nov-20 Mar

Normal price: £32. Dinner £8.50
Short breaks: £30, single £27-£37. Min 2 nights, Mar-May & Jul & Oct

Situated midway along the seafront, between the bandstand and the Wishtower, this long-established family-owned hotel offers comfortable accommodation. All bedrooms have colour television, and most have ensuite facilities. Children under three are not accommodated. There is no parking on the premises.

★★★64% **Wish Tower** King Edward's Parade BN21 4EB ☎ (0323) 22676

Normal price: £75 room. Dinner £13.50-£14.50
Short breaks: £49. Single supplement. Min 2 nights
Credit cards ① ② ③ ④ ⑤

In a prime seafront position opposite the Wish Tower and Gardens this hotel has bedrooms which range from sumptuous to more modest. All have colour television, most have ensuite facilities and some are set aside for non-smokers. A Christmas programme is available.

GH QQQ Wynstay Lewes Road BN21 2BY ☎ (0323) 21550
Closed 12 Oct-31 Mar

Normal price: £15-£17
Short breaks: £13.50-£15.30 excluding dinner. £3 single supplement. Min 3 nights Apr-Sep
✱

A pleasant guesthouse offering friendly and helpful service. All rooms have private facilities and colour television, and there are some family rooms. Children under three are not accommodated.

FOREST ROW   East Sussex   Map 5 TQ43

★★63% **Brambletye** (Inter-Hotels) The Square RH18 5EZ ☎ (0342) 824144

Normal price: £65-£70 room. Dinner £10.50-£17 à la carte
Short breaks: £75 for 2 nights. Single £50 for 2 nights
Credit cards ① ② ③ ⑤

Dating back to the 17th century with a modern annexe at the rear, this hotel has ensuite bedrooms with colour television. The Deerstalker restaurant features English food and friendly service.

HAILSHAM   East Sussex   Map 5 TQ50

★★75% **Olde Forge** Magham Down BN27 1PN ☎ (0323) 842893
Closed 25 Dec-2 Jan

Normal price: £22-£24. Dinner £10.50 and à la carte
Short breaks: £30, single £32.50. Min 2 nights, Oct-Mar
Credit cards ① ② ③ ⑤

A small cottage hotel, situated just outside the town, with a cosy bar and restaurant. Most of the bedrooms have private facilities, all have colour television and one is furnished with a four-poster bed.

HALLAND   East Sussex   Map 5 TQ41

★★66% **Halland Forge** (Inter-Hotels) BN8 6PW ☎ (082584) 456

Normal price: £67 room. Dinner £14.50-£15.50 and à la carte
Short breaks: £80 for 2 people, 2 nights; 3 nights £118; 4 nights £156; 5 nights £189. £10 single supplement
Credit cards ① ② ③ ⑤

Conveniently situated on the A22, this family-run hotel offers a lounge bar, restaurant and a separate coffee shop. All bedrooms are ensuite with colour television, and two rooms have four-poster beds. Children under five are not accommodated.

HASTINGS & ST LEONARDS   East Sussex   Map 5 TQ80

GH QQ Argyle TN34 1EN ☎ (0424) 421294
Closed Christmas

Normal price: £13
Short breaks: £12 excluding dinner. Single £13. Min 3 nights (ex Easter & Bank Holidays)
✱

This homely guesthouse is situated near the seafront and local amenities. Some rooms have private showers, all have tea/coffee making facilities. Children under four are not accommodated. There is no parking on the premises.

★★★73% **Beauport Park** Battle Road TN38 8EA ☎ (0424) 851222

Normal price: £68 room
Short breaks: £72-£84 2 days
Credit cards [1] [2] [3] [5]

This charming Georgian country house is situated in 33 acres of delightful grounds and woodlands. Both restaurant and cocktail bar overlook the Italian sunken garden. Bedrooms are well-equipped and tastefully furnished, and public rooms are spacious and elegant.

QQQQ **Parkside House** 59 Lower Park Road TN34 2LD ☎ (0424) 433096

Normal price: £15-£17
Short breaks: £21, min 2 nights. Single £25

This charming house enjoys a magnificent location overlooking Alexandra Park, and offers well-prepared food and comfortable rooms, including one with a Louis XVI bed.

LEWES   *East Sussex*   Map 5 TQ41

★★★54% **Shelleys** (Mount Charlotte (TS)) High Street BN7 1XS ☎ (0273) 472361

Normal price: £50. Dinner £14.50-£15.50 & à la carte.
Short breaks: £53.50, min 2 nights, Sept-May. Single price £49.50.
Credit cards [1] [2] [3] [5]

This former inn, dating from 1526, was converted into a manor house and became the home of the Shelley family in 1663. Now a hotel with comfortable rooms and pretty restaurant.

★★60% **White Hart** (Best Western) 55 High Street BN7 1XE ☎ (0273) 474676 & 476694

Normal price: £38.50. Dinner £6.90-£11.50.
Short breaks: £46, min 2 nights. Single supplement.
Activity breaks: Golfing Package, £118 including green fees.
Credit cards [1] [2] [3] [5]

Much of the original character and old world charm of this 15th-century town centre hotel has been retained. Facilities include a carvery, conservatory restaurant and coffee shop.

NINFIELD   *East Sussex*   Map 5 TQ71

QQ **Moons Hill Farm** The Green TN33 9LH ☎ (0424) 892645

Normal price: £32-£34
Short breaks: £30 excluding dinner. Oct-May.

This farmhouse with a riding stables and 10 acres of mixed smallholdings has ensuite bedrooms, including a family room with television.

PEASMARSH   East Sussex   Map 5 TQ82

★★66% **Flackley Ash** (Best Western) TN31 6YH ☎ (079721) 651

Normal price: £41.25. Dinner £13.95-£21.50.
Short breaks: £49, min 2 nights. Single supplement.
Activity breaks: Four-Poster Romance, from £105. Jazz
Weekend, from £105, 22 Nov.
Credit cards ① ② ③ ⑤

A Georgian manor house which has been skilfully extended to provide additional bedrooms of a luxurious standard, and good indoor leisure facilities.

PEVENSEY BAY   East Sussex   Map 5 TQ60

QQ Napier The Promenade BN24 6HD ☎ (0323) 768875

Normal price: £14.50, £20.50 including dinner.
Short breaks: £19. Min 3 nights, Apr-May, Sep. Single
supplement.
✱

Right on the beach, this well maintained guest-house provides friendly service and includes a sun lounge and small bar. Bedrooms, which include family rooms, have colour television, and most have private shower. Fishing facilities available.

RYE   East Sussex   Map 5 TQ92

★★★63% **Mermaid Inn** Mermaid Street TN31 7EU ☎ (0797) 223065
Normal price: £90 room and breakfast. Dinner £15-£16.
Short breaks: £94 for 2 people, min 2 nights.
Activity breaks: Sussex Food Weekends, approx £105 for 2
nights, Spring and Autumn. Brass Band Weekends, details
from hotel.
🏌 Credit cards ① ② ③ ④ ⑤

With beams and panelling dating from its 1420 rebuilding, the Mermaid offers good food and warm hospitality. The inn's charm compensates for the lack of space.

QQQ **Old Borough Arms** The Strand TN31 7DB ☎ (0797) 222128
Normal price: £20
Short breaks: £25. Min 3 nights, Sun-Thu.
Credit cards ① ③

This nine-bedroomed family-run hotel on the old town wall partly dates from 1720, including the dining room. The skilfully modernised bedrooms, among them family rooms, all have private shower and colour television.

WADHURST   East Sussex   Map 5 TQ63

★★ 🛏 66% **Spindlewood Country House** TN5 7JG ☎ (0580) 200430
Normal price: £35-£42.50. Dinner £13.50-£15 and à la carte.
Short breaks: £40-£45, min 2 nights, mid Oct-May.
🏌 Credit cards ① ② ③

This small, relaxing, family-run hotel is peacefully situated and furnished with antiques. Imaginative country cooking is complemented by good personal service.

▪ SUSSEX, WEST ▪

AMBERLEY   West Sussex   Map 4 TQ01

✿★★★ 🛏 75% **Amberley Castle** BN18 9ND ☎ (0798) 831992
Normal price: £195
Short breaks: £375 for 2 nights. Not available Xmas or New
Year
🏌 Credit cards ① ② ③ ⑤

This delightful hotel, formerly a 900-year-old castle, has twelve beautifully designed bedrooms with ensuite facilities and colour television, within its battlements and ancient walls. Two bedrooms have four-poster beds. An enthusiastic chef produces some imaginative menus.

ARUNDEL   West Sussex   Map 4 TQ00

★ 🛏 63% **Burpham Country** Old Down, Burpham BN18 9RJ (3m NE off A27) ☎ (0903) 882160
Normal price: £27. Dinner £11.50
Short breaks: £34.50. Single £43.50. Min 2 nights
🏌 Credit cards ① ③

Enjoying a peaceful location, this hotel has ten attractive bedrooms, most with private bath or shower rooms and all with colour television. There is a special Christmas programme. Children under twelve are not accommodated.

★★★67% **Norfolk Arms** (Forestdale) High Street BN18 9AD ☎ (0903) 882101
Normal price: £65 room. Dinner approx £15.75
Short breaks: £90 for 2 people. Single £55-£60

This Georgian coaching inn has been skilfully modernised to retain all its historical features. All bedrooms, including those in the annexe have private bathrooms and colour television, six rooms have four-poster beds and three rooms are set aside for non-smokers. There is a special Christmas programme.

INN QQ Swan High Street BN18 9AG ☎ (0903) 882314

Normal price: £30. Dinner £9 and à la carte
Short breaks: £28.50 Apr-Jun; £34 Jul-Oct; £30 Nov-Feb. £15 single supplement. Min 2 nights
✻ (ex guide dogs) Credit cards ① ② ③ ⑤

This popular 'free house' serves real ale, and there is live entertainment in the bar on some evenings. Bedrooms are modern and are equipped with ensuite facilities and colour television.

ASHINGTON   West Sussex   Map 4 TQ11

★★69% **Mill House** Mill Lane RH20 3BZ ☎ (0903) 892426

Normal price: £35. Dinner from £12.50 and à la carte
Short breaks: £42.50. Min 2 nights, Fri-Sun

A cosy 18th-century mill house has been extended to provide modern accommodation whilst still retaining its charm and character. The majority of bedrooms have ensuite facilities, and all have colour television. Two rooms have four-poster beds. There are special facilities here for children.

BILLINGSHURST   West Sussex   Map 4 TQ02

GH Q Newstead Hall Adversane RH14 9JH ☎ (0403) 783196 & 784734

Normal price: £80 room and breakfast.
Short breaks: £62, min 2 nights, Fri-Sun.
Activity breaks: Details from hotel.
✻ Credit cards ① ② ③ ⑤

An older style house with a new wing of bedrooms, set in a pleasant district with good access.

BOGNOR REGIS   West Sussex   Map 4 SZ99

★62% **Black Mill House** (Minotels) Princess Avenue, Aldwick PO21 2QU ☎ (0243) 821945 & 865596

Normal price: £24.50-£29.50. Dinner from £9
Short breaks: £29-£33. Min 2 nights, except Christmas, Easter, Bank Holidays and Goodwood Week 27 Jul-3 Aug. Single supplement £3
Credit cards ① ② ③ ⑤

A traditional and long established family-run hotel providing a friendly atmosphere and special facilities for children. Most bedrooms have ensuite bath or shower rooms, all have colour television and there are family rooms. There is a special Christmas programme.

BOSHAM   West Sussex   Map 4 SU80

★★67% **Millstream** (Best Western) Bosham Lane PO18 8HL ☎ (0243) 573234

Normal price: £85-£105 room with breakfast. Dinner from £15.50
Short breaks: £48-£56. Min 2 nights
Credit cards ① ② ③ ⑤

A delightful, peaceful hotel in a picturesque setting beside a stream, offering individually-decorated bedrooms all with private facilities and colour television. There are two family rooms and one furnished with a four-poster bed. There is a special Christmas programme.

CHICHESTER   West Sussex   Map 4 SU80

★★★61% **Dolphin & Anchor** (Trusthouse Forte) West Street PO19 1QE ☎ (0243) 785121

Normal price: £41.25. Dinner from £13
Short breaks: £46. Min 2 nights, first night Sun
Credit cards ① ② ③ ④ ⑤

Originally two ancient inns, this charming town centre hotel is situated opposite the cathedral. All the bedrooms have a private bath or shower room and colour television, and some rooms are set aside for families and non-smokers. There is a special Christmas programme.

CUCKFIELD West Sussex Map 4 TQ32

★★ ♨ 55% **Hilton Park** RH17 5EG ☎ (0444) 454555

Normal price: £33. Dinner from £15
Short breaks: £46, single £58. Min 4 nights
Credit cards ① ② ③ ⑤

Attractively and peacefully set in three acres of grounds this hotel offers mainly English home-style cooking. Most of the bedrooms have private bath or shower rooms, and all have colour television.

GATWICK AIRPORT (LONDON) West Sussex Map 4 TQ24

★★★62% **Chequers Thistle** (Mount Charlotte (TS)) Brighton Road, Horley RH6 8PH ☎ (0293) 786992

Normal price: £50.25. Dinner from £14.50 and à la carte
Short breaks: £40 excluding dinner.
✙ Credit cards ① ② ③ ④ ⑤

This former Tudor coaching inn is now a pleasant friendly hotel. All bedrooms are ensuite with colour television, and there are rooms for families and non-smokers. The hotel has an outdoor heated pool.

★★63% **Gatwick Manor** (Berni/Chef & Brewer) London Road, Lowfield Heath, Crawley RH10 2ST
☎ (0293) 26301 & 35251

Normal price: £38. Dinner £8-£15 à la carte
Short breaks: £27.50 excluding dinner. Min 2 nights.
Credit cards ① ② ③ ⑤

Original beamed Tudor buildings in the grounds of this spacious hotel, have been extended to provide modern bedrooms with ensuite facilities and colour television.

★★★65% **George** (Trusthouse Forte) High Street, Crawley RH10 1BS ☎ (0293) 24215

Normal price: £55. Dinner £13.95-£16.
Short breaks: £59, min 2 nights, Thu-Sun, must include Sat. Single price £55.
Activity breaks: Golf Weekend, £106 for 2 nights. Murder Weekends, details from hotel.
Credit cards ① ② ③ ④ ⑤

This historic inn stands in Crawley centre, and combines the old world charm of exposed beams and timbers with modern standards of comfort.

★★★★71% **London Gatwick Airport Hilton** (Hilton) RH6 0LL ☎ (0293) 518080

Normal price: £66.50. Dinner £18.50-£22.50 and à la carte
Short breaks: £60 excluding dinner. Single £75, Fri-Sun

The hotel provides excellent access to the airport, and amenities include a gymnasium, indoor swimming pool and satellite television. Bedrooms are equipped to a high standard with air conditioning and mini-bar; all are ensuite with colour television.

GOODWOOD West Sussex Map 4 SU80

★★★72% **Goodwood Park** PO18 0QB ☎ (0243) 775537

Normal price: Approx £55. Dinner from £17.25.
Short breaks: Approx £55 Fri-Sun, £60 Mon-Thu. Min 2 nights.
Activity breaks: Golf Breaks, £130 for 2 nights including 2 rounds of golf (1990). Golf Tuition Holidays, details from hotel.
Credit cards ① ② ③ ⑤

Originally a coaching inn, recently transformed into a modern leisure complex. A choice of up-to-date bedrooms is complemented by the classic cuisine of Dukes Restaurant.

HORSHAM   West Sussex   Map 4 TQ13

★★69% **Ye Olde King's Head** RH12 1EG ☎ (0403) 53126

Normal price: £36. Dinner £13.50 and à la carte
Short breaks: £32 (1990 prices) Min 2 nights, Fri-Sun
Credit cards ① ② ③ ⑤

This historic coaching inn has a restaurant, coffee shop, bar lounge and Wine Cellar. Bedrooms are comfortable and modern, most have ensuite facilities, and all have colour television.

LOWER BEEDING   West Sussex   Map 4 TQ22

★★★★ 👭 63% **South Lodge** (Prestige) Brighton Road RH13 6PS ☎ (0403) 891711

Normal price: £71.50. Dinner £23-£30 and à la carte.
Short breaks: £90 including champagne, flowers and chocolates. Min 2 nights, Fri-Sun. Single supplement.
🦅 Credit cards ① ② ③ ④ ⑤

South Lodge is set in 90 acres of woodland with a glorious display of rhododendrons and azaleas in season. The interior of the house is splendid.

MIDHURST   West Sussex   Map 4 SU82

★★★67% **Spread Eagle** (Best Western) South Street GU29 9NH ☎ (0730) 816911

Normal price: from £40. Dinner £21.50-£25.50 (1990 price)
Short breaks: £55.60. Min 2 nights, Fri-Sun, except Christmas. £15 single supplement.
Credit cards ① ② ③ ⑤

A former tavern and coaching inn dating back to 1430, this characterful, sympathetically modernised hotel serves imaginative food in the candle-lit restaurant. All bedrooms, some non-smoking, have ensuite facilities and colour television. Christmas breaks are available.

PULBOROUGH   West Sussex   Map 4 TQ01

★★64% **Chequers** (Minotels) Church Place RH20 1AD ☎ (0798) 872486

Normal price: £27.50. Dinner from £12.50 (1990 price)
Short breaks: £35 including morning tea/coffee. Min 2
nights, except Christmas. Single supplement in high
season.
Credit cards ① ② ③ ⑤

This welcoming house with a garden and views over the Sussex Downs serves good traditional food. Well-equipped bedrooms offer private bath or shower rooms and colour television, including two family rooms and one with a four-poster bed.

RUSPER   West Sussex   Map 4 TQ23

★★★71% **Ghyll Manor** (Trusthouse Forte) RH12 4PX ☎ (0293) 871571

Normal price: £82
Short breaks: £67 including set-menu dinner or £20 dinner
allowance. Min 2 nights, Fri-Sun.
Credit cards ① ② ③ ④ ⑤

Set in 40 acres of landscaped gardens, this hospitable Tudor manor house serves good food and has comfortable spacious bedrooms with colour television and private bath or shower, including some with four-poster beds. Leisure facilities include tennis, outdoor swimming pool, sauna and solarium. Christmas breaks are available.

SLINFOLD   West Sussex   Map 4 TQ13

★★★66% **Random Hall** Stane Street RH13 7QX ☎ (0403) 790558 & 790852

Normal price: £37.50. Dinner £13.25 and à la carte.
Short breaks: £42.50, min 2 nights Fri-Sun.
Credit cards ① ② ③

Originally a Tudor farmhouse, this charming road-side hotel has been skilfully modernised to provide attractively furnished, well equipped bedrooms, together with inglenook fireplaces, dark oak beams and flagstone floors.

THAKEHAM (near Storrington)   West Sussex   Map 4 TQ11

❀★★★ ⬧ 74% **Abingworth Hall** Storrington Road RH20 3EF ☎ (0798) 813636

Normal price: £44. Dinner from £27 and à la carte.
Short breaks: £66, min 2 nights.
🎄 Credit cards ① ② ③ ④ ⑤

A charming Edwardian country house hospitably run by its owners, and offering a well balanced selection of good food. Standing in 10 acres of grounds.

TROTTON   West Sussex   Map 4 SU82

★★★65% **Southdowns** (Exec Hotel) GU31 5JN ☎ (073080) 774 & 763

Normal price: £40. Dinner £15-£20 à la carte.
Short breaks: £42.50, min 2 nights.
🎄 Credit cards ① ② ③

Tucked away in four acres of grounds at the foot of the South Downs, this hotel has magnificent views. The restaurant offers a variety of menus.

WEST CHILTINGTON   West Sussex   Map 4 TQ01

★★★61% **Roundabout** (Best Western) Monkmead Lane, RH20 2PF (1.75m S) ☎ (0798) 813838

Normal price: £69.75 room and dinner
Short breaks: £92-£98
Credit cards ① ② ③ ④ ⑤

A Tudor-style hotel in a peaceful rural location. Bedrooms are furnished in dark oak, all have ensuite bath and colour television and four have four-poster beds. There is a special Christmas programme. Children under three are not accommodated.

WORTHING   West Sussex   Map 4 TQ10

★★63% Ardington (Best Western) Steyne Gardens BN11 3DZ ☎ (0903) 30451

Normal price: £27.50-£31.50. Dinner £10.
Short breaks: £30 (1990), min 2 nights, Fri-Sun. Single price £37.50.
Credit cards ① ② ③ ⑤

This established family-run hotel is conveniently situated overlooking Steyne Gardens. The resident proprietors' personal service complements the friendly and informal atmosphere.

★★★67% Beach Marine Parade BN11 3QJ ☎ (0903) 34001

Normal price: £38.75. Dinner from £16 and à la carte
Short breaks: £39.75, Thu-Sun, Oct-Apr. Single £51.50
✕ Credit cards ① ② ③ ④ ⑤

An hotel which commands extensive sea views from its fine position on the front creates a warmly hospitable atmosphere, retaining some traditional services.

GH QQQ Blair House 11 St Georges Road BN11 2DS ☎ (0903) 34071

Normal price: £17
Short breaks: £15 excluding dinner. Min 2 nights, Fri-Sun, Mar, Apr & Oct.
✕ Credit cards ①

This hotel offers a warm, friendly welcome and good home cooked meals. Close to the seafront, Beach House Park and bowling greens.

★★★58% Kingsway Marine Parade BN11 3QQ ☎ (0903) 37542 & 37543

Normal price: £32. Dinner from £14.
Short breaks: £43, min 2 nights weekends, 3 nights midweek. Single price £49 weekends.
Credit cards ① ② ③ ⑤

A hotel in fine seafront position offering traditional hospitality. Guests can relax in the comfortable lounge or cosy bar, and there is a carvery restaurant.

GH QQQ Moorings 4 Selden Road BN11 2LL ☎ (0903) 208882

Normal price: £16.50.
Short breaks: £22, min 2 nights. Single price £24.
✕ Credit cards ① ③

This comfortable and welcoming guesthouse offers a very pleasing lounge and attractive dining room where a good selection of home cooking is offered.

★★61% Windsor House 14-20 Windsor Road BN11 2LX ☎ (0903) 39655

Normal price: £31.50. Dinner from £9 and à la carte
Short breaks: £52-£62, min 2 nights, Thu-Sat, mid Sept-Apr.
✕ Credit cards ① ③ ⑤

This popular hotel is close to the beach and all holiday facilities. Bedrooms are modern, and there is an attractive carvery-style restaurant.

TYNE & WEAR

GATESHEAD   Tyne & Wear   Map 12 NZ26

★★★69% Springfield (Embassy) Durham Road NE9 5BT ☎ 091-477 4121

Normal price: £30. Dinner from £11.95
Short breaks: £38, single £35. Min 2 nights
Credit cards ① ② ③ ④ ⑤

This hotel offers comfortable accommodation; each bedroom has an ensuite bath or shower room and colour television, and there are rooms for families and non-smokers. The restaurant provides a carvery and standard menu. There is a special Christmas programme.

★★★66% **Swallow** (Swallow) High Street West NE8 1PE ☎ 091-477 1105

Normal price: £75 room and breakfast
Short breaks: £85 for 2 nights, Fri-Sun, includes Sunday lunch
Credit cards ① ② ③ ④ ⑤

Situated just off the southern approach to Newcastle this modern hotel offers spacious accommodation in ensuite bedrooms with colour television. Some rooms are for families and non-smokers. Leisure facilities include an indoor heated pool and gymnasium. There is a special Christmas programme.

NEWCASTLE UPON TYNE   Tyne & Wear   Map 12 NZ26

★★★ 🐾 64% **Airport Moat House** (Queens Moat) Woolsington NE13 8DJ ☎ (0661) 24911

Normal price: £42.50
Short breaks: £37.50. Thu-Sun. £10 Single supplement.
Credit cards ① ② ③ ⑤

A modern hotel in a rural setting close to the airport with a cocktail lounge, smart restaurant and well-equipped ensuite, soundproofed bedrooms.

QQQ Chirton House 46 Clifton Road NE4 6XH ☎ 091-273 0407

Normal price: £18
Short breaks: £16 (£19 for single room). Min 2 nights, Fri-Sun.
Credit cards ①

This attractive Victorian house in a peaceful suburban setting provides neat and comfortable accommodation with hot and cold water and colour television in all bedrooms, including 3 family rooms.

★★★63% **County Thistle** (Thistle) Neville Street NE99 1AH ☎ 091-232 2471

Normal price: £45.25
Short breaks: £40 excluding dinner. Single supplement on weekdays.
Credit cards ① ② ③ ④ ⑤

A comfortable city centre hotel opposite the main railway station, with good food served in the attractive Cafe Mozart and all bedrooms (some no-smoking and family rooms) with ensuite facilities and colour television.

★★★55% **Hospitality Inn** (Mount Charlotte) 64 Osborne Road, Jesmond NE2 2AT ☎ 091-281 7881

Normal price: £43.25
Short breaks: £39.50
🐕 (ex guide dogs) Credit cards ① ② ③ ⑤

A comfortable hotel converted from terrace houses and close to the city centre. All bedrooms, including one with a four-poster bed and some family and no-smoking rooms, have private bath and colour television. Dinner is served in the coffee house, open all day.

★★ **Morrach** 82-86 Osborne Road, Jesmond NE2 2AP ☎ 091-281 3361

Normal price: £55
Short breaks: £40 excluding dinner. Fri-Sun.
Credit cards ① ② ③

Modest accommodation is available at this family-run hotel. Dinners represent good value, and there is also a small coffee shop which remains open throughout the day and evening.

★★★58% **Northumbria** (Mount Charlotte) Osborne Road, Jesmond NE2 2BR ☎ 091-281 4961

Normal price: £31.75
Short breaks: £37
🐕 (ex guide dogs) Credit cards ① ② ③ ⑤

Near the city centre, this unpretentious hotel offers pleasant accommodation with ensuite facilities and colour television in all bedrooms, including two family rooms. There is also a garden and sauna.

★★64% **Osborne** Osborne Road, Jesmond NE2 2AE ☎ 091-281 3385

Normal price: £24
Short breaks: £20 excluding dinner. Min 2 nights, Fri-Sun.
Credit cards [1] [3]

Although generally fairly compact and modestly furnished, bedrooms at this friendly hotel are comfortable and well equipped. Sound home cooking is served in the traditional dining room.

★★★59% **Imperial** Jesmond Road NE2 1PR ☎ 091-281 5511

Normal price: £75-£85. Dinner £12.50-£13.50.
Short breaks: £42.50-£45. Min 2 nights, Fri-Sun. Any nights midweek Jul-Aug.
Activity breaks: Christmas Break, £210, 23-27 Dec. New Years Break, £120, 30-31 Dec.
Credit cards [1] [2] [3] [5]

Modernised city centre hotel with open plan public areas and an attractive leisure complex. Restaurant and coffee shop facilities.

SEATON BURN Tyne & Wear Map 12 NZ27

★★★★54% **Holiday Inn** Great North Road NE13 6BP ☎ 091-236 5432

Normal price: £107.90. Dinner from £15.50 and à la carte (1990 prices)
Short breaks: £40 excluding dinner. Min 1 night Fri-Sun. £20 single supplement.
Credit cards [1] [2] [3] [4] [5]

Conveniently close to Newcastle Airport, set in open countryside, this low-rise, purpose-built hotel has spacious, attractive bedrooms and good leisure facilities. Service is generally willing and friendly - especially in the busy carvery restaurant.

SUNDERLAND Tyne & Wear Map 12 NZ35

★★63% **Roker** (Berni/Chef & Brewer) Roker Terrace SR6 0PH ☎ 091-567 1786

Normal price: £27.50. Dinner £8-£15 and à la carte.
Short breaks: £23.50 excluding dinner. Min 2 nights, Fri-Sun.
🏊 Credit cards [1] [2] [3] [5]

Comfortable accommodation and friendly, informal service are offered at this seafront hotel.

★★★63% **Swallow** (Swallow) Queen's Parade, Seaburn SR6 8DB ☎ 091-529 2041

Normal price: £45. Dinner from £14.50.
Short breaks: £42.50, min 2 nights, Fri-Sun.
Credit cards [1] [2] [3] [5]

A well-managed hotel built in the 1930s, overlooking the sandy beaches of Whitburn. Newer bedrooms are more comfortable and up-to-date, but all are well-equipped.

TYNEMOUTH Tyne & Wear Map 12 NZ36

★★★61% **Park** Grand Parade NE30 4JQ ☎ 091-257 1406

Normal price: £33.50. Dinner £9-£11 & à la carte
Short breaks: £27.50 excluding dinner. Min 2 nights, Fri-Sun.
Credit cards [1] [2] [3] [5]

A modern functional hotel situated in a prominent position on the seafront.

WALLSEND   Tyne & Wear   Map 12 NZ26

★★★57% Newcastle Moat House (Queens Moat) Coast Road NE28 9HP ☎ 091-262 8989 & 091-262 7044

Normal price: £37.50-£42.50. Dinner £11.95-£12.95 and à la carte.
Short breaks: £40 (1990) including newspaper. Min 2 nights, Fri-Sun. Any night Jul & Aug.
Credit cards ① ② ③ ⑤

Modern and purpose-built, this hotel offers a small leisure club. Bedrooms, though dated in style, have every facility.

WASHINGTON   Tyne & Wear   Map 12 NZ35

★★★61% Post House (Trusthouse Forte) Emerson District 5 NE37 1LB ☎ 091-416 2264

Normal price: £39. Dinner £10.50-£14.20.
Short breaks: £45, min 2 nights, Fri-Sun.
Credit cards ① ② ③ ④ ⑤

This large modern and well-furnished hotel stands close to the A1(M) on the south side of Newcastle.

★★★68% Washington Moat House (Queens Moat) Stone Cellar Road, District 12 NE37 1PH
☎ 091-417 2626

Normal price: £76-£78 room. Dinner from £12.95.
Short breaks: £45, min 2 nights, including Sat. Single supplement.
Activity breaks: Golfing Breaks, £110 including one round of golf. Snooker Breaks, £110 including three hour's snooker a day.
Credit cards ① ② ③ ⑤

A comfortable hotel featuring extensive leisure facilities which include a golf course and driving range.

WHICKHAM   Tyne & Wear   Map 12 NZ26

★★68% Gibside Arms Front Street NE16 4JG ☎ 091-488 9292

Normal price: £29.50. Dinner £12.50 and à la carte.
Short breaks: £27.50, min 2 nights, Fri-Sun. Jan-Nov.
✷ Credit cards ① ② ③ ⑤

An hotel offering comfortable modern accommodation, interesting menus and friendly service.

WHITLEY BAY   Tyne & Wear   Map 12 NZ37

★★63% Holmedale 106 Park Avenue NE26 1DN ☎ 091-251 3903 & 091-253 1162

Normal price: £23. Dinner £6.95-£10 and à la carte.
Short breaks: £17 excluding dinner. Fri-Sun. Single price £24.
Credit cards ① ② ③ ⑤

A friendly, family-run hotel on a corner site convenient for both the town and sea front. Most bedrooms have ensuite facilities.

GH QQ Lindisfarne 11 Holly Avenue NE26 1EB ☎ 091-251 3954 & 091-297 0579

Normal price: £13-£15.
Short breaks: £12-£14 excluding dinner. Min 2 nights, Fri-Sun, Nov-May.
✷ Credit cards ① ③

The attractive little front garden distinguishes this small guesthouse from the other houses in the terrace. An attractive dining room and friendly service.

★★63% Windsor South Parade NE25 8UT ☎ 091-252 3317

Normal price: £60 room. Dinner £10-£15.
Short breaks: £44 excluding dinner. Fri-Sun.
Credit cards ① ② ③ ⑤

A recently extended and modernised hotel with tastefully appointed public rooms and bedrooms equipped for the business traveller.

■ WARWICKSHIRE ■

ABBOT'S SALFORD   Warwickshire   Map 4 SP05

★★★73% **Salford Hall** (Best Western) WR11 5UT ☎ (0386) 871301

Normal price: £95 room and breakfast. Dinner from £18.95
Short breaks: £55. Min 2 nights.
Activity breaks: Shakespeare Break, £170.50 including
entrance fees to Shakespearean houses and theatre tickets.
Touring in the Cotswolds, with treasure hunt, £145
including entrance fees. Red Carpet for Racegoers, £180
including admission to Member's Enclosures at
Cheltenham, Stratford, Warwick and Worcester. Castles,
Manor & Gardens, £157 including admission fees. Visits to
Kenilworth Castle, Snowhill Manor and Hidcote Manor
gardens among many others. Champagne Balloon
experience, £215 including champagne, balloon flight &
'gift'. Treasures of the Centuries – the best in building,
furniture and art – £145 including entrance fees. All prices
based on 2 nights per person. Hire of chauffeur-driven
Rolls Royce for most of the above breaks from £260 per
day. Champagne picnic hampers from £25 per person.
✶ Credit cards ① ② ③ ⑤

An imposing Tudor manor house offering
modern facilities without sacrificing the
original character. The restaurant serves very
enjoyable meals complemented by a good wine
list.

ALCESTER   Warwickshire   Map 4 SP05

★★57% **Arrow Mill** Arrow B49 5NL (on A435 S of town) ☎ (0789) 762419
Closed 23 Dec-5 Jan

Normal price: £75 room. Dinner from £14
Short breaks: £37.50. Single supplement £15. Min 2 nights
Credit cards ① ② ③ ⑤

This historic building, in a peaceful setting, has
retained much of its charm and character. The
hotel offers facilities for fly fishing, croquet,
archery, clay pigeon shooting and hot air
ballooning. There are eighteen bedrooms, each
with colour television, tea and coffee making
facilities and private bathrooms. There are five
family rooms.

ALDERMINSTER   Warwickshire   Map 4 SP24

★★★★64% **Ettington Park** (Select) CV37 8BS ☎ (0789) 740740

Normal price: £145 room and breakfast. Dinner from £30.
Short breaks: £195 for 2 nights. Fri & Sat only, Jul-Feb. 50%
discount for single occupancy.
Activity breaks: Tennis coaching break, price on
application. Horse riding, £15 per hour. Clay pigeon
shooting, £35 per hour. Theatre break, including visits to
Royal Shakespeare Theatre, price on application.
✶ Credit cards ① ② ③ ⑤

A Victorian mansion in Gothic style with
spacious, ornate bedrooms in the main house
and plainer modern accommodation in a new
wing. The restaurant offers good food.

BAGINTON   *Warwickshire*   Map 4 SP37

★★62% **Old Mill** (Berni/Chef & Brewer) Mill Hill CV8 2BS ☎ (0203) 303588

Normal price: £36.50. Dinner £8-£15 à la carte
Short breaks: £25.50 excluding dinner. Min 2 nights, Fri-Sun.
🕱 (ex guide dogs) Credit cards ①②③⑤

Once a working mill, this hotel has been restyled and refurbished to offer good, modern accommodation. All twenty bedrooms have private baths and colour television, with some rooms set aside for families. There are special facilities for children. Horse riding is available.

BARFORD   *Warwickshire*   Map 4 SP26

★★62% **Glebe at Barford** Church Street CV35 8BS ☎ (0926) 624218

Normal price: £88.50 room with breakfast. Dinner £18.50
Short breaks: £100 for 2 people. Single £55. Min 2 nights, Fri/Sat or Sat/Sun
Credit cards ①②③⑤

A Georgian house in a peaceful village setting adjacent to the church, providing inviting, well-cooked meals. Leisure amenities include heated indoor swimming pool and a gymnasium. All the bedrooms have ensuite facilities and colour television, there are rooms for families and non-smokers, and two rooms have four-poster beds. There is a special Christmas programme.

BILLESLEY   *Warwickshire*   Map 4 SP15

❋★★★ 🏖 74% **Billesley Manor** (Queens Moat) (Prestige) B49 6NF ☎ (0789) 400888

Normal price: £117 room with breakfast. Dinner from £23 and à la carte
Short breaks: £49. Single £64. Min 2 nights
🕱 Credit cards ①②③⑤

This old country mansion 3 miles west of Stratford has oak-panelled rooms, log fires and large grounds. Extensive leisure facilities include a heated indoor swimming pool and tennis courts. There are ensuite facilities and colour televisions in all bedrooms, three are furnished with four-poster beds and there are six family rooms. A special Christmas programme is provided.

BRANDON   *Warwickshire*   Map 4 SP47

★★★61% **Brandon Hall** (Trusthouse Forte) Main Street CV8 3FW ☎ (0203) 542571

Normal price: £56.80. Dinner from £13.50.
Short breaks: £45. Min 2 nights, Fri-Sun.
Activity breaks: Clay Pigeon Shooting, £185 (1990). Music at Leisure, £102 (1990). Details from hotel.
Credit cards ①②③④⑤

Standing in its own wooded grounds in a quaint village, this comfortable hotel offers a range of well-equipped facilities including squash, snooker and pitch and putt.

CHARLECOTE   *Warwickshire*   Map 4 SP25

★★★61% **Charlecote Pheasant Country** (Queens Moat) CV35 9EW ☎ (0789) 470333

Normal price: £80 room. Dinner from £12.95
Short breaks: £41.50. Min 2 nights
Credit cards ①②③⑤

This hotel has a variety of annexe bedrooms converted from former farm buildings, all with private bath or shower rooms and colour television; some have four-poster beds. Leisure amenities include an outdoor heated swimming pool and tennis.

COLESHILL   *Warwickshire*   Map 4 SP28

★★63% **Coleshill** (Lansbury) 152 High Street B46 3BG ☎ (0675) 465527

Normal price: £74 room. Dinner from £14.75 and à la carte
Short breaks: £25 excluding dinner. Min 2 nights, Fri-Sun.
🐕 (ex guide dogs) Credit cards ① ② ③ ⑤

A comfortable modern hotel situated near to junction 4 of the M6. All bedrooms offer colour television and ensuite facilities and there are rooms for non-smokers.

EATHORPE   *Warwickshire*   Map 4 SP36

★★56% **Eathorpe Park** (Exec Hotel) Fosse Way CV33 9QD ☎ (0926) 632245
Closed 25 Dec evening & 26 Dec

Normal price: £55 room and breakfast. Dinner from £15
Short breaks: £30 excluding dinner. Single £20. Min 3 nights, Oct-Mar
🐕 (ex guide dogs) Credit cards ① ② ③ ⑤

This imposing Victorian hotel is situated on the Fosse Way, close to the village centre. All fourteen bedrooms are ensuite with colour television.

HONILEY   *Warwickshire*   Map 4 SP27

★★★68% **Honiley Court** (Lansbury) Honiley CV8 1NP (3m W of Kenilworth on A4117) ☎ (0926) 484234

Normal price: from £80.
Short breaks: £60, min 2 nights, Fri-Sun.
Credit cards ① ② ③ ⑤

A modern hotel, an extension of the Honiley Boot Inn, which combines up-to-date facilities with some character. An ideal venue for leisure guests.

KENILWORTH   *Warwickshire*   Map 4 SP27

★★68% **Clarendon House** Old High Street CV8 1LZ ☎ (0926) 57668

Normal price: £37.50. Dinner from £13.75.
Short breaks: £35, min 2 nights, Fri-Sun.
Credit cards ① ③

The public areas and some bedrooms of this hotel have recently been refurbished to provide comfort and greater convenience. Some rooms are rather compact.

★★★60% **De Montfort** (De Vere) The Square CV8 1ED ☎ (0926) 55944

Normal price: from £44. Dinner from £13.75.
Short breaks: Approx £35.50. Min 2 nights, Fri-Sun.
Activity breaks: Bridge Weekends, from £180 for 4 nights.
Details from hotel.
Credit cards ① ② ③ ⑤

Situated close to the town centre, a hotel offering attractive public areas including a choice of restaurant and coffee shop.

LEAMINGTON SPA (Royal)   *Warwickshire*   Map 4 SP36

★★60% **Abbacourt** 40 Kenilworth Road CV32 6JF ☎ (0926) 451755

Normal price: £30-£35. Dinner £11.
Short breaks: £25-£30 excluding dinner, min 2 nights, Fri-Sun. Single price £40.
Credit cards ① ② ③ ④ ⑤

Resident proprietors, aided by a small helpful team, provide friendly and attentive service at this hotel, a large converted house beside the A452.

★★61% **Beech Lodge** Warwick New Road CV32 5JJ ☎ (0926) 422227

Normal price: £27.50. Dinner £8.50-£14.50 à la carte.
Short breaks: £33. Min 2 nights, Thu-Sun.
Credit cards ① ② ③

Personal service from the proprietors ensures a comfortable stay at this hotel midway between Leamington Spa and Warwick. Cosy public areas and an attractive restaurant.

★(Red) **Lansdowne** 87 Clarendon Street CV32 4PF ☎ (0926) 450505

Normal price: £34.60, £42.90 en suite. Dinner £14.95.
Short breaks: £29.85 and £36.95 as above including
newspaper. Min 2 nights.
Activity breaks: Shakespearean Heritage, £82 for 2 nights
including tickets to Shakespearean buildings and houses.
Medieval Splendour, £78 including free entry to Warwick
Castle, the ruins of Kenilworth Castle and Lord Leycester
Hospital. Cotswold Hills and Country Houses, £77 tour of
the Cotswolds and visits to Sudeley Castle and Ragley Hall.
Pride of the Region Tour, £143 including tour of Cotswolds
and visits to Stratford and Warwick Castle. Champagne
Treasure Hunt, details from hotel. All prices 1990.
✗ Credit cards [1] [3]

An attractive Regency hotel that fits beautifully
into its central location in this pleasant
Warwickshire town. Run by delightful hosts
David and Gillian Allen.

❊★★★(Red) ♠ **Mallory Court** (Relais et Chateaux) Harbury Lane, Bishop's Tachbrook CV33 9QB
(2m S off A452) ☎ (0926) 330214

Normal price: £46-£90. Dinner from £38.50.
Short breaks: £78.33-£90 including early morning tea and
newspaper. Min 3 nights, Nov-Mar.
✗ Credit cards [1] [3]

Lovely gardens surround the mellow stone
manor where guests are certain of receiving a
friendly welcome and luxurious accommodation. The modern French cuisine is
consistently good.

★★★57% **Manor House** Avenue Road CV31 3NJ ☎ (0926) 423251

Normal price: £80 room only
Short breaks: £45. Min 2 nights, Thurs-Sun. Single
occupancy £42-£45. 1990 prices
Activity breaks: Murder weekends £154-£159 room. Bridge
£95 room. Watercolour painting £123 room. Non
participant £90. Garden appreciation £133 room. £30 extra
night.
Credit cards [1] [2] [3] [4] [5]

This large hotel is set in lovely gardens and is
convenient for the railway station and town
centre. Bedrooms are a variety of styles and
sizes, all with ensuite facilities.

★★★62% **Regent** (Best Western) 77 The Parade CV32 4AX ☎ (0926) 427231

Normal price: £37.50. Dinner from £15.
Short breaks: £41.50 weekends, £46.50 midweek. Min 2
nights. Single supplement midweek only.
Activity breaks: England's Historic Heartland, short break
price plus £4.50. A Night To Remember, £61 weekends, £67
midweek, 1 night only.
Credit cards [1] [2] [3] [5]

An hotel with all its original charm and
character intact in spite of undergoing a major
refurbishment programme which has provided
all modern facilities.

NUNEATON   *Warwickshire*   Map 4 SP39

★★61% **Chase** (Porterhouse) Higham Lane CV11 6AG ☎ (0203) 341013

Normal price: £54
Short breaks: £43 excluding dinner. Fri-Sun.
Credit cards [1] [2] [3] [5]

All bedrooms in this modernised hotel with a
garden have ensuite facilities and colour
television.

★★ **Longshoot Toby** (Toby) Watling Street CV11 6JH ☎ (0203) 329711

Normal price: £39.50 Fri-Sat, £49.50 Mon-Thu.
Short breaks: £18.50 (£21.50 single room) excluding dinner.
Min 2 nights, Fri-Sun.
✹ Credit cards ① ② ③ ⑤

A busy motel at the A5/A47 junction, with ensuite facilities and colour television in all bedrooms, which include some family and no-smoking rooms.

OXHILL   Warwickshire   Map 4 SP34

FH QQQ Nolands Farm (SP312470) CV35 0RJ (1m E of Pillarton Priors on A422) ☎ (0926) 640309

Normal price: £15.
Short breaks: £25, min 2 nights Mon-Thu, Oct-1 Apr.
Activity breaks: Clay Pigeon Shooting, Fishing and Rough Shooting Breaks, details from hotel.
✹ Credit cards ①

Most of the farm facilities are in carefully restored outbuildings, including comfortable bedrooms with ensuite facilities.

STRATFORD-UPON-AVON   Warwickshire   Map 4 SP25

★★★59% **Alveston Manor** (Trusthouse Forte) Clopton Bridge CV37 7HP ☎ (0789) 204581

Normal price: £57. Dinner from £17.75 and à la carte.
Short breaks: £56, min 2 nights.
Credit cards ① ② ③ ④ ⑤

An attractive hotel with well-kept gardens just across the river from the theatre and town centre. Afternoon tea can be enjoyed in the cocktail bar with its 16th-century panelling.

GH QQ Ambleside 41 Grove Road CV37 6PB ☎ (0789) 297239 & 295670

Normal price: £15.
Short breaks: £13 excluding dinner. Min 2 nights, Fri-Tues Oct-Apr.
Credit cards ① ③

Facilities at this hotel on the Evesham road are being constantly improved. The hotel offers good value for money, and there is a spacious car park.

GH QQ Avon View 121 Shipston Road CV37 7LW ☎ (0789) 297542

Normal price: £24.50-£28.
Short breaks: 10% reduction, min 2 nights, Nov-Apr.
✹ Credit cards ① ② ③ ⑤

This small private hotel offers ensuite facilities in all bedrooms, and its own car park. Light meals and snacks can be served in the evening on request.

★★64% **Coach House** (Guestaccom) 16-17 Warwick Road CV37 6YW ☎ (0789) 204109

Normal price: £24.50-£27.50. Dinner £9.50-£12.50 and à la carte
Short breaks: £31.50. Single price £38.
✹ Credit cards ① ③

Two adjoining properties, one Georgian and one Victorian, have been merged to create value-for-money, comfortable accommodation with a good range of facilities.

★★★60% **Dukes** Payton Street CV37 6UA ☎ (0789) 69300

Normal price: £47.50. Dinner £13-£18.50
Short breaks: £47.50, min 2 nights, Fri & Sat.
✹ Credit cards ① ② ③ ⑤

The hotel offers attractive accommodation in cosy bedrooms, a spacious lounge and elegant restaurant, and lovingly-tended garden.

★★★55% **Grosvenor House** (Best Western) Warwick Road CV37 6YT ☎ (0789) 269213

Normal price: £36-£41. Dinner £9.95 and à la carte.
Short breaks: £36-£43 (1990), min 2 nights. Single
supplement.
✱ Credit cards 1 2 3 5

This family-run hotel is particularly hospitable,
and a friendly atmosphere prevails. The well-
equipped health centre is now an added
attraction.

QQ Hardwick House 1 Avenue Road CV37 6UY ☎ (0789) 204307

Normal price: £32-£40 room and breakfast.
Short breaks: £14.50-£19.50 (en suite), min 2 nights, Nov-
May.
✱ Credit cards 1 2 3

This spacious, detached Victorian house is
situated within walking distance of river and
memorial theatre. Bedrooms are homely and
well-equipped.

★★★★56% **Moat House International** (Queens Moat) Bridgefoot CV37 6YP ☎ (0789) 414411

Normal price: £49.50. Dinner from £12.95 and à la carte.
Short breaks: £62.50 including early morning tea. Min 2
nights, one must be Sat.
Credit cards 1 2 3 5

Situated on the river by Clopton Bridge, and
close to the theatre, this large hotel offers a
choice of restaurants, shops and a nightclub, as
well as an indoor leisure complex.

GH QQQ Moonraker House 40 Alcester Road CV37 9DB ☎ (0789) 299346

Normal price: £18.
Short breaks: £16.50 excluding dinner. Min 3 nights except
Bank Hols.
Credit cards 1 3

Bedrooms here vary in size, and all have
ensuite facilities, modern fitted furniture and
tasteful colour schemes. Accommodation is
spread over four buildings.

GH QQQ Sequoia House 51-53 Shipston Road CV37 7LN ☎ (0789) 68852

Normal price: £29.50.
Short breaks: £24.50 excluding dinner. Min 2 nights, Nov-
Jun. 10% reduction for singles.
Activity breaks: Royal Shakespeare Theatre Stopover,
details from hotel.
✱ Credit cards 1 2 3 5

This warm and spacious Victorian house is run
by friendly owners who pride themselves on
offering high quality breakfasts.

★★★★57% **Shakespeare** (Trusthouse Forte) Chapel Street CV37 6ER ☎ (0789) 294771

Normal price: £60. Dinner from £17.
Short breaks: £63, min 2 nights, must include Sat.
Activity breaks: Horse Racing Weekend, £190 for 2 nights including racing on Sat, a morning at a local training stable, racing celebrity speaker on Saturday evening, and wine with dinner.
Credit cards ① ② ③ ④ ⑤

A magnificent timbered building dating back to at least 1637. Public areas are comfortable, and there are good standards of service.

★★★53% **Swan's Nest** (Trusthouse Forte) Bridgefoot CV37 7LT ☎ (0789) 66761

Normal price: £47. Dinner £14 and à la carte.
Short breaks: £49, min 2 nights.
Credit cards ① ② ③ ④ ⑤

Standing beside the River Avon, the hotel is handy for both town and theatre. It offers guests comfortable bedrooms and a choice of menus.

★★★★73% **Welcombe** Warwick Road CV37 0NB ☎ (0789) 295252

Normal price: £67.50. Dinner £27.
Short breaks: £80, min 2 nights, Fri-Sun.
Activity breaks: Golf Breaks, £160 including two rounds of golf. Theatre Breaks, £196.

Standing on the outskirts of Stratford in a parkland estate which offers an 18-hole golf course, this Jacobean mansion offers truly traditional service. See advertisement on p285.

★★★50% **White Swan** (Trusthouse Forte) Rother Street CV37 6NH ☎ (0789) 297022

Normal price: £50. Dinner £14 and à la carte.
Short breaks: £50, min 2 nights. Single supplement.
Credit cards ① ② ③ ④ ⑤

Traditional 15th-century inn situated in the town centre.

WARWICK   Warwickshire   Map 4 SP26

★★★57% **Hilton National** A46 Stratford Road CV34 6RE ☎ (0926) 499555

Normal price: £120 room and breakfast
Short breaks: £60, single occupancy £47
Credit cards ① ② ③ ⑤

A popular hotel for both leisure and business guests, with sauna, solarium, pool, and well-furnished bedrooms.

★★58% **Lord Leycester** (Consort) Jury Street CV34 4EJ ☎ (0926) 491481

Normal price: £33. Dinner £12-£15 à la carte.
Short breaks: £37.50, min 2 nights, Fri-Sun.
Credit cards ① ② ③ ⑤

This centrally positioned hotel offers bedrooms which, though in some cases compact, are continually being upgraded to meet modern standards.

WILMCOTE   Warwickshire   Map 4 SP15

★★60% **Swan House** The Green CV37 9XJ ☎ (0789) 67030 due to change to 267030

Normal price: £28.50. Dinner £13.50-£18.35.
Short breaks: £36, min 2 nights. Single supplement.
✖ Credit cards ① ② ③ ④ ⑤

Standing just three miles from Stratford in the little village of Wilmcote, overlooking its green and Mary Arden's House, the hotel offers simply furnished bedrooms.

WIMPSTONE   Warwickshire   Map 4 SP24

FH QQ **Whitchurch** (SP222485) CV37 8NS ☎ (078987) 275 due to change to (0789) 450275

Normal price: £12.
Short breaks: £11 excluding dinner. Min 2 nights.
✖

Lovely Georgian farmhouse built in 1750, and set in parklike surroundings on the edge of the Cotswolds, 4.5 miles from Stratford-upon-Avon.

▪ WEST MIDLANDS ▪

BIRMINGHAM   West Midlands   Map 7 SP08

★★★58% **Apollo** (Mount Charlotte (TS)) 243-247 Hagley Road, Edgbaston B16 9RA ☎ 021-455 0271

Normal price: £89, room with breakfast. Dinner £11.50-£12.75 and à la carte
Short breaks: £23 excluding dinner. Fri-Sun
Credit cards ①②③⑤

This modern motor lodge style hotel has bedrooms in annexe blocks around the main building. All rooms have ensuite baths or showers and colour television, with rooms set aside for families and non-smokers. There is a special Christmas programme.

★★★56% **Grand** (Queens Moat) Colmore Row B3 2DA ☎ 021-236 7951
Closed 4 days at Christmas
Normal price: £45. Dinner £12.50
Short breaks: £35. Min 2 nights, Fri-Sun.
Credit cards ①②③⑤

A city centre hotel with two bars, a carvery and restaurant. The bedrooms offer excellent modern facilities, all rooms have ensuite facilities and colour television and seven rooms are for families. The hotel has no parking facilities but there is a NCP car park a few minutes' walk away.

GH QQ Heath Lodge Coleshill Road, Marston Green B37 7HT ☎ 021-779 2218
Normal price: £37-£45 room with breakfast
Short breaks: £20-£25. Min 3 nights midweek, 2 nights weekends
Credit cards ①③

A licensed hotel with a cosy restaurant, quietly situated just 1½ miles from the NEC. Some of the bedrooms have ensuite facilities, all have colour television and there are two family rooms.

★★60% **New Cobden** (Consort) 166 Hagley Road, Edgbaston B16 9NZ ☎ 021-454 6621
Normal price: £29.25. Dinner £11.75-£14.75 and à la carte
Short breaks: £34.50. Min 2 nights, Fri-Sun.
Credit cards ①②③⑤

Conveniently located on the A456 close to the centre of Birmingham, this hotel has its own leisure centre with a solarium, sauna, swimming pool and gymnasium. All the bedrooms have ensuite facilities and colour television, and there are rooms for non-smokers, and families. There is a special Christmas programme.

★★54% **Norfolk** (Consort) 257/267 Hagley Road, Edgbaston B16 9NA ☎ 021-454 8071
Closed 24 Dec-2 Jan
Normal price: £29.25. Dinner £11.75-£14.75 and à la carte
Short breaks: £34.50. Min 2 nights, Fri-Sun.

A large hotel on the A456, close to the city centre, offering modestly decorated and furnished rooms. Many of the bedrooms have ensuite bath or shower rooms, and all have colour television. Some bedrooms are for non-smokers.

★★★64% **Royal Angus Thistle** (Mount Charlotte(TS)) St Chads, Queensway B4 6HY ☎ 021-236 4211
Normal price: £48.75. Dinner from £13.50 and à la carte
Short breaks: £43.

A modern city centre hotel offering comfortable bedrooms all with ensuite bath or shower rooms and colour television; some rooms are for families and non-smokers.

★★52% **Sheriden House** 82 Handsworth Wood Road, Handsworth Wood B20 2PL ☎ 021-554 2185 & 021-523 5960

Normal price: £31.50. Dinner £10.50-£11 and à la carte
Short breaks: £25 excluding dinner 1 night, £46.50 for 2 nights, £66 for 3 nights. Single rate £29.50 excluding dinner 1 night, £55 for 2 nights, £77.50 for 3 nights. Fri-Sun (except Christmas, Exhibition and Show periods)

A small popular hotel situated in the suburbs quite close to junction 7 of the M6, with a cosy bar and small lounge. All the bedrooms have colour television, most have private facilities and one room has a four-poster bed.

★★★65% **Strathallan Thistle** (Mount Charlotte(TS)) 225 Hagley Road, Edgbaston B16 9RY ☎ 021-455 9777

Normal price: £48.75. Dinner from £15 à la carte
Short breaks: £43.

This striking circular hotel on the main thoroughfare to the city has bedrooms equipped with ensuite bath and shower rooms and colour television; some rooms are for families and non-smokers.

★★★61% **Westmead** (Lansbury) Redditch Road, Hopwood B48 7AL ☎ 021-445 1202

Normal price: £44. Dinner from £14 and à la carte
Short breaks: £36. Min 2 nights, Fri-Sun (except during NEC exhibitions)
Credit cards ① ② ③ ⑤

The hotel is in a peaceful, rural location near junction 2 of the M42, with convenient access to Birmingham. The bedrooms are spacious and well-equipped, all have private baths and colour television, and two are furnished with four-poster beds. Some rooms are set aside for families and non-smokers. There is a special Christmas programme.

★★67% **Wheatsheaf** (Porterhouse) Coventry Road, Sheldon B26 3EH ☎ 021-742 6201 & 021-743 2021
Closed 25 & 26 Dec

Normal price: £65 room and breakfast
Short breaks: £37.50 excluding dinner. Fri-Sun
✻ (ex guide dogs) Credit cards ① ② ③ ⑤

A popular and friendly hotel on the A45 and convenient for the NEC. The rooms are generally spacious and comfortable, all providing ensuite facilities and colour television. Ten are set aside for non-smokers.

BIRMINGHAM AIRPORT   West Midlands   Map 7 SP18

★★★54% **Excelsior** (Trusthouse Forte) Coventry Road, Elmdon B26 3QW ☎ 021-782 8141

Normal price: £78 room only. Dinner £16 and à la carte
Short breaks: £39.50 for 2 people. Max 3 nights, Fri-Sun
Credit cards ① ② ③ ⑤

Situated on the A45 close to the NEC, this hotel offers bedrooms equipped with colour television and ensuite bath or shower rooms. There is a special Christmas programme.

COVENTRY   West Midlands   Map 4 SP37

★★★60% **Novotel Coventry** (Novotel) Wilsons Lane CV6 6HL ☎ (0203) 365000

Normal price: £74 room
Short breaks: £50 for 2 people. Min 2 nights, Fri-Sun.

This modern hotel has a continental-style restaurant which is open throughout the day, a good range of leisure facilities including an outdoor heated swimming pool and special facilities for children. All bedrooms have private baths or showers and colour television.

★★★57% **Post House** (Trusthouse Forte) Rye Hill, Allesley CV5 9PH ☎ (0203) 402151

Normal price: £93 room. Dinner £14.50 and à la carte
Short breaks: £82 for 2 people. Min 2 nights, Thu-Sun.
Credit cards ① ② ③ ④ ⑤

Situated on the A45 close to Coventry, all the bedrooms at this hotel have ensuite facilities and colour television, with some rooms set aside for non-smokers. There is a special Christmas programme.

DUDLEY   West Midlands   Map 7 SO99

★★60% **Station** (Crown & Raven) Birmingham Road DY1 4RA ☎ (0384) 253418

Normal price: £64.45 room.
Short breaks: £36, min 2 nights, Fri-Sun.
Activity breaks: Real Ale Weekend, £84 for 2 nights (1990).
Black Country Weekend. Details from hotel.
Credit cards ① ② ③

The hotel stands close to the town centre, opposite Dudley Zoo, with newly refurbished, modern public rooms and bedrooms.

GREAT BARR   West Midlands   Map 7 SP09

★★★59% **Great Barr** Pear Tree Drive, off Newton Road B43 6HS (1m W of junc A34/A4041)
☎ 021-357 1141

Normal price: £69-£75 room. Dinner from £11.95 and à la carte
Short breaks: £17.50 excluding dinner. Min 2 nights, Fri-Sun.
🛪 (ex guide dogs) Credit cards ① ② ③ ④ ⑤

Pleasantly situated in a residential area, this hotel offers bedrooms with ensuite facilities and colour television.

HOCKLEY HEATH   West Midlands   Map 7 SP17

✿★★★ 🏨 79% **Nuthurst Grange Country House** Nuthurst Grange Lane B94 5NL (off A34, 2m S junc 4
M42) ☎ (05643) 3972

Normal price: £57.40. Dinner £27.50-£32.50
Short breaks: £70. Min 2 nights, Fri-Sun.
Credit cards ① ② ③ ⑤

A luxurious hotel standing in extensive landscaped wooded grounds. Tastefully decorated and furnished, it offers comfortable accommodation and excellent food.

MERIDEN   West Midlands   Map 4 SP28

★★★68% **Manor** (De Vere) CV7 7NH ☎ (0676) 22735

Normal price: £45. Dinner from £15.
Short breaks: £36 (£32.50 Aug). Min 2 nights, Fri-Sun, Jul &
Aug only.
Activity breaks: Chocoholics Weekend, 3-4 May. George
Eliot Weekend, £100-£120, 28-30 Jun. Murder Weekend,
13-15 Sept. Australian Wine Weekend. Details from hotel.
Credit cards ① ② ③ ⑤

An elegant Georgian building conveniently situated for the Midlands motorway network and the NEC. It offers comfortable public areas and the Regency restaurant.

SOLIHULL   West Midlands Map 7 SP17

★★57% **Flemings** 141 Warwick Road, Olton B92 7HW ☎ 021-706 0371

Normal price: £54. Dinner from £10.75.
Short breaks: £35 excluding dinner, weekends only.
Credit cards ①②③⑤

This hotel is particularly popular with business travellers as it offers a home-from-home atmosphere. Situated midway between the NEC and Birmingham, the hotel has been greatly extended. Rooms are a mixture of standards and sizes, and staff are friendly.

★★★63% **George** High Street B91 3RF ☎ 021-711 2121

Normal price: £70. Dinner £16.50-£18.50.
Short breaks: £52, min 2 nights, Fri-Sun.
Credit cards ①②③④⑤

An old coaching inn with modern extensions in the town centre. The main restaurant overlooks the ancient Crown Bowling Green, whilst George's Rotisserie offers a more informal atmosphere.

★★★69% **Regency** Stratford Road, Shirley B90 4EB ☎ 021-745 6119

Normal price: £91.30 room and breakfast. Dinner £13.25 and à la carte.
Short breaks: £50, min 2 nights, Fri-Sun.
Credit cards ①②③

A modern hotel close to the town centre with convenient access to the M42. Accommodation is of a high standard, with a recent extension of 54 new rooms. There are two bars, an attractive restaurant and a leisure centre.

★★★65% **St John's Swallow** 651 Warwick Road B91 1AT ☎ 021-711 3000

Normal price: from £90 room. Dinner £15.
Short breaks: from £95 for 2 nights, Fri-Sat or Sat-Sun.
Includes lunch either Saturday or Sunday.
Credit cards ①②③④⑤

This large, modern hotel set in a residential area close to the town centre, with convenient access to the M42, offers comfortable accommodation. There are extensive conference facilities and a well-equipped leisure centre.

SUTTON COLDFIELD   West Midlands Map 7 SP19

★★65% **Berni Royal** (Berni/Chef & Brewer) High Street B72 1UD ☎ 021-355 8222

Normal price: £32. Dinner £8-£15
Short breaks: £25.50 excluding dinner. Min 2 nights, Fri-Sun.
✱ Credit cards ①②③⑤

Dating from the 19th century, this centrally situated hotel was once the home of William Morris Grundy. There are two bars and a popular Berni restaurant.

★★★68% **Moor Hall** (Best Western) Moor Hall Drive, Four Oaks B75 6LN ☎ 021-308 3751

Normal price: £50. Dinner from £16.95.
Short breaks: £42, min 2 nights, Fri & Sat.
Activity breaks: Romantic Weekends, Theme Park Weekend, Chocolate Lovers Weekend, Health and Fitness Weekend. Details from hotel.
Credit cards ①②③④⑤

This hotel is situated in a residential area, and offers its own fitness centre and an excellent wing of new executive rooms.

★★★★70% **New Hall** (Mount Charlotte (TS)) Walmley Road B76 8QX ☎ 021-378 2442

Normal price: £55. Dinner £19.50-£21.20 and à la carte
Short breaks: £50 excluding dinner. Single supplement weekdays
Credit cards ①②③④⑤

Reputedly the oldest fully moated manor house in England, New Hall's history dates back to the 13th century. A particular feature is the Great Hall, now the dining room.

★★★★55% **Penns Hall** (Embassy) Penns Lane, Walmley B76 8LH ☎ 021-351 3111

Normal price: £55. Dinner from £19.
Short breaks: £45, min 2 nights, Fri-Sun.
Activity breaks: Cadbury Break, £86.50. Details from hotel.
Credit cards ①②③④⑤

The original house dates from the 17th century, but is now considerably extended to include a good leisure centre.

★★★60% **Sutton Court** (Consort) 60-66 Lichfield Road B74 2NA ☎ 021-355 6071

Normal price: from £49 room and breakfast. Dinner from £14.
Short breaks: £36.50, min 2 nights, Fri-Sun.
Activity breaks: Golfing Break, £101, 2 nights including a round of golf at the Belfry Brabazon course – home of the Ryder Cup.
Credit cards ①②③④⑤

A popular hotel, extended over many years and offering good facilities. The restaurant offers an interesting range of dishes.

WALSALL   West Midlands   Map 7 SP09

★★63% **Abberley** 29 Bescot Road WS2 9AD ☎ (0922) 27413

Normal price: £24.15. Dinner £7.95 and à la carte.
Short breaks: £35, min 2 nights, Fri-Sun. Single price £25.
Credit cards ①③

The Stone family have continued to expand and improve this predominantly commercial hotel close to junction 9 of the M6. Bedrooms have excellent facilities including satellite television.

★★60% **Bescot** Bescot Road WS2 9DG ☎ (0922) 22447

Normal price: £25. Dinner from £8.50 and à la carte.
Short breaks: £30 (1990) excluding dinner. Min 2 nights, Fri-Sun.
🦮 Credit cards ①②③⑤

A well run, privately owned hotel where staff create a `home-from-home' atmosphere. Rooms are modest with good modern facilities.

★★69% **Beverley** 58 Lichfield Road WS4 2DJ ☎ (0922) 614967 & 22999

Normal price: £29.50. Dinner from £9.95 and à la carte.
Short breaks: £35 excluding dinner. Min 1 night, Fri-Sun. Single price £32.
🦮 Credit cards ①③

A privately owned and run hotel offering a good standard of accommodation with an excellent range of modern facilities, and a pool room, sauna, solarium and gymnasium.

★★★66% **Friendly** (Consort) 20 Wolverhampton Road West, Bentley WS2 0BS (junc 10, M6) ☎ (0922) 724444

Normal price: £34.25. Dinner £11.75-£14.75 and à la carte.
Short breaks: £37.50, min 2 nights, Fri-Sun.
Credit cards ①②③⑤

This modern hotel provides comfortable accommodation and open-plan public areas. There is a popular carvery restaurant, and a range of leisure facilities.

WOLVERHAMPTON   West Midlands   Map 7 SO99

★★★60% **Goldthorn** Penn Road WV3 0ER ☎ (0902) 29216

Normal price: £37.50-£45. Dinner £10.95-£12.95 and à la carte.
Short breaks: £29.50 including newspaper and courtesy tray. Fri-Sun.
Credit cards ①②③⑤

This large, well-managed hotel offers a wide range of accommodation, two bars and a restaurant popular with guests and non-residents alike. Friendly, attentive staff.

■ WIGHT, ISLE OF ■

FRESHWATER   Map 4 SZ38

★★★50% **Albion** PO40 9RA ☎ (0983) 753631

Normal price: £34. Dinner £15.
Short breaks: £79 for 2 nights, Oct-Mar.
Activity breaks: Bird Watching Weekend, details from hotel.
Credit cards ①②③⑤

This developing hotel stands in a unique seashore position with most of its bedrooms having a balcony or terrace facing the sea.

NITON   Map 4 SZ57

GH QQQ Pine Ridge Country House Niton Undercliff PO38 2LY ☎ (0983) 730802

Normal price: £74 for 2 people including dinner.
Short breaks: £206.50 for 3 nights including car and passengers on ferry. Oct-May.
Activity breaks: Golf Breaks, details from hotel.
Credit cards ①③

Occupying a prime location overlooking the sea, this fine hotel is comfortably furnished and is set in spacious grounds directly off the main road.

RYDE   Map 4 SZ59

★★67% **Biskra House** 17 St Thomas's Street PO33 2OL ☎ (0983) 67913

Normal price: £24
Short breaks: £20. Min 2 nights, Fri-Sun. Not Jul-Aug and Bank Hols.
Credit cards ①③

This small friendly family-run hotel has a choice of two restaurants, a beachside patio, small bar and cosy lounge, while the well-equipped bedrooms have colour television and private bath or shower.

SANDOWN   Map 4 SZ58

GH QQQ Braemar 5 Broadway PO36 9DG ☎ (0983) 403358 & 407913

Normal price: £20-£25.
Short breaks: £44 for 2 nights, £69 for 2 nights including car ferry. Min 2 nights, Sept-Jun, except Bank Hols.
🖈 Credit cards ①②③⑤

Completely refurbished and upgraded, bedrooms are all equipped to the same high standards, and there is an elegant and very comfortable lounge. Menu changed daily.

GH QQQ Culver Lodge Albert Road PO36 8AW ☎ (0983) 403819 & 402902

Normal price: £16.
Short breaks: £13.50, min 4 nights, Oct-May.
✸ Credit cards [1]

This hotel has the benefit of a laundry room and a games room. The staff are friendly and helpful, and the public areas are pleasant.

SEAVIEW *Map 4 SZ69*

✿★★74% **Seaview** High Street PO34 5EX ☎ (0983) 612711

Normal price: From £33. Dinner £14.85-£21.85 and à la carte.
Short breaks: From £47.
Credit cards [1] [2] [3]

The heart of this seaside hotel must be the dining room where unpretentious but innovative food is served. The rest of the hotel has charm too, and bedrooms have many extras.

SHANKLIN *Map 4 SZ58*

GH QQQ Apse Manor Country House Apse Manor Road PO37 7PN ☎ (0983) 866651

Normal price: £23.
Short breaks: £20, min 2 nights, Oct-Feb.

Set in countryside 1.5 miles from the town, this 15th-century manor stands in 2 acres of grounds. A choice of dishes is offered in the dining room, and bedrooms are comfortable.

GH QQQ Aqua The Esplanade PO37 6BN ☎ (0983) 863024

Normal price: £20.
Short breaks: £15, min 3 nights, Apr & Nov. Single price £16.
✸ Credit cards [1] [3]

A modern, well-run friendly hotel enjoying a superb elevated position facing the sea. Some bedrooms have balconies overlooking the sea, and there is live entertainment.

GH QQQQ Chine Lodge East Cliff Road PO37 6AA ☎ (0983) 862358

Normal price: £18.
Short breaks: £16.20, min 2 nights, Fri-Sun, Nov-May except Easter.
✸

The spacious, tastefully appointed bedrooms are a feature of this charming early Victorian house. The house has a warm and friendly atmosphere, and an attractive garden.

★★★58% **Cliff Tops** (Best Western) Park Road PO37 6BB ☎ (0983) 863262

Normal price: £65-£69 room & breakfast.
Short breaks: £50, min 2 nights.
Credit cards [1] [2] [3] [5]

Cliff tops boasts a superb position with glorious sea views from the front bedrooms and balconies. There is a direct lift access to the beach below.

GH QQ Edgecliffe Clarence Garden PO37 6HA ☎ (0983) 862605

Normal price: £25.
Short breaks: £22, min 2 nights, Jan-May, Oct & Nov.
✸ Credit cards [1] [2] [3]

A varied menu is always available at this modern hotel. Several bedrooms have sea views, and the restaurant and ballroom are complemented by a roof-top sun lounge.

★★68% **Fernbank** Highfield Road PO37 6PP ☎ (0983) 862790

Normal price: £28.80 including dinner.
Short breaks: £25 1990 price. Min 2 nights, Oct-May.
Credit cards [1] [3]

Set in an acre of well-tended, sheltered gardens enjoying country and woodland views from its peaceful location yet handy for the old village, a friendly, relaxed hotel.

GH QQQ Hambledon Queens Road PO37 6AW ☎ (0983) 862403

Normal price: £17-£21.
Short breaks: £23, min 2 nights, Oct-May 20.
Credit cards [1] [3]

Children are especially catered for at this hotel which provides a baby-listening service. Bedrooms are comfortable, and local amenities are easily accessible.

GH QQ Harrow Lodge Eastcliff Promenade PO37 6AW ☎ (0983) 862403 & 863651

Normal price: £36-£44.
Short breaks: 15% discount on normal price, Oct-Apr.
Activity breaks: Walking and Golfing Breaks, Oct-Apr.
Details from hotel.
Credit cards [1] [3]

GH QQ Kenbury Clarence Road PO37 7BN ☎ (0983) 862085

Normal price: £17.50.
Short breaks: £16 excluding dinner. Min 2 nights, May & Sept-Oct.
✶ Credit cards [1] [3]

Comfortable accommodation in a small family hotel.

✶✶61% Luccombe Hall (Exec Hotel) Luccombe Road PO37 6RL ☎ (0983) 862719

Normal price: £36. Dinner £13.25-£15.
Short breaks: £33, min 2 nights, Oct-May.
Credit cards [1] [3]

Overlooking the sea and Culver Down, Luccombe Hall is set in a quiet residential area. There are comfortable bedrooms and excellent leisure facilities.

GH QQQ Soraba 2 Paddock Road PO37 6NZ ☎ (0983) 862367

Normal price: £12-£14.50.
Short breaks: £17-£19.50, Jan-Nov.

Within easy reach of the beach, shops and amenities, this Victorian house has simply furnished bedrooms and offers excellent value for money. Wholesome meals served.

TOTLAND BAY Map 4 SZ38

GH QQ Nodes Alum Bay Old Road PO39 0HZ ☎ (0983) 752859

Normal price: £23-£26 including dinner.
Short breaks: £20-£22, min 3 nights, Oct-Mar.

Backing on to Tennyson Down, this country house stands in 2.5 acres of grounds. The courtyard bar is the hub of the hotel which is ideal for young families.

VENTNOR Map 4 SZ57

GH QQQ Lake Shore Road, Bonchurch PO38 1RF ☎ (0983) 852613

Normal price: £19.95.
Short breaks: £17.50, min 4 nights, Mar-May.

Quietly set in 2.5 acres of lovely terraced gardens, this hotel offers a choice of bedrooms, good cooking and friendly service. There are several public rooms and a games room.

GH QQ Macrocarpa Mitchell Avenue PO38 1DP ☎ (0983) 852428

Normal price: £22.60.
Short breaks: £28, min 2 nights, Mar-May, Oct & Nov.
✶ Credit cards [1] [3]

Standing in an acre of gardens, this Victorian house overlooks the Channel and Ventnor, and is next to the bowling green. The young owners and staff give friendly service.

◼ WILTSHIRE ◼

BRADFORD ON AVON   Wiltshire   *Map 3 ST86*

★★★ 🌳 73% **Woolley Grange** Woolley Green BA15 1TX ☎ (02216) 4705

Normal price: £60. Dinner from £24.50.
Short breaks: £87. Min 2 nights, Apr-Sept, Sun-Thu only.
Oct-Mar any nights.
Activity breaks: Riding Breaks, at Widbrook Arabian Stud.
Up to 4 hours trekking or 2 hours tuition. Can include a
pub ride. Clay Pigeon Shooting, 1 hour lesson and
shooting practice. Tennis, half-hour private tuition and 1
hour's court hire. Golf, 2 half-hour private lessons, plus a
round. Other breaks include Pot-Holing/Abseiling, Dry
Skiing, Cycling, Health Spa Sessions, Theatre Royal, Bath
and Antique Hunts. Prices are £130 sharing a small double
room, £160 sharing a medium double room, £190 sharing a
large double room, including early morning tea and
newspaper. Other breaks subject to a supplementary
charge are Champagne Hot Air Balloon Flights, Motor
Racing Driving Instruction, Gliding, Skid Pan and Trial
Flying or Helicopter Lesson.
Credit cards ① ② ③ ⑤

Delightful 17th-century Cotswold stone house
standing in well-kept grounds with open
country views. Public areas are comfortably
furnished in Victorian style.

BURBAGE   Wiltshire   *Map 4 SU26*

★★55% **Savernake Forest** Savernake SN8 3AY (1m NE off A346) ☎ (0672) 810206

Normal price: £32.50. Dinner from £12.50 and à la carte
Short breaks: £39. Min 2 nights. Single room £52
Credit cards ① ② ③ ⑤

In a rural setting beside the Kennet and Avon
Canal, this hotel has well-equipped bedrooms
(some are situated in an annexe) all with
private bath or shower rooms and colour
television. There are two family rooms and one
room has a four-poster bed. The hotel has a
special Christmas programme, and fishing is
available.

CALNE   Wiltshire   *Map 3 ST97*

★★66% **Lansdowne Strand** The Strand SN1 0JR ☎ (0249) 812488

Normal price: £32. Dinner £9.50-£10.50 and à la carte
Short breaks: £34. Min 2 nights, Fri-Sun
Credit cards ① ② ③ ⑤

Dating back to the 16th century, this former
coaching inn maintains many original features.
The ensuite bedrooms have colour television
and many thoughtful extras, and interesting
food is served in the restaurant.

CASTLE COMBE   Wiltshire   *Map 3 ST87*

★★★ 🌳 70% **Manor House** SN14 7HR ☎ (0249) 206782

Normal price: £55-£107.50. Dinner £22.50 and à la carte
Short breaks: £75. Supplement for single occupancy and de
luxe rooms. Min 2 nights, Nov-Mar (ex Christmas and
New Year).

Standing just beyond the busy tourist village
this hotel offers friendly, professional service,
comfortable rooms and a range of leisure
facilities. All bedrooms, including those in the
cottage accommodation, have ensuite facilities
and colour television and some have four-poster
beds. There is a special Christmas programme.

COLERNE   Wiltshire   Map 3 ST87

★★★★75% **Lucknam Park** (Prestige) SN18 8AZ ☎ (0225) 742777

Normal price: £66-£110. Dinner £31.50
Short breaks: £198-£280 for 2 nights
Credit cards ① ③

This magnificent country house offers a very high standard of comfort, service and cuisine. Bedrooms are sited in the main house and the former mews, all are ensuite with colour television, and some have four-poster beds. Extensive leisure amenities include an indoor swimming pool and tennis courts. There is a special Christmas programme.

CORSHAM   Wiltshire   Map 3 ST86

★★66% **Methuen Arms** (Exec Hotel) High Street SN13 0HB ☎ (0249) 714867
Restricted service Sunday

Normal price: £29. Dinner £14.75 and à la carte
Short breaks: 2 nights excluding dinner, £53, 3 nights £73.02. Single price 2 nights £74, 3 nights £105. Fri-Sun.
✸ Credit cards ① ③

Formerly a 15th-century nunnery, this hotel has large oak beams, ancient stonework and mullioned windows. The bedrooms, however, are modern, most have ensuite facilities and all have colour television. Light meals are served in the bars, one of which also houses the skittle alley. There are special facilities for children.

★★★68% **Rudloe Park** Leafy Lane SN13 0PA ☎ (0225) 810555

Normal price: £45. Dinner from £16.50 and à la carte
Short breaks: £55 includes dinner or set price lunch and coffee. Min 2 nights.
Credit cards ① ② ③ ④ ⑤

Refurbishment continues at this small Victorian hotel, where sound standards of service are matched by the quality of the meals. All bedrooms have ensuite facilities and colour television, and one has a four-poster bed. Children under ten are not accommodated. There is a special Christmas programme. See advertisement on p19.

CRUDWELL   Wiltshire   Map 3 ST99

★★68% **Crudwell Court** SN16 9EP ☎ (06667) 7194 & 7195

Normal price: £38.50-£50. Dinner from £17
Short breaks: from £104 for 2 nights. £15 single supplement per night
Credit cards ① ② ③ ⑤

A former vicarage of Cotswold stone set in attractive gardens which include a well-screened heated swimming pool and croquet lawn. All bedrooms have ensuite facilities and colour television. There is a special Christmas programme.

★★66% **Mayfield House** SN16 9EW ☎ (06667) 409 & 7198

Normal price: £27.50. Dinner £9.50-£16 à la carte
Short breaks: £37, including £16 dinner allowance, min 2 nights
Credit cards ① ② ③

This hotel serves a good selection of bar food and an imaginative restaurant menu. Bedrooms are neat and warm, and all have ensuite facilities and colour television.

DEVIZES Wiltshire Map 4 SU06

★★★61% **Bear** Market Place SN10 1HS ☎ (0380) 722444
Closed 25-26 Dec

Normal price: £30. Dinner £14-£15 and à la carte
Short breaks: £40, single £50. Min 2 nights
Credit cards ① ③

Dating from the 16th century, this popular former coaching inn has an attractive restaurant and a grill room. Some rooms have four poster beds, and all are ensuite with colour television.

HOOK Wiltshire Map 4 SU08

★★70% **School House** Hook Street SN4 8EF ☎ (0793) 851198

Normal price: £43. Dinner £16.50-£21.50
Short breaks: £43, single £78. Min 2 nights, Fri-Sun
✻ (ex guide dogs) Credit cards ① ② ③ ⑤

This former school has spacious, modern bedrooms furnished with a Victorian theme, and the lofty schoolroom is now the restaurant. There are special facilities for children and Christmas breaks are available.

LACOCK Wiltshire Map 3 ST96

GH QQQ **At the Sign of the Angel** 6 Church Street SN15 2LA ☎ (024973) 230

Normal price: £45.
Short breaks: £58, min 2 nights, Mon-Wed.
Credit cards ① ② ③

The Levis family have run this inn since 1953 and manage to retain its old world charm while providing all modern facilities including private bathrooms.

LIMPLEY STOKE (near Bath) Wiltshire Map 3 ST76

★★★ ⚬ **Cliffe** (Best Western) Crowe Hill BA3 6HY ☎ (0225) 723226

Normal price: £75-£95 room and breakfast. Dinner £12-£18.
Short breaks: Details from hotel.
Activity breaks: Romantic Breaks, £70 including champagne on arrival, fresh fruit and flowers, and breakfast in bed.
Credit cards ① ② ③ ⑤

A converted country house set in three acres of gardens and grounds with a beautifully landscaped swimming pool - a great attraction in the summer months.

LUDWELL Wiltshire Map 3 ST92

★★66% **Grove House** SP7 9ND (2m E A30) ☎ (0747) 828365

Normal price: £42. Dinner £13.50-£15.
Short breaks: £38, Feb-Nov.
Credit cards ① ③

Attractive gardens are an appealing feature of this friendly, personally-run hotel, with its comfortable lounge with log fire and spacious lounge bar.

MALMESBURY Wiltshire Map 3 ST98

★★★72% **Whatley Manor** Easton Grey SN16 0RB ☎ (0666) 822888

Normal price: from £50. Dinner from £22 (1990 price)
Short breaks: from £60. 2, 3 or 6 nights (must include Sat).
Credit cards 1 2 3 5

A tree-lined drive leads to this charming Cotswold manor house with panelled public rooms and log fires. The spacious bedrooms, some in the annexe, have ensuite facilities and colour television. Leisure facilities include tennis, croquet, heated swimming pool, sauna, solarium and spa bath. Christmas breaks are available.

MARLBOROUGH Wiltshire Map 4 SU16

★★★64% **Castle and Ball** (Trusthouse Forte) High Street SN8 1LZ ☎ (0672) 515201

Normal price: £50.
Short breaks: from £45, min 2 nights.
Activity breaks: Duplicate Bridge, Clay Pigeon Shooting, Fly Fishing, Horse Racing, all from £100. Details from hotel.
Credit cards 1 2 3 4 5

A 17th-century inn with an attractive tile-hung Georgian façade, offering prompt and friendly service. The interior has been completely modernised.

★★★72% **Ivy House** (Best Western) High Street SN8 1HJ ☎ (0672) 515333

Normal price: £73-£120 room. Dinner from £19.50.
Short breaks: £46, min 2 nights.
Activity breaks: Regional Wine Tasting Dinners, £58. Details from hotel.

A listed Georgian hotel overlooking the famous High Street offering meals from the restaurant and a small bistro. Service is attentive, friendly and professional.

MELKSHAM Wiltshire Map 3 ST96

★★56% **Kings Arms** Market Place SN12 6EX ☎ (0225) 707272

Normal price: £48. Dinner £8.50 and à la carte (1990 price)
Short breaks: £55 including £9.50 dinner allowance. Min 2 nights.
Credit cards 1 2 3 5

The service is friendly in this attractive hotel in the town centre which has comfortable well-equipped bedrooms, most with ensuite facilities, and all with colour television.

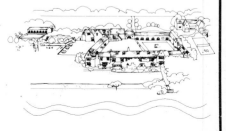

MERE   Wiltshire   Map 3 ST83

QQQ Chetcombe House Chetcombe Road BA12 6AZ ☎ (0747) 860219

Normal price: £43-£45
Short breaks: £28-£29 (less £1 for 3 nights plus). Min 2 nights, Nov-Mar. £31.50 for single occupancy.
Credit cards [1] [3]

Built in 1937, this large detached guesthouse with an extensive garden and views of the countryside has attractive accommodation. All bedrooms are no-smoking and have ensuite facilities and colour television.

★★59% **Old Ship** Castle Street BA12 6JE ☎ (0747) 860258

Normal price: £24. Dinner £10-£17 (1990 price)
Short breaks: £34 (£36 for single occupancy). Min 2 nights.
Credit cards [1] [3] [4]

This 16th-century building with a modern annexe serves a good range of meals in its restaurant. It offers comfortable bedrooms, including 3 family rooms, most with ensuite facilities and all with colour television.

SALISBURY   Wiltshire   Map 4 SU12

QQ Byways House 31 Fowlers Road SP1 2QP ☎ (0722) 28364 due to change to 328364

Normal price: £16.50
Short breaks: £15.50 excluding dinner. Min 2 nights Easter, Christmas & New Year, Bank Holidays. £1.50 single supplement.
Credit cards [1] [3]

A Victorian house offering bed and breakfast with an adjoining coach house which has been fully modernised. It enjoys a central location with views of the distant cathedral.

★★64% **County** Bridge Street SP1 2ND ☎ (0722) 20229

Normal price: £35. Dinner £8-£15 à la carte.
Short breaks: £25.50 excluding dinner. Min 2 nights weekends, 3 nights Mon-Thur.
🍴 Credit cards [1] [2] [3] [5]

A friendly, central hotel built in 1832 alongside the River Avon, with private parking. Bedrooms are well-furnished and comfortable, and there is a Berni restaurant, a separate licensed coffee shop and a spacious bar.

★★★69% **Red Lion** (Best Western) Milford Street SP1 2AN ☎ (0722) 323334

Normal price: from £80 room and breakfast. Dinner £12.50-£13.
Short breaks: from £80 for 2 people, Fri-Sun, £90 midweek, min 2 nights including newspaper. Single price £40-£55.
Activity breaks: Bridge Weekends, from £95 including Sat & Sun lunch. Clay Pigeon Shooting, from £130. Details from hotel.
🍴

Former coaching inn dating from 1320 containing many items of historic interest.

★★★60% **Rose & Crown** Harnham Road, Harnham SP2 8JQ ☎ (0722) 27908

Normal price: £89 room and breakfast. Dinner £11.50-£12.50.
Short breaks: £98.50, min 2 nights Fri-Sun.
Credit cards [1] [2] [3] [5]

This picturesque old coaching inn stands right on the bank of the River Aron, and the Pavilions Restaurant, with its impressive conservatory extension, has a fine view across the meadow to the distant cathedral. Some bedrooms are in the original building, with others in a modern extension, but they have all been refurbished, with ensuite facilities and colour television.

★★63% **Trafalgar** 33 Milford Street SP1 2AP ☎ (0722) 338686

Normal price: From £29 (1990 prices). Dinner from £8.95.
Short breaks: £32, min 2 nights, Fri-Sun. £12 single supplement during weekdays.
Credit cards 1 2 3 5

Originally a pick-up point for the Southampton stagecoach, this hotel dates back to the 15th century. The bedrooms are tastefully decorated, the restaurant offers interesting meals, and snacks are served in the comfortable bar lounge.

★★★63% **White Hart** (Trusthouse Forte) St John Street SP1 2SD ☎ (0722) 27476

Normal price: £40 room only. Dinner from £14 and à la carte.
Short breaks: £50 (1990), min 2 nights.
Credit cards 1 2 3 4 5

The comfortable lounge of this hotel leads to the Wavells bar where open fires enhance traditional decor. The restaurants offers pleasant views across the courtyard and garden.

SWINDON Wiltshire *Map 4 SU18*

★★★★68% **Blunsdon House** (Best Western) Blunsdon SN2 4AD (3m N off A419) ☎ (0793) 721701

Normal price: £46.25-£47.50. Dinner £16.50.
Short breaks: £54 including sherry on arrival and newspapers. Min 2 nights, Fri-Sun.
Activity breaks: Caviar and champagne Breaks, £165. Details from hotel.

Family owned and run hotel where the proprietors take a personal interest in their guests' well being. Supervised creche for younger guests.

★★★53% **Goddard Arms** (Trusthouse Forte) High Street, Old Town SN1 3EW ☎ (0793) 692313

Normal price: £43.50. Dinner from £12.50 and à la carte.
Short breaks: £45, min 3 nights, Fri-Sun.
Credit cards 1 2 3 4 5

The ivy-clad Cotswold-stone building with two modern bedroom annexes is set in 3 acres of grounds. A warm, comfortable atmosphere prevails throughout, and staff are pleasant.

★★★71% **Holiday Inn** Piper's Way SN3 1SH ☎ (0793) 512121

Normal price: £53.45. Dinner £16.50 and à la carte.
Short breaks: £40 for 1 night, £37 per night for 2 or more nights excluding dinner. Fri-Sun. Single price £60 for 1 night, £49.50 for 2 nights or more.
Credit cards 1 2 3 4 5

This is a modern, purpose-built hotel, attractively designed and offering spacious public areas. The young staff provide a friendly style of service.

★★★64% **Post House** (Trusthouse Forte) Marlborough Road SN3 6AQ ☎ (0793) 524601

Normal price: £75 room only. Dinner from £12.50 and à la carte.
Short breaks: £42, min 2 nights Fri-Sun.
Credit cards 1 2 3 4 5

This sprawling, modern, purpose-built hotel offers good health and fitness facilities, and a restaurant serving either à la carte or table d'hôte lunch and dinner.

★★★58% **Quality** Sandy Lane, South Marston SN3 4SL ☎ (0793) 827777

Normal price: £75 room and breakfast. Dinner from £13.95 (1990)
Short breaks: £44, Fri-Sun (£22 for third night)
Activity breaks: Golf Package, £120 for 2 days including golf. Bridge Breaks, details from hotel

The hotel offers extensive indoor leisure facilities, and the sports bar/coffee lounge is used for discos and other entertainment.

TROWBRIDGE Wiltshire Map 3 ST85

★★58% **Polebarn House** Polebarn Gardens, Polebarn Road BA14 7EW ☎ (0225) 777006

Normal price: £32.50-£35. Dinner £8.50-£12 and à la carte. *Short breaks:* £30, min 2 nights, Fri-Sun. Single price £40. ✻ Credit cards ① ③

A Grade II listed building with an impressive façade offers good, simple bedrooms and friendly, helpful service. Disco music makes it popular with local young people.

WARMINSTER Wiltshire Map 3 ST84

★★★★ 🏕 67% **Bishopstrow House** (Relais et Chateaux) BA12 9HH ☎ (0985) 212312

Normal price: from £110 room and continental breakfast. Dinner from £28.
Short breaks: £81 for 2 people, min 2 nights, Fri & Sat. *Activity breaks:* Fishing Breaks, approx £110, mid Apr-mid Oct. Clay Pigeon Shooting, £110 plus £60 half day or £95 full day. Archery Breaks, £110 plus £30 half day or £55 full day.
Credit cards ① ② ③ ⑤

An imposing Georgian house with attractive grounds and excellent leisure facilities. Most bedrooms are spacious although a few are compact.

▪ YORKSHIRE, NORTH ▪

APPLETON-LE-MOORS North Yorkshire Map 8 SE78

★★ 🏕 73% **Dweldapilton Hall** YO6 6TF ☎ (0515) 227 & 452
Closed Jan

Normal price: £41. Dinner £18.50-£21
Short breaks: £52.50 including afternoon tea. Min 3 nights.
Credit cards ① ② ③

Standing in its own attractive grounds, this early Regency/Victorian house has comfortable bedrooms with ensuite facilities and colour television. One room has a four-poster bed. A Christmas programme is available. Children under twelve are not accommodated.

ASKRIGG North Yorkshire Map 7 SD99

★★75% **King's Arms** (Minotels) Market Place DL8 3HQ ☎ (0969) 50258

Normal price: £85-£90. Dinner from £15.
Short breaks: £75-£80, min 2 nights, except Xmas & Bank Holidays. Single supplement.
Activity breaks: Clay Shooting Break, 10 events a year, 2 night stays. Prices on application.
Credit cards ① ③

An 18th-century coaching inn with comfortable bedrooms furnished in period style with some beautiful antiques. Tasty meals from fresh local produce.

BAINBRIDGE North Yorkshire Map 7 SD99

★★68% **Rose & Crown** Village Green DL8 3EE ☎ (0969) 50225

Normal price: £29. Dinner £12.50-£15.50 à la carte
Short breaks: £36, min 2 nights, Oct-Apr. Single room £44
Credit cards ① ③

This 15th-century hotel has attractive, well-cared-for bedrooms all with private baths or showers and colour television. Three rooms have four-poster beds and there is one family room. Fishing is available.

BILBROUGH   North Yorkshire   *Map 8 SE54*

★★★(Red) ♣ **Bilbrough Manor Country House** YO2 3PH ☎ (0937) 83002

Normal price: £85-£135 room with breakfast. Dinner
£19.50-£29.50 à la carte
Short breaks: £53.50-£73.50. Min 2 nights, Oct-Mar
✗ Credit cards ① ② ③ ⑤

A lovely country house standing in extensive grounds just off the A64 only 5 miles from York. There are twelve beautifully appointed and decorated bedrooms with views of the gardens and surrounding countryside; all have ensuite facilities and colour television and one has a four-poster bed. The hotel has a special Christmas programme. Children under twelve are not accommodated.

BOLTON ABBEY   North Yorkshire   *Map 7 SE05*

★★★75% **Devonshire Arms Country House** (Best Western) BD23 6AJ ☎ (075671) 441

Normal price: £47.50-£55. Dinner £23.50.
Short breaks: £57.50-£62.50. Min 2 nights. Single
supplement.
Activity breaks: Fly Fishing, £66. 9 Apr-30 Sept. Five miles
of fishing from either bank of the River Wharfe. Bird-
Watching, £57.50. May-Aug. Walks led by RSPB
representative through Strid Wood on the Bolton Abbey
Estate. Golf, £57.50. Golf at Skipton Golf Club. Clay Pigeon
Shooting, £76. Initial instruction, gun fitting and shooting
at the Beamsley Estate Shooting School.

Beautifully located by the River Wharfe, the hotel is set in the rolling landscape of the Yorkshire Dales near Bolton Abbey. The restaurant offers delicately prepared dishes and sauces.

BOROUGHBRIDGE   North Yorkshire   *Map 8 SE36*

★★★64% **Crown** (Best Western) Horsefair YO5 9LB ☎ (0423) 322328

Normal price: £60 room. Dinner £14.50 and à la carte
Short breaks: £37.50. Min 2 nights, Fri-Sun.
Credit cards ① ② ③ ⑤

This former coaching inn is popular with modern-day coach parties touring the area. All the bedrooms provide ensuite facilities and colour television and there are six family rooms.

BUCKDEN   North Yorkshire   Map 7 SD97

★★67% **Buck Inn** BD23 5JA ☎ (075676) 227
Normal price: £50-£65 room with breakfast, £70-£85 with dinner
Short breaks: £65-£80 for two. Min 2 nights, Sun-Thu.
Credit cards ① ③

Set amid beautiful scenery this charming Dales inn offers a warm friendly welcome. All the bedrooms have ensuite bath or shower and colour television, there are two family rooms and one room with a four-poster bed. There is a special Christmas programme.

BURNT YATES   North Yorkshire   Map 8 SE26

★★68% **Bay Horse Inn** HG3 3EJ ☎ (0423) 770230
Normal price: £25. Dinner £11.95-£13.95 and à la carte
Short breaks: £35.40. Min 2 nights.
Credit cards ① ② ③

Originally an 18th-century coaching inn, the Bay Horse has retained its original atmosphere and provides popular bar food. All bedrooms, including those in the annexe, have private showers and colour television. There is a special Christmas programme.

CARPERBY   North Yorkshire   Map 7 SE08

★★64% **Wheatsheaf** DL8 4DF ☎ (0969) 663216
Normal price: £45-£55 room and breakfast. Dinner £11.50
Short breaks: £55-£60 for 2 people. Min 2 nights, Nov-Mar (ex Bank Holidays)
Credit cards ① ② ③ ⑤

Run in an informal and friendly manner this hotel has prettily decorated bedrooms with ensuite facilities and colour television. Children under twelve are not accommodated.

COPMANTHORPE   North Yorkshire   Map 8 SE54

GH QQ Duke of Connaught Copmanthorpe Grange YO2 3TN ☎ (090484) 318
Closed Christmas week

Normal price: £42 room. Dinner £9
Short breaks: £54 for 2 people. Min 3 nights, single supplement of £2
🛏 (ex guide dogs)

These nicely converted former stables are set in open rural surroundings. All bedrooms have private facilities and colour television with some rooms set aside for non-smokers.

FILEY   North Yorkshire   Map 8 TA18

GH QQ Abbots Leigh 7 Rutland Street YO14 9JA ☎ (0723) 513334
Normal price: £14, £20 with dinner
Short breaks: £18, single £19.80. Min 3 nights, Oct-May.
🛏 (ex guide dogs)

Set in a quiet side road close to the sea this delightful and friendly guesthouse provides bedrooms which are furnished and equipped to a high standard.

GH QQ Seafield 9/11 Rutland Street YO14 9JA ☎ (0723) 513715
Normal price: £16.50. Dinner £3.50
Short breaks: £14. Min 3 nights, Jan-Apr & Oct-Dec
🛏

Bedrooms here are comfortable and bright, all have colour television and most have ensuite facilities. There is an attractive dining room.

GOATHLAND   North Yorkshire   Map 8 NZ80

★★69% **Mallyan Spout** YO22 5AN ☎ (0947) 86206 & 86341

Normal price: £60-£100 room and breakfast. Dinner £17.50-£20 and à la carte
Short breaks: £42.50-£52.50 includes midday bar snack or picnic. Min 2 nights.

An attractive stone building in the centre of the village offering Laura Ashley style bedrooms, most with private bathroom, and enjoyable meals. There is a special Christmas programme.

GRASSINGTON   North Yorkshire   Map 7 SE06

★60% **Black Horse** Garrs Lane BD23 5AT ☎ (0756) 752770

Normal price: £44-£51 room and breakfast. Dinner £10.50-£12.50 and à la carte
Short breaks: £54-£57.50 for 2 nights including one dinner. Single £67. Nov-May.

A family-run hotel with quaint, prettily-decorated bedrooms all with private facilities and colour television. Two rooms have four-poster beds. Meals are wholesome and there is a popular bar menu.

GREAT AYTON   North Yorkshire   Map 8 NZ51

✿★★ ♨70%**Ayton Hall** Low Green TS9 6BW ☎ (0642) 723595

Normal price: £47.50. Dinner from £20.50 and à la carte
Short breaks: £95 for 2 nights, includes Sunday lunch or packed lunch. Fri-Sun. Single £125
🐕 Credit cards ① ② ③ ⑤

A manor house set in six acres of landscaped gardens has been tastefully furnished in the style of a private residence. All nine bedrooms are ensuite with colour television, and three have four-poster beds. A special Christmas programme is available. Children under eleven are not accommodated.

HARROGATE   North Yorkshire   Map 8 SE35

GH QQQQ **Alexa House** 26 Ripon Road HG1 2JJ ☎ (0423) 501988
5 Jan-20 Dec

Normal price: £21
Short breaks: £18.90 excluding dinner. Min 2 nights, Jan-Mar & Oct-Dec

Dating from 1830, this warm, welcoming guesthouse offers very comfortable bedrooms, most with private bath or shower rooms, and all with colour television.

★65%**Alvera Court** 76 Kings Road HG1 5JX ☎ (0423) 505735

Normal price: £25. Dinner from £10 and à la carte
Short breaks: £21 excluding dinner. Min 2 nights (ex conferences and exhibitions)
🐕 (ex guide dogs) Credit cards ① ③

A comfortable and friendly hotel near the conference centre. All of the tastefully decorated bedrooms have ensuite bath or shower room and colour television, and there are some family rooms. Christmas breaks are available.

★★68%**Ascot House** (Minotels) 53 Kings Road HG1 5HJ ☎ (0423) 531005

Normal price: £54 room. Dinner £10.95-£12.45 and à la carte
Short breaks: £32.75, single £38. Min 2 nights, Fri-Sun
Credit cards ① ② ③ ⑤

Situated close to the town centre, this hotel provides value-for-money menus and good service. Most rooms have private facilities, and all have colour television.

GH QQQ Ashwood House 7 Spring Grove HG1 2HS ☎ (0423) 560081
Closed 24 Dec-1 Jan

Normal price: £40 room and breakfast
Short breaks: £36 for 2 people. 10% discount off single rate.
Min 2 nights, Fri-Sun, Nov-Apr
✕

This stylish Edwardian house is situated in a quiet cul-de-sac, close to the town centre and local attractions. It offers high standards of comfort and service and spacious bedrooms.

★★★69% **Balmoral** Franklin Mount HG1 5EJ ☎ (0423) 508208

Normal price: £41. Dinner from £13.50 and à la carte
Short breaks: £44. £5 single supplement, min 2 nights
(must include Sat)
Credit cards ① ② ③

A stylish and elegant hotel close to the town's amenities. There are twenty bedrooms all with private bath or shower room and colour television; some rooms are furnished with four-poster beds.

★71% **Britannia Lodge** 16 Swan Road HG1 2SA ☎ (0423) 508482

Normal price: £29. Dinner £12
Short breaks: £22.50 excluding dinner. Min 2 nights
✕ Credit cards ① ③

A pleasant and friendly family-run hotel serving good home-cooked dinners. There are twelve bedrooms all with private facilities and colour television, and some rooms are for families.

★★★★57% **Crown** (Trusthouse Forte) Crown Place HG1 2RZ ☎ (0423) 567755

Normal price: £57. Dinner from £16.
Short breaks: £51, min 2 nights.
Activity breaks: Antiques Break, £164, Feb & Summer.
Classical Music, £135. Gardening, £170. Archery, £177.
Clay Pigeon Shooting, £205. Golf, £146.
Credit cards ① ② ③ ④ ⑤

An 18th-century building near Valley Gardens and the Royal Baths.

★73% **Gables** 2 West Grove Road HG1 2AD ☎ (0423) 505625

Normal price: £25. Dinner from £9.50 à la carte
Short breaks: £22 excluding dinner. Single £31. Min 2
nights (except major conferences)
✕ Credit cards ① ③

A small, family-run hotel providing a warm welcome and home-cooked food. Most of the bedrooms have ensuite facilities, and all have colour television.

GH Q Gillmore 98 Kings Road HG1 5HH ☎ (0423) 503699

Normal price: £33-£36 room and breakfast. Dinner £7
Short breaks: £30-£33 for 2 people

This comfortable guesthouse has a television lounge and snooker table. Some of the bedrooms have ensuite facilities and colour television.

★★★68% **Grants** 3-11 Swan Road HG1 2SS ☎ (0423) 560666

Normal price: £42.50. Dinner £13.95.
Short breaks: £37.50.
Activity breaks: Golfing Safari, £75 for 2 nights plus £42
green fees. Ski Breaks, £75 for 2 nights plus £25 to include
transport, hire of equipment, private instruction and
practice session. The Green Fingers Special, £77 including
entry to Harlow Car gardens. Theatre-Going Break, £90
including taxi to the theatre, tickets in the dress circle, and
half a bottle of champagne in the interval. Romantic Breaks
£95-£100 for 2 nights including champagne, flowers and
chocolates.

A smart, privately-owned hotel near the town centre with attractive bedrooms, some rather compact. Friendly yet professional staff create a welcoming atmosphere.

★★★64% **St George** (Swallow) 1 Ripon Road HG1 2SY ☎ (0423) 561431

Normal price: £52.50. Dinner £15.25 and à la carte
Short breaks: 2 nights £107, includes 1 lunch.
Credit cards 1 2 3 5

This is a busy hotel with a good leisure suite and a delightful new bar lounge and brasserie. Each bedroom has a private bath or shower room and colour television and there are family rooms. Christmas breaks are available.

★★★64% **Hospitality Inn** (Mount Charlotte (TS)) Prospect Place, West Park HG1 1LB ☎ (0423) 564601

Normal price: £89.50 room and breakfast. Dinner £13.75 and à la carte
Short breaks: £42. Min 2 nights
Credit cards 1 2 3 5

Standing in the city centre this hotel offers comfortable bedrooms with ensuite facilities and colour television. There is a special Christmas programme.

★★★★62% **Majestic** (Trusthouse Forte) HG1 2HU ☎ (0423) 568972

Normal price: £122 room and breakfast. Dinner from £15.50 and à la carte
Short breaks: £116 for 2 people. Single £58. Min 2 nights, Thu-Sun
Credit cards 1 2 3 4 5

An imposing hotel, situated near the new conference centre, with good leisure facilities and modern bedrooms. Christmas breaks are available.

★★★★67% **Moat House International** Kings Road HG1 1XX ☎ (0423) 500000

Normal price: £108 room
Short breaks: £42 including £14.50 dinner allowance. Single occupancy £52
Activity breaks: Gardening weekend. Theatre weekend. Racing weekend. Contact hotel for details.
Credit cards 1 2 3 4 5

This modern, purpose built hotel stands adjacent to the conference centre. Bedrooms are smart and modern, and the restaurant offers high quality cuisine.

GH QQQ Prince's 7 Granby Road HG1 4ST ☎ (0423) 883469

Normal price: £16-£25
Short breaks: £44-£55 for 2 nights. Oct-Jun
✻

A charming Victorian house with individually-styled, comfortable bedrooms, most with ensuite facilities and all having colour television. No children under three are accommodated. There is no parking on the premises.

★★72% **Russell** Valley Drive HG2 0JN ☎ (0423) 509866
Closed 27-30 Dec

Normal price: £28.47. Dinner £14.95 and à la carte
Short breaks: £94 for 2 nights, includes ¹/₂ bottle of wine
✻ (ex guide dogs)

Quietly located overlooking the Valley Gardens, this welcoming hotel offers good service, interesting food and ensuite bedrooms all with colour television. Christmas breaks are available. There is no parking on the premises.

GH QQ Wharfedale House 28 Harlow Moor Drive HG2 0JY ☎ (0423) 522233

Normal price: £31 with dinner
Short breaks: £28. Min 2 nights, Oct-Mar (except Xmas & New Year)

A spacious house, overlooking the Valley Gardens, offering ensuite bedrooms with colour television. Vegetarian meals are available.

HAWES   *North Yorkshire*   Map 7 SD88

70% Herriots Main Street DL8 3QU ☎ (0969) 667536
Closed Nov-mid Feb. Restricted service Feb-Etr
Normal price: £22. Dinner £10.35-£12.85 à la carte
Short breaks: £26. Min 2 nights, Feb-May
✸ Credit cards [1] [3]

Managed by courteous resident proprietors, this small friendly hotel has a restaurant offering excellent value for money and bedrooms with private shower and colour television. Christmas breaks are available. No parking on the premises.

★★**74% Rookhurst Georgian Country House** Gayle DL8 3RT ☎ (0969) 667454
Closed 16 Dec-Jan
Normal price: £34 bed and breakfast, £46 with dinner
Short breaks: £42. Min 2 nights, Nov-Apr. (except Bank Holidays)
✸ (ex guide dogs)

A wonderful welcome awaits guests at this small intimate hotel. Bedrooms are full of character with four-poster and half-tester beds, and the home cooking is of the highest standard. Children are not accommodated.

★★**76% Simonstone Hall** Simonstone, DL8 3LY ☎ (0969) 667255
Normal price: £44.80. Dinner from £18.50.
Short breaks: from £51, min 2 nights.
Activity breaks: Guided Walks, spring and late autumn.
Details from hotel.
Credit cards [1] [3]

The former home of the Earls of Wharncliffe, built in 1733, now a comfortable and elegant hotel with a fine relaxed atmosphere. Service from a friendly young staff.

HELMSLEY   *North Yorkshire*   Map 8 SE68

★★★**76% Black Swan** (Trusthouse Forte) Market Place YO6 5BJ ☎ (0439) 70466
Normal price: £63. Dinner £29.50-£45.
Short breaks: £70, Sun-Thu, £81, Fri-Sat. Min 2 nights.
Activity breaks: Music at Leisure, £215 for 2 nights including two concerts (one at Castle Howard), champagne reception and wine with meals. Gastronomic Weekends, £275 for 2 nights including two gastronomic dinners, wine tasting and lunch at Castle Howard and wine with dinner.
Credit cards [1] [2] [3] [4] [5]

Overlooking the market square, the Black Swan has preserved all of its original character both inside and out. Service by young staff is pleasant and helpful.

★★**67% Crown** Market Square YO6 5BJ ☎ (0439) 70297
Normal price: £38 with dinner
Short breaks: 2 nights £67. 2 Jan-11 May, 11 Oct-23 Dec 1991, 2 Jan-10 May 1992

This 16th-century coaching inn has low beams, log fires and stone floors. Most of the bedrooms have private bath or shower rooms, and all have colour television.

★★★**64% Feversham Arms** (Best Western) 1 High Street YO6 5AG ☎ (0439) 70766
Normal price: £53-£58 with dinner
Short breaks: £43-£53. £10 single supplement. Min 2 nights

This character hotel, in the centre of town, has a tennis court and outdoor heated pool. Some of the comfortable bedrooms have four-poster beds and hand-painted bathroom suites.

★★71% **Pheasant** Harome YO6 5JG (2.5m SE on unclass rd) ☎ (0439) 71241
Closed Christmas, New Year Jan-Feb
Normal price: £48-£52.50 including dinner
Short breaks: £38.50. Min 2 nights, Nov-late May

A very comfortable hotel overlooking the village duck pond. Bedrooms are furnished to a very high standard, and all have private bath and colour television. Children under twelve are not accommodated.

KETTLEWELL   North Yorkshire   Map 7 SD97

QQQ Dale House BD23 5QZ ☎ (075676) 836
Normal price: £30
Short breaks: £68-£72 room, min 2 nights. Oct-May (not Christmas or Bank Hols). £10 single supplement.
Credit cards ① ③

Charming, stone built village house close to the River Wharfe. Christmas programmes available.

GH QQQ Langcliffe House BD23 5RJ ☎ (075676) 243
Closed 4-31 Jan
Normal price: £23
Short breaks: £27. Nov-Mar
Credit cards ① ③

Situated on the edge of the village, this charming, relaxed house offers ensuite bedrooms with colour television.

KILNSEY   North Yorkshire   Map 7 SD96

★★63% **Tennant Arms** BD23 5PS ☎ (0756) 752301
Normal price: £33.25. Dinner £10.95
Short breaks: £66.50 for 2 people, Sun-Thurs. Min 2 nights, Jan-Apr & Nov-Dec
Credit cards ① ③

Situated by the impressive Kilnsey Crags, this is a popular inn with an oak-panelled restaurant. Each bedroom has ensuite facilities and colour television. Fishing is available and there are special Christmas breaks.

KIRKBY FLEETHAM   North Yorkshire   Map 8 SE29

★★★ ♨ 72% **Kirkby Fleetham Hall** (Pride of Britain) DL7 0SU ☎ (0609) 748711
Normal price: £102-£175 room and breakfast. Dinner from £28
Short breaks: £69. Min 2 nights
Credit cards ① ② ③ ④ ⑤

An impressive Georgian house situated in 36 acres of parkland. The bedrooms are spacious and comfortable, all have private facilities and colour television, and some have four-poster beds. There are leisure amenities and Christmas breaks are available.

KIRKBYMOORSIDE   North Yorkshire   Map 8 SE68

★★68% **George & Dragon** 17 Market Place YO6 6AA ☎ (0751) 31637
Normal price: £30. Dinner from £17
Short breaks: £40. Min 2 nights, Nov-Mar
Credit cards ① ③

A welcoming 13th-century inn with modern bedrooms situated in converted stables. Christmas breaks are available.

KNARESBOROUGH North Yorkshire   Map 8 SE35

GH QQQ Newton House 5/7 York Place HG5 0AD ☎ (0423) 863539
Restricted service 25 & 26 Dec

Normal price: £30
Short breaks: £50 for 2 people. Fri & Sat or Sat & Sun,
dinner included Sat night. Min 2 nights, Nov-Mar.
Credit cards ① ② ③

This carefully restored Georgian building provides comfortable accommodation in ensuite bedrooms with mini-bars, colour television and radio alarm.

LEYBURN North Yorkshire   Map 7 SE19

GH Q Eastfield Lodge 1 St Matthews Terrace DL8 5EL ☎ (0969) 23196

Normal price: £15
Short breaks: £18. Min 2 nights, Oct-May (ex Bank
Holidays)
Credit cards ① ② ③ ⑤

A comfortable house offering spacious accommodation and a welcoming atmosphere.

★57% Golden Lion Market PlaceDL8 5AS ☎ (0969) 22161

Normal price: £22.75. Dinner £6.50-£11.50.
Short breaks: £20.23 excluding breakfast. 10% off meals.
Min 2 nights.
Activity breaks: Golf Breaks, £35 per night.
Credit cards ① ③

A good range of both bar meals and \a la carte dinners is served at this busy, popular village inn.

MARKINGTON North Yorkshire   Map 8 SE26

★★★74% Hob Green HG3 3PJ ☎ (0423) 770031

Normal price: £42.50. Dinner from £14.50 (1990 price)
Short breaks: £52.50. Single supplement.
Credit cards ① ② ③ ⑤

With fine views over the rolling countryside, this hospitable country house hotel has open fires and antique furnishings, and its traditionally styled bedrooms all have colour television and ensuite facilities. There is croquet in the lawned garden.

MIDDLEHAM North Yorkshire   Map 7 SE18

★★71% Millers House Market Place DL8 4NR ☎ (0969) 22630

Normal price: £46 including dinner
Short breaks: £40.50 for 2 nights (1990 price). Min 2 nights.
Activity breaks: Racing Breaks, £120 for 2 nights including
enclosure ticket, picnic hamper and wine and visit to local
stables. Wine Weekends, £100-£140 for 2 nights including 2
gourmet banquets, wines, speaker, wine trail and wine
pack gift. 8-10 Nov, 22-24 Nov, 6-8 Dec. Herriot Trails, £100
for 2 nights including picnic hamper and wine with dinner.
Romantic Breaks, £112.50 for 2 nights including bottle of
champagne, roses, and breakfast in bed with smoked
salmon and Bucks Fizz.
🐾 Credit cards ① ③

Friendly attentive service and good cooking using fresh produce can be found at this small Georgian country house hotel in town.

MONK FRYSTON North Yorkshire   *Map 8 SE52*

★★★68% **Monk Fryston Hall** LS25 5DU ☎ (0977) 682369

Normal price: from £38. Dinner £13.25-£14 and à la carte (1990 price)
Short breaks: £46 Mar-Sep, £50 Oct-Mar. Min 2 nights, Fri-Sun & Bank Hol Mon.
Credit cards [1] [2] [3]

Set in beautiful gardens, this historic stone-built house with open fires and oak panelling serves good-quality food and all its bedrooms, including a family room and a four-poster bed, have ensuite facilities and colour television. Christmas breaks are available.

NORTHALLERTON North Yorkshire   *Map 8 SE39*

★★★67% **Solberge Hall** (Best Western) Newby Wiske DL7 9ER (3.25m S off A167) ☎ (0609) 779191

Normal price: £40. Dinner £15-£20 à la carte (1990 price)
Short breaks: £52. Min 2 nights.
Credit cards [1] [2] [3] [5]

This gracious porticoed Victorian house standing in 15 acres of grounds has very comfortable, fully equipped ensuite bedrooms which include 2 four-poster beds and family rooms. Leisure facilities include snooker, croquet and clay pigeon shooting. Christmas breaks are available.

★★★67% **Sundial** Darlington Road DL6 2XF ☎ (0609) 780525

Normal price: £36. Dinner from £13.75 and à la carte (1990 price)
Short breaks: £43. Min 2 nights. £10 single supplement.
Credit cards [1] [2] [3] [5]

This modern hotel a mile north of the town has an elegant restaurant and well-equipped bedrooms, many non-smoking and including some family rooms, with ensuite bath and colour television.

PATELEY BRIDGE North Yorkshire   *Map 7 SE16*

QQQ **Grassfields Country House** HG3 5HL ☎ (0423) 711412

Normal price: £29.50
Short breaks: £21 (1990 prices). Min 3 nights.

Set in 4 acres of grounds, this Georgian house with a pleasant lounge and cosy bar provides good home cooking and comfortable ensuite bedrooms, including a few family rooms.

PICKERING North Yorkshire   *Map 8 SE78*

QQ **Bramwood** 19 Hallgarth YO18 7AW ☎ (0751) 74066

Normal price: £11-£12.50. Dinner £7 (1990 price).
Short breaks: £47-£51.50 for 3 nights, Oct-Apr.
✸ (ex guide dogs) Credit cards [1] [2] [3] [5]

Quietly located close to the town centre, this neat and comfortable guesthouse, for non-smokers only, serves good home-cooked food. All bedrooms, which include 2 family rooms, have washing facilities, one with private shower. No children under 3 are accommodated.

★★68% **Crossways** Eastgate YO18 7DW ☎ (0751) 72804

Normal price: from £20
Short breaks: from £25. Min 2 nights.
Credit cards [1] [3]

This friendly little hotel with a secluded garden has colour television in all bedrooms, which include a few family rooms and some with private shower.

★★68% **Forest & Vale** (Consort) Malton Road YO18 7DL ☎ (0751) 72722

Normal price: £35. Dinner £13 and à la carte (1990 price)
Short breaks: £43 including £13.20 dinner allowance. Min 2
nights. Not available Christmas/New Year.
Credit cards ① ② ③ ⑤

This comfortable country hotel has a well-tended garden and a large restaurant serving mainly English food. All bedrooms, which include some family rooms in the annexe, are ensuite and with colour television.

★★64% **White Swan** Market Place YO18 7AA ☎ (0751) 72288

Normal price: £60-£80 room and breakfast. Dinner from
£13.50
Short breaks: £75, 2 nights min, Nov-March
Activity breaks: Golf Breaks £37.50. Wine appreciation –
contact hotel for details
Credit cards ① ③

The stone-faced White Swan is situated in the town centre and offers well-equipped accommodation and a convivial atmosphere. The restaurant combines an interesting menu with an extensive wine list. There are Christmas and New Year programmes.

REETH   *North Yorkshire* Map 7 SE09

★★64% **Buck** DL11 6SW ☎ (0748) 84210

Normal price: £44
Short breaks: £70 for 2 night weekend break including
Sunday lunch, Fri-Sat, Oct-May. £95 for any 3 nights, Oct-
May. Single supplement.
⊀ Credit cards ① ② ③ ④

This charming former coaching inn serves good value dinners and bar meals and has comfortable bedrooms with ensuite facilities and colour television, including a family room. There is also a garden and children's facilities.

RICHMOND *North Yorkshire* Map 7 NZ10

★★59% **Frenchgate** 59-61 Frenchgate DL10 7AE ☎ (0748) 2087 & 3596

Normal price: £22-£25.25. Dinner from £9 and à la carte
(1990 price)
Short breaks: £27-£30. Min 2 nights, Oct-mid May. Special
rate for single occupancy.
Credit cards ① ② ③ ⑤

This Georgian stone townhouse enclosing a 16th-century cottage provides characterful accommodation; all bedrooms have colour television and over half of them private bath or shower. No children under 7 are accommodated.

★★67% **King's Head** (Consort) Market Square DL10 4HS ☎ (0748) 2311

Normal price: £32.50. Dinner from £10.25 (1990 price)
Short breaks: £37.50-£40. Min 2 nights, except Christmas/
New Year.
⊀ (ex guide dogs) Credit cards ① ② ③ ④ ⑤

This busy inn in the market square has a coffee shop and pizzeria, and ensuite bedrooms, including no-smoking rooms and some family rooms in the annexe, all with colour television and one with a four-poster bed. Christmas breaks are available.

RIPON North Yorkshire Map 8 SE37

QQ Crescent Lodge 42 North Street HG4 1EN ☎ (0765) 2331

Normal price: £17
Short breaks: £13-£16.50 excluding dinner. Min 2 nights.

This early 18th-century town house retains the elegant Georgian staircase and period rooms. Bedrooms include family rooms and all have colour television and wash basins, some with ensuite shower.

★★★64% **Ripon Spa** (Best Western) Park Street HG4 2BU ☎ (0765) 2172

Normal price: £38
Short breaks: £50. Min 2 nights.
Credit cards ① ② ③ ⑤

Standing in large gardens close to the town centre, this extensively refurbished hotel offers comfortable accommodation with attractive bedrooms, all with ensuite facilities and colour television, including a few family rooms, and two with four-poster beds. Christmas breaks are available.

★★56% **Unicorn** (Consort) Market Place HG4 1BP ☎ (0765) 2202

Normal price: £26.50
Short breaks: £34. Min 2 nights. £10 single supplement.
Credit cards ① ② ③ ⑤

Dating to medieval times, this hotel in the market place has a restaurant and bars with some original features, a comfortable lounge and well-fitted bedrooms, including a few family rooms, all with private bath or shower and colour television.

ROSEDALE ABBEY North Yorkshire Map 8 SE79

★★73% **Milburn Arms** (Guestaccom) YO18 8RA ☎ (07515) 312

Normal price: £25-£35. Dinner £14.50.
Short breaks: £42.50 for 2 nights. Min 2 nights.
Activity breaks: Clay Pigeon Shooting, £175 for 2 nights
Credit cards ① ③

A very friendly hotel offering an extensive range of well-prepared bar and restaurant meals, and comfortable accommodation.

★★63% **White Horse Farm** (Minotels) YO18 8SE ☎ (07515) 239

Normal price: £23.50. Dinner £13.50-£15.50 (1990 price)
Short breaks: £20. Min 2 nights, except bank hols.
Credit cards ① ② ③ ⑤

Overlooking unspoilt countryside, this family-run 18th-century converted farmhouse has an attractive bar and dining room, and ensuite bedrooms with colour television, some of them, including two family rooms, situated in the annexe. Christmas breaks are available.

RUFFORTH North Yorkshire Map 8 SE55

QQ Wellgarth House Wetherby Road YO2 3QB ☎ (090483) 592 & 595

Normal price: £13-£17
Short breaks: £19. Min 3 nights, Sun-Thu, Nov-Mar. £2 extra for en suite room.
✻

This large modern house on the edge of the village provides comfortable accommodation with colour television and wash basins in all bedrooms, some with private shower and including a family room.

SCARBOROUGH North Yorkshire Map 8 TA08

Q Avoncroft 5-7 Crown Terrace YO11 2BL ☎ (0723) 372737

Normal price: £16 Mar-early May, end Oct-end Feb; £17 May-mid June, end Aug-25 Oct; £18 mid June-end Aug; 1992 prices.
Short breaks: £20.50 Mar-early May & 26 Oct-end Feb; £21.50 May-14 June & end Aug-25 Oct; £22.50 mid June-end Aug.

Part of an attractive Georgian terrace overlooking Crown Gardens, this is a friendly guest house, simply furnished, with colour television in all the bedrooms.

★★50% Central 1-3 The Crescent YO11 2PW ☎ (0723) 365766

Normal price: £35.50. Dinner £7 and à la carte.
Short breaks: £33.50, min 2 nights, Mon-Thur. £3 single supplement.
Credit cards ①②③⑤

This family-run hotel, overlooking the Crescent gardens, offers basic bedroom accommodation and a wide choice of menus. The restaurant - which features an open display kitchen - serves good, simple meals based on quality ingredients.

★★★63% Esplanade Belmont Road YO11 2AA ☎ (0723) 360382

Normal price: £41.25. Dinner £11 and à la carte.
Short breaks: £33, min 2 nights, Autumn/Winter.
Credit cards ①②③⑤

A large seaside hotel with a superb setting on the South Cliff, overlooking the bay. Bedrooms are attractively decorated and well equipped, and guests can benefit from space in which to relax in the bars, lounges and patio areas.

★★69% Gridley's Crescent The Crescent YO11 2PP ☎ (0723) 360929

Normal price: £30. Dinner from £12.50 and à la carte.
Short breaks: £25 excluding dinner. Min 2 nights, Jan-June & Oct-Dec.
🐾 Credit cards ①③

This attractive listed building has been carefully converted into a very comfortable hotel. All bedrooms are well equipped and nicely furnished, and guests have a choice of restaurants.

★★★★53% Holbeck Hall Seacliff Road YO11 2XX ☎ (0723) 374374

Normal price: £51-£56, min 2 nights, 1990 prices. Dinner from £16.50 and à la carte.
Short breaks: The Champagne Break: £97.50 mid week, min 2 nights, £107.50 weekends, £5 supplement per night for sea view. Weekend Break includes Sunday lunch.
🐾 Credit cards ①②③⑤

A comfortable hotel, full of charm and character, in a superb position overlooking South Bay and the harbour, with three acres of gardens. The elegant lounge and restaurant both enjoy sea views, and the oak panelled reception hall has a minstrels' gallery. The bedrooms are all well equipped, although they vary in size and décor.

★★★64% St Nicholas St Nicholas Cliff YO11 2EU ☎ (0723) 364101

Normal price: £42.50. Dinner from £11.
Short breaks: £47.50, min 2 nights, not available during town conferences. Single supplement Mon-Fri.
Credit cards ①②③⑤

This large seafront hotel, undergoing a continuous programme of upgrading, now offers good conference and leisure facilities.

★★★61% Palm Court Nicholas Cliff YO11 2ES ☎ (0723) 368161

Normal price: from £30. Dinner £10.50-£14 and à la carte.
Short breaks: from £38.
🐾 (ex guide dogs) Credit cards ①②③⑤

Within easy reach of the beach and local amenities, this modernised hotel has ensuite bedrooms with colour television and a heated indoor pool. Christmas breaks are available.

★★66% **Pickwick Inn** Huntriss Row YO11 2ED ☎ (0723) 375787

Normal price: £20. Dinner £9-£10.95 and à la carte.
Short breaks: £27.50, min 2 nights. £3 single supplement.
🗙 Credit cards ① ② ③ ⑤

Conveniently situated for shopping, the hotel provides modern, very comfortable accommodation in attractive, well-equipped bedrooms. A small restaurant serves carefully prepared meals, and the large cosy bar offers an alternative menu.

Q Sefton 18 Prince of Wales Terrace YO11 2AL ☎ (0723) 372310

Normal price: £16.50
Short breaks: £15.50. Min 2 nights, Mar-May & Sep-Nov.
🗙

A Victorian town house with spacious public rooms and some charming bedrooms.

★★61% **Southlands** 15 West Street, South Cliff YO11 2QW ☎ (0723) 361461

Normal price: £40. Dinner £12 and à la carte.
Short breaks: £37.50, min 2 nights, Mar-Dec. Single supplement.
Credit cards ① ② ③ ⑤

A well furnished and comfortable traditional seaside hotel, personally owned and run, offering good home comforts. Situated on South Cliff, near the Esplanade.

★★★ 🏨 64% **Wrea Head Country** Scalby YO13 0PB (3 miles NW off A171) ☎ (0723) 378211

Normal price: £45. Dinner £18.50-£24
Short breaks: £50, min 2 nights.
🗙 Credit cards ① ② ③

A converted Victorian residence standing in 14 acres of landscaped gardens, which include a putting green and croquet lawn.

SCOTCH CORNER   North Yorkshire   Map 8 NZ20

★★★65% **Scotch Corner** Richmond DL10 6NR ☎ (0748) 850900

Normal price: £94 room and breakfast. Dinner £12.50 and à la carte.
Short breaks: £35, min 2 nights, Fri-Sun, except Christmas & New Year. £5 single supplement.
Credit cards ① ② ③ ⑤

Most conveniently located at the junction of the A1/A66, this hotel was recently the subject of extensive refurbishment. The well equipped bedrooms are designed for comfort, and there is a coffee shop which complements the choice of menus offered by the two restaurants.

SELBY North Yorkshire   Map 8 SE63

★★65% **Londesborough Arms** Market Place YO8 0NS ☎ (0757) 707355

Normal price: £26. Dinner £8-£15 and à la carte.
Short breaks: £23.50 excluding dinner. Min 2 nights Fri-Sun.
Credit cards ① ② ③ ⑤

A former coaching inn located in the town centre close to the Abbey, successfully converted to provide comfortable modern facilities whilst retaining its original character and atmosphere. An attractive restaurant overlooking the patio provides an interesting \a la carte menu.

SETTLE North Yorkshire   Map 7 SD86

★★★62% **Falcon Manor** Skipton Road BD24 9BD ☎ (07292) 3814

Normal price: £33. Dinner £14.75 and à la carte.
Short breaks: £41, min 2 nights. £8 single supplement.
Credit cards ① ③ ⑤

This family-run hotel stands in the busy Dales town, which is the gateway to Ribblesdale and the Yorkshire Dales National Park. The food served in the elegant restaurant is well-prepared and includes some typical local specialities.

SHERIFF HUTTON North Yorkshire Map 8 SE66

QQQ Rangers House Sheriff Hutton Park YO6 1RH ☎ (03477) 397

Normal price: £52 room and breakfast.
Short breaks: £38 includes afternoon tea. Min 2 nights, Oct-end Mar, excluding Christmas, New Year and Easter.
✠

A minstrel's gallery forms part of this interesting and unusual house which is set in attractive gardens. The oak-beamed bedrooms are cosy, and most offer ensuite facilities. Guests will enjoy a high standard of cooking.

SKIPTON North Yorkshire Map 7 SD95

INN QQ Red Lion High Street BD23 1DT ☎ (0756) 60718

Normal price: £35 room and breakfast
Short breaks: 3 nights £70 for two. Single £50. Nov-Feb.
✠ Credit cards 1 3

This cosy well-furnished inn has comfortable bedrooms with colour television, and some have ensuite bathroom.

THIRSK North Yorkshire Map 8 SE48

★★65% **Sheppard's** Church Farm, Front Street, Sowerby YO7 1JF ☎ (0845) 523655

Normal price: £27.50-£32.50. Dinner from £16 à la carte.
Short breaks: 10% off room and restaurant. Min 2 nights, Nov-Mar
✠ Credit cards 1 3

A small, family-run hotel set around a central cobbled courtyard. The restaurant, a former stable, serves imaginative dishes, while bedrooms are comfortable and have ensuite facilities. Children under ten are not accommodated.

THORNTON DALE North Yorkshire Map 8 SE88

GH QQ Easthill Wilton Road YO18 7QP ☎ (0751) 74561

Normal price: from £15.50.
Short breaks: £20. Min 2 nights, Oct-Mar (ex Easter)

The majority of rooms at this guesthouse have private bath or shower rooms. It also offers special facilities for children and guests can enjoy a game of tennis or crazy golf.

315

WEST WITTON North Yorkshire *Map 7 SE08*

★★68% **Wensleydale Heifer Inn** (Consort) DL8 4LS ☎ (0969) 22322

Normal price: £30. Dinner from £17.50
Short breaks: £42.50, single £55. Min 2 nights.
Credit cards ① ② ③ ⑤

This 17th-century inn provides attractive and comfortable accommodation in the main building and in two adjacent houses. Some rooms have four-poster beds, and all are ensuite with colour television. Christmas breaks are available.

WHITBY North Yorkshire *Map 8 NZ81*

GH QQQQ **Dunsley Hall** YO21 3TL ☎ (0947) 83437

Normal price: £27-£31
Short breaks: £35 midweek, £37 weekend. Min 2 nights, Mon-Sat, Jan-Jun & Oct-Dec (ex Bank Holidays)
Credit cards ① ③

Standing high above Whitby and Sandsend this magnificent hall offers excellent food, a restful atmosphere and good leisure facilities. Each of the ensuite bedrooms has tea/coffee making facilities and colour television.

★★65% **White House** Upgang Lane, West Cliff YO21 3JJ ☎ (0947) 600469

Normal price: £25. Dinner from £9.50 and à la carte
Short breaks: £30. Min 2 nights
Credit cards ① ③

Located next to the Golf Club and enjoying views over Sandsend Bay, this is a family-run hotel providing comfortable accommodation and a friendly atmosphere. There are special facilities for children and Christmas breaks are available.

WYKEHAM (near Scarborough) North Yorkshire *Map 8 SE98*

★★62% **Downe Arms** YO13 9QB ☎ (0723) 862471

Normal price: £45 room and breakfast. Dinner £10.50.
Short breaks: from £65 for 2 people, min 2 nights.
Activity breaks: Shooting Breaks, Oct-Feb. Details from hotel.
Credit cards ① ② ③ ⑤

A popular old 18th-century coaching inn offering very good value for money. The lounge bar and dining room are very attractive.

YORK North Yorkshire *Map 8 SE65*

GH QQ **Abbingdon** 60 Bootham Crescent YO3 7AH ☎ (0904) 621761
Closed Dec

Normal price: £19
Short breaks: less 10%. Min 3 nights.
🛪 (ex guide dogs)

A friendly guesthouse with pretty bedrooms (some have ensuite showers), a comfortable lounge and snug dining room.

★★63% **Abbots' Mews** 6 Marygate Lane, Bootham YO3 7DE ☎ (0904) 634866

Normal price: £30-£35. Dinner from £12 and à la carte
Short breaks: £40-£42.50. Min 2 nights
🛪

Converted from a coachman's cottage and stables, this city centre hotel offers ensuite bedrooms with colour television. Christmas breaks are available.

GH QQ Aberford 35/36 East Mount Road YO2 2BD ☎ (0904) 622694

Normal price: £18-£26
Short breaks: £16 excluding dinner. Single £17. Min 2 nights, Sun-Thu
🐾 (ex guide dogs) Credit cards ① ② ③

Set in a quiet street close to the town centre this three-storey townhouse has an interesting basement bar and separate sung lounge. All bedrooms have colour television, and some have private showers.

★★62% **Alhambra Court** 31 St Mary's, Bootham YO3 7DD ☎ (0904) 628474

Normal price: £26
Short breaks: £33, single £39. Min 2 nights
🐾

Two town houses were converted to create this hotel which is within walking distance of the Minster. It has a cosy lounge with satellite television, an à la carte restaurant and well-designed bedrooms with modern facilities.

GH QQQ Arndale 290 Tadcaster Road YO2 2ET ☎ (0904) 702424
Closed Christmas & New Year

Normal price: £52 room and breakfast
Short breaks: £48 for two excluding dinner. Min 2 nights
🐾 (ex guide dogs)

This Victorian building retains many original features. It has a beautiful lounge and spacious, well-fitted ensuite bedrooms with colour television.

GH Q Arnot House 17 Grosvenor Terrace, Bootham YO3 7AG ☎ (0904) 641966

Normal price: £14. Dinner £9.50
Short breaks: £11 excluding dinner. Min 2 nights, Nov-Mar
🐾

Only 400yds from the ancient city walls, this spacious house offers a warm welcome, imaginative home-cooked meals and large bedrooms. Children under five are not accommodated.

★★53% **Ashcroft** (Minotels) 294 Bishopthorpe Road YO2 1LH ☎ (0904) 659286
Closed Xmas & New Year

Normal price: from £55 room and breakfast. Dinner from £9.50 and à la carte
Short breaks: £33. Min 2 nights, 29 Mar-30 Jun
Credit cards ① ② ③ ⑤

A large yet quiet house with a restful atmosphere and good home cooking. Each bedroom has a private bath or shower room and colour television and there are some family rooms.

★★69% **Beechwood Close** (Minotels) 19 Shipton Road, Clifton YO3 6RE ☎ (0904) 658378

Normal price: £30. Dinner £13
Short breaks: £39.50. Single £44.25. Min 2 nights
🅇 Credit cards ① ② ③

A converted country house, standing in its own gardens to the north of the city, provides ensuite bedrooms with colour television and some family rooms.

GH QQ Byron House The Mount YO2 2DD ☎ (0904) 32525
Closed 25 Dec-4 Jan

Normal price: £66 room and breakfast
Short breaks: £50 for two excluding dinner. Min 2 nights, Nov-Mar
🅇 (ex guide dogs) Credit cards ① ② ③ ⑤

An impressive early 19th-century building situated close to the race course. Most of the bedrooms have ensuite facilities, and all have colour television.

★65% **Clifton Bridge** Water End, Clifton YO3 6LL ☎ (0904) 610510
Closed 24-31 Dec

Normal price: £30. Dinner £6.75-£11.95 à la carte
Short breaks: £36. Min 2 nights, 31 Oct-Mar

A comfortable hotel on the northern edge of the city and close to the river. The pleasant bedrooms each have private bath or shower room and colour television, and there is one family room.

GH QQQ Collingwood 163 Holgate Road YO2 4DF ☎ (0904) 78333

Normal price: £20
Short breaks: £18 excluding dinner. Min 3 nights, Nov-Feb
🅇 (ex guide dogs) Credit cards ① ② ⑤

Sympathetically restored to retain many period features, this Georgian house has a lounge bar, separate television room and an attractive dining room. Bedrooms are all ensuite with colour television.

GH Q Coppers Lodge 15 Alma Terrace, Fulford Road YO1 4DQ ☎ (0904) 639871

Normal price: £12-£15
Short breaks: £10 excluding dinner. Min 3 nights, Nov-Feb. Single £12

Simple, good value accommodation is available at this former police HQ and jail house just one mile from the town centre.

GH QQ Crescent 77 Bootham YO3 7DQ ☎ (0904) 623216

Normal price: £15.50-£20
Short breaks: £13-£15.50 excluding dinner. Single £15. Min 2 nights, Nov-Jun
🅇 Credit cards ① ② ③ ⑤

Close to the Minster and town centre this guesthouse is situated above shops and has reception and public rooms on the first floor. Bedrooms are full of style and character, all have colour television and some have private facilities.

GH QQQ Curzon Lodge 23 Tadcaster Road YO2 2QG ☎ (0904) 703157
Closed 23 Dec-1 Jan

Normal price: £23-£24
Short breaks: £22-£23 excluding dinner. Min 2 nights. Single £28-£29

This listed building stands close to the racecourse and contains many original features. Bedrooms, some of which are in a converted stable block, are comfortable and well-equipped. Children under 7 are not accommodated.

★★59% **Disraeli's** 140 Acomb Road YO2 4HA ☎ (0904) 781181
Closed 25 Dec-1 Jan

Normal price: £34. Dinner £11.25-£14.50 and à la carte
Short breaks: £38. Single £57
🅇 (ex guide dogs)

This detached Victorian house, in a quiet residential area on the edge of the city, offers ensuite bedrooms with colour television and family rooms. There are special facilities for children.

GH QQ Dray Lodge Moor Lane, Murton YO1 3UH (3m E off A166) ☎ (0904) 489591

Normal price: £22.90
Short breaks: £29.40. Min 2 nights
🛧 (ex guide dogs) Credit cards ①③

This converted 19th-century horse carriage works combines character and modern facilities. Most bedrooms are ensuite, and all have colour television and coffee trays.

★★★59% **Fairfield Manor** (Consort) Shipton Road, Skelton YO3 6XW ☎ (0904) 625621

Normal price: £77 room and breakfast. Dinner £13.50-£15 and à la carte
Short breaks: £38.50. Single supplement £14. Min 2 nights
Credit cards ①②③⑤

An attractive Georgian house on the A19 three miles north of the city centre provides comfortable and generally spacious bedrooms all with ensuite facilities and colour television. Two rooms have four-poster beds. There is a special Christmas programme.

★65% **Fairmount** 230 Tadcaster Road, Mount Vale YO2 2ES ☎ (0904) 638298

Normal price: £25. Dinner £12.50
Short breaks: £35, single £40. Min 2 nights

This attractive Victorian building, close to the racecourse, provides a good standard of accommodation in well-equipped bedrooms. The pleasant restaurant serves enjoyable meals.

GH QQ Greenside 124 Clifton YO3 6BQ ☎ (0904) 623631
Closed 25 Dec

Normal price: £12.50
Short breaks: £17.50 (1990 prices). Min 2 nights, Nov-Mar.

Situated just outside the city walls, this charming detached house has spacious bedrooms with central heating, a television lounge and car park. There are special facilities for children.

GH Q Heworth 126 East Parade YO3 7YG ☎ (0904) 426384

Normal price: £11.50-£14.50
Short breaks: £11 excluding dinner. Min 2 nights, Nov-Apr (except Bank Holidays)
Credit cards ①③

Convenient for the town's facilities, this neat guesthouse offers bedrooms with colour television and tea/coffee trays.

★★70% **Heworth Court** 76-78 Heworth Green YO3 7TQ ☎ (0904) 425156 & 425126

Normal price: £28. Dinner £12.50 and à la carte
Short breaks: £34. Min 2 nights
🛧

Situated on the east side of York about ten minutes' walk from the city walls, this hotel provides a choice of traditional and modern bedrooms and imaginative meals. Christmas breaks are available. See advertisement in colour section.

319

★63% **Holgate Bridge** 106-108 Holgate Road YO2 4BB ☎ (0904) 635971
Closed 24-26 Dec
Normal price: £17.50-£24. Dinner from £8.50 and à la carte
Short breaks: £22.50-£29. Min 2 nights (ex Bank Holidays)

A friendly little hotel, only a short walk from the city centre, with a conservatory-style lounge and a basement dining room serving good meals. Bedrooms are modern, most have ensuite facilities, and all have colour television. See advertisement on p319.

★★62% **Knavesmire Manor** 302 Tadcaster Road YO2 2HE ☎ (0904) 702941
Normal price: £29. Dinner £13.75-£15 and à la carte
Short breaks: £37.50, min 2 nights, (Sun-Thu, Apr-Jun, £34.50)
Credit cards ① ② ③ ⑤

This comfortable Regency villa enjoys views of the racecourse and has an indoor heated swimming pool. Each bedroom has a colour television, most are ensuite and one has a four-poster bed. Christmas breaks are available.

★★★(Red) **Middlethorpe Hall** (Prestige) Bishopthorpe Road YO2 1QB ☎ (0904) 641241
Normal price: £69. Dinner from £26.90 and à la carte
Short breaks: from £80. Min 2 nights, Nov-Apr (ex Bank Holidays)
Credit cards ① ② ③ ⑤

This beautifully restored country house combines grace and elegance with modern comforts. Meals can be taken in the dining room or the basement Grill Room and bedrooms have recently been redecorated and refurbished. Christmas breaks are available. Children under eight are not accommodated.

★65% **Newington** 147 Mount Vale YO2 2DJ ☎ (0904) 625173
Normal price: £58 room and breakfast. Dinner £11-£12.50
Short breaks: £66-£74 for 2 nights. Single £72
✷ Credit cards ① ② ③ ⑤

Situated on the A1036 (south) approach road to the city, this hotel has ensuite bedrooms with colour television, and two rooms have four-poster beds. There is an indoor heated pool and Christmas breaks are available.

★★★64% **Post House** (Trusthouse Forte) Tadcaster Road YO2 2QF ☎ (0904) 707921
Normal price: £47.50. Dinner £10.50-£12.50 and à la carte
Short breaks: £50. Min 2 nights
Credit cards ① ② ③ ④ ⑤

A multi-storey hotel near the racecourse with spacious, attractive lounges and a dining room with a garden patio. Bedrooms are ensuite with colour television, and some rooms are for families and non-smokers. Christmas breaks are available.

GH QQ St Raphael 44 Queen Anne's Road, Bootham YO3 7AF ☎ (0904) 645028
Normal price: from £11
Short breaks: £17.50. Min 2 nights, Oct-Mar
Credit cards ①

A comfortable and homely guesthouse set in a residential area only a short walk from the Minster. All bedrooms have colour television and tea/coffee trays, and some have ensuite showers. No parking on the premises.

★★60% **Savages** 15 St Peters Grove YO3 6AQ ☎ (0904) 610818
Closed 25 Dec
Normal price: £32. Dinner £10.50-£11.50 and à la carte
Short breaks: £37-£39. Min 2 nights.
✷ (ex guide dogs)

A pleasant hotel with a welcoming restaurant and a comfortable lounge with a small bar. Bedrooms offer modern facilities, and most have ensuite bath or shower room. The hotel has a gymnasium and solarium.

★★58% **Sheppard** 63 The Mount YO2 2AX ☎ (0904) 643716
Normal price: £26.50
Short breaks: £33, single £39. Min 3 nights, Sun-Thu, Nov-Mar
🐾 (ex guide dogs)

A centrally-situated hotel with a cellar bar and restaurant. Bedrooms come in a variety of shapes, sizes and decorative styles, most are ensuite with colour television, and six are set aside for non-smokers. Fishing is available.

★★★70% **Swallow Chase** (Swallow) Tadcaster Road YO2 2QQ ☎ (0904) 701000
Normal price: from £92 room and breakfast (1990). Dinner £17-£22 and à la carte
Short breaks: £95-£100 (1990), for 2 nights, includes 1 lunch
Credit cards ① ② ③ ⑤

Ensuite facilities and colour television are available in all rooms at this hotel, and there are rooms for families. Leisure facilities include an indoor heated pool and golf practise net. There is a special Christmas programme.

★★67% **Town House** 100-104 Holgate Road YO2 4BB ☎ (0904) 636171
Normal price: £50 room. Dinner £9.50-£11.50 and à la carte
Short breaks: £32.50, single £40. Min 2 nights, Oct-Feb

Converted from a row of Victorian houses, this hotel provides comfortable bedrooms, a relaxing lounge and a restaurant offering good value menus.

★★★★63% **Viking** (Queens Moat) North Street YO1 1JF ☎ (0904) 659822
Normal price: £90 room and breakfast. Dinner £13.50-£14 and à la carte
Short breaks: £52, single £67. Min 2 nights, Fri-Sun
🐾 (ex guide dogs) Credit cards ① ② ③ ⑤

Situated beside the River Ouse, this is a large modern hotel with a choice of three restaurants and good leisure facilities. Each bedroom has an ensuite bath or shower room and colour television, and there are rooms for families and non-smokers. Christmas breaks are available.

▪ YORKSHIRE, SOUTH ▪

BAWTRY   South Yorkshire   *Map 8 SK69*

★★★66% **Crown** (Trusthouse Forte) High Street DN10 6JW ☎ (0302) 710341

Normal price: £48. Dinner from £14.50 and à la carte
Short breaks: £42, Thu-Sun
Credit cards ①②③④⑤

This coaching inn dating back to the early 17th century provides modern comforts and amenities. All the bedrooms have ensuite bath or shower rooms and colour television, one room is furnished with a four-poster bed, and twelve rooms are set aside for non-smokers. There is a special Christmas programme.

CHAPELTOWN   South Yorkshire   *Map 8 SK39*

★★★64% **Staindrop Lodge** Lane End S30 4UH ☎ (0742) 846783
Closed 25 & 26 Dec

Normal price: £35. Dinner £17.50-£20 and à la carte
Short breaks: £24. Fri-Sun (except Christmas)
Credit cards ①②③⑤

Standing in its own grounds in a quiet area of Sheffield this hotel offers an interesting international menu. All the ensuite bedrooms have colour television and there is a family room.

DONCASTER   South Yorkshire   *Map 8 SE50*

★★★55% **Danum Swallow** High Street DN1 1DN ☎ (0302) 342261

Normal price: £74 room and breakfast. Dinner from £12.50
Short breaks: from £40, includes Sunday lunch. Min 2 nights, Fri-Sun
Credit cards ①②③④⑤

A town centre hotel with a popular lounge bar frequented by guests and residents alike. All bedrooms have ensuite bath or shower and colour television. A Christmas programme is available.

★★★69% **Doncaster Moat House** (Queens Moat) Warmsworth DN4 9UX (2.5m SW on A630 at junc with A1) ☎ (0302) 310331

Normal price: £74 room and breakfast
Short breaks: £72 for 2 people. Min 2 nights, Fri-Sun (ex race days). (1990 prices)
Credit cards ①②③④⑤

An attractively decorated hotel providing a high standard of food, service and hospitality. All seventy bedrooms have private bath or shower rooms and colour television, with some rooms set aside for non-smokers.

ROTHERHAM   South Yorkshire   *Map 8 SK49*

★★69% **Brentwood** Moorgate Road S60 2TY ☎ (0709) 382772

Normal price: £32.50
Short breaks: £17.50 excluding dinner. Fri-Sun.
Credit cards ①②③⑤

This stone-built Victorian residence standing in its own grounds has a modern extension housing about half the bedrooms, all of which have colour television and most with private bath or shower, including one with a four-poster bed.

★★★66% **Rotherham Moat House** (Queens Moat) Moorgate Road S60 2BG ☎ (0709) 364902

Normal price: £68 (room only)
Short breaks: £39. Min 2 nights, Fri-Sun.
Credit cards ① ② ③ ④ ⑤

Close to the town centre and motorways, this modern hotel has comfortable, well-equipped bedrooms, all with ensuite facilities and colour television, including family and no-smoking rooms. The leisure facilities include a sauna, solarium, gymnasium and jacuzzi.

SHEFFIELD   South Yorkshire   Map 8 SK38

★★★65% **Beauchief** 161 Abbeydale Road S7 2QW ☎ (0742) 620500

Normal price: £88 room and breakfast. Dinner from £14 and à la carte
Short breaks: £28 excluding dinner. Fri-Sun.
🦅 Credit cards ① ② ③ ⑤

An original coaching inn, pleasantly set amongst trees, has been extended and modernised to provide a good standard of well appointed accommodation; its restaurant is complemented by the popular Michel's Cellar Bar, and pleasant staff create a lively, friendly atmosphere throughout. Good leisure facilities are also provided.

★★★65% **Hallam Tower Post House** (Trusthouse Forte) Manchester Road, Broomhill S10 5DX ☎ (0742) 670067

Normal price: £79-£89 room and breakfast
Short breaks: £38. Min 2 nights, Fri-Sun. (1990 prices)
Credit cards ① ② ③ ④ ⑤

This modern twelve storey hotel is situated in a residential area and has city views. It has an indoor heated pool and a health and fitness centre. Christmas breaks are available.

★★69% **Rutland** 452 Glossop Road, Broomhill S10 2PY ☎ (0742) 664411

Normal price: £60. Dinner £8.95
Short breaks: £70, min 2 nights, Fri-Sun.
Credit cards ① ② ③ ⑤

Seven detached stone houses, interconnected by walkways, form a modern hotel which is popular with business people. Public rooms include a spacious reception lounge with separate public lounge, writing room and a small, intimate restaurant with adjoining cocktail bar. An excellent bedroom annexe is adjacent.

★★★69% **Sheffield Moat House** Chesterfield Road South S8 8BW ☎ (0742) 375376

Normal price: £50. Dinner £11.95-£13 and à la carte
Short breaks: £38, min 2 nights, Mon-Thur. £8 single supplement.
Credit cards ① ② ③ ⑤

Close to the junction of the A61/A6102 ring road, a new hotel offers attractive bedrooms, all with colour television, a well-equipped leisure centre and extensive facilities for meetings. Efficient room service is provided by friendly staff.

★★★65% **Swallow** Kenwood Road S7 1NQ ☎ (0742) 583811

Normal price: £86. Dinner from £15 and à la carte
Short breaks: £96, Fri-Sun, includes Sunday lunch. Single supplement.
Credit cards ① ② ③ ⑤

A modern hotel situated in its own grounds, close to the city centre. Recently updated public rooms offer comfort and relaxation in pleasant surroundings.

THORNE   South Yorkshire   *Map 8 SE61*

★★67% **Belmont** Horsefair Green DN8 5EE ☎ (0405) 812320

Normal price: £50.50 room and breakfast. Dinner £8.95.
Short breaks: £17.95, min 2 nights, Thu-Sun. Single price
£22.95.
Activity breaks: Swimming and Skating Breaks, £21.95 per
night and weekend.
Credit cards ① ③

A friendly hotel near the town centre offering
good value for money.

TODWICK   South Yorkshire   *Map 8 SK48*

★★★67% **Red Lion** (Lansbury) Worksop Road S31 0DJ ☎ (0909) 771654

Normal price: £82 room and breakfast. Dinner from £14.25
and à la carte
Short breaks: £28 excluding dinner. Fri-Sun
✶ (ex guide dogs) Credit cards ① ② ③ ⑤

A roadside inn offers comfortable accommodation just a short distance from junction 31 of
the M1. All bedrooms have ensuite facilities
and colour television, one has a four-poster bed,
and there are rooms for non-smokers.
Christmas breaks are available.

▦ YORKSHIRE, WEST ▦

BATLEY   West Yorkshire   *Map 8 SE22*

★★65% **Alder House** Towngate Road, off Healey Lane WF17 7HR ☎ (0924) 444777

Normal price: £32. Dinner £10.95-£12.50 and à la carte
Short breaks: £23 excluding dinner. Fri-Sun
Credit cards ① ② ③

A handsome Georgian house dating back to
1730, yet fitted with all today's modern
comforts. All the bedrooms have colour
television, and most have ensuite facilities.
There is one family room.

BRADFORD   West Yorkshire   *Map 7 SE13*

GH QQ **Maple Hill** 3 Park Drive, Heaton BD9 4DP ☎ (0274) 544061

Normal price: £25-£30.
Short breaks: £23-£28 excluding dinner. Single price £34-
£39.
Activity breaks: Celebration Break/Honeymoon, £33-£42
including complimentary celebration toast, 4-poster bed
and breakfast in bed.
Credit cards ① ③

Large comfortable Victorian house with many
original features.

★★★57% **Novotel Bradford** Merrydale Road, BD4 6SA (3m S adjacent to M606) ☎ (0274) 683683

Normal price: £35
Short breaks: £20 excluding dinner. Single £30. Min 2
nights, Fri-Sun

This functional modern hotel offers basic but
clean accommodation. All the bedrooms have
ensuite bath or shower rooms and colour
television, and there are special facilities for
children.

GH QQQ Park Drive 12 Park Drive BD9 4DR ☎ (0274) 480194

Normal price: £22.50 Fri-Sun; £26.50 Mon-Thu
Short breaks: £29.50 Fri-Sun; £33 Mon-Thu. Min 2 nights.
No single supplement at weekends
🏌 Credit cards ① ② ③

Ensuite facilities and colour television are provided in all bedrooms at this comfortable guest house. There is one family room.

★★★★52% **Stakis Norfolk Gardens** Hall Ings BD1 5SH ☎ (0274) 734734

Normal price: £105 room only. Dinner £16.50 and à la carte
Short breaks: £29 excluding dinner (1990 price). Min 2 nights. Single supplement
Credit cards ① ② ③ ④ ⑤

A modern city centre hotel offering good-value buffet meals in addition to the à la carte menu. All the bedrooms have private bath or shower rooms and colour television, and over half the bedrooms are for non-smokers. There is a special Christmas programme.

BRIGHOUSE   West Yorkshire   Map 7 SE12

★★★★62% **Forte** (Trusthouse Forte) Clifton Village HD6 4HW ☎ (0484) 400400

Normal price: £111 room only. Dinner from £17.
Short breaks: £54. Min 2 nights, Thu-Sun. Must include Sat.
Activity breaks: 'Ashley Jackson' Painting Weekends.
Details from hotel.
Credit cards ① ② ③ ④ ⑤

A new hotel built of York stone to blend in with the environment. Bedrooms are comfortable and well-appointed, and there is a health and fitness club.

BOSTON SPA   West Yorkshire   Map 8 SE44

INN QQQ Royal (Berni/Chef & Brewer) High Street LS23 6HT ☎ (0937) 842142

Normal price: £25
Short breaks: £23 excluding dinner. Min 2 nights
🏌 (ex guide dogs) Credit cards ① ② ③ ⑤

The Royal Hotel has nine bedrooms all fitted with ensuite shower rooms and colour television.

HALIFAX   West Yorkshire   Map 7 SE02

★★★73% **Holdsworth House** Holmfield HX2 9TG (3m NW off A629 Keighley Road) ☎ (0422) 240024
Closed 25 & 26 Dec

Normal price: £40. Dinner £18-£25 à la carte
Short breaks: £37.50, Fri-Sun
Credit cards ① ② ③ ⑤

This charming 17th-century house has been extended to provide comfortable accommodation and an intimate restaurant. Each bedroom has a private bath or shower room and colour television, and some rooms have four-poster beds.

★★★67% **Imperial Crown** 42/46 Horton Street HX1 1BR ☎ (0422) 342342

Normal price: £47-£62. Dinner £9.75 and à la carte
Short breaks: £95 for 2 nights including 1 evening meal. Fri-Sun
🏌 Credit cards ① ② ③ ⑤

A comfortable hotel in the centre of town close to the railway station. All the attractive bedrooms have ensuite facilities and colour television. There is a special Christmas programme.

HAWORTH   West Yorkshire   Map 7 SE03

GH QQQ Ferncliffe Hebden Road BD22 8RS ☎ (0535) 43405

Normal price: £40 room and breakfast, £58 with dinner
Short breaks: £46 for 2 people. Single £23. Min 2 nights,
Fri-Sun, Nov-Feb
Credit cards ③

In an elevated position overlooking the Worth Valley this modern house offers bedrooms with private shower and colour television.

★★★58% **Five Flags** (Consort) Cullingworth BD13 5EA ☎ (0274) 834188 & 834594

Normal price: £77.50 weekdays, £63.50 weekends
Short breaks: £25. Single £31
Credit cards ① ② ③ ⑤

A stone building set in a moorland location yet close to Halifax, Keighley and Bradford. Two styles of dining are provided and bedrooms are spacious and well-furnished.

★★64% **Old White Lion** 6 West Lane BD22 8DU ☎ (0535) 42313

Normal price: £42.50 room. Dinner £8-£8.50 and à la carte
Short breaks: £40 for 2 nights including 1 evening meal.
Fri-Mon
🛪 (ex guide dogs)

This stone-built coaching inn has ensuite bedrooms with colour television and tea/coffee making facilities. Christmas breaks are available.

HEBDEN BRIDGE   West Yorkshire   Map 7 SD92

★★67% **Hebden Lodge** (Exec Hotel) New Road HX7 8AD ☎ (0422) 845272
Closed 23-29 Dec

Normal price: £27.50. Dinner £13-£16 à la carte
Short breaks: £37.75. Min 2 nights. Special single rates
available Fri-Sun only
Credit cards ① ② ③

Set in the town centre, close to Rochdale Canal, this family-owned hotel offers comfortable accommodation and a warm welcome. All bedrooms are ensuite with colour television. No parking on the premises.

HUDDERSFIELD   West Yorkshire   Map 7 SE11

★★★61% **Briar Court** Halifax Road, Birchencliffe HD3 3NT ☎ (0484) 519902

Normal price: from £76 room and breakfast. Dinner from
£11.50 and à la carte
Short breaks: £25 excluding dinner. Fri-Sun
🛪 (ex guide dogs) Credit cards ① ② ③ ⑤

A busy, modern hotel near junction 24 of the M62 leading into town. Each bedroom has a private bath or shower room and colour television. A feature of the hotel is the Italian restaurant, renowned for its traditional pizzas.

★★★67% **Pennine Hilton National** (Hilton) HD3 3RH ☎ (0422) 375431

Normal price: £54.95.
Short breaks: £37 excluding dinner. Min 2 nights.
Activity breaks: Hang Gliding, £110 (1990 price) including
two day course with tuition, first flights through to
tethered flights and first solo flight. Knitting Weekend and
Photography Breaks, details from hotel.
🛪 Credit cards ① ② ③ ⑤

Situated just off the M62 at junction 24, this well-furnished modern hotel provides a high standard of comfort and service.

ILKLEY   West Yorkshire   Map 7 SE13

★★★58% **Cow & Calf** Moor Top LS29 8BT ☎ (0943) 607335
Normal price: £32.50. Dinner £13.50 and à la carte
Short breaks: £40 (1990). Min 2 nights
Credit cards [1] [2] [3] [4] [5]

This family-owned hotel is situated on the moor and overlooks the town. It offers efficient service, comfortable accommodation and well-cooked food.

★★76% **Rombalds** 11 West View, Wells Road LS29 9JG ☎ (0943) 603201
Closed 28-30 Dec
Normal price: £42.50. Dinner £17-£25 à la carte
Short breaks: £57-£63, single £68-£82. Min 2 nights, Nov-Aug
Credit cards [1] [2] [3] [5]

A personally-supervised hotel offering comfortable accommodation, friendly service and imaginative food. Bedrooms are all ensuite with colour television. Christmas breaks are available.

KILDWICK   West Yorkshire   Map 7 SE04

★★★60% **Kildwick Hall** BD20 9AE ☎ (0535) 632244
Normal price: £80-£95 room and breakfast
Short breaks: £98-£117 for 2 nights (1990 prices)
Credit cards [1] [2] [3]

A splendid Jacobean manor house, set above the village, with an attractive beamed foyer lounge with an inglenook fireplace. Bedrooms are individually decorated, two have four-poster beds, and all are ensuite with colour television. Christmas breaks are available. See advertisement on p315.

LEEDS   West Yorkshire   Map 8 SE33

★★★★64% **Hilton International** Neville Street LS1 4BX ☎ (0532) 442000
Normal price: £64. Dinner £16 and à la carte
Short breaks: £21 excluding dinner. Min 2 nights, Thu-Sun
Credit cards [1] [2] [3] [5]

A comfortable city-centre hotel offering a very good value buffet in the restaurant. Each bedroom has a private bathroom and colour television, and there are rooms for non-smokers and families.

★★★65% **Parkway** (Embassy) Otley Road LS16 1AG ☎ (0532) 672551
Normal price: £79-£95 room.
Short breaks: £41, min 2 nights including Sat.
Activity breaks: Leisure Learning, details from hotel.
✕ Credit cards [1] [2] [3] [4] [5]

Situated on the A660 just one mile north of the ring road, this hotel offers a choice of restaurants and new leisure facilities.

★★★★61% **Queen's** (Trusthouse Forte) City Square LS1 1PL ☎ (0532) 431323
Normal price: £62. Dinner £13-£14 and à la carte
Short breaks: £40. Min 2 nights, Thu-Sun (must include Sat) (except Xmas & New Year)
Credit cards [1] [2] [3] [4] [5]

A large city centre hotel standing next to the station. It offers well-equipped bedrooms with ensuite bath or shower room and colour television; some rooms are for non-smokers. Christmas breaks are available. There is no parking on the premises.

NORTHOWRAM   West Yorkshire   *Map 7 SE12*

FH QQ Royd (SE107268) Hall Lane HX3 7SN ☎ (0422) 206718

Normal price: £10.
Short breaks: £15, min 2 nights except Sunday. Includes buffet or packed lunch.
Activity breaks: Horse riding, £25 including two-hour ride and buffet lunch. Not Mondays.

This simple farmhouse is found in a quiet lane close to the village, and is personally run by the resident owners.

OTLEY   West Yorkshire   *Map 8 SE24*

★★★66% **Chevin Lodge** Yorkgate LS21 3NU ☎ (0943) 467818

Normal price: £39. Dinner £13.75 and à la carte (1990 price)
Short breaks: £44.75. Min 2 nights, Fri-Sun. £10 single supplement.
Credit cards ① ② ③

Standing in 50 acres of birchwood, this Scandinavian-style hotel has well-equipped ensuite bedrooms with colour television, including some family rooms. The restaurant has a choice of menus and leisure facilities include sauna, solarium, cycling, fishing and children's activities. Christmas breaks are available.

SOWERBY BRIDGE   West Yorkshire   *Map 7 SE02*

★★72% **Hobbit** Hob Lane, Norlands HX6 3QL ☎ (0422) 832202

Normal price: £33.50. Dinner £9.95-£12.95.
Short breaks: £29.50, min 2 nights, Fri-Sun. £6 single supplement.
🛪 Credit cards ① ② ③ ⑤

A charming stone built country inn set on a hillside overlooking the town. It offers delightful bedrooms, a good standard of cooking and friendly service.

WAKEFIELD   West Yorkshire   *Map 8 SE32*

★★★65% **Cedar Court** Denby Dale Road, Calder Grove WF4 3QZ ☎ (0924) 276310

Normal price: £47.50. Dinner £13.50.
Short breaks: £43.75, min 2 nights, Fri-Sun. Single supplement.
Activity breaks: Details from hotel.
Credit cards ① ② ③ ⑤

A large modern hotel situated close to the M1 at junction 39, with a choice of restaurants offering English, French and Italian cuisine.

★★★61% **Post House** (Trusthouse Forte) Queen's Drive, Ossett WF5 9BE ☎ (0924) 276388

Normal price: £39 room. Dinner £13.50 and à la carte
Short breaks: £41. Min 2 nights, Fri-Sun
Credit cards ① ② ③ ④ ⑤

A comfortable, modern hotel situated just off the M1 at junction 40. Bedrooms are well-furnished and have ensuite facilities, some rooms are set aside for non-smokers. There is a special Christmas programme.

★★★61% **Swallow** Queens Street WF1 1JV ☎ (0924) 372111

Normal price: £39. Dinner from £13.50.
Short breaks: £40. Min 2 nights, including one lunch. Mon-Thu
Activity breaks: Sailing Breaks, £120 Easter to Oct. Windsurfing Breaks, £120, Easter-Oct.
Credit cards ① ② ③ ⑤

A popular city-centre hotel with friendly service.

★★★63% **Waterton Park** (Consort) Walton Hall, The Balk, Walton WF2 6PW (3m SE off B6378)
☎ (0924) 257911

Normal price: £62 room and breakfast. Dinner £14.25 and à la carte
Short breaks: £45, min 2 nights, Fri-Sun
✘ Credit cards ① ② ③ ⑤

An unusual converted country house set in a nature reserve at the centre of a lake. Very good leisure facilities include boating, fishing and an indoor heated pool. Some bedrooms have four-poster beds, and all are ensuite with colour television. There are special Christmas breaks.

WETHERBY   West Yorkshire   *Map 8 SE44*

★★★57% **Penguin** Leeds Road LS22 5HE (junc A1/A58) ☎ (0937) 63881

Normal price: £42.50 room. Dinner £10-£30.
Short breaks: £30 excluding dinner. Min 2 nights, Fri-Sun. Single supplement.
Activity breaks: Off-site Paintballing Breaks, Clay Pigeon Shooting, Archery and Hot Air Ballooning. Details from hotel.
Credit cards ① ② ③ ⑤

A modern hotel with good facilities, bars and restaurants, conveniently situated near the A1.

★★★(Red) 🏨 **Wood Hall** (Select) Trip Lane, Linton LS22 4JA ☎ (0937) 67271

Normal price: £52.50. Dinner from £29.50 and à la carte
Short breaks: £75, £35 single occupancy. Min 2 nights, Fri-Sun (except Xmas & New Year)
Credit cards ① ② ③ ④ ⑤

A palatial Yorkshire mansion set in extensive grounds, offering warm hospitality, luxurious accommodation and delectable food. There are facilities for snooker and fishing. Christmas breaks are available.

CHANNEL ISLANDS

▪ JERSEY ▪

ARCHIRONDEL   *Jersey   Map 16*

★★67% **Les Arches** Archirondel Bay ☎ (0534) 53839

Normal price: £55-£78 room and breakfast.
Short breaks: £82 for 2 nights including car hire. Nov-Mar. Single supplement.
Activity breaks: Christmas & New Year Break, £410 for 8 nights including full board from 24-27 & 31 Dec, half board 28-30 Dec, and car hire. Details from hotel.
Credit cards ① ③ ④

A popular and lively hotel with nightclub, offers a choice of modern bedrooms with views of sea, pool or rear garden. There are extensive leisure facilities.

GOREY   *Jersey   Map 16*

★★64% **Moorings** Gorey Pier ☎ (0534) 53633

Normal price: £35.50. Dinner £13-£30
Short breaks: £93, 2 nights including car hire, Nov-Mar (1990 prices)
Credit cards ① ② ③ ④

This small hotel has a long-established restaurant specialising in seafood. Some of the bedrooms overlook the harbour, all have private facilities and colour television. There is a special Christmas programme.

ROZEL BAY   Jersey   Map 16

★★★76% **Chateau La Chaire** Rozel Valley ☎ (0534) 63354

Normal price: £42.50. Dinner £18-£24 and à la carte (1990 price)
Short breaks: from £82 including return flights based on south coast airports and use of hire car. Min 3 nights, Nov-Mar except Christmas/New Year
✻ (ex guide dogs) Credit cards ① ② ③ ⑤

This peaceful and hospitable country house hotel serves good food in the attractive restaurant and has comfortable bedrooms, including a family room and one with a four-poster bed, all with private bathrooms and colour television. No children under 7 are accommodated. Christmas breaks are available.

ST HELIER   Jersey   Map 16

★★★62% **Apollo** St Saviours Road ☎ (0534) 25441

Normal price: £34-£40. Dinner from £8.50
Short breaks: from £25 (1990 prices) Min 2 nights, Fri-Sun, Nov-Mar (except Xmas)

Built around its own quiet courtyard in the heart of St Helier, the Apollo has bright modern bedrooms with private baths and colour television. There is an attractive indoor leisure centre, and a special Christmas programme is available.

★★★63% **Beaufort** Green Street ☎ (0534) 32471

Normal price: £36.50-£40.50. Dinner from £9.50
Short breaks: from £27 (1990 prices) Min 2 nights, Oct-Mar (except Xmas)
✻

Nicely decorated throughout, this hotel has comfortable public rooms, friendly staff and an indoor swimming pool. All the bedrooms have ensuite facilities and colour television. There is a special Christmas programme.

GH QQQ Cornucopia Mont Pinel ☎ (0534) 32646

Normal price: from £19.25, from £26.75 with dinner
Short breaks: from £24.25 with dinner. Single £27.50 Min 3 nights
Credit cards ① ② ③

All bedrooms at this small hotel have ensuite bath or shower room and colour television, and there are family rooms. Leisure amenities include an outdoor heated swimming pool and games room and there are special facilities for children.

★★★★59% **Grand** The Esplanade ☎ (0534) 22301

Normal price: £110 room and breakfast. Dinner £14.50-£17.50 and à la carte.
Short breaks: £61, min 2 nights.
Credit cards ① ② ③ ⑤

The hotel stands facing the sea and offers comfortable public areas and bedrooms varying in style. The restaurant provides a good selection of interesting dishes making it popular with locals, and there is a comprehensive selection of leisure facilities.

QQQ Runnymede Court 46/52 Roseville Street ☎ (0534) 20044

Normal price: £19
Short breaks: 20% reduction, mid Feb-27 April & 6 Oct-mid-Dec.
✻ Credit cards ① ② ③

This extensively refurbished hotel offers a choice of comfortable well-equipped bedrooms, some of which are situated around the rear garden. The beach and shopping centre are within easy reach.

ST LAWRENCE   Jersey   Map 16

★★★74% **Littlegrove** Rue de Hant ☎ (0534) 25321

Normal price: £53.50 (winter) – £71.25 (summer). Dinner £22.50 and à la carte.
Short breaks: £55.50 min 2 nights, 22nd Oct-Easter. Single supplement.
🛪 Credit cards ① ② ③ ⑤

A delightful hotel run in the country house style, with attractive cosy lounges and bar and an elegant restaurant. Interesting and enjoyable food is served in the restaurant, and the staff are polite and attentive throughout the hotel.

ST PETER   Jersey   Map 16

★★★60% **Mermaid** ☎ (0534) 41255

Normal price: £33.50-£41.50. Dinner from £10
Short breaks: £35 half board, weekends only. Min 2 nights, Nov-Mar (except Xmas) (1990 prices)
🛪

Eighteen acres of grounds and gardens surround this hotel which has an extensive range of leisure facilities including an indoor heated swimming pool and an 18-hole golf course. All the bedrooms have private bath and colour television. There is a special Christmas programme.

ST SAVIOUR   Jersey   Map 16

✿★★★★(Red) **Longueville Manor** off St Helier/Grouville Road ☎ (0534) 25501
(Rosette awarded for dinner only)
Normal price: from £52. Dinner £21.50 and à la carte.
Short breaks: £55 (approx), min 2 nights if at a weekend mid Oct-mid Mar, includes a hire car. £15 single supplement.
Credit cards ① ② ③ ⑤

A magnificent part 13th-century hotel which has been sympathetically extended by the present owners. Individually styled bedrooms reflect the good taste shown throughout the hotel, with a welcome attention to detail. Service throughout is highly professional and refreshingly hospitable.

▪ GUERNSEY ▪

FERMAIN BAY   Guernsey   Map 16

★★★63% **La Favorita** ☎ (0481) 35666

Normal price: from £25. Dinner £9.50-£14.
Short breaks: from £30, or £155 for 2 nights, including hire car and return travel from Southampton Airport. Mar-Nov.
Activity breaks: Clay Pigeon Shooting Breaks, £280 (1989). Details from hotel.
🛪 Credit cards ① ③

This privately owned hotel overlooking the bay has been upgraded to a good standard, with some particularly fine public rooms.

PERELLE   Guernsey   Map 16

★★★66% **L'Atlantique** Perelle Bay ☎ (0481) 64056

Normal price: £36. Dinner from £7.25 and à la carte (1990 price)
Short breaks: £200 for 3 nights, Oct-May (except Xmas & Easter), including free car hire and UK flights to and from Southampton.
🛪 (ex guide dogs) Credit cards ① ② ③ ⑤

Overlooking the bay and standing in well-kept gardens with a swimming pool, this modern hotel serves good, varied food and has bright, well-equipped bedrooms, all ensuite and with colour television. Christmas breaks are available.

ST PETER PORT   Guernsey   Map 16

★★★60% **La Collinette** St Jacques ☎ (0481) 710331

Normal price: £25, Nov-end Mar. Dinner £8.50
Short breaks: £120 for 2 people, 2 nights, Nov-end Mar,
excluding Christmas. This includes flights and free hire
car and champagne breakfast.
🎄 Credit cards ⊡ ② ③ ⑤

This friendly, informal hotel under the personal
supervision of the owner, provides modestly
furnished, well-equipped bedrooms and
attentive service. There is a good selection of
leisure facilities.

★★★64% **Moore's** Pollet ☎ (0481) 24452

Normal price: £26. Dinner £10-£12 and à la carte.
Short breaks: £34.50 Fri-Sun, Nov-mid Dec 1991 & Jan-Mar
1992.
Credit cards ⊡ ② ③ ④ ⑤

Situated on the attractive shopping street of Le
Pollet, this Georgian building has undergone
extensive refurbishment. It offers bright, well-
equipped bedrooms and an attractive verandah
restaurant and coffee shop.

ST MARTIN   Guernsey   Map 16

★★★50% **St Martin's Country** Les Merrerimes ☎ (0481) 35644

Normal price: £26.50. Dinner from £7.75 and à la carte.
Short breaks: £23, min 2 nights, Apr & Oct.
Credit cards ⊡ ② ③ ④ ⑤

The hotel is set in 15 acres of grounds and
offers an assortment of bedrooms all furnished
in a contemporary fashion with varying
degrees of comfort. There is a good selection of
recreational facilities.

▪ MAN, ISLE OF ▪

CASTLETOWN   Man, Isle of   Map 6 SC26

★★★63% **Castletown Golf Links** (Best Western) Fort Island ☎ (0624) 822201

Normal price: £73.50. Dinner £14.50-£17.50.
Short breaks: £62.50, min 2 nights. Single supplement.
Activity breaks: Golf Breaks, details from hotel.
Credit cards ⊡ ② ③ ⑤

Popular with golfers because it stands beside
the Castletown golf links, on the edge of
Derryhaven Bay and close to the airport.

A short break is everybody's due. If yours is overdue visit the Isle of Man.

Escape to the Isle of Man and you will enjoy a delightful journey back through time. Set like a rare gem in the Irish Sea, the Island is close but far from everyday cares. There are fewer cars, fewer crowds and more unspoiled scenery, not to mention glorious anachronisms like steam trains and electric and horse-drawn trams. And uncrowded country walks, seven uncrowded golf courses, deserted beaches and cheerful pubs with real local ale.

You'll find a gentler pace of life and warm friendly welcome the moment you set foot on this magic Island, as well as things to see and do that you won't find together anywhere else.

Come. The Manx people are waiting to welcome you.

Start planning now. Then book with the Isle of Man holiday specialists, Everymann Holidays, on 0624 629914 or your local Travel Agent.

Free brochures available.

ISLE of MAN

DOUGLAS   Man, Isle of   Map 6 SC37

★★★64% **Sefton** Harris Promenade ☎ (0624) 26011

Normal price: £25. Dinner £12.50.
Short breaks: from £89 including return air fare from hotel. Min 2 nights, Thu-Sun, except 1st & 2nd week Jun. Single supplement of £10.
Activity breaks: Golf Breaks, £150 for 2 nights including flights and 2 day's golf, Thu-Sun. Theatre Weekends, £135 for 2 nights including flights, theatre tickets, refreshments and tour. Victorian Transport Weekends, £140 for 2 nights including flights, transport and picnic, weekends May-Sept.
✶ Credit cards ① ② ③ ⑤

Overlooking Douglas Bay from its seafront position, this comfortable hotel offers excellent leisure facilities.

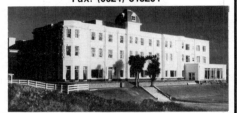
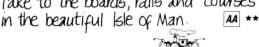

RAMSEY Man, Isle of Map 6 SC49

★★★★61% **Grand Island** Bride Road ☎ (0624) 812455

Normal price: from £74 room and breakfast.
Short breaks: £40. Min 2 nights, Nov-Easter.
🐥 (ex guide dogs) Credit cards ①②③⑤

This friendly hotel has an elegant restaurant with superb views and extremely comfortable bedrooms, including a few family rooms, all ensuite with colour television. The extensive leisure facilities include indoor swimming, snooker, sauna, steam room, solarium, gymnasium, croquet, horse riding and clay-pigeon shooting. Christmas breaks are available.

SCOTLAND

■ BORDERS ■

KELSO Borders Map 12 NT73

★★★60% **Cross Keys** (Exec Hotel) 36-37 The Square TD5 7UL ☎ (0573) 23303

Normal price: £23.50-£26
Short breaks: £22. Min 2 nights
Credit cards ①②③⑤

One of Scotland's oldest coaching inns, this attractive hotel overlooks Kelso's cobbled square. All bedrooms have ensuite facilities and colour television.

★★★ ♨ 76% **Sunlaws House** Heiton TD5 8JZ (2m SW A698) ☎ (05735) 331

Normal price: £107-£120. Dinner £22.50.
Short breaks: £125 Apr-May, £140 Jul-Aug. Min 2 nights. Single supplement.
Activity breaks: Fishing Breaks, £130 for 2 nights, Feb-Aug. Falconry Breaks, £330 for 3 nights. Children's Falconry Weekends, £90-£280. Clay Shooting Breaks, £130 for 2 nights. All 1990 prices. Details from hotel.
🐥

An impressive country house situated 3 miles west of the town amidst woodland and well tended gardens. Owned by the Duke of Roxburgh, the hotel has sporting facilities.

MELROSE Borders (Roxburghshire) Map 12 NT53

★★64% **Burt's** The Square TD6 9PN ☎ (089682) 2285

Normal price: £30. Dinner £12.50-£16 (1990 price)
Short breaks: £42 (£45 for single room), including £14 dinner allowance. Min 2 nights. Not available Easter, 2nd weekend Apr, Christmas & New Year.
Credit cards ①②③⑤

This converted 18th-century town house of architectural interest includes a snooker room and nearby shooting and fishing facilities. All bedrooms have private bath or shower and colour television.

PEEBLES Borders (Peeblesshire) Map 11 NT24

★★ ♨ 77% **Cringletie House** EH45 8PL ☎ (07213) 233

Normal price: £36, £56 including dinner.
Short breaks: £47, min 2 nights. 9 Mar-10 May, 20 Oct-20 Dec. Rest of Year: £53, min 2 nights; £50.50, min 5 nights.
Credit cards ①③

This friendly, family-run country house hotel with romantic turrets and gables serves good traditional food, and all bedrooms have ensuite facilities and colour television. The garden includes hard-court tennis, putting and croquet facilities.

★★★58% **Park** Innerleithen Road EH45 8BA ☎ (0721) 20451

Normal price: from £37. Dinner £12.75-£19.25.
Short breaks: £100.25 for 2 nights including one bar lunch.
Min 2 nights. Single supplement.
Activity breaks: Walk & Cycle Breaks, from £111.25 for 3
nights. Golfing Breaks, from £82 for 2 nights. Fisherman's
Breaks, £35 for 1 night, Oct-Nov. Celebration Break, from
£92.75 for 2 nights.
Credit cards ① ② ③ ⑤

A town centre hotel set in attractive gardens
with pleasant views over the surrounding
countryside. Guests can use the sports and
leisure facilities at the nearby Hydro.

★★★64% **Peebles Hydro** (Consort) EH45 8LX ☎ (0721) 20602

Normal price: from £41.
Short breaks: from £36, min 2 nights, Sun-Thu, Nov-Mar.
Single supplement.
Activity breaks: Walk the Borders Break, £97-£101.50 for 2
nights Mar-Jun & Aug-Oct. A go-as-you-please walking
holiday throush some of the breathtakingly beautiful
countryside of the Borders including a detailed map of the
area and a picnic. Drive Away, £135-£159 for 3 nights, Mar-
Oct, including two full days of golf.
✻

Majestically placed above the town, this elegant
Edwardian hotel has a swimming pool, tennis
courts and a putting green. The supervised
play rooms will appeal to young families.

★★ 🏰 62% **Venlaw Castle** Edinburgh Road EH45 8QG ☎ (0721) 20384

Normal price: £26. Dinner £11.50-£12.50 (1990 price)
Short breaks: £34. Min 2 nights, Apr-Jun, Sep-Oct.
Credit cards ① ② ④ ⑤

Set on a wooded hillside, this country house
hotel in a converted baronial-style castle has
fine views and most of the bedrooms, which
include family rooms, have ensuite facilities; all
have colour television.

ST BOSWELLS   Borders (Roxburghshire)   Map 12 NT53

★★64% **Buccleuch Arms** The Green TD6 0EW ☎ (0835) 22243

Normal price: £32.50. Dinner from £11.25.
Short breaks: £35, min 2 nights. Single price £37.50.
Activity breaks: Fishing, Golf and Shooting Breaks, details
from hotel.
Credit cards ① ② ③ ⑤

A red sandstone hotel on the A68 beside the
village cricket ground with a secluded garden.
Arrangements can be made for guests who
want to hunt, shoot and fish.

WALKERBURN Borders (Peeblesshire) Map 11 NT33

★★ 🏌 66% **Tweed Valley** (Inter Hotels) Galashiels Road EH43 6AA ☎ (089687) 636

Normal price: £47.50 including dinner.
Short breaks: £42 May-Sept. Min 2 nights. Single supplement.
Activity breaks: Salmon Fishing Break, Feb-Nov. Trout Fishing Apr-Sept. Fishing Tuition 10 weeks Apr-Jul, 4 weeks Sept. (Fishing in the Tweed Valley). Walk leaders can be arranged. Art Courses, Sketching, Oils and Watercolours, spring. Golf Packages. Photographic & Archaeology Weekends, spring. Bird Watching and Walking. 1991 prices and details from hotel.
Credit cards [1] [3]

A privately owned and managed hotel with an attractive wood-panelled dining room, which has been recently refurbished.

■ CENTRAL ■

ARDEONAIG Central (Perthshire) Map 11 NN63

★★57% **Ardeonaig** South Loch Tayside FK21 8SU ☎ (05672) 400

Normal price: £37. Dinner £15-£18.
Short breaks: £35, min 2 nights.
Activity breaks: Salmon Fishing, Jan 15-Oct 15. Trout Fishing, Mar 13-Oct 6. Clay Pigeon Shooting, Jan-Nov. Grouse Shooting, Aug-Oct. Prices on application.
Credit cards [1] [2] [3] [5]

A family-run hotel peacefully situated on the south shore of Loch Tay, formerly a coaching inn and still retaining its original character. Modest bedrooms being upgraded.

BRIDGE OF ALLAN Central (Stirlingshire) Map 11 NS79

★★★62% **Royal** Henderson Street FK9 4HG ☎ (0786) 832284

Normal price: £69-£80 room with breakfast. Dinner £15.25-£17.25 & à la carte
Short breaks: £42.50 Min 2 nights, Fri-Sun, Oct-Apr
Credit cards [1] [2] [3] [5]

Right in the centre of town, this hotel has a smart restaurant and bedrooms each with private facilities and colour television. A special Christmas programme is available.

CALLANDER Central (Perthshire) Map 11 NN60

★59% **Pinewood** Leny Road FK17 8AP ☎ (0877) 30111

Normal price: £17.50-£20. Dinner £12.50-£13.50.
Short breaks: £15.75-£18, excluding dinner. Nov-May except Christmas & New Year period.
Activity breaks: Fishing, Shooting, Walking and Cycling Breaks arranged to order.
Credit cards [1] [2] [3]

A family-run hotel set in its own grounds beside the main road on the edge of town, offering a friendly atmosphere, comfortable public rooms and functional bedrooms.

★★★ ⚓ 68% **Roman Camp** FK17 8BG ☎ (0877) 30003

Normal price: £164
Short breaks: £116.66. Min 3 nights, Apr-Oct
Credit cards ①②③⑤

This delightful hotel, set in twenty acres of grounds, offers elegant and comfortable accommodation. Bedrooms are individual in shape, style and size, all have ensuite facilities and colour television and one is furnished with a four-poster bed. Guests can enjoy fishing and croquet and there is a special Christmas programme.

DUNBLANE   Central (Perthshire)   Map 11 NN70

✳★★★(Red) ⚓ **Cromlix House** (Pride of Britain) Kinbuck FK15 9JT (3m NE B8033) ☎ (0786) 822125

Normal price: £100 including dinner.
Short breaks: £125-£150 including lunch and tea. 15 Oct-15 Mar. Single price £75 weekdays, £95 weekends.
Activity breaks: Clay Pigeon Shooting, £45 extra per day. Game Shooting, from £90 extra per day, 12 Aug-31 Jan. Trout Fishing, £16 extra per day, 15 Mar-6 Oct. Salmon & Sea Trout Fishing, £16 extra per day, 15 Mar-31 Oct.
Credit cards ①②③⑤

A charming Victorian and Edwardian country house with fine prints and paintings, porcelain, silver and other antiques much in evidence. Set in a beautiful 5,000-acre family estate.

POLMONT   Central (Stirlingshire)   Map 11 NS97

★★★62% **Inchyra Grange** (Best Western) Grange Road FK2 0YB ☎ (0324) 711911

Normal price: £42.50-£55
Short breaks: £40-£45 excluding dinner. Min 2 nights, Fri-Sun.
Credit cards ①②③⑤

This much extended country house has well-equipped bedrooms, all ensuite with colour television, and extensive leisure facilities which include an indoor swimming pool, snooker, sauna, solarium, gymnasium, jacuzzi, steam room and beauty therapy room.

STRATHBLANE   Central (Stirlingshire)   Map 11 NS57

★★66% **Kirkhouse Inn** (Minotels) G63 9AA ☎ (0360) 70621

Normal price: £50 including dinner.
Short breaks: £37.50, min 2 nights, Fri-Sun.
Activity breaks: Golf, Fishing and Shooting Breaks, details from hotel.
Credit cards ①②③⑤

A friendly, hospitable roadside inn at the foot of the Campsie Fells. The hotel features a restaurant with a very good local reputation serving mainly continental cuisine.

■ DUMFRIES & GALLOWAY ■

ANNAN   Dumfries & Galloway (Dumfriesshire)   Map 11 NY16

★★65% **Warmanbie** DG12 5LL ☎ (04612) 4015

Normal price: £59.90 room and breakfast. Dinner from £12.95
Short breaks: Weekender Breaks £31.50-£42.50, single £45.50-£54.75. Min 2 nights, must include Sat. Inflation Beater: 5 nights bed and breakfast for the price of 3. 15 Nov-30 Mar. Not available for single rooms
Credit cards ①②③

A modernised country house, on the outskirts of town, run in an informal manner. There are seven bedrooms all with ensuite facilities and colour television. With its own stretch of water, the hotel is popular with fishermen, and guests can also enjoy clay pigeon shooting. There is a special Christmas programme.

AUCHENCAIRN   Dumfries & Galloway (Kirkcudbrightshire)   Map 11 NX75

★★★ ♨ 69% **Balcary Bay** DG7 1QZ ☎ (055664) 217 & 311
Closed Nov-Feb

Normal price: from £42. Dinner £16 and à la carte
Short breaks: from £35. Min 2 nights, Mar-May & Oct-Nov
Credit cards ① ③

This delightful hotel has grounds which run down to the water's edge. Bedrooms are bright and airy, all have colour television and most have ensuite bath or shower rooms. There is a snooker table for guests' use.

BEATTOCK   Dumfries & Galloway (Dumfriesshire)   Map 11 NT00

★★59% **Beattock House** DG10 9QB ☎ (06833) 403 & 402

Normal price: from £47.50 room and breakfast
Short breaks: £60 for 2 nights, Nov-20 Dec & 5 Jan-20 Mar. 1990 prices.

This converted Victorian house is family run, and still retains some of its original large washbasins and baths. Some rooms have private showers and colour television and there are two family rooms. There is a small caravan park in the 6-acre grounds, along with fishing and putting.

CARRUTHERSTOWN   Dumfries & Galloway (Dumfriesshire) Map 11 NY17

★★★64% **Hetland Hall** (Best Western) DG1 4JX ☎ (0387) 84201

Normal price: £74 room and breakfast. Dinner £14
Short breaks: £48. £6 single supplement. Min 2 nights
Credit cards ① ② ③ ⑤

A spacious country house providing friendly, informal service. Each bedroom has an ensuite bath or shower room and colour television, with rooms set aside for families and non-smokers. Leisure amenities include fishing, snooker, badminton and a gymnasium. There is a special Christmas programme.

CASTLE DOUGLAS   Dumfries & Galloway (Kirkcudbrightshire)   Map 11 NX76

★★62% **Imperial** King Street ☎ (0556) 2086 & 3009
Restricted service 25-26 Dec & 1-2 Jan

Normal price: £21. Dinner £7.50-£8.50 and à la carte
Short breaks: £26, single £28.50
Credit cards ① ③

This former coaching inn is situated in the main street and has a popular lounge bar. Most of the bedrooms have private bathrooms, whilst all have colour television. There are facilities for sailing and water-skiing.

COLVEND   Dumfries & Galloway (Kirkcudbrightshire)   Map 11 NX85

★★63% **Clonyard House** DG5 4QW ☎ (055663) 372

Normal price: £39. Dinner £10-£15 à la carte
Short breaks: £30. Min 2 nights, Nov-Mar.

Peacefully situated in seven acres of woodland, this pleasant family-run small hotel has a comfortable bar serving light meals at lunch-time and in the evening. All rooms have colour television and ensuite facilities, and some are situated on the ground floor. There are special facilities for children.

CROSSMICHAEL Dumfries & Galloway (Kirkcudbrightshire) Map 11 NX76

★★ 🏨 59% **Culgruff House** DG7 3BB ☎ (055667) 230
Restricted service Oct-Etr

Normal price: £54 room and breakfast. Dinner £11 and à la carte
Short breaks: £51.50. Min 3 nights
Credit cards ①②③⑤

Genuine warmth and hospitality can be found at this baronial mansion, furnished with many antiques. Some of the bedrooms have ensuite baths and colour television.

DUMFRIES Dumfries & Galloway (Dumfriesshire) Map 11 NX97

★★★66% **Cairndale** (Inter-Hotels) English Street DG1 2DF ☎ (0387) 54111

Normal price: £66. Dinner from £12.95.
Short breaks: £40, min 2 nights.
Activity breaks: Golfing Breaks, £100 for 2 nights including golf on a choice of six courses. Mar-Nov. Scottish Ceilidh Weekends, £80 including dinner/dance and Scottish entertainment night. Apr-Oct.

A traditional hotel with comfortable bedrooms, interesting good value menus and friendly service. Conveniently close to the town centre.

★★★64% **Station** (Consort) 49 Lovers Walk DG1 1LT ☎ (0387) 54316

Normal price: £70 room and breakfast. Dinner £17.50
Short breaks: £65 for 2 people, single £45. Min 2 nights, Fri-Sun.
Credit cards ①②③⑤

Convenient for the station and town centre, this hotel, dating from 1896, provides attractive and comfortable accommodation. All bedrooms are ensuite with colour television.

ESKDALEMUIR Dumfries & Galloway (Dumfriesshire) Map 11 NY29

★★67% **Hart Manor** DG13 0QQ ☎ (03873) 73217
Closed 25 Dec

Normal price: £24
Short breaks: £22 excluding dinner. Min 3 nights

Set in beautiful countryside this small hotel offers courteous, attentive service and good value dinners. Most bedrooms are ensuite with colour television. Fishing is available.

GATEHOUSE OF FLEET   Dumfries & Galloway (Kirkcudbrightshire) Map 11 NX55

★★★★64% **Cally Palace** DG7 2DL ☎ (05574) 341
Closed 3 Jan-Feb

Normal price: £45. Dinner from £16.50
Short breaks: £40 midweek, min 3 nights; £45 weekends, min 2 nights (lunch included at weekends) Mar-May & Oct-Dec

Set in its own grounds, this impressive country house has spacious bedrooms with ensuite bathroom and colour television. Leisure amenities include tennis and fishing, and there is a special Christmas programme. The hotel is popular with family parties.

KIRKBEAN   Dumfries & Galloway (Dumfriesshire)   Map 11 NX95

QQQQ **Cavens House** DG2 8AA ☎ (038788) 234

Normal price: £32
Short breaks: £30, Oct-Mar
Credit cards [1] [3]

A converted licensed mansion house set within acres of gardens and woodland on the Solway Coast. The bedrooms are well furnished and spacious, and the freshly cooked 4-course dinner offers a choice of good value.

KIRKCUDBRIGHT   Dumfries & Galloway (Kirkcudbrightshire)   Map 11 NX65

★★65% **Selkirk Arms** Old High Street DG6 4JG ☎ (0557) 30402

Normal price: from £45. Dinner from £12.50 and à la carte
Short breaks: £42, min 2 nights Christmas and New Year
Credit cards [1] [2] [3] [5]

Dating back to 1770 and reputedly the place where Burns wrote The Selkirk Grace, this popular hotel has been completely refurbished to provide attractive, comfortable bedrooms and public areas. Efficient house keeping ensures good levels of service throughout.

LOCKERBIE   Dumfries & Galloway (Dumfriesshire)   Map 11 NY18

★★64% **Dryfesdale** DG11 2SF ☎ (05762) 2427 and 2121

Normal price: £60 room and breakfast. Dinner £12.50 and à la carte (1990 prices)
Short breaks: £49.50, min 2 nights
Credit cards [1] [2] [3]

A peacefully situated former mansion offering comfortable accommodation, personally managed by the resident proprietors. In the attractive restaurant, guests can enjoy not only well-prepared meals, but also fine views of the surrounding countryside.

★★67% **Queens** Anna Road DG11 2RB ☎ (05762) 2415 and 3005

Normal price: £55 room and breakfast
Short breaks: £65
Credit cards ① ③

Conveniently situated adjacent to the A74, this sturdy Victorian house has been extended and improved to provide well-equipped, modern bedrooms, a leisure complex and conference facilities.

MOFFAT Dumfries & Galloway (Dumfriesshire) Map 11 NT00

QQ Barnhill Springs DG10 9QS ☎ (0683) 20580

Normal price: £12.50-£13.50
Short breaks: £20. Min 3 nights

A quiet and friendly small country house guesthouse offering good plain food. Bedrooms with hot and cold water facilities include a family room.

★★70% **Beechwood Country House** Harthorpe Place DG10 9RS ☎ (0683) 20210

Normal price: £31.15. Dinner £14.95 (1990 price)
Short breaks: £127.50 for 3 nights. Single supplement.
Credit cards ① ② ③

Set on a hillside above the town, this small friendly hotel with a garden and conservatory/lunch room has an imaginative menu and wine list, and mostly spacious bedrooms with private facilities and colour television. Christmas breaks are available.

★★★60% **Moffat House** (Exec Hotel) High Street DG10 9HL ☎ (0683) 20039

Normal price: £30. Dinner £11.50-£19 and à la carte (1990 price)
Short breaks: £35-£38 including £12 dinner allowance. Min 3 nights. Single supplement.
Credit cards ① ② ③ ⑤

This fine 18th-century Adam mansion with a 2¹⁄₂ acre garden provides attentive service and has attractive well-equipped bedrooms, including family rooms, all with private bath or shower and colour television. There are special facilities for children. See advertisement in colour section.

★★70% **Star** 44 High Street DG10 9EF ☎ (0683) 20156

Normal price: £21. Dinner £3.50-£8 (1990 price)
Short breaks: £63-£85 for 3 nights
Credit cards ① ③

This central family-run hotel, reputedly Britain's narrowest, has an attractive dining room and lounge bar. Most of the first-floor bedrooms have colour television and private shower.

❀★77% **Well View** Ballplay Road DG10 9JU ☎ (0683) 20184

Normal price: £35. Dinner £10.50-£13 (1990 price)
Short breaks: £33. Min 3 nights
Credit cards ① ③

This small friendly hotel with a garden includes a family room and no-smoking rooms among the bedrooms, all with colour television and most with private bath or shower; there is also a four-poster bed. Christmas breaks are available.

NEWTON STEWART Dumfries & Galloway (Wigtownshire) Map 10 NX46

★★★57% **Bruce** 88 Queen Street DG8 6JL ☎ (0671) 2294

Normal price: £40. Dinner £12.50-£14.95 (1990 price)
Short breaks: £35 (£40 for single room). Min 2 nights
Credit cards ① ② ③ ⑤

This informal family-run hotel with an attractive lounge bar serves freshly prepared meals and all bedrooms, including 2 family rooms, have private bath and colour television. There is a solarium and gymnasium, nearby golf and special facilities for children.

★★65% **Creebridge House** (Consort) DG8 6NP ☎ (0671) 2121

Normal price: £45. Dinner £12.95-£14.50 (1990 price)
Short breaks: £41. Min 2 nights, except Christmas/New
Year. £10 single supplement.
Credit cards ① ③

This country-house style hotel serves well-prepared dinners and has attractive bedrooms with private bath and colour television, including 2 family rooms. Christmas breaks are available.

PORTPATRICK   Dumfries & Galloway (Wigtownshire)   Map 10 NX05

✿★★(Red) ♨78% **Knockinaam Lodge** (Pride of Britain) DG9 9AD (2m S on unclass rd)
☎ (077681) 471

Normal price: £75-£85 including dinner
Short breaks: 10% off normal tariff for 2 nights; 15% off for 3
or more nights. Min 2 nights, 15 Mar-Gd Fri, Nov-23 Dec.
Credit cards ① ② ③ ⑤

Set in wooded grounds with cliffs on three sides and a private beach, this peaceful out-of-the-way hotel serves outstanding food. The ten bedrooms, one with a four-poster, are all en suite with colour television. Christmas breaks are available.

★★56% **Portpatrick** (Mount Charlotte (TS)) DG8 8TQ ☎ (077681) 333

Normal price: £32.50. Dinner from £11.50.
Short breaks: £37.50, min 2 nights, Mar-Nov. Single
supplement.
Activity breaks: Golf Competitions, £42.50 including green
fees. Every Thu, May-Oct.
Credit cards ① ② ③ ⑤

Large cliff-top resort hotel with good amenities for families with children.

PORT WILLIAM   Dumfries & Galloway (Wigtownshire)   Map 10 NX34

★★★ ♨63% **Corsemalzie House** (Inter-Hotels) DG8 9RL ☎ (098886) 254

Normal price: £48 including dinner.
Short breaks: £44.50 for 2 nights. Single supplement.
Activity breaks: Golf breaks, as short breaks plus free golf.
Game Fishing Breaks, £140 for 3 nights.
Credit cards ① ③

Very peaceful 19th-century country mansion surrounded by extensive wooded grounds. Sporting pursuits can be arranged, and the young staff are friendly and efficient.

POWFOOT   Dumfries & Galloway (Dumfriesshire)   Map 11 NY16

★★61% **Golf** Links Ave DG12 5PN ☎ (04617) 254

Normal price: £28.50. Dinner from £11 and à la carte (1990
price)
Short breaks: £34. 2 or 3 nights, Nov-15 Mar, except Xmas/
New Year. Single supplement.
✼ Credit card ①

Next to a golf course on the Solway coast, this helpful hotel has spacious public areas and a modern wing of comfortable bedrooms, many with private bath or shower and some with colour television. Golfing and fishing facilities are available. Christmas breaks are available.

ROCKCLIFFE   Dumfries & Galloway (Kirkcudbrightshire)   Map 11 NX85

★★★68% **Baron's Craig** DG5 4QF ☎ (055663) 225

Normal price: £40-£47. Dinner from £16 (1990 price)
Short breaks: £145 including dinner and afternoon tea for 3
nights, Apr-May, Oct. £165 for 3 nights, Jun-Sep. Single
supplement.
Credit cards ① ③

Set in woodland with views over the Solway and Rough Firths, this handsome country house hotel has a smart cocktail bar and comfortable ensuite bedrooms with colour television and modern amenities. The gardens include a putting green.

THORNHILL   Dumfries & Galloway (Dumfriesshire)   Map 11 MX89

★★53% Bucclench & Queensberry Drumlaurig Street DG3 5LU ☎ (0848) 30215

Normal price: £25. Dinner £5-£9
Short breaks: £33, min 4 nights
🦅 Credit cards ⬚1 ⬚3

Very friendly service and good-value menus are attractive features of this modest High Street hotel.

▪ FIFE ▪

ABERDOUR   Fife   Map 11 NT18

★64% Fairways 17 Manse Street ☎ (0383) 860478

Normal price: from £19. Dinner £4.50-£7.50
Short breaks: from £23. Single £29. Min 2 nights, Sep-May.
Credit cards ⬚1 ⬚3

Friendly resident proprietors have created a cosy hotel where guests can enjoy home-cooked meals. Two of the ten bedrooms have private bathrooms, and all have colour television.

★★66% Woodside High Street ☎ (0383) 860328

Normal price: £63.50
Short breaks: £65, Fri-Sun. Single room £40
Credit cards ⬚1 ⬚2 ⬚3 ⬚4 ⬚5

This beautifully restored hotel has attractive bedrooms, all equipped with private facilities and colour television. Three bedrooms have four-poster beds. A sauna is available for guests' use.

ANSTRUTHER   Fife   Map 12 NO50

★★★60% Craws Nest Bankwell Road KY10 3DA ☎ (0333) 310691

Normal price: £85 room and breakfast
Short breaks: £64 for 2 people. Min 2 nights, Nov-Apr.
Single supplement £8
🦅 (ex guide dogs) Credit cards ⬚1 ⬚2 ⬚3 ⬚4 ⬚5

This popular hotel has a superior annexe of spacious, comfortable bedrooms, all with colour television and private facilities. There are four rooms for families and two rooms with four-poster beds. The hotel has a solarium and a games room. A special programme is arranged for Christmas.

INN Q Royal 20 Rodger Street KY10 3DU ☎ (0333) 310581

Normal price: £14.50. Dinner £6-£14 and à la carte
Short breaks: £20. Min 2 nights

A family-run inn with a friendly, homely atmosphere. The bedrooms are bright and airy and two have ensuite facilities. Well-prepared meals are served in the dining room.

DUNFERMLINE   Fife   Map 11 NT08

★★61% City Bridge Street KY12 8DA ☎ (0383) 722538
Restricted service 1 & 2 Jan

Normal price: £26-£28. Dinner £10.50-£11.50 and à la carte
Short breaks: £30. Min 2 nights, Fri-Sat
Credit cards ⬚1 ⬚3

Situated in the town centre this hotel has neat well-equipped bedrooms, all with ensuite facilities and colour television. One room has a four-poster bed.

★★76% **Elgin** Charlestown KY11 3EE ☎ (0383) 872257
Normal price: £27. Dinner £6.50-£12 and à la carte
Short breaks: £30. Min 2 nights. Fri-Sun, Jan-May & Sep-Dec
✝ (ex guide dogs) Credit cards ① ③

Good value, freshly-cooked meals are served at this delightful hotel. All the comfortable bedrooms are ensuite with colour television.

★★★64% **Keavil House** (Best Western) Crossford KY12 8QW (2m W A994) ☎ (0383) 736258
Normal price: from £65 room and breakfast. Dinner £14.50-£16.50
Short breaks: from £45. Min 2 nights. No single supplement at weekends

This converted fortified mansion has an elegant new bedroom wing and two attractive restaurants. All rooms are ensuite with colour television and one is furnished with a four-poster bed. There is a special Christmas programme.

★★★67% **King Malcolm Thistle** (Mount Charlotte (TS)) Queensferry Road, Wester Pitcorthie KY11 5DS ☎ (0383) 722611
Normal price: £36.75. Dinner from £11.95 and à la carte
Short breaks: £31 excluding dinner. No single supplement at weekends.
Credit cards ① ② ③ ④ ⑤

A purpose-built hotel, located on the southern outskirts of town, offering friendly service and well-equipped bedrooms.

★★★62% **Pitfirrane Arms** Main Street, Crossford KY12 8NJ (0.5m W A994) ☎ (0383) 736132
Normal price: £47-£54. Dinner £8.50-£18 and à la carte
Short breaks: £33. Fri-Sun
✝ (ex guide dogs) Credit cards ① ② ③

This modern hotel was originally an old coaching inn. All rooms have colour television, tea and coffee making facilities and bath or shower ensuite. A special Christmas programme is provided.

FREUCHIE Fife Map 11 NO20

★★62% **Lomond Hills** (Exec Hotel) Parliament Square KY7 7EY ☎ (0337) 57329 & 57498
Normal price: £47-£55 room and breakfast. Dinner £12.50
Short breaks: £69, 2 nights
Credit cards ① ② ③ ⑤

Set in the centre of this small village, this former coaching inn has well-equipped bedrooms which very in size and style; all are ensuite with colour television and one has a four-poster bed.

GLENROTHES Fife Map 11 NO20

★★★72% **Balgeddie House** Balgeddie Way KY6 3ET ☎ (0592) 742511
Closed 1 & 2 Jan
Normal price: £45. Dinner £12 and à la carte
Short breaks: £36.50, single £42.50. Min 2 nights, Fri-Sun
✝ (ex guide dogs) Credit cards ① ② ③

This is a large privately-owned mansion, dating from 1936, standing on a hillside in six acres of land. All rooms are ensuite with colour television. Guests can enjoy horse riding and there is a pool table.

★★75% **Rescobie** Valley Drive, Leslie KY6 3BQ ☎ (0592) 742143
Normal price: £30-£32.50. Dinner £13.50 and à la carte
Short breaks: £37-£42. Single £50-£52. Min 3 nights
Credit cards ① ② ③ ⑤

Delightful service and good value menus of freshly prepared dishes are features of this hotel. Bedrooms are comfortable with ensuite bath or shower room and colour television. There are special facilities for children.

KINGHORN   Fife   Map 11 NT28

QQQ Longboat 107 Pettyour Road KY3 9RU ☎ (0592) 890625

Normal price: £16.47. Dinner from £7.95 and à la carte
Short breaks: £19.95, min 2 nights
Credit cards 1 2 3 5

A large, modern villa overlooking the Firth of Forth, decorated and furnished to the highest standard.

NORTH QUEENSFERRY   Fife   Map 11 NT18

★★★70% **Queensferry Lodge** St Margaret's Head KY11 1HP ☎ (0383) 410000

Normal price: £33 (1990)
Short breaks: £25 (1990) excluding dinner. Fri-Sun.
Credit cards 1 2 3

Modern and purpose-built, the hotel provides a choice of eating styles - formal, informal and coffee shop - which can all be recommended. There are tastefully decorated public areas and very comfortable, well appointed bedrooms. A friendly staff renders courteous service under the personal supervision of the owners.

ST ANDREWS   Fife   Map 12 NO51

QQ Albany 56 North Street KY16 9AH ☎ (0334) 77737

Normal price: £14-£24 (en suite)
Short breaks: £75 (en suite) 3 nights, Mon-Fri, Jan-Mar & Nov-Dec, £85 Apr & Oct (except Easter)
Credit cards 1 3

A neat and compact terraced house with functional, well-equipped bedrooms.

QQ Craigmore 3 Murray Park KY16 9AW ☎ (0334) 72142 & 77963

Normal price: £12-£20
Short breaks: Normal tariff less 10%, min 4 nights, dinner not included
✖

A smartly decorated, comfortable guesthouse conveniently situated for town centre and the Old Course.

★★65% **Parklands** Kinburn Castle, Double Dykes Road KY16 9DS ☎ (0334) 73620

Normal price: £57.50 room and breakfast. Dinner from £12.50 and à la carte.
Short breaks: £95 for 3 days, £65 for 2 days Oct-Apr.
✖ Credit cards 1 3

A friendly, quiet hotel set back from the road. There are two dinner menus including a gourmet menu offering first class cooking by the chef/proprietor. There is a comfortable cocktail lounge.

★★★★60% **Rusack's** (Trusthouse Forte) Pilmour Links KY16 9JQ ☎ (0334) 74321

Normal price: £166 room only. Dinner £24.50-£32.
Short breaks: £81, min 2 nights.
Activity breaks: Golf Breaks, £92.50 for 2 nights including two rounds of golf but excluding dinner. Music at Leisure Breaks, details from hotel.
Credit cards 1 2 3 4 5

An ideal base for golfers and their families, this hotel overlooks the 1st and 18th fairways of the famous Links Golf Course towards the expanse of beach beyond.

WORMIT   Fife   Map 11 NO32

★★58% Sandford Hill Newport-on-Tay DO6 8RG ☎ (0382) 541802

Normal price: £50, including dinner £17.50-£20
Short breaks: £38, May-Sep, £35 Jan, Apr, Oct and Dec, min
2 nights. £10 supplement for single occupancy
Credit cards ① ② ③ ⑤

Located 3 miles south of the Tay Road Bridge, this well-established hotel is popular with both business people and tourists. The modern bedrooms are well-equipped. Leisure facilities include, tennis and clay pigeon shooting.

▨ GRAMPIAN ▨

ABERDEEN   Grampian (Aberdeenshire)   Map 15 NJ90

★★★70% Caledonian Thistle (Mount Charlotte (TS)) 10 Union Terrace ☎ (0224) 640233

Normal price: £50.25
Short breaks: £45. There is no single supplement at weekends

Set in the heart of Aberdeen this hotel has a café-bar, an attractive restaurant and a cocktail lounge. It offers a choice of bedrooms, all with colour television and ensuite facilities and two with four-poster beds.

★★★67% Copthorne 122 Huntly Street ☎ (0224) 630404

Normal price: £105 room only. Dinner from £12.95 and à la carte
Short breaks: £60. Fri-Sun. Single supplement.
Credit cards ① ② ③ ④ ⑤

All of the bedrooms at this hotel have private facilities and colour television, and some have been set aside for non-smokers. The menu offers a choice of French and Scottish dishes.

GH QQQ Corner House 385 Great Western Road AB1 6NY ☎ (0224) 313063

Normal price: £23
Short breaks: £18, single room £26. Fri-Sun
Credit cards ① ③

Conveniently situated in the West End, this hotel offers a relaxed atmosphere and good service. All the bedrooms have private facilities and colour television.

★★★62% New Marcliffe 51-53 Queen's Road AB9 2PE ☎ (0224) 321371

Normal price: £54. Dinner £17.50-£23.50 and à la carte
Short breaks: £35. Available Fri-Sun. £10 single supplement.
✕ (ex guide dogs) Credit cards ① ② ③ ⑤

This small, elegant hotel built of granite, has attractive bedrooms with ensuite facilities and colour television.

★★★★51% Skean Dhu Altens (Mount Charlotte (TS)) Souter Head Road, Altens (3m S off A956)
☎ (0224) 877000 Restricted service Christmas week

Normal price: £50. Dinner from £14
Short breaks: £38. Min 2 nights. £17.50 single supplement.
Credit cards ① ② ③ ④ ⑤

This spacious hotel stands on the main route to Aberdeen Harbour. Some bedrooms have views across the city towards the coast, and all rooms have private facilities and colour television. There are some rooms for non-smokers. The outdoor heated swimming pool is open May-September.

★★★63% Stakis Treetops 161 Springfield Road ☎ (0224) 313377

Normal price: £107 (room). Dinner £12.50-£15 and à la carte
Short breaks: £45. Min 2 nights. £12 single supplement.
(1990 prices)
Credit cards ① ② ③ ⑤

An indoor heated swimming pool, tennis courts and a small gymnasium are among the leisure amenities at this large hotel. All the bedrooms have ensuite facilities and colour television, and some rooms are set aside for non-smokers. A special Christmas programme is held.

★★★57% **Swallow Imperial** Stirling Street ☎ (0224) 589101

Normal price: £39. Dinner £12.95 and à la carte
Short breaks: £34.50 including lunch on day of departure.
Single room £62 for 2 nights including lunch on day of departure
Credit cards ①②③⑤

This hotel is situated close to the station and the city centre shops. Most bedrooms have a private bath or shower room and all have colour television. No parking.

ABERDEEN AIRPORT   Grampian (Aberdeenshire)   Map 15 NJ81

★★★★67% **Holiday Inn** Riverview Drive, Farburn AB2 0AZ ☎ (0224) 770011

Normal price: £100 room. Dinner £15-£30 and à la carte
Short breaks: £40 excluding dinner (1990). Min 1 night, Fri-Sun
Credit cards ①②③④⑤

This hotel has a good range of leisure amenities, and a combined coffee shop/restaurant which features well-cooked dishes. Bedrooms are all ensuite with colour television, and some rooms are for families and non-smokers. There is a special Christmas programme.

★★★63% **Skean Dhu Dyce** (Mount Charlotte (TS)) Farburn Terrace AB2 0DW (off A947)
☎ (0224) 723101

Normal price: £44. Dinner from £13.45 and à la carte
Short breaks: £22 excluding dinner. £8 single supplement.
Min 2 nights, weekends only
Credit cards ①②③⑤

This friendly hotel has a coffee shop, restaurant and some leisure amenities. The modern bedrooms are all ensuite with colour television, with rooms set aside for families and non-smokers. There is a special Christmas programme.

BALLATER   Grampian (Aberdeenshire)   Map 15 NO39

★★60% **Monaltrie** (Inter-Hotels) 5 Bridge Square AB3 5QJ ☎ (03397) 55417

Normal price: £28. Dinner £15.25 and à la carte
Short breaks: £40.50. Min 2 nights

This 19th-century hotel has been extensively modernised and has a spacious bar and popular restaurant. The bedrooms are well equipped and several overlook the River Dee; most have ensuite facilities, all have colour television, and three are family rooms. There is a special Christmas programme.

BANCHORY   Grampian (Kincardineshire)   Map 15 NO69

★★★★ 🏴 71% **Invery House** (Prestige) Bridge of Feugh AB3 3NJ ☎ (03302) 4782
Closed 5-25 Jan

Normal price: £92.50. Dinner £29.50
Short breaks: £75. Min 2 nights, Oct-Mar
✗ (ex guide dogs)

An elegant and luxurious mansion near the River Feugh, with fishing rights on the river and shooting parties organised. It is popular with sportsmen and those seeking peace and quiet. There are fourteen spacious bedrooms, all with ensuite facilities and colour television. There is a special Christmas programme. Children under eight are not accommodated.

★★★ ♨ 75% **Raemoir** AB3 4ED ☎ (03302) 4884

Normal price: £45. Dinner £19.50.
Short breaks: £47.50. Min 2 nights. Singles only as part of a double booking.
Activity breaks: Golf Break, £47.50, 9-hole mini golf course. Clay Pigeon Shooting, price on application. Hill Walking Break, £47.50. Walking on the hotel estate. All Weather Tennis, £47.50 plus £1 per person per session.
Credit cards [1] [2] [3] [5]

Elegant 18th-century mansion magnificently set in 3,500 acres, and furnished throughout with antiques. The friendly service is complemented by the personal involvement of the owner.

★★★62% **Tor-Na-Coille** AB3 4AB ☎ (03302) 2242

Normal price: £85 room and breakfast.
Short breaks: £49.50. Min 2 nights, Fri, Sat & Sun.
Activity breaks: Squash, Indoor Bowls and Snooker Breaks available. Hunting, Shooting and Fishing can be arranged. Details on application.
Credit cards [1] [2] [3] [5]

Currently being dramatically upgraded, this hotel offers elegant and spacious bedrooms. Guests can enjoy table d'hôte and à la carte meals with a Scottish flavour.

BANFF   *Grampian (Banffshire)*   Map 15 NJ66

★★★56% **Banff Springs** (Consort) Golden Knowes Road AB4 2JE ☎ (02612) 2881

Normal price: £27.50. Dinner £12.50 and à la carte
Short breaks: £32.50, Fri-Sat

A popular modern, purpose-built hotel on the edge of town overlooking the Moray Firth. The bedrooms are comfortable and well-equipped, and all have ensuite facilities and colour television, including the family rooms. There is a special Christmas programme.

★★58% **County** (Guestaccom) 32 High Street AB4 1AE ☎ (02612) 5353

Normal price: £45 room with breakfast. Dinner £10-£12 and à la carte
Short breaks: £22.50. Min 2 nights, Nov-Mar (except Xmas and Easter)
✷ (ex guide dogs) Credit cards [1] [2] [3] [5]

A charming Georgian house in the town centre with special facilities for children. Bedrooms, in keeping with the rest of the house, are in period style. All have colour television, some have ensuite facilities, there are two family rooms and two with four-poster beds. The hotel offers a special Christmas programme.

BRAEMAR   *Grampian (Aberdeenshire)*   Map 15 NO19

★★67% **Braemar Lodge** Glenshee Road AB3 5YQ ☎ (03397) 41627
Closed Dec & Apr

Normal price: £30. Dinner £15-£19.50
Short breaks: £30. Min 5 nights, Sun-Thu, Jan-Mar (ski season)
Credit cards [1] [3]

A granite-built lodge providing willing and friendly service and good food. There are eight bedrooms, all have colour television and six have ensuite showers.

BUCKIE   Grampian (Banffshire)   Map 15 NJ46

★★57% **Cluny** 2 High Street AB5 1AL ☎ (0542) 32922
Closed 1-2 Jan

Normal price: £39 room and breakfast, £57 including
dinner
Short breaks: £52 for 2 people. Single £28. Min 5 nights or
weekends.
Credit cards 1 2 3 5

Conveniently situated in the town centre this
hotel offers good value practical accommodation. Most rooms have private facilities, and
all are equipped with colour television.

ELGIN   Grampian (Morayshire)   Map 15 NJ26

★★★57% **Eight Acres** (Consort) Sheriffmill IV30 3UN ☎ (0343) 543077

Normal price: £30. Dinner from £13.
Short breaks: £34.95, min 2 nights, Fri-Sun.
Activity breaks: Rambling Breaks, £90 including transport.
Horse Riding, £99. Water Sports/Water Skiing, £125 plus
£30 for water-skiing. Golf Breaks, £95. Shooting, £120. All
breaks include 2 nights full board.

This purpose-built hotel stands on the A96, on
the western outskirts of the town. Bedrooms
built in 1985 with the sports and leisure
complex are very attractive.

★★★71% **Mansion House** The Haugh IV30 1AW ☎ (0343) 548811

Normal price: £45. Dinner £15-£20 and à la carte
Short breaks: £37.80-£45, 2-7 nights
🐾 Credit cards 1 3

A comfortable, small hotel with a smart new
leisure centre. Each bedroom has an ensuite
bathroom and colour television, and some have
four-poster beds. Christmas breaks are
available.

FORRES   Grampian (Morayshire)   Map 14 NJ05

GH QQQQ **Parkmount House** St Leonards Road IV36 0DW ☎ (0309) 73312

Normal price: £20-£23.
Short breaks: £18.50-£21.50 excluding dinner, min 4 nights
Sept-Jun.
Activity breaks: Golf Breaks, £270. Details from hotel.
Credit cards 1 3

A charming mid 19th-century town house with
well-kept gardens. A choice of simple, honest
dishes is offered at dinner.

★★56% **Royal** Tytler Street IV36 0EL ☎ (0309) 72617
Normal price: £18-£23. Dinner £3.75-£14 à la carte
Short breaks: £13.50-£16.50 excluding dinner. Min 2 nights,
Fri-Sun
Credit cards ① ② ③

A substantial Victorian building situated in the west end and convenient for the railway station. All bedrooms have colour television, and some have ensuite bath or shower room.

INVERURIE   Grampian   Map 15 NJ72

★★★64% **Strathburn** Burghmuir Drive AB5 9GY ☎ (0467) 24422
Normal price: £29
Short breaks: £23.50. Fri-Sat. Single supplement.
Credit cards ① ② ③

This small family-run hotel overlooks Strathburn Park and play area, and there are excellent facilities for golf and fishing nearby. Comfortable bedrooms offer ensuite facilities and colour television.

KILDRUMMY   Grampian   Map 15 NJ41

★★★ ♠ 75% **Kildrummy Castle** (Best Western) AB3 8RA ☎ (09755) 71283
Normal price: £62
Short breaks: £45. Min 2 nights. 3 Jan-16 May and 1 Oct-21
Dec. Single supplement £11
Credit cards ① ② ③ ④

This elegant hotel overlooks the ruins and beautiful gardens of the 13th-century Kildrummy Castle. The impressive interior features Victorian fireplaces and tapestry-covered walls. Spacious bedrooms all have colour television and ensuite facilities.

MACDUFF   Grampian (Banffshire)   Map 15 NJ76

★★★51% **Highland Haven** Shore Street AB4 1UB ☎ (0261) 32408
Normal price: £24.45. Dinner £11.65.
Short breaks: £55 for 2 nights. Min 2 nights, Thu-Mon.
Activity breaks: Golfing Breaks, £100-£115 for 3 nights.
Bowling Breaks, £10 extra per week.
Credit cards ① ③ ④

A good range of leisure facilities is available at this small family-run commercial and tourist hotel which overlooks the harbour from a waterfront location.

MARYCULTER   Grampian (Aberdeenshire)   Map 15 NO89

★★★68% **Maryculter House** (Minotels) AB1 6BB ☎ (0224) 732124
Normal price: from £85.
Short breaks: £25 excluding dinner, min 2 nights, Fri-Sun.
Single £30.
Activity breaks: Golf or Fishing Breaks, details from hotel.
🎋 Credit cards ① ② ③ ⑤

Set in five acres of grounds on the south bank of the River Dee some eight miles from Aberdeen, this comfortable hotel offers friendly service throughout.

PETERHEAD   Grampian (Aberdeenshire)   Map 15 NK14

★★★67% **Waterside Inn** (Consort) Fraserburgh Road AB4 7BN ☎ (0779) 71121
Normal price: £37. Dinner from £10.95 (1990 price)
Short breaks: £38.50 including £12 dinner allowance. Min 2
nights. Not available Christmas/New Year.
Credit cards ① ② ③ ⑤

This courteous, well-equipped modern hotel with a choice of restaurant and bar has comfortable bedrooms all with private facilities and colour television. Extensive leisure facilities include snooker, indoor swimming pool, gymnasium, sauna, solarium and steam room.

TYNET   Grampian (Banffshire)   Map 15 NJ36

★★56% **Mill House** AB5 2HJ ☎ (05427) 233

Normal price: £21.
Short breaks: £18 excluding dinner, min 4 nights May-Jun.
Activity breaks: Golf Breaks, £25 pp pn. Ten local courses
played twice over five consecutive days.
Credit cards ① ② ③ ⑤

This former meal mill, now a roadside hotel, offers good value practical accommodation.

▪ HIGHLAND ▪

ACHARACLE   Highland (Argyll)   Map 13 NM66

FH QQ Dalilea House (NM735693) PH36 4JX ☎ (096785) 253

Normal price: £22-£26.
Short breaks: £20-£24, min 3 nights, Mar-May, Oct-Nov.
Activity breaks: Fishing Package, £202.50 per week.

Delightfully situated on the shore of Loch Shiel, this fine turreted 15th-century farmhouse is an ideal base for the touring holidaymaker.

ACHNASHEEN   Highland (Ross & Cromarty)   Map 14 NH15

★★ 👭 70% **Ledgowan Lodge** (Best Western) IV22 2EJ ☎ (044588) 252
Closed 29 Oct-Mar

Normal price: £32.50-£37.50. Dinner £17.50-£19.75 and à la
carte
Short breaks: £48 for 2 nights, single room £53. Min 2
nights, Apr-Oct

This former shooting lodge offers friendly service and good wholesome country cooking. There are thirteen bedrooms all with private bathrooms and colour television; four of the rooms are for families.

ARISAIG   Highland (Inverness-shire)   Map 13 NM68

★★★(Red) 👭 **Arisaig House** (Relais et Châteaux) Beasdale PH39 4NR (3m E A830) ☎ (06875) 622
Closed 11 Nov-8 Mar

Normal price: £93.50-£121. Dinner £33
Short breaks: £83-£105. Min 3 nights, mid Mar-mid May &
Oct-mid Nov. Single room 20% off.
🐾 (ex guide dogs) Credit cards ① ③

Guests will receive a warm welcome at this elegant, comfortable country house hotel. Most of the fifteen bedrooms have ensuite bathrooms, and all have colour television. There is a splendid 2nd-floor billiards room and a croquet lawn. Children under ten are not accommodated.

AULTBEA   Highland (Ross & Cromarty)   Map 14 NG88

★★66% **Aultbea** IV22 2HX ☎ (044582) 201

Normal price: £36.50-£39.50
Short breaks: £30-£33 including lunch. Min 2 nights
Credit cards ① ③

Delightfully situated on the shore of Loch Ewe, this small friendly family-run hotel is an ideal base for touring holidaymakers. Seven of the eight bedrooms have ensuite facilities, all have colour television and one room is set aside for families. The hotel has special facilities for children.

AVIEMORE   Highland (Inverness-shire)   Map 14 NH81

GH QQQ Corrour House Inverdruie PH22 1QH ☎ (0479) 810220
Closed Nov-26 Dec

Normal price: £36-£44 room and breakfast
Short breaks: £33-£36
Credit cards [1] [3] [5]

A stone-built house standing in its own grounds half a mile east of Aviemore on the B970. Most of the eight bedrooms have ensuite bath or shower rooms, all have colour television and there are two rooms for families. Children under one are not accommodated.

BALLACHULISH   Highland (Argyllshire)   Map 14 NN05

★★★60% Ballachulish (Inter-Hotels) PA39 4JY ☎ (08552) 606

Normal price: £52. Dinner £17
Short breaks: £29.50. Min 2 nights, Nov-Apr. Single occupancy £35.50.
Activity breaks: Ski Lochaber, £29.50 per night. Dec-May. Details on application.

A Scottish baronial-style hotel with good views of Loch Linnhe and the surrounding mountain scenery. Service provided by a team of friendly young staff.

BEAULY   Highland   Map 14 NH54

QQ Arkton Westend IV4 7BT ☎ (0463) 782388

Normal price: £48
Short breaks: £42

Close to the village square, this small guesthouse caters mostly for the touring holidaymaker. It has a friendly atmosphere and offers good value, practical accommodation.

★★63% Priory (Inter-Hotels) The Square IV4 7BX ☎ (0463) 782309

Normal price: £49.50. Dinner £8.50-£16.50.
Short breaks: £62.50 for 2 nights. Min 2 nights, Fri-Sun.
Activity breaks: Golf Break, £112.50 for 3 days including green fees for 2 days golf. £169.50 for 5 days including green fees for 4 days golf.
Credit cards [1] [2] [3]

Modern hotel standing in the town square serving meals and refreshments throughout the day. There are plans to refurbish the ground floor and add more bedrooms.

BRORA   Highland (Sutherland)   Map 14 NC90

★★★58% Links (Best Western) Golf Road KW9 6QS ☎ (0408) 21225

Normal price: £57.50 including dinner.
Short breaks: £53, min 2 nights. Single supplement.
Activity breaks: Golf Week, £330. May 26-31. Fishing Breaks, details from hotel.
Credit cards [1] [2] [3] [5]

Holiday hotel next to an 18-hole golf course, with fine uninterrupted sea views. The traditionally furnished bedrooms vary in size but are well-equipped.

★★62% Royal Marine Golf Road KW9 6QS ☎ (0408) 21252

Normal price: £56. Dinner £15-£16.
Short breaks: 55, min 2 nights.
Activity breaks: Loch Fishing, Apr-mid Oct. Curling, Oct-Apr. Golf. Details from hotel.
Credit cards [1] [2] [3] [5]

Popular holiday hotel with good range of leisure facilities including golf, fishing and curling. Bedrooms are comfortable and log fires burn in public areas.

CROMARTY   Highland (Ross & Cromarty)   Map 14 NH76

★★62% **Royal** Marine Terrace IV11 8YN ☎ (03817) 217

Normal price: £22. Dinner from £13.95.
Short breaks: £39.50 for 2 nights. Nov-Apr.
Activity breaks: Walking Wonderland Break. Including hill walks of varying difficulty, detailed maps and specialist guidance. Fishing Fantasy, river or sea fishing. Shooting Short Stay, includes one day's basic gun training. Opportunities for wild geese shooting, rough shooting and stalking. All breaks £99 for 3 days.
Credit cards 1 2 3

An hospitable hotel overlooking the harbour and Cromarty Firth with a very good reputation for its cooking. Guests can relax in the sheltered gardens.

DALWHINNIE   Highland (Inverness-shire)   Map 14 NN68

★★56% **Loch Ericht** (Inter-Hotels) PH19 1AF ☎ (05282) 257

Normal price: £45 room and breakfast. Dinner £5-£10
Short breaks: £20 excluding dinner.
Credit cards 1 2 3

Set amidst splendid scenery in the Highlands' highest village, this former lodge provides modern bedrooms with ensuite facilities. Meals are available all day. There are facilities for fishing, shooting and ski-ing. A Christmas programme is available.

DORNOCH   Highland   Map 14 NH78

★★60% **Dornoch Castle** (Inter-Hotels) Castle Street IV25 3SD ☎ (0862) 810216

Normal price: £26. Dinner from £14.50.
Short breaks: £79 for 2 nights, mid Apr-Oct. Single price £87 for 2 nights.
Activity breaks: Golf Breaks, £72 including one round of golf, 2 nights, mid-Apr-15 May and all Oct. (1990 prices)
Credit cards 1 2 3

A town centre hotel, popular as a base for golfers and tourists. The best bedrooms are in the older part of the castle, those in the wing being modern in style.

★★★53% **Royal Golf** Grange Road IV25 3LG ☎ (0862) 810283

Normal price: £54.
Short breaks: £35, min 2 nights, Mar-Oct. Single supplement.
Activity breaks: Golf Holidays, details from hotel.
🎣

Set in its own grounds overlooking the famous links course this popular golfing hotel is enjoying widespread upgrading.

FORT AUGUSTUS   Highland (Inverness-shire)   Map 14 NH30

★★63% **Caledonian** PH32 4BQ ☎ (0320) 6256
Closed Oct-Mar

Normal price: £37.50 room and breakfast. Dinner £12-£14
Short breaks: £56 for 2 people. Min 3 nights, April-September

This family-run, small Highland holiday hotel is especially noted for its warm and friendly hospitality. It offers enjoyable home cooking and good value accommodation, and some rooms have ensuite facilities.

★★63% **Inchnacardoch Lodge** (Consort) Loch Ness PH32 4BL ☎ (0320) 6258
Closed Dec-1 Apr

Normal price: £30. Dinner £16-£20
Short breaks: £33. Min 2 nights, Apr-Jun & Sep-Nov
Credit cards ① ② ③ ⑤

This converted hunting lodge overlooking Loch Ness offers good food and good-sized bedrooms, most with ensuite facilities and colour television.

FORT WILLIAM Highland (Inverness-shire) Map 14 NN17

★★★58% **Alexandra** The Parade PH33 6AZ ☎ (0397) 2241

Normal price: £42. Dinner £6.50-£16.
Short breaks: £45, min 2 nights. Single supplement.
Activity breaks: Skiing Break, from £172 for 4 nights including 5-day ski hire, lift and tuition. Jan-Apr. Connoisseur Collection, from £120 for 4 nights including first class rail tickets and excursions by luxury mini coach. Mar-Apr & Oct-Nov.

A traditional hotel situated close to the main shopping area. The popular Great Food Shop provides meals and snacks from 9.30am until 11pm supplementing the main restaurant.

★★59% **Grand** Gordon Square PH33 6DX ☎ (0397) 2928

Normal price: £22.50-£32. Dinner from £13.95
Short breaks: £35. Min 3 nights, all year (except Easter & Christmas)
Credit cards ① ② ③ ⑤

A three-storey hotel on a corner site at the west end of the shopping centre and adjacent to the Pier. There are thirty-three bedrooms, all with colour television and ensuite facilities.

★★61% **Imperial** Fraser's Square PH33 6DW ☎ (0397) 2040 & 3921
Closed 3-31 Jan

Normal price: £40-£66 room and breakfast. Dinner £12.59-£14.50 and à la carte
Short breaks: £20 excluding dinner. Min 3 nights, Oct-May.

Enjoying views of Loch Linnhe from its town centre position, this long-established hotel has modern bedrooms with ensuite bath or shower rooms and colour television. There is a special Christmas programme.

★★55% **Milton** North Road PH33 6TG ☎ (0397) 2331

Normal price: £37. Dinner £6.50-£14.
Short breaks: £40, min 2 nights. Single supplement.
Activity breaks: Skiing Breaks, from £164 for 4 nights including ski school, hire and lift pass for 5 days, Jan-Apr. Leisure Packages, from £99, 4 nights including rail ticket from home town, and two excursions to Skye and Glencoe. Mar, Oct & Nov.
Credit cards ① ② ③ ④ ⑤

A busy holiday hotel overlooking Ben Nevis which has benefitted from extensive refurbishment in recent years and offers good-value accommodation. Popular with tour groups.

★★★65% **Moorings** (Exec Hotel) Banavie PH33 7LY (3m N of Fort William off A830) ☎ (03977) 797 due to change to (0397772) 797

Normal price: £56-£76 room and breakfast. Dinner £17 and à la carte
Short breaks: £132 for 3 nights
Credit cards ①②③⑤

This professionally-managed, family-run hotel has a spacious new lounge, bar and wine bar. Bedrooms are modern in style, all are ensuite with colour television and one has a four-poster bed. There is a special Christmas programme. Children under ten are not accommodated.

GAIRLOCH   Highland (Ross & Cromarty)   Map 14 NG87

★★62% **Old Inn** Flowerdale IV21 2BD ☎ (0445) 2006

Normal price: £45-£59 room and breakfast. Dinner from £14.50
Short breaks: £114-£129, 3 nights for 2 people, includes free tickets to Inverewe Gardens
Credit cards ①②③

Set back from the road, this charming 18th-century former coaching inn overlooks the fishing harbour. The atmosphere is welcoming and the bedrooms are ensuite with colour television. There are special facilities for children and there is a special Christmas programme.

GARVE   Highland (Ross & Cromarty)   Map 14 NH 36

★★64% **Inchbae Lodge** Inchbae IV23 2PH ☎ (09975) 269

Normal price: £49 room and breakfast. Dinner £15.95
Short breaks: £32. Min 3 nights

This former hunting lodge is now a comfortable, family-run hotel providing imaginative, well-cooked food and spacious public areas. Most of the bedrooms have ensuite facilities. Fishing and clay pigeon shooting are available, and there is a special Christmas programme.

GLENSHIEL (Shiel Bridge)   Highland (Ross & Cromarty)   Map 14 NG91

★★63% **Kintail Lodge** IV40 8HL ☎ (059981) 275
Closed 24 Dec-2 Jan. Restricted service Nov-Mar

Normal price: £37-£42 with dinner
Short breaks: £66 for 2 nights. Mid Oct-mid May (except Bank Holidays)
Credit cards ①③

This former hunting lodge is situated on the shores of Loch Duich. Bedrooms vary in shape and size but are generally comfortable, all have colour television and most have ensuite showers. Home-cooked meals are served in the dining room.

GRANTOWN-ON-SPEY   Highland (Morayshire)   Map 14 NJ02

GH QQQ **Umaria** Woodlands Terrace PH26 3JU ☎ (0479) 2104
Jan-Oct

Normal price: £20.50
Short breaks: £58 3 nights, Sep-Jun

A warm and friendly welcome awaits guests at this large Victorian house. Some of the bedrooms are large enough for families.

INVERNESS   Highland (Inverness-shire)   Map 14 NH64

QQ Ardmnir House 16 Ness Bank IV2 4SF ☎ (0463) 231151

Normal price: £18.25
Short breaks: £25, min 3 nights. £4 single supplement.

Standing on the River Ness, this comfortable guesthouse has good all round comfort and service.

★★★ 🛏 73% Bunchrew House Bunchrew IV3 6TA (3m W off A862) ☎ (0463) 234917

Normal price: From £50
Short breaks: From £45. Min 3 nights.
Credit cards ① ② ③ ④

This beautifully furnished 17th-century castle stand in 15 acres of garden and woodland on the shores of the Beauly Firth. It features a very comfortable lounge with open log fire and bedrooms of individual design, all with ensuite facilities and colour television. Salmon fishing in grounds.

★★★65% Caledonian (Embassy) IV1 1DX ☎ (0463) 235181

Normal price: £68. Dinner from £15.75.
Short breaks: £51 Apr-Nov, £37 Nov-Mar, min 2 nights. Single supplement midweek.
Activity breaks: Indoor Bowling, £69 for 2 nights. Oct-Apr.
Credit cards ① ② ③ ⑤

A smart town centre hotel with an extended range of services and facilities including a new leisure club and a pleasant restaurant with views over the river.

★★★73% Craigmonie (Best Western) 9 Annfield Road IV2 3HX ☎ (0463) 231649

Normal price: £52.50 with dinner.
Short breaks: £48-£58, min 2 nights, Mon-Thu.
Activity breaks: Golf Breaks, Mar-Oct. Shooting Breaks, Nov-Feb. Stalking Breaks. Fishing Breaks. Details from hotel.
🐎 Credit cards ① ② ③ ⑤

A splendid indoor leisure complex and pool have recently been added to this very comfortable personally-run hotel, with its elegant restaurant and first class service.

★★ 🛏 74% Dunain Park IV3 6JN ☎ (0463) 230512

Normal price: £55. Dinner £22.50.
Short breaks: £220 for 3 nights.
Credit cards ① ② ③ ⑤

A delightful country house set in six acres of secluded grounds close to Loch Ness. The charming bedrooms have ensuite facilities and colour television. Congenial hosts Ann and Edward Nicoll offer fine traditional cuisine served in comfortable surroundings.

★★71% Glen Mhor 10 Ness Bank IV2 4SG ☎ (0463) 234308

Normal price: £65-£80.
Short breaks: £80. Min 2 nights, Sat and Sun only. Oct-Apr.
Credit cards ① ② ③ ⑤

Overlooking the River Ness, this hotel offers bedrooms equipped to a very high standard including ensuite facilities in most and colour television in all.

★★57% Loch Ness House Glenurquhart Road IV3 6JL (Consort) ☎ (0463) 231248

Normal price: £32.50
Short breaks: £29.50. Min 2 nights, Fri-Sun, Oct-May. Single room supplement from £8.
Credit cards ① ② ③

This family-run hotel is situated on the edge of town beside the Caledonian Canal. Bedrooms are compact and practical in design, all with colour television.

★★★58% **Mercury** Nairn Road IV2 3TR (junc A9/A96) (Mount Charlotte (TS)) ☎ (0463) 239666

Normal price: £41.50
Short breaks: £37.50. Min 2 nights. Single supplement £15.
Credit cards ① ② ③ ⑤

Situated on the outskirts of town, with convenient access to the A9, this modern hotel provides a high standard of comfort. All bedrooms have ensuite facilities and colour television.

★★★56% **Palace** Ness Walk IV3 5NE ☎ (0463) 223243

Normal price: £42. Dinner £6.50-£16.
Short breaks: £45, min 2 nights. Single supplement.
Activity breaks: Skiing Breaks, from £20. All inclusive package breaks, from £99 including rail from hometown and two full day excursions.

Situated near the river, a hotel catering for business and tourist trade. The atmosphere is friendly and informal.

★62% **Redcliffe** 1 Gordon Terrace IV2 3HD ☎ (0463) 232767

Normal price: £18.50
Short breaks: £26. Min 3 nights. Single supplement £2.
Credit cards ① ② ③

A small, family-run hotel standing in a quiet residential area close to the town centre. Resident owners ensure that guests' needs are met efficiently, and all of the bedrooms have colour television.

INVERMORISTON   Highland   Map 14 NH41

★★68% **Glenmoriston Arms** IV3 6YA ☎ (0320) 51206

Normal price: £32.50
Short breaks: £33. Min 2 nights, Oct-Apr.
Credit cards ① ③

A traditional Highland hotel offering friendly service and a fine selection of malt whiskies. There are colour televisions in all bedrooms.

KINGCRAIG   Highland (Inverness-shire)   Map 14 NH80

QQ **March House** Laggamlia, Feshie Bridge PH21 1NG ☎ (05404) 388

Normal price: £21 (£23 with private bath)
Short breaks: £60 (£63 with private bath) for 3 nights excluding Easter and New Year. £2 single supplement

Secluded in the free-studded Glen Feshie, this modern house provides friendly service, interesting meals and magnificent views.

KINGUSSIE   Highland (Inverness-shire)   Map 14 NH70

★★67% **Columba House** Manse Road PH21 1JF ☎ (0540) 661402

Normal price: £24. Dinner £12-£14.
Short breaks: £84 low season, £108 high season for 3 nights.
Activity breaks: Unlimited Golf Breaks, £120 low season, £135 high season for 3 nights.

A warm, friendly and hospitable hotel standing in a slightly elevated position to the north of town, with a large garden for guests to relax in.

KINLOCHBERVIE   Highland   Map 14 NH06

★★★60% **Kinlochbervie** IV27 4RP ☎ (097182) 275
Restricted services Jan & Feb

Normal price: £35. Dinner £25.
Short breaks: £55-£60 room. Min 3 nights. Single supplement.
Credit cards ① ② ③ ⑤

There are fine views of the harbour and out to sea from this modern hotel. All of the comfortable bedrooms boast smart bathrooms and colour television. Guests can eat in the informal bistro or in the attractive candle-lit restaurant where the menu features fresh local produce.

KIRKHILL   Highland   Map 14 NH54

★66% **Inchmore** IV5 7PX (at junc A862/B9164) ☎ (0463) 83296

Normal price: £17.50-£20
Short breaks: £20. Min 3 nights. Single supplement £5.
Credit cards ① ③

There is a relaxed and informal atmosphere at this small, family-run hotel. Compact bedrooms offer ensuite facilities and colour television.

KYLE OF LOCHALSH   Highland   Map 13 NG72

★★65% **Kyle** Main Street IV40 8AB ☎ (0599) 4204

Normal price: £27-£29
Short breaks: £23. Min 3 nights, Fri-Sun only, Sep-May.
Credit cards ③

Conveniently situated close to the railway station and to the ferry terminal for the Isle of Skye, this hotel offers compact, comfortable bedrooms with ensuite facilities and colour television.

LATHERON   Highland (Caithness)   Map 15 ND13

FH Q Upper Latheron KW5 6DT ☎ (05934) 224

Normal price: £9-£10.
Short breaks: Approximately 10% discount.
Activity breaks: Pony Trekking Holidays, £90 for 3 nights, Jun-Aug.
✼

Two-storey farmhouse in elevated position with fine views across the North Sea. The farm runs its own Ponies of Britain Pony Trekking Centre.

LOCHINVER   Highland   Map 14 NC02

★★★76% **Inver Lodge** IV27 4LU (Best Western) ☎ (05714) 496

Normal price: £71
Short breaks: £56. Min 2 nights. May, Oct & Nov only.
Single supplement £19.
Credit cards ① ② ③ ⑤

This modern hotel enjoys a commanding position above the village overlooking Inver Bay. Spacious bedrooms have ensuite facilities and colour television. Service is friendly and efficient.

MALLAIG   Highland (Inverness-shire)   Map 13 NM69

★★58% **Marine** PH41 4PY ☎ (0687) 2217

Normal price: £40-£48. Dinner from £11.50 (1990 price)
Short breaks: Apr-Oct: 10%, min 3 nights. Nov-Mar: £45, min 2 nights. Extra for private facilities.
Credit cards ① ② ③

Close to the harbour and the railway station, this is a well-run hotel; most of its bedrooms have colour television and some have private bath or shower.

NAIRN   Highland (Nairnshire)   Map 14 NH85

★★★★51% **Newton** (Consort) Inverness Road IV12 4RX ☎ (0667) 53144

Normal price: £45. Dinner £12.50 (1990 price)
Short breaks: £44.50. Min 2 nights. Single supplement.
Credit cards 1 2 3 5

A baronial hall set in 27 secluded acres with views of the Moray Firth, this efficient hospitable hotel serves good-quality food and the bedrooms, with a four-poster bed and several family rooms, are all ensuite with colour television. Leisure facilities include tennis, sauna, solarium and putting. Christmas breaks are available.

★★★★55% **Golf View** Seabank Road IV12 4HG ☎ (0667) 52301

Normal price: from £38. Dinner from £17.50 (1990 price).
Short breaks: £57. Min 2 nights. £8 single supplement.
Credit cards 1 2 3 5

Overlooking the Moray Firth, this hotel provides fine food and well-equipped bedrooms with ensuite facilities and colour television, including family rooms and one with a four-poster bed. The leisure facilities include an outdoor swimming pool, tennis, sauna, gymnasium, putting green and regular entertainment. Christmas breaks are available.

ONICH   Highland (Inverness-shire)   Map 14 NN06

★★★65% **Lodge On The Loch** Creag Dhu PH33 6RY ☎ (08553) 237

Normal price: £46. Dinner £16.50.
Short breaks: £36.50, min 2 nights, Feb-Apr & Oct.
Activity breaks: Painting in Watercolour, £316 for 6 nights including tuition and materials, 7-13 Apr, £364 29 Sept-5 Oct.
Credit cards 1 3

Relaxing, family-run hotel with magnificent views of Loch Linnhe and surrounding mountains from most bedrooms. A ground floor bedroom has been specially designed for the disabled.

★★65% **Onich** (Consort) PH33 6RY ☎ (08553) 214 and 266

Normal price: £29.50. Dinner £13.50-£15 (1990 price)
Short breaks: £37.50. Min 2 nights, Oct-May. Price includes one jacuzzi and solarium session per person. Dinner served in lounge bar Nov-Feb.
Credit cards 1 2 3 5

This comfortable family-run hotel whose gardens run down to the lochside has bedrooms with private bath or shower and colour television, including some family rooms. Facilities include solarium, gymnasium, jacuzzi and games room. See advertisement on p355.

PLOCKTON   Highland (Ross & Cromarty)   Map 14 NG83

★★76% **Haven** IV52 8TW ☎ (059984) 223 & 334

Normal price: £36. Dinner £13.50-£15 (1990 price)
Short breaks: £33. Min 3 nights, Feb-May, Oct-Dec.
Credit cards 1 3

This small and friendly owner-run hotel, close to the islands of Skye and Raasay, serves good homely food and provides comfortable accommodation with colour television in all bedrooms, most of them also having private bathrooms. No children under 7 are accommodated.

ROY BRIDGE   Highland (Inverness-shire)   Map 14 NN28

★★57% Glenspean Lodge PH31 4AW ☎ (039781) 223

Normal price: £45.
Short breaks: £39.
Activity breaks: Fishing Holidays from £135 for 3 days including packed lunch, Mar-Sept. Hunt with a Camera, £167 for 3 nights, Mar-Oct.

Attractively situated in an elevated position two miles east of Roy Bridge offers informal service from friendly staff, and a number of sporting activities can be arranged.

SCOURIE   Highland   Map 14 NC14

★★68% Eddrachilles Badcall Bay IV27 4TH ☎ (0971) 2080 & 2211

Normal price: £27.30-£31.65
Short breaks: £34.50-£38.55. Min 3 nights, Mar-Oct.

This former manse enjoys wonderful views of island-studded Badcall Bay from the peaceful setting of its own extensive grounds. Compact and modern, the bedrooms have ensuite facilities and colour television.

SPEAN BRIDGE   Highland (Inverness-shire)   Map 14 NN28

QQ Coireglas PH34 4EU ☎ (039781) 272

Normal price: £12-£14.50 (en suite)
Short breaks: £63 for 3 nights, £150 for 7 nights

A well-equipped modern bungalow with a private garden, situated 50 yards back from the A86.

QQQ Inverour PH34 4EU ☎ (039781) 218

Normal price: £13-£15.50 (en suite)
Short breaks: £12.50-£14.50. Min 4 nights, Mar-Oct excluding dinner.

An alternative roadside house in a central position with a pleasant lounge featuring an open fire.

★★57% Spean Bridge PH34 4ES ☎ (039781) 250

Normal price: £30. Dinner £14-£16
Short breaks: £126 for 2 people, 3 day break. £117 single
Credit cards ① ③ ⑤

A family-run roadside hotel with a modern, purpose-built annexe, ten chalets and a choice of original hotel bedrooms all furnished in contemporary style.

STRUY   Highland   Map 14 NH33

★★73% Cnoc Erchless Castle Estate IV4 7JU ☎ (046376) 264

Normal price: £24
Short breaks: £22. Min 3 nights. Jan-Apr & Oct-Dec.
Activity breaks: These can be arranged to suit guests. Please enquire for details.
Credit cards ① ③

This friendly little hotel is ideal for anglers. There are attractive, spacious public areas and comfortable bedrooms with ensuite facilities.

TONGUE Highland (Sutherland) Map 14 NC55

★★58% **Ben Loyal** IV27 4XE ☎ (084755) 216

Normal price: £20-£26.50. Dinner from £8.50.
Short breaks: £78-£95 for 3 nights, Apr-18 Oct, £55-£65 for
2 nights from 19 Oct.
Activity breaks: Loch Fishing Break, £152-£220 for 7 nights
including rod fee. Tuition available.
Credit cards [1] [3]

Small and friendly family-run tourist hotel.

WICK Highland Map 15 ND35

★★58% **Mackay's** Union Street KW1 5ED ☎ (0955) 2323

Normal price: £52
Short breaks: £40 excluding dinner. Min 2 nights, Fri-Sun.
Single supplement.
Credit cards [1] [3]

A family-run hotel situated in the town centre
on the banks of the River Wick. Service is
friendly and all bedrooms have colour
television. Free golf all year.

▪ LOTHIAN ▪

ABERLADY Lothian (East Lothian) Map 12 NT47

★★64% **Kilspindie House** Main Street EH32 0RE ☎ (08757) 682

Normal price: £78. Dinner from £11.
Short breaks: £60, min 2 nights, Oct-Mar
Activity breaks: Golf package, £290 (1990 price). Details
from hotel.
Credit cards [1] [3] [5]

A friendly family hotel, popular with both
business guests and golfers. Improvements
include a wing of comfortable bedrooms, but
the Golf Addict's Bar remains the same.

DUNBAR Lothian (East Lothian) Map 12 NT67

★★66% **Redheugh** Bayswell Park EH42 1AE ☎ (0368) 62793

Normal price: £22-£27.50. Dinner £10 and à la carte
Short breaks: £29.50. Min 2 nights, Fri-Sun

Friendly service and home-cooked meals are
provided by this hotel quietly situated in a
residential area. Bedrooms are comfortable
with ensuite bath or shower rooms and colour
television.

EAST LINTON Lothian Map 12 NT57

★★62% **Harvesters** Station Road EH40 3DP ☎ (0620) 860395

Normal price: £32. Dinner £6-£10 and à la carte
Short breaks: £40, (children 14 and under sharing family
room with 2 adults charged for meals only, children's
menu available). Min 2 nights, Fri-Sun
Credit cards [1] [2] [3] [5]

Conveniently located south of Edinburgh and
close to the A1, the hotel offers good-value
menus and friendly service. All the bedrooms
have colour television, and most have ensuite
facilities. Fishing is available.

EDINBURGH Lothian (Midlothian) Map 11 NT27

QQQ Ashdene House 23 Fountainhall Road EH9 2LN ☎ 031-667 6026

Normal price: £18
Short breaks: £28-£32 for 2 nights, £41-£45 for 3 nights,
Nov-Easter

This hotel has well-appointed, comfortable rooms, with colour television, hairdryers and telephones. Children under 2 are not accommodated.

★★★67% **Barnton Thistle** (Mount Charlotte (TS)) Queensferry Road, Barnton EH4 6AS ☎ 031-339 1144

Normal price: from £48. Dinner from £12
Short breaks: £38 excluding dinner. Min 2 nights
Credit cards ①②③④⑤

On the western outskirts of the city, this hotel has two restaurants and well-equipped bedrooms with ensuite facilities and colour television. There are rooms for families and non-smokers.

★★★56% **Braid Hills** 134 Braid Road, Braid Hills EH10 6JD (2.5m S A702) ☎ 031-447 8888

Normal price: £78 room and breakfast. Dinner from £14.95
Short breaks: £35. Min 2 nights, Jul & Aug
Credit cards ①②③⑤

A popular hotel offering an interesting blend of the old and the new. Bedrooms are modern with ensuite facilities and colour television, two rooms have four-poster beds and others are set aside for non-smokers. There is a special Christmas programme.

★★★63% **Bruntsfield** (Best Western) 69/74 Bruntsfield Place EH10 4HH ☎ 031-229 1393

Normal price: from £75 room. Dinner £14.50-£16 and à la carte
Short breaks: from £42. Min 2 nights. No single supplement at weekends

A new leisure complex is under development at this hotel situated just south of the city centre, which also offers a choice of bars and restaurants. Bedrooms are all ensuite with colour television, and one has a four-poster bed. There is a special Christmas programme.

★★51% **Cairn** 10-18 Windsor Street EH7 5JR ☎ 031-557 0175

Normal price: £45-£75 room and breakfast. Dinner £10.50 and à la carte
Short breaks: £28.50, single occupancy £35

This informal hotel at the east end of the city has been refurbished to provide bright public areas and bedrooms with ensuite facilities and colour television. No parking.

★★★★★65% **Caledonian** (Queens Moat) (Pride of Britain) Princes Street EH1 2AB ☎ 031-225 2433

Normal price: £87.50. Dinner £18.75 and à la carte
Short breaks: £65 excluding dinner.
🐾 (ex guide dogs) Credit cards ①②③④⑤

The hotel stands at one end of Princes Street and is overlooked by Edinburgh Castle. It offers friendly, efficient service, a choice of restaurants and ensuite bedrooms with colour television. Christmas breaks are available.

★★★67% **Capital Moat House** (Queens Moat) Clermiston Road EH12 6UG ☎ 031-334 3391

Normal price: £78 room and breakfast. Dinner £14.95-£16.95 & à la carte
Short breaks: £39.50. Min 2 nights, Fri-Sun
Credit cards ①②③④⑤

A comfortable, modern hotel in the west end of the city, offers a choice of restaurants, good leisure facilities and smart, well-equipped bedrooms with ensuite facilities and colour television. There is a special Christmas programme.

GH QQ Galloway 22 Dean Park Crescent EH4 1PH ☎ 031-332 3672

Normal price: £15
Short breaks: £15 including free city tour/coastal tour, discount voucher, and a Glayra liquer on arrival

This cheerful, informal establishment forms part of a Victorian terrace. Most bedrooms are spacious, and those with private facilities are particularly comfortable. Guests may have to share tables at breakfast time.

★★61% Lady Nairne (Berni/Chef & Brewer) 228 Willowbrae Road EH8 7NG ☎ 031-661 3396

Normal price: £69. Dinner £8-£15.
Short breaks: £23 Fri & Sat, £11 Sun, excluding dinner. Min 3 nights.
🦊 Credit cards ① ② ③ ⑤

A welcoming village inn has been converted to provide comfortable accommodation with cosily inviting lounge and bars. Service is warm and friendly throughout.

★★★57% Royal Scot (Swallow) 111 Glasgow Road EH12 5NF ☎ 031-334 9191

Normal price: £120 room and breakfast
Short breaks: £100 for 2 people for 2 days, including dinner and 1 lunch (1990 prices)
Credit cards ① ② ③ ⑤

A large, purpose-built hotel convenient for the airport, with a choice of restaurants and a leisure centre. All bedrooms have ensuite bath or shower room and colour television.

★★★58% Stakis Grosvenor Grosvenor Street EH12 5EF ☎ 031-226 6001

Normal price: £60. Dinner £12.50-£13.50.
Short breaks: £45-£60, min 2 nights.
Activity breaks: Christmas & New Year Party, 23 Dec-2 Jan. Details from hotel.
Credit cards ① ② ③ ⑤

A recently refurbished hotel catering for business and coach tour markets with a choice of two attractive restaurants.

GH QQQ Teviotdale House 53 Grange Loan, Grange EH9 2ER ☎ 031-667 4376

Normal price: £44 room and breakfast
Short breaks: £36 for two excluding dinner. Min 2 nights, Nov-Feb
🦊 (ex guide dogs) Credit cards ① ② ③

A carefully renovated Victorian house south of the city centre offering attractive bedrooms and superb breakfasts. This is a 'no smoking' establishment. No parking.

GH QQQ Thrums 14 Minto Street, Newington EH9 1RQ ☎ 031-667 5545
Closed Christmas & New Year

Normal price: £23.50-£25
Short breaks: £21.50-£26.50. Min 2 nights, Oct-Apr

Situated to the south of the city centre, this comfortable guesthouse has tastefully decorated bedrooms; those in the annexe have private shower rooms and are particularly spacious.

HUMBIE   Lothian (East Lothian) Map 12 NT46

★★★ 🏨 66% Johnstounburn House (Mount Charlotte (TS)) EH36 5PL (1m S on A6137)
☎ (087533) 696

Normal price: £57.50
Short breaks: £49.50 excluding dinner. Single £64.50. Min 2 nights
Credit cards ① ② ③ ⑤

A charming 17th-century house set in secluded grounds and gardens. Bedrooms are individually styled, and all are ensuite with colour television. There are special facilities for children. Clay pigeon shooting is available.

NORTH BERWICK   Lothian (East Lothian)   Map 12 NT58

★★★64% **Marine** (Trusthouse Forte) Cromwell Road EH39 4LZ ☎ (0620) 2406

Normal price: £55 including dinner.
Short breaks: £45-£55, min 2 nights. Single supplement in summer.
Activity breaks: Golf Weeks, £450 for 6 nights including golf, tuition, prizes and entertainment. Mar, Apr, Jun & Oct. Golf Breaks, £125 for 2 nights including golf. Murder Weekends, £165 for 2 nights. Feb, Mar, Apr & Nov. Art/Painting Breaks, £130 for 2 nights including instruction and some equipment. Jun, Nov & Apr.
Credit cards ① ② ③ ④ ⑤

A popular golfing hotel standing beside the championship golf links overlooking the Firth of Forth. The comfortable bedrooms have mostly been upgraded.

SOUTH QUEENSFERRY   Lothian (West Lothian)   Map 11 NT17

★★★60% **Forth Bridges Moat House** Forth Bridge EH30 ☎ 031-331 1199

Normal price: £48. Dinner from £13 and à la carte.
Short breaks: £39.50, min 2 nights, Fri-Sun. £7 single supplement.
Credit cards ① ② ③ ⑤

A popular business and tourist hotel overlooking the Firth, substantially refurbished to provide comfortable modern accommodation, combined with an excellent selection of recreational facilities.

▪ STRATHCLYDE ▪

APPIN   Strathclyde (Argyllshire)   Map 14 NN04

★★★ ♨ 73% **Invercreran Country House** Glen Creran PA38 4BJ ☎ (063173) 414 & 456
Closed Dec-Feb

Normal price: £42.50. Dinner £22.50
Short breaks: from £60. Min 2 nights, Mar-Apr and Oct-Nov
✿ (ex guide dogs) Credit cards ① ③

A small, select country house hotel offering the best of Scottish seafood, meat and game. All seven bedrooms have ensuite facilities and colour television, there are three family rooms and one room is set aside for non-smokers. A seasonal programme is offered at Christmas. Children under five are not accommodated

ARDUAINE   Strathclyde (Argyllshire)   Map 10 NM80

★★★68% **Loch Melfort** PA34 4XG ☎ (08522) 233
Closed mid Oct-Etr

Normal price: £42.50
Short breaks: from £47.50. Min 2 nights. Available end Sep-28 Dec (excluding Xmas and New Year) and Mar-2 May
Credit cards ①

A family-owned hotel enjoying superb views of the sea and islands. Most of the bedrooms are situated in the Cedar Wing and have balconies or patios, and ensuite bathrooms. A few rooms have colour television. In addition to the restaurant, guests can eat in the Chart Room Bar which serves food for most of the day.

AYR   Strathclyde (Ayrshire)   Map 10 NS32

★62% **Aftongrange** 37 Carrick Road KA7 2RD ☎ (0292) 265679

Normal price: £21
Short breaks: £24. Min 3 nights, Oct-Mar

Situated on the south side of town this small family-run hotel is popular for the generous portions served in the dining room. All bedrooms have colour television, most enjoy ensuite facilities and there are two family rooms.

★★★56% **Caledonian** (Embassy) Dalblair Road KA7 1UG ☎ (0292) 269331

Normal price: £56.50. Dinner from £14.50.
Short breaks: £46. Min 2 nights. Single breaks weekends only.
Activity breaks: Golf Break, details from hotel.
Credit cards ① ② ③ ⑤

The bright, spacious public areas of this centrally-located, modern hotel include a terrace cafe open from 7am to 11pm. Many bedrooms have sea views.

★★★61% **Pickwick** 19 Racecourse Road KA7 2TD ☎ (0292) 260111

Normal price: £80 (room). Dinner £12.95-£14.95 and à la carte
Short breaks: £190 for 2 people, including lunch on day of departure. Min 2 nights
Credit cards ① ② ③ ⑤

Friendly, personally-run hotel in a Victorian mansion with good parking facilities. There is a putting green and fishing is available. All the bedrooms have colour television and ensuite bath or shower rooms, three are for families and one room has a four-poster bed. The hotel has special facilities for children.

BARRHILL   Strathclyde (Lanarkshire)   Map 10 NX28

❀★★★ 🐾 77% **Kildonan** KA26 0PU ☎ (046582) 360

Normal price: £55. Dinner £21.95-£25 and à la carte
Short breaks: £65, single £75. Min 2 nights (ex Bank Holidays)
Credit cards ① ② ③ ⑤

Located off the beaten track this country house offers a haven for those seeking solitude in beautiful surroundings. Most of the bedrooms are spacious, all have private facilities and colour television, and there are seven family rooms. One has a four-poster bed. Leisure amenities include an indoor heated swimming pool, 9-hole golf course, tennis and gymnasium. There is a special Christmas programme.

BIGGAR   Strathclyde (Lanarkshire)   Map 11 NT03

★★★ 🐾 75% **Shieldhill** Quothqan ML12 6NA ☎ (0899) 20035

Normal price: £45.50. Dinner from £19.95 and à la carte
Short breaks: £57.50. Min 2 nights, Oct-15 Dec & 3 Jan-Apr. Single £99

This charming, elegant hotel is comfortably furnished and enhanced by lovely antiques and fresh flowers. All the bedrooms have ensuite facilities and colour television, and four are furnished with four-poster beds. All are non-smoking. Guests can enjoy croquet and bowls. Children under fifteen are not accommodated.

★★★64% **Tinto** Symington ML12 6PQ ☎ (08993) 454

Normal price: £28. Dinner £10-£20 à la carte
Short breaks: £25.20 excluding dinner. Single £34.20. Min 3 nights.
Credit cards ① ② ③ ⑤

Situated within attractive gardens and close to Tinto Hill, this hotel offers keenly-priced light meals throughout the day and evening. All the bedrooms including the two family rooms have ensuite facilities and colour television, and one has a four-poster bed. There is a solarium and pool table for guests' use. A Christmas programme is available.

CAMPBELTOWN   Strathclyde (Argyllshire)   Map 10 NR72

★61% **Ardshiel** Kilkerran Road PA28 6JL ☎ (0568) 52133

Normal price: £50 room and breakfast
Short breaks: £30, min 3 nights
Credit cards ① ③

A friendly family-run hotel, where all the bedrooms have ensuite facilities and colour television, including the family rooms.

★65% **Seafield** Kilkerran Road PA28 6JL ☎ (0568) 54385

Normal price: £44 room and breakfast. Dinner £10.50-£13.50 and à la carte
Short breaks: 10% discount on room and breakfast. Min 3 nights
Credit cards ① ③

A small, homely family-run hotel with a cosy little lounge bar. Most of the ensuite bedrooms are situated in a modern bungalow at the rear, and all are equipped with colour television.

CLACHAN-SEIL   Strathclyde (Argyllshire)   Map 10 NM71

★★65% **Willowburn** (Guestaccom) PA34 4JT ☎ (08523) 276
Closed Nov-mid Mar

Normal price: £35 including dinner
Short breaks: £88 for 3 days, mid Mar-May & mid Sep-Oct
Credit cards ① ③

Bar lunches are available at this small hotel which is situated in its own garden. All rooms have ensuite facilities and colour television.

COLMONELL   Strathclyde (Ayrshire)   Map 10 NX18

FH QQ **Burnfoot** KA26 0SQ ☎ (046588) 220 & 265
Apr-Oct

Normal price: £22 room with breakfast
Short breaks: £20. Dinner £6. Min 3 nights (except Jun-Aug)

This welcoming farmhouse is in a peaceful country setting beside the River Stinchar. The bedrooms have tea and coffee making facilities and there is full central heating.

CONNEL   Strathclyde (Argyllshire)   Map 10 NM93

★★64% **Falls of Lora** (Inter-Hotels) PA37 1PB ☎ (063171) 483
Closed Xmas & New Year

Normal price: £35-£91 room and breakfast. Dinner from £14.50
Short breaks: £29.50, single £39.50. Min 2 nights, 15 Oct-15 May (except Bank Holidays)

This spacious hotel has lovely views of Loch Etvie and a pleasant, relaxing atmosphere. All the bedrooms, both those in the main house and in the modern wing, have colour television and ensuite bathrooms. One room has a four-poster bed.

DOLPHINTON   Strathclyde (Lanarkshire)   Map 11 NT14

★★★ ♨ 64% **Dolphinton House** EH46 7AB ☎ (0968) 82268
Normal price: £57. Dinner £24.95.
Short breaks: £60
Activity breaks: Cross Country Equestrian Event, 12 Aug.
Details from hotel.
Credit cards ① ② ③ ④ ⑤

A 19th-century sandstone house standing in 186 acres of parkland and woods, carefully converted to provide up to date facilities while retaining many original Victorian features.

DUNLOP   Strathclyde (Ayrshire)   Map 10 NS44

FH QQQ Struther Newmill Road KA3 4BA ☎ (0560) 84946
Closed 2 weeks Spring & Autumn, restricted service Sun

Normal price: £25 room and breakfast
Short breaks: £21. Min 2 nights

A large farmhouse situated in its own gardens on the outskirts of the village. Some of the comfortable bedrooms are for families.

DUNOON   Strathclyde (Argyllshire)   Map 10 SN17

★★78% **Enmore** Marine Parade, Kirn PA23 8HH ☎ (0369) 2230 & 2148
Closed Christmas & New Year. Restricted service Nov-Feb

Normal price: £55-£71
Short breaks: £43-£65. Min 2 nights, Nov-1 May
Credit cards ① ③ ⑤

This attractive hotel is run in the style of a country house. Bedrooms are individually styled and thoughtfully equipped, and there are rooms with waterbeds and four-poster beds. Special facilities are available for children.

EAST KILBRIDE   Strathclyde (Lanarkshire)   Map 11 NS65

★★★60% **Stuart** 2 Cornwall Way G74 1JR ☎ (03552) 21161
Closed 25 Dec-1 Jan

Normal price: £27
Short breaks: £22 excluding dinner, single occupancy
£34.40.
Credit cards ① ② ③ ⑤

A town centre hotel with ensuite bedrooms, all with colour television and one with a four-poster bed. There is weekly entertainment and a Christmas programme is available. No parking.

GIFFNOCK   Strathclyde (Renfrewshire)   Map 11 NS55

★★★67% **Macdonald Thistle** (Mount Charlotte (TS)) Eastwood Toll G46 6RA ☎ 041-638 2225
Normal price: £45.25. Dinner from £12.95 and à la carte
Short breaks: £40 excluding dinner. No single supplement
at weekends
Credit cards ① ② ③ ④ ⑤

Situated on the southern outskirts of Glasgow at the Eastwood Toll roundabout (A77), this modern hotel has a good range of leisure facilities. All bedrooms are ensuite with colour television.

GLASGOW   Strathclyde (Lanarkshire)   Map 11 NS56

★★★★61% **Holiday Inn Glasgow** Argyle Street, Anderston G3 8RR ☎ 041-226 5577
Normal price: £62.25. Dinner £16.25 and à la carte
Short breaks: £37.50 excluding dinner. Single occupancy
£49.50
Credit cards ① ② ③ ④ ⑤

A large city-centre hotel offering a good range of leisure facilities, including an indoor heated pool, and comfortable ensuite bedrooms. A pianist plays in the cocktail bar in the evenings. Christmas breaks are available.

★★★62% **Kelvin Park Lorne** (Queens Moat) 923 Sauchiehall Street G3 7TE ☎ 041-334 4891

Normal price: £40.48. Dinner £11.95.
Short breaks: £34, min 2 nights, Fri-Sun.
Activity breaks: Classics Weekends. Details from hotel.
Credit cards [1] [2] [3] [4] [5]

Totally refurbished hotel offering an elegant restaurant, comfortable public areas and two styles of bedrooms.

★★58% **Sherbrooke** 11 Sherbrooke Avenue, Pollokshields G41 4PG ☎ 041-427 4227

Normal price: £65 room and breakfast
Short breaks: £30 excluding dinner, single occupancy £40. Fri-Sun
Credit cards [1] [2] [3] [5]

An attractive red sandstone building located in a residential area close to the M77. The annexe wing offers a more modern style of accommodation; bedrooms throughout the hotel are ensuite with colour television, and there are rooms for families and non-smokers.

★★★59% **Stakis Ingram** (Stakis) Ingram Street G1 1DQ ☎ 041-248 4401

Normal price: £83 room and breakfast. Dinner £11.95-£12.95
Short breaks: £35 excluding dinner. £6 single supplement. Min 2 nights, Fri-Sun
Credit cards [1] [2] [3] [5]

A city centre hotel close to George Square. The comfortable bedrooms are all ensuite with colour television, with rooms set aside for non-smokers. There is a special Christmas programme.

★★★66% **Tinto Firs Thistle** (Mount Charlotte (TS)) ☎ 041-637 2353

Normal price: £45.25. Dinner from £12.50 and à la carte
Short breaks: £40 excluding dinner. No single supplement at weekends
Credit cards [1] [2] [3] [4] [5]

A modern purpose-built hotel, set in a residential area on the south of the city, with comfortable ensuite bedrooms equipped with colour television. There are rooms for families and non-smokers.

GLASGOW AIRPORT   Strathclyde (Renfrewshire)   Map 11 NS46

★★★60% **Dean Park** (Queens Moat) 91 Glasgow Road PA4 8YB (3m NE A8) ☎ 041-886 3771

Normal price: £39. Dinner £9.95 and à la carte (1990 prices)
Short breaks: £34. Min 2 nights, Fri-Sun. £10 single supplement.
Credit cards [1] [2] [3] [5]

This comfortable well-equipped hotel with a garden has private bathrooms and colour television in all bedrooms, which include a few family rooms. Christmas breaks are available.

★★★58% **Glynhill** (Consort) Paisley Road PA4 8XB (2m E A741) ☎ 041-886 5555

Normal price: £40. Dinner £11.45-£15.95 and à la carte (1990 prices)
Short breaks: £45 including weekend entertainment. Fri-Sun
Credit cards [1] [2] [3] [5]

This much-extended hotel has a smart bar, carvery restaurant and leisure complex with an indoor swimming pool, gymnasium, sauna, steam room, solarium and snooker. All bedrooms, which include family rooms and two with four-poster beds, are ensuite with colour television. Christmas breaks are available.

IRVINE   Strathclyde   Map 10 NS33

★★★63% **Hospitality Inn** (Mount Charlotte (TS)) Annick Road, Annickwater KA11 4LD ☎ (0294) 74272

Normal price: £47.30
Short breaks: £53.50 (£10 less for twin room). Min 2 nights. Single supplement.
Credit cards [1] [2] [3] [4] [5]

A popular business and tourist hotel conveniently situated close to the A78. A feature of one of the restaurants is a spectacular tropical lagoon. Bedrooms are comfortable and offer ensuite facilities and colour television.

LANGBANK   Strathclyde (Renfrewshire)   Map 10 NS37

★★★ 🏨 **Gleddoch House** PA14 6YE ☎ (047554) 711

Normal price: £125 room and breakfast.
Short breaks: £68, min 2 nights, Fri-Sun. Single price £75.
Activity breaks: Golf Breaks, £136 for 2 nights including golf. Tuition available by arrangement. Skeet Shooting, as for golf break plus shooting charge.
Credit cards ① ② ③ ⑤

A fine hotel with many of the features of a private country house, and fine views across the Clyde. Menus based on top quality Scottish produce.

LARGS   Strathclyde   Map 10 NS25

★★59% **Springfield** Greenock Road KA30 8QL ☎ (0475) 673119

Normal price: £32.50-£36.50
Short breaks: £25.50-£28.50, Oct-Mar
Credit cards ① ② ③ ⑤

This seafront hotel has spacious public rooms and comfortable bedrooms, all with colour television and most with ensuite facilities.

MILNGAVIE   Strathclyde (Dunbartonshire)   Map 11 NS57

★★★59% **Black Bull Thistle** (Thistle) Main Street G62 6BH ☎ 041-956 2291

Normal price: £37.75
Short breaks: £32 excluding dinner. Single supplement.
Credit cards ① ② ③ ④ ⑤

Beamed ceilings, polished oak and tapestries feature in this tastefully restored former coaching inn, where all bedrooms, including 2 family rooms, have ensuite facilities and colour television. Occasional musical entertainment.

OBAN   Strathclyde (Argyllshire)   Map 10 NM83

✿★★76% **Manor House** Gallanach Road PA34 4LS ☎ (0631) 62087

Normal price: £70 including dinner
Short breaks: £35-£39. Min 2 nights, Oct-Dec, Feb-Mar
Credit cards ① ③

This small, relaxing hotel on the waterfront provides good food and comfortable bedrooms, including two no-smoking rooms, all with ensuite bathrooms and colour television. No children under 5 accommodated.

RHU Strathclyde (Dunbartonshire) Map 10 NS28

★★★55% **Rosslea Hall** G84 8NF ☎ (0436) 820684

Normal price: £79 room and breakfast
Short breaks: £87 for two excluding dinner. Single occupancy £60
Credit cards ① ② ③ ⑤

This mansion, which dates back to 1849, is situated on the shore of the Gareloch, a popular Clyde anchorage. It has recently been extended to offer a range of eating and function facilities.

TAYNUILT   Strathclyde   Map 10 NN03

★★66% **Brander Lodge** Bridge of Awe PA35 1HT (Consort) ☎ (08662) 243 & 225

Normal price: £20.50-£28.50
Short breaks: £32. Min 2 nights, Oct-Apr.
Credit cards ① ② ③ ⑤

Small family-run hotel with a relaxing atmosphere. Comfortable bedrooms boast ensuite facilities and colour television.

TROON Strathclyde (Ayrshire) Map 10 NS33

★★★★65% **Marine Highland** (Scottish Highland) KA10 6HE ☎ (0292) 314444

Normal price: £60. Dinner £17.50.
Short breaks: £65, min 2 nights.
Activity breaks: Golf Breaks, £95 per day.

With Troon's championship golf course on its doorstep this hotel is popular with golfers. It offers good leisure facilities.

★★57% **South Beach** South Beach Road KA10 6EG ☎ (0292) 312033

Normal price: From £27.50
Short breaks: £35-£39.50. Min 3 nights.
Credit cards ① ② ③

A seafront hotel, popular with families, with a recently-completed leisure centre. All bedrooms have ensuite facilities and colour television.

TURNBERRY Strathclyde Map 10 NS20

★★★66% **Malin Court** KA26 9PB ☎ (0655) 1457

Normal price: £39.55
Short breaks: £39.50. Min 2 nights. Oct-Apr.
Credit cards ① ② ③ ④ ⑤

Situated on the coast, just north of the famous golf course, this small modern hotel forms an integral part of a home for the elderly. Recently refurbished, the bedrooms offer ensuite facilities and colour television.

TAYSIDE

ABERFELDY Tayside Map 12

★★61% **Weem** PH15 2LD ☎ (0887) 20381

Normal price: £46 room and breakfast. Dinner £12.50 and à la carte
Short breaks: £36 for two excluding dinner. 2-4 nights 22 Oct-28 Mar
Credit cards ② ③ ⑤

A friendly roadside inn with a fascinating history. The hotel offers practical, well-equipped bedrooms and traditional comforts. It is a popular base for touring holidaymakers. Christmas/Hogmanay programmes. Golf, fishing and shooting are all available.

ARBROATH Tayside (Angus) Map 12 NO64

★★★66% **Letham Grange** (Best Western) Colliston DD11 4RL ☎ (024189) 373

Normal price: £40. Dinner from £16.
Short breaks: £58 includes golf. Min 2 nights. Prices subject to review
🕷 (ex guide dogs) Credit cards ①②③⑤

This handsome Victorian mansion, set in 200 acres of wooded grounds, offers a range of leisure facilities including an 18-hole championship golf course, a 4-sheet curling rink, putting, and pool tables. All bedrooms have private baths and colour television, one has a four-poster bed, and there are four family rooms. A special Christmas programme is available.

AUCHTERARDER   Tayside (Perthshire) Map 11 NN91

★★★★★(Red) **Gleneagles** PH3 1NF ☎ (0764) 62231

Normal price: £82-£97. Dinner from £27.50.
Short breaks: £120 (1990 price). Min 2 nights, Fri-Sat, May-Oct, any 2 nights from Nov.
Activity breaks: Golf Breaks, playing on championship courses. Clay Target Shooting at the Gleneagles Jackie Stewart Shooting School. Riding at the Mark Phillips Equestrian Centre. Health and Beauty, including treatments at the Champneys Health Spa. Country Club with swimming pool, jacuzzi, turkish baths, sauna, solarium, squash, tennis, croquet and bowls. Prices on application.
Credit cards ①②③④⑤

Unrivalled leisure and recreational facilities at this hotel include 2 fine golf courses, a shooting school and an equestrian centre. The hotel and restaurant are admirably run.

BLAIRGOWRIE   Tayside (Perthshire) Map 15 NO14

★★58% **Angus** (Consort) 46 Wellmeadow PH10 6NQ ☎ (0250) 2838

Normal price: £61. Dinner £12.50-£17.
Short breaks: £67.50 for 2 nights, including Sunday bar lunch. Min 2 nights.
Activity breaks: Skiing, from £120, 5 nights, Jan. Golf, from £210, 5 nights.
Credit cards ①②③

A popular town centre holiday hotel with bright modern public rooms and a good range of leisure facilities.

★★60% **Rosemount Golf** Golf Course Road, Rosemount PH10 6LJ ☎ (0250) 2604

Normal price: £22.50 bed and breakfast, £33 with dinner
Short breaks: £28.50 including £11.50 dinner allowance. £5 single supplement. Min 2 nights, Nov-Apr.
Credit cards ①③

Popular with golfers, this family-run hotel stands in its own spacious grounds not far from the Rosemount Course. There are twelve bedrooms all with private facilities and colour television, with two rooms set aside for families.

COMRIE Tayside (Perthshire) Map 11 NN72

★★63% **Royal** Melville Square PH6 2DN ☎ (0764) 70200
Restricted service Oct-Mar

Normal price: £24. Dinner £14 and à la carte
Short breaks: £74 2 days full board, £80 single occupancy
(except Easter, Christmas & New Year)
Credit cards ① ② ③

Originally a famed hostelry with historic connections, this hotel offers courteous service and comfortable accommodation. Most of the bedrooms have private baths, and all have colour television. Fishing is available and there is a snooker table. At Christmas there is a special programme.

CRIEFF Tayside (Perthshire) Map 11 NN82

★60% **Gwydyr House** Comrie Road PH7 4BP ☎ (0764) 3277
Closed Nov-Etr

Normal price: £14.50. Dinner £8.50 and à la carte
Short breaks: £13 excluding dinner.

A small, family-run hotel to the west of town, with a friendly atmosphere and good value accommodation. All rooms have colour television and some are set aside for families.

DUNDEE Tayside (Angus) Map 11 NO43

★★★61% **Angus Thistle** (Mount Charlotte (TS)) 10 Marketgait DD1 1QU ☎ (0382) 26874

Normal price: £42.75. Dinner from £12.95 and à la carte
Short breaks: £37 excluding dinner. No single supplement at weekends
Credit cards ① ② ③ ④ ⑤

This busy hotel is situated in the city centre. All bedrooms are ensuite with colour television, two have four-poster beds and some are set aside for non-smokers. There is a games room.

★★★66% **Stakis Earl Grey** (Stakis) Earl Grey Place DD1 4DE ☎ (0382) 29271

Normal price: £92 room. Dinner £14.75.
Short breaks: £34, excluding dinner, min 2 nights.
Activity breaks: Golfing Breaks, Clay Pigeon Shooting Breaks, Fishing Breaks, details from hotel.
🏌 Credit cards ① ② ③ ④ ⑤

A modern hotel on the banks of the River Tay with commanding panoramic views, offering a small leisure complex.

DUNKELD Tayside (Perthshire) Map 11 NO04

★★★63% **Birnam** (Consort) Birnam PH8 0BQ ☎ (03502) 462

Normal price: £31.50. Dinner £14.95-£16.95
Short breaks: £37.50, single £44.50. Min 2 nights.
Credit cards ① ② ③ ⑤

A comfortable, friendly, family-run hotel situated just off the A9, with a spacious lounge, first-floor dining rooms and ensuite bedrooms with colour television.

★★★★62% **Stakis Dunkeld House** PH8 0HX ☎ (03502) 771

Normal price: from £60. Dinner from £22.50.
Short breaks: from £120 for 2 nights. Single supplement.
Activity breaks: Christmas House Party, from £330 for 3 nights. New Year House Party, from £550 for 4 nights. (1990 prices). Clay Pigeon Shooting, from £170, Mon-Sat. Salmon/Trout Fishing, from £150. Archery Breaks, from £140.
🏌 Credit cards ① ② ③ ⑤

Set in its own extensive grounds on the banks of the River Tay, the house has been sympathetically extended, and offers an extensive range of leisure and sporting activities.

GH QQ Waterbury PH8 0BG ☎ (03502) 324

Normal price: £24
Short breaks: £22 excluding dinner, 3-6 nights, £21 7 nights

This family-run guesthouse stands in the main street of the village of Birnham. It offers comfortable accommodation and a friendly atmosphere. There are two family rooms.

EDZELL Tayside (Angus) Map 15 NO56

★★★58% **Glenesk** High Street DD9 7TF ☎ (03564) 319

Normal price: £30. Dinner £10.50
Short breaks: £39. Min 2 nights, Oct-Mar & Jul
Credit cards ②③⑤

A family-run hotel by the golf course at the edge of the village, popular with holiday makers and golfers. Most bedrooms are ensuite with colour television. There is a good range of leisure facilities and a Christmas programme is available.

FORGANDENNY Tayside (Perthshire) Map 11 NO01

FH QQQ Craighall PH2 9DF (0.5m W off B935 Bridge of Earn/Forteviot Road) ☎ (0738) 812415

Normal price: £12.50-£14
Short breaks: £12-£13.50 excluding dinner. Min 6 nights
🛏

This large bungalow-type farmhouse is situated in 1000 acres of farmland. Two of the bedrooms have ensuite shower rooms. Smoking is not allowed in the bedrooms.

GLENFARG Tayside (Perthshire) Map 11 NO11

★★60% **Bein Inn** PH2 9PY ☎ (05773) 216

Normal price: 2 days £140, 3 days £200, 4 days £280. All prices room with breakfast. Dinner £15-£25 à la carte
Short breaks: 2 days £150, 3 days £220, 4 days £300. All prices for 2 people. Single occupancy £95
🛏 (ex guide dogs) Credit cards ①③

This former Drovers Inn is a popular base for tourists and sporting enthusiasts. It offers an interesting blend of the old and new, and has a relaxed atmosphere. The best bedrooms are in the annexe. There is a special Christmas programme.

KILLIECRANKIE   Tayside   Map 14 NN96

★★67% **Killiecrankie** PH16 5LG ☎ (0796) 3220

Normal price: £37.75
Short breaks: £46.75. Min 2 nights. 13 May-30 Sep.
Activity breaks: Golf (all year) and Shooting (from 12 Aug)
breaks are available. Please enquire for details.
Credit cards ① ③

Set in four acres of wooded grounds, close to the famous Pass of Killiecrankie, this charming hotel has a friendly, informal atmosphere. All of the attractive bedrooms have colour television. Meals make imaginative use of fresh local produce.

KINROSS   Tayside (Kinross-shire)   Map 11 NO10

★★★62% **Green** (Best Western) 2 The Muirs KY13 7AS ☎ (0577) 63467

Normal price: £36.50-£40. Dinner £14.50-£16.
Short breaks: £50, min 4 nights. Single price £60.
Activity breaks: Golfing Breaks, £110 any 2 days. Curling
Weekends, £80. Details from hotel.

A friendly atmosphere prevails at this popular hotel with its wide range of sporting facilities. Bedrooms are compact and practical.

★★★66% **Windlestrae** The Muirs KY13 7AS (Consort) ☎ (0577) 63217

Normal price: £32.50-£35
Short breaks: £48-£52.50. Min 2 nights. Single supplement.
Credit cards ① ② ③ ⑤

A comfortable hotel with an attractive split-level bar. All bedrooms have colour television.

KIRKMICHAEL   Tayside   Map 15 NO06

★★58% **Aldchappie** PH10 7NS ☎ (025081) 224

Normal price: £17-£20
Short breaks: £26. Min 2 nights.
🐾 (ex guide dogs) Credit cards ① ② ③

An attractive hotel by the River Ardle which caters for tourists in summer and ski enthusiasts in winter. The cosy Malt Room bar is noted for its extensive range of malt whiskies.

★55% **Strathlene** Main Road PH10 7NT ☎ (025081) 347

Normal price: £15
Short breaks: £21. Min 3 nights. All year except Christmas
and New Year. Rooms with private facilities £2 per person
per night extra.
Credit cards ① ③

A family-run hotel located at the centre of this picturesque village. All bedrooms have colour television.

MONTROSE   Tayside (Angus)   Map 15 NO75

★★★58% **Park** 61 John Street DD10 8RJ ☎ (0674) 73415

Normal price: £38. Dinner £12.50.
Short breaks: £23, Thu-Sun. Single price £35.
Activity breaks: Golf Weekends, £110.
Credit cards ① ② ③ ⑤

An hotel just a few minutes' walk from both the town centre and the beach, offering standard or superior bedrooms.

PERTH   Tayside (Perthshire)   Map 11 NO12

★★★60% **Lovat** 90 Glasgow Road PH2 0LT ☎ (0738) 36555

Normal price: £32. Dinner from £9.50 and à la carte (1990 price)
Short breaks: £34 including hotel dance when available. Min 2 nights, Fri-Sun. £39 for single occupancy.
🌟 (ex guide dogs) Credit cards ① ② ③

Just south of the city centre, this popular hotel has ensuite facilities and colour television in all bedrooms. One bar is reserved for non-smokers and regular dinner dances are held. Christmas breaks are available.

★★★57% **Newton House** (Inter-Hotels) Glencarse PH2 7LX ☎ (073886) 250

Normal price: £32. Dinner £19 and à la carte
Short breaks: from £44. Single supplement from £11. Min 2 nights.
Credit cards ① ③ ⑤

Set back from the busy A85, in its own grounds, this small hotel has dinner and lunch menus which feature well-prepared Scottish produce. Each bedroom has a private bath or shower room and colour television. There are special facilities for children and a Christmas programme is available.

★★★63% **Queens** Leonard Street PH2 8HB ☎ (0738) 25471

Normal price: £72 room and breakfast
Short breaks: £37. Min 2 nights, Fri-Sun. £45 for single occupancy.
🌟 Credit cards ① ② ③

Near the station and city centre, this refurbished hotel has leisure facilities which include an indoor swimming pool, sauna, solarium and gymnasium. All bedrooms, some of them family rooms, are ensuite with colour television.

★★★58% **Royal George** (Trusthouse Forte) Tay Street PH1 5LD ☎ (0738) 24455

Normal price: £75 room only (1990).
Short breaks: £47, min 2 nights (1990). Single supplement.
Credit cards ① ② ③ ④ ⑤

This popular hotel by the river and close to the town centre has ensuite bath and colour television in all bedrooms, which include some no-smoking rooms. Christmas breaks are available.

★★★59% **Stakis City Mills** West Mill Street PH1 5QP ☎ (0738) 28281

Normal price: from £86 room only. Dinner £8-£10.50 and à la carte (1990 price)
Short breaks: from £39. Min 2 nights. £12 single supplement.
Credit cards ① ② ③ ⑤

This imaginatively converted watermill has a choice of bars and restaurants, and all bedrooms, over half of which are non-smoking, have ensuite facilities and two with four-poster beds. Christmas breaks are available.

PITLOCHRY   Tayside   Map 14 NN95

★★★58% **Atholl Palace** (Trusthouse Forte) Atholl Road PH16 5LY ☎ (0796) 2400

Normal price: £50. Dinner £13.50-£14.50 and à la carte (1990 price)
Short breaks: £52, Apr-Jun, Oct-Dec. £57, Jul-Sep. Min 2 nights.
Credit cards ① ② ③ ④ ⑤

Set in 48 acres of grounds, this popular hotel has comfortable public rooms and extensive leisure facilities including snooker, outdoor swimming, tennis, pitch and putt, sauna, solarium and gymnasium. The practical bedrooms are ensuite with colour television and include family and no-smoking rooms. Christmas breaks are available.

★★64% **Birchwood** (Inter-Hotels) 2 East Moulin Road PH16 5DW ☎ (0796) 2477

Normal price: from £37. Dinner £14.50.
Short breaks: from £35, min 3 nights. Single supplement.
Activity breaks: Golf Week, £280 including green fees, tuition and entertainment. 27 Apr-4 May. Golf Breaks, £200 for 5 days including green fees for unlimited golf. Apr-Oct.
Credit cards 1 3

An attractive Victorian house set in its own grounds and providing a popular base for tourists seeking quiet relaxation.

★★★63% **Green Park** Clunie Bridge Road PH16 5JY ☎ (0796) 3248

Normal price: £45 including dinner.
Short breaks: £38. Min 2 nights, 26 Mar-4 May.
✚ Credit cards 1

This country house hotel on the banks of Loch Faskally has private facilities and colour television in all bedrooms. Leisure facilities include fishing, putting, table tennis and bar billiards.

★71% **Knockendarroch House** Higher Oakfield PH16 5HT ☎ (0796) 3473

Normal price: £21 low season, £28 high season. Dinner £11 (1990 price)
Short breaks: £31.50 low season, £38.50 high season. Min 2 nights, 1 Apr-14 Nov.
Credit cards 1 2 3 5

This small family-run hotel with pleasant grounds serves good local food and has bright, airy bedrooms with private facilities and colour television, including a family room and two with four-poster beds.

★★★68% **Pine Trees** Strathview Terrace PH16 5QR ☎ (0796) 2121

Normal price: £35
Short breaks: £26-£30 excluding dinner. Min 2 nights, Jan-May, Oct-Nov.
✚ (ex guide dogs) Credit cards 1 3

Set in 14 acres of grounds which include a putting green, this attractive family-run country house hotel has elegant public rooms and well-equipped bedrooms with private bathrooms and colour television, including some family rooms.

★★★58% **Scotland's** (Best Western) 40 Bonnethill Road PH16 5BT ☎ (0796) 2292

Normal price: £27-£39. Dinner from £12.50.
Short breaks: £41.50-£45.50. Min 2 nights.
Activity breaks: Curling Weekends, £90 approx. Jan, Feb & Mar.
Credit cards 1 2 3 5

A busy hotel with a friendly atmosphere and good value practical accommodation. A new leisure centre is due to open in the spring.

SCONE   Tayside (Perth)   Map 12 NO12

❋★★★ 🏨 **Murrayshall Country House** New Scone PH2 7PH ☎ (0738) 51171

Normal price: £52.50-£57.50. Dinner £35-£40.
Short breaks: £85 (1990 price). £10 single supplement.
Activity breaks: Gourmet weekends, Christmas & New Year breaks. Contact hotel for details.
Credit cards 1 2 3 5

A country-house hotel just north of Perth, Murrayshall has its own golf course and separate club house so that golfing parties do not intrude on the quiet atmosphere. The major attraction, however, is the excellent cooking of master chef Bruce Sangster. The 4-course table d'hôte menu provides a choice at each course and displays a subtlety and skill rarely encountered outside London and the Home Counties. A pianist and harpist provide entertainment in the evenings, creating a relaxing atmosphere for diners. Accommodation, especially in the main house, is spacious, though rooms in the new wing are more compact.

SCOTTISH ISLANDS

■ ARRAN, ISLE OF ■

LAMLASH Arran, Isle of (Strathclyde)   Map 10 NS03

★★66% **Glenisle** KA27 8LS ☎ (07706) 559 & 258

Normal price: £29.50-£34.50
Short breaks: £25. Min 3 nights. Nov-Mar.
Credit cards ① ③

This small, comfortable hotel is set on the seafront overlooking Holy Isle. The popular restaurant provides enjoyable meals featuring fresh local produce.

■ COLONSAY, ISLE OF ■

SCALASAIG Colonsay, Isle of (Argyllshire)   Map 10 NR30

★71% **Colonsay** PA61 7YP ☎ (09512) 316 and 353

Normal price: £45. Dinner £15.
Short breaks: £43, min 2 nights, Mar, Apr, 1-14 May, Sept & Oct.
Activity breaks: Wildlife Weekends, £43 per day, Mar & Oct. Wildlife and archaeological walking tours with a guide.
Credit cards ① ② ③ ⑤

Kevin Byrne, the owner of this delightful island hotel, has a warm welcome for guests, and meets them personally from the hotel. Good home cooking.

■ HARRIS, ISLE OF ■

TARBERT Western Isles   Map 13 NB10

★★60% **Harris** PA85 3DL ☎ (0859) 2154

Normal price: £55.50 room and breakfast.
Short breaks: £64.50-£73.50 for 2 people. Jan-May and Sep-Dec. Single supplement.
Credit cards ① ③

Conveniently situated for the ferry terminal, this long-established family-run hotel offers traditional standards of hospitality and service with good home cooking.

■ ISLAY, ISLE OF ■

PORT ASKAIG Strathclyde (Argyllshire)   Map 10 NR46

★★59% **Port Askaig** PA46 7RD ☎ (049684) 245 & 295

Normal price: £25. Dinner from £10 (1990 price)
Short breaks: £165 for 3 nights, including return ferry tickets for car & 2 people. £172 for single occupancy.

Overlooking the pier in the hamlet of Port Askaig, this modernised old Highland inn incorporates the original 16th-century bar. All bedrooms, some with private bathrooms, are on the first floor and have colour television.

▨ LEWIS, ISLE OF ▨

STORNOWAY   *Western Isles*   *Map 13 NB43*

★★★64% **Caberfeidh** (Best Western) PA87 2EU ☎ (0851) 2604

Normal price: £69 room and breakfast
Short breaks: £78 for 2 nights.
Credit cards ① ② ③ ④ ⑤

This comfortable hotel is situated on the southern approach of the town. Rooms are modern and well-equipped and have ensuite facilities. Service is friendly and attentive.

▨ MULL, ISLE OF ▨

CRAIGNURE   *Strathclyde (Argyllshire)*   *Map 10 NM73*

★★★58% **Isle of Mull** (Scottish Highland) PA65 6BB ☎ (06802) 351
Closed 2 Nov-24 Mar

Normal price: £39. Dinner £13-£14
Short breaks: £41-£46. Min 2 nights
Credit cards ① ② ③ ⑤

Conveniently placed for the ferry terminal and enjoying spectacular sea views, this hotel has bedrooms with ensuite baths and colour television. There are some family rooms.

▨ SHETLAND ▨

BRAE   *Map 16 HU36*

★★★ ♨ 67% **Busta House** (Consort) ZE2 9QN ☎ (080622) 506
Closed 23 Dec-2 Jan

Normal price: £29. Dinner £18.25-£21.50
Short breaks: £65 for 2 people. Single £42. Fri-Sun. Nov-22 Dec & Jan-Feb
Credit cards ① ② ③ ⑤

An 18th-century mansion house situated on the western shores of Busta Voe with its own little harbour and offering facilities for sea fishing and water sports. All the bedrooms have ensuite bath or shower and colour television.

LERWICK   *Map 16 HU44*

★★★58% **Lerwick** South Road ZE1 0RB ☎ (0595) 2166

Normal price: £30
Short breaks: £42. Min 5 nights (ie: 2 nights on Aberdeen-Lerwick ferry plus 3 nights at hotel. Single supplement £7 per night.
Credit cards ① ② ③

There are fine views across the bay from this purpose-built tourist/commercial hotel. All rooms have ensuite facilities and colour television.

★★★66% **Shetland** Holmsgarth Road ZE1 0PW ☎ (0595) 5515

Normal price: £33
Short breaks: £240 (1990). Min 3 nights. Apr-Sep. Single supplement £10. Inclusive travel package available from Aberdeen airport (enquire for details).
Credit cards ① ② ③ ④ ⑤

This modern hotel overlooks the car ferry terminal. All of the spacious bedrooms have ensuite facilities and colour television.

▪ SKYE, ISLE OF ▪

BROADFORD   Highland (Inverness-shire)   Map 13 NG62

★★54% **Broadford** IV49 9AB ☎ (04712) 204 & 414
Restricted service Nov-Mar

Normal price: £29
Short breaks: £25-£27 excluding dinner. Single £35-£37, Jun-Sep. Min 3 nights.
Credit cards [1] [3]

Formerly an inn dating back to 1611, this extended and modernised hotel offers accommodation in well-equipped, compact bedrooms with ensuite bath or shower room and colour television. The hotel has a gymnasium and there are facilities for fishing.

ISLE ORNSAY   Highland   Map 13 NG61

★★66% **Duisdale** IV43 8QW ☎ (04713) 202

Normal price: £23-£29
Short breaks: £67-£84 for 2 nights (weekend). £98.50-£123 for 3 nights (weekday). Single supplement £4.
Credit cards [1] [3]

A former hunting lodge, surrounded by pleasant gardens, with views over the Sound of Sleat to the mountains beyond. The spacious and comfortable lounge boasts a welcoming log fire, and the home-cooked meals are prepared using fresh local ingredients.

PORTREE   Highland (Inverness-shire)   Map 13 NG44

★★69% **Rosedale** IV51 9DB ☎ (0478) 3131

Normal price: £27.50-£33. Dinner £13.50-£14 (1990 price)
Short breaks: from £125 for 3-day break, including free entrance to local places of interest, mid May-Sep.

This helpful holiday hotel overlooking the harbour serves good honest meals and has characterful public rooms and modest but comfortable bedrooms with private bath or shower room and colour television.

★★65% **Royal** IV51 9BU ☎ (0478) 2525

Normal price: £25-£28
Short breaks: £32. Min 2 nights, Jan-May, Sep-Dec, except bank hols & Easter.

This traditional town centre hotel provides accommodation in a modern extension with bedrooms, including family rooms, having private bath or shower and colour television.

TEANGUE   Highland   Map 13 NG60

★★65% **Torvaig House** IV44 8RJ ☎ (0471) 231

Normal price: £27
Short breaks: £38. Min 3 nights, Etr-Oct. Single supplement.
Credit cards [1] [3]

This small, family-owned hotel stands in eight acres of attractive grounds. There are colour televisions and ensuite facilities in all of the individually decorated bedrooms.

WALES

■ CLWYD ■

ABERGELE   Clwyd   *Map 6 SH97*

★★63% **Kinmel Manor** St Georges Road LL22 9AS ☎ (0745) 832014

Normal price: £46. Dinner £13.50 and à la carte
Short breaks: £37.50. Single occupancy £42.50. Min 2 nights, except Bank Holidays
Credit cards ①②③④⑤

Set in open countryside one mile east of the town centre, this extended country house offers a range of leisure facilities which include indoor heated swimming pool, gymnasium, spa bath and solarium. There are twenty-five bedrooms, all with private bath or shower room and colour television. The hotel offers a Christmas programme.

COLWYN BAY   Clwyd   *Map 6 SH87*

GH Q Alwyn House (formerly Southlea Hotel) 4 Upper Promenade LL28 4BS ☎ (0492) 532004

Normal price: £11 bed and breakfast, £17 with dinner
Short breaks: £13 or £10 excluding dinner. Single £18.50. Min 3 nights, Sep-May.

A small and friendly guesthouse just off the main promenade, offering comfortable rooms and home-cooked meals. Pets are made as welcome as families. No parking.

★★64% **Ashmount** (Minotels) 18 College Avenue, Rhos-on-Sea LL28 4NT ☎ (0492) 45479 & 44582

Normal price: £62. Dinner £9.50-£10.25 à la carte
Short breaks: £55.80. Single occupancy £63.20. Nov-20 May (except Christmas & Bank Holidays). 1990 prices

This large detached late Victorian house is now a family-run hotel, situated in a quiet residential road close to the seafront. All bedrooms are ensuite with colour television. There is a special Christmas programme.

★★64% **Edelweiss** (Consort) Lawson Road LL29 8HD ☎ (0492) 532314

Normal price: £28. Dinner from £11.50
Short breaks: £55 for 2 nights.
Credit cards ①②③⑤

Conveniently close to the town centre and seafront, this large Victorian detached house has its own car park. All bedrooms have ensuite facilities and colour television and there are some leisure amenities. There is a special Christmas programme.

★★★58% **70 Degrees** (Best Western) Penmaenhead LL29 9LD (2m E A547) ☎ (0492) 516555

Normal price: £37.50. Dinner £15.75-£18.75.
Short breaks: £42.50. Min 2 nights. Single price £52.50.
Activity breaks: Golf Breaks, £59 for 2 nights.

A large, purpose-built hotel enjoying panoramic views of town and sea from its cliff-top position east of Colwyn Bay. Equally suitable for holiday-makers and business people.

★64% **Marine** West Promenade LL28 4BP ☎ (0492) 530295
Closed Nov-Feb

Normal price: £23. Dinner from £6
Short breaks: £21. Min 2 nights. Single occupancy £23
Credit cards ②⑤

A well-maintained family-run hotel on the Promenade, with its own car park. The town centre and leisure centre are within easy reach. Most bedrooms have colour television and ensuite facilities.

★★★68% **Norfolk House** Princes Drive LL29 8PF ☎ (0492) 531757

Normal price: £29
Short breaks: £34 including £11 dinner allowance. Single midweek £44.50, weekend £35. Min 2 nights.
Credit cards ① ② ③ ⑤

A friendly privately-owned hotel conveniently situated for the town centre and the beach. Bedrooms are comfortable and have ensuite facilities and colour television.

GH QQQ **Northwood** 47 Rhos Road, Rhos-on-Sea LL28 4RS ☎ (0492) 49931

Normal price: £16 bed and breakfast, £22 with dinner
Short breaks: £19.50-£20.50. Min 2 nights

Just a short walk from the village and promenade stands this detached Edwardian hotel. Most of the bedrooms have ensuite bath or shower rooms and all have colour television.

★55% **Stanton House** Whitehall Road, Rhos-on-Sea LL28 4ET ☎ (0492) 44363

Normal price: £34. Dinner £7.50-£7.95.
Short breaks: £83 for 2 nights, including one lunch.
Activity breaks: Golf Breaks, Pony Trekking, Sea Fishing and Water Sports. Details from hotel.
Credit cards ① ③

This small, simple and homely hotel, though situated in a quiet residential road, is within easy reach of both sea shore and shopping centre.

★67% **West Point** 102 Conway Road LL29 7LE ☎ (0492) 530331
Closed last 2 weeks Dec & 1st 2 weeks Jan

Normal price: £52 room and breakfast. Dinner from £12
Short breaks: £45 for 2 people. Min 3 nights
Credit cards ① ③

A comfortable, family-run hotel within walking distance of the town centre and the sea front. Most of the bedrooms have ensuite baths or showers and all have colour television.

★65% **Whitehall** Cayley Promenade, Rhos-on-Sea LL28 4EP ☎ (0492) 47296
Closed Nov-Etr

Normal price: £20.50
Short breaks: £18. Min 3 nights, Mar-May & Oct
Credit cards ① ③

A small, pleasant family-run hotel on the Promenade at Rhos-on-Sea, with its own car park. Most bedrooms have private facilities, all have colour television.

GLYN CEIRIOG Clwyd Map 7 SJ23

★★★58% **Golden Pheasant** LL20 7BB ☎ (069172) 281

Normal price: £31.50. Dinner £16.95
Short breaks: £90 for 2 nights, Mon-Thu
Credit cards ① ② ③ ⑤

Enjoying beautiful country views, this tranquil hotel, with the character of an inn, is ideal for a relaxing break. Horse riding is available along with game shooting during the season. There are spacial facilities for children and a Christmas programme is provided. Bedrooms are ensuite with colour television.

HANMER Clwyd Map 7 SJ44

FH QQ **Buck** SY14 7LX ☎ (094874) 339

Normal price: £15.50
Short breaks: £47.40 2 nights. Apr-Jun & Sep-Oct. Single occupancy £48.40

A small, friendly house offering a relaxed atmosphere and comfortable bedrooms. Smoking is discouraged.

LLANDEGLA Clwyd Map 7 SJ15

★★ 🐎 74% **Bod Idris Hall** (WR) LL11 3AL ☎ (097888) 434
Normal price: £32.50. Dinner £10-£15.50.
Short breaks: £37.50, min 2 nights.
Activity breaks: Pheasant and Grouse Shooting Weekends,
Aug 12-Feb 28. Clay Target Shooting, Wed, Sat & Sun.
Trout Fishing Breaks. Horse Riding and Pony Trekking
Breaks. Prices from hotel.
🏃 Credit cards ① ② ③

A beautifully preserved old house steeped in
history, set in a secluded situation surrounded
by hills and moorland. Bedrooms are spacious
and comfortable.

LLANDRILLO Clwyd Map 6 SJ03

★★ 🐎 76% **Tyddyn Llan Country House** (WR) LL21 0ST ☎ (049084) 264
Normal price: £60-£67 room and breakfast. Dinner £17.
Short breaks: £88-£99 for two, min 2 nights. Single price:
£51-£55.
Activity breaks: Fishing & Shooting Breaks, details from
hotel. Guided Walks, £10 on tariff. Christmas House Party,
£300, 24-26 Dec. New Years Party, £78 excluding dinner, 1
night.
Credit cards ① ③

A delightful Georgian country house in its own
lovely gardens. It has a deservedly high
reputation for food, and the short but
imaginative menu takes advantage of fresh
local produce.

MARCHWIEL Clwyd Map 7 SJ34

★★65% **Cross Lanes** Cross Lanes LL13 0TF ☎ (0978) 780555
Normal price: £37.50. Dinner £12.95.
Short breaks: £39, min 2 nights. Single supplement.
Activity breaks: Bridge Breaks, Fishing, Gardening, Racing,
£100-£120. Details from hotel.
Credit cards ① ② ③ ⑤

A Victorian country house set in seven acres of
grounds beside the A525 about three miles
south east of Wrexham.

MARFORD Clwyd Map 7 SJ35

★65% **Trevor Arms** Springfield Lane LL12 8TA ☎ (0244) 570436
Normal price: £16.50 including continental breakfast
Short breaks: £15 including full English breakfast excluding
dinner. Min 2 nights.
🏃 (ex guide dogs) Credit cards ① ③

This village inn with beams and open fires
dates from the early 1800s and has comfortable
bedrooms with colour television and ensuite
shower. Varied meals are served.

MOLD Clwyd Map 7 SJ26

★★63% **Bryn Awel** Denbigh Road CH7 1BL ☎ (0352) 58622
Normal price: £23
Short breaks: £16. Single occupancy £20. Min 2 nights,
Fri-Sun
Credit cards ① ③

A family-run hotel, with well-equipped
bedrooms and pleasant public areas, situated
on the A541 on the north-west outskirts of the
town. It is equally popular with tourists and
travelling business people.

NORTHOP HALL   Clwyd   Map 7 SJ26

★★★58% **Chequers** (Inter) Chester Road CH7 6HJ ☎ (0244) 816181

Normal price: £30. Dinner £11.95 and à la carte (1990 price)
Short breaks: £30. Min 2 nights, Fri-Sun
Credit cards ① ② ③ ⑤

Set in wooded parkland, this old manor house has some Welsh dishes on the extensive menu and all bedrooms, including a four-poster and 2 non-smoking and family rooms, have ensuite facilities and colour television.

NORTHOP   Clwyd   Map 7 SJ26

★★★ 🏨 76% **Soughton Hall** (Welsh Rarebits) CH7 6AB ☎ (035286) 811

Normal price: £50. Dinner £19.50.
Short breaks: £130 for 2 weekend nights, (summer).
Activity breaks: Dinner Weekends including Clay Pigeon Shooting. Beaujolais Weekend. Details from hotel.
🐕 Credit cards ① ② ③

A lovely old building standing in landscaped grounds just over the Welsh border from Cheshire. It is run in very personal style by the Rodenhurst family.

REDBROOK MAELOR   Clwyd   Map 7 SJ54

★★64% **Redbrook Hunting Lodge** (Inter) Wrexham Road SY13 3ET ☎ (094873) 204 & 533

Normal price: £27.50. Dinner from £8.50 and à la carte (1990 price)
Short breaks: £35. Min 2 nights, exc bank hols.
Credit cards ① ② ③ ⑤

This small family-run hotel at a busy road junction is peacefully set in well-tended gardens and includes some family rooms among the bedrooms, all with private bath or shower and colour television and two with four-poster beds. Christmas breaks are available.

ROSSETT   Clwyd   Map 7 SJ35

★★★73% **Lyndir Hall** LL12 0AY ☎ (0244) 571648

Normal price: £37.50-£47.50, including continental breakfast. Dinner £16.50 and à la carte (1990 price)
Short breaks: £49. Min 2 nights, Thur-Sun. £25 single supplement.
🐕 (ex guide dogs) Credit cards ① ② ③ ⑤

This peaceful country house hotel and restaurant set in grounds which include a croquet lawn provides comfortable accommodation, with attractive public rooms, well-equipped ensuite bedrooms with colour television and a new leisure centre. Christmas breaks are available.

RUTHIN   Clwyd   Map 6 SJ15

★★★62% **Ruthin Castle** (Best Western) LL15 2NU ☎ (08242) 2664

Normal price: £34.50. Dinner from £14.50.
Short breaks: £44, min 2 nights. Single price £49. Medieval banquet £5.
Activity breaks: Honeymoon/Anniversary, £130. Motor Safari, £155. Details from hotel.
🐕

An authentic castle set in thirty acres of delightful grounds, yet only a short walk from the town centre. It caters well for holidaymakers. See advertisement in colour section.

★★★67% **St Andrews Golf** 40 The Scores KY16 9AS ☎ (0334) 72611
Normal price: £56. Dinner £18.50.
Short breaks: £44, min 2 nights, Nov-Mar. Single price £52.
Activity breaks: Golf Breaks, from £170 for 3 days including
2 rounds of golf.

This comfortable hotel continues to improve under the personal supervision of the proprietor.

ST ASAPH   Clwyd   Map 6 SJ07

★★★61% **Oriel House** Upper Denbigh Road LL17 0LW ☎ (0745) 582716
Normal price: £30.80. Dinner £11 and à la carte.
Short breaks: £38.75, min 2 nights, Fri-Sun.
Credit cards [1] [2] [3] [5]

A popular hotel set in large grounds leading down to the River Elwy. Facilities include easy function rooms, a restaurant and an extensive snack bar menu.

★★66% **Plas Elwy** The Roe LL17 0LT ☎ (0745) 582263 & 582089
Normal price: £22.50. Dinner £12 and à la carte
Short breaks: £33, min 2 nights, Fri-Sun, Sep-Jun. £10 single supplement.
🕇 Credit cards [1] [2] [3] [5]

A small, family-run hotel on the outskirts of St Asaph. The bedrooms are compact but well-equipped and the bar has character with an informal atmosphere.

★★★68% **Taldardy Park** The Roe LL17 0HY ☎ (0745) 584957
Normal price: £37.50. Dinner from £3.50 and à la carte
Short breaks: £34.25, £70.75 Fri-Mon. Closed over Christmas.
🕇 Credit cards [1] [2] [3] [5]

A busy and hospitable hotel situated on the outskirts of the town. Bedrooms are spacious, warm and well-equipped. There is a brasserie-style restaurant and a modern, bright lounge bar, and at the rear of the hotel, with separate access, is a premier nightclub.

▒ DYFED ▒

ABERPORTH   Dyfed   Map 2 SN25

★★55% **Highcliffe** (Minotels) SA43 2DA ☎ (0239) 810534
Normal price: £22.50 bed and breakfast, £32 including dinner
Short breaks: £29.50. Single supplement £8. Min 2 nights, except 2 weeks at Xmas
Credit cards [1] [2] [3] [5]

Conveniently situated above the town centre and a short walk from two sandy beaches, is this friendly, family-run hotel. Some of the bedrooms are situated in an annexe, most have ensuite facilities and all have colour television. A Christmas programme is available.

ABERYSTWYTH   Dyfed   Map 6 SN58

★★55% **Cambrian** Alexandra Road ☎ (0970) 612446
Closed 25 Dec
Normal price: £26-£28
Short breaks: £22-£24. Min 3 nights. 10% discount for single occupancy
Credit cards [1] [3]

A small, mock-Tudor hotel in the centre of town, opposite the station, with friendly, helpful staff. All of the bedrooms have colour television, and some have private baths or showers. No parking.

★★★ 🛥 66% **Conrah** (Welsh Rarebits) Ffosrhydygaled, Chancery SY23 4DF ☎ (0970) 617941
Closed 24-31 Dec

Normal price: £32.50-£42.50. Dinner £17-£18.50 and à la carte
Short breaks: £45-£54, Min 2 nights, Apr-Jun & Oct-May; 3 nights Jul-Sep. Single room £60, min 2 nights.
🦮 Credit cards ① ② ③ ⑤

A Georgian-style country mansion set in pleasant lawns and gardens just south of the town. The restaurant has a good local reputation. Leisure amenities include a heated indoor swimming pool, table tennis and croquet. Most of the bedrooms, including those in the annexe, have private facilities, all with colour television. Children under five are not accommodated.

★★61% **Groves** (Minotels) 42-46 North Parade SY23 2NF ☎ (0970) 617623
Closed Christmas

Normal price: £24-£25. Dinner from £8.50 and à la carte
Short breaks: £29. Single room £36-£41. Min 2 nights
🦮 (ex guide dogs) Credit cards ① ② ③ ⑤

A family-run hotel at the centre of town with an à la carte restaurant and cosy lounge bar. There are eleven bedrooms all with ensuite facilities and colour television. One room is 'no-smoking'. Children under three are not accommodated.

★★57% **Queensbridge** Promenade, Victoria Terrace SY23 2BX ☎ (0970) 612343 & 615025
Closed 1 week at Christmas

Normal price: £21
Short breaks: £28.50, min 2 nights, Nov-May
Credit cards ① ② ③ ⑤

Standing near the foot of Constitution Hill, within easy walking distance of the town centre, this small family-run hotel has an attractive basement restaurant and a cosy bar and lounge. All bedrooms have ensuite facilities and colour television. No parking.

AMMANFORD   Dyfed   Map 2 SN61

★★67% **Mill at Glynhir** (Exec Hotel) Glyn-Hir, Llandybie SA18 2TE (3m NE off A483) ☎ (0269) 850672
Restricted service 24-28 Dec

Normal price: £58 room. Dinner £12 and à la carte
Short breaks: £69-£73. Single £34.50-£36.50. Min 2 nights, spring and autumn, 4 nights summer (not available Christmas)
Credit cards ① ③

This comfortable hotel, probably a former flour mill, serves enjoyable meals in the attractive restaurant. All the bedrooms have ensuite facilities and colour television, and leisure amenities include fishing, golf and an indoor heated swimming pool. Children under eleven are not accommodated.

BORTH   Dyfed   Map 6 SN68

GH QQ Glanmor Princess Street SY24 5JP ☎ (0970) 871689

Normal price: £21.45
Short breaks: £17.25. Min 2 nights, Nov-Feb

Situated opposite a safe, sandy beach this hotel offers comfortable accommodation and good food. Two rooms have private showers and there are three family rooms. The hotel has an 18-hole golf course.

CARMARTHEN   Dyfed   *Map 2 SN42*

★★★64% **Ivy Bush Royal** (Trusthouse Forte) Spilman Street SA31 1LG ☎ (0267) 235111

Normal price: £42. Dinner from £12.50 and à la carte
Short breaks: £37 Min 2 nights, Thu-Sun
Credit cards ① ② ③ ④ ⑤

This large, popular hotel is ideally situated for touring West Wales. Each bedroom has ensuite bath or shower room and colour television, and there are rooms for families and non-smokers. The hotel has a sauna and there is a special Christmas programme.

CRUGYBAR   Dyfed   *Map 3 SN63*

★★ 🏨 69% **Glanrannell Park** (WR) SA19 8SA ☎ (0558) 685230

Normal price: £39.50. Dinner from £12.50.
Short breaks: £37, Apr-Oct. Single price £41.
Activity breaks: Fishing Breaks, Jul-Sept. Bird Watching Breaks. Pony-trekking Breaks. Welsh Cob Week, third week October. Details from hotel.

Mr and Mrs Davies extend a warm welcome to their guests at this hotel run by the same family for over twenty years. Bedrooms are sparkling and bright, and the food consistently enjoyable.

CWMDUAD   Dyfed   *Map 2 SN33*

GH QQQ Neuadd-Wen SA33 6XJ ☎ (026787) 438

Normal price: £11.50, £16.50 with dinner
Short breaks: 2 nights £31, 3 nights £46, 4 nights £60. Nov-Feb, except Xmas and New Year.

A welcoming, family-run guesthouse in a village providing special facilities for children. There are family rooms, and the lounge has a colour television.

CROESGOCH   Dyfed   *Map 2 SM83*

FH QQ Torbant SA62 5JN ☎ (03483) 276 due to change to (0348) 831276
Restricted service Oct-Etr

Normal price: £14-£16
Short breaks: £36 for 2 nights, 13 Apr-18 May

This larger than average farm guesthouse is in a pleasant position overlooking open country and has special facilities for children. Some of the bedrooms have ensuite facilities and there is a television lounge.

GWAUN VALLEY   Dyfed   *Map 2 SN03*

FH QQQ Tregynon SA65 9TU (4m E of Pontfaen, off unclass road joining B4313) ☎ (0239) 820531
Closed 2 wks winter

Normal price: from £29.50 including dinner
Short breaks: from £26. Min 2 nights, Nov-21 Mar (except Christmas)
✱

A comfortable, beamed 16th-century farmhouse at the foothills of the Preseli mountains. All bedrooms have private facilities and colour television, and vegetarian and wholefood meals are a speciality.

HAVERFORDWEST   Dyfed   Map 2 SM91

★★59% **Mariners** Mariners Square SA61 2DU ☎ (0437) 763353
Closed 26-27 Dec & 1 Jan

Normal price: £60-£74 room. Dinner £10-£12 and à la carte
Short breaks: from £37, Fri-Sun. £5 single supplement
Credit cards ①②③⑤

This historic hotel has thirty-two bedrooms with colour television, most with ensuite facilities. The food is good and staff are friendly.

LAMPETER   Dyfed   Map 2 SN54

★★★63% **Falcondale Country House** SA48 7RX ☎ (0570) 422910

Normal price: £47.50. Dinner £15
Short breaks: £42.50, min 2 nights, Jan-end Apr and Oct-20 Dec, £40 for each extra day. Single supplement.
✼ Credit cards ①③

An Italianate mansion set in fourteen acres of park and woodland, with its own kitchen gardens supplying most of the produce. It offers comfortably furnished, well-equipped bedrooms, enjoyable food and helpful service. See advertisement in colour section.

LAMPHEY   Dyfed   Map 2 SN00

★★★ 🏤 64% **Court** (Best Western) SA71 5NT ☎ (0646) 672273

Normal price: £39-£50. Dinner £14.50.
Short breaks: £42-£51, min 2 nights. Single supplement.
Activity breaks: Yacht Charter, Apr-Oct. Golf Breaks. Details from hotel.
Credit cards ①②③⑤

Several acres of pleasant lawns, gardens and woodlands surround this family-run hotel where guests enjoy friendly, attentive service and the use of an excellent leisure centre.

LLANDOVERY   Dyfed   Map 3 SN73

QQ Llwyncelyn SA20 0EP ☎ (0550) 20566

Normal price: from £14.80
Short breaks: £13.33-£14.20, min 2 days, £18.90-£20.15, min 3 days, except Christmas. Single supplement.
✼

Alongside the river and the A40, just on the Llandeito side of the town, this pleasant establishment has been run by the same family for forty-one years. Their hospitality is warm, and the accommodation is of good quality.

LLANELLI   Dyfed   Map 2 SN50

★★★59% **Diplomat** Felinfoel SA15 3PJ ☎ (0554) 756156

Normal price: £59
Short breaks: £40, min 2 nights
Credit cards ①②③⑤

A popular and busy family-run hotel in a quiet, residential part of town with modern bedrooms furnished to a high standard, a coffee shop and conference/function facilities. There is also an excellent range of leisure facilities including a Turkish bath and indoor pool.

★★★56% **Stradey Park** Furnace SA15 4HA ☎ (0554) 758171

Normal price: £27.50. Dinner £10.75-£11.95 and à la carte
Short breaks: £32, min 1 night, Fri-Sun. £22.50 single occupancy
Credit cards ①②③④⑤

A large, well run hotel in an elevated position with fine views over the bay. The purpose-built accommodation designed for business clients is in the process of being upgraded.

MANORBIER   Dyfed   Map 2 SS09

★★59% **Castle Mead** SA70 7TA ☎ (0834) 871358
Closed Nov-Easter

Normal price: £36. Dinner £9 (1990 price)
Short breaks: £32.50. Min 2 nights.
Credit cards ①②③

A small family-run hotel at the head of a wooded valley running down to the beach, with modest but cosy bedrooms, including 2 family rooms, all with colour television and ensuite bath.

MILTON   Dyfed   Map 2 SN00

★★61% **Milton Manor** (Exec Hotel) SA70 8PG ☎ (0646) 651398

Normal price: £49. Dinner from £8.50 and à la carte (1990 price)
Short breaks: £57-£64. Min 2 nights, Sep-May. £10 single supplement.
Credit cards ①③

Set in 7 acres of woodlands, this family-run Georgian manor house serves good-quality food. All bedrooms, including a family room, have private bath or shower and colour television. There is a putting green in the garden. Christmas breaks are available.

NANTGAREDIG   Dyfed   Map 2 SN42

QQQ **Cwmtwrch Farm** SA32 7NY ☎ (0267) 290238

Normal price: £19
Short breaks: £30. Min 2 nights, Nov-Mar, (ex Christmas/New Year)

A carefully modernised early 19th-century stone farmhouse, with 30 acres of mixed land. Bedrooms, all with ensuite facilities and half with colour television, include 2 family rooms.

NARBERTH   Dyfed Map 2 SN11

★★61% **Plas-Hyfryd** (Guestaccom) Moorfield Road SA67 7AB ☎ (0834) 860653

Normal price: £17
Short breaks: £22.50. Fri-Mon.
Credit cards ①②③⑤

This family-run hotel in an 18th-century former rectory has colour television in all bedrooms, including a family room and no-smoking rooms, most with private bath or shower. There is a putting green and outdoor swimming pool.

NEW QUAY   Dyfed   Map 2 SN35

★★60% **Black Lion** SA45 9PT ☎ (0545) 560209

Normal price: £25. Dinner £6-£15 à la carte (1990 price)
Short breaks: £20 excluding dinner. Min 2 nights, Oct-Dec, Mar.
Credit cards ①②③⑤

Built in 1830 of the same stone as the harbour, this small locally popular hotel overlooking the bay serves good food and has comfortable accommodation. Nearly all bedrooms, including some family rooms, have private bath or shower and colour television.

FH QQQ Ty Hen Farm Llwyndafydd SA44 6BZ (S of Cross Inn, A486) ☎ (0545) 560346

Normal price: £23 (1990).
Short breaks: 20% off normal price, Feb-May (not Easter/Whit), Oct-Jan (not Christmas/New Year). Swimming lessons available for a fee.
Credit cards ①③

This period farmhouse in quiet sheep-farming land serves good food and has comfortable bedrooms, many of them family rooms, and all with ensuite shower and colour television; plus an indoor swimming pool, sauna, solarium, gymnasium and special children's facilities. No-smoking throughout.

PEMBROKE Dyfed Map 2 SM90

★★59% **Coach House Inn** (Exec Hotel) 116 Main Street SA71 4HN ☎ (0646) 684602

Normal price: £23. Dinner £10.25-£18 à la carte (1990 price)
Short breaks: £27.50, min 2 nights. £35 for single occupancy.
🦮 (ex guide dogs) Credit cards ① ② ③ ⑤

This extended and modernised old coach house serves good food and has comfortable, pine-fitted bedrooms, including a few family rooms. All have ensuite facilities and colour television. There is also a garden and a solarium.

ST DAVID'S Dyfed Map 2 SM72

GH QQ Ramsey Lower Moor SA62 6RP ☎ (0437) 720321

Normal price: £13.80-£16.10. Dinner £9.90.
Short breaks: £24-£26, min 2 nights, Oct-Mar. Single price £27.30.
Activity breaks: Car Treasure Hunts, £48, 8-10 Nov, 7-9 Mar. Microwave Cookery Classes, £59, 22-24 Nov, 28 Feb-2 Mar. Details from hotel.

Run by the friendly Thompson family, this bright cosy guesthouse lies just outside the town with easy access to the cathedral.

★★61% **St Non's** St Catherine's Street SA62 6RJ ☎ (0437) 720239

Normal price: from £39.50. Dinner £13.50-£14.85
Short breaks: from £32.50
Credit cards ① ② ③

A short walk from the cathedral, this very popular hotel has well equipped bedrooms, all with colour television. Free golf is available nearby for residents.

★★★64% **Warpool Court** SA62 6BN ☎ (0437) 720300

Normal price: from £40. Dinner £20-£28 and à la carte.
Short breaks: £50, min 2 nights. £5 single supplement.
Credit cards ① ② ③ ④ ⑤

Originally built in the 1860's as St David's Cathedral Choir School, this country house hotel overlooks St Bride's Bay from seven acres of Italian gardens. The bedrooms are stylish, the public rooms comfortable and the restaurant of a good standard. There is a comprehensive selection of leisure facilities.

SAUNDERSFOOT Dyfed Map 2 SN10

QQ Jalna Stammers Road SA69 9HH ☎ (0834) 812282

Normal price: £45-£49
Short breaks: £42, min 2 nights, Mar-May and Sep
Credit cards ① ③

A well-maintained, family-run hotel situated just above the harbour. It provides modern and well-equipped bedrooms, a cosy bar and a comfortable lounge.

★★65% **Rhodewood House** St. Brides Hill SA69 9NU ☎ (0834) 812200

Normal price: £30 Oct-Apr. Dinner £7-£8.25 and à la carte.
Short breaks: £24, min 2 nights, Fri-Sat, Oct-Apr, £32 May-Sep. £5 single supplement May-Sep.
Credit cards ① ② ③ ⑤

Situated just above the harbour and sandy beach, the restaurant views are exceptional. The public rooms are spacious and comfortable, the staff are friendly, and the food is constantly enjoyable.

★★★65% **St Brides** (Inter-Hotels) St Brides Hill SA69 9NH ☎ (0834) 812304

Normal price: £40. Dinner £14.95-£17.50.
Short breaks: £35 Oct-Mar, £43 Apr-Sept, Fri-Sat. Single supplement Apr-Sept.
Activity breaks: Golfing Breaks, £120 for 2 nights including two days golf. Deep Sea Fishing, £120 for 2 nights including two days deep sea fishing from Saundersfoot Harbour and tackle. Horse Riding Holiday Break, £120 for 2 nights including six hours riding. Mix and Match Activity Break, £120 for 2 nights, and a choice of two activities from those listed above plus one day guided walk in the Pembrokeshire Coast National Park, or Carve Your Own Love Spoon.

Situated just above the harbour and sandy beach, the restaurant views are exceptional. The staff are friendly and efficient, and the food is constantly enjoyable.

QQQ Sandy Hill Sandy Hill Road/Tenby Road SA69 9DR ☎ (0834) 813165

Normal price: £17
Short breaks: £16.50, min 2 nights, Mar, Apr, May & Sept.

A friendly, family-run guesthouse on the A478 approaching Saundersfoot. The bedrooms are pretty and cosy, the home cooking is good value and there is a comfortable lounge and bar. Guests are also offered the use of a pleasant outdoor pool.

QQQ Vine Farm The Ridgeway SA69 9LA ☎ (0834) 813543

Normal price: £15-£16.50 (1990 prices)
Short breaks: £20-£21.50, min 3 nights, Apr-mid Jul, Sep & Oct.

A spacious lounge with a cheerful open fire, and good value, enjoyable food are offered at this old farmhouse. The bedrooms are comfortable and well-equipped, all with colour television.

TENBY Dyfed Map 2 SN10

★★69% **Atlantic** Esplanade SA70 7DU ☎ (0834) 2881 and 4176
Normal price: £24. Dinner from £11
Short breaks: from £65, min 2 nights, Oct-May. £10 single
supplement.
Credit cards 1 3

Overlooking the South Beach from a superb situation, this Victorian family holiday hotel offers good, comfortable accommodation, lounge and a spacious restaurant looking onto the heated indoor pool. See advertisement on p391.

★★68% **Fourcroft** The Croft SA70 8AP ☎ (0834) 2886
Normal price: £34-£48. Dinner £13.50-£15
Short breaks: £40-£44, min 2 nights. £4 single supplement.
Credit cards 1 3

A family holiday hotel overlooking North Beach and the harbour offering a new attractive pool, and good selection of recreational facilities. Well-equipped accommodation is provided with friendly, attentive service.

QQ **Seabreezes** 18 The Norton SA70 8AA ☎ (0834) 2753
Normal price: £24
Short breaks: £22, min 3 nights, Mar-Jul and Sep-Nov. Bar service is restricted except June-Sep.
✕

A guesthouse with a popular residents bar, near the harbour and North Beach. The service is friendly and hospitable.

TREGARON Dyfed Map 3 SN65

QQ **Neuadd Las Farm** SY25 6LG ☎ (0974) 298905
Normal price: £16
Short breaks: £20, min 2 nights, Fri-Sat, Oct-Mar

Set in its own grounds, with panoramic views to the Cumbrian mountains, this cosy guesthouse is 1 mile from the town, off the Aberystwth Road. Private fishing is available, and the Cors Caron Nature Reserve is nearby.

▨ GLAMORGAN, MID ▨

BRIDGEND Mid Glamorgan Map 3 SS97

★★★71% **Coed-y-Mwstwr** (WR) Coychurch CF35 6AF ☎ (0656) 860621
Normal price: £63 bed and breakfast, £88 with dinner
Short breaks: £132, 2 nights, weekends; £185, 3 nights, weekdays.
✕ (ex guide dogs) Credit cards 1 2 3 5

Service is friendly and attentive at this Victorian mansion set in woodland. Each bedroom has a private bath or shower room and colour television and the hotel has an indoor swimming pool, snooker table and tennis court. Children under seven are not accommodated.

MERTHYR TYDFIL   Mid Glamorgan   Map 3 SO00

★★★62% **Baverstock** The Heads of Valley Road CF44 0LX ☎ (0685) 6221

Normal price: £55. Dinner from £9.50 (1990 price)
Short breaks: £64. Min 2 nights, Fri-Sun, not Christmas week. £7 single supplement.
🌟 (ex guide dogs) Credit cards ① ② ③ ⑤

Just north of the town, this comfortable modern hotel has ensuite facilities and colour television in all bedrooms, including 2 family rooms. There is a garden, and snooker and pool tables. Christmas breaks are available.

★★64% **Tregenna** Park Terrace CF47 8RF ☎ (0685) 723627 & 82055

Normal price: £24.50. Dinner from £7 and à la carte (1990 price)
Short breaks: £27.50, £35 single occupancy. Min 2 nights, Thu-Sun.
Credit cards ① ② ③

This cheerful modern hotel close to the town centre has a good value, wide-ranging menu and well-equipped bedrooms, all with ensuite facilities and colour television, including family rooms in the annexe. Christmas breaks are available.

PORTHCAWL   Mid Glamorgan   Map 3 SS87

★63% **Rose & Crown** (Berni/Chef & Brewer) Heol-y-Capel, Nottage CF36 3ST ☎ (065671) 4850

Normal price: £27
Short breaks: £25.50 excluding dinner. Min 2 nights, Fri-Sun.
🌟 (ex guide dogs) Credit cards ① ② ③ ⑤

This small friendly inn, a short drive from the sea and town centre, has a choice of bars and a good-value carvery restaurant, while the comfortable compact bedrooms all have private bathrooms and colour television.

★★★57% **Seabank** (Lansbury) The Promenade CF36 3LU ☎ (065671) 2261

Normal price: £38. Dinner £11.50 and à la carte.
Short breaks: £38. Min 2 nights, Fri-Sun.
Credit cards ① ② ③ ⑤

Overlooking the Bristol Channel, this characterful hotel has spacious public rooms, a small leisure complex with a sauna, solarium, gymnasium and jacuzzi, and comfortable ensuite bedrooms with colour television. Christmas breaks are available.

▪ GLAMORGAN, SOUTH ▪

BARRY   South Glamorgan   Map 3 ST16

★★★53% **Mount Sorrell** (Consort) Porthkerry Road CF6 8AY ☎ (0446) 740069

Normal price: £94 for 2 people with dinner for 2 nights
Short breaks: £74 for 2 people for 2 nights, Fri-Sun

In an elevated position above the Bristol Channel and Barry, this hotel has a gymnasium, indoor heated swimming pool and sauna. Ensuite bath or shower rooms and colour television are provided in all the bedrooms, and there are three family rooms. A special programme is provided at Christmas.

CARDIFF   South Glamorgan   Map 3 ST17

★★★★66% **Holiday Inn** Mill Lane CF1 1EZ ☎ (0222) 399944

Normal price: £60. Dinner £12-£14.50
Short breaks: from £40 excluding dinner. Fri-Sun
Credit cards ① ② ③ ④ ⑤

A modern city centre hotel with good leisure facilities. The ensuite bedrooms all have colour television, and some rooms are set aside for families and non-smokers. There is a special Christmas programme.

★★57% **Lincoln** 118 Cathedral Road CF1 9LQ ☎ (0222) 395558

Normal price: £27.75
Short breaks: £19.75 excluding dinner. Min 2 nights, Fri-Sun, most weekends (not Christmas, New Year and Rugby Internationals)
✻ (ex guide dogs)

Only a few minutes' walk from the castle and city centre, this converted Victorian hotel offers comfortable, modern accommodation and friendly service. All rooms have private facilities and colour television.

★★★59% **Post House** (Trusthouse Forte) Pentwyn Road, Pentwyn CF2 7XA ☎ (0222) 731212

Normal price: £87 room and breakfast. Dinner £12.50
Short breaks: £38 (1990). Min 2 nights, Fri-Sat.
Credit cards ① ② ③ ④ ⑤

A busy hotel, situated alongside the city's Eastern Avenue bypass, with good leisure facilities and a coffee shop. All the bedrooms have private bathrooms and colour television, with rooms set aside for non-smokers and families.

★★★56% **Royal** (Embassy) Saint Mary's Street CF1 1LL ☎ (0222) 383321

Normal price: £42-£52 room and breakfast. Dinner £12.50-£14.50 and à la carte
Short breaks: £35. Min 2 nights, Fri-Sun (not Xmas, New Year and Rugby Internationals)
Credit cards ① ② ③ ④ ⑤

This city centre hotel has a range of popular bars and comfortable public areas. All the bedrooms have colour television, some have ensuite facilities with some rooms for families and non-smokers. There is a special Christmas programme.

LLANTWIT MAJOR South Glamorgan Map 3 SS96

★★67% **West House** West Street CI6 9SP ☎ (0446) 792406 & 793726

Normal price: £23.50. Dinner £9.50 and à la carte
Short breaks: £28.75, min 2 nights, Fri-Sun. £10 single supplement.
Credit cards ① ② ③

Comfortable and relaxing hotel facilities are now provided at this converted 250-year-old farmhouse. Bedrooms are well-equipped and a Victorian conservatory has recently been completed. Meals are consistently good, and staff are friendly.

▨ GLAMORGAN, WEST ▨

LANGLAND BAY West Glamorgan Map 2 SS68

★★66% **Langland Court** Langland Court Road, Swansea SA3 4TD ☎ (0792) 361545

Normal price: £64 Jan-end May, £68 Jun-end Dec. Dinner £13.50-£14.45 and à la carte
Short breaks: from £42, min 2 nights, Mon-Sat, from £21 including Sun. £15 single supplement Mon-Thu.
Credit cards ① ② ③ ⑤

Set in small but attractive gardens in a quiet residential area with good views over the Bay, this personally-run hotel offers comfortable, well-equipped bedrooms, individually decorated. This Tudor-style country house, with a galleried staircase and an oak-panelled dining room, provides a reliable standard of cooking and prompt, friendly service.

★★★59% **Osborne** Rotherslade Road, Swansea SA3 4QL ☎ (0792) 366274

Normal price: £37.50. Dinner from £14 and à la carte
Short breaks: £37, min 2 nights
Credit cards ① ② ③ ④ ⑤

A popular hotel on the cliff top, offering a warm welcome and friendly service, with colour television in all the bedrooms.

NEATH   West Glamorgan Map 3 SS79

★★64% **Castle** (Lansbury) The Parade SA11 1RB ☎ (0639) 641119 & 643581

Normal price: £35. Dinner £7-£12 à la carte
Short breaks: £33. Min 2 nights, Fri-Sun.
Credit cards [1] [3]

All bedrooms have ensuite facilities and colour television, one with a four-poster bed, in this friendly hotel; also a sauna and solarium.

OXWICH   West Glamorgan   Map 2 SS58

QQ **Oxwich Bay** Gower SA3 1LS ☎ (0792) 390329 & 390491

Normal price: £26-£38
Short breaks: £54.95-£72.95 for 2 nights, £83.95-£105.95 for 3 nights, £109.95-£130.95 for 4 nights, including cream tea on arrival, lunch and £10.95 dinner allowance.
✷ Credit cards [1] [2] [3] [5]

This small and friendly family holiday hotel just by the beach has a restaurant and bars. All bedrooms, including two family rooms, are ensuite with colour television and modern facilities.

PENMAEN   West Glamorgan   Map 2 SS58

★★65% **Nicholaston House** Nicholaston SA3 2HL ☎ (0792) 371317

Normal price: £32.50
Short breaks: £16 excluding dinner. Oct-Mar.
Credit cards [1] [3]

This friendly family-run hotel in a 19th-century house has well-equipped bedrooms, all with ensuite bath and colour television, and many with sweeping views of Oxwich Bay. There is also snooker and a putting green.

PORT TALBOT   West Glamorgan   Map 3 SS79

★★★51% **Aberafan** (Consort) Aberavon Beach SA12 6QP ☎ (0639) 884949

Normal price: £24.50. Dinner from £10 and à la carte (1990 price)
Short breaks: £31.50. Min 2 nights, Fri-Sun. Single supplement.
Credit cards [1] [2] [3] [5]

This modern hotel on the seafront offers a good choice of meals and has open-plan public areas. Comfortable bedrooms offer private bathrooms and colour television, including some family rooms. Christmas breaks are available.

SWANSEA   West Glamorgan   Map 3 SS69

★★★63% **Fforest** Pontardulais Road, Fforestfach SA5 4BA (on A483 1.5m S of M4 junction 47)
☎ (0792) 588711

Normal price: £41. Dinner from £14 and à la carte
Short breaks: £33, min 2 nights, Fri-Sun.
Credit cards [1] [2] [3] [5]

A busy commercial hotel with comfortable well-equipped bedrooms, a small fitness centre and extensive conference/function facilities. The attractive restaurant serves a good à la carte menu, and bar meals are also available.

★★★★64% **Hilton National** Pheonix Way, Swansea Enterprise Park SA7 9EH (1m S M4 junctions 44 and 45, SW of Llansamlet) ☎ (0792) 310330

Normal price: £53.50. Dinner £12.50-£14.25 and à la carte
Short breaks: £38 excluding dinner. Min 2 nights
Credit cards ① ② ③ ⑤

A modern commercial hotel situated within the Swansea Enterprise Zone. Good accommodation is offered in well-equipped bedrooms, and open-plan public rooms are spacious and comfortable. There is a popular carvery in addition to an à la carte menu, and a good selection of conference and leisure facilities is also available.

★65% **Parkway** 253 Gower Road, Sketty SA2 9JL ☎ (07992) 201632

Normal price: £22. Dinner £7.50 and à la carte
Short breaks: £24, min 2 nights, Fri-Sun. £3.50 single supplement
Credit cards ① ② ③ ⑤

Situated in a residential suburb, this extended house offers attractive open-plan public areas and modern, well-equipped bedrooms, with friendly service.

QQQ Tredilion House 26 Uplands Crescent, Uplands SA2 0PB

Normal price: £33.50, includes dinner
Short breaks: £30.15, min 3 nights, Fri-Sun, except Bank Hols
🏌 Credit cards ① ③

Well situated, this Victorian town house has been tastefully refurbished to provide excellent accommodation. Bedrooms are furnished in pine, with every modern facility, and a very comfortable modern lounge is available.

■ GWENT ■

ABERGAVENNY Gwent Map 3 SO21

★★★57% **Angel** (Trusthouse Forte) Cross Street NP7 5EW ☎ (0873) 7121

Normal price: £35 room only. Dinner £12.95.
Short breaks: £45, min 2 nights.
Activity breaks: Pony trekking, Mar-Oct. Details from hotel.
Credit cards ① ② ③ ④ ⑤

A popular town-centre hotel dating from the 17th century with extensive conference facilities and friendly, helpful service. Bedrooms being upgraded.

★★70% **Llanwenarth Arms** Brecon Road NP8 1EP ☎ (0873) 810550

Normal price: £29, single room £48
Short breaks: £23, single room £36. Min 2 nights, Fri-Sun.
🏌 Credit cards ① ② ③ ⑤

Situated on the banks of the River Usk, just 2½ miles west of the town centre, this hotel enjoys spectacular views across the valley. There are eighteen bedrooms, all with colour television and ensuite facilities.

CHEPSTOW Gwent Map 3 ST59

★★66% **Castle View** 16 Bridge Street NP6 5EZ ☎ (02912) 70349

Normal price: £28.75. Dinner £12-£13.50
Short breaks: £39.50. Single £49.50. Min 2 nights

Situated opposite the castle, this ivy-clad hotel is 300 years old. All the bedrooms have ensuite bath or shower room and colour television, including the family rooms. Home-made food is served in the restaurant and bar.

★★55% **George** (Trusthouse Forte) Moor Street NP6 5DB ☎ (0291) 625363
Normal price: £52
Short breaks: £45. Fri-Sun (except Christmas, New Year and Easter)
Credit cards ① ② ③ ④ ⑤

This small friendly hotel has comfortable bedrooms all with ensuite bath or shower rooms and colour television; some rooms are for non-smokers. A special Christmas programme is available.

LLANGYBI Gwent Map 3 ST39

★★★★67% **Cwrt Bleddyn** Usk NP5 1PG ☎ (0633) 49521
Normal price: £42.50. Dinner £17.95 and à la carte
Short breaks: £55, min 2 nights, Fri-Sun
Credit cards ① ② ③ ⑤

Originally a small country manor house set in fine gardens, the hotel has been extensively but sympathetically extended over the years, and there is a wide selection of recreational facilities.

LLANTILIO CROSSENNY Gwent Map 3 SO31

FH QQ **Little Treadam** Abergavenny NP7 8TA ☎ (060085) 326
Normal price: £28
Short breaks: £26, Nov-Feb
✱

This delightful 16th-century farmhouse is set amidst beautiful open countryside, overlooking the Black Mountains, 5 miles from Abergremmy. The accommodation is comfortable, and there is good home cooking from fresh produce.

MONMOUTH Gwent Map 3 SO51

★★★63% **Kings Head** Agincourt Square NP5 3DY ☎ (0600) 2177
Normal price: £41. Dinner £20-£22.
Short breaks: £47.50, min 2 nights. Single supplement.
Activity breaks: Golf Breaks, £135 for 2 nights including early morning tea, newspaper, golf and green fees.
Credit cards ① ② ③ ⑤

A comfortable 17th-century inn professionally run by the Gough family for over two decades, with good food.

★★68% **Riverside** (Minotels) Cinderhills Street NP5 3EY ☎ (0600) 5577 & 3236
Normal price: £29.
Short breaks: £24.75. Min 2 nights, Fri-Mon. Single price £33.
Activity breaks: Golf Breaks, short breaks plus green fees from £7.50. Riding Breaks, short breaks plus riding from £5.
✱ Credit cards ① ③

NEWPORT Gwent Map 3 ST38

★★★★63% **Celtic Manor** Coldra Woods NP6 2YA ☎ (0633) 413000
Normal price: £79 room. Dinner £20.
Short breaks: £125 Fri-Sat, £110 Sat-Sun.
Activity breaks: Clay Pigeon/Lazer Shooting, £100/£40. Ballooning, £500-£1,000. Archery, £40-£80. Details from hotel.
✱

A 19th-century manor house, once used as a maternity home, offers elegant public rooms and two good restaurants. See advertisement in colour section.

★★★55% **Hilton National** (Hilton) The Coldra NP6 2YG ☎ (0633) 412777

Normal price: £55
Short breaks: £38. Min 2 nights, Fri-Sun.
Credit cards [1] [2] [3] [5]

This busy commercial hotel has refurbished ensuite bedrooms with colour television, including many family and no-smoking rooms, plus a leisure complex with indoor swimming pool, sauna, gymnasium and steam room. Christmas breaks are available.

RAGLAN Gwent *Map 3 SO40*

★★67% **Beaufort Arms** High Street NP5 2DY ☎ (0291) 690412

Normal price: £22.50
Short breaks: £29. Min 2 nights. Single supplement.
✦ (ex guide dogs) Credit cards [1] [2] [3] [5]

Overlooking the church in the centre of Raglan, this comfortable hotel has characterful public rooms and modernised bedrooms, including two family rooms, all ensuite and with colour television. Christmas breaks are available.

TINTERN Gwent *Map 3 SO50*

★★★68% **Beaufort** Chepstow NP6 6SF ☎ (0291) 689777

Normal price: £40. Dinner £14.95-£16.95
Short breaks: £46, min 2 nights; single occupancy only available at weekends
Credit cards [1] [2] [3] [4] [5]

A busy, popular hotel situated in the picturesque Wye Valley, opposite the Abbey, with magnificent views. Standards of comfort are good, and residential conferences are something of a speciality.

★★57% **Parva Farmhouse** Chepstow NP6 6SQ ☎ (0291) 689411

Normal price: £19.50. Dinner £14
Short breaks: £30, min 2 nights, £10 single supplement
Credit cards [1] [2] [3] [5]

Set close to the bank of the River Wye, this small, friendly, family-run hotel provides well-equipped bedrooms and good meals. There is an 'honesty bar' arrangement in the comfortable lounge.

★★63% **Royal George** Chepstow NP6 6SF ☎ (0291) 689205

Normal price: £29.43. Dinner £14.75 and à la carte
Short breaks: £35.75, min 2 nights, Mon-Thur, £39.95 Fri-Sun. £15.64 single supplement
Credit cards [1] [2] [3] [5]

Standing beside the A466 in the picturesque Wye Valley, this is a family-run hotel whose history as an inn dates back to the 17th-century. It offers well-equipped accommodation, the majority of rooms in annexes overlooking delightful gardens.

USK Gwent *Map 3 SO30*

★74% **Glen-Yr-Afon** Pontypool Road ☎ (02913) 2302

Normal price: £51.50 room and breakfast. Dinner £12.50-£20 and à la carte
Short breaks: £33.75, for 2 people, min 2 nights, Fri-Sun, Sep-end May. £6.25 single supplement. Includes newspaper and morning tea.
Credit cards [1] [3]

Situated on the edge of town in attractive grounds, this lovely old house provides good quality, well-equipped accommodation and pleasant, comfortable public areas.

WHITEBROOK   Gwent   Map 3 SO50

★★65% Crown at Whitebrook (Exec Hotel) ☎ (0600) 860254

Normal price: £50. Dinner £21.50-£24.
Short breaks: £45, min 3 nights.
Activity breaks: Canoeing, Abseiling, Climbing and Caving Breaks, details from hotel.
Credit cards ①②③④⑤

This pleasant 'restaurant with rooms' stands in a quiet wooded valley yet conveniently near major roads, and offers small comfortable bedrooms.

▨ GWYNEDD ▨

ABERDOVEY   Gwynedd   Map 6 SN69

★★66% Harbour LL35 0EB ☎ (065472) 250 & 7792

Normal price: £45. Dinner £15-£17.
Short breaks: £35, not Sat or Sun, Mar-Oct only.
Activity breaks: Details from hotel.
Credit cards ①②③⑤

In a central position on the seafront, this well-furnished hotel offers a homely atmosphere, pleasant bedrooms and good food.

★66% Maybank 4 Penhelig Road, Penhelig LL35 0PT ☎ (065472) 500 due to change to (0654) 767500

Normal price: £18-£25.95, Dinner £16.50-£19.
Short breaks: £32-£36. Min 2 nights. Single supplement.
Activity breaks: Watersports breaks, including sailing, water skiing, wind surfing and fishing. Clay pigeon shooting and rough shooting breaks. Golfing breaks. RSPB breaks including visits to sanctuaries and reserves. All prices on application. Most require up to three months advance booking.
Credit cards ①③

The charming little restaurant of this small, well-run hotel overlooking the sea offers a very high standard of home-cooked dishes and accommodation of a comparable quality.

GH QQQQ Morlan LL35 0SE ☎ (065472) 7706

Normal price: £18
Short breaks: £25-£26
✵ (ex guide dogs)

Close to the coastguard station, Morlan enjoys views over the golf course and sand dunes to Cardigan Bay. There are four modern, light airy bedrooms with ensuite facilities and colour television. All bedrooms are 'no smoking'. Children under sixteen are not accommodated.

★★68% Penhelig Arms LL35 0LT ☎ (065472) 215 due to change to (0654) 767215
Closed 4 days at Christmas

Normal price: £28-£32. Dinner £14.50
Short breaks: £37-£45. Min 2 nights, available all year except Bank Holidays.
Credit cards ①③

This delightfully furnished hotel overlooking the harbour provides a cosy lounge, bars and good food. All eleven bedrooms have private bath or shower rooms and colour television.

ABERSOCH   Gwynedd   Map 6 SH32

★★61% Deucoch LL53 7LD ☎ (075881) 2680

Normal price: £28.50-£30.50. Dinner from £11.
Short breaks: £75 for 3 nights (1990 prices). Single
supplement.
Activity breaks: Golf Breaks, from £90. Details from hotel.
Credit cards [1] [2] [3] [5]

A friendly, family-run hotel in an elevated
position with panoramic views across Cardigan
Bay from Snowdonia to mid-Wales.

★★76% Neigwl Lon Sarn Bach LL53 7DY ☎ (075881) 2363

Normal price: £25. Dinner £15-£16.
Short breaks: £33.33, min 3 nights, Sept-May.
Activity breaks: Golfing Breaks, £125 per person, 3 nights
including golf at three courses. Sept-May.
🛪 Credit cards [1] [3] [5]

There are excellent views across Cardigan Bay
to the Cambrian Mountains from this
impeccable family-run hotel, which offers
imaginative food, attentive service and
comfortable bedrooms.

★★★ ⚓ 65% Porth Tocyn Bwlch Tocyn LL53 7BU ☎ (075881) 3303
Closed end Nov-21 Mar

Normal price: from £43.50
Short breaks: from £39. Min 3 nights during low season.
Single room 10% off normal rate for 3 days or more, 15% off
for 7 days or more
Credit cards [1]

Standing in 25 acres of farmland with superb
views over Cardigan Bay, this hotel has a
relaxing informal atmosphere. Sports facilities
include a swimming pool, tennis courts and
windsurfing. All the bedrooms have ensuite
facilities and colour television.

BALA   Gwynedd   Map 6 SH93

GH QQ Frondderw LL23 7YD ☎ (0678) 520301

Normal price: £11-£13
Short breaks: £16.70-£18.70. Min 3 nights, Mon-Thu, Mar-
May & Oct, Nov
🛪 (ex guide dogs)

Set on a hillside overlooking the town this
charming period mansion provides good food
and service. Two of the bedrooms have ensuite
facilities and there are three family rooms.

★★57% Plas Coch High Street LL23 7AB ☎ (0678) 520309

Normal price: £47. Dinner £10.50-£12.25.
Short breaks: £29.75, min 2 nights. Single supplement.
Activity breaks: Golf Break, usual tariff plus £2.50 per day.
Driving Tuition, usual tariff plus £60 per day, including
intensive driving course. Water Sports Break, usual tariff
plus various watersports fees.
Credit cards [1] [2] [3] [5]

Grade II listed building dating from 1790 set in
a 29-acre estate with a terraced swimming pool
and a 9-hole golf course leading to the south
shore of Bala Lake.

GH Q Plas Teg Tegid Street LL23 7EN ☎ (0678) 520268

Normal price: £14
Short breaks: £12.50 excluding dinner, Oct-Mar

Pleasantly situated on the outskirts of town,
this guesthouse has a comfortable lounge with
colour television and six bedrooms suitable for
families.

BANGOR   Gwynedd   Map 6 SH57

★★68% **Menai Court** Craig y Don Road LL57 2BG ☎ (02483) 354200
Closed 26 Dec-7 Jan

Normal price: £36. Dinner £16 and à la carte
Short breaks: £36 Fri-Sun, £42 Mon-Thu. Single £50, Fri-Sun only.
Credit cards ①③

A delightful, well-furnished hotel offering good food and friendly service. All the comfortable bedrooms have ensuite facilities and colour television and there are two family rooms. There is a special Christmas programme.

BARMOUTH   Gwynedd   Map 6 SH61

★63% **Bryn Melyn** Panorama Road LL42 1DQ ☎ (0341) 280556
Closed Dec-Feb

Normal price: £22.50. Dinner from £10.75
Short breaks: £29.50. Min 2 nights
Credit cards ①③

A small family-run hotel in an elevated position east of the town. The majority of bedrooms have ensuite showers and colour television, and there are family rooms.

GH QQ Cranbourne 9 Marine Parade LL42 1NA ☎ (0341) 280202

Normal price: £18
Short breaks: £49.50 for 2 nights. Oct-Mar
✵ (ex guide dogs) Credit cards ①③

A well-furnished small family-run hotel overlooking the sea. Most of the bedrooms have ensuite facilities and all have colour television. There are six family rooms.

★★65% **Ty'r Graig** Llanaber Road LL42 1YN ☎ (0341) 280470
Closed Nov-Feb

Normal price: £26.50. Dinner from £11.50 and à la carte
Short breaks: £34, single £40. Min 2 nights, Mar-May & Sep-Oct
✵ (ex guide dogs) Credit cards ①③

Standing in its own grounds overlooking the beach and Cardigan Bay is this late Victorian house. All twelve bedrooms have ensuite facilities and colour television, two rooms are furnished with four-poster beds. The hotel has facilities for windsurfing, yachting and sea fishing.

BEDDGELERT   Gwynedd   Map 6 SH54

★★★63% **Royal Goat** LL55 4YE ☎ (076686) 224 & 343

Normal price: £50. Dinner £16.
Short breaks: £43. Min 2 nights, Oct-Apr. Single occupancy £47.
Activity breaks: Fishing Breaks, £43. Details from hotel.

A well-furnished family-run hotel in the village centre, lying amidst spectacular scenery.

★ 🏨 69% **Sygun Fawr Country House** LL55 4NE ☎ (076686) 258

Normal price: £56 room with breakfast
Short breaks: £104, including £9 dinner allowance, 2 days
Nov-Apr (ex Easter); £210, including £9 dinner allowance,
4 days all year. Single £52, 2 days Nov-Apr (ex Easter);
£105, 4 days

This small country house hotel has seven bedrooms, the majority with ensuite bath or shower rooms and one room for families. The hotel has a sauna and there is a special Christmas programme.

★59% **Tanronen** (Frederic Robinson) LL55 4YB ☎ (076686) 347

Normal price: £26
Short breaks: £49.50 for 2 days, £71 for 3 days.
🍴 Credit cards ① ③ ⑤

This small friendly hotel and public house stands beside the river bridge in the middle of the village. Bedrooms are warm and comfortable with colour television, and there is a cosy lounge. There is a special Christmas programme.

BENLLECH BAY   Gwynedd   *Map 6 SH58*

★★59% **Bay Court** Beach Road LL74 8SW ☎ (0248) 852573

Normal price: £16.50
Short breaks: £16.50 including £11.50 dinner allowance.
Min 2 nights, Jul & Aug & Bank Holidays
Credit cards ① ② ③ ⑤

A modern hotel just 200 yards from the beach. Some bedrooms have ensuite facilities and colour television and there are five family rooms. There is a special Christmas programme.

BETWS-Y-COED   Gwynedd   *Map 6 SH75*

★★★ 🏨 63% **Craig-y-Dderwyn Country House** (Minotels) LL24 0AS ☎ (06902) 293

Normal price: £30. Dinner from £15 and à la carte
Short breaks: £40, min 2 nights. Single £55

This half-timbered house is situated beside the River Conwy on the edge of town. All the bedrooms have private facilities and colour television, some rooms have four-poster beds, and family rooms are available. The hotel has special facilities for children and there is a Christmas programme.

★★★ 🏨 64% **Plas Hall** (Minotels) Pont-y-Pant, Dolwyddelan LL25 0PJ ☎ (06906) 206

Normal price: £39.50. (£49.50 after May 1991).
Short breaks: £36 including a packed lunch, morning tea or coffee and newspaper. Min 2 nights.
Activity breaks: Bridge Weekends, £85, details from hotel.
🍴

A delightful Welsh stone building standing in its own grounds on the banks of the River Lleds. The attractive restaurant uses local produce in its high standard cuisine.

QQQQ Tan-y-Foel Capel Garman LL26 0RE ☎ (06902) 507

Normal price: £35-£40
Short breaks: £42.50 for 2 nights, £40 for 3 nights. Includes dinner, sherry, petite fours, after dinner coffee, flowers in rooms.
Activity breaks: Photography tuition. Oct-Mar weekends/ by arrangement. £60 per day including tuition, use of darkroom and transport to shoot locations.

Tan-y-Foel is a 16th-century manor house perched high on a hillside, and is being lovingly restored by Hazel and Barrie Michael. The views are outstanding, tranquility and hospitality are made perfect by the good dinners - there is a set menu - which are served at a huge refectory table in what was the original dairy. Tan-y-Foel was the winner for Wales of the AA's Best Newcomer award for 1989/90.

★★69% Ty Gwyn (Best Western) LL24 0SG ☎ (06902) 383 & 787

Normal price: £17-£32.50. Dinner £12.95 and à la carte
Short breaks: £29.95-£45.45. Min 2 nights
Credit cards ① ③

A stone-built coaching inn standing beside the A5 close to Waterloo Bridge. Most of the individually styled and furnished bedrooms have ensuite facilities and colour television, and some have four-poster beds. There is a special Christmas programme.

★★★69% Waterloo (Consort) LL24 0AR ☎ (06902) 411
Closed Christmas

Normal price: £48
Short breaks: £42.50. Min 2 nights, Nov-Mar, Apr-Jun

This hotel has a coffee shop and a leisure/ fitness complex with an indoor pool and a fully supervised gymnasium. All the bedrooms have a private bathroom and colour television and there are two family rooms. Fishing is available.

BONTDDU   Gwynedd   Map 6 SH61

★★★65% **Bontddu Hall** LL40 2SU ☎ (034149) 661
Closed Jan-Etr. Restricted service Nov-Dec

Normal price: £52.50. Dinner £17.50 and à la carte
Short breaks: £90 for 2 nights. £10 single supplement for 2 nights
Credit cards ⊡ ⊡ ⊡ ⊡

Standing in two acres of lovely grounds this charming, delightful hotel furnished in the style of a Victorian country house, provides comfortable bedrooms all with ensuite facilities and colour television. One room has a four-poster bed and others are set aside for families. Children under three are not accommodated.

CAERNARFON   Gwynedd   Map 6 SH46

★62% **Chocolate House** Plas Treflan, Caeathro LL55 2SE ☎ (0286) 672542

Normal price: £16-£18.50. Dinner from £11.50 à la carte
Short breaks: £24.50-£29 for 2 nights Apr-Oct. Single supplement £6

This hotel offers accommodation with ensuite shower rooms and colour television. There is a solarium for guests' use. Children under ten are not accommodated.

★64% **Menai Bank** North Road LL55 1BD ☎ (0286) 673297

Normal price: £38 room and breakfast. Dinner £9-£10
Short breaks: £24. Min 2 nights, Jun-Sep
Credit cards ⊡ ⊡

This family-run hotel stands just north of the town centre overlooking the Menai Straits. All the comfortable bedrooms have colour television and most have ensuite facilities.

FH QQQ Plas Tirion Llanrug LL55 4PY (Llanrug 3m E A4086) ☎ (0286) 673190
May-Oct

Normal price: £18
Short breaks: £15. Min 3 nights, May, Jun, Sep & Oct (except Bank Holidays)

A warm and friendly welcome awaits guests at this traditional Welsh farmhouse. It offers a good standard of accommodation, and some bedrooms have ensuite showers and colour television.

CONWY   Gwynedd   Map 6 SH77

★★59% **Castle** (Trusthouse Forte) High Street LL32 8DB ☎ (0492) 592324

Normal price: £75 room. Dinner £12.50.
Short breaks: £52, £56 Jul, Aug & Sept. Min 2 nights.
Activity breaks: Golf Breaks, £95-£109. Pony Trekking Breaks, £110-£128.
Credit cards ⊡ ⊡ ⊡ ⊡ ⊡

An early coaching house hotel, parts of which date back to the 15th century, standing beside the castle walls close to the quay. Warm and comfortable throughout.

★★72% **Castle Bank** Mount Pleasant LL32 8NY ☎ (0492) 593888
Closed Jan. Restricted service Dec & Feb

Normal price: £46 room and breakfast. Dinner from £13
Short breaks: £59-£65 for 2 people. £4 single supplement. Min 2 nights
🐾 Credit cards ⊡ ⊡

Situated just outside the ancient town walls this early Victorian house overlooks the estuary of the River Conwy. Most of the bedrooms have ensuite showers, and all have colour television.

★★★65% **Sychnant Pass** Sychnant Pass Road LL32 8BJ ☎ (0492) 70009

Normal price: £33-£42. Dinner £13.95-£18.95
Short breaks: £29.50-£38 including £13.95 dinner allowance.
Single supplement £5-£10. Min 2 nights (except Christmas
& Bank Holidays)

This delightful house is situated at the foot of the Pass amidst beautiful scenery. It offers well-equipped, modern accommodation, and all bedrooms have colour television and private bath or shower rooms. There is a special Christmas programme.

CRICCIETH Gwynedd Map 6 SH43

★65% **Abereistedd** West Parade LL52 0EN ☎ (0766) 522710
Closed 30 Oct-Feb

Normal price: £24. Dinner from £8
Short breaks: £21. Min 2 nights
Credit cards ⬜1

Situated on the seafront, with views across Cardigan Bay this is a small, well-maintained family-run hotel. All the bedrooms have colour television, some have ensuite showers, and there are family rooms.

★★★ 🛥 66% **Bron Eifion Country House** (Inter-Hotels) LL52 0SA ☎ (0766) 522385

Normal price: from £64 room. Dinner from £14.50 and à la carte
Short breaks: from £76 for 2 people. Min 3 nights

Built in the 1870s, this large country house stands in spacious grounds on the edge of town. All bedrooms offer ensuite facilities and colour television, and some are furnished with four-poster beds. There is a special Christmas programme.

GH Q Min-y-Gaer Porthmadog Road LL52 0HP ☎ (0766) 522151
Mar-Oct

Normal price: £13.50-£17
Short breaks: £20-£23. Min 2 nights

This small, friendly Victorian house overlooks the sea and offers good value for money. All the bedrooms have colour television and most have ensuite showers.

★★66% **Parciau Mawr** High Street LL52 0RP ☎ (0766) 522368
Closed Nov-Feb

Normal price: £23. Dinner £8
Short breaks: £23. £4 single supplement. Min 2 nights, Mar-May & Sep-Oct.
Credit cards ⬜1 ⬜3

A pleasant, family-run hotel on the edge of the village offering a good standard of home cooking. Bedrooms are warm and well furnished with ensuite facilities and colour television. Children under five are not accommodated.

DEGANWY   Gwynedd   Map 6 SH77

★★66% Bryn Cregin Garden (Exec Hotel) Ty Mawr Road LL31 9UR ☎ (0492) 585266

Normal price: £32. Dinner from £14.50.
Short breaks: £42, min 2 nights. Not Jan. Single price £55.
Activity breaks: Golf Breaks, £98 for 2 days. Golf Weekend,
£110 for 2 nights. (1990 prices)
🅧 Credit cards [1] [3]

Standing in its own grounds overlooking the Conwy Estuary, this warm, comfortable and well furnished hotel was once the home of a successful sea captain.

DOLGELLAU   Gwynedd   Map 6 SH71

★63% Clifton House Smithfield Square LL40 1ES ☎ (0341) 422554

Normal price: £19-£23. Dinner £7-£12.
Short breaks: £30-£34, min 2 nights, Oct-Etr.
Activity breaks: Special Walking Weekends, £90-£100 for 3
nights including sherry reception and packed lunches, and
an experienced guide. Single supplement. Walking in the
southern Snowdonia range.
🅧 Credit cards [1] [3]

Attractive stone building in the centre of town where the basement restaurant was once the local gaol, although the atmosphere is warm and friendly today.

★★63% Dolserau Hall (Minotels) LL40 2AG ☎ (0341) 422522

Normal price: £32.50. Dinner from £15 and à la carte
Short breaks: £35-£40. Min 2 nights, mid Sep-mid May.

Standing in its own delightful grounds this Victorian building has fourteen rooms all with colour television, and most have ensuite facilities. There is a special Christmas programme.

★★67% George III Penmaenpool LL40 1QD ☎ (0341) 422525
Closed 24 Dec-7 Jan Restricted service May Day

Normal price: £46. Dinner £12-£28 à la carte
Short breaks: £53.25. Min 2 nights, Nov-Apr (except Bank
Holidays)
Credit cards [1] [2] [3]

A friendly informal hotel set on the banks of the Mawddach estuary. Some of the bedrooms are situated in a lodge that was once part of a railway station; all rooms have colour television, and most have ensuite facilities. Fishing is available.

★★64% Royal Ship (Frederic Robinson) Queens Square LL40 1AR ☎ (0341) 422209

Normal price: £25.75. Dinner £10.50
Short breaks: 2 days £49; 3 days £71

A coaching inn built at the beginning of the 19th-century and set at the centre of town. Most of the bedrooms have ensuite facilities, and all have colour television. There is a special Christmas programme.

FAIRBOURNE   Gwynedd   Map 6 SH61

Q Sea View LL38 2NX ☎ (0341) 250388

Normal price: £14.50
Short breaks: £12.50. Min 2 nights, Jan-June, Sept-Dec

Located in the tiny hamlet of Friog, this stone-built house has pleasant gardens. The accommodation is simple and comfortable.

GANLLWYD Gwynedd Map 6 SH72

★★★ 🏨 66% **Dolmelynllyn Hall** LL40 2HP ☎ (034140) 273
Restricted service Dec-Feb

Normal price: £85-£105 for 2 people, including dinner
Short breaks: £80-£100 for 2 people. Min 3 nights, Apr-Nov
Credit cards ① ② ③

Parts of this very pleasant country house hotel date back to the 16th century. Public rooms are very elegant and comfortable, whilst bedrooms are all ensuite with colour television; some rooms are set aside for non-smokers. Fishing is available. Children under ten are not accommodated.

HARLECH Gwynedd Map 6 SH53

GH QQQQ Castle Cottage Pen Llech LL46 2YL ☎ (0766) 780479

Normal price: from £18.50.
Short breaks: £31.50 for 2 people. Min 2 nights, Oct-Mar. (except Bank Holidays). Single occupants get £2 discount on dinner.
Credit cards ① ③

In a central position, this family-run hotel has cottage-style bedrooms and a character restaurant. There is no parking on the premises.

★57% **Noddfa** Lower Road LL46 2UB ☎ (0766) 780043

Normal price: £30.50 room and breakfast. Dinner from £16
Short breaks: 10% reduction.
Activity breaks: Medieval Break, £53 including guided tour of Harlech Castle and two archery lessons.
🏹 Credit cards ① ③

Personally run by the owners, and commanding fine sea views from its position next to the famous castle, the hotel provides warmth and comfort.

LLANBEDR Gwynedd Map 6 SH52

★★ 🏨 60% **Cae Nest Hall** LL45 2NL ☎ (034123) 349

Normal price: £23. Dinner from £11.50
Short breaks: £32, min 2 nights
🏹

This 15th-century stone-built manor house stands in 3 acres of grounds. Pleasantly furnished, it offers welcoming, friendly service and the owner, a talented pianist and organist regularly entertains guests in the evenings.

LLANDDEINIONLEN   Gwynedd   Map 6 SH56

QQQQ Ty'n-Rhos Farm Saion Caernarfon LL55 3AE ☎ (0248) 670489

Normal price: £30-£38, includes dinner.
Short breaks: £29-£35, min 2 nights.
🏋

Half a mile north on an unclassified road, this farm has been extended to provide modern hotel comforts, whilst retaining its original atmosphere. Imaginative country cooking using fresh produce is provided.

LLANDUDNO   Gwynedd   Map 6 SH78

★★★(Red) ♣ 81% **Bodysgallen Hall** (on A470 Llandudno link road) LL30 1RS ☎ (0492) 584466

Normal price: £75.50. Dinner £25.50
Short breaks: £90, min 3 nights, May-Aug, excluding Bank Hols. £5 single supplement. Includes newspaper and morning tea.
Credit cards ⊡ ⊡ ⊡ ⊡

This 17th-century house was restored and converted by Historic House Hotels Ltd., and recently celebrated its 10th anniversary. The public rooms still reflect the origins of the Hall, with fine oak panelling, large fireplace and many pieces of period furniture. The bedrooms combine the air of the bygone age with all the expected 20th-century modern comforts. The restaurant is famous in North Wales, and the chef uses local produce to provide a good choice on a fixed price menu, supplemented by an extensive wine list. Surrounding the hotel are beautifully maintained gardens set in 200 acres of parkland, with magnificent views. Children under 8 not accommodated.

★★64% **Bromwell Court** LL30 1BG ☎ (0492) 78416 and 874142

Normal price: £21. Dinner from £9
Short breaks: £25, min 2 nights, Apr, May, Oct-Dec 1991, Jan-May 1992. £2 single supplement
Credit cards ⊡ ⊡

This small and friendly family-run hotel is situated on the Promenade to the east of the town centre. Bedrooms are thoughtfully designed and equipped, and public areas are comfortable.

★★65% **Bryn-y-Bia Lodge** Craigside LL30 3AS ☎ (0492) 49644 & 40459

Normal price: £35.50. Dinner £16.
Short breaks: £29, Nov-Mar.
Activity breaks: Dry Slope Skiing, £86 (£64 under 15), 1990/91. Dry skiing on the slopes of the Great Orme overlooking Llandudno Bay.
Credit cards ⊡ ⊡ ⊡

A delightful detached house set in its own grounds on the Coastal Road near the Little Orme. Good food, ably prepared by the resident owner.

QQ Bryn-y-Mor North Parade LL30 2LP ☎ (0492) 76790

Normal price: £37-£47 room and breakfast
Short breaks: £24, min 2 nights, Nov-Mar
🏋 Credit cards ⊡ ⊡ ⊡ ⊡

This large and beautifully maintained early 18th-century house, standing close to the pier, commands excellent views of the bay, the beach and the promenade from its elevated position. Nearby street parking is available.

QQ Cranberry House 12 Abbey Road LL30 2EA ☎ (0492) 879760

Normal price: £40
Short breaks: £37, min 3 nights, Apr and May
🏋 Credit cards ⊡ ⊡

Good quality accommodation is offered at this charming Victorian house, which caters for non-smokers only. Conventionally situated for access to the town centre, it has its own car park.

★64% **Crickleigh** Lloyd Street LL30 2YG ☎ (0492) 75926
Normal price: £14.50-£17.90 (en suite). Dinner £7.40
Short breaks: £14.25-£16.90 (en suite), min 2 nights, Oct-Dec 29th and Jan-beg Apr
✶ Credit cards ① ③

A friendly, family-run hotel, centrally located for both beach and shopping.

★★★73% **Empire** Church Walks LL30 2HE ☎ (0492) 860555
Normal price: from £30. Dinner £14.95
Short breaks: from £32.50, min 2 nights, includes Sunday lunch
Credit cards ① ② ③ ④ ⑤

Family owned and run, this large well-furnished hotel offers an extensive range of facilities including indoor and outdoor pools, a sauna and solarium. Bedrooms contain antiques, complemented by every modern amenity, and good food is served in the delightful restaurant.

GH QQQ Epperstone 15 Abbey Road LL30 2EE ☎ (0492) 78746
Normal price: £16.50.
Short breaks: £43 for 2 nights, Fri & Sat, Oct-Dec, Feb-Apr. £60 for 3 nights (senior citizens only), Sun-Thu.
Activity breaks: Golfing Weekends, £100 for 2 nights including two rounds of golf. Fishing, Skiing and Dancing, details from hotel.

A high standard of accommodation and good cooking are to be found at this elegant, detached Edwardian house which is surrounded by well-tended gardens.

★★59% **Esplanade** Glyn-y-Nor Parade, Promenade LL30 2LL ☎ (0492) 860300
Normal price: £27.50-£31.50. Dinner £10.50-£17.50
Short breaks: £30, min 2 nights, Jan-end Apr and Nov-end Dec, except Christmas. Includes Sunday lunch, Nov-end Apr.
Credit cards ① ② ③ ⑤

A large hotel on the promenade, overlooking the pier. The simple but well-equipped bedrooms are popular with holidaymakers, and coach parties are catered for.

★★★64% **Gogarth Abbey** West Shore LL30 1QY ☎ (0492) 76211
Normal price: £100. Dinner from £17
Short breaks: £85, min 2 nights
✶ Credit cards ① ② ③ ⑤

This large, attractive house was built in 1862, and is now a well-furnished, comfortable hotel, which enjoys splendid views across the Country Estuary of Snowdonia and Anglesey. The public areas are quiet and relaxing, and the bedrooms well-equipped. Additional facilities include an indoor pool, sauna and solarium.

★★66% **Gwesty Leamore** 40 Lloyd Street LL30 2YG ☎ (0492) 75552

Normal price: £17.50. Dinner £7-£8.
Short breaks: £16, min 2 nights.
✗

A pleasant, well maintained family-run hotel, conveniently situated for the town centre, beaches and theatres. Accommodation is modest but well equipped, and the proprietors are friendly and hospitable.

GH QQ **Heath House** Central Promenade LL30 1AT ☎ (0492) 76538

Normal price: £16-£20.
Short breaks: £20.70-£24.30. Min 4 nights, Nov-Apr. Single supplement.
Activity breaks: Christmas Package, £210 (£260 en suite), 24-28 Dec.
✗

Privately owned hotel enjoying a position on the promenade overlooking the bay.

★61% **Hilbre Court** Great Ormes Road, West Shore LL30 2AR

Normal price: £23.50. Dinner £6.50-£7.50
Short breaks: £20, min 2 nights, Mar-May, Sep and Oct, excluding Bank Holidays
Credit cards 1 2 3

Situated in a quiet side road on the West Shore, this family-run hotel offers friendly service and good house comforts.

★★★64% **Imperial** The Promenade LL30 1AP ☎ (0492) 77466

Normal price: £75. Dinner £15.50-£19.50 and à la carte
Short breaks: £47.50, min 2 nights, not Christmas and New Year. £10 single supplement
Credit cards 1 2 3 5

This large hotel offers many attractions for visitors, and is conveniently located for the pier and shopping centre. Bedrooms are well-equipped and the public areas offer a choice of bars and a large, attractive, restaurant. There is a good selection of leisure facilities, including an indoor pool, gym and hairdressing salon.

QQ **Kinmel** 12 Mostyn Crescent LL30 1AR ☎ (0492) 76171

Normal price: £23
Short breaks: £18, min 2 nights, Apr and May, excluding Bank Holidays
Credit cards 1 3

This privately-owned, friendly hotel stands on the promenade overlooking the bay and beach. Many rooms have ensuite facilities and all have colour television.

★59% **Min-y-Don** North Parade LL30 2LP ☎ (0492) 76511

Normal price: £17.50. Dinner from £6
Short breaks: £17.50, min 2 nights, Mon-Fri, Mar-Oct. £2 single supplement.
✗ Credit cards 1 3

A traditional resort hotel situated on the promenade, near the shops, with simply furnished, comfortable rooms and friendly proprietors.

★★66% **Plas From Deg** 48 Church Walks LL30 2HL ☎ (0492) 77267 and 860226

Normal price: £37.50, includes dinner
Short breaks: £25, min 3 nights
✗ Credit cards 1 3 5

A beautifully presented and maintained Victorian house in a well-situated position, fronted by a large terraced garden. Bedrooms are comfortable, and well-equipped, and friendly proprietors provide informal but attentive service.

★63% **Quinton** Church Walks LL30 2HN ☎ (0492) 76879 & 75086

Normal price: £44 room and breakfast.
Short breaks: £40, Mar-May, Sept-Nov.
Activity breaks: Golfing Holidays. Details from hotel.
Credit cards 1

Homely, personally-run hotel situated north-west of the town centre between the two beaches. Popular with golfing parties.

★66% **Ravenhurst** West Parade LL30 2BB ☎ (0492) 75525

Normal price: £22. Dinner £8
Short breaks: £25-£28, min 2 nights, mid Oct-mid May
Credit cards 1 3 5

A pleasant, privately owned and run hotel on the town's West Shore offering well-maintained accommodation with good facilities.

★★★61% **Risboro** (Inter-Hotels) Clement Avenue LL30 2ED ☎ (0492) 76343

Normal price: £45. Dinner £15.
Short breaks: £40, min 2 nights.
Activity breaks: Golf Breaks, £150 for 3 nights, including 3 green fees. Ski-Swim Breaks, £99 for 2 nights, including 2 hours skiing per day.

A family-owned and run hotel in a residential area, with a pleasant atmosphere and friendly staff.

★★59% **Royal** Church Walks LL30 2HW ☎ (0492) 76476

Normal price: £28. Dinner £11.50.
Short breaks: £50 for 2 nights weekend break. £48 midweek. Oct-Etr.
Activity breaks: Golf Breaks, from £92 for 2 nights.
✶

Close to the sea, yet standing in a quiet side road, this family-run hotel offers value-for-money accommodation.

★★67% **Sandringham** West Parade LL30 2BD ☎ (0492) 76513 and 76447

Normal price: £27-£30. Dinner £9
Short breaks: £26, min 2 nights, excluding May 26th-end Sep
🏋 Credit cards ①③

Excellent views of the Country Estuary can be enjoyed from this pleasant, family-run hotel on the West Shore. All the bedrooms are well-furnished, with ensuite facilities.

QQ **Sunnyside** Llewelyn Avenue LL30 2ER ☎ (0492) 77150

Normal price: £16
Short breaks: £14, Apr-end Oct

Set between Great Orme and the town centre, a few minutes from the seafront, this guesthouse offers well-kept rooms, some with ensuite facilities. The bar and lounge areas are attractive and relaxing.

LLANFAIR PWLLGWYNGYLL   Gwynedd   Map 6 SH57

★★★63% **Carreg Bran Country** Church Lane LL61 3YH ☎ (0248) 714224

Normal price: £31.75. Dinner £13.74
Short breaks: £41, min 2 nights, Jan-Nov. £4 single supplement
Credit cards ①②③⑤

This former country house provides modern, well-equipped accommodation and pleasant public areas. It is situated on the Menai Straits close to the Britannia Bridge and is convenient for the A5.

LLANWNDA   Gwynedd   Map 6 SH45

★★★61% **Stables** Caernarron LL54 5SD ☎ (0286) 830711 and 830935

Normal price: £32. Dinner £8.95 (1990 prices)
Short breaks: £30, min 2 nights, Fri-Sun, Apr-Jun and Sep-Mar. £6 single supplement
Credit cards ①②③

The modern, well-equipped bedrooms are located in a purpose-built single storey motel-style block. The restaurant, which serves good food, is situated in converted stables. There is also a pleasant suite situated in the original Victorian building.

LLANRWST   Gwynedd   Map 6 SH76

★★67% **Meadow Sweet** Station Road LL26 0DS

Normal price: from £28-£40. Dinner £16.50-£27.50 and à la carte
Short breaks: £45-£55
Credit cards ①③

Situated on the A470 just north of the town centre, this small family-run hotel offers imaginative cuisine, complemented by an extensive selection of wines.

★★★ 🏨 63% **Plas Maenan Country House** Maenan LL26 0YR ☎ (049269) 232

Normal price: £30. Dinner £13.50
Short breaks: £30, min 2 nights
🏋 Credit cards ①③⑤

Overlooking the beautiful Conwy Valley, this large elegant country mansion, located just off the A470, is set in 20 acres of grounds. Bedrooms, although a little dated, are spacious and comfortable, and a good choice of food includes Welsh and vegetarian specialities.

NEFYN   Gwynedd   Map 6 SH34

★60% **Caeau Capel** Rhodfar Mor LL53 6EB ☎ (0758) 720240

Normal price: £23
Short breaks: £28. Min 3 nights.
Credit cards ① ③

Set in its own grounds in a quiet cul-de-sac, this holiday hotel has private bath or shower in many of the bedrooms, which include family rooms. There is a grass tennis court and putting green.

★★★68% **Nanhoron Arms** Ffordd Dewi Sant LL53 6EA ☎ (0758) 720203

Normal price: £60.50. Dinner £13.50-£16.
Short breaks: £61, min 2 nights including Sat.
Activity breaks: Clay Shooting, £165 (1990). Shooting ground set in 80 acres of natural surroundings. Golfing, £125 (1990) excluding green fees. Riding Break, £148 (1990) including four hour's riding. Breaks are for 2 nights, and include welcome drink, two lunches and afternoon tea.
🔨 Credit cards ① ② ③ ⑤

A fine example of Edwardian architecture near the town centre offering friendly, obliging service throughout.

PENNAL   Gwynedd   Map 6 SH60

★★60% **Llugwy Hall** SY20 9JX ☎ (065475) 228

Normal price: £32.50 (1990)
Short breaks: £32. Min 2 nights, Fri-Sun.
Credit cards ① ② ③ ⑤

The hall stands beside the Dovey River, and guests enjoy modern comforts, friendly service and good cooking. Part of the building has been converted into an Outdoor Pursuits Centre.

PWLLHELI   Gwynedd   Map 6 SH33

❋★★ 🏨 75% **Plas Bodegroes** LL53 5TH (1.5m W on Nefyd Rd)

Normal price: £45-£55. Dinner £14-£20 and à la carte (1990 price)
Short breaks: £40-£50. Min 2 nights, except Sat & Tue. Mar-Jun, Nov-Dec.
Credit cards ① ③

This elegant Georgian country house, set in 6 acres of grounds which include a croquet lawn, serves high quality food and has comfortable ensuite bedrooms, most with colour television and two with four-poster beds. Christmas breaks are available.

ROWEN   Gwynedd   Map 6 SH77

★ 🏨 64% **Tir-y-Coed** LL32 8TP ☎ (0492) 650219

Normal price: £18. Dinner £8.50 (1990 price)
Short breaks: £25.50. Min 2 nights, Oct-Apr. £26.75 for single occupancy.

This detached Edwardian house in a peaceful little village has a garden and children's facilities, and all bedrooms, which include a family room, have private bath or shower and colour television.

TALSARNAU   Gwynedd Map 6 SH63

★★(Red) 🏨 **Maes Y Neuadd** (Pride of Britain) LL47 6YA (2m SE on unclass rd off B4573)
☎ (0766) 780200

Normal price: £49-£59. Min 2 nights.
Short breaks: £64.50-£78.50, Apr-Oct. £57-£71, Nov-Mar 92.
Single price £58.50-£95.
Activity breaks: Wine Weekends, Welsh Musical Weekend,
Gourmet Weekends, Japanese Cooking, Jazz Evenings,
details from hotel.
Credit cards ① ② ③ ⑤

A historic old property, part dating back to the 14th century, which has been steadily improved over the past eight years. Set amidst fine Welsh scenery.

★★64% **Trefwylan** LL47 6YG ☎ (0766) 770424

Normal price: £20.50. Dinner £9.75
Short breaks: £26.50, min 3 nights, Feb-Jun, Sep-Oct.
🍴 Credit cards ① ③

A farmhouse built in 1906 has been extended to create a comfortable, family-run hotel offering a warm Welsh welcome. There is a cosy lounge and bar, and the varied menu offers a choice of good food. It is a friendly place to stay, with superb views over Cardigan Bay from its own grounds.

TAL-Y-BONT (near Conwy) Gwynedd Map 6 SH76

★★63% **Lodge Conwy** LL32 8YX ☎ (049269) 766

Normal price: £22.50-£25 (1990). Dinner from £11.
Short breaks: £22.50-£25, min 2 nights.
Credit cards ① ③

Resident owners offer a friendly reception at this small village hotel in the beautiful Conwy Valley. Bedrooms are in a modern, single-storey block at the back of the main building, and have good facilities.

TAL-Y-LLYN Gwynedd Map 6 SH70

★(Red) **Minffordd** Minffordd Tywyn LL36 9AJ ☎ (0654) 761665

Normal price: from £82-£92 room and breakfast. Dinner
£14.75
Short breaks: £66 for two excluding dinner. Min 2 nights,
Mar-May and Oct-Dec. Available Fri and Sat only Nov and
Dec. Dinner £14.75.
🍴 Credit cards ① ③ ⑤

This charming hotel stands at the head of the Dysynni Valley in magnificent scenery, but near to the A487/B4405 junction. All the bedrooms offer quite comfortable accommodation, and although mostly small, are individually decorated and furnished. The owner's son is in charge of the cooking and he produces high quality, well prepared food.

TREARDDUR BAY Gwynedd Map 6 SH27

★★★62% **Beach** Holyhead LL65 2YT ☎ (0407) 860332

Normal price: £55. Dinner £10-£20
Short breaks: £44, min 2 nights. £5 single supplement
Credit cards ① ② ③ ⑤

An imposing, privately-owned hotel close to the beach and ideally suited for the family holidaymaker. Bedrooms are quite well-equipped, and there is a choice of restaurants and bars. There is also an indoor leisure centre with a small pool, 2 squash courts and 9 full-sized snooker tables.

QQ Highground off Ravenspoint Road LL65 2YY ☎ (0407) 860078

Normal price: £16
Short breaks: £22.50
✗ Credit cards [1] [3]

Enjoying a superb location overlooking the sea, this hotel is privately owned and offers comfortable accommodation and value for money.

TREFRIW Gwynedd Map 6 SH76

★★73% **Hafod House** LL27 0RQ ☎ (0492) 640029

Normal price: £42.50, includes dinner £14.95
Short breaks: £37.50, min 2 nights, Apr-Oct, £32.50 Oct 91-Apr 92. £7 single supplement. 3 night breaks are also available, details from hotel.
✗ Credit cards [1] [2] [3] [5]

A delightful small 17th-century farmhouse, carefully restored and extended to provide very good standards of both hospitality and cuisine. Personally run, the chef/proprietor offers good food based on local produce, and the rural location on the edge of the village commands excellent views over the Conwy Valley.

POWYS

BERRIEW Powys Map 6 SJ10

★★65% **Lion** SY21 8PQ ☎ (0686) 640452 & 640844

Normal price: £27.50-£30. Dinner from £15 and à la carte
Short breaks: £25-£28 excluding dinner. Min 2 nights.

A charming 17th-century inn offering a good choice of bar meals or an à la carte menu. There are seven bedrooms all with colour television and ensuite facilities, one room has a four-poster bed and one is for families. Fishing is available.

BRECON Powys Map 3 SO02

GH Q Beacons 16 Bridge Street LD3 8AH ☎ (0874) 3339

Normal price: £20-£22
Short breaks: £19.50-£21.50. Min 2 nights.
Credit cards [1] [3]

A Georgian house set in a secluded garden beside the River Usk. Six of the bedrooms have ensuite shower rooms, and there are three family rooms.

★★58% **Castle of Brecon** (Consort) Castle Square LD3 9DB ☎ (0874) 4611

Normal price: £25-£32.50. Dinner from £12.50 and à la carte
Short breaks: £35-£42.50. Min 2 nights
Credit cards [1] [2] [3] [4] [5]

A traditional coaching inn near the town centre, with comfortable bedrooms all equipped with private bath or shower rooms and colour television. One room is furnished with a four-poster bed and there are family rooms. A special Christmas programme is provided.

★65% **Lansdowne** 39 The Watton LD3 7EG ☎ (0874) 3321

Normal price: £20.50. Dinner £6-£14.50.
Short breaks: £32.50, including pre-dinner drink and glass of wine. Min 2 nights.
Activity breaks: Pony Trekking and Golf Breaks. Details from hotel.
Credit cards [1] [2] [3] [5]

This small, personally run hotel combines character with charm and friendly service. Comfortable bedrooms with modern private facilities.

★★67% **Wellington** (Inter-Hotels) The Bulwark LD3 7AD ☎ (0874) 5225

Normal price: £56. Dinner £7-£15 à la carte
Short breaks: £66. Min 2 nights
Credit cards ① ② ③ ⑤

Conveniently located right in the town centre, this Georgian hotel has a bistro and an all-day coffee shop. The modern well-equipped bedrooms all have private bathrooms and colour television. There is a special Christmas programme.

BRONLLYS Powys *Map 3 SO13*

GH QQ Beacons Edge Pontithel LD3 0RY ☎ (0874) 711182

Normal price: £24
Short breaks: £25. Min 2 nights, Oct-May (except Bank Holidays)
Credit cards ① ③

This cosy family-run inn, set beside the A438 Brecon to Hereford road, has a good steak bar. All the bedrooms have ensuite bath or shower rooms and colour television and there is one family room. There are special facilities for children.

BUILTH WELLS Powys *Map 3 SO05*

★★56% **Lion** Broad Street LD2 3DT ☎ (0982) 553670

Normal price: £42-£62 room and breakfast. Dinner from £9.
Short breaks: £42-£62. Min 2 nights, Jul, Aug & Bank Hols.
Activity breaks: Golf and Fishing Breaks, details from hotel.
Credit cards ① ③

Traditional hotel situated near the River Wye at the centre of the busy market town, and attracting much local trade to its bar. Bedrooms retain old world character.

★★64% **Pencerrig Country House** (Consort) LD2 3TF ☎ (0982) 553226

Normal price: £32. Dinner £16.50.
Short breaks: £35, min 2 nights. Single supplement.
Activity breaks: Bridge Breaks, Nov-Mar. Details from hotel.
Credit cards ① ② ③ ⑤

A former gentleman's residence off the A483 offering good food and comfortable modern bedrooms. It is also a popular meeting place for locals.

CRICKHOWELL Powys *Map 3 SO21*

GH QQ Dragon House High Street NP8 1BE ☎ (0873) 810362

Normal price: £45-£50 room and breakfast
Short breaks: £40-£50 for 2 people. Min 2 nights (except Bank Holidays).

A friendly, informal hotel serving vegetarian meals. Some of the bedrooms have ensuite bath or shower and colour television, and rooms are set aside for non-smokers.

★★ ♣ 72% **Gliffaes Country House** NP8 1RH ☎ (0874) 730371
Closed Jan-9 Mar

Normal price: £25.50-£34.50. Dinner £15.30 and à la carte
Short breaks: £45-£55. Min 2 nights.
✕ (ex guide dogs) Credit cards ① ② ③ ⑤

Set amid thirty acres of magnificent grounds, this distinctive hotel has an informal friendly atmosphere and offers good home cooking. The character bedrooms are well equipped with modern facilities, most have ensuite bath or shower rooms, and some have colour television. Leisure amenities are available and the hotel has special facilities for children.

HAY-ON-WYE   Powys Map 3 SO24

★★★66% **Swan** (Best Western) Church Street HR3 5DQ ☎ (0497) 821177 & 821188

Normal price: £40. Dinner £10-£25.
Short breaks: £45, min 2 nights except Bank Holidays.
Single price £50.
Activity breaks: Salmon Fishing, £55, min 2 days.
Credit cards 1 2 3 5

A Georgian hotel which has been completely refurbished and offers modern facilities. The lounge is particularly elegant, and the two bars offer a choice of atmosphere.

KNIGHTON   Powys Map 7 SO27

★★71% **Milebrook House** Milebrook LD7 1LT ☎ (0547) 528632

Normal price: £26.50. Dinner £12.50-£19.50 and à la carte
Short breaks: £36, min 3 nights, except Bank Holidays and Dec 21st-Jan 1st
🛪 Credit cards 1 3

This 18th-century manor house to Stanmage Castle is 2 miles east of the town, alongside the A4113. Bedrooms are attractive and comfortable and public rooms cosy and relaxing. A mile stretch of fly fishing is available to guests, and the grounds are very attractive and include a productive kitchen garden.

LLANDRINDOD WELLS   Powys Map 3 SO06

★★★63% **Metropole** Temple Street LD1 5DY ☎ (0597) 822881

Normal price: £49, includes dinner £15
Short breaks: £44, min 2 nights. £10 single supplement
Credit cards 1 2 3 4 5

This large, well-run town centre hotel, which has been in the same family for over 100 years, has recently been refurbished. There are good conference facilities, an excellent leisure complex including an indoor pool, and staff are friendly and helpful.

QQQ Three Wells Chapel Road, Howey LD1 5PB (Howey 2m A483 then unclassified road, E 1m)
☎ (0597) 824427 and 822484

Normal price: £14-£19.
Short breaks: £14-£19, Nov-Apr.
🛪

The Bufton family have run this relaxing 'Farm Hotel' for many years, and an excellent standard of accommodation is maintained. Good food is served, there is colour television in all bedrooms, and fishing and riding are available.

LLANFYLLIN   Powys Map 6 SJ11

★★ **Bodfach Hall** SY22 5HS ☎ (069184) 272

Normal price: £55. Dinner from £13.50 and à la carte
Short breaks: from £66, min 2 nights, Mar-mid Nov
Credit cards 1 2 3 5

Set back from the main road just north of the town, this is an elegant 17th-century house with ornate ceilings, wood-panelled halls and some original William Morris wallpaper. Bedrooms and public areas are comfortable and well-equipped, food is good and the hotel is personally run by its friendly owners.

LLANGAMMARCH WELLS   Powys *Map 3 SN94*

❀★★★ ♨ 76% **Lake** LD4 4BS ☎ (05912) 202 and 474

Normal price: £50-£60. Dinner £19.50
Short breaks: £65, min 2 nights
Credit cards ① ② ③

An elegant and hospitable Victorian house standing in 50 acres of beautiful grounds. Individually styled bedrooms combine character with comfort, and the innovative cooking uses local produce to great effect. A very extensive range of recreational facilities is available.

LLANGURIG   Powys   *Map 6 SN98*

★★69% **Glansevern Arms** Pant Mawr, Llanidloes SY18 6SY (4m W on Aberystwyth Road) ☎ (05515) 240

Normal price: £42. Dinner from £16
Short breaks: £35, min 2 nights

Comfortable modern facilities, good food, and a welcome as warm as its log fires are the hallmarks of this cosy inn, set just above the River Wye on the main A44 road.

QQQ Old Vicarage SY18 6RB ☎ (05515) 280

Normal price: £21.50-£24.50
Short breaks: £20.50-£23.50, min 3 nights.

Run by the very friendly Rothings family, this pleasant guesthouse is in a cul-de-sac just off the main road. The modern bedrooms are well-equipped and there are two comfortable lounges.

LLANWDDYN   Powys   *Map 6 SJ01*

★★★ ♨ 71% **Lake Vyrnwy** (WR) SY10 1LY ☎ (069173) 692

Normal price: from £25.50 room.
Short breaks: from £39.85, min 2 nights. Single price £50.
Activity breaks: Helicopter Safaris, Clay Shooting Breaks, Sailing Breaks and Fly Fishing Breaks, details from hotel.
Credit cards ① ② ③ ④ ⑤

Set in 24,000 acres of the foot of the Berwyn Mountains this country house, with its country sports facilities, provides elegant public rooms and a carefully selected menu.

MACHYNLLETH   Powys   *Map 6 SH70*

QQQ White Lion Heol Pentrerhedyn SY20 8ND ☎ (0654) 703455

Normal price: £37-£52 (en suite)
Short breaks: £27.98, min 2 nights
Credit cards ① ② ③ ⑤

In the centre of the busy market town, this former coaching inn offers attractive prime furnished bedrooms and a comfortable bar. There is a good range of food, and the staff are friendly and helpful.

PRESTEIGNE   Powys   *Map 3 SO36*

★★64% **Radnorshire Arms** (Trusthouse Forte) High Street LD8 2BE ☎ (0544) 267406

Normal price: £33.50-£38.50 room only
Short breaks: £94 for 2 nights. Min 2 nights. £10 supplement for superior room.
Credit cards ① ② ③ ④ ⑤

Set amid lawns and gardens, this half-timbered inn has characterful public rooms and modernised bedrooms, half of them in an annexe, all with ensuite bathrooms and colour television. Christmas breaks are available.

RHAYADER   Powys *Map 6 SN96*

★★66% **Elan** West Street LD6 5AF ☎ (0597) 810373

Normal price: £33-£35.
Short breaks: £29.50-£30.50. Min 2 nights.
Credit cards ① ③

This family-run hotel in the centre of a small market town has comfortable, newly modernised bedrooms, including family rooms, some with private bath.

TALYBONT-ON-USK   Powys   *Map 3 SO12*

★★67% **Aberclydach House** Aber, Brecon LD3 7YS (2m SW) ☎ (087487) 361

Normal price: £29. Dinner from £15.50
Short breaks: £36, min 2 nights Fri-Sun (Not Bank Holidays, weekends, Easter and Christmas). £5 single supplement.
🛪 Credit cards ① ③

An elegant 18th-century house, set in a wooded valley within the Brecons National Park, has been carefully modernised to provide well-equipped bedrooms and comfortable public areas. Meals are of a high standard and there are good facilities for small conferences.

WELSHPOOL   Powys   *Map 7 SJ20*

★★64% **Royal Oak** SY21 7DG ☎ (0938) 552217

Normal price: £30. Dinner £10-£11
Short breaks: £32.50, min 2 nights, Fri-Sun. £5 single supplement
🛪 Credit cards ① ② ③

Situated in the heart of the small market town, this 18th-century hotel provides a popular function suite and a good choice of bars and lounges. Many bedrooms have recently been modernised, and good choice is available in the timbered restaurant.

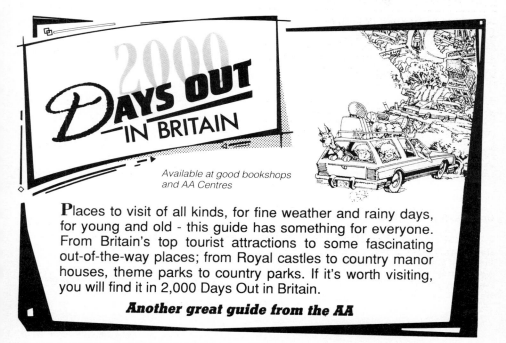

Available at good bookshops and AA Centres

Places to visit of all kinds, for fine weather and rainy days, for young and old - this guide has something for everyone. From Britain's top tourist attractions to some fascinating out-of-the-way places; from Royal castles to country manor houses, theme parks to country parks. If it's worth visiting, you will find it in 2,000 Days Out in Britain.

Another great guide from the AA

INDEX
of Special Interest Breaks

AIRBORNE SPORTS

Abbot's Salford, WARWKS: Salford Hall: ▪ *Ballooning*
Amberley, GLOS: Amberley Inn: ▪ *Ballooning, Gliding*
Bradford on Avon, WILTS: Woolley Grange:
▪ *Ballooning, Gliding,*
Helicopter Flying Lessons
Bushey, HERTS: Hilton National: ▪ *Gliding*
Charlbury, OXON: Bell: ▪ *Ballooning, Gliding*
Eastleigh, HANTS: Crest: ▪ *Flight Training*
Grimston, NORFOLK: Congham Hall: ▪ *Ballooning,*
Helicopter Flying Lessons
Hereford, H & W: Netherwood: ▪ *Ballooning, Flying,*
Gliding, Hang-gliding, Micro-gliding,
Paragliding, Powerchuting
Huddersfield, W YORKS: Pennine Hilton: ▪ *Hang-*
gliding
Llanwddyn, POWYS: Lake Vyrnwy: ▪ *Helicopter Safari*
Longhorsley, NTHUMB: Linden Hall: ▪ *Ballooning*
Newport, GWENT: Celtic Manor: ▪ *Ballooning*
Rochester, KENT: Bridgewood Manor: ▪ *Flying Lessons*
Ross-on-Wye, H & W: Glewstone Court: ▪ *Ballooning*
Rotherwick, HANTS: Tylney Hall: ▪ *Ballooning*
Tetbury, GLOS: Calcot Manor: ▪ *Ballooning*
Hare & Hounds: ▪ *Ballooning, Gliding*
Tewkesbury, GLOS: Tewkesbury Hall: ▪ *Ballooning*
Tormarton, AVON: Compass Inn: ▪ *Ballooning*
Wetherby, W YORKS: Penguin: ▪ *Ballooning*

ART AND ANTIQUES

Alconbury, CAMBS: Alconbury House: ▪ *Antiques*
Ascot, BERKS: Berystede: ▪ *Arts and Antiques*
Beverley, HUMB: Beverley Arms: ▪ *Treasures of*
Yesteryear
Bournemouth, DORSET: Norfolk Royale: ▪ *Antiques*
Cambridge, CAMBS: University Arms: ▪ *Antiques*
Canterbury, KENT: Chaucer Arms: ▪ *Arts and Antiques*
Fort William, HIGHLAND: Alexandra: ▪ *Connoisseur*
and Collection
Harrogate, N YORKS: Crown: ▪ *Antiques*
Grants: ▪ *Antiques Browsing*
Hereford, H & W: Netherwood: ▪ *English Furniture*
1660-1830, 18th and 19th Century
English Porcelain
Hintlesham, SUFFOLK: Hintlesham Hall: ▪ *Antiques*
Lowestoft, SUFFOLK: Rockville House: ▪ *Antiques*
Newby Bridge, CUMBRIA: Crown: ▪ *Antiques*
Shrewsbury, SHROPS: Lion: ▪ *Art and Antiques*
Woodstock, OXON: Bear: ▪ *Arts and Antiques*

ARTS AND CRAFTS

Bamburgh, NTHUMB: Victoria: ▪ *Wildlife Painting*
Betws-y-Coed, GWYNEDD: Tan-y-Foel: ▪ *Photography*
Bideford, DEVON: Pines at Eastleigh: ▪ *Painting*
Yeoldon House: ▪ *Painting*
Bloxham, OXON: Olde School: ▪ *Painting*
Brighouse, W YORKS: Forte Hotel: ▪ *Painting*
Bushey, HERTS: Hilton National: ▪ *Patchwork*
Cambridge, CAMBS: University Arms: ▪ *Water Colour*
Painting
Cheriton Fitzpaine, DEVON: Brindiwell Farm House:
▪ *Painting*
Clawton, DEVON: Court Barn: ▪ *Painting and Drawing*
Hereford, H & W: Netherwood: ▪ *Basket Making,*
Calligraphy, Drawing and
Watercolours, Flower Arranging,
Needlecraft, Oil Painting, Photography,
Pottery, Rural Surprises, Wood Turning
Hintlesham, SUFFOLK: Hintlesham Hall: ▪ *Flower*
Arranging
Huddersfield, W YORKS: Pennine Hilton: ▪ *Knitting,*
Photography
Keswick, CUMBRIA: Red House: ▪ *Painting*
Richmond House: ▪ *Photography*
Skiddaw: ▪ *Art Holidays*
Lynmouth, DEVON: Bath: ▪ *Water Painting*
Malvern, H & W: Colwall Park: ▪ *Painting*
Newby Bridge, CUMBRIA: Swan: ▪ *Flower Arranging*
North Berwick, LOTHIAN: Marine: ▪ *Art and Painting*
Onich, HIGHLD: Lodge on the Loch: ▪ *Painting*
Padstow, CNWLL: Metropole: ▪ *Water Colours*
Roy Bridge, HIGHLD: Glenspean Lodge: ▪ *Photography*
– Hunt with a Camera
Stroud, GLOS: Bear of Rodborough: ▪ *Botanical*
Drawing
Totnes, DEVON: Old Forge: ▪ *Blacksmithing Courses*
Walkerburn, BORDERS: Tweed Valley: ▪ *Art Courses,*
Photography
Weymouth, DORSET: Crown: ▪ *Painting*
Woolacombe, DEVON: Watersmeet: ▪ *Painting*
Lizard The, CNWLL: Kynance Bay House:
▪ *Photographic Courses*

BRIDGE AND OTHER GAMES

Aldeburgh, SUFFOLK: Brudenell: ▪ *Bridge*
Betws-y-Coed, GWYNEDD: Plas Hall: ▪ *Bridge*
Bovey Tracey, DEVON: Coombe Cross: ▪ *Bridge*
Builth Wells, POWYS: Pencerrig: ▪ *Bridge*
Eastbourne, E SUSSEX: Lansdowne: ▪ *Bridge (contract)*
Great Yarmouth, NORFOLK: Palm Court: ▪ *Bridge*
Kenilworth, WARWKS: De Montfort: ▪ *Bridge*
Macclesfield, CHES: Park Villa: ▪ *Bridge*

Marchwiel, CLWYD: Cross Lanes: ■ *Bridge*
Marlborough, WILTS: Castle & Ball: ■ *Duplicate Bridge*
Mildenhall, SUFFOLK: Riverside: ■ *Bridge*
Newquay, CNWLL: Riviera: ■ *Bridge*
Paignton, DEVON: Sunhill: ■ *Bridge*
Petty France, AVON: Petty France: ■ *Bridge*
Ross-on-Wye, H & W: Royal: ■ *Bridge*
Salcombe, DEVON: Tides Reach: ■ *Bridge*
Salisbury, WILTS: Red Lion: ■ *Bridge*
Sidmouth, DEVON: Royal York & Faulkner: ■ *Bridge and Chess*
Swindon, WILTS: Quality: ■ *Bridge*
Templecombe, SOMSET: Horsington House: ■ *Bridge*
Tiverton, DEVON: Tiverton: ■ *Bridge*
Weymouth, DORSET: Crown: ■ *Bridge*
Rex: ■ *Bridge*
Woolacombe, DEVON: Watersmeet: ■ *Bridge*

FOOD AND DRINK

Ambleside, CUMBRIA: Kirkstone Foot: ■ *Wines of the World*
Appleby-in-Westmorland, CUMBRIA: Appleby Manor: ■ *Whisky Tasting*
Bath, DEVON: Somerset House: ■ *Swiss Cuisine*
Bideford, DEVON: Yeoldn House: ■ *Wine Tasting*
Bournemouth, DORSET: Norfolk Royale: ■ *Wine Appreciation*
Brockenhurst, HANTS: Careys Manor: ■ *Gourmet*
Broxted, ESSEX: Whitehall: ■ *Gourmet*
Church Stretton, SHROPS: Mynd House: ■ *Wine Tasting*
Dudley, W MIDS: Station: ■ *Real Ale*
Helmsley, N YORKS: Black Swan: ■ *Gastronomic*
Hereford, H & W: Orchard Farm: ■ *Wine and Cider Tasting*
Hintlesham, SUFFOLK: Hintlesham Hall: ■ *Cookery Classes*
Ilfracombe, DEVON: Ilfracombe Carlton: ■ *Taste of the West Country*
Ipswich, SUFFOLK: Marlborough: ■ *Tutored Wine*
Marlborough, WILTS: Ivy House: ■ *Wine Tasting*
Marlow, BUCKS: Compleat Angler: ■ *Gourmet*
Meriden, W MIDS: Manor: ■ *Australian Wines*
Middleham, N YORKS: Millers House: ■ *Wine*
Northop, CLWYD: Soughton Hall: ■ *Beaujolais*
Nutfield, SURREY: Nutfield Priory: ■ *Wine, Gourmet*
Oxford, OXON: Randolph: ■ *Gourmet*
Perth, TAYSIDE: Murrayshall: ■ *Gourmet*
Petty France, AVON: Petty France: ■ *Wine Tasting*
Rugby, WARWKS: Dun Cow: ■ *Wine Tasting*
Rye, E SUSSEX: Mermaid Inn: ■ *Sussex Food*
St David's, DYFED: Ramsey House: ■ *Microwave Cookery Classes*
Talsarnau, GWYNEDD: Maes y Neuadd: ■ *Gourmet, Wine*
Thurlestone, DEVON: Thurlestone: ■ *Wine Tasting*
Torquay, DEVON: Roseland: ■ *Gourmet*
Worcester, H & W: Fownes: ■ *Cider Trail*

GARDENS AND GARDENING

Bovey Tracey, DEVON: Coombe Cross: ■ *Gardening*
Falmouth, CNWLL: Westcott: ■ *House and Garden*
Harrogate, N YORKS: Crown: ■ *Gardening*
Grants: ■ *Gardening*
Leeds, W YORKS: Parkway: ■ *Gardens of Yorkshire and Harrogate, Flower Show*
Marchwiel, CLWYD: Cross Lanes: ■ *Gardening*
Newquay, CNWLL: Trevone: ■ *Wild Flowers and Gardening*
Oxford, OXON: Randolph: ■ *Gardens*
St Austell, CNWLL: Carlyon Bay: ■ *Gardens*
Shrewsbury, SHROPS: Lion: ■ *Gardens*
Thurlestone, DEVON: Thurlestone: ■ *National Trust Gardens*

HEALTH AND FITNESS

Auchterarder, TAYSIDE: Gleneagles: ■ *Health and Beauty*
Bagshot, SURREY: Pennyhill Park: ■ *Stress Management*
Bath, AVON: Somerset House: ■ *Herbs for Health and Happiness*
Brockenhurst, HANTS: Careys Manor: ■ *Health/Fitness Assessment*
Great Driffield, HUMB: Bell: ■ *Nautilus Fitness*
Hereford, H & W: Merton: ■ *Self-awareness*
Looe, CNWLL: Kantara: ■ *Reflexology, Positive thinking, Self awareness, Counselling*
Port Isaac, CNWLL: Archer Farm: ■ *Health and Beauty*
Stockton-on-Tees, CLEVE: Parkmore: ■ *Health and Fitness*
Tunbridge Wells, KENT: Spa: ■ *Fitness*

HERITAGE

Abbot's Salford, WARWKS: Salford Hall: ■ *Castles, Manors and Gardens, Touring in the Cotswolds*
Aylesbury, BUCKS: Hartwell House: ■ *Historic Houses*
Banbury, OXON: Whately Hall: ■ *Historic Houses*
Bath, AVON: Somerset House: ■ *Georgian Bath, Roman Bath, Brunel, Jane Austen, Canal*
Blandford Forum, DORSET: Crown: ■ *Thomas Hardy*
Bridgwater, SOMSET: Friarn Court: ■ *Taste of Somerset*
Bury St Edmunds, SUFFOLK: Angel: ■ *Literary*
Canterbury, KENT: Chaucer: ■ *Heritage*
Chesterfield, DERBYS: Chesterfield: ■ *Heritage*
Church Stretton, SHROPS: Mynd House: ■ *Industrial Heritage, Countryside Heritage*
Cleobury Mortimer, SHROPS: Redfern: ■ *Steam*
Douglas, I O M: Sefton: ■ *Victorian Transport*
Dudley, W MIDS: Station: ■ *Black Country*
Dumfries, D & G: Cairndale: ■ *Scottish Ceilidh*
Glasgow, STRATH: Kelvin Park Lorne: ■ *Heritage*
Grantham, LINCS: Angel & Royal Hotel: ■ *Medieval*

MISCELLANEOUS

MURDER AND MYSTERY

MUSIC AND THEATRE

NATURE AND COUNTRY PURSUITS

SPORT AND ADVENTURE

Silloth, CUMBRIA: Golf: ■ *Golf*
Southport, MERSYD: Prince of Wales: ■ *Golf*
      Scarisbrick: ■ *Golf*
Stratford-upon-Avon, WARWKS: Shakespeare:
      ■ *Horse-racing*
      Welcombe: ■ *Golf*
Strathblane, CENTRAL: Kirkhouse Inn: ■ *Golf*
Sutton Coldfield, W MIDS: Sutton Court: ■ *Golf*
Swindon, WILTS: Quality: ■ *Golf*
Talland Bay, CNWLL: Talland Bay: ■ *Golf, Tennis*
Tetbury, GLOS: Hare & Hounds: ■ *Golf*
Tewkesbury, GLOS: Tewkesbury Park: ■ *Golf*
Titchwell, NORFOLK: Titchwell Manor: ■ *Golf*
Torpoint, CNWLL: Whitsand Bay: ■ *Golf*
Troon, STRATH: Marine Highland: ■ *Golf*
Tynet, GRAMPIAN: Mill House: ■ *Golf*
Walkerburn, BORDERS: Tweed Valley: ■ *Golf*
Washington, TYNE & WEAR: Washington Moat House:
      ■ *Snooker, Golf*
Weedon, NTHANTS: Crossroads: ■ *Motor Racing Tuition*
Wells, SOMSET: Swan: ■ *Golf Tuition*
Weston-super-Mare, AVON: Beachlands: ■ *Learn to*
      Play Golf
Whitebrook, GWENT: Crown: ■ *Canoeing, Caving,*
      Climbing, Abseiling
Windermere, CUMBRIA: Wild Boar: ■ *Golf*
Workington, CUMBRIA: Cumberland Arms: ■ *Golf*
Wroxton St Mary, OXON: Wroxton House: ■ *Learn to*
      Race at Silverstone

WATER SPORTS

Aberdovey, GWYNEDD: Maybank: ■ *Sailing, Water-*
      skiing
Bala, GWYNEDD: Plas Coch: ■ *Water Sports*
Bideford, DEVON: Yeoldon House: ■ *Water-skiing*
Bishopsteignton, DEVON: Cockhaven Manor: ■ *Sailing*
Bournemouth, DORSET: Norfolk Royale: ■ *Motor*
      Cruising
Colwyn Bay, CLWYD: Stanton: ■ *Water Sports*
Elgin, GRAMPIAN: Eight Acres: ■ *Water Sports*
Falmouth, CNWLL: Green Lawns: ■ *Sailing, Diving*
      Royal Duchy: ■ *Sailing*
Hereford, H & W: Netherwood: ■ *Sailing, Windsurfing,*
      Canoeing
Kingsteignton, DEVON: Passage House: ■ *Rowing,*
      Water-skiing, Windsurfing
Lamphey, DYFED: Court: ■ *Yacht Charter*
Llanwddyn, POWYS: Lake Vyrnwy: ■ *Sailing*
Reading, BERKS: Caversham: ■ *Boating*
Talland Bay, CNWLL: Talland Bay: ■ *Water-skiing*
Wakefield, W YORKS: Swallow: ■ *Sailing, Windsurfing*
Windermere, CUMBRIA: Low Wood: ■ *Windsurfing,*
      Water-skiing

Reader's Report

Please use this form to record your comments on any hotel, guesthouse, farmhouse or inn at which you stay. We shall be most interested to hear about any recommendations of establishments not included in our Guide, or about any criticisms or complaints. All complaints will be treated seriously and passed on to our Inspectorate, but we do urge you to take up any complaint in the first instance with the owner or manager of the establishment to give them the chance to put things right.

Please post to: Editorial Department
Automobile Association
Fanum House,
Basingstoke
Hants RG21 2EA

Your name (block capitals): _____

Your address (block capitals): _____

AA Membership Number: _____

Comments: _____

Reader's Report

Please use this form to record your comments on any hotel, guesthouse, farmhouse or inn at which you stay. We shall be most interested to hear about any recommendations of establishments not included in our Guide, or about any criticisms or complaints. All complaints will be treated seriously and passed on to our Inspectorate, but we do urge you to take up any complaint in the first instance with the owner or manager of the establishment to give them the chance to put things right.

Please post to: Editorial Department
Automobile Association
Fanum House,
Basingstoke
Hants RG21 2EA

Your name (block capitals): _____

Your address (block capitals): _____

_____

AA Membership Number: _____

Comments: _____

_____

_____

_____

_____

_____

_____

_____

_____

_____

_____

_____

_____

READER'S REPORT

Reader's Report

Please use this form to record your comments on any hotel, guesthouse, farmhouse or inn at which you stay. We shall be most interested to hear about any recommendations of establishments not included in our Guide, or about any criticisms or complaints. All complaints will be treated seriously and passed on to our Inspectorate, but we do urge you to take up any complaint in the first instance with the owner or manager of the establishment to give them the chance to put things right.

Please post to: Editorial Department
Automobile Association
Fanum House,
Basingstoke
Hants RG21 2EA

Your name (block capitals): _____

Your address (block capitals): _____

_____

AA Membership Number: _____

Comments: _____

_____

_____

_____

_____

_____

_____

_____

_____

_____

_____

_____

_____

READER'S REPORT

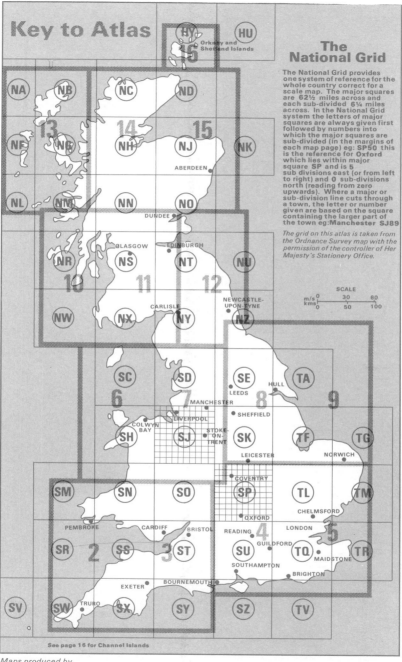

Key to Atlas

The National Grid

The National Grid provides one system of reference for the whole country correct for a scale map. The major squares are 62½ miles across and each sub-divided 6¼ miles across. In the National Grid system the letters of major squares are always given first followed by numbers into which the major squares are sub-divided (in the margins of each map page) eg: **SP50** this is the reference for **Oxford** which lies within major square **SP** and is 5 sub-divisions east (or from left to right) and 0 sub-divisions north (reading from zero upwards). Where a major or sub-division line cuts through a town, the letter or number given are based on the square containing the larger part of the town eg:**Manchester SJ89**

The grid on this atlas is taken from the Ordnance Survey map with the permission of the controller of Her Majesty's Stationery Office.

SCALE

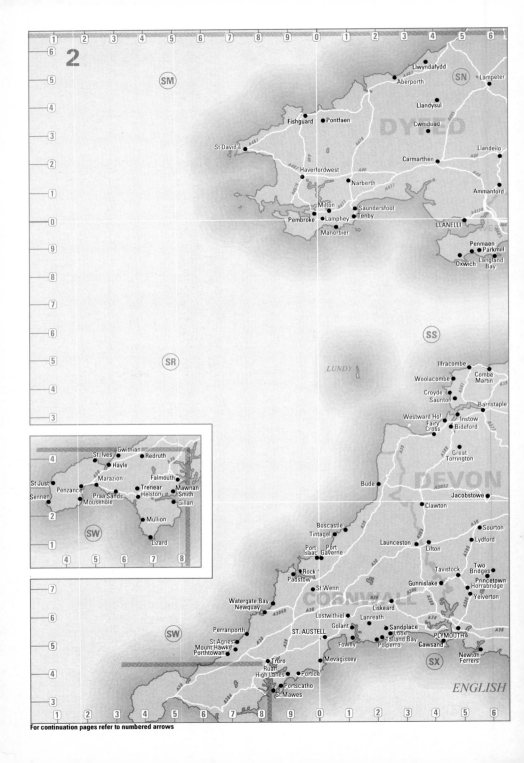

2

SM

SN

SR

SS

SW

SW

SX

LUNDY

DYFED

DEVON

CORNWALL

ENGLISH

Llwyndafydd
Aberporth
Lampeter
Llandysul
Cwmduad
Fishguard
Pontfaen
Carmarthen
Llandeilo
St David's
Haverfordwest
Narberth
Ammanford
Milton
Saundersfoot
Pembroke
Lamphey
Tenby
LLANELLI
Manorbier
Penmaen
Parkmill
Oxwich
Langland
Bay

Ilfracombe
Woolacombe
Combe
Martin
Croyde
Saunton
Barnstaple
Westward Ho!
Instow
Fairy
Cross
Bideford
Great
Torrington
Bude
Jacobstowe
Clawton
Boscastle
Tintagel
Sourton
Port
Isaac
Port
Gaverne
Launceston
Lydford
Lifton
Rock
Tavistock
Two
Bridges
Padstow
St Wenn
Princetown
Horrabridge
Gunnislake
Yelverton
Watergate Bay
Newquay
Lostwithiel
Lanreath
Liskeard
Perranporth
Golant
Sandplace
St Agnes
Looe
PLYMOUTH
Mount Hawke
Fowey
Talland Bay
Cawsand
Porthtowan
Polperro
Newton
Ferrers
Truro
Mevagissey
Ruan
High Lanes
Portloe
Portscatho
St Mawes
ST. AUSTELL

Gwithian
St. Ives
Redruth
Hayle
Marazion
Falmouth
St Just
Penzance
Trenear
Mawnan
Smith
Praa Sands
Helston
Sennen
Mousehole
Gillan
Mullion
Lizard

For continuation pages refer to numbered arrows

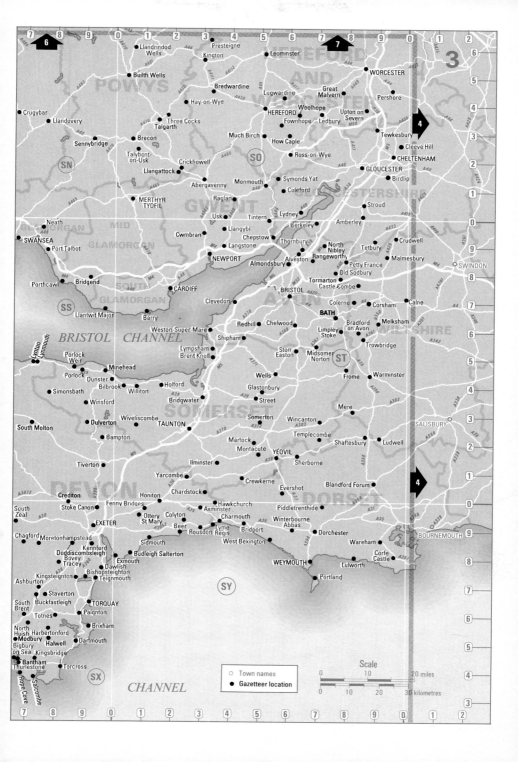

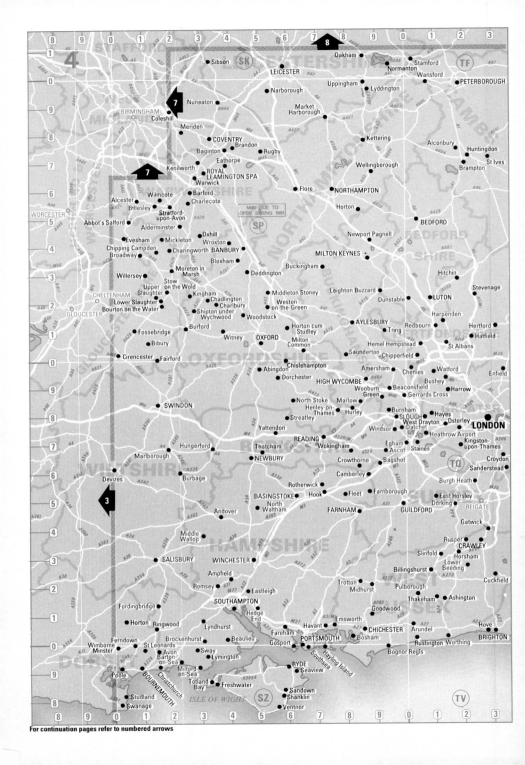

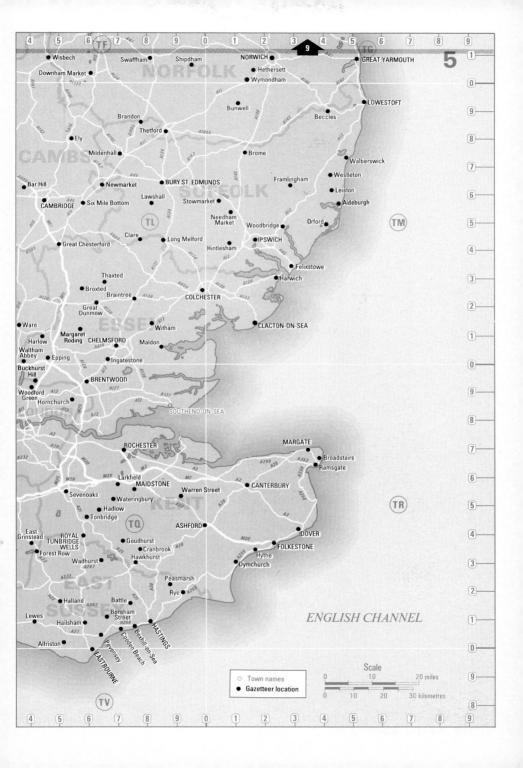

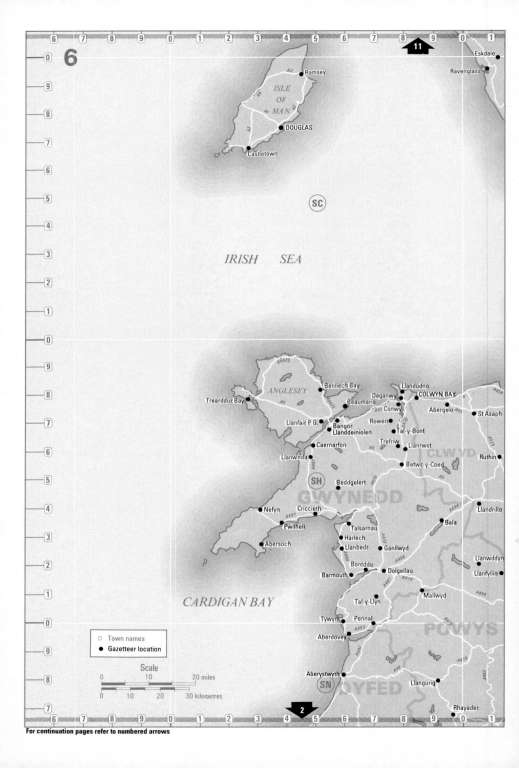

11

Eskdale

Ravenglass

Ramsey

ISLE
OF
MAN

DOUGLAS

Castletown

(SC)

IRISH   SEA

ANGLESEY

Benllech Bay

Llandudno

Deganwy   COLWYN BAY

Trearddur Bay

Beaumaris

Conwy

Abergele   St Asaph

Llanfair P.G.

Bangor   Rowen

Llanddeiniolen   Tal-y-Bont

Caernarfon   Trefriw

Llanrwst   CLWYD

Llanwnda   Betws-y-Coed   Ruthin

(SH)   Beddgelert   GWYNEDD

Nefyn   Criccieth   Llandrillo

Pwllheli   Bala

Abersoch   Talsarnau   Llanwddyn

Harlech

Llanbedr   Ganllwyd   Llanfyllin

Bontddu

Barmouth   Dolgellau

CARDIGAN BAY   Mallwyd

Tal-y-Llyn

Tywyn   Pennal   POWYS

Aberdovey

○ Town names

● Gazetteer location

Scale

0   10   20 miles

0   10   20   30 kilometres

Aberystwyth

(SN)   DYFED   Llangurig

Rhayader

2

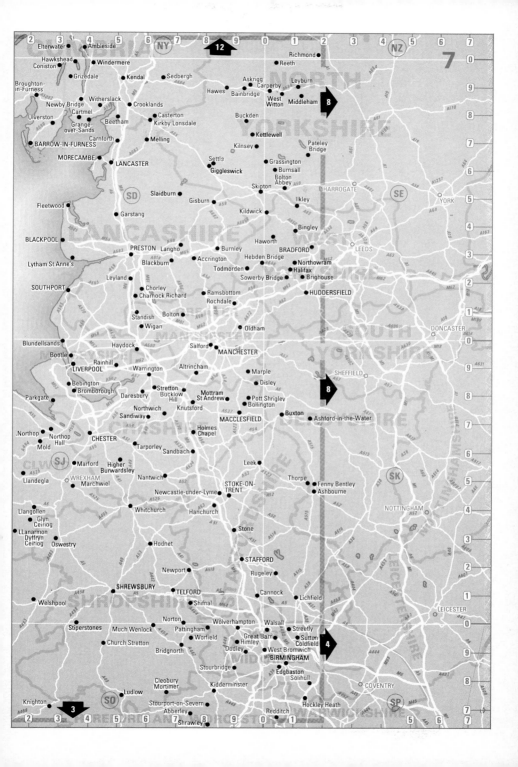

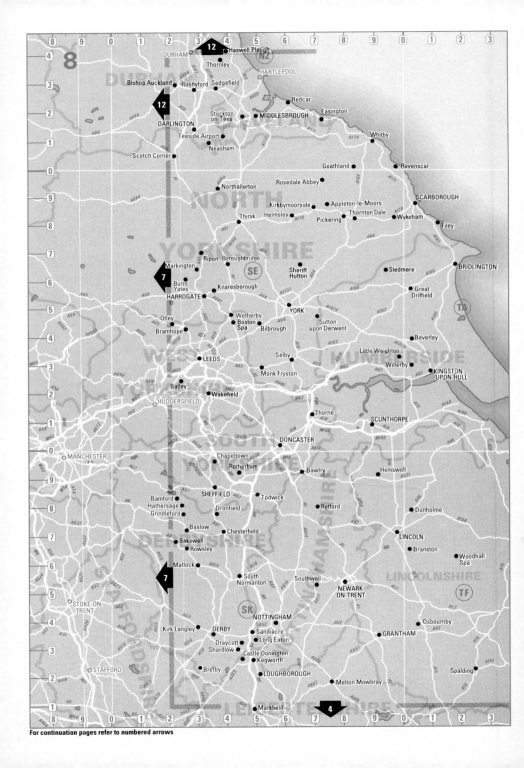

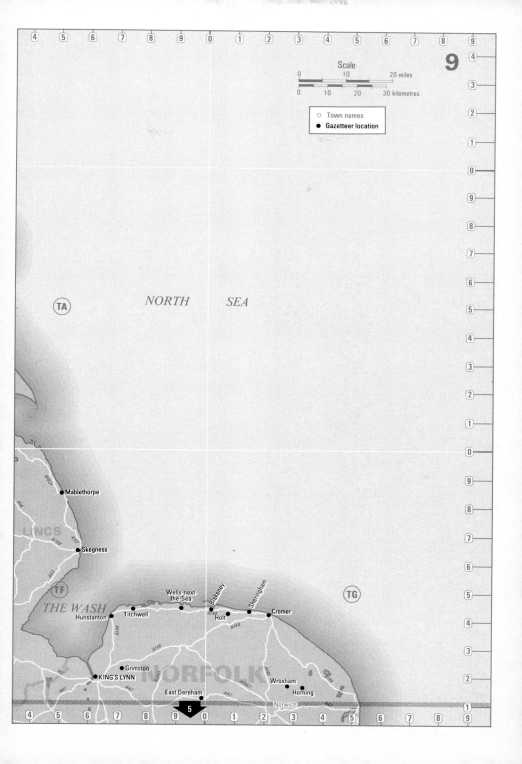

Scale

0   10   20 miles

0   10   20   30 kilometres

○ Town names
● Gazetteer location

NORTH   SEA

TA

TF

THE WASH

LINCS

NORFOLK

● Mablethorpe

● Skegness

Wells-next-
the-Sea

● Titchwell

Hunstanton ●

● Blakeney

● Holt

Sheringham ●

Cromer ●

TG

● Grimston

● KING'S LYNN

Wroxham ●

Horning ●

East Dereham ●

Norwich

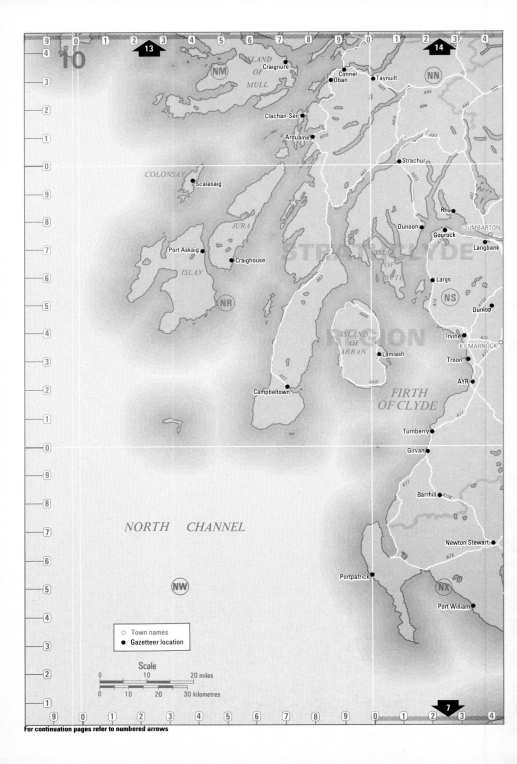

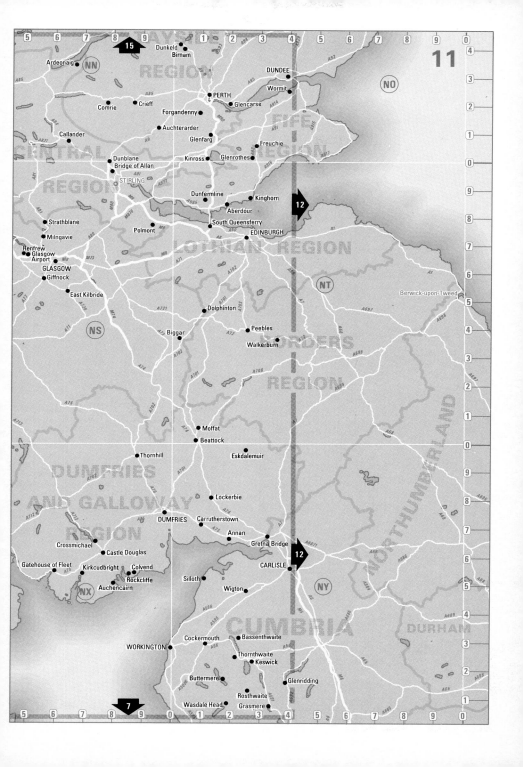

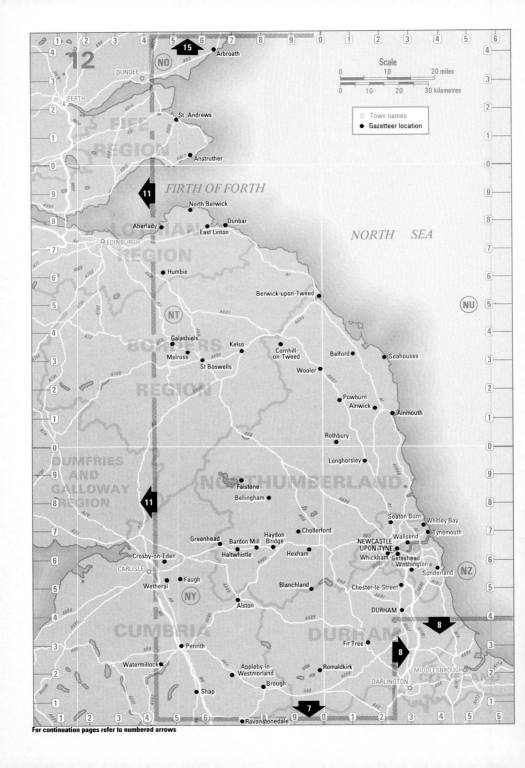

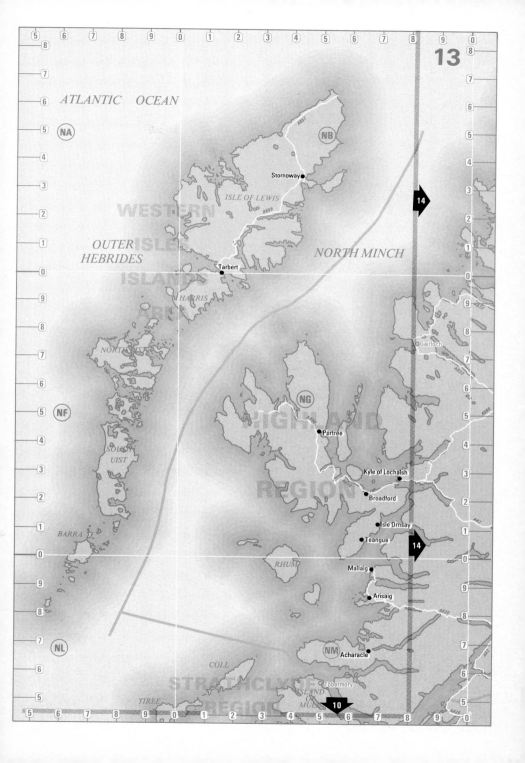

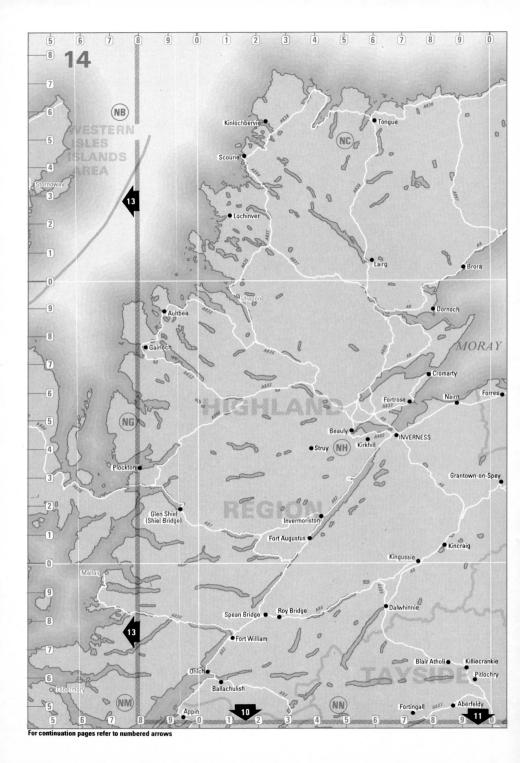

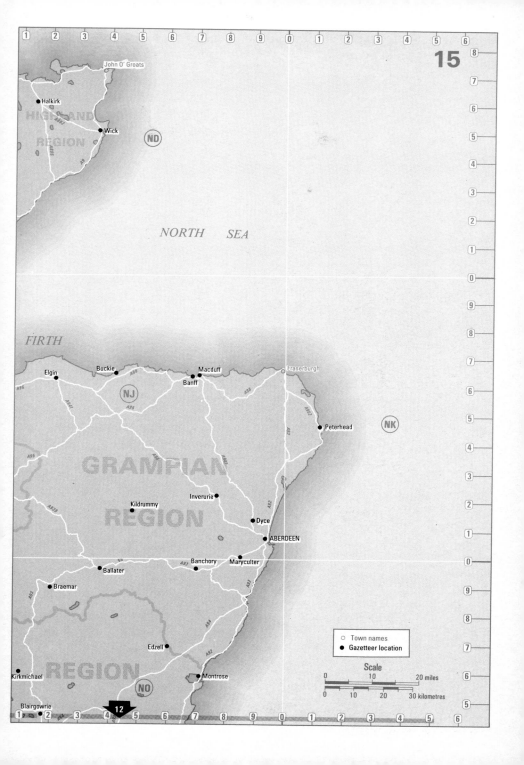

16

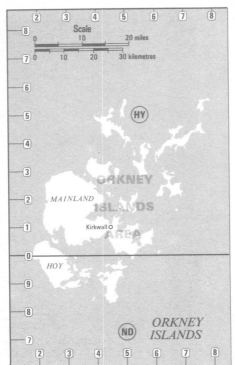

For continuation pages refer to numbered arrows